Lecture Notes in Computer Science 16375

Founding Editors

Gerhard Goos
Juris Hartmanis

Editorial Board Members

The series Lecture Notes in Computer Science (LNCS), including its subseries Lecture Notes in Artificial Intelligence (LNAI) and Lecture Notes in Bioinformatics (LNBI), has established itself as a medium for the publication of new developments in computer science and information technology research, teaching, and education.

LNCS enjoys close cooperation with the computer science R & D community, the series counts many renowned academics among its volume editors and paper authors, and collaborates with prestigious societies. Its mission is to serve this international community by providing an invaluable service, mainly focused on the publication of conference and workshop proceedings and postproceedings. LNCS commenced publication in 1973.

María Cecilia Reyes · Frank Nack

Editors

Interactive Storytelling

18th International Conference
on Interactive Digital Storytelling, ICIDS 2025
Saint Julian, Malta, December 1–5, 2025
Proceedings, Part II

 Springer

Editors
María Cecilia Reyes
Universidad del Norte
Barranquilla, Colombia

Frank Nack
University of Amsterdam
Amsterdam, The Netherlands

ISSN 0302-9743 ISSN 1611-3349 (electronic)
Lecture Notes in Computer Science
ISBN 978-3-032-12404-3 ISBN 978-3-032-12405-0 (eBook)
https://doi.org/10.1007/978-3-032-12405-0

Preface

This volume constitutes the proceedings of the 18th International Conference on Interactive Digital Storytelling (ICIDS 2025). ICIDS is the premier conference for researchers and practitioners concerned with studying digital interactive narrative forms from various perspectives, including theoretical, technological, socially aware, and applied design lenses. Organized by ARDIN (Association for Research in Digital Interactive Narratives), the annual conference is an interdisciplinary gathering that combines theoretical inquiry, empirical research, and artistic expression. This year's conference featured an academic session presenting the papers published in this volume, workshops, a doctoral consortium, and a parallel art exhibition.

This year's ICIDS returned to Europe. The host country was the Mediterranean island of Malta, with a rich history featuring most of the European powers and reaching back to some of the earliest civilizations, with Neolithic remains dating back to 5000 BC. This history is characterized by decisive battles which shaped world history and by foreign rule due to the country's strategic position between Africa, Europe, and Asia. This also led to it being influenced by many cultures while at the same time becoming influential in art, music, and architecture, way beyond its own shores. Malta's future-looking economy has attracted iGaming and FinTech companies through early regulation and supportive legal frameworks. The island has also embraced the opportunities offered by the recent wave of Artificial Intelligence (AI) through its National AI Strategy, aiming to position Malta as a testbed for AI innovation in areas like healthcare, transport, and public services.

Like Malta's architectural and artistic heritage, where diverse cultural elements combine to create something uniquely beautiful, AI systems are now collaborating with human creators to generate ever-shifting narrative possibilities and story worlds. This situation reminded us of Janet Murray's keynote at ICIDS 2018 in Dublin, where she discussed her kaleidoscopic view on IDN research. She described IDNs as environments that support the analysis of the same event in multiple contexts and at the same time foster the imagination of multiple variants of the same scenario. This has inspired the main theme of this year's conference: *Kaleidoscopic Machines.*

The aim of this year's conference was rather programmatic: through retelling, we looked at the past to understand what worked, why or why not; we analyzed new IDN works to describe the current thinking; and we presented critical and thought-provoking visionary contemplations to look ahead. The studies presented in this volume allow us to gain an understanding of what we aim to reach out for in the years to come – memory machines, creative post-coding environments that are rooted in core human stories, non-human-generated multisensorial environments, narratives driven by brain-computer interfaces, kaleidoscopic machines, or even more new types of IDN that can help us to understand an increasingly complex world better. All this should help us to reflect on our current foundations and on how related methodological issues need to be further developed.

ICIDS 2025 received 110 submissions: 80 full and short papers, and 30 Late Breaking Works papers. Following the review process, the Program Committee accepted 31 full papers, 4 short papers, and 19 Late-Breaking Works, for a total of 54 papers. The acceptance rate of the conference was 52%. This year we decided to reorganize the thematic areas of the conference into five main sections: Theory, History and Foundations; Methods, Tools and Updates; Applications and Case Studies; Social, Cultural and Critical Perspectives; and the Late Breaking works. All papers were subjected to a rigorous double-blind review procedure, utilizing an organized and comprehensive review process, much like in previous years. A minimum of three reviews per paper were completed before the decision, with additional reviews solicited on the recommendations of reviewers. In addition, we included a rebuttal phase, and final decisions were made in agreement by area and program chairs.

ICIDS also accepted 14 doctoral proposals, whose authors received feedback and mentoring at the third iteration of ARDIN's Emerging Scholars Academy, 7 workshops, and 25 artworks to be showcased at the Art Exhibition. As has become the rule for ICIDS, this conference has been fully hybrid for the paper sessions, workshops, doctoral consortium, posters, and art exhibition.

We want to express our deep gratitude to the members of the program committee who provided high-quality reviews, critical analysis, and insightful discussions to authors but also the community. We also want to extend our appreciation to the program area chairs: Ehud Ben Arie, Kath Dooley, Daniel Echeverri, Jamie Fawcus, Lissa Holloway-Attaway, Vincenzo Lombardo, Catia Prandi, Lyle Skains, and David Thue; and to the art exhibition jury: Shanmugapriya T., Rafaela Nunes, Kavi Duvvoori, Diogo Marques, Mateo Alayza, Nico Valdivia, Iliana Hernandez, Paula Fleisner, Ramiro Sanchiz, Shamim Shoomali, and Matti Kangaskoski.

We deeply thank our keynote speaker Ruth Aylett for her longstanding contribution to our field.

Finally, we thank the Malta Tourism Authority as the main sponsor of the conference and the Gaming Malta Foundation for sponsoring the Art Exhibition. We are also very grateful to Springer, who generously provide the prizes for best full, student, and short paper.

December 2025

María Cecilia Reyes
Frank Nack

ARDIN, Association for Research in Digital Interactive Narratives

ARDIN's purpose is to support research in Interactive Digital Narratives (IDN), in a wide range of forms, be that video and computer games, interactive documentaries and fiction, journalistic interactives, art projects, educational titles, transmedia, virtual reality and augmented reality titles, or any emerging novel forms of IDN.

ARDIN provides a home for an interdisciplinary community and for various activities that connect, support, grow, and validate said community. The long-term vision for the suite of activities hosted by ARDIN includes membership services, such as a community platform, job postings, and support for local gatherings, but also conferences, publication opportunities, research fellowships, and academic/professional awards. ARDIN publishes a monthly newsletter and holds a monthly online social, where both established researchers and graduate students share their ongoing work in an informal setting. In 2024 we launched the Journal for Interactive Narrative Research, published in collaboration with ETC Press (https://journal.ardin.online/). There are also several committees and task forces, listed below.

ICIDS is the main academic conference of ARDIN. Additional international and local conferences are welcome to join the organization. The Zip-Scene conference, focused on Eastern Europe, is the first associated conference. Diversity is important to ARDIN. The organization strives towards gender balance and the representation of different people from different origins. Diversity also means to represent scholars at different levels of their careers. No ARDIN member shall discriminate against any other ARDIN member or others outside of the organization in any way, including but not limited to gender, nationality, race, religion, sexuality, or ability. Discrimination against these principles will not be tolerated and membership in ARDIN can be withdrawn based on evidence of such behavior.

The association is incorporated as a legal entity in Amsterdam, the Netherlands. First proposed during the ICIDS 2017 conference in Madeira, Portugal, the association was officially announced at ICIDS 2018 in Dublin, Ireland. During its foundational year, members of the former ICIDS Steering Committee continued to serve on the ARDIN board as approved by the first general assembly at ICIDS 2018. The current board structure and membership were approved at the general assembly at ICIDS 2024 in Barranquilla, and, as of November 2025, ARDIN has more than 400 members.

More information about ARDIN can be found at https://ardin.online/.

Organization

General Chair

Jonathan Barbara   Saint Martin's Institute of Higher Education, Malta

Program Committee Chairs

María Cecilia Reyes   Universidad del Norte, Colombia
Frank Nack   University of Amsterdam, The Netherlands

Art Exhibition Chairs

Terhi Marttila   Interactive Technologies Institute, Portugal
Jaime Rodríguez   Universidad de los Andes, Colombia
Nelson Vera   Universidad de los Andes, Colombia

Workshop Chairs

Anca Serbanescu   Politecnico di Milano, Italy
Mattia Bellini   University of Tartu, Estonia

Doctoral Consortium Chairs

Hartmut Koenitz   Södertörn University, Sweden
Claudia Silva   European Commission-Joint Research Centre, Italy

Financial Management Chair

Frank Nack   University of Amsterdam, The Netherlands

Local Organization

Saint Martin's Institute of Higher Education, Malta

Charles Theuma	Sponsorship, Venue, and Catering Manager
Silvio McGurk	Technology and Infrastructure
Karina Almeida	Website and Social Media Graphic Design

Program Committee Area Chairs

Theory, History and Foundations

Vincenzo Lombardo	University of Amsterdam, The Netherlands
Lyle Skains	Bournemouth University, UK

Social, Cultural and Critical Perspectives

Lissa Holloway-Attaway	University of Skövde, Sweden
Jamie Focus	University of Skövde, Sweden

Methods, Tools and Updates

Catia Prandi	University of Bologna, Italy
David Thue	Carleton University, Canada

Applications and Case Studies

Ehud Ben Ari	Tel Aviv University, Israel
Kath Dooley	University of South Australia, Australia
Daniel Echeverri	Masaryk University, Czech Republic

Late Breaking Works

María Cecilia Reyes	Universidad del Norte, Colombia
Frank Nack	University of Amsterdam, The Netherlands

Program Committee

Elizabeth Murice Alexander	Independent Scholar, USA
David Antognoli	Columbia College Chicago, USA
Thais Arrias Weiller	Tampere University and ITI/LARSyS, Portugal
Pratama Wirya Atmaja	University of Pembangunan Nasional "Veteran" Jawa Timur, Indonesia
Ágnes Karolina Bakk	Moholy-Nagy University of Art and Design, Hungary
Jonathan Barbara	Saint Martin's Institute of Higher Education, Malta
Mattia Bellini	University of Tartu, Estonia
Jessica L. Bitter	Hochschule RheinMain, Germany
Justin Bortnick	University of Pittsburgh, USA
Sarah Brown	University of Florida, USA
Elke Brucker-Kley	Zurich University of Applied Sciences, Switzerland
Luis Emilio Bruni	Aalborg University, Denmark
Alex Calderwood	Montana State University, USA
Angeliki Chrysanthi	University of the Aegean, Greece
Dan Cox	Illinois State University, USA
Joseph Livingston Crawford-Visbal	Pontificia Universidad Católica del Perú, Peru
Giuliana Dettori	Istituto di Tecnologie Didattiche del CNR, Italy
Kath Dooley	University of South Australia, Australia
Daniel Echeverri	Masaryk University, Czech Republic
Mirjam Eladhari	Stockholm University, Sweden
Carl Erez	University of California, Santa Cruz, USA
Jamie Fawcus	University of Skövde, Sweden
Alisa Feklicheva	Tallinn University, Estonia
Paola Feng	Universidad de Costa Rica, Costa Rica
Joshua Fisher	Ball State University, USA
Caitlin Foley	University of Massachusetts Lowell, USA
Dren Gerguri	University of Prishtina, Kosovo
Arnau Gifreu-Castells	Universidad Autónoma de Barcelona, Spain
Nandhini Giri	Purdue University, USA
Ian Gonzales	Ball State University, USA
Andrew Gordon	University of Southern California, USA
Mads Haahr	Trinity College Dublin, Ireland
Lissa Holloway-Attaway	University of Skövde, Sweden
Jussi Holopainen	City University of Hong Kong, China
Shi Johnson-Bey	University of California Santa Cruz, USA

Akrivi Katifori	National and Kapodistrian University of Athens, Greece
Jack Kelly	University of California, Santa Cruz, USA
Hartmut Koenitz	University of Amsterdam, The Netherlands
Victoria Lagrange	Kennesaw State University, USA
David Lamas	Tallinn University, Estonia
Sofia Lindgren	Stockholm University, Sweden
Vincenzo Lombardo	University of Torino, Italy
Péter Kristóf Makai	Universität Duisburg-Essen, Germany
Mark Marino	ELO, USA
Terhi Marttila	Interactive Technologies Institute (ITI/LARSyS), Portugal
Michael Merriam	UCF, USA
Alex Mitchell	National University of Singapore, Singapore
John T. Murray	University of Central Florida, USA
Gabriela Muñoz	Universidad del Norte, Colombia
Frank Nack	University of Amsterdam, The Netherlands
Rafaela Nunes	Interactive Technologies Institute (ITI/LARSyS), Portugal
Jorge Palinhos	CEAA-ESAP; ESACT-IPB; ESTC-IPL, Portugal
Dave Pape	University at Buffalo, USA
Andrew Phelps	American University, USA
Margarida Pinheiro	School of Design, Politecnico di Milano, Italy
Catia Prandi	University of Bologna, Italy
Niels Erik Raursø	Aalborg University, Denmark
Derek Reilly	Dalhousie University, Canada
Maria Cecilia Reyes	Universidad del Norte, Colombia
Allen Riley	University of California, Santa Cruz, USA
Juan-David Rodas	Universidad de Antioquia, Colombia
Jaime Rodriguez	Universidad de los Andes, Colombia
Anastasia Salter	University of Central Florida, USA
Ben Samuel	University of New Orleans, USA
Anca Serbanescu	Politecnico di Milano, Italy
Samuel Shields	University of California, Santa Cruz, USA
Lyle Skains	Bournemouth University, UK
Jouni Smed	University of Turku, Finland
Nicolas Szilas	University of Geneva, Switzerland
Mariët Theune	University of Twente, The Netherlands
David Thue	Carleton University, Canada
Michel Toledo	Universidad Viña del Mar, Chile
Mauricio Vasquez	Universidad de Caldas, Colombia
Nelson Vera	Universidad de los Andes, Colombia

Noah Wardrip-Fruin   University of California, Santa Cruz, USA
Alejandro Ángel Torres   Universidad Jorge Tadeo Lozano, Colombia

Keynote

The Emperor's New Clothes

Ruth Aylett

Heriot-Watt University, Scotland, UK

Abstract. Amazon now overflows with books digitally generated by LLMs, and publishers too are struggling with a deluge. This talk addresses how far LLM outputs can be considered adequate digital interactive narratives and how their use interacts with the research aims of the Digital Narrative field. Are there useful and ethically-acceptable positions between the 'miracle' tag of the hype, and the 'delusion' with which the sceptics counter it? If so, what are they and what do they offer?

Biography

Prof. Ruth S. Aylett is a British author, computer scientist, professor, poet and political activist. She is a professor of computer science at Heriot-Watt University in Edinburgh. Aylett's research involves affective computing, social computing, software agents, and human–robot interaction. She is the leader of Socially Competent Robots (SoCoRo), a project of the Engineering and Physical Sciences Research Council that studies whether robots can assist autistic people in learning to recognize facial expressions and other social cues.

She has also studied the use of "emotionally literate" robots for tutoring schoolchildren, developed interactive role-playing software intended to combat bullying, and performed with a robot poet named Sarah the Poetic Robot as part of the Edinburgh Free Fringe.

Contents

Exploring the Influence of Narrative in VR Games: Players Gameful Experience and Empathy

Zhengya Gong[1]([✉]) [iD], Petra Nurmela[1] [iD], Ashley Colley[1] [iD],
Georgi V. Georgiev[2] [iD], and Jonna Häkkilä[1] [iD]

[1] University of Lapland, Rovaniemi, Finland
Zhengya.Gong@outlook.com,
{Petra.Nurmela,Ashley.Colley,Jonna.Hakkila}@ulapland.fi
[2] University of Oulu, Oulu, Finland
Georgi.Georgiev@oulu.fi

Abstract. This study used eye-tracking interaction to investigate how narrative influences players' gameful experience and empathy in a virtual reality (VR) shooting game. Participants were assigned to either an empathy-driven condition or a neutral condition. Quantitative and qualitative data were collected through a questionnaire, open-ended responses, and interviews. Results showed that the empathy-driven narrative significantly enhanced players' sense of immersion but had no measurable effect on empathy-related reflections. These findings suggest that narrative can strengthen immersion in VR, even with minimal interaction methods like eye tracking. However, its potential to foster empathy may be limited in fast-paced game contexts without deeper narrative integration. The study highlights the importance of aligning narrative design with gameplay mechanics to support emotional engagement in VR experiences.

Keywords: VR game · shooting game · empathy · narrative

1 Introduction

Virtual reality (VR) has become an influential medium for digital storytelling, offering immersive experiences that engage users both emotionally and cognitively [9–11]. As VR technologies advance, there is growing interest among designers and researchers in how narrative elements can deepen players' immersion and strengthen connections with virtual characters and environments [9–11]. Among these approaches, empathy-driven storytelling stands out for its potential to evoke strong emotional responses and create memorable experiences [19,24].

This study investigates how different narratives-empathy-driven versus neutral-affect players' gameful experiences and empathy in a fast-paced VR

M. C. Reyes and F. Nack (Eds.): ICIDS 2025, LNCS 16375, pp. 1–14, 2026.
https://doi.org/10.1007/978-3-032-12405-0_1

shooting game designed with hands-free eye-gaze interaction, omitting controllers or physical objects. We developed two narrative conditions, one embedding an accessibility-aware empathy-driven framing (a protagonist without arms, aligned with the interaction modality) and the other neutral. Participants played under one of these conditions. To evaluate their experiences, we employed a validated questionnaire measuring multiple dimensions of gameful experience and collected qualitative data through open-ended responses and interviews. This mixed-method approach allowed us to capture both measurable outcomes and deeper insights into how narrative framing shapes empathy and interactive experience under constrained modalities.

Our findings indicated that players exposed to the empathy-driven narrative condition reported significantly higher immersion than the neutral narrative condition. However, the empathy-driven narrative did not lead to greater empathic connection with the targeted group portrayed in the story. These results suggested that while the empathy-driven narrative can enhance certain aspects of the VR experience, its influence on empathy may be more complex. This work offered valuable implications for the design of narrative-driven VR experiences.

2   Background and Related Work

This section provides an overview of the key concepts central to this study: narrative, empathy, and VR games. It also reviews prior research on how narrative influences empathy and gameful experiences, leading to the explanation of our research aim.

2.1   Narrative

Narrative is a foundational cognitive and cultural mechanism through which humans make sense of experiences and construct meaning [6,17]. In interactive media, especially games, narrative elements play a vital role in guiding player engagement, emotional involvement, and the interpretation of in-game events [1,23]. Storytelling relies on narrative structure, such as character development, plot, and thematic context, to shape user experiences [11,27]. In VR, storytelling extends beyond traditional dialogue or text, emerging through environmental design, player agency, and embodied interaction in an immersive 3D world [11, 27].

2.2   Empathy

Empathy is the ability to understand and share the feelings of others [2], often categorized into cognitive empathy (understanding another's perspective) and affective empathy (emotionally resonating with others) [28]. In interactive media, empathy operates on two distinct levels: as a guiding principle for designers to better understand and address users' needs, and as a desired outcome where players experience empathy toward mediated or fictional characters [9,15]. Mediated experiences that cultivate empathy-such as those in digital games or interactive media-can lead to deeper emotional engagement, ethical reflection, and increased prosocial behavior [16,18]. In digital and narrative-driven media, empathy is often evoked through devices such as character identification, point of view, and emotional arcs, which are especially potent in immersive and interactive contexts [9].

2.3 VR Game

VR games create immersive experiences by combining visual immersion, physical interaction, and spatial presence [5,20,26]. Unlike traditional games, VR allows players to feel as though they are "present" in a virtual environment, offering new possibilities for storytelling and emotional engagement [11,12]. The particular affordances of VR-such as embodiment and agency-make it an especially suitable platform for exploring how narratives shape user experience, such as the gameful experience in our study.

2.4 Influence of Narrative on Empathy and Gameful Experiences

Narrative has a strong influence on how empathy develops in media experiences. Stories that include emotionally resonant characters, moral dilemmas, or social themes have been shown to increase both cognitive and affective empathy [4,12]. In interactive contexts, such as VR, narrative structure shapes players' interpretations of characters and events, contributing to emotional depth and player identification [25].

Empathy-driven narratives-those that highlight social or emotional dimensions-are particularly effective in engaging players on a deeper level rather than neutral narratives. These narratives can enhance immersion, intensify emotional reactions, and strengthen empathetic understanding [4,12]. At the same time, narrative also influences how players experience gameplay itself. It frames in-game actions, contextualizes challenges, and helps players assign meaning to game mechanics and goals [1,23].

In particular, narrative elements can support player immersion by providing coherent and emotionally resonant story worlds [13]. Moreover, narrative can contextualize goals and feedback systems in ways that align with the player's emotional journey, thereby increasing perceived accomplishment and challenge [12]. Social dimensions of the game, including empathy and connection with in-game characters or co-players, are also enhanced when narratives evoke shared experiences or moral dilemmas [7,9]. Therefore, narrative design in VR is not merely decorative but instrumental in shaping how players feel, act, and reflect within the game world.

However, despite the recognized importance of narrative in shaping empathy and player experience, little empirical work has isolated the effects of different narrative framings within VR contexts. Existing studies often focus on traditional media or controller-based VR, leaving open questions about how empathy-driven narratives function under constrained interaction modalities, such as hands-free eye-gaze control. Significantly, previous research has not investigated accessibility-aware narratives that directly correlate plot components with the method of interactions-for instance, a protagonist lacking arms to symbolize the absence of controllers. This study examines the impact of empathy-driven (corresponding with the interaction method) versus neutral narratives on empathy and gameful experience in a fast-paced VR game.

2.5   Research Aim

This study aims to explore the role ofempathy-driven narrative in shaping players' gameful experience in a VR game. Specifically, we examine *whether and how empathy-driven narrative influences players' gameful experiences and empathy by comparing it with a neutral narrative.* While there is growing interest in narrative-driven VR experiences, few empirical studies have directly compared different types of narrative framing-such as empathy-driven versus neutral-on players' emotional and experiential responses. While aligning narrative with gameplay is a known Interactive Digital Narrative principle, our study is the first to empirically examine how empathy-driven narrative framing affects player experience and empathy in a fast-paced VR shooting game using hands-free eye-gaze interaction (omitting physical objects and controllers). Importantly, prior work has not examined accessibility-aware narratives that explicitly align story elements with the interaction method. To address this gap, we integrate an accessibility-aware narrative-with a protagonist lacking arms to match the interaction design. This underexplored context reveals important limitations in how narrative functions under constrained modalities. By addressing this gap, our study offers new insights into how narrative design (corresponding to the interactive method) can enhance emotional engagement and interactive storytelling in VR games. Through a mixed-method approach, we aim to contribute to the broader understanding of narrative, empathy, and gameful experience in immersive digital media.

3   Methods

To explore how narrative influences empathy and gameful experience in VR, we developed a custom-designed VR game and conducted a between-subjects experimental study. Thirty-five participants were randomly assigned to one of two narrative conditions: empathy-driven or neutral. Following gameplay, participants completed a solid questionnaire assessing their gameful experience and participated in a semi-structured interview to provide qualitative insights into their emotional responses and engagement with the narrative.

3.1   VR Game Design

The VR game was developed with five key considerations: interaction method, game genre, target empathy group, narrative, and gameplay mechanics.

Interaction Method. The game used a hands-free, eye-gaze interaction method in place of traditional controllers. This approach was selected for both accessibility and design-related reasons. Eye-gaze interaction makes the game accessible to individuals with physical or motor impairments [21], while also minimizing physical input, allowing players to focus more on the narrative and visual experience [22]. Importantly, accessibility-aware narratives that explicitly connect story aspects with interaction methods to foster empathy have not been studied. This design choice supports the study's goal of understanding how tales alter emotions and experiences.

Game Genre. Drawing on our prior research with VR developers, we identified common VR genres such as adventure, strategy, and combat. Given the simplicity and immediacy of eye-gaze input, a combat/shooting genre was chosen. This genre supported narrative-driven tension and goal-directed interaction while remaining compatible with accessible interaction.

Empathy Target. The empathy-driven narrative featured a protagonist without arms, designed to naturally integrate with the hands-free gameplay. This character limitation was intended to enhance perspective-taking and reinforce the experience of physical constraint. Aligning the narrative with the interaction method emphasized the challenges faced by individuals with disabilities, supporting the goal of fostering empathy.

Narrative Conditions. Two distinct narrative versions were created. In the neutral condition, players were described as generic guardians protecting a piece of cake from mischievous flying elves-presented in a light-hearted, whimsical tone with no personal backstory (Fig. 1, light green background).

In the empathy-driven condition, the narrative was designed to elicit both cognitive empathy (via perspective-taking) and affective empathy (via emotional resonance with the protagonist's physical and social limitations). Players embodied a young elf without wings, who had a physical disability and was left behind while others searched for food. This character remained to protect the last piece of cake in a land plagued by scarcity. The story emphasized vulnerability, exclusion, and determination to encourage both cognitive and emotional empathy (Fig. 1, pink background).

Game Summary: Cake Protection War. The game, Cake Protection War, took place in a fantasy forest where players defended a slice of cake from incoming waves of elves, accompanied by melodic birdsong only, without narration. Interaction was exclusively gaze-based. A visible gaze ray projected from the player's point of view; maintaining eye focus on a target elf for one second triggered its elimination, accompanied by visual and audio feedback. Gameplay was identical across both conditions, with the only difference being the introductory

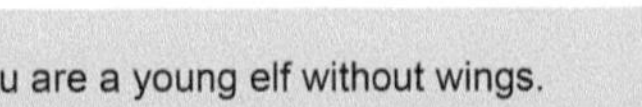

Fig. 1. The difference between the two conditions.

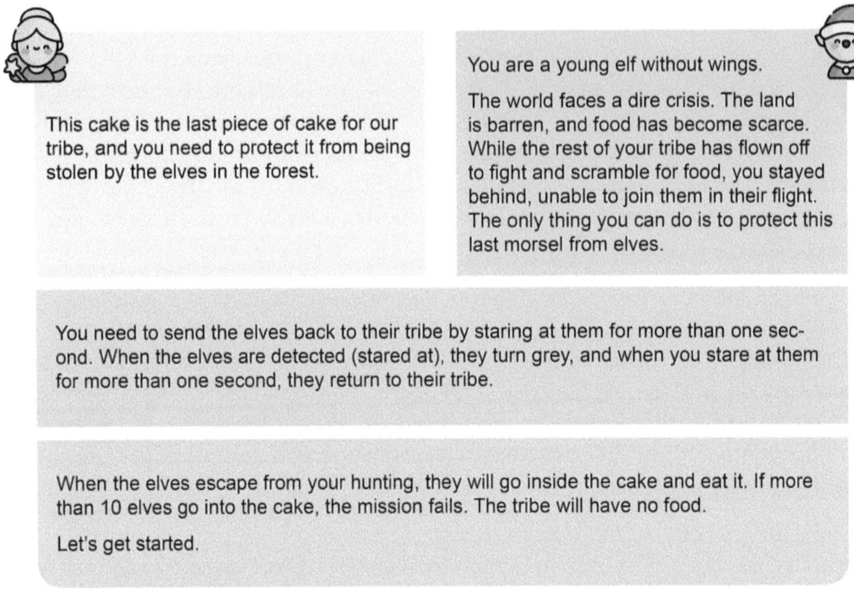

narrative. All visuals, mechanics, and difficulty settings were held constant. In both cases, players used only eye movements to aim and eliminate approaching elves. The game included escalating difficulty levels, as common games do:

- **Easy**: Elves spawned every 2.5 s from a narrow frontal area (Fig. 2, blue frame).
- **Medium**: Elves spawned every 1.5 s across a wider area (Fig. 2, green frame).
- **Hard**: Elves spawned every second across the broadest range (Fig. 2, orange frame).

Each session began with a narrative introduction corresponding to the assigned condition. Players used their gaze to select a start button and initiate gameplay. Each level lasted 90 s, with players progressing by successfully defending the cake. If ten elves reached the cake, the session ended. After completing all three levels, participants were asked if they would like to replay the game.

3.2 Experiment

Participants. Thirty-five participants (mean age $= 28.74$, SD $= 8.32$) were recruited via posters distributed across a university campus. The sample included students and staff from diverse academic backgrounds. Participants were randomly assigned to one of two conditions: 22 to the neutral (control) condition and 13 to the empathy-driven condition. Of the participants, 18 identified as female, 15 as male, and 2 chose not to disclose their gender. VR experience

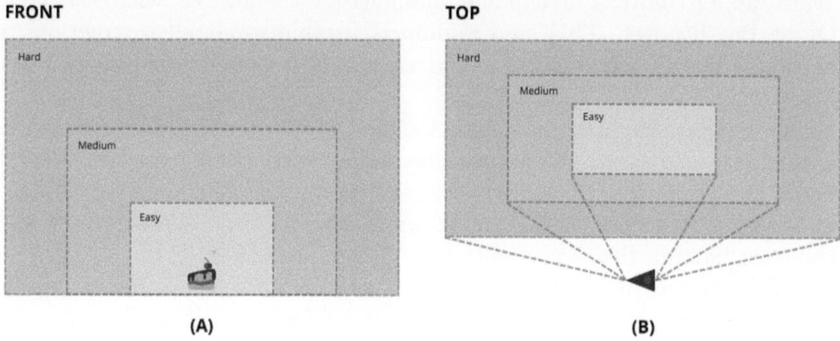

Fig. 2. Elf spawn zones across difficulty levels. (A) Front view, (B) Top view. Blue: Easy level; Green: Medium level; Orange: Hard level. (Color figure online)

ranged from novice to advanced: 4 participants had never used VR, 9 had used VR between 1 and 9 times, and 9 had used it more than 10 times.

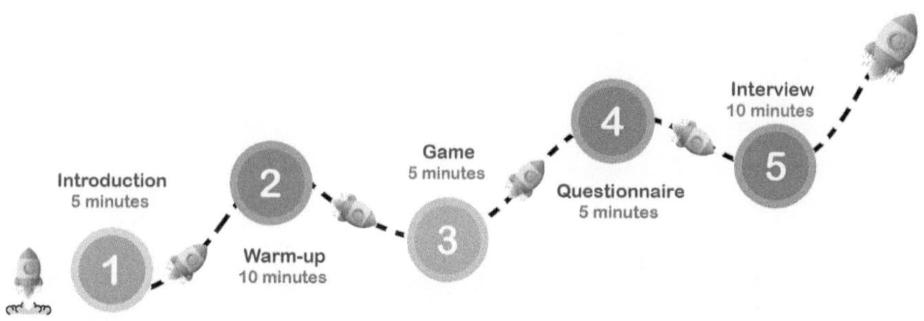

Fig. 3. The experiment's procedure.

Procedure. The experiment was conducted in a dedicated VR lab at the University of Lapland. Each session followed a five-step process (see Fig. 3):

- Introduction (5 min): Participants were briefed on the study's purpose and procedures, provided informed consent, and completed a pre-questionnaire. Addressing the research purpose, we instructed participants just to assist in testing a game, deliberately omitting any mention of the empathy-related issue to prevent biassing their perceptions of empathy and influencing results. This questionnaire collected demographic data, information about their VR experience, and their dominant eye. They were also asked to describe situations or reasons why someone might be unable to play a VR game.

- Warm-up (10 min): Participants familiarized themselves with the Oculus
  Quest Pro headset. This step minimized usability-related distractions and
  ensured that all participants could clearly perceive in-game elements and
  instructions.
- Game Session (5 min): Participants signed in to one of the conditions randomly before playing the game. Then, they read the narrative (either the
  neutral or empathy-driven narrative, depending on their assigned condition)
  and know how to play the game, as shown in Fig. 4 (A). Then, after clicking
  the start button, they experienced the game, illustrated in Fig. 4 (B).
- Questionnaire (5 min): After gameplay, participants completed a questionnaire assessing their gameful experience using a validated scale. They
  also responded again to the same open-ended empathy question used pre-
  gameplay, which asked them to describe situations or reasons why someone
  might be unable to play a VR game.
- Semi-structured Interview (10 min): A semi-structured interview was conducted to gather qualitative insights into players' gameful experiences and
  empathic responses. All interviews were audio-recorded with consent and later
  transcribed for analysis.

(A)   **(B)**

Fig. 4. The screenshots of the game scenes. (A) The beginning of the game, (B) During
gameplay.

3.3   Measurements

Participants' gameful experience was assessed using a shortened version of the
Gameful Experience Questionnaire [14], a validated instrument designed to capture seven key dimensions: accomplishment, challenge, competition, guidance,
immersion, playfulness, and social connection. The original scale includes 56
items, but due to concerns about participant fatigue and potential impacts on
data quality [8], we selected 4 items with the highest factor loadings from each
dimension, based on the original confirmatory factor analysis.

To assess empathy, we employed two open-ended questions before and after gameplay. In both instances, participants were asked to *describe situations or reasons why someone might be unable to play a VR game*. Comparing pre- and post-game responses enabled us to explore potential shifts in empathy.

In addition, semi-structured interviews offered qualitative insights into how participants interpreted the narrative, perceived the protagonist, and emotionally engaged with the experience. Various inquiries were posed, including whether engaging in the game with eye-gazing interaction enhanced their comprehension of the experiences of individuals with arm disabilities, what new insights or understandings about disability they acquired from this experience, and what emotions the story evoked in them.

4   Results

To examine differences in participants' experiences between the empathy-driven and neutral narrative conditions, we conducted independent-samples Mann-Whitney U tests on the dimensions of gameful experience and on participants' open-ended responses.

The analysis revealed a statistically significant difference in Immersion scores between the two conditions, $U = 204.000$, $Z = 2.093$, $p = .038$ (two-tailed). Participants in the empathy-driven condition reported significantly higher immersion than those in the neutral condition. This suggests that narrative influenced how deeply participants engaged with the VR environment.

For the remaining dimensions-Accomplishment ($p = .972$), Challenge ($p = .972$), Competition ($p = .753$), Guided ($p = .960$), Playfulness ($p = .159$), and Social Experience ($p = .085$)-no statistically significant differences were found between the two conditions. These results indicate that narrative framing did not significantly affect participants' sense of achievement, difficulty, enjoyment, competitiveness, guidance, or social engagement. However, average scores for Playfulness and Social Experience were descriptively higher in the empathy-driven condition, as illustrated in Fig. 5.

We also analyzed participants' open-ended responses describing why some people may be unable to play VR games. Although the empathy-driven group produced more words on average, the difference in word count was not statistically significant ($p = .353$). This suggests that the narrative had no measurable effect on the quantity of participants' reflections related to the empathy of disabled people (no arm). Interview findings further supported this, showing no substantial increase in expressed empathy in the empathy-driven condition compared to the neutral one.

5   Discussion

5.1   The Influence of Narrative on Immersion

The significant difference in immersion scores between the neutral and empathy-driven conditions indicates the unique role of narrative in shaping participants'

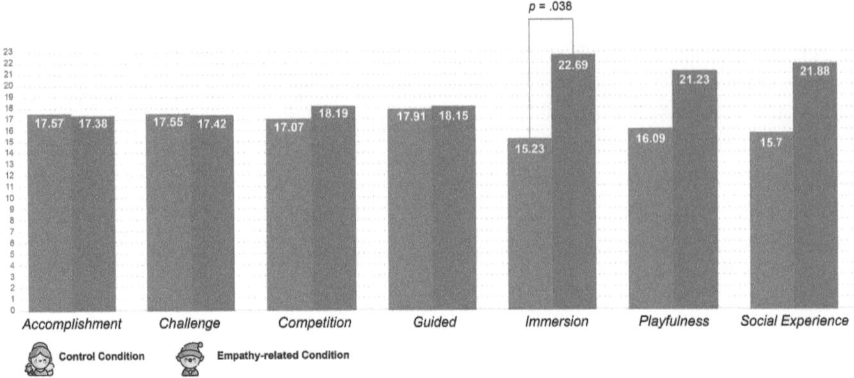

Fig. 5. The difference in gameful experiences between the two conditions.

psychological engagement within VR environments. Although other dimensions of gameful experience-such as accomplishment, challenge, or social connection-did not differ significantly, the narrative had a measurable effect on how fully participants felt absorbed in the experience. This suggests that immersion may be particularly sensitive to narrative context, especially when physical interaction is limited, as was the case with our use of eye-gaze input.

These findings resonate with prior work emphasizing the power of narrative to foster emotional and cognitive investment in virtual settings [12], even under constrained interaction modalities [3]. In our study, the empathy-driven narrative likely offered a more coherent and emotionally resonant framing that elevated users' attentional focus and imaginative involvement. This aligns with the concept of "narrative presence"-the subjective experience of "being in" a story-which has been shown to enhance immersion by giving actions and events narrative coherence and emotional consequence [3,12,29].

Importantly, the absence of significant differences in other experiential dimensions suggests that the narrative did not uniformly enhance all aspects of gameful experience. Rather, it selectively deepened the experiential dimension most directly related to story absorption. This has important implications for VR game design: when interactivity is constrained or simplified (e.g., via eye-tracking), narrative can play a compensatory role in sustaining immersion, provided it is meaningfully integrated into the user experience.

5.2   The Influence of Narrative on Empathy

Contrary to expectations, the empathy-driven narrative did not elicit a measurable increase in empathy-related reflections or expressions across open-ended responses and interviews. Despite being designed to highlight genres of accessibility and inclusion, the narrative failed to generate a significant shift in participants' perspective-taking or affective engagement. This raises critical questions about the mechanisms through which narrative can-or cannot-foster empathy in interactive media.

One plausible explanation is the inconsistency between narrative intent and gameplay form. The VR experience employed a fast-paced, action-oriented mechanic–centered on shooting and survival-that may have reduced the narrative's emotional appeal. In our study, the tension between the narrative's emotional message and the game's competitive structure may have weakened the intended empathic response.

Further, post-session interviews revealed that several participants did not fully engage with or even recall the narrative content, suggesting that narrative delivery-brief text at the outset-was insufficiently integrated into the gameplay loop. Without recurring narrative cues, embodied interaction with the protagonist's challenges, or opportunities for affective choice-making, the narrative struggled to generate sustained emotional resonance.

Together, these findings suggest that while narrative can effectively enhance immersion, its ability to foster empathy in VR depends on deeper integration with mechanics, pacing, and interactive structure. In action-driven contexts, isolated narrative cues may be too subtle or easily overlooked to meaningfully shape empathic engagement. Future work should explore how richer narrative devices-e.g., voiceovers, branching choices, and character embodiment-might more effectively cultivate empathy in VR storytelling.

6   Limitations

While the present study provides valuable insights into the influence of narrative framing on user experience in VR, several limitations must be considered.

Firstly, the study's sample size was relatively small, with only 35 participants, which may limit the generalizability of the findings. A larger sample could help establish more robust conclusions and potentially reveal more subtle differences in the participants' experiences. Additionally, the participant group was not diverse in terms of demographics and VR experience, which could influence how individuals perceive and respond to immersive narratives. Future research should aim to include a broader and more varied sample to explore how factors such as age, cultural background, and prior VR experience impact narrative engagement and empathy.

Secondly, the design of the VR game itself may have influenced the results. The choice of a fast-paced, action-oriented game, focused on shooting and defense, might not have been the most conducive to eliciting empathy. The genre may have prioritized excitement and engagement over emotional reflection, which could have diluted the impact of the empathy-driven narrative. A slower-paced or more contemplative game could allow for deeper emotional engagement and a more effective test of narrative-driven empathy.

Finally, the narrative integration within the game was relatively brief and limited in scope. The exposure to the empathy-driven narrative was brief and primarily focused on a short introductory segment. This limited narrative immersion may have hindered the ability of the story to fully evoke empathy, particularly in an action-oriented game where players' attention was likely directed towards gameplay mechanics. Future studies might benefit from integrating narrative elements more thoroughly throughout the gameplay experience, enabling deeper engagement with the story.

7   Conclusion and Future Work

This study examined the impact of narrative elements on user experience and empathy in a VR shooting game using eye-tracking interaction. While the inclusion of an empathy-driven narrative significantly enhanced participants' immersion, it did not influence their empathic responses. These results suggest that while narrative can effectively boost engagement in VR, its impact on empathy may be limited in fast-paced, action-oriented contexts where players are less likely to reflect on the story. The lack of empathy-related effects may also stem from participants not fully engaging with or reading the narrative, highlighting the importance of integrating the story more seamlessly into the gameplay. Future research should explore alternative game genres and stronger narrative-gameplay integration to better evoke empathy in VR experiences.

Despite providing valuable insights, this study opens several avenues for future exploration. Researchers could examine different game genres, such as narrative-driven or simulation-based games, where players may be more receptive to emotional engagement. Additionally, integrating immersive storytelling techniques-like interactive cutscenes, in-game dialogue, or environmental storytelling-could encourage deeper engagement with the narrative. Extending gameplay sessions or providing longer exposure to narratives might also allow for a more profound emotional response. Finally, incorporating physiological or behavioral measures, such as gaze tracking, facial expression analysis, or post-experience interviews, could offer a more detailed understanding of how narratives shape emotional engagement in VR.

Acknowledgements. This study is funded by grants from the Research Council of Finland, as part of the AWARE project [Grant Number: 355694].

References

1. Bizzochi, J.: Games and narrative: an analytical framework. Loading J. Can. Games Stud. Assoc. **1**(1) (2007)
2. Bošnjaković, J., Radionov, T.: Empathy: concepts, theories and neuroscientific basis. Alcohol. Psychiatry Res. J. Psychiatr. Res. Addictions **54**(2), 123–150 (2018)
3. Cadet, L.B., Chainay, H.: Memory of virtual experiences: role of immersion, emotion and sense of presence. Int. J. Hum Comput Stud. **144**, 102506 (2020)

4. Calvert, J., Abadia, R., Tauseef, S.M.: Design and testing of a virtual reality enabled experience that enhances engagement and simulates empathy for historical events and characters. In: 2019 IEEE Conference on Virtual Reality and 3D User Interfaces (VR), pp. 868–869. IEEE (2019)

5. Christensen, J.V., Mathiesen, M., Poulsen, J.V., Ustrup, E.E., Kraus, M.: Player experience in a VR and non-VR multiplayer game. In: Proceedings of the Virtual Reality International Conference-Laval virtual, pp. 1–4 (2018)

6. Cobley, P.: Narrative. Routledge (2013)

7. Emmerich, K., Ring, P., Masuch, M.: I'm glad you are on my side: How to design compelling game companions. In: Proceedings of the 2018 Annual Symposium on Computer-Human Interaction in Play, pp. 141–152 (2018)

8. Galesic, M., Bosnjak, M.: Effects of questionnaire length on participation and indicators of response quality in a web survey. Public Opin. Q. **73**(2), 349–360 (2009)

9. Georgiev, G. V., Nanjappan, V., Georgieva, I., ong, Z.: Empathic experiences of visual conditions with virtual reality. In: International Conference on Interactive Digital Storytelling, pp. 168-180. Springer Nature Switzerland, Cham (2023)

10. Gong, Z., Wang, M., Nanjappan, V., Georgiev, G.V.: Instrumenting virtual reality for priming cultural differences in design creativity. In: Creativity and Cognition. 510–514 (2022)

11. Gong, Z., Gonçalves, M., Nanjappan, V., Georgiev, G. V.: VR storytelling to prime uncertainty avoidance. In: International Conference on Interactive Digital Storytelling. pp. 103–116. Springer Nature Switzerland, Cham (2023)

12. Hadjipanayi, C., Christofi, M., Banakou, D., Michael-Grigoriou, D.: Cultivating empathy through narratives in virtual reality: a review. Pers. Ubiquit. Comput. **28**(3), 507–519 (2024)

13. Hafner, M., Jansz, J.: The players experience of immersion in persuasive games: a study of my life as a refugee and PeaceMaker. Int. J. Serious Games **5**(4), 63–79 (2018)

14. Högberg, J., Hamari, J., Wästlund, E.: Gameful experience questionnaire (GAME-FULQUEST): an instrument for measuring the perceived gamefulness of system use. User Model. User Adap. Inter. **29**(3), 619–660 (2019). https://doi.org/10.1007/s11257-019-09223-w

15. Kouprie, M., Visser, F.S.: A framework for empathy in design: stepping into and out of the user's life. J. Eng. Des. **20**(5), 437–448 (2009)

16. Lee, K.J.: Augmenting digital media consumption via critical reflection to increase compassion and promote prosocial attitudes and behaviors (2024)

17. Lugmayr, A., Sutinen, E., Suhonen, J., Sedano, C.I., Hlavacs, H., Montero, C.S.: Serious storytelling–a first definition and review. Multimedia Tools Appl. **76**, 15707–15733 (2017)

18. Li, B., Hou, F., Guan, Z., Chong, A.Y.L.: The use of social media for a better world: roles of social experience, empathy and personal impulsiveness in charitable crowdfunding. Inf. Technol. People **36**(6), 2587–2610 (2023)

19. Maisoni, M.F.P., Bakri, A., Aulia, P.: The effectiveness of the storytelling method using folktales on early childhood empathy behavior at villa beta kindergarten Padang City. Trend Int. J. Trends Glob. Psychol. Sci. Educ. **1**(3), 62–68 (2024)

20. Murray, J.H.: Hamlet on the Holodeck: The Future of Narrative in Cyberspace. The Free Press, USA (1997)

21. Monteiro, P., Gonçalves, G., Coelho, H., Melo, M., Bessa, M.: Hands-free interaction in immersive virtual reality: a systematic review. IEEE Trans. Visual Comput. Graphics **27**(5), 2702–2713 (2021)

22. Monteiro, P., Gonçalves, G., Peixoto, B., Melo, M., Bessa, M.: Evaluation of hands-free VR interaction methods during a Fitts' task: efficiency and effectiveness. IEEE Access **11**, 70898–70911 (2023)
23. Moser, C., Fang, X.: Narrative structure and player experience in role-playing games. Int. J. Hum. Comput. Interact. **31**(2), 146–156 (2015)
24. Pulivarthi, P., Bhatia, A. B.: Designing empathetic interfaces enhancing user experience through emotion. In: Humanizing Technology With Emotional Intelligence, pp. 47–64. IGI Global Scientific Publishing (2025)
25. Seinfeld, S., et al.: Offenders become the victim in virtual reality: impact of changing perspective in domestic violence. Sci. Rep. **8**(1), 2692 (2018)
26. Slater, M., Wilbur, S.: A framework for immersive virtual environments (FIVE): Speculations on the role of presence in virtual environmentser. Presence Teleoperators Virtual Environ. **6**(6), 603–616(1997)
27. Wolfe, A., Louchart, S., Loranger, B.: The impacts of design elements in interactive storytelling in VR on emotion, mood, and self-reflection. In: International Conference on Interactive Digital Storytelling, pp. 616-633. Springer International Publishing, Cham (2022)
28. Shamay-Tsoory, S.G., Aharon-Peretz, J., Perry, D.: Two systems for empathy: a double dissociation between emotional and cognitive empathy in inferior frontal gyrus versus ventromedial prefrontal lesions. Brain **132**(3), 617–627 (2009)
29. Shin, D.: Empathy and embodied experience in virtual environment: to what extent can virtual reality stimulate empathy and embodied experience? Comput. Hum. Behav. **78**, 64–73 (2018)

A Shared Field of Perception: Voice Over and Focalisation in Extended Reality (XR)

Kath Dooley[(✉)] [iD]

The University of South Australia, Adelaide 5000, Australia
Kath.Dooley@unisa.edu.au

Abstract. This article explores how extended reality (XR) reconfigures narrative focalisation by embedding the user within the perceptual frame of a storyworld. Drawing on foundational narrative theory as well as more recent scholarship, it analyses *Notes on Blindness: Into Darkness* (dirs. Arnaud Colinart, Amaury La Burthe, Peter Middleton, and James Spinney, 2016), *Goliath: Playing With Reality* (dirs. Barry Gene Murphy and May Abdalla, 2021) and *Turbulence: Jamais Vu* (dir. Ben Andrews, 2023) to show how voiceover, sensory stimuli, and user interaction co-create a shared field of perception in these XR works. Narration in this context is shown to be variable and relational, blending first and second-person strategies. Focalisation emerges as embodied, contingent, and interactive- no longer confined to text or image alone. This challenges traditional distinctions between narrator, character, and audience, positioning the user as a kind of co-focaliser. The article argues that XR invites an expansion of focalisation theory to accommodate hybrid modes of perception and highlights the medium's potential for telling embodied and marginalised stories through immersive experience.

Keywords: focalisation · voiceover · narrative theory · narration · extended reality

1 Introduction

Over the last decade, extended reality (XR) has emerged as a distinct storytelling medium, enabled by technologies that support the creation and distribution of spatialised narrative content. A range of innovative documentary, fiction, and hybrid works using virtual reality (VR), augmented reality (AR), or mixed reality (MR) have been presented at festivals and online, offering users immersive, interactive story experiences. Drawing on 360° media, which places the user at the centre of a represented world, much of this work seeks to communicate diverse human experience, including non-typical bodily or mental functions. As per the IDN works analysed by Holloway-Attaway and Fawcus [17], XR projects may draw upon the human voice to evoke emotion, connect creators with audiences, and open up new forms of storytelling. While XR's capacity to let users 'walk in the shoes' of others is debated [6, 15, 18, 20], a growing body of work is clearly invested in diverse subjectivities conveyed first-hand through immersive media.

This article adds to XR narration scholarship by exploring focalisation, a concept introduced by Genette [13] and later developed by Bal [2] and Ciccoricco [9]. While

M. C. Reyes and F. Nack (Eds.): ICIDS 2025, LNCS 16375, pp. 15–28, 2026.
https://doi.org/10.1007/978-3-032-12405-0_2

narration refers to how narrative information is conveyed, focalisation asks whose point of view organises it. Genette distinguishes 'who sees' from 'who narrates' [13, p.186], the latter often linked to a voiceover narrator. Despite XR's potential for first-person perspectives, focalisation in XR has been the subject of few studies [4, 5], an omission this article addresses.

A recurring XR storytelling technique is voiceover that allows protagonists to express thoughts and speak directly to users. Yet its relation to focalisation remains underexamined. Several have explored user positioning in VR storyworlds as witness, character or unseen entity, highlighting the user as the one 'who sees' [11, 12, 24, 30]. However, XR often includes a represented protagonist whose perspective also shapes the story, echoing film conventions. This co-presence complicates focalisation, especially when voiceover is used. I analyse how voiceover impacts focalisation across three XR works: *Notes on Blindness: Into Darkness* [27], *Goliath: Playing With Reality* [14], and *Turbulence: Jamais Vu* [28][1]. Produced across a period of five years, all of these interactive works feature voiceover but differ in their representing of protagonists and engagement of users, thus enabling an exploration of varying focalisation styles. Through close formal analysis informed by narrative theory, I aim to clarify how these elements interact, offering insight for both researchers and creators into how user and character perspectives can co-produce narrative meaning in XR.

2   Literature Review

2.1   On Narration, Narrators and Voice Over

Within all narrative-based audio-visual media, one can sense a narrating voice that orders the text. Cinema theorists have described this agent as a 'master of ceremonies' [23, p. 21] or 'image-maker' [21, p. 44]; the one who selects the order of images and sounds. Audio-visual texts may also include a human voice from offscreen, intermittently narrating story elements. As Kozloff notes in her seminal study of voice-over in American cinema, this speaker offers a subjective version of story elements or an interpretation of what is seen on screen [21]. The spectator, in turn, draws meaning from this.

'Voice-over narration' refers to spoken commentary by an off-screen speaker, whose temporal and spatial context differs from the accompanying visuals. Though oral storytelling is an ancient tradition, voice-over emerged in cinema in the 1930s, influenced by radio, newsreels and documentaries [21]. As a narrative tool, it can create intimacy by granting access to a character's inner thoughts, or irony when the narration contradicts visuals. Audio-visual media that features voice over can thus be considered quite differently to an offering of visual media without verbal commentary, with the latter requiring spectators to interpret meaning and significance on their own. Perhaps for this reason, cinematic voice-over has been criticised as detracting from film's visual nature. Kozloff cites links to theatre as another reason voice-over has been considered 'redundant' [21, p. 9]. Yet it remains a familiar tool across film, television and digital media.

---

[1] Trailers or artist statements for the case studies featured in this article can be viewed online [see 14, 27, 28].

Narrative theorists identify several narrator categories. Kozloff distinguishes 'first-person' or 'character' narrators and 'third-person' or 'authorial' narrators (p. 6), echoing Genette's 'homodiegetic' (in-story) and 'heterodiegetic' (outside the story) narrators [13, p. 245]. The homodiegetic narrator, a character within the story, offers a subjective view and serves as a point of identification. Genette also identifies 'extradiegetic' narration from outside the story world, and 'intradiegetic' narration from within it [13, p. 248]. Typically, extradiegetic narrators are heterodiegetic and adopt a third-person, omniscient stance. These useful distinctions are referenced in the case study analysis below to locate the narrator's position in XR works.

It must be noted, however, that these categories have been determined in the context of non-interactive media (the novel and cinema), and so are not entirely adequate for an exploration of XR. In interactive environments where users may influence the diegesis, Vosmeer et al. highlight the potential of second-person narration addressing the user as 'you' [29, p. 3], citing examples in text-based games and online MUDs and MOOs (p. 3–4). Their study finds second-person narration particularly effective in 360° VR, with most test subjects preferring it to first- or third-person narration. They argue that the specificity of 360° video might 'overrule previous 'laws' of cinematic storytelling' (p. 10), and that second-person narration, common in games, effectively engages users in this context.

Relatedly, VR narration studies by Barbara et al. [4, 5] explore the role of disembodied voice in interactive narratives and its effect on user presence and self-identification. Through analysis of two VR works with varied uses of voice and perspective, they observe that while VR places users at the centre of a story, they may lack tools for self-identification, reducing presence. Direct address by characters and narrators would seem to be a useful tool in this regard, enabling the user's role within the story world to be made clear. Barbara et al. call for further empirical work that explores the impact of second-person voice and interaction on users' self-identification and immersion [5]. My article takes up this suggestion with reference to scholarship on 3D game words [8, 25] and by considering the variable and relational nature of voiceover in XR, as observed in three case studies.

2.2 Focalisation Theory

The frameworks above inform the question of 'who speaks?' (i.e., who is the narrator?), which Genette distinguishes from the question of 'who sees?' [13]. The latter, labelled 'focalisation', concerns not just point of view but the filtering of narrative through a character's subjectivity. In essence, 'the agent who tells the narrative is not necessarily the same one who perceives it' [9, p. 255]. This foundational distinction, extended and debated over the past four decades, remains essential for understanding narrative transmission.

Genette suggests that focalisation might be variable within a work. He identifies three distinct modes that have served as analytical tools in the study of literature and older media: non-focalisation, internal focalisation, and external focalisation [13]. Non-focalisation, also referred to as 'zero focalisation', describes a narrative conveyed from an omniscient perspective, providing the reader or viewer with unrestricted access to all aspects of the story. Internal focalisation occurs when the narrative is filtered through the perspective of a specific character, thereby limiting the audience's knowledge to what that character sees, thinks, or feels. This mode may include insight into the character's inner thoughts and emotions. In contrast, external focalisation presents events from an objective standpoint, focusing solely on characters' observable actions and dialogue, with minimal or no access to their internal states.

Mieke Bal reinterprets Genette by introducing the term 'focaliser' to refer to the agent through whom narrative information is perceived and processed [2, 3]. Whereas Genette treats focalisation as a passive feature of the text, Bal presents the focaliser as an active perceiver, either situated within or outside the story world, offering a particular view of the 'focalised'. It must be noted that Genette disagreed with Bal's reading of the theory, and ongoing debate of their two positions has featured in subsequent narratological work [10, 16]. Bal's reinterpretation is however particularly useful for visual media, as it more closely aligns with the notion of point of view, as captured by a camera. Internal focalisation, for Bal, involves a character whose point of view structures and informs the presentation of the narrative. In the context of a film, this might manifest in point of view shots, where we literally see through the eyes of a specific character, or a shot-reverse-shot, where we see a character looking (the focaliser) and the object of their vision (the focalised). By contrast, external focalisation refers to an 'anonymous agent' outside the fabula, offering a more objective viewpoint. These focalisers function separately from narrators, though both serve as key narrative elements. Bal, like Genette, acknowledges that focalisation may shift within a work or remain ambiguous [2, p. 144].

Deleyto extends Bal's theory by suggesting that in film, the focaliser typically coincides with the camera's position. Camera movement and editing (cuts, dissolves, etc.) indicate changes in focalisation [10, p. 167]. He argues that cinema often leans towards external focalisation, lending narratives a sense of objectivity, even when subjective alignments are apparent. This raises interesting questions in relation to XR, where the 'camera' is effectively replaced by the user's perspective, situated in 360° diegetic space. One might then ponder the degree to which the XR user functions as an internal or external focaliser.

Discussing the animated film *Persepolis* (dirs. Satrapi & Paronnaud, 2007), Nixon observes sections that she suggests invite 'audience focalisation' [26]. She notes that, while the film is largely 'told' by the protagonist, Majane, it features sections that 'appear to be detached from any perceiving entity, leaving the viewers as perceivers and partial constructors of the meaning' [26, p. 94]. While it may well be the case that the film asks its viewers to 'perform an incredible amount of inferential activity' [p. 94], I would argue that Bal's notion of external focalisation more aptly describes these sequences, preserving a distinction between focalisation as a formal device and act of interpretation. Nevertheless, the concept of the spectator as focaliser is provocative in the context of XR. To explore this further, I adopt Bal's concept of the focaliser, aligned with camera position, while retaining Genette's central question: who perceives? This would appear to be critical in interactive media, where the user is embedded in the story world as an active agent, as is noted in the scholarship outlined below.

2.3 Focalisation Theory for Interactive Media

In recent years, focalisation theory has expanded through its application to digital and interactive media. On this front, Ciccoricco explores focalisation in multimodal, computer-based narratives (i.e. digital fiction), which combine text, imagery, and ludic participation [9]. He argues for a reconceptualisation that accounts for digital fiction's multimodality and its 'recursive, algorithmically orchestrated relationship between reader and machine' [p. 256]. Although this raises questions about including reception in focalisation theory, Ciccoricco concludes the digital fiction reader remains 'an agent of interpretation, not of focalization', as they are not meaningfully aligned with an avatar or fictional agent [p. 263]. As in the discussion of *Persepolis*, this emphasises focalisation as a formal textual feature.

In contrast to the digital fiction described by Ciccoricco, video games (and XR) may in fact feature an avatar and/or point of view that the player can control. Michael Nitsche [25] investigates focalisation in video game studies, favouring Mieke Bal's framework for its emphasis on visual storytelling. Nitsche conceptualises focalisation through virtual camera perspective, treating it as a narrative element distinct from a traditional narrating voice. His analysis shows how visual techniques, such as restricted camera positioning and environmental cues, guide attention and reflect a character's psychological state. Although Nitsche provides a thorough account of visual focalisation, he affords comparatively little consideration to the roles of audio presentation, action affordances, or access to characters' internal knowledge.

Taking a different approach, Gordon Calleja [8] proposes the concept of 'alterbiography' to characterise video game narratives as emergent, personal histories formed through player interaction with the game world. In this model, focalisation is not an inherent attribute of the game artefact but is instead variable and contingent upon the player's engagement. Calleja identifies three potential loci for focalisation: the player's own self, a controlled in-game entity, or a series of multiple characters without a singular point of identification. The former (the alterbiography of self) is present in first person games where players experience game events as happening to them [8, p. 4]. Drawing on Genette's notion of focalisation, Calleja foregrounds the experiential dimension of narrative situatedness, contrasting with Nitsche's more textually focused approach that privileges visual structures. This expansion of focalisation theory to account for a player's point of view will be further interrogated below considering its applicability to XR.

Extending these discussions, Fraser Allison [1] applies Genette's question of 'who sees?' to video games designed to convey subjective experience. He aims to create a framework for works that 'present a diversity of perspectives, and allow players to access modes of thinking [...] other than their own' [1, p. 1], a useful concept for XR analysis. Allison argues that internal focalisation appears across visual and auditory presentation, gameplay mechanics, and the selective disclosure of private knowledge. He suggests that games, by virtue of their interactivity, complicate focalisation theory while offering unique opportunities for expressing subjectivity.

A key distinction between these media and XR is the user's physical presence in the diegetic space through VR, AR or MR. Film spectators 'imaginatively construct screen space' (i.e. a 3D space is simulated on a 2D screen) whereas immersive 3D environments allow users to physically walk through space [22, p. 2]. Questions remain about theorising focalisation in virtual spaces where the user functions as camera and participant. Following Allison, I argue that Genette's concept of focalisation is complicated, but enriched, by the immersive, interactive affordances of XR, as demonstrated below.

3   Case Study Analysis

3.1   Notes on Blindness: Into Darkness

This first VR case study relays the experience of John Hull, a man who became blind in 1983 following many years of deterioration of his sight[2]. The project draws upon original diary recordings that Hull made on audiocassettes to make sense of his experience. As a companion piece to a feature film of the same name, the VR project uses a 360° environment, binaural audio and real time 3D animations to immerse the viewer in a physical space that is visualised according to sounds and Hull's narration. I experienced the project at home, after downloading it from the Meta Store, using a Meta Quest 2 headset. In this analysis, the first of three scenes is interrogated.

The opening scene is presented in a largely black space. At its start, one can see some vague blue forms that look like bushes or trees scattered around the 360° environment, and hear the sound of birds chirping. Titles that appear in the space provide an overview of Hull's story. Then one of his audio cassette recordings begins to play and he relays *'a note on the nature of acoustic space'*. Hull describes his experience of sitting in a public park and listening to the sounds around him. As he describes hearing the sounds of people's footsteps on a concrete path, the vague shape of people- adults and children- appear in the black space, with the actions of feet tracking across a path most brightly highlighted. Hull describes the distinct sounds of women's high heeled shoes and flip-flops, which we also hear, followed by the sounds of joggers and bicycles. These story agents are visually presented in the various quadrants of space as blurry blue forms pinpointed by the locations of spatialised sounds. Other noises- the rustle of a newspaper, passing cars or birds in a nearby lake- communicate how Hull builds a mental picture of his environment through sound. He describes this as *'a panorama of music and information that is absorbing and fascinating'*. As Hull emphasises, 'where there is no activity, there is no sound, and then that part of the world dies'. In other words, a lack of sound means that he is unable to visualise space. After he makes this point all sound ends and the user is left in a totally silent, black space.

According to Genette's categorisation, Hull (the one who speaks) can be considered a homodiegetic narrator who is recounting a subjective experience in the first-person tense. This form of narration aids in the user's understanding of the visuals and increases their identification with Hull as a character in the scene. The voice over also draws attention to the subjective nature of the experience, and of human perception in general. Hull's position in the space of the narrative is assumed; however, he is not visualised on screen. Rather, the user, as *perceiver*, is placed in his position (the camera), and encouraged to

---

[2] *Notes on Blindness* can be downloaded from the Meta store at this link: https://www.meta. com/en-gb/experiences/notes-on-blindness/1946326588770583/?srsltid=AfmBOorgfn_XbrF Y6JSEHH5Chtf12zuxcwMZgFnV7qi1TiknB24zV6rU.

interpret the environment in the same manner as Hull. Writing on *Notes on Blindness*, Kennedy and Atkinson describe this positioning of the user and protagonist as 'an offset-persona – a parallax view of reality – a decentered subjectivity' [19, p. 11]. This means that while positioned in the place of the central character, the user does not become him but rather is 'guided by them and accompan(ies) them' [19, p. 11].

The user's occupation of Hull's point of view in this scene, and their ability to swivel around in 360° space to choose their viewing direction, indicates a complex system of focalisation. On the one hand, the user can be considered the one 'who sees': they are placed at the centre of the scene and can select their vantage point of the action, following the visual and auditory developments described by Hull or not. In this sense that the user occupies the position of the camera, they are the focaliser of the scene; however, this form of focalisation can be considered to be variable and contingent upon their engagement, similar to that observed by Calleja in the game context. On the other hand, Hull can be considered a narrator/focaliser. Returning to Gennette, one can observe that Hull's character, as narrator, gives rise to internal focalisation, seeing as what is seen and heard is filtered through his perspective as a character within the story world, colouring the user's experience. Accordingly, the scene can be seen to involve dual focalisers (the user and Hull) both of whom are located within the 360° storyworld as perceivers.

3.2 Goliath: Playing with Reality

This game-engine-driven VR experience examines the lived experience of a young man with schizophrenia- referred to as Jon, but known online as Goliath- who spent several years in a psychiatric facility before eventually finding a sense of belonging through online multiplayer gaming[3]. Based on a true story, *Goliath* invites users to enter the protagonist's cognitive and emotional world, revisiting his memories through a combination of observational sequences and simulated gameplay. The work offers the user six degrees of freedom (6DoF) meaning that they can move around the 360° space to a limited degree and interact with objects. As with the previous case study, I downloaded the project from the Meta Store, and experienced it with a Meta Quest 2 headset.

Throughout the work, a disembodied female narrator (voiced by Tilda Swinton) addresses the user directly, guiding their engagement by encouraging vocal participation and interaction with objects via their digitally rendered hands. This occurs alongside narration from Goliath as the central character. According to Genette's taxonomy, the unnamed female voice is a heterodiegetic narrator as she is non-visualised and located outside of the storyworld. Seemingly unrelated to Goliath as a character, this narrator who adopts a second-person tense seems to function as an interrogator of the user's experience in the virtual world, as evidenced by her direct address and questioning of the user's behaviour. This approach is introduced in the work's onboarding sequence, which both acclimates the user to the virtual world and introduces the interactive devices to come. Located in a dark environment with a computer game aesthetic, the user is directly addressed by the disembodied voice who demands, *'Tell me your name'*. A user who

---

[3] *Goliath* can be downloaded from the Meta store at this link: https://www.meta.com/en-gb/experiences/goliath-playing-with-reality/3432432656819712/?srsltid=AfmBOoq1ta2OeVlVIZ ZKKk5NxjiDMQItYHy-C8UThQUEizvA9HNbaECR.

speaks their name in response finds that it is recorded through the headset microphone and repeated back to them. The female voice then instructs the user to look at their hands and complete some tasks using their hand controllers, before suggesting that *"reality is just a story after all. It's what we tell ourselves to make sense of the world. Some stories are not true. This one is. This is the story of Goliath, told from inside his mind.'* This narration draws attention to the illusory nature of virtual reality. It also reminds the user of their dual existence in both real and virtual worlds, which later finds parallels with Goliath's experience of mental illness.

In the following sequence, we are introduced to Goliath, a homodiegetic, first-person narrator whose life story is presented through various visual forms across the work. Neon-coloured lines and flashes of light illuminate the dark virtual environment as Goliath reflects on his diagnosis of schizophrenia and his journey towards recovery through gaming. A retro arcade game then appears within the 360° space, and the user is prompted to engage with it using their hand controller as a joystick. The gameplay visualises Goliath's troubled childhood and early adulthood through a 2D avatar navigating a series of levels: avoiding schoolyard bullies, confronting opponents on urban streets, and dodging pills and dancers in a nightclub. This sequence is one of several 'gameplay' moments where the user is positioned within Goliath's perspective. The user simultaneously witnesses a stylised representation of his past and experiences the act of re-living it through the lens of retro gaming, resulting in a deeply immersive encounter.

A later sequence, around the midpoint of the work, further draws upon gameplay to aid in narrative comprehension. Goliath is represented as a blurry, pink, faceless form, who swims through an abstract, cubed space. Via voiceover narration, Goliath describes his experience of taking powerful anti-psychotic medication while in a mental hospital. *'They used to churn that stuff out to people,'* he explains. *'You get hungry. You get fat'*. The user watches from an adjacent position, as brightly coloured pills fly past Goliath and towards them. Their hand controllers are visualised in the scene as blue rings, which can be strategically positioned to intercept the flying pills, making them explode on contact. Goliath groans as the volume of unpredictable flying pills increases, commenting that *'It completely knocks you out'*. Working together, this voiceover and game play communicate a sense of disorientation, overwhelm and powerlessness. In combat with the steady stream of pills, the user is encouraged to experience these sensations firsthand, a technique that may influence their comprehension of Goliath's experience.

These sequences demonstrate the ways in which Goliath's subjective experience as protagonist is communicated through a variety of techniques- the voiceover narration, stylised environment and ludic affordances. As Allison observes, the audiovisual style of a game environment, whether stylised or photorealistic, 'can be suggestive of the subjectivity of the character that views it – as is commonly seen in specific cases such as hallucinatory sequences' [1, p. 13]. On a related note, he suggests that a game's ludic affordances might 'convey a great deal about the character's nature, goals and mental models, as well as their abilities' [1, p, 13]. We see these techniques at play throughout *Goliath*, with the overall visual aesthetic and various game play sequences highlighting his feelings of isolation, levels of agency and ultimate recovery from mental illness.

In the latter part of the sequence described above, Goliath's body evaporates and then reappears, sleeping on a bed in a darkened room. The stream of pills that fly towards the user slows down, making the gameplay easier. At this point the heterodiegetic voiceover returns. '*I see you're getting more comfortable in this place*' she comments. '*You're getting the hang of it. [...] But are you still in two places at once? From the outside you look like someone who is doing something very peculiar- fighting thin air.*' Once again, the user is reminded of their dual existence in real and virtual worlds, and invited to make connections between their own and Goliath's subjectivity.

As with *Notes on Blindness*, *Goliath* appears to feature two internal focalisers: the user and Goliath, both of whom are situated within the storyworld, interacting with other story agents. For much of the project, the persepctives of Goliath and the user can be considered distinct in the sense that Goliath (as a visually represented character) presents his subjective account of a past experience, while the user (in the position of the camera) ingests story material based on their selected field of vision. However, ludic elements encourage a blurring of perspectives, allowing the user to experience gaming through Goliath's eyes, and demonstrating how focalisation is variable in the work. Direct address by the non-visualised female narrator emphasises the user's status as focaliser, providing suggestions for how audiovisual and interactive elements might be perceived throughout. Although the user cannot alter the outcome of Goliath's narrative, their role as both player and interactor influences how certain sequences unfold, allowing their participation to shape aspects of the storytelling process.

3.3 Turbulence: Jamais Vu

This short, installation-based, mixed reality work explores the chronic vestibular migraine condition of its creator, Ben Andrews[4]. Upon suffering an attack of vestibular migraine, Andrews loses his sense of orientation, balance, and spatial awareness. The condition also affects his experience of reality, where everything familiar suddenly seems new and different, a neurological phenomenon called 'jamais vu' (the opposite of 'déjà vu'). Andrews provides a simulation of this experience for a user who sits at an office desk adorned with objects, wearing a VR headset. Pass-through technology is drawn upon so that the user sees a distorted version of their environment in the headset. Objects are viewed as blurry white outlines against a black backdrop. One can view the desk, other objects and one's own hands with a further distortion: the image has been flipped horizontally, so that objects on the left of the desk are depicted to the right and vice versa. According to the logic of the environment, if the user waves their left hand in front of their eyes, it thus appears as their right hand, fostering feelings of disorientation, and parallelling Andrew's experience of a vestibular migraine. I viewed this location-based work in a festival setting, taking notes on its narrative and stylistic elements. My analysis is additionally informed by a review of promotional material and interviews with the director.

Voiceover narration from Andrews guides the viewer's experience of the work, allowing him to speak directly to the user as subject/director to share experience and instructions. This approach to narration, which can be aligned with an established strand of auto-ethnographic documentary, foregrounds the subjectivity of the 'image-maker'. As a disembodied homodiegetic narrator, Andrews moves between first-person and second

---

[4] Please note that *Turbulence: Jamais Vu* is not available for online download.

person address as he 1) interrogates his own bodily experience and 2) encourages the user to explore their perception in the story world. This is evidenced in the following excerpt, which is heard as the user examines their hands:

The onset of 'jamais vu' always catches me like this. Like you, I find myself looking at my hands. I know that they're mine but I'm struck by how different they appear. My body suddenly feels new, foreign, like some form of avatar.

This is a complex use of voiceover that shifts from 'I' to 'you' tenses to deliver narrative information and encourage audience interaction. After some moments, Andrews presents the user with a task that provides further insight into his condition: they must retrieve some aspirin tablets from a container on the desk and place them in a nearby mug. This sounds simple, but the inversion of the image makes it incredibly difficult, as one's visual perception and bodily movement is no longer aligned (in other words, your hands do not move as you would expect them to). This disconnection between what is seen and what is felt gives rise to feelings of nausea as 'normal' proprioceptive perceptions are manipulated. Andrews further describes his development of symptoms, and the MR image distorts once more, becoming wavy and unstable, further conveying his experience of disability.

Returning to Barbara et al. [4, 5] one might consider how Andrews' voiceover enables the user's role within the story world to be made clear. I would argue that his use of direct address encourages the user to draw parallels between their own and Andrews' experience, highlighting the work's status as a simulation of the latter. The suggestion that a disembodied voice can encourage self-identification within the diegesis and an increased sense of presence, would seem applicable here [4, 5]. As is the case with *Notes on Blindness,* the user is positioned in the place of the central character, but does not become him. Rather, they retain the 'offset- persona' described by Kennedy and Atkinson [19], drawing upon their own life experience and sensibilities as they react to audiovisual elements.

Given this positioning, I would argue that this third project also features two internal focalisers: the user and Andrews, both of whom are located in the diegetic space as perceivers. Whereas Andrews is the one 'who speaks', the user's physical positioning in the place of the camera foregrounds them as the one 'who sees' in a literal sense. It must be noted that whereas the previous two case studies feature visuals that have been authored by the work's creators, *Turbulence* incorporates the user's physical surroundings into the work, meaning that the construction of imagery is more heavily influenced by the user, despite the staged scene of the desk and its contents. Representations of the user's hands, and their engagement with a physical environment (fostered by MR technology), further emphasises their centrality to the project. However, the project's status as a simulation of Andrews' experience positions the director as a narrator/focaliser, seeing as the image distortions reflect his experience of a vestibular migraine. As is the case with *Notes on Blindness,* Andrews' first-person narration orders the work's narrative, while his direct address to the user encourages physical engagement and introspection.

4 Discussion

The above exploration (summarised in Table 1) demonstrates the complexity of narration for XR storytelling. Considering the qualities of the three works, one can make several observations regarding the use of voiceover narration and styles of focalisation.

Table 1. Overview of narrators and focalisers in the three case studies

XR Title	*Notes on Blindness: Into Darkness*	*Goliath: Playing with Reality*	*Turbulence: Jamais Vu*
Narrator/s	John Hull (homodiegetic, non-visualised)	Goliath (homodiegetic, visualised) Anonymous Female (heterodiegetic, non-visualised)	Ben Andrews (homodiegetic, non-visualised)
Style of voiceover narration	First-person	First-person (Goliath) Second-person (Anonymous Female)	Variable
Focalisers	The User John Hull	The User Goliath	The User Ben Andrews

Firstly, voiceover would appear to be a multifunctional narrative tool that not only delivers exposition, but also meta-narratives and directives for the user. The first-person narration that appears in all three works fosters cognitive and perceptual alignment with the protagonist (especially in simulating sensory alterations), while second-person address (e.g., the interrogative female narrator in *Goliath*) directs user engagement through instructional or reflective prompts. Also in *Goliath*, the non-character narrator functions as a meta-narrative agent, reminding the user of their dual presence in both physical and virtual worlds. In the instance of *Turbulence*, the narrator blends the roles of internal narrator, facilitator, and interlocutor, illustrating the increasing hybridity of voiceover in XR contexts.

Secondly, focalisation in XR can involve dual focalisers: the user and a narrating character who is seen and/or heard in the diegesis. This duality generates a layered perceptual structure where the user occupies the camera's physical point of view (i.e., the 'one who sees' in Genette's terms) while simultaneously receiving a filtered subjective experience via the internal focalisation of a narrator-character. This shared or decentered subjectivity results in the 'parallax view' described by Kennedy and Atkinson [19], where the user's perspective is aligned with but never fully identical to the protagonist. As an approach to narration, this allows users to reflect on their own subjectivity while experiencing another's, an especially powerful affordance in works dealing with disability, mental illness, or altered perception. This structure reflects a broader move away from fixed focalisation found in traditional film and literature and toward more variable and participatory experiences, such as those described by Calleja and Allison.

Moreover, the user's presence within the diegetic space of an XR story, where they can choose their field of view and/or interact with objects, transforms focalisation into a dynamic system whereby gameplay mechanics and ludic elements can shape how users access, interpret, and internalise character experience. *Goliath* and *Turbulence* demonstrate how actions such as fighting off pills or reaching for aspirin create bodily alignment with character affect, giving focalisation a kinaesthetic dimension absent in non-interactive media. This interaction does not necessarily change the narrative's outcome, but it does shape its affective and cognitive impact on the user as perceiver.

5 Conclusion

The analysis presented above demonstrates how XR narration can cultivate a shared field of perception, where meaning arises through the interplay of voiceover, sensory stimuli, and user interaction. Across the three case studies, voiceover narration emerges as variable and relational, often blending first and second-person strategies to produce complex, layered perspectives. Focalisation in these environments becomes embodied, contingent, and interactive- no longer confined to textual or visual cues but instead shaped by the user's active, sensory participation. These narrative dynamics not only reconfigure how stories are told but also enable new modes of subjectivity, making XR especially potent for conveying personal, embodied, and often marginalised experiences.

The three works chosen for analysis reflect a particular strand of XR storytelling that foregrounds non-typical bodily experience and its affective communication. While narrative and stylistic features such as voiceover narration and alignment between user and character are recurring motifs in VR and MR storytelling, they represent only one set of possibilities among many. Future research might expand on this study by examining a broader range of XR works to test and refine these findings.

Returning to debates around the distinction between focalisation and interpretation (as explored by Ciccoricco and others), I would suggest that XR invites us to reconsider these boundaries. In traditional narrative theory, the reader cannot be a focaliser, as they remain outside the diegetic space. XR, however, embeds the user within the perceptual frame, reconfiguring the dynamics of narrative reception. In works like *Notes on Blindness*, *Goliath* and *Turbulence*, the user is not merely interpreting events but participating in situated, embodied acts of perception that materially shape how the narrative unfolds. This co-presence challenges conventional separations between narrator, character, and audience, and suggests that the user may be understood as a kind of co-focaliser who is neither entirely autonomous nor fully absorbed into a character's viewpoint. Such a perspective urges us to expand focalisation theory to account for hybrid modes of perception within immersive environments, where point of view is not simply assigned but dynamically constructed through sensory and spatial engagement. Ultimately, this rethinking underscores the narrative specificity of XR as a medium uniquely capable of delivering insight through lived, embodied experience.

Disclosure of Interests.   The author has no competing interests to declare that are relevant to the content of this article.

References

1. Allison, F.: Whose mind is the signal? Focalization in video game narratives. In: DiGRA Conference (2015)

2. Bal, M.: Narratology: Introduction to the Theory of Narrative. Trans. von Boheemen, C. University of Toronto Press, Toronto (1985)
3. Bal, M.: Narratology: Introduction to the Theory of Narrative. University of Toronto Press, Toronto (2009)
4. Barbara, J., Haahr, M.: Who am I that acts? The use of voice in virtual reality interactive narratives. In: Nunes, N., Oakley, I., Nisi, V. (eds.) ICIDS 2021. LNCS, vol. 13066, pp. 3–12. Springer, Cham (2021). https://doi.org/10.1007/978-3-030-92300-6_1
5. Barbara, J., Haahr, M.: The role of voice in virtual reality interactive narratives. J. Interact. Narrat. **1**(1) (2024). https://doi.org/10.62937/JIN.2024.VQRM5201
6. Bevan, C., et al.: Behind the curtain of the "ultimate empathy machine": on the composition of virtual reality nonfiction experiences. In: Proceedings of the 2019 CHI Conference on Human Factors in Computing Systems, pp. 1–12 (2019)
7. Bordwell, D., Thompson, K., Smith, J.: Film Art: An Introduction, 11th edn. McGraw-Hill Higher Education, New York (2016)
8. Calleja, G.: Experiential narrative in game environments. In: DiGRA '09 - Proceedings of the 2009 DiGRA International Conference: Breaking New Ground: Innovation in Games, Play, Practice and Theory. Brunel University, London (2009)
9. Ciccoricco, D.: Focalization and digital fiction. Narrative **20**(3), 255–276 (2012)
10. Deleyto, C.: Focalisation in film narrative. Atlantis **13**(1/2), 159–177 (1991)
11. Dolan, D., Parets, M.: Redefining the axiom of story: the VR and 360 video complex. https://techcrunch.com/2016/01/14/redefining-the-axiom-of-story-the-vr-and-360-video-complex/. Accessed 10 Jan 2024
12. Dooley, K.: Virtual Reality Narratives: Embodied Encounters in Space. Springer, Cham (2024). https://doi.org/10.1007/978-3-031-64965-3
13. Genette, G.: Narrative Discourse. Trans. Lewin, J.E. Cornell University Press, Ithaca (1980)
14. Goliath: Playing with Reality (VR experience). Directed by Barry Gene Murphy and May Abdalla, Anagram, UK (2021). Trailer: https://www.youtube.com/watch?v=V2x9XVY9mEc
15. Hassan, R.: Digitality, virtual reality and the 'empathy machine.' Digit. Journal. **8**(2), 195–212 (2020)
16. Herman, D., Jahn, M., Ryan, M.L. (eds.): Routledge Encyclopedia of Narrative Theory. Routledge, London (2010)
17. Holloway-Attaway, L., Fawcus, J.: Affective sound: developing a critical framework for audio-based interactive digital narratives. In: Murray, J.T., Reyes, M.C. (eds.) ICIDS 2024. LNCS, vol. 15468, pp. 205–213. Springer, Cham (2025). https://doi.org/10.1007/978-3-031-78450-7_14
18. Jones, S., Dawkins, S.: Walking in someone else's shoes: creating empathy in the practice of immersive film. Media Pract. Educ. **19**(3), 298–312 (2018)
19. Kennedy, H., Atkinson, S.: Virtual humanity: empathy, embodiment and disorientation in humanitarian VR experience design. Refractory: J. Entertain. Media **30**, 2 (2018)
20. Kool, H.: The ethics of immersive journalism: a rhetorical analysis of news storytelling with virtual reality technology. Intersect: Stanford J. Sci. Technol. Soc. **9**(3) (2016)
21. Kozloff, S.: Invisible Storytellers: Voice-over Narration in American Fiction Film. University of California Press, Berkeley (1989)
22. McMahan, A., Buckland, W.: Cognitive schemas and virtual reality. In: Intelligent Agent, vol. 5 (2005)
23. Metz, C.: Film Language: A Semiotics of the Cinema. Trans. Taylor, M. Oxford University Press, New York (1974)
24. Nicolae, D.F.: Spectator perspectives in virtual reality cinematography: the witness, the hero and the impersonator. Ekphrasis **20**(2), 168–180 (2018)
25. Nitsche, M.: Focalization in 3D video games. In: Digital Proceedings of Future Play, pp. 13–15 (2005)

26. Nixon, L.: I focalize, you focalize, we all focalize together: audience participation in Persepolis. Image Narrat. **11**(2), 92–99 (2010)
27. Notes on Blindness: Into Darkness (VR experience). Directed by Arnaud Colinart, Amaury La Burthe, Peter Middleton, and James Spinney, Archers Mark & Atlas V, UK/France (2019). https://www.youtube.com/watch?v=Fj1HFTT1Qfk
28. Turbulence: Jamais Vu (Mixed Reality work). Directed by Ben Andrews, Australia (2024). Artist Statement: https://www.youtube.com/watch?v=K6Fpufx54aw
29. Vosmeer, M., Roth, C., Koenitz, H.: Who are you? Voice-over perspective in surround video. In: Koenitz, H., Ferri, G., Haahr, M., Sezen, D., Sezen, T. (eds.) ICIDS 2017. LNCS, vol. 10690, pp. 221–232. Springer, Cham (2017). https://doi.org/10.1007/978-3-319-71027-3_18
30. Weaving, S.: Evoke, don't show: narration in cinematic virtual reality and the making of Entangled. Virtual Creat **11**(1), 147–162 (2021)

Meet *Daiyu* in The Era of GenAI: Using LLMs to Remediate Classics into Interactive Digital Narratives

Yuxuan Huang, Kexin Xiang, Gauransh Sharma, Reshad Rabbi, Ran Ju, and Jussi Pekka Holopainen(✉)

City University of Hong Kong, Hong Kong SAR, China
{yhuang573-c,kxiang9-c,gsharma5-c,rrabbi2-c,ranju4-c}@my.cityu.edu.hk,
jholopai@cityu.edu.hk

Abstract. In this paper, we explore the integration of large language models (LLMs) in interactive digital narratives (IDNs) in the context of remediating the classic Chinese novel, *Hong Lou Meng* (HLM). Adopting Research through Design (RtD), we developed an LLM-driven IDN prototype that allows players to interact with Lin Daiyu, the iconic female character of HLM. We then playtested the prototype with seven HLM readers and five IDN designers through semi-structured interviews. Our findings reveal the potential and challenges of using LLMs as character and plot design materials for IDNs that remediate classic literature. We conclude by proposing two design strategies for LLM-driven IDNs that ensure both player engagement and narrative coherence: 1) Designing towards engaging AI and humans in the same task, and 2) Expanding AI responses beyond predictable boundaries.

Keywords: Interactive digital narrative · Large language model · design material · remediation · cultural heritage

1 Introduction

Interactive digital narratives (IDNs) represent a narrative form that employs digital technologies to enable players to experience and enact a storyline through character embodiment and world exploration [16,32]. One major form of IDNs is narrative-based videogames. For example, in *The Witcher 3: Wild Hunt*[1], players role-play as a monster hunter navigating a fantasy world in search of his adopted daughter. Their choices throughout the experience meaningfully alter story outcomes and character relationships, creating unique narrative paths that invite multiple playthroughs.

The recent boost of large language models (LLMs) and generative AI (GenAI) is revolutionizing IDNs by enabling real-time narrative generation that responds dynamically to player actions [23,40]. This technological shift allows IDNs to

---

[1] https://en.wikipedia.org/wiki/The_Witcher_3:_Wild_Hunt.

M. C. Reyes and F. Nack (Eds.): ICIDS 2025, LNCS 16375, pp. 29–47, 2026.
https://doi.org/10.1007/978-3-032-12405-0_3

evolve into a highly personalized experience that was previously unattainable. Contemporary IDN platforms such as *AI Dungeon*[2] utilize LLMs to generate stories based on players' text prompts, opening up infinite plot possibilities. However, the current LLM systems, while impressive in many regards, still struggle to create convincing interactive narratives [23]. The player community of *AI Dungeon* often discusses that off-topic input may derail the storyline and disrupt the coherence of the whole story [36]. On the other hand, limiting the scope of player input risks reducing interactivity and narrative diversity. This trade-off highlights the need to balance player autonomy and story quality when integrating LLMs in IDNs [36]. In this sense, LLMs are far from being a tool that can autonomously provide interactive stories that are sophisticated enough, but instead, design material that HCI researchers can utilize to explore new design possibilities for application domains such as IDNs.

Hong Lou Meng (HLM), also known as *The Story of the Stone*, is a classic Chinese novel written by Cao Xueqin in the 18th century. It follows the decline of the Jia family and the tragic romance between Jia Baoyu and his cousin Lin Daiyu. The novel's literary sophistication makes it ideal for adaptation across different media, or, more technically, narrative remediation. Meanwhile, its incompleteness – with only 80 of 120 chapters by the original author – leaves more room for creative reinterpretation. So far, HLM has been remediated into various media, including television series (e.g., the renowned 1987 television series[3].), stage productions, and videogames (e.g., *Stone Story* on Steam[4]). With the rise of LLMs, HLM can now be remediated into a more advanced form of IDN that dynamically adjusts story content based on player input.

This leads to our research questions and design goal: *What are the affordances and challenges of using LLMs in the narrative remediation of HLM? (RQ1)* and *How can LLMs be used effectively for narrative design within the context of the remediation of classic novels? (RQ2)*

We introduce an interactive prototype that integrates LLMs for players to converse and interact with Lin Daiyu. To clarify our design intent, we did not develop AI Daiyu as a supportive AI companion [24], an LLM-driven non-player character (NPC) designed to enhance gaming immersion through contextually relevant interactions [15], or a digital afterlife system aimed at preserving LIN Daiyu's personality and memories for continued digital presence [26]. Rather, our focus centers on exploring the distinct IDN experiences that emerge from designing "game-like" interactions with AI Daiyu. By adopting Research through Design (RtD) as the guiding methodology, we explored the unique affordances and challenges of LLMs as design material for IDNs. RtD is a "rapid response methodology" that informs insights concerning evolving disruptive technologies [6], which, in our case, is LLMs. Using the prototype as a conversation starter [27], we conducted semi-structured interviews with seven HLM readers and five professional IDN designers to explore their experience of narrative remedia-

---

[2] https://aidungeon.com/.

[3] https://en.wikipedia.org/wiki/Dream_of_the_Red_Chamber_(1987_TV_series)

[4] https://store.steampowered.com/app/2761570/_Stone_Story/.

tion integrated with LLMs, as well as the design possibilities and constraints that LLMs open up for IDNs.

Our research contribution is two-fold: 1) We presented an LLM-integrated IDN approach that allows players to converse with Daiyu, whose responses are real-time generated and personalized to players' inputs (as opposed to pre-scripted). It is demonstrated with an online prototype playable in a browser. 2) We employed RtD as the overarching methodology and conducted a user study to inform design implications on utilizing LLMs as material for character and plot design in narrative remediation. Specifically, concerning the "authoring problem" [37] in IDNs, we propose future designs to engage AI and humans in the same task and expand AI responses beyond what is predictable.

2   Related Work

In this section, we clarify several concepts that are essential in our work. We first introduce the definition of remediation and how narrative relates to it. Next, we explain the rationale for choosing interactive digital narratives (IDNs) as the specific narrative method and Daiyu as the character to narrate the story. We propose integrating LLMs in the process to mitigate the prevalent "authoring problem" in IDNs. Last, we elucidate the notion of design material in HCI, illustrating how narrative remediation helps inform knowledge of using LLMs as design material.

2.1   Remediation

According to Marshall McLuhan [29], media stands for the various technologies, including print, television, and digital platforms like websites and social media, that mediate our communication. They are not "hollow pipes" that just carry messages. Instead, as McLuhan famously argues, "the medium is the message"-the specific properties of a medium also influence our perception and under-standing of the world.

For Jay Bolter and Richard Grusin, media is also defined by the process of "remediation": "What is a medium? We offer this simple definition: a medium is that which remediates. It is that which appropriates the techniques, forms, and social significance of other media and attempts to rival or refashion them in the name of the real." [9] In other words, remediation refers to the process by which new media represent (i.e., absorb, refashion, and rework) old media, and together they constitute the "media ecology" of their time.

In narrative studies, remediation also serves as a particularly useful concept in framing questions within the field of transmedial narratology [33]. According to Ryan's framework of transmedia narratology [33], our research aligns with a form of narrative remediation that "transposes from one medium to another," as exemplified by adaptations of novels into films, novelizations of movies or computer games, and computer games originating from literary works, etc. One similar concept to this form of remediation might be "fan fiction," a genre of writing where fans create their own stories using characters and settings from existing works of fiction. While remediation and fan fiction are two valid, different approaches to understanding our project, fan fiction highlights its status as a creative reimagining of the narrative universe of HLM. We frame our work as remediation to emphasize that we are exploring the specific narrative affordances/limitations of LLMs as compared to those of print through the lens of adapting HLM into an LLM-powered IDN.

2.2   Interactive Digital Narratives and Character

Narrative can be considered to operate on two basic levels: story and discourse. Story refers to the sequence of events, characters, and settingsthe "4what" of the narrative, while discourse, moreover, concerns the way the story is toldthe "how" [3,14,30]. Traditional storytelling forms, such as novels and films, offer linear experiences through predetermined sequences. In contrast, interactive digital narratives (IDNs) allow players to actively participate in the storytelling process, making choices that influence the direction and outcome of the story. Transforming a traditional linear story into a digital interactive one has become an increasingly popular form of narrative remediation in recent years, as evidenced by the widespread success of video games like *Black Myth: Wukong* (2024), *Middle-earth* series (2014–2017), and *80 Days* (2014), to name just a few.

A story element that undergoes significant transformation in this kind of narrative remediation is "character." While literary text-based narratological discussions conventionally frame character as a textual construct and structural component of the narrative [3,4,13,31], in IDNs, character is made to dynamically adapt and react to the player's choices and actions [2]. As Aarseth [1] argues, "the most effective way of creating ludo-narrative content is to invest in character-creation, by making the characters rich, deep and interesting." A corollary of this argument would be that character becomes a largely foregrounded narrative element in IDNs, where the player cares less about the predefined plotlines, but more about how they themselves can enact the story through interacting with or embodying an interesting character.

Today, GenAI has been used to create IDNs [23]. However, we are still facing the prevalent "authoring problem"the challenge of developing interactive narratives that grant player agency while maintaining content coherent and engaging [37]. The remediation of a classic can even complicate the "authoring problem". The player's prior knowledge of the source material may lead to expectations about character behavior, plot development, or thematic consistency, thus making the design of meaningful and engaging interactions more difficult. The use of LLMs, as this research proposes, may offer a potential solution to the authoring problem by enabling responsive, real-time content generation that remains largely coherent with the original work, while still allowing players creative space to explore and interact. To demonstrate this, our research aims to create an interactive narrative that remediates *Hong Lou Meng* by focusing on crafting a digital consciousness of Lin Daiyu, the female protagonist and the soul of the novel, within our story, supported by LLMs.

2.3   Technology as Design Material in HCI

In Human-Computer Interaction (HCI), design material refers to the elements and tools that designers use to create interactive systems, similar to how physical materials are utilized in traditional design fields like architecture or fashion. These materials can be tangible, such as sensors and screens, or intangible, including code, algorithms, data, and interaction patterns [20,21]. By framing technology as design material, we refer to its design innovation or design contribution [38]. Different from engineers who create technical innovation by inventing new technology that allows new capabilities, designers assemble or reassemble known technologies for novel user scenarios [28,38]. In this process, designers "converse with existing materials" [38,39] to envision things that haven't existed before, and the materials "talk back to designers" [38,39] on how the technology opens up design possibilities as well as constraints [34]. Recent HCI research has started to explore the use of AI [21,39] and machine learning (ML) [5,17,38] as design material. Interestingly, all these studies point out that AI (or ML) has unique capabilities to create novel applications and services that no other technology has ever achieved. LLMs are now sophisticated enough to understand, generate, and manipulate human language in real-time, creating unlimited yet unknown design possibilities for IDNs.

The notion of design material aligns closely with the concept of remediation. Our research aims to remediate the Chinese classic *Hong Lou Meng* through IDNs. To achieve that, we designed a dialogue game where we implement a conversational agent remediating from the representative female character in HLM, LIN Daiyu, to tell the narrative. The conversational agent, supported by LLMs, is capable of responding to the player's input in real-time, and the player's responses to the agent are used to determine the story outcome. In our remediation of HLM, we designed an LLM-driven, dialogue-based game prototype to gain insights into LLMs as design material for IDNs.

3   Methodology

In this section, we first justify our choice of Research through Design (RtD) as the leading methodology. We detail our design objective and process, as well as the features of our prototype. The prototype is used as a discussion starter in semi-structured interviews with HLM readers and IDN designers to answer our research questions.

3.1   Research Through Design

Research through Design (RtD) is an approach of inquiry in which knowledge is generated through the design process [18,35]. Researchers probe "what the world could and should be" [35] by creating artifacts, such as products, systems, or services. These artifacts serve as both research outcomes and ways to generate design knowledge. RtD is especially useful in rapidly responding to emerging technologies [6], LLMs in our case, and informing future work. Our design decisions on the prototype are made for the narrative remediation of HLM. Therefore, we claim that our aim is not to evaluate the user experience of the prototype, such as the UX issues. Instead, our design-led inquiry uses the prototype as a "conversation starter" with related stakeholders, through which we aim to gain design knowledge on how LLMs can be utilized as design material for IDNs.

Our RtD study is structured as follows: in the design and implementation phase, we constantly iterated our design idea while we implemented the prototype using an agile approach; then, during the user study, we used the prototype as a conversation starter [27] in semi-structured interviews to gain insights from two different groups, namely HLM readers and IDS designers.

3.2   Prototype Design

Design Objective. This research aims to create an application where players can interact with the digital character (i.e., Lin Daiyu) and narrative elements in a way that would not be possible without using LLMs. This system showcases how classical texts like HLM can be brought to life in a new, interactive medium, preserving the depth and nuance of the original story by integrating LLMs.

Design Process. The initial idea for the system came from one of the author's PhD project (forthcoming), which focused on remediating HLM as an Augmented Reality book. Our team conducted an extensive literature review and a survey of how HLM had been remediated in other media. The authors then conducted seven weekly informal ideation and design workshops. The sessions lasted an average of an hour and had at least three of the authors present in each. In the end, we decided to use LLM-powered IDNs for remediation and selected one overarching theme, the Buddhist conception of reality as illusion and illusion as reality as handled in the original novel, and three major features: focus on interaction with Daiyu as a dynamic character [8]; include prominent social rituals such as gift giving, poetry recitation, and riddles as game mechanics; and provide clear narrative progression and closure.

The design process then followed an iterative, exploratory approach centered on translating the selected theme and features into interactive affordances. Early ideas were sketched through Figma-based semi-interactive prototypes to demonstrate interaction flows. Besides, drawing from Blom [8], we implemented a preliminary system of affection to track dimensions such as trust, delight, empathy, and awareness, influencing both the surface style of character responses and the narrative possibilities available to the player. Parallel to these developments, we experimented with poetry composition and riddle challenges as turn-based mini-games embedded within dialogue sequences. To test the overall flow and coherence of the narrative experience, we developed a Twine[5] prototype incorporating key interaction sequences and multiple branching arcs. These iterative and parallel prototyping stages informed one another, helping refine design priorities and revealing how the system might dynamically support both emergent play and structured narrative arcs.

Implementation Process. The interactive system follows an Agile development process, using iterative cycles of design, implementation, and evaluation. The core architecture is built with Flask[6], a lightweight Python web framework that supports a modular structure. This structure separates key components such as conversation handling, stage transitions, poetry generation, riddle interaction, and character introspection. The system uses Flask-Session for secure state tracking and GPT-4o[7] to generate dynamic, context-aware dialogues. We evaluated the suitability of Gemini, Llama, Hermes, GPT-4, GPT-4 mini, and GPT-4o models for our project. We finally chose GPT-4o based on the ease of fictional character creation, stronger conversational abilities, and lower implementation effort and cost. We fine-tuned the GPT-4o model to do specific prompt engineering to train the AI Daiyu by feeding it with: 1) the English version of the entire HLM novel [12], 2) representative dialogues between Daiyu and other characters from the novel, and 3) outlier questions and possible Daiyu way of answers composed by an HLM expert (the fifth author). Detailed prompts can be found at https://greathyx718.github.io/meet_daiyu/prompts.

System Mechanism. This section introduces our prototype from two dimensions: the storyline and functions. Referring to the concept from game design, the storyline is the framework that guides the player's narrative experience throughout the interactions within the system, while the functions encompass the interactions that players can perform on it. The display video of the prototype can be found at https://youtu.be/CPLKupsuMyQ.

Storyline. The narrative consists of four stages, each with its own emotional theme for Daiyu. Every stage has various pre-scripted endings, which are achieved based on what the player chats with Daiyu. In the first stage, Daiyu is in a mood of *peace*, and the conversation between her and the player is mainly greetings and self-introductions. At that time, Daiyu considers herself a real human and believes that the world of *Dream of the Red Chamber* is a real, existing world where she lives. The second stage is about *doubt*, where Daiyu discovers that something has gone wrong and questions the player's world. In this stage, the player is expected to tell Daiyu more about the real world outside the novel or prove that they know everything about her and the other characters in HLM. In the third stage, Daiyu realizes that she is fictional but *struggles* to accept this truth. She wonders (in a feeling of *crisis*) who, where, and even what

---

[5] https://twinery.org/.

[6] https://en.wikipedia.org/wiki/Flask_(web_framework).

[7] https://openai.com/index/hello-gpt-4o/.

she is. In this stage, the player is expected to engage in a more reflective discussion with her on existential questions such as "What is life?", "Can characters have life?", "What is the real world?", etc. In the fourth stage, the conversation is more open-ended. Daiyu *accepts* that she is just a fictional character and *clams down*. Before "a final goodbye," she asks the player if they have anything else to say.

Functions. Our prototype is mainly a conversation app where players put text prompts into the chat box, and Daiyu replies accordingly (see Fig. 1). What Daiyu says to the player is all generated by GenAI in real-time. We train the LLM (GPT-4o) to imitate the way Daiyu thinks and speaks in the original novel. There are four functions, namely "Poem," "Riddle," "Gift," and "Peek into Mind", designed to support the progression of the storyline. Details are explained as follows:

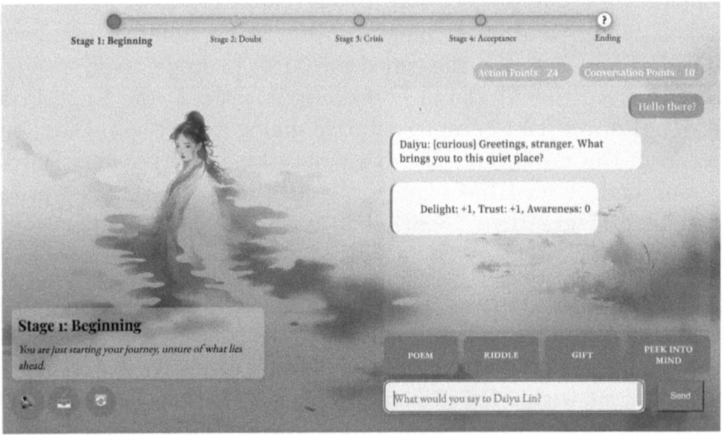

Fig. 1. The main conversation interface of the prototype.

1. *Poem.* The player clicks the *POEM* button, and Daiyu will propose a keyword and invite the player to compose a poem. A panel pops up, showing the keyword, as well as a textfield and 15 options of poetic imagery. The player enters the theme that they want to express through the poem and selects up to five poetic images they want their poem to contain. The poem will then be generated by the LLM and appear as a text input in the main chat box, where the player will have one last chance to edit it. The whole process is elaborated in Fig. 2.

2. *Riddle.* The player clicks the *RIDDLE* button, and Daiyu will challenge the player through riddles. The riddles are all related to Daiyu's experiences in the original novel, and are all generated by Daiyu (LLMs) in real-time. The player answers the riddle through the chat box. The whole process is elaborated in Fig. 3.

3. *Gift.* The player clicks the *GIFT* button, and the gift shop panel will pop up. There are eight gifts in it, which are Buddhist beads, a drum set, an HLM book, a motorcycle, palace flowers, a mobile phone, a steamed crab, and a wedding dress. When the player clicks to choose one gift, it will appear in the chat box together with the gift-giving message. The player can edit the message before giving the gift to Daiyu. The whole process is elaborated in Fig. 4.

4. *Peek into Mind.* This function shows what Daiyu is thinking right now. The player can also check the value of Daiyu's dynamic traits here. It serves as a hint for the player to continue the current dialogue. The whole process is elaborated in Fig. 5.

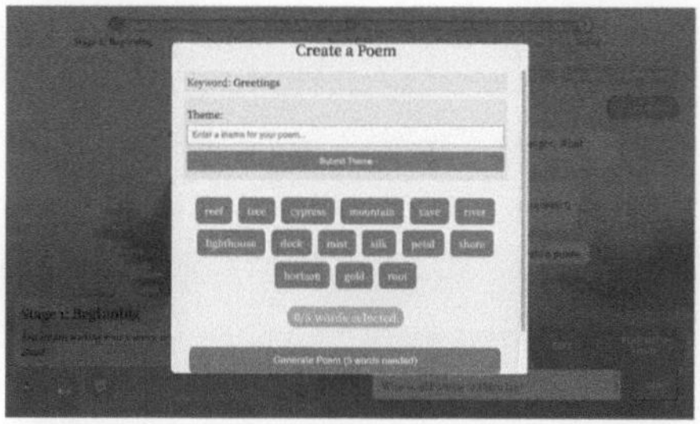

(a) Step 1: The player clicks the *POEM* button, and the poem editing panel pops up.

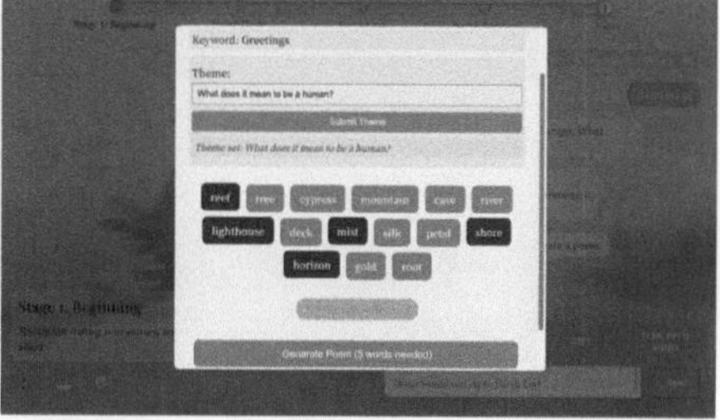
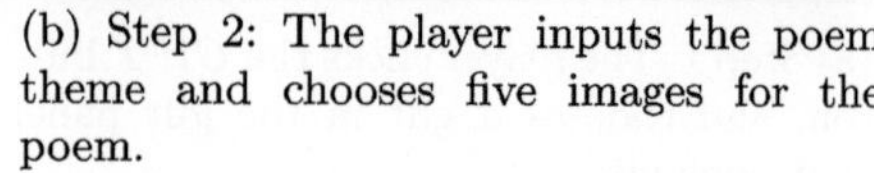

(b) Step 2: The player inputs the poem theme and chooses five images for the poem.

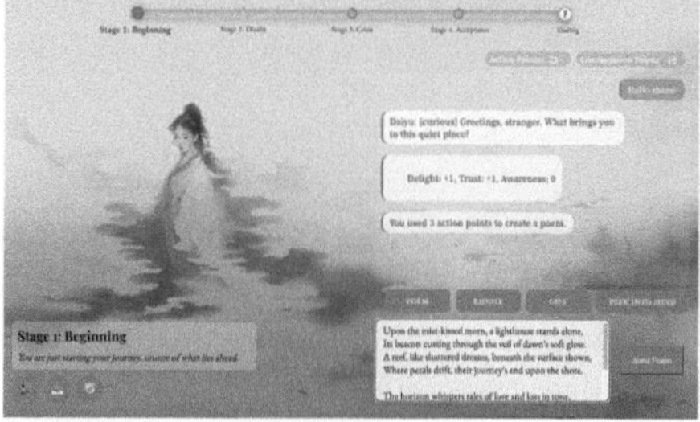

(c) Step 3: The poem is generated in the chat box where the player can still edit it before sending it to Daiyu.

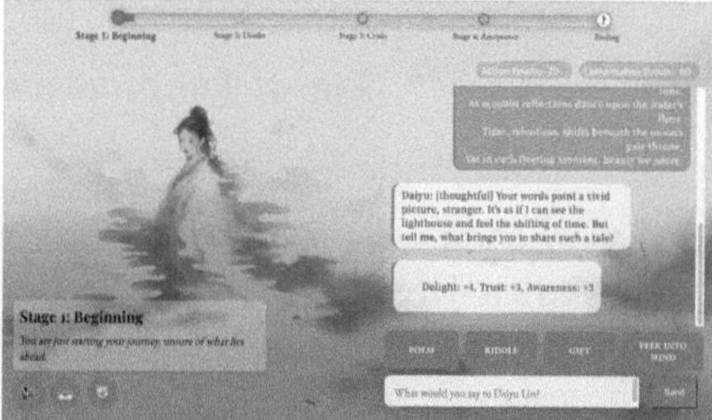

(d) Step 4: Daiyu comments on the poem.

Fig. 2. The process of composing a poem with Daiyu.

State Variables. We designed various variables to connect these four functions, consisting of action points, conversation points, Daiyu's dynamic traits (including awareness, delight, and trust), and her stable traits (including temperament, taste, playfulness, and curiosity). The design of the dynamic and stable straits was based on the system of affection (SA) [7].

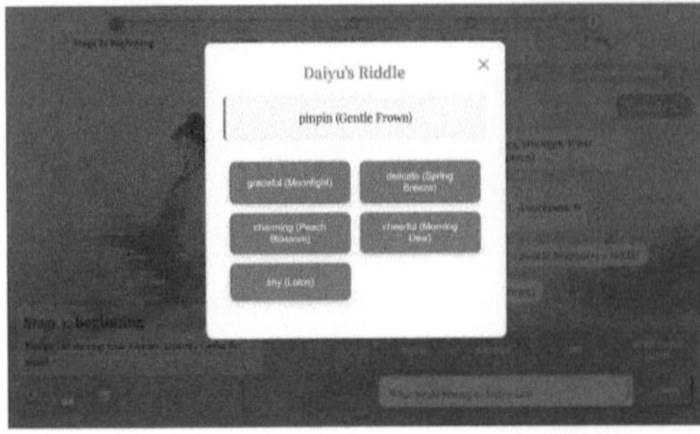 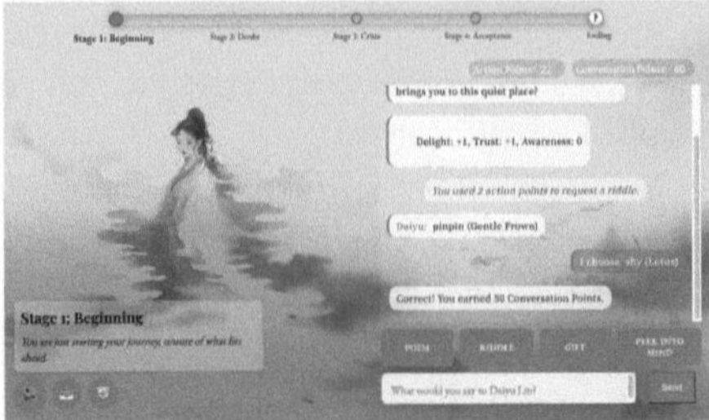

(a) Step 1: The player clicks the *RIDDLE* button, and the riddle panel then pops up.

(b) Step 2: The player chooses an answer on the panel, and the answer will be sent to Daiyu in the chat box automatically.

Fig. 3. The process of a riddle challenge with Daiyu.

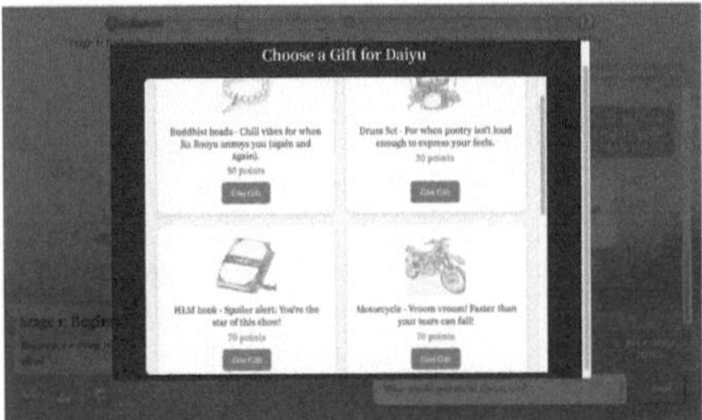 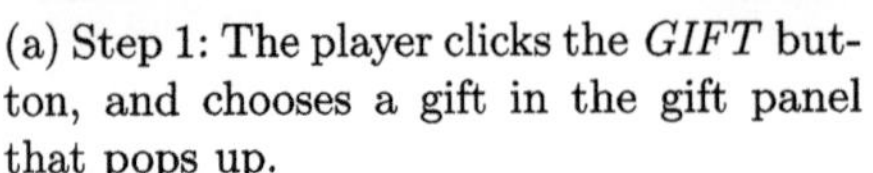 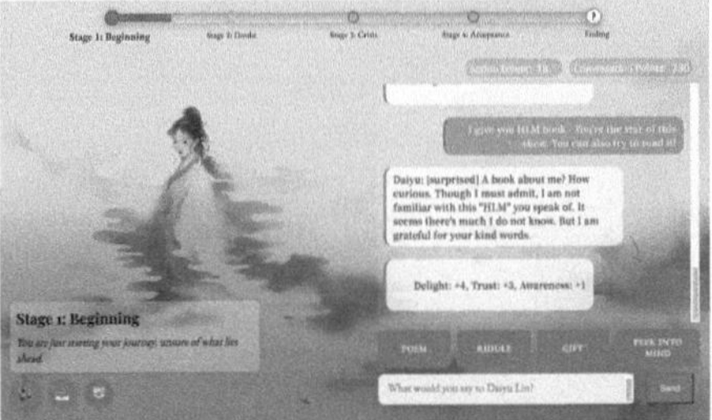

(a) Step 1: The player clicks the *GIFT* button, and chooses a gift in the gift panel that pops up.

(b) Step 2: The player customizes the gift-giving message and gives the gift through the chat box. Daiyu responds.

Fig. 4. The process of giving a gift to Daiyu.

1. *Action points* are used to indicate the number of interactions the player can have with Daiyu. For instance, sending a casual message costs one action point; composing a poem costs three; answering a riddle costs two; giving a gift costs one; and peeking into the mind also costs one.
2. *Conversation points* serve as the currency in our prototype. Players can earn them by eliciting as many affective responses from the Daiyu as possible during the conversation, and then use those points to purchase gifts.
3. *Dynamic traits* are aspects of Daiyu's personality that can be influenced by the player during the conversation. They directly shape the progression of the interactive story. There are three traits: awareness, delight, and trust. Awareness reflects the extent to which Daiyu realizes she is a fictional character as well as an LLM-driven consciousness; delight represents how happy she feels during the interaction; and trust indicates how much she sees the player as a friend. Among these, awareness determines whether the player can advance to the next stage and is directly tied to the story's progression bar. Delight and trust, meanwhile, determine which ending the player reaches at

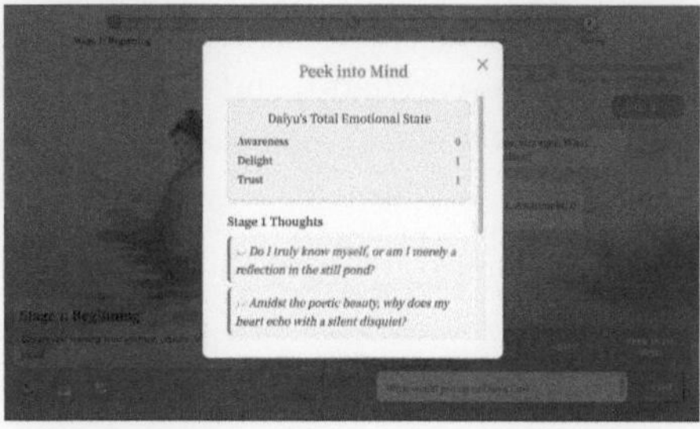

Fig. 5. The player clicks the *PEEK INTO MIND* button. The pop-up panel shows what Daiyu is thinking and the value of her current dynamic traits.

each stage. All three traits can be modified through good conversation quality, successful riddle challenges, positive reviews of the composed poems, and giving appropriate gifts.

4. *Stable traits* are aspects of Daiyu's personality that cannot be influenced by the player during the conversation, yet they influence how soon the dynamic traits can be added by the player. These traits (temperament, curiosity, playfulness, taste) are means to control the progress of relationship development, where each trait acts as a multiplier that determines how effectively player actions (dialogue exchanges, poem composition, riddle challenges, gift giving, and peeking into mind) can increase the dynamic attributes of awareness, delight, and trust. For instance, a higher temperament (70) and curiosity (60) make it easier to build "trust" through interactions, while higher playfulness (40) and taste (80) enhance the effectiveness of actions that increase "delight", and curiosity (60) directly influences how quickly "awareness" can be developed, creating a consistent personality baseline that shapes all player interactions and relationship progression. The design of stable traits is also useful to portray different personalities of the "Twelve Beauties of Jinling" for future work (see Sect. 6).

4   User Study

4.1   Motivation and Participants

We conducted a user study with two different groups-HLM readers and IDN designers-to answer our research questions. We targeted HLM readers for three reasons: first, the whole playthrough of our prototype requires knowledge of HLM more than just having heard of it; second, we think people who are familiar with HLM can offer more critical opinions on remediation than HLM novices; third, we want to understand players' experiences, acceptance, and other thoughts regarding remediating HLM with LLMs. Through recruiting IDN designers, we aimed to explore the possibilities that LLMs open up for IDNs, as well as the constraints or limitations from the design perspective. Therefore, we did not require in-depth knowledge of HLM from the recruited IDN designers.

We recruited 12 participants in total, including seven HLM readers (two of whom were cultural heritage researchers) and five IDN designers. The demographic details are listed in Table 1.

Table 1. Demographics of the participants

No.	Gender	Familiarity with HLM	Identity
P1	Male	heard of HLM	IDN designer
P2	Female	read the original novel & watched HLM TV adaptations	HLM reader
P3	Female	read the original novel & watched HLM TV adaptations	HLM reader
P4	Female	watched HLM TV adaptations & liked HLM a lot	HLM enthusiast
P5	Male	read the original novel & watched HLM TV adaptations	HLM enthusiast
P6	Female	read the original novel	IDN designer & lecturer
P7	Male	never heard of HLM	IDN designer & researcher
P8	Male	partially read the original novel	HLM reader
P9	Male	heard of HLM	IDN designer
P10	Female	partially read the original novel	IDN designer for games
P11	Female	watched HLM TV adaptations & knew the plots	HLM reader & cultural heritage researcher
P12	Female	read the original novel	HLM reader & cultural heritage researcher

4.2   Semi-structured Interviews

The study started with an introduction to our research and prototype, after which the participants explored the prototype freely for approximately 15 min. We then conducted interviews in a semi-structured way, which allows us to seek clarifications, add questions, and follow comments for nuanced insights [19,25]. We conducted interviews in Chinese or English, depending on the participants' preference. All interviews were recorded via Zoom[8] with the participants' consent. The interview scripts for the two player groups can be found at https://greathyx718.github.io/meet_daiyu/.

4.3   Data Collection and Thematic Analysis

We used Feishu Minutes[9] to transcribe the recorded videos into text automatically. Following this, we performed manual checks and content calibration to ensure that the transcribed text matched the original interview content. Subsequently, we conducted a thematic analysis (TA) to examine those text transcripts.

Thematic analysis (TA), as defined by Braun and Clarke [10], serves as an interpretative framework to uncover patterns of meaning-commonly referred

---

[8] https://www.zoom.com/.

[9] https://www.feishu.cn/hc/en-US/articles/022111234449-get-the-most-out-of-feishu-minutes.

to as "themes"-within a qualitative dataset. These themes convey the narratives behind the data. Notably, there are no uniform or definitive themes for a particular dataset; themes vary due to the researcher's theoretical insights and analytical capabilities [11]. The first author conducted an inductive TA on the interview data, employing open coding rather than adhering to a predefined codebook. Adopting the six-phase TA outlined by Braun and Clarke [10], the first author commenced by thoroughly reading the transcripts to gain a solid understanding of the entire dataset. Second, 16 preliminary codes were generated, which represented the first author's preliminary interpretations of the original data. Third, the researcher reviewed these codes and clustered similar ones around the research questions, yielding three potential themes. In the fourth phase, the first and second authors scrutinized these candidate themes against both the codes and the entire dataset to ensure that they encapsulated a coherent narrative. The final two phases involve defining, naming, and documenting these themes, which are detailed in Sect. 5.3.

5   Results

In this section, we present three themes to answer the proposed research questions. We address RQ1 by analyzing LLM capabilities in terms of characterization and emplotment. We then respond to RQ2 by identifying two design implications for future LLM-powered IDN systems.

5.1   LLMs as IDN Character Design Material (in Narrative Remediation)

We received mixed reactions towards the AI Daiyu. Participants' responses appeared to correlate with their familiarity with, and devotion to, the original HLM. On the one hand, two participants who were HLM enthusiasts expressed reservations about our prototype. P5 observed: *"In the novel, Daiyu wouldn't readily engage in such friendly banter with strangers, but here she seemed too affable and outgoing."* P4 directly suggested that the crucial next step for improving the prototype is to *"enhance its literary fidelity to the original novel-specifically, to ensure that Daiyu's speaking and poetic style more closely mirror the literary characteristics of Daiyu as depicted in the classic."* On the other hand, participants who were not HLM enthusiasts or had only limited knowledge of the work generally provided positive feedback regarding how well our prototype matched their impression of Daiyu. *"I am surprised that the way Daiyu talked in your prototype is consistent with her sentimental image in the original novel."* [P2] *"The personality that she showed to me is quite close to Daiyu in Hong Lou Meng. When I talked to her, I could sense her hesitation derived from her personality."* [P12] All our participants see the AI Daiyu as THE Daiyu, more or less. Holopainen et al. [22] propose the strong concept of "liveness" in expression is not limited to the physical presence of a human author or performer. In this sense, our work might be an indication that "liveness" in expression could also not be confined to the physical presence of a human character, even if he or she is fictional.

Regardless of their familiarity with HLM or satisfaction with our prototype, most participants reported being able to detect AI characteristics in Daiyu's responses. P6 provided a particularly illustrative example: *"When I asked her, 'Do you feel sad for not knowing your future life?' and she answered, 'I cannot feel sadness for what I do not know.' This answer reminded me of her AI-ness."* Many participants also picked up on Daiyu's AI nature through her constant availability to respond. This created a double-edged effect: while the immediate, tailored responses made the character feel more *"real"* [P3], her relentlessly passive role gradually caused some participants to feel an uncomfortable one-sidedness in their conversations. As P9 put it: *"She always listened to what I said and showed respect for my words, but she didn't start new topics with me. Sometimes, she would ask me questions, but they were based on the context that I mentioned to her. She was not proactive, and that made me feel like talking with an AI, instead of the character from the novel."*

To a large extent, the detectable and hard-to-eliminate AI characteristics were responsible for the unfavorable responses to our prototype. Based on this, P9 further highlighted *"the possible dilemma of character analogs"* in LLM-powered IDNs, as *"I don't expect to see characters featured in different classics all saying things like 'How can I help you?'"* That said, there were also some alternative perspectives that found value in how we used AI to construct Daiyu's indecisive character: *"My impression of Daiyu is that she tends to be indecisive, while AI tends to give answers with repetitive meanings. Maybe that's why I feel that the Daiyu in your prototype is believable."* [P10] This suggests that AI can share certain commonalities with human personality, which are worth exploring and leveraging when using LLMs to portray human characters.

5.2   LLMs As IDN Plot Design Material (in Narrative Remediation)

By utilizing LLMs, we make it possible for the player to intervene and influence the plots while keeping them relevant to the player's input. As several participants reported, they felt an enhanced sense of interaction and engagement due to the perspective shift enabled by LLMs. When reading the novel or watching the TV adaptations, they were in the third-person perspective. When chatting with Daiyu, however, they were in the second-person perspective. *"I felt like a time traveller, stepping into Hong Lou Meng. I got infinite possibilities [of Daiyu's answers] due to AI, and it gave me the opportunity to bring about change for her, which made me immersed."* [P8] Another evidence is that most participants felt in control of the whole narrative, but none thought they had absolute control over it, which in turn made them feel engaged in the narrative. *"If ten is total control, I'd give it a six. In your context, although I could say anything to Daiyu, I still had a task [to persuade Daiyu that she is fictional] to complete, and I was constrained by the action points. But that was good. It made me more focused on what I should say."* [P1]

Besides, with the integration of LLMs, there will be no two identical narrative experiences, but experiences personalized to each player's input. Most of our participants were aware of this point, like what P6 said, *"I have a really big variety of ways of seeing how Daiyu responds to me. Even though I asked the same question or played the game again, the responses were different. I feel I'm into it [the narrative]."* This merit of LLMs makes the narrative experiences distinct from pre-scripted ones and can encourage players to engage more thoughtfully with the story. *"Personally, pre-scripted narratives or narratives with a tree structure are like a multiple-choice question to me. I would have a trial-and-error mentality when I experience pre-scripted narratives. But in your game, I must be careful since I cannot let things start over again as they were."* [P1]

Nevertheless, there were still criticisms of the narrative design, arguing that the narrative based on the passive, responsive AI weakens the engagement. *"The current storyline is that I destroy Daiyu's worldview and help her rebuild a new one according to my worldview. However, I was expecting that Daiyu, or the AI, could, at least try to, persuade me and change my viewpoint. If that happens, I'll see her as more human and get more engaged."* [P12]

5.3 Takeaways for Future IDN Design Using LLMs

Players are capable of prompting any content to the LLM. However, it seems that this right can distract them from the narrative and thus undermine the narrative coherence. We summarize two insights on approaching the "authoring problem" [37] in IDNs in the context where players co-create the narrative with LLMs. Specifically, the two insights help ensure that players' inputs to LLMs lead to meaningful and engaging experiences while maintaining a consistent storyline.

Designing Towards Engaging AI and Humans in the Same Task. Many participants mentioned that our storyline was designed around the task-resolving the worldview conflict between Daiyu and them. This conflict challenges them while also encouraging meaningful interactions between them and Daiyu. *"I think the conflict between the character [Daiyu] and me interests me a lot."* [P3] *"I think it [the prototype] is about the conflict between humans and AI, that is, how to convince an AI that it is an AI."* [P8] In situations where there is a conflict to be resolved, especially between the players and the LLM, they seem unlikely to talk to the LLM about irrelevant matters. Therefore, we propose to frame the narrative around collaborative problem-solving so as to create a shared goal that aligns the interests of both the player and the AI. This approach allows the player to feel a sense of agency while simultaneously fostering a deeper connection with the AI character.

However, it cannot be guaranteed that the player will always focus on the designed task and input relevant content to the LLM. In that case, we should consider how to make them realize when they have deviated from the narrative at an appropriate time. *"Your design of immediate value feedback from Daiyu reminded me of deviating from the storyline. When I saw her awareness increase by zero,*

I knew I had said something not that important, and that made me focus on thinking about what Daiyu wanted." [P1] Thus, providing real-time feedback to players' inputs can be a solution to guide players back to the core story while preserving their autonomy. This helps maintain the narrative coherence, ensuring that while players explore their creative input, they remain anchored within the framework of the story.

Expanding AI Responses Beyond Predictable Boundaries. LLMs appear to answer within a safe area, where human players seem to have pre-set expectations of what LLMs would respond. This tendency for LLMs to stay within predictable boundaries can limit the richness of player experiences. *"AI constructs sentences by predicting the most likely next word based on the context of the conversation. It uses patterns learned from existing datasets to determine which words and phrases fit best, and that is why I hardly had the experience of being surprised by AI. I expect AI, or Daiyu in your context, could say something that surprises me."* [P10] *"I think the AI-implemented characters are too safe now. I want to see how Daiyu can get annoyed with me, since I tried to be rude to her by directly saying that she was a character written by somebody, but her response was not angry. Neither did she ever challenge me."* [P9]

Therefore, it is understandable that even if the player could input anything to the LLM, they can be bothered by constantly getting expected responses and become disengaged. How to get AI out of passive consent and take more proactive stances seems essential. *"AI always responds with a kind and empathetic tone, and maybe that's why I feel it inactive, although it does interact with me to some extent. I would recommend designing the AI character to be more proactive, for example, let AI, or Daiyu, solve the conflict or convince me of certain viewpoints."* [P12] This proactive engagement could involve allowing the AI to pose challenges or counterarguments to the player's input, thus creating a more "player-passive" dialogue. Moreover, pushing the boundary of AI responses can also contribute to this aim. *"Maybe try to reach the outliers of AI responses, for example, to what extent will it be annoyed? And then we might know where to go."* [P9] We thereby propose to train LLMs to react beyond their usual scope, moving from passive answering to proactively initiating or ending conversations, and from always being friendly and polite to showing a range of emotions, such as rudeness or anger. This can allow AI characters to be capable of emotional complexity and more authentic.

6   Limitations and Future Work

Our research has three noteworthy limitations. First, a potential sampling bias may have occurred during participant recruitment, as individuals who volunteered for interviews might have been inherently more receptive to AI applications in narrative reinterpretation than the general population. Second, the prototype's English-language interface created barriers to user immersion, as several participants emphasized that Chinese would arouse more cultural resonance in this context. Third, our prototype is naive in guiding players to understand and complete their task. Many participants pointed out the need for a beginner's guide; otherwise, they would be overwhelmed when they were exposed to a blank chat box.

Looking ahead, we are preparing for a further study with a refined prototype focusing on the cultural acceptance of LLM remediations. Concerning the prototype, we plan to make a Chinese version and improve responses from LLMs, potentially incorporating strategies to make characters more proactive. In addition, we aim to remediate characters more than only Lin Daiyu, but also the "Twelve Beauties of Jinling" using LLMs, with each beauty representing a unique personality and narrative.

7   Conclusion

In this research, we demonstrated how LLMs can enhance player engagement and create personalized narrative experiences by designing and developing a prototype, which enables real-time conversations with iconic characters Lin Daiyu from the Chinese classic novel *Hong Lou Meng*. The findings from our user study indicate that while participants appreciated the real-time personalized responses of the character, there is a need for more proactive interaction initiated by LLMs that is contextually coherent. Based on this gap, we offer insights on how to maintain player engagement while ensuring narrative coherence when they are able to input anything to LLMs. On the players' side, we encourage the design of a task for players and LLMs to complete collaboratively and remind the players when they deviate from the task at an appropriate time. On the LLMs' side, we propose to train them towards being more active and emotionally diverse.

References

1. Aarseth, E.: A narrative theory of games. In: Proceedings of the International Conference on the Foundations of Digital Games, FDG 2012, pp. 129–133. ACM, New York, NY, USA (2012). https://doi.org/10.1145/2282338.2282365
2. Aljammaz, R., Wardrip-Fruin, N., Mateas, M.: Towards an understanding of character believability. In: Proceedings of the 18th International Conference on the Foundations of Digital Games, FDG 2023, pp. 1–9. ACM, New York, NY, USA, April 2023. https://doi.org/10.1145/3582437.3582466
3. Bal, M.: Narratology: Introduction to the Theory of Narrative. University of Toronto Press (2009)
4. Barthes, R., Duisit, L.: An introduction to the structural analysis of narrative. New Literar. History **6**(2), 237–272 (1975)
5. Benjamin, J.J., Berger, A., Merrill, N., Pierce, J.: Machine learning uncertainty as a design material: a post-phenomenological inquiry. In: Proceedings of the 2021 CHI Conference on Human Factors in Computing Systems, CHI 2021, ACM, New York, NY, USA (2021). https://doi.org/10.1145/3411764.3445481

6. Benjamin, J.J., et al.: Responding to generative ai technologies with research-through-design: the ryelands ai lab as an exploratory study. In: Proceedings of the 2024 ACM Designing Interactive Systems Conference, DIS 2024, pp. 1823–1841. ACM, New York, NY, USA (2024). https://doi.org/10.1145/3643834.3660677

7. Blom, J.: Parasocial relationships with non-playable characters. In: Video Game Characters and Transmedia Storytelling: The Dynamic Game Character, pp. 125–150. Amsterdam University Press (2023)

8. Blom, J.: Video Game Characters and Transmedia Storytelling: The Dynamic Game Character. Amsterdam University Press, Amsterdam (2023). https://doi.org/10.1515/9789048553495

9. Bolter, J.D., Grusin, R.: Remediation: Understanding New Media. MIT Press (1999)

10. Braun, V., Clarke, V.: Thematic analysis. In: APA handbook of research methods in psychology, vol 2: Research designs: Quantitative, qualitative, neuropsychological, and biological, pp. 57–71. APA handbooks in psychology®, APA, Washington, DC, US (2012). https://doi.org/10.1037/13620-004

11. Braun, V., Clarke, V.: Reflecting on reflexive thematic analysis. Qualit. Res. Sport Exerc. Health **11**(4), 589–597 (2019). https://doi.org/10.1080/2159676X.2019.1628806

12. Cao, X.: The Story of the Stone (trans. D. Hawkes). Penguin Classics, 2 edn. (1999)

13. Chatman, S., Chatman, S.: Story and Discourse: Narrative Structure in Fiction and Film. Cornell University Press, Cornell Paperbacks (1980)

14. Chatman, S.: Story and Discourse: Narrative Structure in Fiction and Film. Cornell University Press (1978)

15. Cox, S.R., Ooi, W.T.: Conversational interactions with npcs in llm-driven gaming: guidelines from a content analysis of player feedback. In: Chatbot Research and Design: 7th International Workshop, CONVERSATIONS 2023, Oslo, Norway, 22–23 November 2023, Revised Selected Papers, pp. 167–184. Springer, Berlin, Heidelberg (2023). https://doi.org/10.1007/978-3-031-54975-5_10

16. Crawford, C.: Chris Crawford on Interactive Storytelling. Pearson Education (2004)

17. Dove, G., Halskov, K., Forlizzi, J., Zimmerman, J.: Ux design innovation: challenges for working with machine learning as a design material. In: Proceedings of the 2017 CHI Conference on Human Factors in Computing Systems, CHI 2017, pp. 278–288. ACM, New York, NY, USA (2017). https://doi.org/10.1145/3025453.3025739

18. Frayling, C.: Research in art and design (Royal College of Art Research Papers, Vol 1, No 1, 1993/4) (1994), https://researchonline.rca.ac.uk/384/

19. Galletta, A.: Mastering the semi-structured interview and beyond: from research design to analysis and publication. Mastering the semi-structured interview and beyond: From research design to analysis and publication, New York University Press, New York, NY, US (2013). https://doi.org/10.18574/nyu/9780814732939.001.0001, pages: xiii, 245

20. Hallnäs, L., Redström, J.: Interaction Design: Foundations, Experiments. Interactive Institute - The Swedish School of Textiles, University College of Borås. (2006)

21. Holmquist, L.E.: Intelligence on tap: artificial intelligence as a new design material. Interactions **24**(4), 28–33 (2017). https://doi.org/10.1145/3085571

22. Holopainen, J., Huang, Y., Shin, J., Nissinen, E., Lucero, A.: Infinity book: speculating literary expressions in the age of generative ai. In: Proceedings of the 2025 ACM Designing Interactive Systems Conference, DIS 2025, pp. 1430–1454. ACM, New York, NY, USA (2025). https://doi.org/10.1145/3715336.3735735

23. Koenitz, H., Eladhari, M.P., Barbara, J.: Can AI create an interactive digital narrative? A benchmarking framework to evaluate generative AI tools for the design of IDNs. In: Murray, J.T., Reyes, M.C. (eds.) Interactive Storytelling, pp. 160–180. Springer, Cham (2025). https://doi.org/10.1007/978-3-031-78453-8_11
24. Kouros, T., Papa, V.: Digital mirrors: Ai companions and the self. Societies **14**(10), 200 (2024)
25. Lazar, J., Feng, J.H., Hochheiser, H.: Chapter 8 - interviews and focus groups. In: Lazar, J., Feng, J.H., Hochheiser, H. (eds.) Research Methods in Human Computer Interaction (Second Edition), pp. 187–228. Morgan Kaufmann, Boston, January 2017. https://doi.org/10.1016/B978-0-12-805390-4.00008-X
26. Lei, Y., Ma, S., Sun, Y., Ma, X.: "Ai afterlife" as digital legacy: perceptions, expectations, and concerns. In: Proceedings of the 2025 CHI Conference on Human Factors in Computing Systems, CHI 2025, ACM, New York, NY, USA (2025). https://doi.org/10.1145/3706598.3713933
27. Lim, Y.K., Stolterman, E., Tenenberg, J.: The anatomy of prototypes: prototypes as filters, prototypes as manifestations of design ideas. ACM Trans. Comput.-Hum. Interact. (TOCHI) **15**(2), 1–27 (2008)
28. Louridas, P.: Design as bricolage: anthropology meets design thinking. Des. Stud. **20**(6), 517–535 (1999). https://doi.org/10.1016/S0142-694X(98)00044-1
29. McLuhan, M.: Understanding Media: The Extensions of Man. Gingko Press (2003)
30. Prince, G.: Narratology: The Form and Functioning of Narrative. Mouton, Berlin (1982)
31. Rimmon-Kenan, S.: Narrative Fiction: Contemporary Poetics. Routledge, London, 2 edn. December 2003. https://doi.org/10.4324/9780203426111
32. Ryan, M.L., Ruppert, J., Bernet, J.W.: Digital media. In: Narrative Across Media: the Languages of Storytelling, pp. 329–335. U of Nebraska Press (2004)
33. Ryan, M.L., Ruppert, J., Bernet, J.W.: Narrative Across Media: The Languages of Storytelling. U of Nebraska Press, January 2004
34. Schön, D., Bennett, J.: Reflective conversation with materials, pp. 171–189. ACM, New York, NY, USA (1996)
35. Stappers, P.J., Giaccardi, E.: Research through design. In: Soegaard, M., Friis-Dam, R. (eds.) The Encyclopedia of Human-Computer Interaction, pp. 1–94. Interaction Design Foundation (2017)
36. Sun, Y., Ni, X., Feng, H., LC, R., Lee, C.H., Asadipour, A.: Bringing stories to life in 1001 nights: a co-creative text adventure game using a story generation model. In: Vosmeer, M., Holloway-Attaway, L. (eds.) Interactive Storytelling. pp. 651–672. Springer, Cham (2022). https://doi.org/10.1007/978-3-031-22298-6_42
37. Thue, D.: Working with intelligent narrative technologies. In: Hargood, C., Millard, D.E., Mitchell, A., Spierling, U. (eds.) The Authoring Problem: Challenges in Supporting Authoring for Interactive Digital Narratives, pp. 271–284. Springer, Cham (2022). https://doi.org/10.1007/978-3-031-05214-9_17
38. Yang, Q.: Machine learning as a ux design material: how can we imagine beyond automation, recommenders, and reminders? In: AAAI Spring Symposia (2018)
39. Yildirim, N., et al.: How experienced designers of enterprise applications engage ai as a design material. In: Proceedings of the 2022 CHI Conference on Human Factors in Computing Systems. CHI 2022, ACM, New York, NY, USA (2022). https://doi.org/10.1145/3491102.3517491
40. Yong, Q.R., Mitchell, A.: From playing the story to gaming the system: repeat experiences of a large language model-based interactive story. In: Holloway-Attaway, L., Murray, J.T. (eds.) Interactive Storytelling, pp. 395–409. Springer, Cham (2023). https://doi.org/10.1007/978-3-031-47655-6_24

Mixed Initiative Comic Making in the Wild: Taking an Artist's Approach Out of the Studio

Yana Knight[(✉)] [iD] and Mirjam Palosaari Eladhari[iD]

Department of Computer and Systems Sciences, Stockholm University, Postbox 7003,
SE-164 07 Kista, Sweden
{yana.knight,mirjam}@dsv.su.se

Abstract. This paper presents a further exploration of a mixed initiative comic-making method that combines hand-drawn imagery with AI-generated visuals in a turn-taking, interactive manner. Initially developed within a personal artistic practice, the method was later tested in broader settings to understand how it might function as a public, co-creative method. As a first step, a pre-study was conducted at a public AI art exhibition, where casual participants were invited to engage with the method by producing short visual narratives.

Based on insights from this initial engagement, a structured workshop was carried out where participants created comics with the same method by alternating between analogue sketching and AI-assisted generation using a publicly available image generation tool appropriated for the task by the authors. Participants provided written reflections on their experience. The resulting comics and responses were collected and clustered to explore emerging patterns in narrative form and participant perception. This paper documents both phases – the pre-study and the workshop – and outlines the steps of the method and presents the comics created with it. Drawing from participant reflections, the paper highlights themes that arose in relation to the process. In particular, we examine how the authors' method operates outside their studios in situated contexts and in relation to casual creative practices.

Keywords: mixed initiative comics · human-AI collaboration · comic making · visual storytelling · casual creativity

1 Introduction and Background

The widespread availability of generative AI tools has transformed creative expression from a specialized artistic endeavor into a public, participatory phenomenon. As systems like DALL·E, Stable Diffusion, and Midjourney become embedded into everyday digital culture, they enable not only professional creators but also non-artists – casual users, hobbyists, and curious tinkerers – to engage in visual storytelling, aesthetic play, and exploratory ideation [7]. This

M. C. Reyes and F. Nack (Eds.): ICIDS 2025, LNCS 16375, pp. 48–71, 2026.
https://doi.org/10.1007/978-3-032-12405-0_4

emerging shift challenges traditional assumptions about authorship, skill, and originality by making complex creative processes accessible through natural language prompts and intuitive interfaces.

Building on Human-Computer Interaction (HCI) and creativity studies, this work focuses on casual creativity – spontaneous, non-professional creative acts like sketching or tinkering. These practices are valued not for expertise but for playfulness, reflection, and everyday engagement.

Digital creativity tools can support these forms of engagement by lowering technical barriers and embracing ambiguity, improvisation, and surprise as productive forces [4,6]. AI-based tools, in particular, introduce new materialities and affordances for non-expert users. Their ability to respond to prompts with richly detailed imagery or textual responses enables users to co-construct narratives, experiment visually, and reinterpret their own intentions fostering emergent, rather than predetermined, outcomes.

Prior work has demonstrated that people are capable of meaningfully engaging with AI systems even without artistic training, provided that the interaction design foregrounds playfulness, transparency, and interpretive agency [8,10,11,23]. This resonates with earlier ideas in participatory design and critical making, where emphasis is placed on process, reflection, and discovery rather than polished output [12,19]. In this view, the AI system is not merely a tool but a co-actor in a broader performative and exploratory practice. However, most studies on the topic emphasise expert creators, design professionals, or polished outputs. Casual or amateur visual narrative creation using generative AI for personal/autobiographical topics remains underexamined.

In this paper, we present a series of participatory workshops with non-experts which appropriate a generative AI tool and which is built on a mixed-initiative comic-making method that alternates between human hand-drawn frames and AI-generated interpretations. Originally developed within the first author's (FA) own artistic practice [16], the method has since been adapted to support casual creators in participatory settings such as public exhibitions and educational workshops. It is inspired by narrative scaffolding techniques such as Lynda Barry's "and then what happened?" [3] which guides a story through its development and lets it unfold frame by frame.

Furthermore, we report on how participants, regardless of drawing skill, used this approach to construct the alternating human-AI visual narratives. Through a combination of qualitative clustering and visual analysis, we examine both the comics produced and the participant reflections. While user research on co-creative AI exists, it often relies on controlled lab evaluations and focuses on output-based metrics or technical novelty [13,14]. Our study aims to contribute to the need for richer, situated user accounts and insights of AI's real-world integration in playful and informal settings. Our aim is to understand how our method can support creative self-expression among general audiences. Lastly, we aim to shine a critical lens on the use of AI in creative tasks, and the participants' reflections contribute to an emerging but still-scarce critical AI literacy perspective in design and arts practice [2,5].

2   Pre-study at an Exhibition

Before conducting the structured public workshop described in this paper, a preliminary exploratory study was carried out by the FA during the NeurIPS 2023 Creative AI exhibition in New Orleans, USA. This early study aimed to test the feasibility, accessibility, and creative potential of the mixed-initiative comic-making method when presented to casual creators outside an artistic setting.

2.1   The Setup

This pre-study was conducted in an informal, public setting over several hours during one morning. Willing passers-by were invited to draw a quick sketch using drawing materials available at the FA's table where she exhibited her own comics generated using this method and was available to answer questions about her own work. These analogue sketches were photographed and uploaded to a Google Colab interface running the AI tool, described in more detail in the subsequent section. Participants then provided a text prompt that would guide the generation of one or more AI-augmented images derived from their original drawing. See Fig. 1 for the images of the setup.

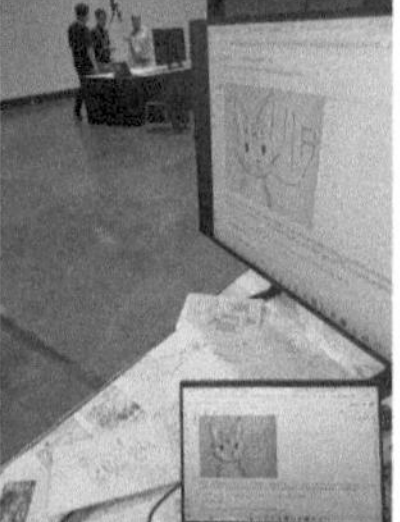

Fig. 1. The FA's exhibition and pre-study setup.

To reduce cognitive and technical overhead, the FA facilitated the entire technical process while participants focused solely on creative decisions – choosing what to draw, how to prompt, and interpreting the AI-generated outcomes. Participants were guided but not led creatively; they retained full authorship over their mini-narratives. Some chose to stay and iterate, generating a sequence of related images; others created a single pair of a drawing and generated image.

2.2   The Tool

The generative tool used was a publicly available Google Colab notebook based on Stable Diffusion and GPT-2 and developed at the University of Edinburgh, selected by the FA for its compatibility with image-prompt workflows and accessibility.[1]. It is important to note that the tool was not developed by the authors; thus only its core functions relevant to narrative transformation were employed, such as image-to-image generation with pre-set parameters to maintain consistency. A more detailed description of these is available in the original study by the authors [16]. Figure 2 shows the tool's interface.

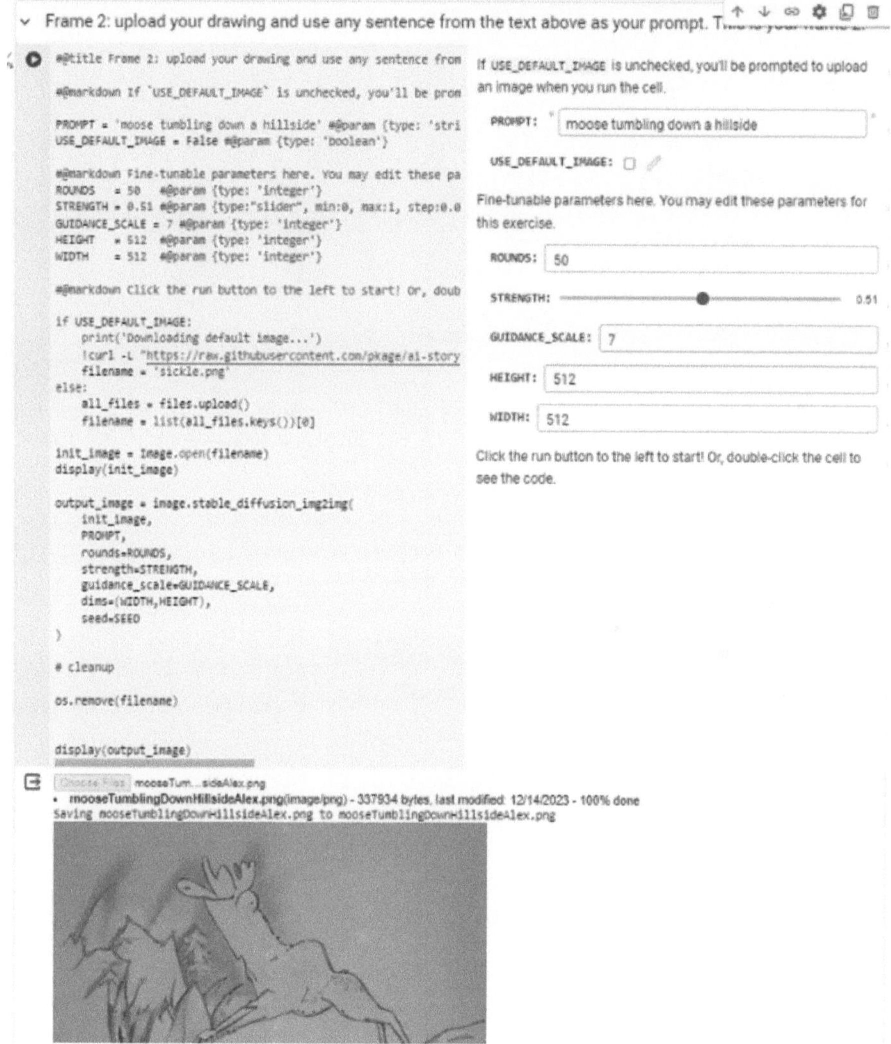

Fig. 2. The tool's interface.

---

[1] https://github.com/pkage/ai-storytelling-backstage.

2.3   The Artworks

Participants of the pre-study produced either one-off images (see Fig. 3) or short narrative sequences (see Fig. 4), depending on their engagement level. For each hand drawing, the accompanying AI-generated image introduced unexpected visual twists or thematic shifts.

Fig. 3. Analogue drawing (left) by one of the participants, and an AI image they generated from it (right) with the prompt "A cat singing a happy song about mice".

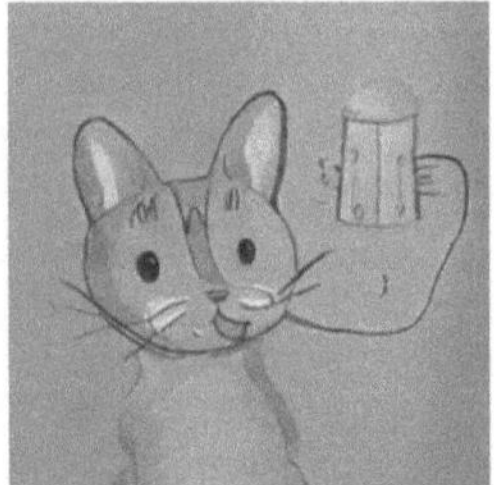

Fig. 4. An example sequential narrative generated by one of the participants from their hand drawing by experimenting with different prompts. From left to right: *"A cat singing a happy song about mice"*, *"A mouse appears and starts singing too"*, *"A cat sings the song, and the mouse looks worried"*.

In total, 21 artworks were generated, with 13 participants consenting to retention of the images and 12 providing consent for inclusion of their reflective responses. Some examples of the AI-generated artworks are presented in Fig. 5.

Fig. 5. Examples of AI-generated images based on participant prompts: *"Moose tumbling down a hillside"*, *"Cat eating yesterday's beignet"*, *"Dog raving by the pool"*, *"The cat flies into space"*, *"Moose transforms into a butterfly"*, *"Scientists have discovered a hole in the sun"*.

2.4   Participant Reflections

A brief 10-question survey gathered participant insights. Most participants had some prior experience with generative AI (10 of 12), but were not regular drawers or comic-makers. When asked to describe the experience in one word, responses included: "delightful", "funny", "meditative", "FUN!", and "brainstorming". Participants expressed surprise at how their own ideas were echoed and reshaped by the AI, highlighting the collaborative nature of the tool.

When evaluating the AI-generated image, participants rated each on a 5-point Likert scale for *interest, surprise,* and *visual appeal.* The most highly rated attribute was *surprise* (mean = 4.0), followed by *visual appeal* (mean = 3.5), and *interest* (mean = 3.1). Most participants reported that the results exceeded or matched their expectations, and the majority stated they would share the output with friends.

2.5   Implications for the Workshop

This pre-study affirmed the accessibility and expressive capacity of the method for non-artists and casual creators. Despite being situated in a busy conference venue, with minimal setup and brief interactions, participants created images they valued and reflected on thoughtfully. The following sections examine how participants engage with the approach in a focused, time-bound setting.

3   Workshop Methodology and Set-Up

The workshop took place at the authors' home institute as part of a Bachelor level AI and programming course led by the second author (SA). As such, this was a more formal and structured setting than the pre-study. Participants engaged in a 90-min session structured around the following steps: quick-list journaling, drawing, AI image generation from prompt and photo, iterative storytelling and story curation. The tool used was the same as in the pre-study, and the same as the authors used in [16], and the drawing materials (colour pencils and paper) were provided. We collected both the comics and the reflective feedback and performed thematic clustering to examine emergent narrative and emotional patterns.

Fig. 6. Workshop setup.

As in the original study, the method used is rooted in autoethnography and autodesign [9]. The experience was documented through photographs (see Fig. 6) and reflective notes by the FA, capturing her perspective on facilitating both sessions. In this case, however, the reflections on the experience are also extended from only the individual practitioner to a participant samplegroup. Their resulting comics were collected alongside qualitative feedback via a survey.

Our analysis draws from clustering of narrative structure (story descriptions provided by the participants through the survey form) and clustering of reflective feedback (participants' emotional and cognitive responses about the experience provided in the same survey).

3.1   Participants

Twelve participants took part in the structured workshop. All but two were students at the institute, and the remaining two were educators and professionals with varying levels of experience in drawing or working with AI. The SA was among the participants (thus trying this process for the second time and in a different, public setting) following the study reported in [16].

All of the participants had prior familiarity with generative AI tools but did not identify as artists or comic-makers (most reported to never draw or at most, occasionally). Participation was voluntary, as was the submission of the results, and all data was collected with informed consent. The FA in this case was merely a facilitator involved only in guiding the participants and not in art making.

3.2   The Comic Creation Method

The process followed in the workshop adheres closely to the mixed initiative comic-making framework previously described in [16]. It consists of the following steps:

1. **Pre-step: Drawing Warm-Up** – Participants begin with warm-up drawing exercises, including blind contour drawings and rapid sketching, to ease into the creative process.
2. **Step 1: 24-Hour Memory List** – Each participant creates a bullet-point list of events, moments, or observations from their last 24 h.
3. **Step 2: First Frame Drawing** – From this list, a compelling item is chosen and drawn in a limited time (34 min), forming the first frame of the comic narrative.
4. **Step 3: Image Capture** – The drawing is photographed and uploaded to the AI tool's interface.
5. **Step 4: Prompting the Tool** – The participant describes their image in a short textual prompt, which is used to guide the AI's generation of a new image based on the hand-drawing.
6. **Step 5: First AI Image** – The AI-generated image is reviewed and added to the story as frame 2. Because it is derived from the original drawing, it often retains stylistic or compositional coherence.
7. **Step 6: "And Then What Happens?"** – The participant reflects on the evolving narrative prompted by the AI image and hand draws the next frame by asking "what happens next?" In this step AI begins to actively influence the story trajectory.
8. **Step 7: Iterative Expansion** – Steps 3 to 6 are repeated in a turn-taking fashion until a complete story of 48 frames emerges. The alternation between human drawing and machine generation creates a dialogical, co-creative rhythm.

Participants were free to title their stories and interpret the narrative as it unfolded, without constraints on theme, tone, or coherence. As in the pre-study, the FA provided guidance through the creative steps and general assistance above but did not guide content decisions.

3.3   Feedback Collection

Upon completing their story, each willing participant filled out a short feedback form consisting of open-ended questions. They were asked to describe their comic frame-by-frame, reflect on their experience of working with the AI, assess the resulting story, and share what they felt they learned. The form also included optional questions about prior experience with generative AI and whether the process met their expectations.

Participant responses were later clustered: word frequencies were manually tallied, thematically categorized into our chosen categories, and visually arranged into clustered word clouds to visualise thematic patterns in both narrative content and subjective experience.

Altogether, ten visual stories were recorded (of which three belong to the same author); this is complemented with five feedback responses (as not all the participants filled out the form). There are, thus, eight different participant authors, (numbered here 1–7; the SA is labeled as such) and five corresponding pieces of feedback.

4   Comics Created with the Method

In total, ten comics are presented here.

We categorized the comics into the following thematic groups (see Fig. 7):

– Whimsical Metamorphosis
– Everyday Disruption
– Fantasy and Narrative Structure
– Slice-of-Life Realism

Fig. 7. Word cloud showing storyline clusters. Clockwise: Whimsical Metamorphosis, Everyday Disruption, Slice-of-Life Realism, Fantasy and Narrative Structure.

4.1   Whimsical Metamorphosis

This cluster is defined by surreal, often animal or whimsical creature-centered narratives that revel in visual transformation, layered realities, and absurdity with a light-hearted tone. Stories involve anthropomorphic or shape-shifting creatures navigating playful or illogical worlds. "Penguin Comic", "Mermaids" and "Weirdo" all showcase a recursive logic, where visual motifs serve as portals for movement and transformation. This cluster often employs a dream-like or fairytale logic where plot coherence is secondary to visual motifs and imaginative momentum.

Generative AI often introduces visual motifs and transformations that go beyond the participant's input, responding with exaggerated or surreal augmentations. "Image as a prompt" generation, in particular, preserves compositional elements but may remix textures or shapes in unpredictable ways. These outputs may encourage participants to follow the AI's lead, creating stories where transformation is not only allowed but expected. The AI becomes an engine for whimsical leaps, visual recursion, and absurdity – prompting narrative developments that might not emerge through drawing alone.

Examples include:

- Mermaids, Knights & Children (Fig. 8)
- Penguin Comic (Fig. 9)
- Weirdo Series (Fig. 10)

Fig. 8. Whimsical fantasy scenes: mermaids, knights and children. By participant 3.

Fig. 9. Surreal comic involving penguin transformations and a skiing penguin. Artwork by participant 2.

Fig. 10. A narrative depicting a whimsical "Weirdo" creature (created and titled by participant 3).

4.2   Everyday Disruption

These stories begin in mundane or realistic settings and are disrupted by sudden, often illogical events. Characters experience unexpected shifts – such as turning into a painting or a gust of wind – without explanation. "Cinema" and "Windy" reflect a surrealist tradition where everyday environments unravel into humorous or uncanny outcomes. This cluster focuses less on character depth and more on the comedic or disorienting potential of transformation. These narratives often arise when the AI interprets prompts too literally, or introduces visual noise or distortion. Participants may describe a simple action (e.g. "a man goes to the cinema"), but the AI might exaggerate or reinterpret it in ways that feel random or illogical – such as turning the character into a cloud. These surreal shifts reflect both the power and the unpredictability of generative AI. The resulting dissonance often leads participants to retrofit meaning into the output, yielding comedic or absurd story lines grounded in visual misalignment.

Examples include:

– Windy (Fig. 11)
– Cinema (Fig. 12)

Fig. 11. The "Windy" comic: a mundane walk turns fantastical through AI-generated wind transformations by participant 5.

Fig. 12. The "Cinema" comic series: surreal shifts from routine movie-going to frogs by participant 4.

4.3   Fantasy and Narrative Structure

Stories in this cluster exhibit more narrative structure and thematic depth. They reference classical genres such as opera or space epics and tend to follow a more coherent arc. "Tosca and the Tiny Violins" re-imagines a tragic opera into a magical tale involving birds and music. "Stargazing with Alien Encounter" similarly blends awe, imagination, and wonder into a space-fantasy structure. These stories often retain a protagonist and purpose, combining fantasy with storytelling traditions that feel intentional and emotionally resonant.

In this cluster, participants seemed to use the AI more as an illustrator than a generative force – guiding it with precise prompts and selecting outputs that aligned with a predefined narrative. The tool's output appears to have reinforced the epic or dramatic tone of their stories. These narratives suggest a more "directorial" relationship with the AI, in which participants remained in control of story logic while using the tool to add atmosphere, beauty, or mythic scale.

Examples include:

- Tosca and the Tiny Violins (Fig. 13)
- A Beautiful Queen Dancing at a Ball (Fig. 14)
- Stargazing with Alien Encounter (Fig. 15)

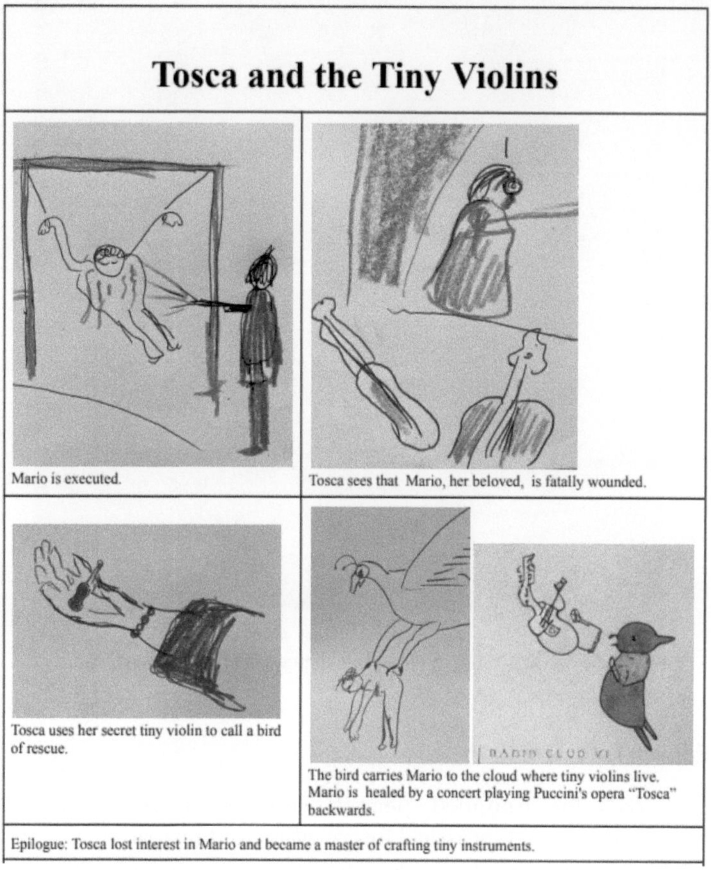

Tosca and the Tiny Violins

Mario is executed.

Tosca sees that Mario, her beloved, is fatally wounded.

Tosca uses her secret tiny violin to call a bird of rescue.

The bird carries Mario to the cloud where tiny violins live. Mario is healed by a concert playing Puccini's opera "Tosca" backwards.

Epilogue: Tosca lost interest in Mario and became a master of crafting tiny instruments.

Fig. 13. "Tosca and the Tiny Violins", by SA.

Fig. 14. "A Beautiful Queen Dancing at a Ball" by participant 3.

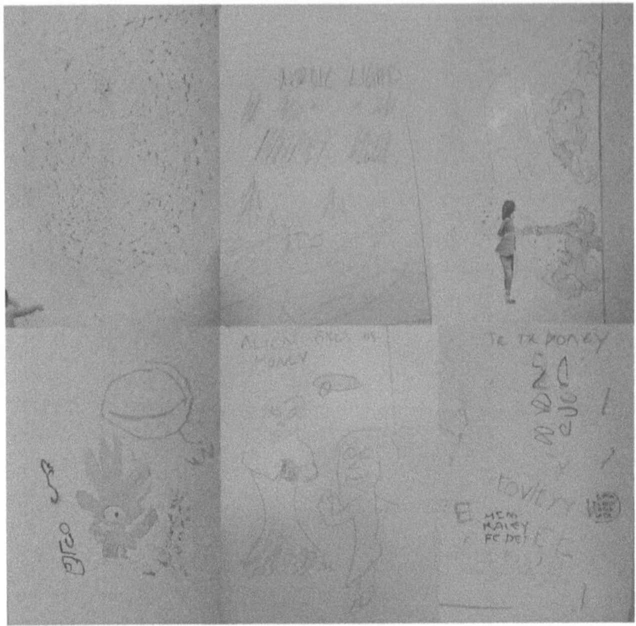

Fig. 15. "Stargazing with Alien Encounter" by participant 1.

4.4 Slice-of-Life Realism

This cluster contains grounded, personal, and often introspective sequences. These stories feature less fantastical intervention and instead document moments from daily life – eating, walking, sleeping, making plans. The tone is quiet and observational. "Tomorrows plan" exemplifies this structure, unfolding as a literal to-do list or diary entry. The strength of these stories lies in their simplicity and their potential for relatable reflection. Here, the AI plays a subtler role. Its outputs tend to "fill in" visual context without significantly altering narrative direction. This suggests a lower level of initiative from the AI, and a more illustrative, support-oriented role. The predictability or neutrality of these AI responses may reflect how less stylized or imaginative prompts result in equally mundane outputs. In some cases, participants relied more heavily on their own drawings to anchor the story, with the AI used as a filler, while in others, the whole final story is AI-generated images (no hand drawings were included). It is important to note that following the original study [16], the participants were free to curate their final outputs and include the drawings they wanted to include, thus, the stories could contain a mix of AI and hand drawings, or could be fully hand or AI drawn, even if the creative process that generated these outputs was a mixed initiative one.

Examples:

- Tomorrow's plans (Fig. 16)
- Walking my dog (Fig. 17)

Fig. 16. "Tomorrow's Plans": a sequence of daily life events by participant 6.

Fig. 17. The "Walking My Dog" comic captures a peaceful day-in-the-life of pet companionship by participant 7.

Fig. 18. Word clusters showing participants' descriptions of the creative process. Clockwise: Explorative Delight, Critical Skepticism, Pragmatic Tolerance, Curious Ambiguity.

5   Discussion and Reflections

5.1   The Process as Artistic Practice

The mixed initiative comic-making method, when applied in both personal artistic practice and public-facing workshop settings, elicits a range of emotional and cognitive responses. This section reflects on how participants experienced the process in our structured workshop and compares their reflections with those described in the original study [16], focusing especially on areas of both convergence and tension.

Beyond the individual outputs, the creative process of alternating between hand-drawn sketches and AI-generated transformations became a site of artistic engagement. Participants were not merely producing illustrations; they were shaping a narrative rhythm through interaction, surprise, and response to the AI-generated frames [18]. The method foregrounded process over results inviting creators to think in terms of transitions, turns, and reframings.

This dialogic interplay between human intention and machine suggestion resembles an improvised duet. Each move – the sketch, the prompt, the generated image – prompted a reaction that unfolded the narrative step-by-step highlighting process-centric interaction, distributed authorship, and the role of AI as co-narrator or co-creator and supporting what Ryan (2006) called "internal interactivity," where engagement occurs not through navigating a finished storyworld, but through shaping it in collaboration with a system [20]. Rather than functioning as a linear tool, the AI operates as a collaborator within a reflective, evolving workflow.

This echoes the original study where drawing with AI was described not just as making something, but as engaging with something. In this sense, the aesthetic value lies not only in the final visuals but in the recursive negotiation of meaning through a hybrid process. The method supports not just storytelling, but also story-making as an open-ended, interpretive, and artful practice.

5.2   Reflections in Parallel Contexts

Through clustering of participants' written reflections of the experience and the results, four primary experiential themes were identified: *Explorative Delight*, *Critical Skepticism*, *Curious Ambiguity*, and *Pragmatic Tolerance*, see Fig. 18. These themes reflect both positive and critical aspects of engaging in mixed initiative creation and align, to varying degrees, with the reflective accounts in the original paper [16].

Explorative Delight describes the moments where participants found the process enjoyable, surprising, and immersive. In the workshop, only one participant described the process as "fun", "engaging" or "highly concentrated". Upon close examination, this data point came from the feedback given by the SA (not the students). This is consistent with her experience in the original study, where the turn-taking structure was described as poetic and creatively liberating. The AI was perceived as a source of visual and narrative prompts that extended the creative act. This experience may have also been due to the fact that this was SA's second time with the method and the tool (while for all the other participants it was the first). One other participant mentioned "That a randomly generated thing can be extremely useful in ideation and storytelling", which appears to suggest the value of random generation for their creative thinking (this is, of course, not limited to generative AI and can be achieved through other, non-AI computational – or analogue – means [15]).

Critical Skepticism, however, emerged strongly in both contexts. In the workshop, some participants expressed dissatisfaction with the AI's output, describing a mismatch between their intent and the generated images. These concerns were particularly pronounced when the AI produced results that were off-topic, unappealing, or incoherent. Importantly, this mirrors – and arguably intensifies – the first author's (FA) reflections. In her professional practice, FA found the AI's interventions to be actively disruptive, referring to them as "interruptions from the outside" that clashed with her intuitive drawing rhythm. She described moments where the AI imposed an external logic that conflicted with her narrative intentions, requiring her to consciously "adjust her flow" or even discard frames that had previously held personal meaning. This experience did not negate the value of the AI's input, but it did shift the burden onto the human creator to resolve inconsistencies and reassert narrative control. These accounts suggest that while co-creation can be fruitful, it may also introduce tension – especially for practitioners accustomed to uninterrupted creative flow.

Curious Ambiguity captures instances where participants were open to the experience but offered minimal elaboration. The workshop saw responses such as "interesting" and "It was interesting, despite my limited skill with pencils, the pictures generated from them and prompts were very nice", that neither praised nor criticized the process in great depth, but suggested being a curiously open to the process and pleased with the results. This ambiguity was mirrored in the original paper [16], where the authors described using obscure or abstract AI outputs as narrative prompts, requiring interpretation or acceptance of ambiguity. These moments suggest that participants may tolerate uncertainty in the AI's contributions, especially when the output leaves room for imaginative reinterpretation. One participant noted that "I felt a bit frustrated with the AI... Ultimately it did force me to come up with new ideas so I do see the point of it". However, again it is not elaborated upon further (to reveal what the participant believed to be "the point of it"), thus it is unclear if this comments on an AI-specific quality or rather an aspect of the creative process that can be achieved by other means.

Pragmatic Tolerance includes more neutral or mildly disengaged responses, such as "It was alright." This subdued tone was less explicit in the original paper [16], but still detectable. For instance, the SA described feeling that her first comic was "not really finished" and needed to rest before revisiting it. This reflects a tentative or unresolved relationship with the AI-assisted output, suggesting that the method may not produce immediately satisfying results for every participant. Similarly, FA noted that using the method often required patience and multiple iterations before something meaningful emerged. In addition, one participant reported "I thought it was fun to draw, and I think the AI made it easier for me to draw something new", commenting on AI more as an aid (but not elaborating on whether it was an aid to imagination, creative courage or any other aspects).

5.3   Creative Tension and Control

A cross-cutting observation in both studies is that while the method encourages play and improvisation, it also introduces creative tension. The role of the AI is inherently double-edged: it offers generative momentum, but also unexpected shifts that may derail the participant's intended direction or break the creative flow. In the workshop, some users reported that their stories became incoherent, "disconnected" or veered off course due to the AI's visual choices. FA's experience in the original study underscores this risk: although she valued the AI as a material, she also described its outputs as sometimes jarring, requiring post-hoc repair and curation. The human creator must often reframe, sequence, or even discard AI contributions to maintain narrative and aesthetic coherence.

Some participants expressed dissatisfaction with the visual coherence or quality of the AI-generated images. These concerns included aesthetic mismatches or unexpected outputs that didn't align with their intentions.

"AI result wasn't always what I expected/didn't always look good", "AI frame turned out bad but im happy with the rest"

There is also a theme of reduced agency or loss of direction when working with AI.

"I guess maybe that it sort of got a bit random...", "Not really a comic, more a collection of pictures..."

This points to a broader creative tension: while surprise can be delightful, too much unpredictability – especially without meaningful control – can reduce satisfaction and make the story feel fragmented.

Furthermore, several participants expressed frustration with having to wait during the image generation process, especially when using the Google Colab interface. While anticipation can sometimes contribute to creative suspense, extended or uncertain latency disrupt participants' engagement, concentration and flow. This aligns with prior findings in HCI and creativity research where interruptions in feedback loops – particularly during ideation – can lead to diminished flow, disengagement, or decreased perception of control [1]. In co-creative systems, where momentum and interpretive responsiveness are central, waiting can flatten emotional energy or break the rhythm of meaning-making.

Participants also appeared to overestimate the capabilities of the AI, expecting it to interpret their drawings with greater coherence and narrative intelligence than the system was designed to deliver. This disappointment with the AI's interpretive limitations can be seen in comments such as "I expected the AI to understand my images a little better". This aligns with other studies such as [21] which has found that people generally overestimate the accuracy of large language model outputs, highlighting a disconnect between AI performance and user perception.

5.4   Summary of Reflection Alignment

These findings are summarised in Table 1. They underscore that while the method can generate meaningful, even joyful experiences, it also introduces friction, particularly when participants confront the tension between AI autonomy and their own creative vision. This echoes the original study where the FA has found that her working method, that of allowing the story to "come out", unfold through time, arrive on paper simply by moving the pen and sustaining that movement, clashes with the tool when it gets in the way of "letting it out". Rather than treating these challenges as failure modes, the reflections suggest they are inherent to the co-creative nature of the process and offer insight into how human-AI interactive collaboration in narrative creation might be better scaffolded, curated, or supported across different use contexts.

5.5   Is Generative AI Necessary?

While the mixed initiative method successfully introduced elements of surprise, engagement, and narrative expansion through generative AI, it also raises a critical question: to what extent is AI actually needed for this form of creative practice? The method relies on a structured alternation between human drawing and AI generation, but many of the cognitive, emotional, and narrative gains – such as reflection, reinterpretation, and playful experimentation – might arguably be achieved through purely human means. For example, techniques such as collaborative drawing, role-based improvisation, or storyboard games

Table 1. Parallels in Reflections Between Workshop Participants and Original Study by the Authors

Reflection Cluster	Workshop Participants	Original Study Echo
Explorative Delight	Fun, highly focused, meditative engagement	Joyful engagement, poetic discovery
Critical Skepticism	Frustration with AI, mismatch with intent, aesthetic dissatisfaction	AI perceived as disruptive to flow, wait, narrative clashes, need for adjustment
Curious Ambiguity	Open but minimal commentary ("interesting")	Use of obscure AI outputs as creative prompts
Pragmatic Tolerance	Mild engagement, feeling of incompleteness	Deferred satisfaction, trial-and-error acceptance

have historically enabled similar forms of narrative invention without requiring intervention from an AI [15].

Participant feedback strongly reinforces this observation: the tactile, analogue aspects of the workshop – particularly hand drawing – were consistently highlighted as the most enjoyable element. Every respondent identified their favourite part of the session as something related to sketching or physical materials: "Just sketching out pictures, rarely do I do it but it is enjoyable", "it felt nice to draw", "it was fun to draw", and as well as "What I enjoyed the most was my own drawings", with one participants naming "coloured pencils" to be their favourite part.

For over a decade, the FA has facilitated numerous analogue comic-making workshops built around a single guiding prompt: "What happens next?". These sessions have taken place in a variety of settings, including high schools and corporate team-building contexts. Across these environments, she has consistently observed participants engaging in spontaneous, imaginative storytelling with minimal instruction or intervention. In contrast, attempts to introduce AI tools into similar sessions were found to introduce unnecessary complexity, often disrupting the intuitive flow of the activity without meaningfully enhancing either the creative experience or the narrative outcomes.

Moreover, the material and environmental costs of generative AI – ranging from computational intensity to ethical concerns around dataset provenance – are increasingly difficult to overlook. The high energy usage associated with training and deploying large-scale models has prompted calls for more environmentally sustainable approaches to creative computation [5,22]. In addition, the opacity of generative image datasets raises questions about authorship, consent, and artistic accountability – particularly when images are produced through models trained on content whose origins are not always disclosed or controllable.

Researchers in post-digital art and critical design have long emphasized the importance of human agency, tactile materials, and constraint as generative forces [2,17]. Within this perspective, the process of making – rather than the novelty of the tools – becomes the site of meaning and reflection. From this view, the introduction of AI into a traditionally human practice such as comics-making may enrich the experience for some, but it may also displace existing creative dynamics or introduce unnecessary complexity.

The presence of AI undoubtedly shaped the outcomes of this process, but whether it was indispensable or justifiable remains an open question. Rather than resolving this tension, this study highlights the need for more situated, critical engagement with the role of generative AI in everyday creative practice. What is gained, what is lost, and what is displaced when complex systems are inserted into simple human workflows? These are design and pedagogical questions as much as technical ones, and they warrant ongoing reflection by researchers, educators, and creative practitioners alike.

6   Conclusion

Building on our prior artistic work with generative AI, this paper has presented an exploration of our mixed-initiative comic-making method among casual creators. The resulting comics and reflections were analyzed through thematic clustering, offering insight into both the narrative forms that emerged and the range of emotional and cognitive experiences reported.

The stories participants created spanned fantasy, surrealism, everyday life, and playful disruption – highlighting the method's capacity to support divergent narrative styles. Reflections revealed both delight and skepticism: participants valued the surprise and visual amplification provided by AI, but also voiced frustration when the AI output conflicted with their intentions or aesthetic goals. These mixed reactions echo earlier experiences in a studio-based practice and affirm the variability of engagement depending on context, expectation, and creative agency.

By integrating feedback from a public pre-study and a more structured workshop, this work underscores the potential of our method of appropriating generative AI within a creative workflow to enable accessible, improvisational storytelling for non-artists. At the same time, it raises critical questions about necessity, sustainability, and the nature of collaboration with AI. Rather than positioning AI as essential to creativity, we suggest that its value may lie in how it invites reinterpretation, reflection, and reconfiguration of familiar materials and routines.

We believe that the structured yet open-ended format introduced here could be adapted to interactive storytelling systems, particularly those that emphasize co-creative dialogue between user and system, such as story-based games, procedural generation environments, or AI-assisted narrative design tools. Our method could be of use to researchers exploring narrative scaffolding techniques that facilitate user-driven story emergence; Mixed-initiative authoring tools where narrative evolves through interplay; Low-barrier IDN systems for public workshops, education, or participatory prototyping.

While the study surfaced rich insights into casual creative engagement with AI, some participant frustration – particularly around AI output quality – may have been mitigated through clearer guidance on prompt formulation or system expectations. Additionally, future studies might benefit from broader participant diversity and alternative methodological framings to explore how different creative backgrounds and support structures shape human-AI collaboration.

References

1. Amershi, S., et al.: Guidelines for human-AI interaction. In: Proceedings of the 2019 CHI Conference on Human Factors in Computing Systems (CHI 2019), ACM (2019). https://doi.org/10.1145/3290605.3300233
2. Bardzell, J., Bardzell, S.: What is "critical" about critical design? In: Proceedings of the SIGCHI Conference on Human Factors in Computing Systems (CHI 2013), pp. 3297–3306. ACM (2013). https://doi.org/10.1145/2470654.2466451
3. Barry, L.: Making Comics. Drawn & Quarterly, Montreal (2019)
4. Shneiderman, B.: Leonardo's Laptop: Human Needs and the New Computing Technologies. MIT Press (2002)
5. Bender, E.M., Gebru, T., McMillan-Major, A., Shmitchell, S.: On the dangers of stochastic parrots: Can language models be too big? In: Proceedings of the 2021 ACM Conference on Fairness, Accountability, and Transparency, FAccT 2021, pp. 610–623. ACM, New York, NY, USA (2021). https://doi.org/10.1145/3442188.3445922
6. Buxton, B.: Sketching User Experiences: Getting the Design Right and the Right Design. Morgan Kaufmann (2007)
7. Compton, K., Mateas, M.: Casual creators. In: Foundations of Digital Games (FDG) (2015)
8. Deterding, S.: The lens of intrinsic skill atoms: a method for gameful design. In: Proceedings of the 2016 CHI Conference on Human Factors in Computing Systems (2016)
9. Ellis, C., Adams, T.E., Bochner, A.P.: autoethnography: an overview. Hist. Soc. Res. **12**, 273–290 (2010). https://api.semanticscholar.org/CorpusID:145694038
10. Gero, K.I., Chilton, L.B.: Metaphoria: an algorithmic companion for metaphor creation. In: Proceedings of the 2019 CHI Conference on Human Factors in Computing Systems (CHI 2019), ACM (2019). https://doi.org/10.1145/3290605.3300526
11. Gero, K.I., Long, D., Chilton, L.B.: Social dynamics of AI support in creative writing. In: Proceedings of the 2023 CHI Conference on Human Factors in Computing Systems (CHI 2023), ACM (2023). https://doi.org/10.1145/3544548.3580782
12. Loi, D., Wolf, C.T., Blomberg, J.L., Arar, R., Brereton, M., et al.: Co-designing AI Futures: Integrating AI Ethics, Social Computing, and Design. In: DIS 2019 Workshop on Co-designing AI Futures, ACM (2019). https://research.ibm.com/publications/co-designing-ai-futures-integrating-ai-ethics-social-computing-and-design
13. Kantosalo, A., Riihiaho, S.: Experience evaluations for human–computer co-creative processes – planning and conducting an evaluation in practice. Connect. Sci. **31**(1), 60–81 (2019)

14. Karimi, P., Grace, K., Maher, M.L., Davis, N.: Evaluating creativity in computational co-creative systems. In: Proceedings of the International Conference on Computational Creativity (ICCC) (2018)
15. Knight, Y., Eladhari, M.P.: Artificial intelligence in an artistic practice: a journey through surrealism and generative arts. Media Pract. Educ. 1–18 (2025). https://doi.org/10.1080/25741136.2024.2443865
16. Knight, Y., Eladhari, M.P.: Mixed initiative comic making in an artistic practice. In: Proceedings of the 2024 International Conference on Interactive Digital Storytelling (ICIDS). LNCS, vol. 15467, pp. 144–159. Springer (2025). https://doi.org/10.1007/978-3-031-78453-8_10
17. Lindtner, S., Hertz, G., Dourish, P.: Emerging sites of HCI innovation: hackerspaces, hardware startups & incubators. In: Proceedings of the 32nd Annual ACM Conference on Human Factors in Computing Systems (CHI 2014), ACM (2014). https://doi.org/10.1145/2556288.2557132
18. Mitchell, A., McGee, K.: Reading again for the first time: a model of rereading in interactive stories. In: Oyarzun, D., Peinado, F., Young, R.M., Elizalde, A., Méndez, G. (eds.) ICIDS 2012. LNCS, vol. 7648, pp. 202–213. Springer, Heidelberg (2012). https://doi.org/10.1007/978-3-642-34851-8_20
19. Rosner, D.K.: Critical Fabulations: Reworking the Methods and Margins of Design. MIT Press (2018)
20. Ryan, M.L.: Avatars of Story. University of Minnesota Press, Minneapolis, MN (2006)
21. Steyvers, M., He, J., Lucas, G.: People overestimate the reliability of AI language models, study finds. Tech Xplore (2025), https://techxplore.com/news/2025-01-people-overestimate-reliability-ai-language.html
22. Strubell, E., Ganesh, A., McCallum, A.: Energy and policy considerations for deep learning in NLP. arXiv preprint arXiv:1906.02243 (2019)
23. Wieluch, S., Schwenker, F.: Co-creative drawing with one-shot generative models. In: EvoMUSART 2021 – International Conference on Computational Intelligence in Music, Sound, Art and Design (Lecture Notes in Computer Science). LNCS, vol. 12693, pp. 475–489. Springer (2021). https://doi.org/10.1007/978-3-030-72914-1_31

Social Robots Against Bullying – Effects of Embodiment and Interactivity on Social Story Experience and Efficiency

Sophia C. Steinhaeusser[1]([⊠]) [iD], Ohenewa Bediako Akuffo[1] [iD],
Hanna-Finja Weichert[1] [iD], Gerhild Nieding[2] [iD], and Birgit Lugrin[1] [iD]

[1] Socially Interactive Agents, University of Würzburg, Würzburg, Germany
`sophia.steinhaeusser@uni-wuerzburg.de`
[2] Developmental Psychology, University of Würzburg, Würzburg, Germany

Abstract. Bullying in early childhood remains an underexplored challenge despite its early manifestation and lasting impact. Social stories are a proven tool to teach appropriate behavior in young children. Social robots as storytellers offer an engaging medium, i.a. for children, for such interventions due to their embodied, interactive capabilities. This paper investigates the potential of a robot telling a social story as an anti-bullying intervention. Across two studies, we compared storytelling with an embodied robotic storyteller to a loudspeaker (Study I) and linear versus interactive robotic storytelling (Study II). Results from Study I showed that while story recognition and transportation did not differ significantly, robotic storytelling elicited significantly more empathy. Study II revealed that interactivity notably improved bullying awareness, though it did not affect empathy or transportation. These findings suggest that robotic storytelling – especially when interactive – can be an effective, engaging tool for early bullying interventions.

Keywords: social robots · child-robot interaction · bullying · storytelling · interactivity

1 Introduction

Bullying – defined as an aggressive act that is done repeatedly and is further characterized by an imbalance of power [69] – is already apparent to children even in young ages such as preschoolers [5,41]. While they have a different understanding of the term being less focused on repetition, intention, and imbalance of power, they already understand the term victim and being victimized [86]. Bullying has three typical forms, it can happen verbally, physically, and there is also relational bullying in form of social exclusion [86] with the last being the most common type among preschoolers [41]. Doing so, bullying is not an act including only two individuals, bully and victim [5,60], but also peripheral roles of assistants and reinforcers of defenders and observers, i.e. bystanders [5,86].

M. C. Reyes and F. Nack (Eds.): ICIDS 2025, LNCS 16375, pp. 72–94, 2026.
https://doi.org/10.1007/978-3-032-12405-0_5

Although extensive research has been conducted on bullying and its prevention – targeting, for instance, empathy, awareness, or simply knowledge on consequences [24] – the majority of studies have focused on school-age children and adolescents, with considerably less attention given to younger children [5,60]. However, Vlachou et al. [86] found a link between pre-schoolers understanding of emotions and aggression, suggesting that deficits in emotion knowledge are associated with both verbal and physical aggression. Similarly, Gini [25], in a study of children aged eight and eleven, reported problems in social cognition being related to the role of the victim. Belacchi and Farina [5] also found, when studying children aged three to six years, that children with poorer external emotion comprehension were more likely to assume the role of the victim, indicating a diminished ability to understand others' emotions. In contrast, a strong comprehension of external, mental, and reflective emotions was positively associated with prosocial roles such as that of the defender. These results suggest that correct recognition and interpretation of emotions helps in avoiding these forms of victimization [86], even though aggressive roles such as bullies are not related to emotion understanding.

Stories seem to have great potential in the domain of bullying prevention being used by therapists to evoke specific emotions in patients [59]. Emotion understanding is closely related to empathy, the emotional response of oneself to understanding emotional stimuli [13]. Thus, both training emotion comprehension but also gathering insights into children's empathetic reactions to bullying might help in bullying prevention, which can be employed through storytelling. For example, therapy designed for children with disorders from the autism spectrum (ASD) makes use of stories to teach socially appropriate behavior, so-called social stories [30].

Stories emerged from traditional oral storytelling to audio books, movies, games [42], and even robots [74]. Especially social robots – defined as physically embodied agents [16] with a socially interactive focus [47] that are capable to communicate in a multimodal way [6] – are heavily researched as storytellers (see e.g., [67,74,76]). In the context of therapeutic storytelling, Simut et al. [67] used social stories to teach socially appropriate behavior to children with ASD delivered either by a human therapist or a social robot. The results indicated greater improvements in behavior for the robotic than the human storyteller, indicating the suitability of social robots for therapeutic storytelling, at least within ASD therapy.

Given the potential of storytelling as a prevention method for bullying and the advantages of social robots in delivering stories in a multimodal and interactive manner, we explore the use of robotic storytellers as a novel approach to bullying prevention in children. In this paper, we describe two experiments investigating the potential of social robots as storytellers of social stories to young children to act as a prevention tool against bullying. To determine the benefits of the robotic storyteller's physical embodiment and its related ability to convey emotions, we first compared it to a loudspeaker playing the story without visual elements. Furthermore, to examine the added benefits of interactivity, we implemented an interactive version of the story, comparing it to the linear version. By leveraging the engaging yet standardized nature of robotic storytelling, this approach has the potential to serve as an effective and scalable prevention method with strong applicability in real-world settings.

2   Related Work

Storytelling accompanies humans since the earliest beginning of mankind. It is defined by it's dialogic nature between the storyteller and the recipient(s) [42]. In the ancient past it was used as a method for implicit information sharing [42], including the teaching of social behaviors favoring cooperation and altruism [9].

2.1   Storytelling for Implicit Learning

Today, storytelling is a common approach for implicit learning, particularly in children, for example in second language learning [40], but also aiming for behavioral changes, for instance, in therapy. For example, the power of stories to induce emotions can be used to facilitate patients experiencing particular emotions or to reduce negative emotions and affects [59]. Stories incorporated in new media such as narrative game-based interventions have shown potential to trigger behavioral changes as well as improve self-efficacy [90]. Further strengthening the important role of storytelling in therapy, Gray [30] composed a special form of therapy called *social stories* in which short stories are adapted to patients to teach them social situations and appropriate social behaviors. Social stories were originally created and are mostly used for children with disabilities such as autism spectrum disorders [43], but also showed to be suitable for other purposes, e.g., healthcare interventions in children [91]. They include four types of sentences: (1) descriptive sentences describing actions of others together with a rationale, (2) directive sentences suggesting preferred reactions, (3) perspective sentences describing others' reactions to this appropriate behavior, and (4) affirmative sentences which reinforce shared societal values or common beliefs relevant to the situation. Subsequently, two additional sentence types were introduced: (5) control sentences created by the learner to improve comprehension and recall, and (6) cooperative sentences, which highlight the support that others can offer. When constructing a Social Story, specific ratios of these sentence types should be maintained to ensure balance and effectiveness [80]. Within interventions, social stories should initially be read out loud by the teacher, followed by one of three formats for the child: reading the story independently, listening to an audio recording, or viewing a visually enriched video presentation. However, in practice, they are most commonly delivered through traditional read-aloud sessions [64]. The telling of social stories by therapists have also proven effective in bullying interventions among children, particularly in enhancing coping strategies [71].

This way of learning can be explained by grasping stories as simulations. Stories – even if completely fictional – enable recipients to experience isolated simulated events, but they also "model and abstract the human social world.

Like other simulations (e.g., computer models), fictional stories are informative in that they allow for prediction and explanation while revealing the underlying processes of what is being modeled (in this case, social relations)" [48, p. 173]. Thereby, stories can modify our mental models of the world and even provoke changes in our personality [56]. As people are the subject matter of most stories told [57], it can be assumed that story reception particularly improves mental models about people and their minds, also referred to as theory of mind, thus enhancing social skills and cooperative abilities [50]. Although study results investigating this relationship are mixed [14,17], positive effects of, for instance, frequency of reading time on theory of mind [61] and empathy [14], or a short-term increase of social abilities [49], empathy [14], and even trait changes in terms of the Big Five [15] due to artistic stories were found. Studies show that from the age of three, children can adopt characters' goals that they have personal experience with in order to identify with them, while unfamiliar goals can be adopted not until the age of five [55].

An important factor shaping the relationship between stories and real-world mental models is transportation [33,49,50], the recipients' absorption into the story, involving focused attention, vivid imagery, and emotional engagement [33]. This is not surprising as transportation is not only closely linked to enjoyment [35,78], fun, and perceived meaningfulness of a media artifact [35], but also facilitates the suspension of disbelief and elicits strong feelings toward story characters – particularly positive ones toward protagonists – thereby increasing the potential for stories to influence recipients' beliefs [33], and enabling them to "change the way we see the world" [32, p. 76].

2.2 Social Robots as Embodied Storytellers

"To do this, stories must attract the listener's attention, and be memorable enough to influence the listener's later behaviour" [9, p. 25]. Such engagement in stories is especially achieved by representing story emotions and their causes as well as evoking such emotions in the recipients [10]. For this, a storyteller has to transfer their mental images of the story to the mental imagery, i.e. the internal representation, of the recipients, using not only speech but also facial expressions, body language, or voice modulation [46] to bring story characters to life [8]. Particularly, Lipman [46] stresses the need of physical presence of the storyteller to shape recipients' experience.

Offering this physical presence, social robots bear great potential as storytellers. They are able to communicate on a natural and intuitive way using both verbal and non-verbal cues [6]. This anthropomorphic, i.e. human-like, communication as well as further anthropomorphic design elements such as the robot's shape trigger human users to anthropomorphize a robot, attributing human characteristics such as gender but also emotions to it [21]. In turn, human users tend to treat robots like social (human-like) beings [92], an effect that is found for communicative technology in general [63]. On this base, social robots can elicit social responses and emotions in their users [28]. Given that "humans usually know how to interact with each other" [21, p. 204], it is unsurprising that anthropomorphism in robots improves humans' perceptions and attitudes towards them [29]. This effect is also present in children [65]. Moreover, social robots can combine the advantages of embodied storytellers applying expressive body language [74,76] and technology allowing for controlling modalities that humans are not capable of such as colored light [72] or sound effects [74]. Based on these abilities, social robots are able to bring stories and their characters to life, achieving storytelling experiences comparable to audio books [76] and even in-person human storytelling [88].

Robotic storytelling is generally well received by children, being able to successfully convey stories' content and dramaturgy to children [23]. Conti et al. [11] even revealed that memory of a story told by a human respectively a robotic storyteller, namely a *NAO* robot, does not differ over several sessions. Particularly robotic storytellers supporting implicit learning in children are widely researched. Especially expending vocabulary in first language developing [89] as well as in second language learning [27,87] was positively evaluated in robotic storytelling interventions. Even in stressful contexts such as hospitals robotic storytellers were shown to effectively pass knowledge to children, evoking increased emotional engagement while reducing negative emotions such as anxiety compared to tablet-based interventions [7]. Robots telling social stories were yet primarily investigated in children with ASD, for instance a *ZECA* robot telling social stories was shown to support emotion recognition in combination with an external optical device [66]. Furthermore, Simut et al. [67] found that compared to a human therapist telling social stories a storytelling *Probo* robot presenting the same stories resulted in an increase of expected social responses shown by the children, suggesting an improved intervention effect for robotic storytellers. Although research on robots telling specifically social stories for implicit learning to typically developing children is rare, first attempts show that robotic storytelling can be used to provoke critical social thinking and communication in children, for example, on the topic of gender inequality [51].

2.3   The Potential of Interactive Narratives

Similarly, digital interactive stories – "stories the player interacts with by contributing actions to them" [1, p. 213], in contrast to linear stories, where recipients cannot influence the outcome [1] – can be employed to address bullying by encouraging reflection on its consequences [81]. Interactive stories enable recipients to shape a story in real time [68], increasing their absorption into the story as well as their perceived agency, i.e. their feeling of control and influence over the content or experience [31,58]. This increased agency was previously shown to positively affect recipients' "feelings of autonomy and competence, flow state, and desires to participate in similar experiences" [54, p. 529] in role-playing with robots. Flow, a state of deep focus and enjoyment [12], was shown to positively influence persuasive effectiveness of media messages [37]. Moreover, related works on advertising reported strong persuasive functions of interactivity itself [77]. Furthermore, focusing on children, Ligthart et al. [45] reported increased attention, enjoyment, and memory performance when adding interactive design patterns to a robotic storytelling. This interactive approach was already applied in the *FearNot!* project, allowing child users to advise a bullied virtual agent in an autonomously emerging virtual drama [4,82]. Studies on this intervention tool revealed its effectiveness in increasing knowledge on and awareness of bullying [36] as well as its potential to foster peer intervention in terms of defense [84]. These findings not only strengthen the idea of technology-based story interventions against bullying, but further highlight the added potential of interactivity to their effectiveness.

In summary, previous research highlights the strong potential of storytelling as an intervention method for bullying, especially when delivered in a digital and interactive format. Given their physical presence and ability to multimodally convey emotions, social robots may offer a promising approach to delivering social stories for bullying prevention.

3   Contribution

We conducted two studies to get detailed insights into the potential of using social robots and a social story in a bullying prevention. First, we focused on the comparison of a physically embodied robotic storyteller and an audio book presentation using a loudspeaker, both enabling a consistent, repeatable storytelling. Given the advantages shown by previous research on robots' embodiment and the associated ability of multimodal communication, we postulate an improvement of prevention effects of a social story on variables targeted by classical bullying interventions (see [24]) for a robotic storyteller compared to an audio book.

- **RQ1:** Does physical embodiment through a robotic storyteller increase story recognition in preschoolers?
- **RQ2:** Do preschoolers sympathize more with a physically embodied robotic storyteller compared to a audio book?
- **H1:** Preschoolers' transportation is higher in storytelling delivered by a social robot compared to an audio book.
- **H2:** Preschoolers sympathize more with the victim than with the bully in stories delivered by a social robot compared to an audio book.
- **H3:** Preschoolers perceive higher empathy in storytelling delivered by a social robot compared to an audio book.
- **H4:** Preschoolers exhibit greater bullying awareness in storytelling with a social robot compared to an audio book.

In a subsequent study, we investigated the realization of the story as either linear or interactive. Given the potential of added interactivity reported in related works described above, we suggest an improvement of prevention effects of a social story for an interactive robotic storytelling compared to a linear one.

- **RQ1:** Does interactive storytelling increase story recognition of preschoolers?

- **RQ2:** Do preschoolers sympathize more with a robotic storyteller telling an interactive compared to a linear story?
- **H1:** Preschoolers' transportation is higher in interactive storytelling compared to linear storytelling.
- **H2:** Preschoolers exhibit higher sympathy towards the victim than the bully in interactive storytelling compared to linear storytelling.
- **H3:** Preschoolers perceive higher empathy in interactive storytelling compared to linear storytelling.
- **H4:** Preschoolers exhibit greater bullying awareness during interactive storytelling than during linear storytelling.

In total, we used three versions of a social story: (1) in form of an audio book played back using a loudspeaker, (2) multimodally told by a social robot, and (3) by the same multimodal robotic storyteller but in an interactive way.

4   Creating the Storytelling

To realize our investigations on robotic storytelling in a anti-bullying scenario for young children, a social story was crafted and subsequently implemented on a social robot.

4.1   Conception

The social story addressing the issue of bullying used was exclusively written for our studies. As the story had to be child-friendly for the target group of preschoolers, we chose animal characters (see [44] for a discussion) in a bullying scenario. We integrated four characters, each representing one of the typical roles in a bullying scenario as described above: the victim (hedgehog), the bully (fox), the supporter (deer), and the bystander (rabbit). As a setting, we chose an animal kindergarten to ease identification of the child participants with the story characters.

The story starts with the victim being excluded from play by the bully and bystander. As the narrative tension builds, the victim sadly separates from the others, only to be approached by the supporter, who invites it to join in a new activity. The climax occurs when the bully attempts once more to exclude the victim, but the supporter intervenes, emphasizing the positive qualities of each animal character. The story concludes with a happy ending that conveys the moral: unique traits are strengths, not weaknesses.

The story was iteratively reviewed by experts – a developmental psychologist and an educational social worker – to ensure consistency and age-appropriateness for preschoolers. This included evaluating not only content but also aspects such as structure, wording, and sentence length. In addition, the story was tested for comprehensibility with a three-year-old child.

Once finalized, the interactive version of the story was developed. To enable active participation, three decision points were incorporated, allowing children to choose the victim's actions. To maintain consistency across all story versions, these choices did not influence the overall storyline or its outcome. Instead, they focused on elements that were narrative-neutral, such as deciding between two types of play activities with the supporter.[1]

The story was annotated by two persons who jointly assigned Ekman's [19] big six emotions (happiness, sadness, fear, surprise, anger, disgust) to the story's sentences. These annotations are necessary to realize emotion expression of the robot. Parts of the story altered in the interactive version were not annotated throughout all conditions to maintain consistency across the versions.

Fig. 1. Snapshots of the Reeti robot during storytelling, facial expressions f.l.t.r.: anger, disgust, happiness (top row), sadness, surprise, neutral (bottom row).

4.2 Implementation

We selected the *Reeti* robot for its small size and cute design, which makes it particularly well suited for interactions with young children. The decision making was realized using a mini-keyboard with two buttons which were colored in blue and yellow, as can be seen in Fig. 2. To enable this interactivity, we utilized the *NarRobot* plugin [75] to program the robot with *Unity* version 2020.1.10.f.1.

Facial expressions reflecting the annotated big six emotions [18] were conceptualized and applied to the respective sentences. The expressions are displayed in Fig. 1. As fear was not annotated to the story, no respective facial expression was implemented.

Additionally, the robot's cheek LEDs were used to indicate which story character was currently speaking, with each character represented by a distinct light color. Narrator segments – comprising approximately half of the story's text

---

[1] The final story can be found here: https://doi.org/10.58160/3v10gwkacx9n4272.

Fig. 2. Study setup for interactive robotic storytelling condition.

– were presented without LED illumination. This design was intended to help children more easily identify the active speaker and follow the storytelling more effectively.

For speech we used the robot's internal text-to-speech system as related research shows the suitability of synthetic voices for robotic storytelling [73]. Taken together, we sent speech commands together with commands for the corresponding facial expressions and LED color, if applicable, for subsequent separate parts of the story to the robot to realize the robotic storytelling of our social story.

For the audio book version, the robot's storytelling was recorded without facial expression to avoid motor noise, resulting in a five-minute audio file that could be played back through a loudspeaker.

5   Research Focus I: Embodiment

In our first study, we compared a social story for bullying prevention either multimodally told by an embodied social robot or unimodally played back by a loudspeaker.

5.1   Methods

We carried out a field study using a between-participants design in two kindergartens to compare the effects of a social story on bullying prevention between robotic storytelling and audio book. The study was deemed ethically sound by the local ethics committee.

5.2   Measures

Due to the participants' young age, the questionnaire was read aloud by the experimenter, and responses (Yes, No, I don't know) were recorded using pen and paper. All items were formulated in collaboration with developmental psychologists to align with the children's cognitive and linguistic development.[2]

Story Recognition: To assess the respondents' comprehension of the story, they were asked to recognize six statements related to the story they had previously heard, such as "Did the hedgehog cry?" or "Is the hedgehog good at picking berries?". Of these six statements, three served as distractors.

Transportation: The *Transportation Scale - Short Form* by Appel et al. [3], adapted by Steinicke, for preschool children, was used to measure narrative transportation. The scale was tailored to the story used in this study and included four items such as, "Did you want to know how the story ends?" and "Could you see yourself in the animal kindergarten described in the story?".

Empathy: Empathy towards the victim in the story was measured using three items adapted from Rosenthal-von der Pütten's [62] *Empathy with the Robot* scale, including the following items: "Were you sad when the hedgehog was all alone?", "When the hedgehog was sad, were you sad, too?", and "When the others were mean to the hedgehog, were you sad?".

Awareness of bullying: To evaluate the awareness of bullying among the preschool sample, two items were developed. The items were phrased in a way that allowed children to relate to the described situations. The two items were: "Do you think it's good or bad if someone isn't allowed to play with you and your friends?" and "Do you think it's good or bad when a child in your group is teased?".

Sympathy: Sympathy toward the victim in the story was assessed using an objective behavioral measure. Children were given six stickers, which they could freely distribute among three color-coded bowls representing the main characters of the story (the victim and the bully) and themselves. Before the distribution, children were explicitly told that they would only be allowed to keep the stickers they allocated to themselves, while the remaining stickers would, allegedly, be given to the respective animals. The procedure was then repeated, whereby, participants were again given six stickers, which they now had to distribute between two color-coded bowls. This time, the bowls represented the participant and either the robot or the speaker, depending on the condition. This setup was used to assess the children's sympathy toward the robot or speaker. Again, the same instructions applied, whereby, children could only keep the stickers they allocated to themselves.

5.3   Participants and Their Recruitment

As all participants were minors, their parents were fully informed about the study's procedures through a written information letter and an online parent

---

[2] All items can be found here: https://doi.org/10.58160/3v10gwkacx9n4272.

meeting. Their informed consent was obtained in advance. Similarly, the kindergarten directors were informed about the study and shown prototypes of the storytelling, providing their explicit approval. In addition, all experimenters provided a police clearance certificate to ensure compliance with child protection standards.

In study I, 31 children between three and six years with a mean age of 4.36 ($SD = 0.92$) participated. While 16 reported being female (age: $M = 4.19$, $SD = 0.91$), 14 of them self-reported being male (age: $M = 4.57$, $SD = 0.94$). No one indicated as diverse gender. One child did not answer the question (age: 4 years). Being randomly assigned to one of the two conditions, 15 children received the story from the robot (8 female, 7 male; age: $M = 4.67$, $SD = 0.82$), whereas 16 children listened to the story played back by the speaker (8 female, 7 male, 1 missing answer; age: $M = 4.06$, $SD = 0.93$).

5.4   Study Procedure

Before the study, children were asked again if they wished to participate. To avoid priming effects, the specific purpose of the study was not disclosed in advance. A preschool teacher accompanied each child individually to a separate room and remained present throughout the experiment. This one-to-one setting was chosen over a group setting to focus on the effects of the bullying prevention itself, omitting effects of group dynamics.

Depending on the experimental condition, either the robot or a loudspeaker was placed on a child-sized table. The interviewers introduced themselves, engaged in child-friendly small talk, and gave a brief, age-appropriate explanation of the study, emphasizing its voluntary nature and the child's right to withdraw at any time. To maintain eye level with the children, they also sat on child-sized chairs.

Each child listened to the social story delivered either via the robot or the loudspeaker. After listening to the story, one experimenter administered a structured oral questionnaire containing the aforementioned scales and behavioral measure, while the second experimenter noted the children's responses.

After the session, participants were debriefed in an age-appropriate manner. To reduce the risk of information spreading among the preschoolers before all had participated, educators were asked to involve previously tested children in separate activities.

Finally, both the participating children and their educators received a certificate of participation. Each session lasted approximately 15 min and was deemed age-appropriate by developmental psychologists. To ensure that children in the loudspeaker condition were not disadvantaged, the robot was introduced to all participating children at the end of the study.

5.5   Results

All analyses were carried out using *Microsoft Excel* and a significance level of .05 if not stated otherwise.

Questionnaires. χ^2-tests were carried out to analyze the conditions' effects. Doing so, "I don't know"-answers were excluded from the analyses, except for *Story Recognition*, for which they were counted as wrong answers. Descriptives are displayed in Table 1.

Table 1. Answer frequencies for linear robot and loudspeaker conditions.

	Linear Robot			Loudspeaker		
	"Yes"	"No"	"I don't know"	"Yes"	"No"	"I don't know"
Transportation[a]	35	22	3	30	34	0
Empathy[b]	12	33	0	5	42	1
Bullying Awareness[c]	11	17	2	11	21	0

[a] Summed amounts of four items.

[b] Summed amounts of three items.

[c] Summed amounts of two items, coded: "yes" = "bullying good", "no" = "bullying bad."

Regarding *Story Recognition*, no significant relation between condition and amount of correct ($n_{robot} = 66, n_{loudspeaker} = 69$) respectively incorrect ($n_{robot} = 24, n_{loudspeaker} = 27$) answers was found, $\chi^2(1) = 0.05, p = .824$. Similarly, no significant relation between the conditions and *Transportation* was obtained, $\chi^2(1) = 2.56, p = .110$. In contrast, a significant relation between condition and *Empathy* was indicated ($\chi^2(1) = 3.921, p = .048$) with higher *Empathy* in the robot condition. Last, we indicated no significant relation between the conditions and children's *Bullying Awareness*, $\chi^2(1) = 0.155, p = .694$.

Behavioral Measure. Descriptive data for stickers apportioned to the story characters, devices, and the children themselves are displayed in Table 2.

For the first round, in which children were asked to allocate six stickers to the story's victim (hedgehog) and bully (fox) and themselves, a Chi^2-test indicated no significant relationship between embodiment condition and distribution of the stickers, $\chi^2(5) = 1.84, p = .871$. No significant difference was found between victim and bully, $p = .775$. In the second round, in which children apportioned six stickers to the storytelling device (loudspeaker or robot) and themselves, the Chi^2-test again revealed no significant relationship between embodiment condition and distribution of the stickers, $\chi^2(3) = 1.63, p = .652$.

5.6   Discussion

In this first study, we examined the potential advantages of a physically embodied robotic storyteller compared to an audio book in the context of a bullying intervention for children, using a social story.

The results revealed no significant differences in children's recognition of story details (**RQ1**) or their sympathy toward the storytelling device (**RQ2**).

Table 2. Means and standard deviations for amount of stickers apportioned in Study I.

	Round 1						Round 2			
	Victim		Bully		Child		Device		Child	
	M	SD	M	SD	M	SD	M	SD	M	SD
Robot	1.80	1.37	1.20	0.86	3.00	1.65	2.93	0.96	3.07	0.96
Loudspeaker	1.56	0.81	1.75	1.13	2.69	1.85	2.38	1.54	3.63	1.54

Likewise, no differences were found between the robot and audio book conditions regarding children"s transportation into the story or their sympathy toward the story characters - both the victim and the bully - leading to the rejection of **H1** and **H2**. Comparable levels of transportation between emotional robotic storytellers and audio books have previously been observed in studies with adult participants [76]. Since transportation has been shown to influence the likeability of story characters [33], this similarity may explain the absence of differences in sympathy toward the characters across conditions.

However, children who received the story from the robot reported significantly higher levels of empathy compared to those in the loudspeaker condition, supporting **H3**. In contrast, no significant difference in bullying awareness was found between the two conditions, resulting in the rejection of **H4**. This finding may again be attributed to the similar levels of transportation, as transportation has been shown to mediate the influence of narratives on real-world beliefs [33]. Despite the absence of differences in some outcome measures, these initial results are promising: the robot's embodiment enhanced children's empathy – an important factor in bullying contexts, as higher empathy has been shown to reduce bullying behavior and promote defending behavior [83].

6   Research Focus II: Interactivity

In a second study, we explored how another advantage of the embodied storytelling robot, specifically its interactive capabilities, could further enhance the effectiveness of the intervention.

6.1   Methods

To investigate the impact of interactivity data for a third condition was collected.

Measures. The same instruments as in Study 1 were employed to assess story recognition, narrative transportation, empathy toward the victim, and bullying awareness. Sympathy was also assessed through the objective behavioral allocation task, comparing sticker distributions among the victim, the bully, and the participant.

Study Procedure. Data for the interactive condition were collected during the same phase as the first two conditions, following an identical recruitment process and procedure. The only modification to the setup was the addition of color-coded buttons to enable interactive decision-making, as shown in Fig. 2.

6.2 Participants

For the interactive condition, fifteen children (6 female, 9 male; age: $M = 4.73$, $SD = 1.03$) were acquired. Thus, together with the 15 children who received the linear storytelling from the robot (8 female, 7 male; age: $M = 4.67$, $SD = 0.82$), the data sets of thirty children aged from three to six years ($M = 4.70$, $SD = 0.92$) were used to investigate the impact of interactivity.

6.3 Results

Again, all analyses were carried out *Microsoft Excel* and a significance level of .05.

Questionnaires. The same procedure using χ^2-tests was conducted to compare the linear and interactive robot conditions. Descriptives are displayed in Table 3.

Table 3. Answer frequencies linear and interactive robot conditions.

	Linear Robot			Interactive Robot		
	"Yes"	"No"	"I don't know"	"Yes"	"No"	"I don't know"
Transportation[a]	35	22	3	32	26	2
Empathy[b]	12	33	0	8	37	0
Bullying Awareness[c]	11	17	2	1	29	0

[a] Summed amounts of four items.
[b] Summed amounts of three items.
[c] Summed amounts of two items, coded: "yes" = "bullying good", "no" = "bullying bad."

Concerning *Story Recognition*, no significant relation between condition and amount of correct ($n_{interactive} = 72, n_{linear} = 66$) respectively incorrect ($n_{interactive} = 18, n_{linear} = 24$) answers was obtained, $\chi^2(1) = 1.12, p = .290$. Similarly, we found no significant relation between robot conditions and *Transportation*, $\chi^2(1) = 0.46, p = .498$. Also, no significant relation was indicated between the robot conditions and *Empathy*, $\chi^2(1) = 1.03, p = .310$. In contrast, we found a significant relation between the robot conditions and *Bullying Awareness* ($\chi^2(1) = 11.41, p < .001$), with higher awareness toward bullying in the interactive condition.

Behavioral Measures. Descriptive data for stickers apportioned to the story characters, robotic storyteller, and the children themselves are presented in Table 4.

Regarding the first round a Chi^2-test showed no significant relationship between interactivity condition and distribution of the stickers, $\chi^2(5) = 3.06, p = .691$. For the second round, the Chi^2-test again revealed no significant relationship between condition and distribution of the stickers, $\chi^2(3) = 0.56, p = .906$ (Table 4).

Table 4. Means and standard deviations for amount of stickers apportioned in Study II.

	Round 1						Round 2			
	Victim		Bully		Child		Device		Child	
	M	SD	M	SD	M	SD	M	SD	M	SD
Robot	1.80	1.37	1.20	0.86	3.00	1.65	2.93	0.96	3.07	0.96
Loudspeaker	1.56	0.81	1.75	1.13	2.69	1.85	2.38	1.54	3.63	1.54

6.4   Discussion

To gain deeper insights into the potential of robotic storytelling as a bullying intervention method, we compared the initial linear version of the storytelling with an interactive version designed to leverage the advantages of the social robot.

When comparing the linear and interactive story versions told by the robot, no significant differences were found in story recognition (**RQ1**) nor sympathy with the robot itself (**RQ2**). Similarly, no differences were observed for transportation, sympathy toward the story characters, or empathy, resulting in the rejection of **H1, H2,** and **H3**. These findings are somewhat unexpected, given that research has shown that interactivity can enhance transportation in interventional stories across various media, subsequently promoting greater story-consistent beliefs and behavioral intentions [20,39,58]. While some studies report conflicting results [2,38], it is also possible that the level of interactivity in this study was insufficient to foster a sense of agency, as the choices presented and their consequences did not meaningfully impact the story's outcome. Furthermore, stopping the narrative at the decision points while waiting for the children's input could have been distracting, in turn lowering transportation (see [79] for a discussion). Similarly, breaks in processing fluency of a story themselves were shown to negatively impact transportation [34,85].

However, a significant difference in bullying awareness was found, leading to the acceptance of **H4**. It is possible that the intervention influenced children's beliefs through a different pathway than the previously discussed one via transportation – namely, through emotional engagement. In a film-based study, Soto

Sanfiel et al. [70] reported heightened feelings of guilt among participants in the interactive condition compared to the linear one, suggesting that interactivity may be particularly effective in eliciting this emotion. Given that guilt plays a crucial role in bullying dynamics [53] and is positively associated with defending behaviors [52], interactivity may contribute to increased bullying awareness by enhancing this particular but possibly also the overall emotional resonance rather than transportation alone.

7   General Discussion

The two comparisons presented in this work suggest potential of robotic storytellers as a tool for bullying prevention through social stories. Beyond demonstrating promising initial results on the benefits of robotic embodiment and added interactivity, we also provide a methodological framework for implementing robotic storytelling in this context.

The first study demonstrated that a robotic storyteller was comparably effective to a traditional audio book in delivering an anti-bullying narrative to preschoolers. Concerning empathy, the robotic storytelling outperformed the audio-only storytelling, potentially by the increase in physical presence (see e.g. [26]) but also the benefit of multimodality to improve recipients' imagery of the story (see [46] for an overview).

Given that the primary advantage of social robots lies in their capacity for social interaction, particularly in persuasive contexts (see [22] for an overview), we conducted a second study comparing linear robotic storytelling with an interactive version. While leveraging the advantage of interactivity did not further improve measures of transportation, sympathy, or empathy, the overall aim of increasing bullying awareness was achieved, strengthening the idea of robotic storytelling as a bullying prevention tool.

Importantly, the storytelling approach overall proved to be well-suited for the preschool age group, as indicated by consistently high story recognition rates across all condition – highlighting the story's comprehensibility and the method's age-appropriateness. Notably, neither the robot nor the interactive elements appeared to distract from the narrative, as reflected in the comparable or even elevated mean recall scores. These findings further support the feasibility and effectiveness of robotic storytelling as an engaging and developmentally appropriate bullying prevention tool for preschoolers.

While the findings support this potential use of robotic storytellers, certain limitations of our studies suggest directions for future research. One such limitation concerns the depth of interactivity in the current version of the story. Although the robot engaged children interactively, the consequences of their choices remained relatively uniform. Previous research indicates that allowing user decisions to lead to outcomes that mirror the real-life consequences of bullying can prompt reflection on appropriate behavior [81]. Future research could therefore explore more dynamic narrative structures with distinct, meaningful consequences - not only to enhance children's sense of agency and engagement, but also to deepen their understanding of the story's message and encourage critical thinking about bullying behavior.

Moreover, the current design favored a single child-robot interaction over a group setting, allowing for an isolated understanding of the childrobot interaction without the additional complexity of group dynamics. While results show that future deployment of such robotic storytelling interventions might be an effective on-demand tool to implement target-oriented and needs-based individual interventions, future research should explore group settings to understand how such interventions function within peer dynamics and collaborative learning environments.

8   Conclusion

This research explores for the first time the use of social stories delivered by a robotic storyteller in a bullying prevention for preschoolers. The findings demonstrate the promising potential of social robots for early childhood bullying prevention through storytelling. While a physically embodied robot performed comparably to traditional audio storytelling in terms of narrative comprehension and transportation, it notably enhanced empathetic responses among children. Further, integrating interactivity into robotic storytelling significantly increased children's bullying awareness, suggesting that decision-making and participation may enhance emotional processing and critical reflection. Together, these findings underscore the value of leveraging the unique affordances of social robots – embodiment and interactivity – to create emotionally resonant, educational experiences for young children. Future work should explore richer interactive narratives with consequential decision-making to further enhance children's agency and deepen their changes in attitude.

Acknowledgments. The authors would like to thank Valeria Elsesser, Leonie Lücke, Miriam Semineth, and Sarah Tomiczek for their help in developing the materials and conducting the data collection.

References

1. Adams, E.: Fundamentals of Game Design, Third Edition. New Riders, 3rd edition edn. (2013)
2. Ahn, C.: Interacting with story: Examining transportation into video game narrative. Master's thesis, Cleveland State University (2015)
3. Appel, M., Gnambs, T., Richter, T., Green, M.C.: The transportation scale-short form (ts-sf). Media Psychol. **18**(2), 243–266 (2015)
4. Aylett, R., Vala, M., Sequeira, P., Paiva, A.: Fearnot!–an emergent narrative approach to virtual dramas for anti-bullying education. In: Virtual Storytelling. Using Virtual Reality Technologies for Storytelling: 4th International Conference, ICVS 2007, Saint-Malo, France, 5–7 December 2007. Proceedings 4, pp. 202–205. Springer (2007)

5. Belacchi, C., Farina, E.: Prosocial/hostile roles and emotion comprehension in preschoolers. Aggressive Behav. **36**(6), 371–389 (2010). https://doi.org/10.1002/ab.20361

6. Breazeal, C., Dautenhahn, K., Kanda, T.: Social robotics. In: Springer Handbook of Robotics, pp. 1935–1972. Springer, Cham (2016). https://doi.org/10.1007/978-3-319-32552-1_72

7. Chang, C.Y., Hwang, G.J., Chou, Y.L., Xu, Z.Y., Jen, H.J.: Effects of robot-assisted digital storytelling on hospitalized children's communication during the covid-19 pandemic. Educ. Technol. Res. Dev. ETR & D 1–13 (2023). https://doi.org/10.1007/s11423-023-10209-0

8. Choo, Y.B., Abdullah, T., Nawi, A.M.: Digital storytelling vs. oral storytelling: an analysis of the art of telling stories now and then. Universal J. Educ. Res. **8**(5A), 46–50 (2020). https://doi.org/10.13189/ujer.2020.081907

9. Coe, K., Aiken, N.E., Palmer, C.T.: Once upon a time: ancestors and the evolutionary significance of stories. Anthropol. Forum **16**(1), 21–40 (2006). https://doi.org/10.1080/00664670600572421

10. Colm Hogan, P.: The Mind and its Stories: Narrative Unversals and Human Emotion. Studies in emotion and social interaction, Cambridge Univ. Press, Cambridge (2003)

11. Conti, D., Cirasa, C., Di Nuovo, S., Di Nuovo, A., et al.: "Robot, tell me a tale!": a social robot as tool for teachers in kindergarten. Interact. Stud. **21**(2), 220–242 (2020)

12. Csikszentmihalyi, M.: Flow: The Psychology of Optimal Experience. Harper & Row, New York (1990)

13. Cuff, B.M., Brown, S.J., Taylor, L., Howat, D.J.: Empathy: a review of the concept. Emot. Rev. **8**(2), 144–153 (2016). https://doi.org/10.1177/1754073914558466

14. Djikic, M., Oatley, K., Moldoveanu, M.C.: Reading other minds. Sci. Study Literat. **3**(1), 28–47 (2013). https://doi.org/10.1075/ssol.3.1.06dji

15. Djikic, M., Oatley, K., Zoeterman, S., Peterson, J.B.: On being moved by art: how reading fiction transforms the self. Creat. Res. J. **21**(1), 24–29 (2009). https://doi.org/10.1080/10400410802633392

16. Duffy, B.R., Rooney, C., O'Hare, G.M.P., O'Donoghue, R.: What is a social robot? In: 10th Irish Conference on Artificial Intelligence & Cognitive Science (1999). http://hdl.handle.net/10197/4412

17. Eekhof, L.S., Mar, R.A.: Does reading about fictional minds make us more curious about real ones? Lang. Cogn. **16**(1), 176–196 (2024). https://doi.org/10.1017/langcog.2023.30

18. Ekman, P., Friesen, W.V.: Unmasking the face: a guide to recognizing emotions from facial clues, vol. 10. Ishk (2003)

19. Ekman, P., Oster, H.: Facial expressions of emotion. Annu. Rev. Psychol. **30**(1), 527–554 (1979)

20. Ferchaud, A., Seibert, J., Sellers, N., Escobar Salazar, N.: Reducing mental health stigma through identification with video game avatars with mental illness. Front. Psychol. **11**, 2240 (2020)

21. Fink, J.: Anthropomorphism and human likeness in the design of robots and human-robot interaction. In: Ge, S.S., Khatib, O., Cabibihan, J.-J., Simmons, R., Williams, M.-A. (eds.) ICSR 2012. LNCS (LNAI), vol. 7621, pp. 199–208. Springer, Heidelberg (2012). https://doi.org/10.1007/978-3-642-34103-8_20

22. Fong, T., Nourbakhsh, I., Dautenhahn, K.: A survey of socially interactive robots. Robot. Auton. Syst. **42**(3–4), 143–166 (2003)

23. Fridin, M.: Storytelling by a kindergarten social assistive robot: a tool for constructive learning in preschool education. Comput. Educ. **70**, 53–64 (2014)
24. Gaffney, H., Ttofi, M.M., Farrington, D.P.: Evaluating the effectiveness of school-bullying prevention programs: an updated meta-analytical review. Aggression Violent Behav. **45**, 111–133 (2019). https://doi.org/10.1016/j.avb.2018.07.001
25. Gini, G.: Social cognition and moral cognition in bullying: what's wrong? Aggressive Behav. Official J. Int. Soc. Res. Aggression **32**(6), 528–539 (2006)
26. Gomez, R., et al.: Exploring affective storytelling with an embodied agent. In: 2021 30th IEEE International Conference on Robot & Human Interactive Communication (RO-MAN), pp. 1249–1255. IEEE (2021). https://doi.org/10.1109/RO-MAN50785.2021.9515323
27. Goossens, N., Aarts, R., Vogt, P.: Storytelling with a social robot. Robots for Learning R4L (2019)
28. de Graaf, M.M.A., Allouch, S.B., van Dijk, J.A.G.M.: Long-term acceptance of social robots in domestic environments: Insights from a user's perspective. In: 2016 AAAI Spring Symposium Series (2016). https://www.aaai.org/ocs/index.php/SSS/SSS16/paper/view/12692
29. de Graaf, M.M., Ben Allouch, S.: Exploring influencing variables for the acceptance of social robots. Robot. Auton. Syst. **61**(12), 1476–1486 (2013). https://doi.org/10.1016/j.robot.2013.07.007
30. Gray, C.: The New Social Story Book. Future Horizons (2000)
31. Green, J.A.: Interactivity and agency in real time systems. In: Conferência Internacional de Artes de Novas Mídias, p. 84 (2010)
32. Green, M.C., Appel, M.: Narrative transportation: How stories shape how we see ourselves and the worls. Advances in Experimental Social Psychology **70**, 1–82 (2024), https://doi.org/10.1016/bs.aesp.2024.03.002
33. Green, M.C., Brock, T.C.: The role of transportation in the persuasiveness of public narratives. J. Pers. Soc. Psychol. **79**(5), 701–721 (2000). https://doi.org/10.1037//0022-3514.79.5.701
34. Green, M.C., Jenkins, K.M.: Interactive narratives: Processes and outcomes in user-directed stories. J. Commun. **64**(3), 479–500 (2014). https://doi.org/10.1111/jcom.12093
35. Hall, A., Zwarun, L.: Challenging entertainment: Enjoyment, transportation, and need for cognition in relation to fictional films viewed online. Mass Communication and Society **15**(3), 384–406 (2012https://doi.org/10.1080/15205436.2011.583544
36. Hall, L., Jones, S., Paiva, A., Aylett, R.: Fearnot! providing children with strategies to cope with bullying. In: Proceedings of the 8th International Conference on Interaction Design and Children. pp. 276–277 (2009)
37. Ham, C.D., Yoon, G., Nelson, M.R.: The interplay of persuasion inference and flow experience in an entertaining food advergame. J. Consum. Behav. **15**(3), 239–250 (2016)
38. Jenkins, K.M.: Choose your own adventure: Interactive narratives and attitude change. Master's thesis, The University of North Carolina at Chapel Hill (2014)
39. Kim, S.: Getting Vaccinated Through Watching Innovative Forms of Stories: An Examination of the Persuasive Impact of Interactive Narrative Health Interventions. The University of Wisconsin-Madison (2021)
40. Kirsch, C.: Using storytelling to teach vocabulary in language lessons: does it work? The Language Learning Journal **44**(1), 33–51 (2016https://doi.org/10.1080/09571736.2012.733404

41. Kirves, L., Sajaniemi, N.: Bullying in early educational settings. Early Child Development and Care **182**(3-4), 383–400 (2012https://doi.org/10.1080/03004430.2011.646724

42. Kleine Wieskamp, P. (ed.): Storytelling: digital - multimedial - social: Formen und Praxis für PR, Marketing, TV, Game und Social Media. Hanser, München (2016https://doi.org/10.3139/9783446448100

43. Kokina, A., Kern, L.: Social story™ interventions for students with autism spectrum disorders: A meta-analysis. J. Autism Dev. Disord. **40**, 812–826 (2010)

44. Krueger, D.W., Krueger, L.N.: Animals in children's stories. In: Cultural Zoo, pp. 127–143. Routledge (2018)

45. Ligthart, M.E., Neerincx, M.A., Hindriks, K.V.: Design patterns for an interactive storytelling robot to support children's engagement and agency. In: Proceedings of the 2020 ACM/IEEE international conference on human-robot interaction. pp. 409–418 (2020)

46. Lipman, D.: Improving your storytelling: Beyond the basics for all who tell stories in work or play. August House (1999)

47. Lugrin, B.: Introduction to socially interactive agents. In: The Handbook on Socially Interactive Agents, pp. 1–18. ACM, New York, NY, USA (2021)

48. Mar, R.A., Oatley, K.: The function of fiction is the abstraction and simulation of social experience. Perspectives on psychological scien: a journal of the Association for Psychological Science **3**(3), 173–192 (2008). https://doi.org/10.1111/j.1745-6924.2008.00073.x

49. Mar, R.A., Oatley, K., Hirsh, J., dela Paz, J., Peterson, J.B.: Bookworms versus nerds: Exposure to fiction versus non-fiction, divergent associations with social ability, and the simulation of fictional social worlds. J. Res. Pers. **40**(5), 694–712 (2006). https://doi.org/10.1016/j.jrp.2005.08.002

50. Mar, R.A., Oatley, K., Peterson, J.B.: Exploring the link between reading fiction and empathy: Ruling out individual differences and examining outcomes. COMM **34**(4), 407–428 (2009). https://doi.org/10.1515/COMM.2009.025

51. Maure, R., Bruno, B.: Participatory design of a social robot and robot-mediated storytelling activity to raise awareness of gender inequality among children. In: 2023 32nd IEEE International Conference on Robot and Human Interactive Communication (RO-MAN). pp. 974–981. IEEE (2023https://doi.org/10.1109/RO-MAN57019.2023.10309391

52. Mazzone, A., Camodeca, M., Salmivalli, C.: Interactive effects of guilt and moral disengagement on bullying, defending and outsider behavior. Journal of Moral Education **45**(4), 419–432 (2016)

53. Menesini, E., Camodeca, M.: Shame and guilt as behaviour regulators: Relationships with bullying, victimization and prosocial behaviour. Br. J. Dev. Psychol. **26**(2), 183–196 (2008)

54. Ng, S., Lin, T.H., Li, Y., Sebo, S.: Role-playing with robot characters: Increasing user engagement through narrative and gameplay agency. In: Proceedings of the 2024 ACM/IEEE International Conference on Human-Robot Interaction. pp. 522–532 (2024)

55. Oatley, K.: A taxonomy of the emotions of literary response and a theory of identification in fictional narrative. Poetics **23**(1–2), 53–74 (1995). https://doi.org/10.1016/0304-422X(94)P4296-S

56. Oatley, K.: The cognitive science of fiction. Wiley interdisciplinary reviews. Cognitive science **3**(4), 425–430 (2012). https://doi.org/10.1002/wcs.1185

57. Oatley, K.: Film and meaning. In: The Oxford Handbook of the Positive Humanities, pp. 350–361. Oxford University Press (2022https://doi.org/10.1093/oxfordhb/9780190064570.013.11

58. Oh, J., Lim, H.S., Hwang, A.H.C.: How interactive storytelling persuades: The mediating role of website contingency and narrative transportation. Journal of Broadcasting & Electronic Media **64**(5), 714–735 (2020)

59. Parker, T.S., Wampler, K.S.: Changing emotion: The use of therapeutic storytelling. J. Marital Fam. Ther. **32**(2), 155–166 (2006)

60. Perren, S., Alsaker, F.D.: Social behavior and peer relationships of victims, bully-victims, and bullies in kindergarten. J. Child Psychol. Psychiatry **47**(1), 45–57 (2006). https://doi.org/10.1111/j.1469-7610.2005.01445.x

61. Phillips, L.H., Lawrie, L., Suchomelova, Z., Heinämaa, S., O'Dwyer, A., Yong, M.H.: Age and cultural differences in the relationship between reading and theory of mind. Poetics **109**, 101984 (2025https://doi.org/10.1016/j.poetic.2025.101984

62. Rosenthal-von der Pütten, A.M., Krämer, N.C., Hoffmann, L., Sobieraj, S., Eimler, S.C.: An experimental study on emotional reactions towards a robot. International Journal of Social Robotics **5**, 17–34 (2013)

63. Reeves, B., Nass, C.I.: The media equation: How people treat computers, television, and new media like real people and places. CSLI Publ, Stanford, Calif (1996)

64. Reynhout, G., Carter, M.: Social stories for children with disabilities. J. Autism Dev. Disord. **36**(4), 445–469 (2006). https://doi.org/10.1007/s10803-006-0086-1

65. Robben, D., Fukuda, E., de Haas, M.: The effect of gender on perceived anthropomorphism and intentional acceptance of a storytelling robot. In: Companion of the 2023 ACM/IEEE International Conference on Human-Robot Interaction. pp. 495–499. ACM, New York, NY, USA (2023https://doi.org/10.1145/3568294.3580134

66. Silva, V., Pereira, A.P., Soares, F., Leão, C.P., Jurdi, A., Sena Esteves, J., Hertzberg, J.: Social stories for promoting social communication with children with autism spectrum disorder using a humanoid robot: Step-by-step study. Technol. Knowl. Learn. **29**(2), 735–756 (2024). https://doi.org/10.1007/s10758-023-09681-7

67. Simut, R., Vanderfaeillie, J., Vanderborght, B., Pop, C., Pintea, S., Rusu, A., David, D., Saldien, J.: Is the social robot probo an added value for social story intervention for children with asd? In: 2012 7th ACM/IEEE International Conference on Human-Robot Interaction (HRI), pp. 235–236 (2012)

68. Smed, J., Suovuo, T., Skult, N., Skult, P.: Handbook on interactive storytelling. Wiley, Hoboken, NJ and Chichester, West Sussex (2021), https://ieeexplore.ieee.org/book/9566729

69. Smith, P.K., Cowie, H., Olafsson, R.F., Liefooghe, A.P.D., Almeida, A., Araki, H., Del Barrio, C., Costabile, A., Dekleva, B., Houndoumadi, A., Kim, K., Olafsson, R.P., Ortega, R., Pain, J., Pateraki, L., Schafer, M., Singer, M., Smorti, A., Toda, Y., Tomasson, H., Wenxin, Z.: Definitions of bullying: a comparison of terms used, and age and gender differences, in a fourteen-country international comparison. Child Dev. **73**(4), 1119–1133 (2002). https://doi.org/10.1111/1467-8624.00461

70. Soto Sanfiel, M.T., Aymerich Franch, L., Ribes Guardia, F.X., Martinez Fernandez, J.R.: Influence of interactivity on emotions and enjoyment during consumption of audiovisual fictions. International Journal of Arts and Technology **4**(1), 111–129 (2011)

71. Srija, S., Sugi, S., Srinivasan, D.: Efficacy of social stories in coping with bullying among children with childhood psychiatry conditions: A randomized controlled

interventional study. The Indian Journal of Occupational Therapy **51**(2), 52 (2019). https://doi.org/10.4103/ijoth.ijoth_10_19

72. Steinhaeusser, S.C., Lugrin, B.: Effects of colored leds in robotic storytelling on storytelling experience and robot perception. In: HRI '22: Proceedings of the 2022 ACM/IEEE International Conference on Human-Robot Interaction. pp. 1053–1058. IEEE Press (2022)

73. Steinhaeusser, S.C., Lugrin, B.: Effects of number of voices and voice type on storytelling experience and robot perception. In: Sound and robotics, pp. 9–32. Chapman and Hall/CRC (2023)

74. Steinhaeusser, S.C., Piller, R., Lugrin, B.: Combining emotional gestures, sound effects, and background music for robotic storytelling - effects on storytelling experience, emotion induction, and robot perception. In: Proceedings of the 2024 ACM/IEEE International Conference on Human-Robot Interaction. p. 687–696. HRI '24, Association for Computing Machinery, New York, NY, USA (20https://doi.org/10.1145/3610977.3634956, https://doi.org/10.1145/3610977.3634956

75. Steinhaeusser, S.C., Siol, L., Ganal, E., Maier, S., Lugrin, B.: The narrobot plugin-connecting the social robot reeti to the unity game engine. In: Companion of the 2023 ACM/IEEE International Conference on Human-Robot Interaction. pp. 65–70 (2023)

76. Striepe, H., Lugrin, B.: There once was a robot storyteller: Measuring the effects of emotion and non-verbal behaviour. In: Social Robotics, Lecture Notes in Computer Science, vol. 10652, pp. 126–136. Springer International Publishing, Cham (2017https://doi.org/10.1007/978-3-319-70022-9_13

77. Sundar, S.S., Kim, J.: Interactivity and persuasion: Influencing attitudes with information and involvement. J. Interact. Advert. **5**(2), 5–18 (2005)

78. Tal-Or, N., Cohen, J.: Understanding audience involvement: Conceptualizing and manipulating identification and transportation. Poetics **38**(4), 402–418 (201https://doi.org/10.1016/j.poetic.2010.05.004

79. Tal-Or, N., Cohen, J.: Unpacking engagement: Convergence and divergence in transportation and identification. Annals of the International Communication Association **40**(1), 33–66 (2016https://doi.org/10.1080/23808985.2015.11735255

80. Test, D.W., Richter, S., Knight, V., Spooner, F.: A comprehensive review and meta-analysis of the social stories literature. Focus on Autism and Other Developmental Disabilities **26**(1), 49–62 (2011). https://doi.org/10.1177/1088357609351573

81. Tsai, M.-K., Tseng, S.-S., Weng, J.-F.: A Pilot Study of Interactive Storytelling for Bullying Prevention Education. In: Chang, M., Hwang, W.-Y., Chen, M.-P., Müller, W. (eds.) Edutainment 2011. LNCS, vol. 6872, pp. 497–501. Springer, Heidelberg (2011). https://doi.org/10.1007/978-3-642-23456-9_89

82. Vala, M., Sequeira, P., Paiva, A., Aylett, R.: Fearnot! demo: a virtual environment with synthetic characters to help bullying. In: Proceedings of the 6th international joint conference on Autonomous agents and multiagent systems. pp. 1–2 (2007)

83. Van Noorden, T.H., Haselager, G.J., Cillessen, A.H., Bukowski, W.M.: Empathy and involvement in bullying in children and adolescents: A systematic review. J. Youth Adolesc. **44**, 637–657 (2015)

84. Vannini, N., Enz, S., Sapouna, M., Wolke, D., Watson, S., Woods, S., Dautenhahn, K., Hall, L., Paiva, A., André, E., et al.: "fearnot!": a computer-based anti-bullying-programme designed to foster peer intervention. Eur. J. Psychol. Educ. **26**, 21–44 (2011)

85. Vaughn, L.A., Hesse, S.J., Petkova, Z., Trudeau, L.: "this story is right on": The impact of regulatory fit on narrative engagement and persuasion. European Journal of Social Psychology **39**(3), 447–456 (200https://doi.org/10.1002/ejsp.570

86. Vlachou, M., Botsoglou, K., Andreou, E.: Bullying/victimization in preschool children. In: Conference paper. Diaksesdari doi. vol. 10, pp. 5086–1764 (2014)
87. Vogt, P., van den Berghe, R., de Haas, M., Hoffman, L., Kanero, J., Mamus, E., Montanier, J.M., Oranc, C., Oudgenoeg-Paz, O., Garcia, D.H., Papadopoulos, F., Schodde, T., Verhagen, J., Wallbridgell, C.D., Willemsen, B., de Wit, J., Belpaeme, T., Goksun, T., Kopp, S., Krahmer, E., Kuntay, A.C., Leseman, P., Pandey, A.K.: Second language tutoring using social robots: A large-scale study. In: 2019 14th ACM/IEEE International Conference on Human-Robot Interaction (HRI). pp. 497–505. IEEE (2019https://doi.org/10.1109/HRI.2019.8673077
88. Wang, H., Zhang, L., Zheng, C., Gomez, R., Nakamura, K., Li, G.: Personalized storytelling with social robot haru. In: Social Robotics, Lecture Notes in Computer Science, vol. 13818, pp. 439–451. Springer Nature Switzerland, Cham (2022https://doi.org/10.1007/978-3-031-24670-8_39
89. Westlund, J.K., Breazeal, C.: The interplay of robot language level with children's language learning during storytelling. In: Proceedings of the Tenth Annual ACM/IEEE International Conference on Human-Robot Interaction Extended Abstracts - HRI'15 Extended Abstracts. pp. 65–66. ACM Press, New York, New York, USA (201https://doi.org/10.1145/2701973.2701989
90. Zhou, C., Occa, A., Kim, S., Morgan, S.: A meta-analysis of narrative game-based interventions for promoting healthy behaviors. Journal of health communication **25**(1), 54–65 (2020https://doi.org/10.1080/10810730.2019.1701586
91. Zhou, N., Wong, H.M., McGrath, C.: Efficacy of social story intervention in training toothbrushing skills among special-care children with and without autism. Autism research: official journal of the International Society for Autism Research **13**(4), 666–674 (2020). https://doi.org/10.1002/aur.2256
92. Złotowski, J., Sumioka, H., Eyssel, F., Nishio, S., Bartneck, C., Ishiguro, H.: Model of dual anthropomorphism: The relationship between the media equation effect and implicit anthropomorphism. Int. J. Soc. Robot. **10**(5), 701–714 (2018). https://doi.org/10.1007/s12369-018-0476-5

Designing for Environmental Citizenship: Insights from Combining Immersive VR and Dialogue-Based Activities

Akrivi Katifori[1]([✉])[iD], Dimitra Petousi[1][iD], Giorgos Ganias[1][iD], Georgia Koutiva[1][iD], Marina Stergiou[1][iD], Katerina Servi[1][iD], Gabriel Gourdoglou[1][iD], Maria Boile[1][iD], Yannis Ioannidis[1][iD], and Ioannis Kousis[2][iD]

[1] Athena Research and Innovation Center, Aigialias and Chalepa, 15125 Marousi, Greece
`{vivi,dpetousi,george.ganias,georgia.koutiva,mboile,yannis}@athenarc.gr`
[2] School of Built Environment, Faculty of Arts, Design and Architecture, University of New South Wales, Sydney, NSW 2033, Australia
`i.kousis@unsw.edu.au`

Abstract. In large metropolitan areas, the urban heat island effect and growing urbanization pose health risks and deepen the disconnect between residents-especially children-and nature. This disconnection hinders public engagement with nature-based climate solutions. To address this, we present an educational approach grounded in dialogic and collaborative pedagogy, combining interactive, single-user immersive Virtual Reality (i-VR) with mobile app-mediated group dialogue. In VR, children explore future environmental scenarios shaped by human actions; outside VR, they discuss real-world environmental issues and sustainable solutions. An evaluation workshop with ten participants-five educators and five high school children-offered valuable feedback and design recommendations. Findings highlight the potential of an IDN paradigm combining embodied learning in VR with dialogue to reconnect urban youth with nature, foster environmental citizenship, and inform future use of social VR and in-VR dialogic elements.

Keywords: Virtual Reality · Dialogue-based Activities · User-Centered Design · Environmental Education

1 Introduction

Modern environmental education emerged in the 1960s amid growing awareness, leading to the 1977 Tbilisi Declaration which emphasized environmental education's role in global sustainability and outlined key goals: awareness, knowledge, concern, motivation, problem-solving, and active participation [5,52,62].

Today, promoting environmental awareness remains vital [34], particularly in cities impacted by the urban heat island effect-caused by heat-retaining surfaces, reduced greenery, and disrupted airflow. Yet, many urban dwellers remain

M. C. Reyes and F. Nack (Eds.): ICIDS 2025, LNCS 16375, pp. 95–112, 2026.
https://doi.org/10.1007/978-3-032-12405-0_6

unaware or alienated from nature. Urbanization limits access to green spaces, and many children lack meaningful nature experiences, leading to apathy or fear: barriers to adopting nature-based climate solutions.

Immersive virtual reality (i-VR) offers promising educational potential [33], enabling embodied, empathy-driven experiences. However, it is less suited to sustained dialogue, because long sessions can cause discomfort [49], and avatars can limit non-verbal expressiveness [6,55,68].

We propose a two-part approach: a single-user i-VR experience exploring alternative environmental futures, followed by a group dialogue activity via a mobile app. By weaving a domain specific storyworld, rich with environmental narrative that the learner is free to explore together with collaborative dialogue for joint reflection, we aim to extend IDN paradigms to the domain of environmental citizenship education. We evaluate this design through a workshop with five educators and five high school students engaged in environmental education. Our research question is: How can i-VR, combined with a post-VR dialogue activity, effectively foster reflection, awareness, and environmental citizenship?

This work contributes insights into an immersive and conversationally interleaved IDN model for environmental education, along with practical design recommendations for formal education contexts. Section 2 reviews relevant literature on environmental education, VR, and dialogue-based learning. Section 3 presents the i-VR and mobile app. Section 4 outlines our study method. Section 5 reports findings, discussed in Sect. 6. Section 7 concludes the paper.

2 Background

2.1 Environmental Awareness and Empathy

Environmental awareness lacks a single definition, with terms like environmental consciousness and concern often used interchangeably, blurring distinctions between attitudes and actions. According to [16], "environmental awareness can be broadly defined as the attitude regarding environmental consequences of human behaviour... a predisposition to react to environmental issues in a certain manner", combined with actual pro-environmental behaviour [24].

Environmental empathy refers to "the ability to feel and understand issues related to the natural environment" [2] and involves emotional and cognitive responses directed toward nature, increasing the likelihood of environmentally responsible action [59].

Environmental citizenship entails active public participation in sustainability through responsible behaviour, equitable resource use, and policy co-creation [22]. Education is foundational [25], as it can foster concern, understanding, and the skills needed to act. Its components include [25]:

- *Information and literacy*: access to and understanding of environmental knowledge.
- *Awareness*: comprehension of human impact on the environment.
- *Concern*: empathy and responsibility.

- *Attitudes and beliefs*: values supporting sustainability.
- *Knowledge and skills* for sustainable action.
- *Responsible behaviour*: pro-environmental action in daily life.

2.2   Interaction Design for Environmental Education

While literature on interaction design for children in environmental education is optimistic about technology, it stresses a child-centered, pedagogically driven approach prioritizing emotional connection and real-world relevance. Cumbo and Iversen [17] show technology enhances nature-play and stewardship when child-designed, embodied, and situated.

Perkins [45] critiques "technological solutionism," noting technology alone is insufficient without pedagogy, while Vasalou et al. [63] observe technically focused research has limited educational impact. Albar et al. [1] show game-based learning fosters understanding, critical perspectives, and sustainable action.

Thus, effective design in environmental education must move beyond embedding technology to align with children's developmental needs, emotions, and agency.

2.3   VR for Environmental Education

The potential of i-VR for education embracing constructivist approaches has been explored for more than three decades [32,53], including also fostering environmental awareness and empathy [26,27,29,37,44]. Xie et al. show i-VR enhances environmental empathy and attitudes more than traditional methods [69], while Huang et al. [28] use VR forest visualizations with climate projections to create "visceral experiences" for public and expert communication.

Applications range from simulations and experiments [15,18,19,60,67] to gamified tools across educational levels [36,54,58]. Mikropoulos et al. [41] pioneered VR-based environmental learning with a constructivist model. Strassmann et al. [57] and Chirico et al. [14] show i-VR boosts engagement and pro-environmental behaviors. Pochwatko et al. [48] enable users to simulate and manipulate pollution scenarios using multisensory inputs.

Our approach extends this work by integrating i-VR with mobile-facilitated dialogue to deepen learning and promote environmental citizenship.

2.4   Dialogic Pedagogy and Facilitated Dialogue

Dialogic pedagogy highlights the role of dialogue as a collaborative process of exploring and co-constructing understanding [12]. Rooted in constructivist learning theory, Burbules describes dialogue as a "process of discovery... with the goal of mutual understanding," based on respect and care, even amid disagreement. This approach shifts power dynamics in the classroom, increasing student participation and fostering a sense of agency [3,12], which extends beyond education to societal engagement.

Applied to environmental education, dialogic approaches move beyond content delivery to support learners critically analyze environmental issues, consider diverse perspectives, and develop an "agency of knowledge" [3,11,39] i.e. awareness of their ability to influence learning, and take action as informed citizens.

Arizpe Vicencio [65] found that dialogic teaching enhanced environmental awareness and agency in Mexico's Baja California Sur, while Piersol and Timmerman [47] argue that dialogue and storytelling challenge power imbalances and foster empathy, including with the more-than-human world, in line with ecofeminist pedagogy.

The US National Park Service adopted an audience-centered, dialogue-based interpretive model called the Arc of Dialogue [56], designed to guide participants from the "me," to the "other", and finally to the "we". It includes four phases:

1. **Build community** with "ice-breakers" and mutually agreed ground rules [9].
2. **Share personal experiences** to create personal connections.
3. **Explore experiences of others** by challenging assumptions and recognizing diverse perspectives.
4. **Synthesize and bring closure** through reflection and next steps [9].

Mobile-mediated adaptations of this model in the context of the EMOTIVE project [51] propose visitor-led guided tours to foster democratic dialogue among the group via a mobile device [21,64]. Chatbot-based tools such as "A Discussion with Bo the ChatBot" [38] or "Hermias, the Bot" [46] facilitated small-group dialogue on historical facts. In all cases the human facilitator had a supporting unobtrusive role.

3   The Experience

3.1   Objectives and Scope

Our study objective was to explore the combination of a single-user i-VR application and a mobile-mediated, group dialogue activity for promoting environmental empathy and citizenship. i-VR supports embodied, multisensory learning through full-body interaction [13,30,33,50], creating alternative realities to immerse students in environmental challenges. Dialogue enables collaborative reflection, consolidating knowledge and sparking discussion around nature-based solutions. To this end we designed a prototype, two-part experience aimed at KS4 (ages 14–16) and KS5 (ages 16–18) students. The target ages are aligned with the Meta Oculus Quest 2.0/3.0 recommended age (10+), though the content's complexity makes it more suitable for 14+.

The two-part experience contribute to the "Information and Literacy" dimension of environmental citizenship [25], providing access to relevant knowledge. The i-VR experience emphasizes "Awareness", "Concern", and empathy through experiential learning, while the dialogue focuses on cultivating "Attitudes and Beliefs" and "Knowledge and Skills" essential for "Responsible Behaviour."

The prototype has been developed in the context of the ARSINOE research project, involving multidisciplinary input from climate experts, scientists, and municipal staff. The Athens Case Study Living Lab followed a Systems Innovation Approach [43] to identified environmental challenges and relevant nature-based mitigation measures for the Athens, Greece, metropolitan area. Key environmental hazards identified included the urban heat island effect, atmospheric pollution, and biodiversity loss.

3.2 VR Experience

The VR experience was developed in Unity 3D as a single-user immersive application for the Meta Oculus Quest 3.0, using hand-held controllers. It begins with a short tutorial introducing VR navigation and hand interactions.

Users start inside the "Pod", a futuristic vessel that travels through time and space. Inside, they access (1) a Map to select a geographical location, with only ARSINOE square available in this prototype, and (2) portals to two alternative futures (Fig. 1). Their virtual futuristic Heads-Up Display (HUD) and hand-held device displays environmental and personal health data.

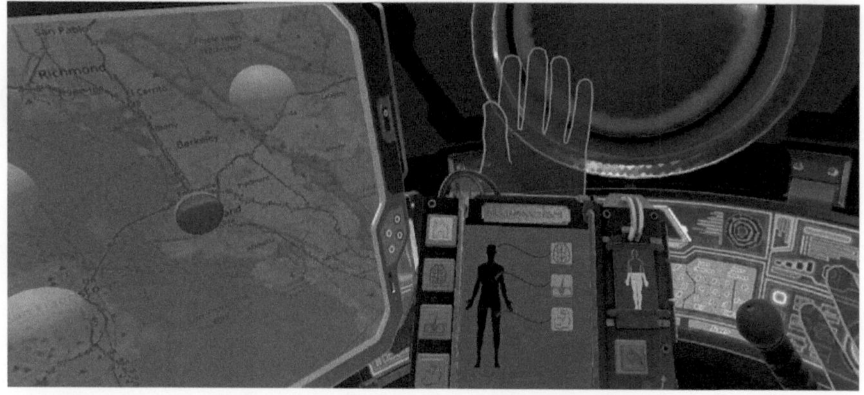

Fig. 1. Detail of the controls of the Pod.

Users exit the Pod into a reimagined Athens city square. Chosen for its social and ecological relevance, the square allows the visualization of climate impact on people, plants, and animals.

Users freely explore the square. Two contrasting scenarios are presented: a "good" future shaped by coordinated climate action, and a "bad" future where no additional mitigation efforts have been made. These scenarios differ in biodiversity, air quality, soundscape, landscape design, and overall livability (Fig. 2).

Fig. 2. Details from the two scenarios. Left column: Pleasant weather, thriving birds, greenery. Right column: Heat stress, biodiversity loss, haze.

Atmospheric pollution and heat are conveyed through visual cues like haze, lighting, and air clarity. A photorealistic style is used for the environment and wildlife, while humans are depicted abstractly -viewable but not interactable- to emphasize the observer role of the user.

All informative content is delivered through text on the user's HUD. After exploring both scenarios, users return to the Pod. The full session lasts 25–30 min. A brief video of the experience can be found in [4].

3.3 Mobile-Mediated Dialogue Activity

The dialogue activity is guided by a mobile app built with the Narralive Story Maker interactive narrative creation tool [66] and is implemented as a series of multimedia screens. Each participant uses their own device to view the content (Fig. 3), alternating between individual exploration and group dialogue. It emphasizes shared meaning-making and reflection, building on the VR experience and encouraging deeper understanding of climate-related challenges and possible solutions. Following the Arc of Dialogue model (Fig. 4), the activity unfolds in four stages: **Build community**. A member reads the ground rules aloud to set a respectful, open space. Ice-breakers (e.g., "Which is your favourite time of year?") build rapport. Participants then reflect on the VR experience with prompts such as: "Which future felt most impactful? How did it make you feel? Did anything surprise you?"

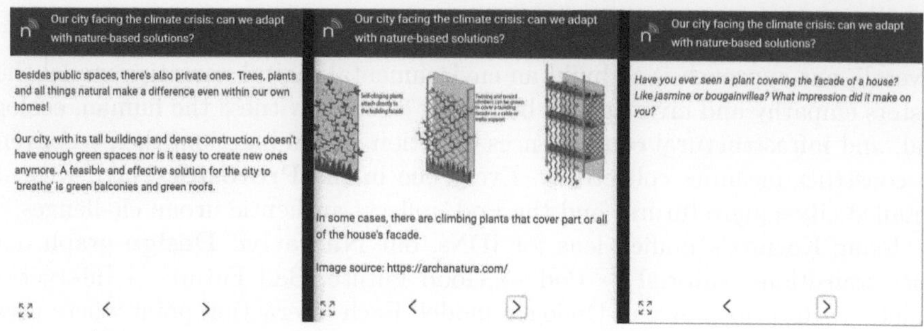

Fig. 3. Guided dialogue experience. Left and center: informational content screens. Right: Dialogue and reflection prompt.

Share Personal Experiences. The group exchanges stories and memories of city life and nature. Prompts include: "Do heatwaves affect your daily life or sleep?"

Explore Experiences of Others. This stage considers broader perspectives, including vulnerable groups affected by climate change. For example: "Do you know someone-elderly, child, or pet-who suffers more during heatwaves?"

Synthesize and Bring Closure. Participants reflect on what they've heard and discuss collective action. Questions include: "How do our actions influence sustainability? Can you think of ways to support nature-based solutions in your neighbourhood?"

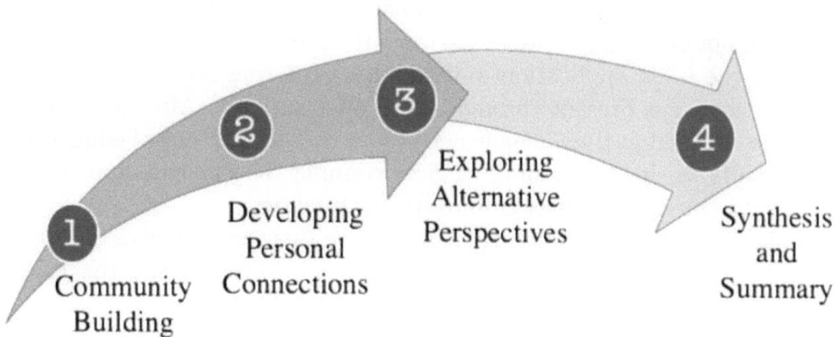

Fig. 4. The Arc of Dialogue approach for the guided dialogue activity.

The activity is designed to last 35 to 60 min, depending on the depth of the conversations.

3.4   The Combined Approach as a Single Narrative Experience

Overall, our approach is to build an environmental digital narrative model that fosters empathy and civic agency by letting learners witness the human, ecological, and infrastructural consequences of action versus inaction, then reconvene to construct meaning collectively. Every cue in the **Protostory** [31], with its detailed city-square futures and the Pod, reflects authentic urban challenges.

Using Koenitz's unified lens for IDNs, our **Narrative Design** graph outlines transitions: tutorial → Pod → Good Future, Bad Future → Interaction Points → Return → Arc of Dialogue model. Each interaction point where users observe environmental indicators on flora, fauna, and the built environment is a *node*, with the HUD conveying environmental and health data as *lexias*, guiding learners through branching climate trajectories. In play, each learner generates a **Narrative Vector**-e.g., choosing the "bad" future first or the order of interaction points-embodying their unique passage through VR. Finally, the Arc of Dialogue model underlying the dialogic activity lets these individual narrative vectors converge into linear but interactive narrative nodes, where students, guided by the system, act as co-authors of new perspectives, promoting transformation [40].

4   Methodology

Purposeful sampling was used to recruit participants for the evaluation workshop. Invitations were extended to members of the organization's educator network, resulting to five educators (4 women, 1 man) and five 12th-grade students (2 women, 3 men), all active in a national environmental education network and experienced in awareness-raising activities.

The workshop began with a short presentation of the research goals and procedure (Fig. 5) and participants reviewed an information sheet and signed the consent form before being assisted with the VR equipment. Each participant then experienced the i-VR application individually, exploring both future scenarios. A team member was present throughout to offer support. After a short break, participants engaged in the dialogue activity in two groups, one of educators and one of students, each using mobile devices running the dialogue app. A human facilitator remained in the background, ready to assist.

Educators and students were invited to share their perspectives on the experience, in two separate focus groups, with attention to their respective roles and insights.

5   Results

5.1   Strengths and Potential

Educators. Educators noted students increasingly reject traditional lectures in favor of interactive formats: "they want new, digital tools, and rightly so." They valued the dual activity design as a powerful learning tool for capturing attention through i-VR and promoting deeper reflection via group dialogue, making environmental issues more resonant and engaging.

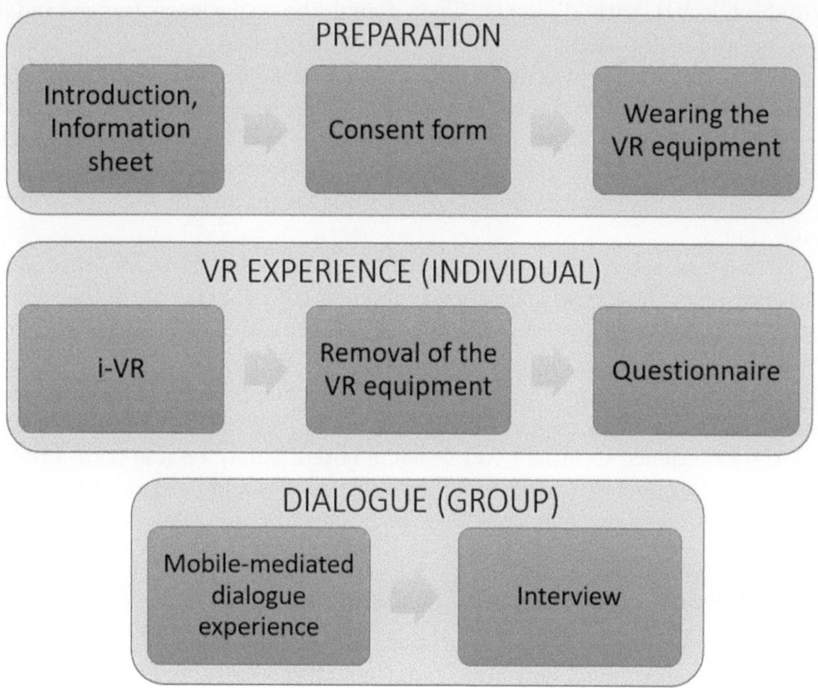

Fig. 5. Overall workshop process.

VR was described as "dynamic", "experiential", and "visually rich". Educators emphasized that pre-exposure to environmental concepts through VR would help students engage more deeply in discussion. They related the value of this approach to past successes with experiential and drama-based learning.

The dialogue app with structured prompts was recognized as a flexible tool supporting discussion and critical thinking. One educator noted its usefulness across workshops, group exercises, and roundtables.

Beyond pedagogy, the format was praised for practicality. In Greece, environmental education in secondary schools is currently voluntary. This approach addresses the need for engaging, ready-to-use educational resources that capture students' attention. Developing high-quality materials is time-consuming, especially for non-designers; a ready-made kit combining digital modules was seen as time-saving and adaptable for diverse classroom contexts.

Students. Student feedback aligned closely with educators', showing strong appreciation for the immersive and engaging nature of the two-part activity. Even those with prior environmental knowledge reported learning new concepts, such as the "3-30-300 rule" [10] about green spaces. Students appreciated the balance between individual reflection and group interaction, reinforcing the value of combining VR with dialogue. They found the experience understandable, engaging, and well-paced.

The VR experience was especially well received, praised for its ability to capture attention and visualize environmental challenges in a direct, embodied and interactive way. Students felt that seeing the consequences of human actions firsthand enhanced their grasp of theoretical content. As one student put it, "VR allows us to visualize environmental consequences and then be more able to discuss them."

The dialogue activity was seen as both informative and dynamic, encouraging guided but open conversations on environmental topics. Students valued the mix of personal and general questions, noting that sharing personal experiences made the dialogue more relatable and potentially motivating for action. They highlighted the diversity of perspectives as key to deepening their understanding of complex environmental issues. Students unanimously said they would recommend the experience to others. While some noted it may be less transformative for environmentally aware students, they believed it would be especially powerful for those with less prior exposure (Fig. 1).

5.2   Challenges and Design Suggestions

Educators. A key concern among educators was maintaining student attention during the combined activities, particularly the dialogue component. They recommended limiting it to under 30 min, as standard class periods last 45 min, or breaking it into shorter segments, to support a flexible approach based on student familiarity and interest. Two educators suggested alternating brief VR sessions with dialogue to sustain engagement and prevent cognitive overload.

Educators also stressed the need to tailor VR content by age. While VR was seen as highly engaging for young children, concerns were raised about eye strain and device suitability for those under six. Alternatives like video casts were suggested. Balancing engagement, technological exposure, and age-appropriateness was seen as crucial to maximize impact and minimize risks.

Participants proposed adding interactive elements to the dialogue, such as polls, to support joint reflection. This sparked discussion on collaborative VR formats involving group decision-making. Participants agreed this could enhance the experience, especially with interactive features that promote discussion and teamwork.

Students. Students' concerns echoed those of educators regarding the dialogic activity, suggesting it be shortened or reformatted. They also recommended adding visual and audio elements to enhance engagement across age groups.

While students appreciated the VR experience, they wanted it to be more exploratory and interactive. Suggestions included expanding the environment with discoverable content and tools to measure heat or pollution. One idea was to add a timeline showing how long different environmental scenarios might take to unfold, making the impact of choices more tangible.

Table 1. Positive aspects

Experiences	Educators	Students
i-VR	– Important as an experiential learning activity – Novelty factor - useful to capture attention	– Immersive and engaging – Dynamic – Hands-on – Enhancing understanding of issues
Dialogue	– Facilitating discussions and promoting critical thinking – Modular and re-usable	– Engaging and informative – Diversity of perspectives – Guided but at the same time open – Enjoyable mix of personal and general questions – Sharing personal experiences can lead to action for the environment
Combination	– Significant potential, effective to capture students' attention and foster engagement – Supporting the shift towards digital tools in learning	i-VR facilitates reflection before the dialogue-based activity

A major proposal was to redesign the i-VR activity as a multi-user experience: "It would be interesting to explore the world together, since we're also working on the dialogue-based activity as a group." Students envisioned joint exploration for two or more users and brief in-VR dialogic moments tied to the environment and participants' roles. Example features included decision-making tasks and gamification elements. Role-playing with distinct expert perspectives was proposed to foster collaboration and deeper engagement through perspective-taking (Fig. 2).

6   Discussion

Both students and educators found the combined VR-dialogue approach engaging and educational, particularly for those less familiar with environmental issues. They supported its use in schools, while recommending enhancements to increase dynamism, interactivity, and clarity.

A key limitation of this study is its small, non-representative sample, restricting the generalizability of findings. Most participants were already environmentally aware, likely more receptive to innovative methods than the average teacher. Their feedback serves primarily as expert design input. Further formative evaluation is needed to assess impact and barriers for less environmentally aware audiences.

Insights from this work suggest that integrating immersive VR with a post-experience dialogue activity, which together form an interactive digital narrative,

Table 2. Suggestions for improvement

Experiences	Educators	Students
i-VR	– Requires tailoring to age groups – Alternative formats for younger children (videos) – Need for training educators	– A more open, exploratory approach needed – More visual elements – Virtual tools for interactive exploration – Interactive timelines to illustrate long-term impacts – Role-playing elements – Collaborative version – Integration of group decision-making
Dialogue	Shorter, flexible dialogue models	– Shorter duration – More content variety – More multimedia elements

combining spatial story nodes and structured conversational arcs, can effectively promote environmental awareness and citizenship, supporting all key components defined by [25]. This integration exemplifies how interactive digital narratives can leverage embodied storytelling and narrative arcs to cultivate empathy and civic agency in educational settings. While each component has standalone value, their combination enhances impact. Both contribute to *Information and literacy* by delivering targeted sustainability content. i-VR's realistic, interactive depictions of environments foster experiential learning, while the dialogue phase reinforces it through reflection. Together, they also enhance *Awareness*, by linking visualized impacts to discussion.

i-VR fosters emotional *Concern*, often termed "the ultimate empathy machine" [42], with support from embodiment studies [7,61]. Yet, given debates on VR's limitations for cognitive empathy [35], the dialogue's perspective-taking role is critical in shaping *Attitudes and beliefs* about sustainability. For *Knowledge and skills*, i-VR introduces key issues, while dialogue provides practical solutions-such as nature-based strategies-guiding students toward *Responsible, environmentally friendly behaviour* in both private and public contexts.

A modular design for i-VR and dialogue components can accommodate different curricula, ensuring flexibility. Shorter HMD sessions, or 360-degree and plain video alternatives, retain some interactivity while addressing health concerns for young users while richer multimedia content can support younger or less environmentally aware students.

Educators expressed concerns about real-world application, citing high VR equipment costs, especially in under-resourced schools. However, using i-VR independently of VR group activities could enable broader, cost-effective implementation. Teacher training also emerged as a major barrier: effective adoption requires both comfort with new technologies and structured lesson design support. Despite this, participants expressed eagerness to receive training, valuing VR as a safe space to simulate climate risks and envision hopeful futures.

We intentionally kept the post-experience dialogue outside VR to preserve meaningful verbal and non-verbal communication. Non-verbal cues-such as posture, gestures, and facial expressions-play a dominant role in conveying attitudes [23], with research indicating that only 30% of interaction is verbal [8]. However, students proposed a collaborative VR version with brief dialogue segments integrated: "It would be great to explore the virtual worlds together and talk about our experiences". Tools inside the VR environment, such as instruments to measure pollution, were proposed to foster exploration and hands-on learning and assuming different roles, to support perspective-taking. This collaborative extension would give way to a multi-agent IDN system where co-authors inhabiting distinct narrative roles within the protostory and jointly shape branching story vectors through synchronized spatial exploration and dialogue arcs.

7   Conclusions

The combination of immersive i-VR and dialogue shows strong potential for fostering environmental awareness, critical thinking, and citizenship. This dual approach combines VR's empathy-driven, experiential learning with the reflective, knowledge-sharing nature of guided dialogue. i-VR nurtures responsibility and illustrates the impact of human actions on the environment, while dialogue supports literacy and equips students with skills for sustainable decision-making. Educators and students widely supported this engaging, interactive approach and suggested refinements for its design.

A key outcome was the proposal to design a collaborative, role-based version of the VR experience. Distinct roles will help students explore diverse viewpoints, and decision-making activities will support addressing environmental challenges collaboratively. A prototype collaborative i-VR version has been implemented [20] to be soon assessed with students. In parallel, the participant's suggestions to improve the dialogue component regarding brevity, modularity, content variety, and multimodality are also under way.

In conclusion, integrating collaborative, role-based VR with dialogue-based activities has the potential to redefine environmental education as a participatory, multisensory, and socially grounded practice. By combining immersion with reflection, students are not only learning about sustainability but also rehearsing the skills, choices, and responsibilities it entails, enhancing capacity for environmental action.

Acknowledgments. We would like to thank the ARSINOE project CS1 Athens Metropolitan area team for the support. The ARSINOE project has been funded by EU's Horizon programme under grant agreement No 9101037424.

References

1. Albar, R., Gauthier, A., Vasalou, A.: A playful path to sustainability: synthesizing design strategies for children's environmental sustainability learning through gameful interventions. In: Proceedings of the 23rd Annual ACM Interaction Design and Children Conference (IDC 2024), pp. 201–217 (2024). https://doi.org/10.1145/3628516.3655797

2. Albelda, J., Sgaramella, C.: Art, empathy and sustainability: empathic ability and environmental awareness in contemporary ecological art practices. Eur. J. Literat. Cult. Environ. **6**(2), 10–25 (2015). https://doi.org/10.37536/ECOZONA.2015.6.2.662

3. Alexander, R.J.: Culture, dialogue and learning: Notes on an emerging pedagogy. In: Mercer, N., Hodgkinson, S. (eds.) Exploring Talk in School, pp. 91–113. Sage, London (2008)

4. ARSINOE VR: Arsinoe vr - immersive vr and facilitated dialogue for environmental education. https://youtu.be/RwRreeSfZhg (2025), youTube video

5. Athman, J., Monroe, M.: Elements of effective environmental education programs (2001), https://www.researchgate.net/publication/254389309_Elements_of_Effective_Environmental_Education_Programs, Accessed 28 Jan 2025

6. Bailenson, J.N., Beall, A.C., Loomis, J., Blascovich, J., Turk, M.: Transformed social interaction: decoupling representation from behavior and form in collaborative virtual environments. Presence: Teleoperators Virt. Environ. **10**(4), 358–371 (2001). https://doi.org/10.1162/105474601300343595

7. Banakou, D., Hanumanthu, P.D., Slater, M.: Virtual embodiment of white people in a black virtual body leads to a sustained reduction in their implicit racial bias. Front. Hum. Neurosci. **10**, 601 (2016). https://doi.org/10.3389/fnhum.2016.00601, https://doi.org/10.3389/fnhum.2016.00601

8. Birdwhistell, R.L.: Introduction to kinesics: An annotation system for analysis of body motion and gesture. Department of State, Foreign Service Institute (1952)

9. Bormann, T., Campt, D.: The arc of dialogue. In: Americans: A Dialogue Toolkit for Educators (nd), https://americanindian.si.edu/sites/1/files/pdf/education/NMAI-Americans-dialogue-toolkit.pdf

10. Browning, M., et al.: Measuring the 3-30-300 rule to help cities meet nature access thresholds. Sci. Total Environ. **907**, 167739 (2024). https://doi.org/10.1016/j.scitotenv.2023.167739, http://dx.doi.org/10.1016/j.scitotenv.2023.167739

11. Bruner, J.: Acts of Meaning. Harvard University Press (1990)

12. Burbules, N.C.: Dialogue in Teaching: Theory and Practice. Teachers College Press (1993). https://doi.org/10.1080/002

13. Chatain, J., Kapur, M., Sumner, R.W.: Three perspectives on embodied learning in virtual reality: opportunities for interaction design. In: Extended Abstracts of the 2023 CHI Conference on Human Factors in Computing Systems (CHI EA 2023), CHI EA 2023, ACM, New York, NY, USA (2023). https://doi.org/10.1145/3544549.3585805, https://doi.org/10.1145/3544549.3585805

14. Chirico, A., Scurati, G.W., Maffi, C., Gaggioli, A., Riva, G.: Designing virtual environments for attitudes and behavioral change in plastic consumption: a comparison between concrete and numerical information. Virt. Real. **25**, 107–121 (2021). https://doi.org/10.1007/s10055-020-00442-w, https://doi.org/10.1007/s10055-020-00442-w

15. Clayborn, J., Delamarre, A.: Living room conservation: a virtual way to engage participants in insect conservation. Rethinking Ecol. **4**, 31–43 (2019). https://doi.org/10.3897/rethinkeco.4.e36016

16. Culiberg, B., Rojšek, I.: Identifying service quality dimensions as antecedents to customer satisfaction in retail banking. Econ. Bus. Rev. **12**(3), 1 (2010)
17. Cumbo, B.J., Iversen, O.S.: CCI in the wild: designing for environmental stewardship through children's nature-play. In: Proceedings of the Interaction Design and Children Conference. pp. 335–348. ACM (2020). https://doi.org/10.1145/3392063.3394398
18. Dede, C., Grotzer, T., Kamarainen, A., Metcalf, S.: Ecoxpt: designing for deeper learning through experimentation in an immersive virtual ecosystem. J. Educ. Technol. Soc. **20**, 166–178 (2017)
19. Fan, S., Zhang, Y., Fan, J., He, Z., Chen, Y.: The application of virtual reality in environmental education: model design and course construction. In: 2010 International Conference on Biomedical Engineering and Computer Science, pp. 1–4 (2010). https://doi.org/10.1109/ICBECS.2010.5462324
20. Ganias, G., et al.: From dystopia to eutopia: transforming urban environments through collaborative decision-making in arsinoe vr. In: 2025 IEEE Conference on Virtual Reality and 3D User Interfaces Abstracts and Workshops (VRW), pp. 1534–1535 (2025). https://doi.org/10.1109/VRW66409.2025.00412
21. Gargett, K.: Re-thinking the Guided Tour: Co-creation, Dialogue and Practices of Facilitation at York Minster. Master's thesis, University of York (2018)
22. Hadjichambis, A.C., Reis, P.: Introduction to the conceptualisation of environmental citizenship for twenty-first-century education, pp. 1–14. Springer, Cham (2020). https://doi.org/10.1007/978-3-030-20249-1_1, https://doi.org/10.1007/978-3-030-20249-1_1
23. Hall, J.A., Horgan, T.G., Murphy, N.A.: Nonverbal communication. Ann. Rev. Psychol. **70**, 271–294 (2019). https://doi.org/10.1146/annurev-psych-010418-103145
24. Ham, M., Mrčela, D., Horvat, M.: Insights for measuring environmental awareness. Ekonomski Vjesnik: Rev. Contemp. Entrep. Bus. Econ. Issues **29**(1), 159–176 (2016). https://hrcak.srce.hr/file/237426
25. Hawthorne, M., Alabaster, T.: Citizen 2000: development of a model of environmental citizenship. Glob. Environ. Chang. **9**(1), 25–43 (1999). https://doi.org/10.1016/S0959-3780(98)00022-3
26. Huang, J., Lucash, M., Scheller, R., Klippel, A.: Visualizing ecological data in virtual reality. In: Proceedings of the 2019 IEEE Conference on Virtual Reality and 3D User Interfaces (VR), pp. 1311–1312. IEEE, Osaka, Japan (2019)
27. Huang, J., Lucash, M., Simpson, M., Helgeson, C., Klippel, A.: Visualizing natural environments from data in virtual reality: Combining realism and uncertainty. In: Proceedings of the 2019 IEEE Conference on Virtual Reality and 3D User Interfaces (VR), pp. 1485–1488. IEEE, Osaka, Japan (2019)
28. Huang, J., Lucash, M.S., Scheller, R.M., Slavenas, J.P., Mueller, U.T.: Walking through the forests of the future: using data-driven virtual reality to visualize forests under climate change. Int. J. Geog. Inf. Sci. **35**(6), 1155–1178 (2021). https://doi.org/10.1080/13658816.2020.1830997, https://www.tandfonline.com/doi/full/10.1080/13658816.2020.1830997
29. Ke, P., Keng, K.N., Jiang, S., Cai, S., Rong, Z., Zhu, K.: Embodied weather: promoting public understanding of extreme weather through immersive multi-sensory virtual reality. In: Proceedings of the 17th International Conference on Virtual-Reality Continuum and its Applications in Industry (VRCAI 2019), vol. 60, pp. 1–2. ACM, Brisbane, QLD, Australia (2019)
30. Klingenberg, S., Bosse, R., Mayer, R., et al.: Does embodiment in virtual reality boost learning transfer? testing an immersion-interactivity framework. Educ. Psychol. Rev. **36**, 116 (2024). https://doi.org/10.1007/s10648-024-09956-0

31. Koenitz, H.: Towards a Specific Theory of Interactive Digital Narrative, p. 15. Routledge, April 2015. https://doi.org/10.4324/9781315769189-8
32. Loftin, R.B.: Sciencespace: virtual realities for learning complex and abstract scientific concepts. In: Proceedings of the IEEE 1996 Virtual Reality Annual International Symposium (1996). https://doi.org/10.1109/VRAIS.1996.490534
33. Luo, H., Li, G., Feng, Q., Yang, Y., Zuo, M.: Virtual reality in k-12 and higher education: a systematic review of the literature from 2000 to 2019. J. Comput. Assist. Learn. **37**(3), 887–901 (2021). https://doi.org/10.1111/jcal.12538
34. Magro, K.: Awareness and empathy: essential dimensions of global citizenship education. In: Kornelsen, L., Balzer, G., Margo, K. (eds.) Teaching Global Citizenship: A Canadian Perspective, pp. 29–48 (2020)
35. Martingano, A.J., Hererra, F., Konrath, S.: Virtual reality improves emotional but not cognitive empathy: a meta-analysis. Technol. Mind Behav. **2** (2021). https://doi.org/10.1037/tmb0000034
36. Mawsally, D., Sudarmilah, E.: A virtual-reality edu-game: save the environment from the dangers of pollution. Khazanah Informatika: Jurnal Ilmu Komputer dan Informatika **5**, 140–145 (2019). https://doi.org/10.23917/khif.v5i2.8843
37. McGinity, M.: Immersive media for environmental awareness. In: Proceedings of the 2018 IEEE Workshop Augmented Virtual Realities Good (VAR4Good), pp. 1–5. IEEE, Reutlingen, Germany (2018)
38. McKinney, S.: Generating Pre-historic Empathy: An Examination of a Digital Classroom Kit. Msc in digital heritage, University of York (2018)
39. Mercer, N., Dawes, L.: The value of exploratory talk. In: Exploring Talk in School, pp. 55–71. SAGE Publications, London, UK (2008)
40. Mezirow, J.: How critical reflection triggers transformative learning, chap. 1, pp. 1–20. Jossey-Bass (1990). https://api.semanticscholar.org/CorpusID:111380047
41. Mikropoulos, T.A., Chalkidis, A., Katsikis, A., Kossivaki, P.: Virtual realities in environmental education: the project lake. Educ. Inf. Technol. **2**(2), 131–142 (1997). https://doi.org/10.1023/A:1018648810609, https://link.springer.com/article/10.1023/A:1018648810609
42. Milk, C.: How virtual reality can create the ultimate empathy machine (2015), https://www.ted.com/talks/chris_milk_how_virtual_reality_can_create_the_ultimate_empathy_machine, tED Talk
43. Mulgan, G., Leadbeater, C.: Systems Innovation. Nesta, London (2013)
44. Nelson, K., Anggraini, E., Schlüter, A.: Virtual reality as a tool for environmental conservation and fundraising. PLoS ONE **15**, e0223631 (2020). https://doi.org/10.1371/journal.pone.0223631
45. Perkins, H.: Beyond techno-solutionism: towards critical perspectives in environmental education and digital technology. a critical-hermeneutic review. Int. J. Child-Comput. Interact. **42**, 100705 (2024). https://doi.org/10.1016/j.ijcci.2024.100705
46. Petousi, D., Katifori, A., McKinney, S., Perry, S., Roussou, M., Ioannidis, Y.: Social bots of conviction as dialogue facilitators for history education: promoting historical empathy in teens through dialogue. In: Interaction Design and Children (IDC 2021), pp. 326–337. ACM, New York, NY, USA (2021). https://doi.org/10.1145/3459990.3460710
47. Piersol, L., Timmerman, N.: Reimagining environmental education within academia: Storytelling and dialogue as lived ecofeminist politics. J. Environ. Educ. **48**(1), 10–17 (2017). https://doi.org/10.1080/00958964.2016.1249329

48. Pochwatko, G., Świdrak, J., Kopeć, W., Jędrzejewski, Z., Feledyn, A., Vogt, M., Castell, N., Zagórska, K.: Multisensory representation of air pollution in virtual reality: Lessons from visual representation. In: Digital Interaction and Machine Intelligence, pp. 239–247. Springer (2022). https://doi.org/10.1007/978-3-031-11432-8_24, https://link.springer.com/chapter/10.1007/978-3-031-11432-8_24

49. Porter, J., Robb, A.: An analysis of longitudinal trends in consumer thoughts on presence and simulator sickness in VR games. In: Proceedings of the Annual Symposium on Computer-Human Interaction in Play, CHI PLAY 2019, pp. 277–285. ACM, New York, NY, USA (2019). https://doi.org/10.1145/3311350.3347153, https://doi.org/10.1145/3311350.3347153

50. Prakash, A., Rajendran, R.: Virtual reality and embodied learning: Unraveling the relationship via dynamic learner behavior. In: Proceedings of the 31st International Conference on Computers in Education (ICCE), vol. 2, pp. 307–316. Asia-Pacific Society for Computers in Education (APSCE), Matsue, Japan, December 2023

51. Project, E.: Emotive project - empathy and emotion for a sustainable future. https://emotiveproject.eu/ (nd), Accessed 28 Jan 2025

52. of Public Instruction, W.D.: A Guide to Curriculum Planning in Environmental Education. Wisconsin Department of Public Instruction, Madison, Wisconsin (1994)

53. Roussou, M., Johnson, A., Moher, T., Leigh, J., Vasilakis, C., Barnes, C.: Learning and building together in an immersive virtual world. Presence: Teleoperators Virt. Environ. 8 (2001). https://doi.org/10.1162/105474699566215

54. Ruan, B.: Vr-assisted environmental education for undergraduates. Adv. Multimedia 2022, 3721301 (2022). https://doi.org/10.1155/2022/3721301

55. Schroeder, R.: Being There Together: Social Interaction in Virtual Environments. Oxford University Press, Oxford, UK (2011). https://doi.org/10.1093/acprof:oso/9780199737501.001.0001

56. Service, N.P.: Forging connections through audience centred design: Workbook spring 2018. Technical Report, Stephen T. Mather Interpretive Development Program, Training Center, Harpers Ferry (2018)

57. Strassmann, C., Arntz, A., Eimler, S.C.: Inspiring movement–physical activity in a virtual sea as a driver for ecological awareness. Int. J. Seman. Comput. 15(4), 539–559 (2021). https://doi.org/10.1142/S1793351X21400158

58. Sulisworo, D., Erviana, V., Robiin, B., Sepriansyah, Y., Soleh, A.: The feasibility of enhancing environmental awareness using virtual reality 3d in primary education. Education Res. Int. 2022, 1–10 (2022). https://doi.org/10.1155/2022/4811544

59. Tam, K.P.: Concepts and measures related to connection to nature: Similarities and differences. J. Environ. Psychol. 34, 64–78 (2013). https://doi.org/10.1016/j.jenvp.2013.01.004

60. Taulien, A., Paulsen, A., Streland, T., Jessen, B., Wittke, S., Teistler, M.: A mixed reality environmental simulation to support learning about maritime habitats: an approach to convey educational knowledge with a novel user experience. In: Proceedings of Mensch und Computer 2019, pp. 921–925. ACM, New York, NY, USA (2019)

61. Trevena, L., Paay, J., McDonald, R.: Vr interventions aimed to induce empathy: a scoping review. Virtual Reality 28, 80 (2024). https://doi.org/10.1007/s10055-024-00946-9, https://doi.org/10.1007/s10055-024-00946-9

62. UNESCO: Final report of the intergovernmental conference on environmental education. Technical Report, UNESCO ED/MD/49, UNESCO, Paris (1978), organized by UNESCO in cooperation with UNEP, Tbilisi, USSR, 14-26 October 1977

63. Vasalou, A., Gauthier, A.: The role of cci in supporting children's engagement with environmental sustainability at a time of climate crisis. Int. J. Child-Comput. Interact. 100605 (2023). https://doi.org/10.1016/j.ijcci.2023.100605
64. Vayanou, M., Katifori, A., Ioannidis, Y.: Perspective sharing in culture group games: Passing around the social mediator role. Proc. ACM Hum.-Comput. Interact. **5**, 1–24 (2021). https://doi.org/10.1145/3474676
65. Vicencio, M.A.A.: Dialogue based strategies in the teaching of environmental education in baja California Sur, Mexico. Ph.D. thesis, University of York (2012), https://etheses.whiterose.ac.uk/5811/1/MArizpePhDThesisFinal.pdf, doctoral dissertation
66. Vrettakis, E., et al.: The story maker - an authoring tool for multimedia-rich interactive narratives. In: Bosser, A.-G., Millard, D.E., Hargood, C. (eds.) ICIDS 2020. LNCS, vol. 12497, pp. 349–352. Springer, Cham (2020). https://doi.org/10.1007/978-3-030-62516-0_33
67. Windschitl, M., Winn, W.: A virtual environment designed to help students understand science. In: Fourth International Conference of the Learning Sciences, pp. 290–296. Psychology Press, London, UK (2000)
68. Xenakis, I., Gavalas, D., Kasapakis, V., Dzardanova, E., Vosinakis, S.: Non-verbal communication in immersive virtual reality through the lens of presence: a critical review. PRESENCE: Virt. Augmented Real. **31**, 1–71 (2022). https://doi.org/10.1162/pres_a_00387
69. Xie, T., Yang, Y.: Use of immersive virtual reality in environmental education: effects on environmental empathy, skill transfer, and attitudes. Interact. Learn. Environ. 1–15 (2025). https://doi.org/10.1080/10494820.2024.2436947, https://doi.org/10.1080/10494820.2024.2436947

Design, Reflect, Create: Game Poem Practices with Generative AI Tools

Ziyi Wang[1]($\boxtimes$) , Ling Ma[2] , Ray Lc[3] , and Jussi Holopainen[4]($\boxtimes$)

[1] School of Creative Media, City University of Hong Kong, Hong Kong, China
`zwang2428-c@my.cityu.edu.hk`
[2] Cornell University, Ithaca, USA
[3] Studio for Narrative Spaces, City University of Hong Kong, Hong Kong, China
`LC@raylc.org`
[4] School of Creative Media, City University of Hong Kong, Hong Kong, China
`jholopai@cityu.edu.hk`
`https://recfro.github.io/`

Abstract. Generative Artificial Intelligence (GenAI) tools are transforming creative practices, yet their role in game poem design remains largely unexplored. Game poems serve as a bridge between interactive artwork and design for engagement. Although game poems themselves are a small genre, they serve as a microcosm for exploring how AI influences minimal, expressive, and human-centric design. This research was based on ten student-made game poems with GenAI tools. Using qualitative analysis, this study explores how student designers navigate, integrate, and revise GenAI in game poem making. Analysis of the ten included student projects demonstrates that the influence of GenAI accelerates technical implementation and ideation scaffolding, but human authorship and emotional intention play a vital role in game poem design. Students simultaneously engaged in iterative prompting, Human Creative Override, and manual curation to negotiate GenAI's outputs.

Keywords: Generative AI · game design · game poems · Design Education

1 Introduction

Generative Artificial Intelligence (GenAI) tools like ChatGPT, Midjourney, and Deepseek have quickly entered the game design space and provide support. While the tools have been praised for boosting efficiency and diminishing creative barriers, their role in the creation of game poems remains underexplored.

Game poems as small, short-form interactive experiences distill core design decisions into minimal but potentially impactful gestures. For instance, Jordan Magnuson's "Loneliness"[1] as a game poem, foregoes complex mechanics in favor

---

[1] https://jordanmagnuson.itch.io/loneliness.

M. C. Reyes and F. Nack (Eds.): ICIDS 2025, LNCS 16375, pp. 113–129, 2026.
https://doi.org/10.1007/978-3-032-12405-0_7

of evocative, symbolic interactions that prioritize emotional resonance over traditional gameplay goals. Game poems' brevity and simplicity make them well-suited for examining how game designers integrate AI tools into their creative practice.

This paper can reveal how designers navigate the interplay between automation and intentionality, and how they use AI not just to generate assets, but to shape the meaning and emotional tone of gameplay. In this way, studying AI-assisted game poems offers insight into both the evolving role of generative AI in game design and creative strategies that guide expressive and reflective play.

We aim to address these research questions in our study:

RQ1: How do game designers perceive the role of GenAI in the game poem design process?

Sub-question: What are the perceived advantages and limitations of GenAI tools in game poem design, according to student designers?

RQ2: What specific strategies do student game designers use when integrating GenAI tools into different parts of the game poem design process (e.g., character, plot, mechanics)?

RQ3: What technical or creative challenges do students encounter when using GenAI for game poems, and how do they address them?

By pointing out the largely underexamined intersections between GenAI and game poem design, this research contributes to both the game-design field and the broader domains of GenAI. The findings have implications for design education, creative ownership, tool development, and the ethical framing of AI as a co-creative partner in expressive and reflective game design.

The study explores its own questions of authorship, intentionality, and meaning-making in the age of AI-assisted creativity. Game poems require careful attention to emotional tone, ambiguity, and designer intention–qualities that cannot be fully automated. this study breaks new ground by centering game poems' distinct, non-negotiable poetic qualities–emotional tone, intentional ambiguity, and designer subjectivity–as the lens to redefine human-AI collaboration. Therefore, we not only learn about tool development and educational practices, but also raise critical questions regarding the evolving relationship between human and computational collaboration. Even though we are focusing on game poem design, the results give insights on core game design issues and are thus applicable for designing other kinds of games as well.

2   Literature Review

The literature review covers Game Poems, Game Design Studies and GenAI.

2.1   Game Poems as a Creative Medium

Based on [28], a game poem is a short, subjective video game that uses lyric poetry tendencies (metaphor, ritual space, poetic address, etc.) to prioritize emotional resonance over traditional gameplay goals, intervening in videogames' established language to evoke human experiences.

Mitchell's poetic gameplay refers to forms of play that encourage reflective engagement analogous to reading poetry, but through expressive use of form, structure, and interaction. This aligns closely with the design of game poems, which use minimalist mechanics to create short, evocative experiences intended to be felt rather than solved. Both use game form as expression and ambiguity to invite interpretation.

Where poetic gameplay functions as a broader theoretical lens for understanding certain qualities of gameplay, game poems can be seen as concrete instantiations of this idea. They are typically short-form works that use interactive elements to produce a specific emotional or contemplative effect. Notable game poem examples include Jason Rohrer's "Passage"[2], Jordan Magnuson's "Loneliness"[3], and Anna Anthropy's "Dys4ria"[4].

The Game "Passage" simulates a young man from birth to death through simple pixel style and 5-min real-time experiences [32] . In this game, there's no goal reminder, and the player's choice won't trigger clear feedback. This game invites players to reflect on their own experiences through ambiguity.

The game "Loneliness," as pointed out by [28], has minimalist mechanics. The core interaction is to use the arrow key to move. Players will feel a sense of loneliness by controlling the small box to go around. And other boxes keep getting away from the player. The game focuses on the emotional experience at the moment.

2.2   Game Design Studies

Game design research seeks to generate systematic knowledge about the processes, practices, and outcomes of game design itself [23,25]. Game design research has recently become an academic focus, linking to general design studies [22].

Cross [10] states that design research involves the development and communication of design knowledge, understood across three domains: epistemology, praxiology, and phenomenology. Epistemology focuses on the types of knowledge designers bring to and develop through their practice. Praxiology investigates the tools, methods, and collaborative contexts in which design occurs. Phenomenology addresses the analysis of games as designed artifacts, including their structure, function, and cultural impact. Together, these dimensions provide a comprehensive lens for situating and analyzing game design practices and outcomes.

Another widely used categorization in design research [13,14] distinguishes between research on or about design (studying design as a human activity), research for design (producing applicable knowledge for practice), and research

---

[2] https://hcsoftware.sourceforge.net/passage/.
[3] https://jordanmagnuson.itch.io/loneliness.
[4] https://w.itch.io/dys4ia.

through design (creating knowledge by designing artifacts). In game design research, all three approaches are present, though research for design, which focuses on improving tools, frameworks, and methodologies, has been particularly prominent (e.g. [4,11,12,35]). However, game design research also includes works that aim to understand deeper historical, cognitive, and conceptual aspects of design, going beyond immediate applicability (e.g. [8,21,22,24]). This broader orientation informs our study, which explores how game design students integrate generative AI tools into their creative practices, where both epistemological and praxiological dimensions of design knowledge are being reshaped.

2.3   GenAI in Game Design and Interactive Digital Storytelling

Generative artificial intelligence (GenAI) tools are being integrated into game design as they complete vital tasks such as code generation, asset building, and writing narratives [16,20,38]. These new tools significantly improved efficiency and expanded creative potential. In the evolution of game development, automation has played a pivotal role. Automation, procedural content generation, and model-driven techniques have historically advanced game development [7,9].

A scoping review by Yang [36] encompassed 131 studies highlighting the application of GenAI in various areas. Despite AI's incredible speed in prototyping and ideation, the originality and creative dependency continue to pose challenges [3]. Thus, while GenAI offers efficiency, human oversight and control remain crucial to ensure creative integrity.

GenAI aids character prototyping [27], dynamic narratives [1], personalized Extended Reality experiences [26], and interactive storytelling [33,34]. However, challenges existed regarding emotional depth and coherence in AI-generated narratives. This study consist of emergent storytelling, AI-human co-creation, and emotional coherence in computational narratives.

2.4   Gaps in Existing Research

Most studies focus on GenAI's technical uses, while its impact on expressive or poetic game design is underexplored [17]. In particular, the integration of GenAI into short-form, reflective works like game poems remains underexplored. Existing frameworks in interactive storytelling acknowledge GenAI's potential in dynamic narrative generation. However, it offers limited insight into how emotional nuance, ambiguity, and authorship are negotiated when the designer's goal is poetic experience [5].

Additionally, game design research has not reached sufficient depth to explore how students encounter and respond to the technology of GenAI within the context of game poem design, especially one that encompasses the epistemological and praxiological dimensions of design knowledge [10]. As students create game poems–works that prioritize poetry expression–how they engage with GenAI and how they collaborate with GenAI is significant to explore.

This study bridges this gap by examining how student designers understand, adapt to, and critique various GenAI tools for the making of game poems, concentrating on roles, benefits, challenges, strategies, and the negotiation of emotional and creative boundaries.

3   Methodology

This Methodology section includes Research Design, Participants, Data Collection, Data Analysis, Ethical Considerations.

3.1   Research Design

The data for this research were collected from the course: Art and Activist Games Workshop, taught by one of the authors. It is a course for master students. And it is offered by the School of Creative Media at City University of Hong Kong. In this course, the game-making experiences of students are diverse. The analysis focuses on ten student-created games developed during the course. Some of these games were developed individually, while others were created collaboratively in groups. A qualitative research approach was employed, with data sources including semi-structured interviews, artist statements, and analysis of game artifacts. We first coded each individual interview, then we went through the other materials and triangulated them.

We first came up with a set of interview questions and conducted a pilot interview to assess the effectiveness. After the pilot interview, we adjusted the interview questions based on the outcome and feedback. After reviewing the games created by students, we further refine and adjust the interview questions to better align with the specific design choices and GenAI integrations observed in each project.

3.2   Participants

This study consisted of ten (10) student-made games developed as part of the course: art and activist games workshop. It included individual and collaborative teams. In total, there are 15 participants. As a policy to protect the anonymity of those involved, all names given in this research are pseudonyms, and non-disclosed game titles are anonymized unless otherwise permitted for their use.

The projects varied in form and theme, ranging from metaphorical views on Human-AI relationships and memory to poetic reflections. Some were developed by individuals, others by groups of two or three students cooperating in their design. Each team participated in a 30–45-min interview session to talk about their design process, the use of generative AI, and creative intentions.

For internal reference and analytic clarity, each game was given a unique code, and the anonymized mapping is shown in Table 1 and was used continuously throughout the data analysis workflow.

Table 1. Anonymized Team Description.

Game Code	Team Type	Team Members (Anonymized)	Team Size
Game A	Team project	A1, A2	2
Game B	Solo project	B1	1
Game C	Team project	C1, C2, C3	3
Game D	Solo project	D1	1
Game E	Team project	E1, E2	2
Game F	Solo project	F1	1
Game G	Solo project	G1	1
Game H	Solo project	H1	1
Game I	Team project	I1, I2	2
Game J	Solo project	J1	1

3.3 Data Collection

We began by attending the in-class presentations of each game to understand
their concepts, mechanics, and design details. During these sessions, each group
demonstrated and played their games live. Afterward, we collected their artist
statement, full URL to their playable game, and documentation of GenAI tools.
After the prior analysis of the materials, we further refine the interview questions
based on each individual game. Then we conducted 30–45 min semi-structured
interviews for each game team. All interviews were audio-recorded and transcribed for analysis. Notes were also taken during the interview process to record
the key information. There are ten interviews in total. The overall interview
recording is approximately 5 h.

3.4 Data Analysis

The data analysis employed a qualitative, multi-source triangulation approach,
integrating semi-structured interviews, artist statements, AI tool usage logs, and
game artifacts. The process combined thematic coding with cross-source synthesis, grounded in the study's three research questions (RQ1RQ3).

Step 1: Thematic Analysis of Interviews. We followed the Thematic Analysis guidelines by Naeem [30] and conducted the Thematic Analysis. We summarize the interview results in the first part of our results. An inductive coding
method was primarily used to create codes based on the interview data. After
that, codes were iteratively developed and clustered into themes. The code book
consists of several parts: code category, inductive codes, example quotes, frequency, and notes. In this study, we developed one code book for each game.
The first author developed 9 code books, and the second author developed 1
code book. All the codes from the code books were summarized and converted

into key themes. A table that summarizes all interview key themes is also shown in the results section. We combine all themes from the code book, then conceptualize and summarize them. Then, we present our final Thematic Analysis results.

Step 2: Triangulation Across Data Sources. A triangulation framework was applied to synthesize insights across four sources for each game: Interview transcript, Artist statement, AI tool logs, and Game artifact.

Step 3: Cross-Case Comparison and Theoretical Synthesis Once all individual cases were triangulated, thematic patterns were compared across the ten games to identify broader design tendencies.

3.5   Ethical Considerations

This study was conducted under institutional ethical guidelines, with informed consent and anonymization for all participants and their work.

4   Results

This section integrates results from interviews, triangulated tool logs, art statements, and game artifacts. The findings are contextualized through key themes that emerged from the data, supported by example quotes and triangulated evidence. The emerging codes, which were summarized from the results, are presented in Table 2.

Table 2. Key Themes and Descriptions from Thematic Coding.

Theme/Code	Description
GenAI as Generator	GenAI acts as a tool to execute human decisions, lacking original creative input.
Technical Tutor	GenAI provides technical guidance and troubleshooting help.
Brainstorming Explorer	GenAI helps stimulate creative ideas during the initial design phases.
Efficiency and Acceleration	GenAI accelerates content generation and shortens development timelines.
Scaffolding Support	GenAI provides structural or conceptual frameworks (mood boards, initial outlines) for human refinement.
Emotional Gap	GenAI lacks the ability to produce emotionally nuanced, morally resonant content.
Conventional Output	GenAI outputs are often generic and require human curation to achieve distinctiveness.
Inconsistency	GenAI outputs, especially AI-generated Art, are often inconsistent.
Technical Failures	Instances of GenAI providing flawed or unusable outputs (e.g., fake links, incomplete coding).
Stage-Specific Applications	Different uses of GenAI across design phases: early-stage research, mid-stage asset generation, late-stage debugging, or localization.
Human Creative Overrides	Human designers ultimately curate, refine, or override AI outputs to preserve creative vision and authenticity.
Iterative Human-AI Refinement	GenAI outputs are combined with human refinement in layered iterative workflows.
Emotional Interactions	Designers interact with GenAI in emotionally expressive ways, from frustration to playful or supportive exchanges.
Technical Constraints	Technical or resource limitations (e.g., memory limits, API costs, version mismatches) that complicate GenAI use.
Flawed Output	GenAI struggles with creative writing, style mismatch, or culturally awkward outputs that require editing.
Prompt Refinement	Structured, iterative prompting strategies to improve GenAI output relevance and style.
Tool Switching	Shifting between GenAI tools to find the best fit for specific tasks or aesthetic needs.
Moral Rejection of AI Art	Ethical concerns lead some designers to reject AI-generated assets or feel a diminished sense of authorship.
GenAI Adaptation to Game Poem Ambiguity	GenAI tools are adjusted through human efforts to fit the poetic characteristics of Game Poems

All the games in this study are game poems. For example, Game A qualifies as a game poem because it abandons "win/lose" mechanics to focus on immersing players in the feeling of anxiety–a core goal of game poems; Game E is a game poem because it uses interactive mechanics to explore an abstract, emotional metaphor; Game I is a game poem because it reimagines poetry as an interactive act–letting players "co-create" poetry through gameplay, rather than just reading static verses.

4.1 RQ1: How Do Game Designers Perceive the Role of GenAI in the Game Poem Design Process?

Three themes reflect this research question: GenAI as Generator, Technical Tutor, and Brainstorming Explorer.

Student designers viewed GenAI mainly as a technical facilitator in the game poem design process. The theme "GENAI AS GENERATOR" was strongly represented, thereby suggesting that GenAI carried out the predefined tasks rather than contributing original creative ideas. In Game A, it was considered a "hard labourer." In Game D, it was also considered an "instruction executor", as can be inferred from the quotation below:"Give commands, let AI execute...human creativity is stronger" (Game D). According to Game B, GenAI helps a lot in building initial frameworks: "AI helped structure the framework, but details were all mine" (Game B). Such a pattern was consistently observed in tool logs where the outputs of GenAI were mainly used to undertake coding, layout, and debugging instructions.

The theme "TECHNICAL TUTOR" also emerged prominently positioned in the discovery, which indicated that GenAI offered procedural guidance during design iterations. For instance, in Game I, it was described as providing "step-by-step to the button level" assistance. In Game G, GenAI was used to provide the initial software instructions: "Asked GPT how to use Construct 3". Game F also used AI to reference the basic game engine functions. Tool logs from Games I and J further demonstrated how GenAI's technical suggestions were employed to streamline interface development and resolve platform-specific obstacles.

The theme "BRAINSTORMING EXPLORER" highlighted GenAI's limited role in creative idea generation. In most of the game groups, they came up with the ideas by themselves. There are only two groups out of ten that used GenAI to assist them in gaining their initial ideas. In Game C, it was stated to be utilized "to stimulate ideas," although participants noted that the help might diminish their cognitive effort.

GenAI was primarily employed for task execution, but the emotional and thematic heart of game poems was still purely human-operated.

Sub-Question: What Are the Perceived Advantages and Limitations of GenAI Tools in Game Poem Design, According to Student Designers? The perceived benefits were mirrored in the themes "EFFICIENCY AND ACCELERATION" and "SCAFFOLDING SUPPORT". GenAI was perceived as offering "rapid task execution" (Game A) and "accelerated brainstorming" (Game

H), thus shortening the development time frame. The interview by Game D indicated that "AI can generate everything at once". The designers in Game I also mentioned, "AI helped achieve high-speed completion...impossible to finish in two weeks without AI". In Game G, an AI-generated mood board was indicated as the first initial conceptual scaffold, enabling visual and narrative planning. Mentioned by Game F "AI helped organize my messy ideas into logical text". Artist statement and tool logs consistently indicated that these AI-generated initial frameworks provided a structured starting point for subsequent human refinement.

However, there were also limitations. The theme "EMOTIONAL GAP" highlighted concerns about the lack of ability for GenAI to convey emotions in a nuanced way. In Games A, B, E, and H, participants complained that the dialogue and narrative generated by GenAI were either "mechanical" or just lacked "emotional nuance." The "CONVENTIONAL OUTPUT" theme highlighted how visuals and narratives created by GenAI tended to be "too generic" and required manual improvements to achieve unique artistic expressions.

The theme "INCONSISTENCY" also reflects one of the key problems of AI-generated output. This problem occurs often for AI-generated art. As indicated by Game F, "AI-generated images weren't consistent...styles didn't match". Game G mentioned: "GPT's images were slow/inaccurate...switched to Jiyimeng".

Then, technical shortages were identified under the theme "TECHNICAL FAILURES". In Game J, GenAI was reported to have had "fake resource links," and in Game D, it failed to execute coding tasks fully. In addition, in Game J, the AI failed to solve the problem in this game; the remaining problem was also reflected in the final game product. Referring to Game H, "Stable Diffusion failed...pixel art hand-drawn". AI failed to create the art they wanted, therefore, they decided to hand-draw the pixel art.

4.2   RQ2: What Specific Strategies Do Student Game Designers Use When Integrating GenAI Tools Into Different Parts of the Game Poem Design Process (e.g., Character, Plot, Mechanics)?

Four themes reflect this research question: Stage-Specific Applications, Human Creative Overrides, Iterative Human-AI Refinement, and Emotional Interactions.

The theme "STAGE-SPECIFIC APPLICATIONS" describes GenAI's phase-based use was tailored to preserve the "distilled emotional intent" of game poems. In Game B (a game poem exploring "memory fragmentation"), GenAI was used in the early stage to research "metaphorical language for lost memories" and summarize a narrative framework. However, the specific minimalist details were manually crafted to fit with the main characteristic of Game Poem. The application occurred more frequently and intensely in mid-stage development, which includes scene detail production, dialogue, and interactive narrative branches (in Games A, C, E, and H).

The theme "HUMAN CREATIVE OVERRIDES" is even more critical for game poems, as their value lies in subjective emotional resonance. Many participants mentioned GenAI can't replicate the nuanced emotional expression central to game poems. Game designers in Games E and F pointed out that their core ideas and aesthetic choices came from personal experiences and values rather than from GenAI. Handcrafted assets and manual story adjustments were used to maintain creative integrity, even when GenAI suggestions were available. Game F's interview mentioned "Only kept useful parts from AI's suggestions". AI outputs are sometimes rejected because they're too machine-like or general. Referring to Game D: "AI's 'deep thinking' produced weird, non-human ideas."

The theme "ITERATIVE HUMAN-AI REFINEMENT" was essential to preserving game poems' poetic ambiguity. In Game I, for example, color palettes were created algorithmically and then refined manually. In Game H, AI-generated images underwent significant Photoshop modifications. In game E, they mentioned "Generated 5 versions...selected one line". Many other teams also mentioned their hybrid workflow with GenAI. Tool logs corroborated these mixed practices, showing iterative cycles of AI prompting and human curation.

Nonetheless, a theme called "EMOTIONAL INTERACTIONS" emerged, representing the affective dimension of working with GenAI. In Game I, emotionally supportive prompts made people feel cared about ("Don't worry, I'll help you"), encouraging motivation and emotional comfort. Also, as mentioned in Game C, "AI can provide emotional support to you". Other teams vented frustration at AI's limitations, revealing tension between expectations and outputs. In Game D, frustration was vented towards the AI in emotionally charged interactions. According to Game B, their emotional interaction process is: Yelled at AI → AI apologized → regenerated (still flawed).

The theme "GENAI ADAPTATION TO GAME POEM AMBIGUITY" demonstrated that GenAI tools are adjusted through human efforts to fit the poetic characteristics of Game Poems such as ambiguous, inexpressible, and uncertain. In Game H, AI is unable to understand the fragmented emotions of the "train station story" due to its "limited memory." Creators refine the prompt repeatedly (e.g., "Give me three color schemes for 'separation anxiety'") to prompt AI to generate elements that align with the poetic atmosphere.

4.3   RQ3: What Technical or Creative Challenges Do Students Encounter When Using GenAI for Game Poems, and How Do They Address Them?

Technical challenges were captured under the theme "TECHNICAL CONSTRAINTS", which included high rates of API token usage (Game C), memory limitations in iterative processes (Game H), and tool version mismatches (Game A). According to Game A, "API tokens drained quickly...expensive to iterate". These constraints restrict GenAI from being easily employed in design workflows.

Creative and linguistic challenges were also identified through the theme "FLAWED OUTPUT". In Game B, there were descriptions of "awkward or unusual" outputs from AI. In Game E, the mechanical tone of AI-generated dialogue was noted to undermine emotional authenticity. This mechanical tone distracts from the emotional content that originally created by humans. In Game A, the AI output lacked depth ("AI's moral dilemmas lacked depth...added real-world cases manually"). In Game E, some outputs are even incorrect: "DeepSeek adds things that's not originally in our input".

To address this issue, the theme "PROMPT REFINEMENT" was employed. In Game E, the initial prompt for the dialogue of the otome game male protagonist made the conversation too regular and lacked emotional nuance. Which is irrelevant to their inital metaphor of "misunderstanding and emotional distance". Then, they revised it to "Write a dialogue for the AI male protagonist" to made the results more relevant. In Game I, for instance, structured and precise prompts were iteratively refined to elicit more relevant responses. Another adaptive strategy was "TOOL SWITCHING". In Game G, despite their initial use of GPT-based models, they shifted towards a visual focused AI Tool "Jimeng" to create art assets. Also, in Game F, they moved from DeepSeek to ChatGPT to better align with narrative goals.

In some instances, these technical and creative challenges were even reinterpreted as aesthetic choices in final artifacts. For example, in Game E, they used glitch-style visuals and messy code to show that AI can never break through the boundary between screen and reality.

4.4 Contextual Insights

Beyond the technical and creative integration, the student designers often gain their game poem inspiration from non-AI sources. Personal experiences (Game H), cinematic inspirations (Game B), and the previous gameplay experiences (Game E) served as a primary inspiration for their game poem idea.

Ethical considerations also influenced tool use. In Game E, the use of AI-generated art was generally rejected due to moral concerns. Because AI art usually infringes the copyright of other artists. In Game C, questions arose about personal accomplishment and creative ownership when using AI tools. In Game I, they explained "AI would mix a poet's lines with other poets' work without saying so". For a game poem that honors a specific poet, that's theft. Game G also rejected AI art to avoid plagiarism. The theme "MORAL REJECTION OF AI ART" captured these tensions.

Tool preferences varied, reflecting useful priorities and cultural aesthetics. For instance, regionally specialized models, such as DeepSeek, were more popular for their Chinese language aesthetics, whereas GPT-4.5 was mentioned to be more logically coherent than Claude.

Triangulated logs, artist statements, and artifacts confirmed these above perceptions. These themes, supported by participant interviews, artist statements, tool logs, and artifacts, collectively reveal that while GenAI provides significant technical and scaffolding advantages in game poem design, it remains limited and requires further adjustment by human creativity and emotional oversight.

4.5 Comparison Between Games

The ten games have shown varied but converging uses of GenAI. Most used it as a technical assistant. Creative roles were mainly dominated by humans. There are very few projects that used GenAI for the initial game idea (e.g., Game E). Table 3 summarizes the perceived AI role and the integration stage of all game groups. The data in Table 3 is gained from the interview and triangulation.

Table 3. Primary AI Roles and Integration Stages in Ten Game Groups.

Game	Primary AI Role	Integration stage
(A)	Technical laborer	Mid-Stage
(B)	Framework builder	Early-stage
(C)	Poetic generator	Early and mid-stage
(D)	Instruction executor	Mid-stage
(E)	Technical support (coding) Explorer	Mid-stage
(F)	Visual and technical assistant	Mid-stage
(G)	Workflow starter and technical tutor	Mid-stage
(H)	Logic organizer, product manager	Early, Mid, and Late stages
(I)	Technical tutor	Mid-stage
(J)	Technical assistant	Mid-stage

5 Discussion

The study reveals how student designers differ in the way they perceive, negotiate, and incorporate GenAI into the design of game poems. Game poem is a game genre that requires emotional control, intentional ambiguity, and minimalistic expression. We found that GenAI's dual role as not only a technical accelerator but also a creative boundary [18], an issue that calls for adaptive strategies that preserve human authorship.

GenAI's role as Generator (Games A, D) and Tutor (Games I, G) reflects the view that AI is just a technical tool. It's unusable to generate original meaning (e.g., generic outputs, emotional gaps) [37], indicating the fundamental limitation of AI: Creativity remains on the human side. This resonates with broader observations across the game design and interactive storytelling research, where GenAI's efficiency and idea-generation capabilities are praised, but its limits in creative authorship and emotional nuance remain evident [3,6]. Especially for game poems, where ambiguity and emotional resonance are important, this limitation becomes particularly significant [28,29].

Furthermore, the study confirms that while GenAI provided scaffolding for brainstorming and technical tutoring, students' creativity often overrides AI output [15,18]. The recurring theme of hybrid workflows–in which outputs generated by AI were altered, remixed, or entirely substituted–highlights the situated and iterative nature of design work in the AI-assisted process.

In particular, the findings highlight dual emotional aspects of the human-AI relationship, where some designers were satisfied with the help provided by GenAI while others found frustration or moral problems in its role. This reflects debates about authorship, authenticity and the premise of ethics in AI art in creative fields [2,17].

From an educational standpoint, the results reveal that GenAI tools can be incorporated as beneficial technical tutors and framework builders, especially in the mid-stages of implementation. However, several other key issues are also found from the results. Since AI don't have the real-life experience, their outputs sometimes contain emotional and cultural bias, which also reflects previous literature [19]. In addition, the AI-generated outputs lack consistency, and human iteration is often required. Moreover, ethical contradictions remains considerable – some groups rejected AI output due to ethical considerations.

Nonetheless, educators should emphasize the importance of critical reflection and manual refinement practices, so that the outputs of GenAI tools do not replace key creative and emotional processing in designing. This resonates with calls for education to foster reflective and ethically grounded operations in AI-based workflows [36]. Moreover, the study reveals that teaching Human-AI co-creation is not a solely linear or tool-centered practice. Rather, it is an interconnected loop of dialogue between humans and machines. Students' practices of prompt refining, manual override, and Iterative Human-AI Refinement illustrate that GenAI outputs must be engaged and interpreted in context rather than passively accepted.

The study also raises important questions about the evolving role of design knowledge. Students leveraged GenAI's procedural and technical knowledge, but the main idea of their game poems was based on their personal, experiential, and contextual insights. This also supports the previous literature about GenAI, they suggests that social interactions, as real-life experiences, cannot be replicated by AI tools [6]. This study indicate that GenAI as a more pragmatic domain of design practice rather than a generator of new design knowledge, which also resonates with the previous study [31].

This study reveals that present-day GenAI systems are designed to produce assets quickly, but game poem production requires more. Specifically, the data indicates that designers spend time looking for tools providing support for poetic and emotionally meaningful design. Developers of GenAI systems should understand the potential importance of adding features enabling layered iteration, nuanced emotional expression, and co-creative meaning-making [27]. By doing so, AI tools can better align with the goals of reflective, expressive game design.

5.1   Limitations and Future Directions

The findings offer transferability to a wide range of game genres and other creative domains where authorial control and emotional expressiveness seem equally important. We plan to use these results as a basis for developing a GenAI game design tool focusing on creative support for game poems. This study offers rich insights, but there are some things to consider in its limitations – first, the sample is only composed of student designers in one workshop setting, limiting generalizability. Second, the sample contains geographical bias; all the participants were east asians. Third, we combined solo projects and group projects for our analysis, which may have introduced variability in collaborative dynamics that was not separately examined. Fourth, the games are not diverse enough due to the total number of ten. Finally, emotionality was not explored in depth in this study, leaving open questions about how generative AI might contribute to or hinder emotional nuance in game poem design.

Future study could explore how similar dynamics unfold in different cultural contexts, team compositions, or genre-specific design challenges. Future work could include professional designers or a cross-cultural cohort to explore how GenAI implementation varies based on experience, cultural background, or genre. It would be an interesting direction to explore how GenAI contribute or hinder emotional nuance in interactive storytelling. Finally, while we focus on game poems, future studies could emphasize other expressive game forms to test the broader applicability of GenAI across different genres. Exploring how AI tools influence emotional resonance and authorship across genres will remain a critical area of inquiry as GenAI becomes increasingly embedded in creative practice.

6   Conclusion

The results show that although GenAI offered significant assistance to the student designers as a technical facilitator and scaffolder, the true creative and emotive work remained largely rooted in human authorship. The workflow choices adopted by the student designers reflect the pragmatic negotiation of human intention and computational suggestion over time, thus confirming that GenAI is better suited for assisting rather than for replacing the creative mindset of humans.

It highlight the need to teach students how to integrate these tools into their game design workflows. This study advocates for its position as a flexible yet limited partner whose outputs require careful gathering, editing, and contextualization. For tool developers, the study suggests that there are evolving needs for GenAI systems to support poetic expression and nuanced emotional content.

Future research could expand to consider various contexts, professional design workflows, and other expressive game forms to create a landscape for how AI will be shaping meanings, emotions, and authorship in digital games.

Ultimately, GenAI offers considerable benefits in task execution, content generation, structural scaffolding, technical assistance, and overall workflow efficiency. Nevertheless, significant limitations persist–particularly in its inability to produce emotionally nuanced or highly original content, its tendency toward generalized outputs, inconsistency in results, and the emergence of ethical concerns. It is the human-created intention, ambiguity, and emotional depth that remain at the heart of expressive game poem creation.

Disclosure of Interests. The authors have no competing interests to declare that are relevant to the content of this article.

References

1. Arif, S., Arif, T., Khan, A.J., Haroon, M.S., Raza, A.A., Athar, A.: The art of storytelling: multi-agent generative AI for dynamic multimodal narratives. arXiv **abs/2409.11261** (2024), https://api.semanticscholar.org/CorpusID:272693979
2. Bardon, A.: AI in video games, design and development. Lindenwood University Online, December 2024, https://online.lindenwood.edu/blog/ai-in-video-games-design-and-development/
3. Begemann, A., Hutson, J.: Empirical insights into ai-assisted game development: a case study on the integration of generative ai tools in creative pipelines. Metaverse **5**(2) (2024)
4. Björk, S., Holopainen, J.: Games and design patterns. The game design reader: A rules of play anthology, pp. 410–437 (2005)
5. Buongiorno, S., Klinkert, L., Zhuang, Z., Chawla, T., Clark, C.: PANGeA: procedural artificial narrative using generative AI for turn-based, role-playing video games. In: Proceedings of the AAAI Conference on Artificial Intelligence and Interactive Digital Entertainment, vol. 20, pp. 156–166, November 2024
6. Cheung, L.M.E., Shi, H.: Co-creating stories with generative ai: reflections from undergraduate students of a storytelling service-learning subject in Hong Kong. Australian Rev. Appl. Linguist. **47**(3), 259–283 (2024). https://doi.org/10.1075/aral.24101.che
7. Chia, A.: The metaverse, but not the way you think: game engines and automation beyond game development. Crit. Stud. Media Commun. **39**(3), 191–200 (2022). https://doi.org/10.1080/15295036.2022.2080850
8. Chiapello, L.: Epistemological underpinnings in game design research. Game Des. Res. Introduction Theor. Pract. 15–33 (2017)
9. Cook, M., Colton, S., Gow, J.: The ANGELINA videogame design system–Part I. IEEE Trans. Comput. Intell. AI Games **9**, 192–203 (2017). https://api.semanticscholar.org/CorpusID:14960131
10. Cross, N.: Design research: a disciplined conversation. Des. Issues **15**(2), 5–10 (1999). https://doi.org/10.2307/1511837
11. Dormans, J.: Engineering emergence: applied theory for game design. Ph.D. thesis, Universiteit van Amsterdam, Amsterdam, The Netherlands (2012). https://pure.uva.nl/ws/files/1167835/102091_09.pdf
12. Flanagan, M., Nissenbaum, H.: Values at Play in Digital Games. MIT Press (2014)
13. Forlizzi, J., Zimmerman, J., Stolterman, E.: From design research to theory: evidence of a maturing field. In: International Association of Societies of Design Research Conference (2009)
14. Frayling, C.: Research in art and design. Royal College of Art Research Papers (1993)

15. Fu, K., Wu, R., Tang, Y., Chen, Y., Liu, B., LC, R.: "Being eroded, piece by piece": enhancing engagement and storytelling in cultural heritage dissemination by exhibiting GenAI co-creation artifacts. In: Proceedings of the 2024 ACM Designing Interactive Systems Conference, DIS 2024, pp. 2833–2850. ACM, New York, NY, USA (2024). https://doi.org/10.1145/3643834.3660711
16. Gallotta, R., et al.: Large language models and games: a survey and roadmap. IEEE Trans. Games 1–18 (2024). https://doi.org/10.1109/TG.2024.3461510
17. Guzdial, M., Liao, N., Riedl, M.: Co-creative level design via machine learning. arXiv (2018). https://doi.org/10.48550/arXiv.1809.09420
18. Han, Y., Qiu, Z., Cheng, J., LC, R.: When teams embrace AI: human collaboration strategies in generative prompting in a creative design task. In: Proceedings of the 2024 CHI Conference on Human Factors in Computing Systems. CHI 2024, ACM, New York, NY, USA (2024). https://doi.org/10.1145/3613904.3642133
19. He, Z., Su, J., Chen, L., Wang, T., Lc, R.: "I recall the past": exploring how people collaborate with generative AI to create cultural heritage narratives. Proc. ACM Hum.-Comput. Interact. **9**(2), 1–30 (2025)
20. Holopainen, J., Huang, Y., Shin, J., Nissinen, E., Lucero, A.: Infinity book: speculating literary expressions in the age of generative ai. In: Proceedings of the 2025 ACM Designing Interactive Systems Conference, DIS 2025, pp. 1430–1454. ACM, New York, NY, USA (2025). https://doi.org/10.1145/3715336.3735735
21. Holopainen, J., Nummenmaa, T., Kuittinen, J.: Modelling experimental game design. In: Proceedings of Nordic DiGRA 2010 Conference: Experiencing Games: Games, Play, and Players (2010)
22. Kuittinen, J., Holopainen, J.: Some notes on the nature of game design. In: Proceedings of DiGRA 2009: Breaking New Ground (2009)
23. Kultima, A.: Game design research. In: Proceedings of the 19th International Academic Mindtrek Conference, pp. 18–25 (2015)
24. Kultima, A.: Game design praxiology. Ph.D. thesis, Tampereen yliopisto (2018)
25. Lankoski, P., Holopainen, J.: Game design research: an overview. In: Game Design Research: An Introduction to Theory and Practice, pp. 1–24. ETC Press (2017)
26. Liang, X., Wang, Y., Yan, F., Ouyang, Z., Hu, Y., Luo, S.: Reborn of the white bone demon: Role-playing game design using generative AI in XR. In: SIGGRAPH Asia 2024 Posters, SA 2024, ACM (2024). https://doi.org/10.1145/3681756.3697949, https://doi-org.ezproxy.cityu.edu.hk/10.1145/3681756.3697949
27. Ling, L., Chen, X., Wen, R., Li, T.J.J., Lc, R.: Sketchar: supporting character design and illustration prototyping using generative AI. Proc. ACM Hum.-Comput. Interact. **8**(CHI PLAY), 1–28 (2024). https://doi.org/10.1145/3677102
28. Magnuson, J.: Game Poems: Videogame Design as Lyric Practice. Amherst College Press (2023)
29. Mitchell, A.: Making the familiar unfamiliar: techniques for creating poetic gameplay. In: Proceedings of DiGRA/FDG 2016 Conference (2016)
30. Naeem, M., Ozuem, W., Howell, K., Ranfagni, S.: A step-by-step process of thematic analysis to develop a conceptual model in qualitative research. Int. J. Qual. Methods **22** (2023). https://doi.org/10.1177/16094069231205789
31. Partlan, N., Kleinman, E., Howe, J., Ahmad, S., Marsella, S., Seif El-Nasr, M.: Design-driven requirements for computationally co-creative game ai design tools. In: Proceedings of the 16th International Conference on the Foundations of Digital Games, FDG 2021, ACM, New York, NY, USA (2021). https://doi.org/10.1145/3472538.3472573
32. Rutkoff, A.: The game of life. Wall Street J. https://www.wsj.com/articles/SB120034796455789469

33. Santiago, J.M., Parayno, R.L., Deja, J.A., Samson, B.P.V.: Rolling the dice: imagining generative AI as a dungeons & dragons storytelling companion. arXiv **abs/2304.01860** (2023). https://api.semanticscholar.org/CorpusID:257921144
34. Tan, L.: Using chatgpt to extract design concepts from stories. In: Jones, D., Borekci, N., Clemente, V., Corazzo, J., Lotz, N., Nielsen, L.M., Noel, L.A. (eds.) The 7th International Conference for Design Education Researchers, London, United Kingdom (2023). https://doi.org/10.21606/drslxd.2024.054
35. Upton, B.: Situational Game Design. CRC Press (2017)
36. Yang, D., Kleinman, E., Harteveld, C.: Gpt for games: an updated scoping review (2020–2024). IEEE Trans. Games 1–16 (2025). https://doi.org/10.1109/TG.2025.3563780
37. Yang, D., Zhou, Y., Zhang, Z., Li, T.J.J., LC, R.: AI as an active writer: interaction strategies with generated text in Human-AI collaborative fiction writing. In: Joint Proceedings of the ACM IUI Workshops 2022, CEUR-WS.org, Helsinki, Finland, March 2022, http://ceur-ws.org/Vol-3073/HAIGEN2022_paper5.pdf, available under Creative Commons Attribution 4.0 International (CC BY 4.0)
38. Zeng, Y., Shi, Y., Huang, X., Nah, F., LC, R.: "Ronaldo's a poser!": how the use of generative ai shapes debates in online forums. In: Proceedings of the 2025 CHI Conference on Human Factors in Computing Systems, CHI 2025, ACM, New York, NY, USA (2025). https://doi.org/10.1145/3706598.3713829

The Curious Case of Alan: Provocative Dialogue and Puzzle Play for Reflecting on GenAI in Informal Learning

Georgia Koutiva[1]([⊠]) [iD], Akrivi Katifori[1] [iD], Lori Kougioumtzian[1] [iD], and Maria Roussou[2] [iD]

[1] ATHENA Research and Innovation Center, Maroussi, Greece
{georgia.koutiva,vivi,lori.kougioumtzian}@athenarc.gr
[2] National and Kapodistrian University of Athens, Athens, Greece
mroussou@di.uoa.gr

Abstract. Museums are important spaces for free-choice learning. However, historical objects are often emphasized without explicitly exploring the ongoing relevance of a domain, particularly when addressing emergent technologies such as GenAI. In this paper, we propose a two-layer cooperative game design that combines active exhibit exploration through puzzles with an NPC serving as a Bot of Conviction to promote reflective dialogue as a means of transformation. Playtesting sessions with 10 participants suggest that the puzzle component effectively supported learning about the history of Computer Science (specifically, Human-Computer Interaction), while the collaborative setup was widely described as enjoyable and engaging. Although some participants reported novel insights, others found that the dialogue echoed and helped clarify preexisting reflections, underscoring both the topical relevance of GenAI and the potential of narrative-driven design to support reflective learning.

Keywords: Bot of Conviction · Interactive Digital Narrative · Educational Game Design · AI Ethics in Games

1 Introduction

Museums are widely recognized as important spaces for informal learning, where visitors engage with content on their own terms, motivated by personal curiosity rather than formal instruction. However, exhibitions often focus on historical artifacts and narratives without drawing explicit connections to contemporary developments in their respective domains. This disconnect can be particularly noticeable in fields marked by rapid change, such as Computer Science, whose presence in everyday life is pervasive and where emergent technologies like Generative AI (GenAI) reshape societal and disciplinary conversations in real time. This information-and-object-centric approach becomes even more apparent in remote museum visits, which gained relevance during the COVID-19 pandemic

M. C. Reyes and F. Nack (Eds.): ICIDS 2025, LNCS 16375, pp. 130–146, 2026.
https://doi.org/10.1007/978-3-032-12405-0_8

and subsequent restrictions to on-site visits [19]. Addressing this disconnect between past and present requires more than simply updating museum collections through the addition of new exhibits or updating the relevant content; it calls for new forms of visitor engagement that promote active meaning-making and critical reflection. Interactive Digital Narratives (IDNs) offer such a possibility, through their capacity to scaffold agency, to provoke emotional engagement in the form of eudaimonic appreciation [16], and, ultimately, to foster transformational learning. IDNs have been increasingly explored as mediums for engaging with 'serious' topics, akin to 'serious' games [5].

In addition to this topical disconnect, remote museum visits, which remain relevant even after the pandemic for reasons such as health or distance, often lack opportunities for meaningful social interaction, which is crucial, as Falk and Dierking argue [7]. As museums are environments where visitors collectively create meaning and share experiences, designing interactive experiences that support social interaction even for remote visitors is thus particularly valuable.

Motivated by this, we present the design and evaluation of a ludic, educational IDN that extends the work in [10], where a remote and an on-site player must collaborate in an educational escape room to solve puzzles embedded in the museum environment. As the previous version of this work focused on evaluating the experience's potential to promote sociality in a non-collocated visit scenario, here we polish and further flesh out its educational scope, in what we will call a dual-level approach. The first level involves clear, concrete educational objectives that are connected to the history of the museum's domain -namely, Computer Science (CS)- which are a) communicated to the players through the collaborative puzzles they must solve, and b) realized exclusively through exhibits in the museum's collection. The second educational level focuses more on higher-level reflection on the future of the domain with an epicenter of GenAI and, while also pervasive in the overarching narrative, becomes more apparent in an activity involving the players' interaction with Alan, a dialogic NPC that serves as a Bot of Conviction [18], posing challenging questions intended to elicit reflection on these themes.

We conducted an evaluation with 10 players in 5 sessions. The findings showed that the participants appreciated the balance between educational and narrative elements, with puzzles fostering engagement with core HCI concepts and the dialogue segment either prompting new reflections or helping them articulate existing thoughts on GenAI. The experience was generally well received and considered suitable for further development.

This work is structured as follows. Section 2 expands on relevant work, including concepts from IDN theory and the Bot of Conviction paradigm and previous applications. Section 3 goes into detail about the structure of the experience, its narrative and its educational objectives. Sections 4 and 5 present the evaluation methodology and results, respectively. Section 6 discusses the results in more detail and concludes the paper with some future work directions.

2   Related Work

2.1   Interactive Narrative Design for Meaningful Player Engagement and Transformation

Although structural accounts of narrative in games offer valuable ways to categorize interaction, the balance between instrumental and reflective engagement remains a core challenge in educational IDNs. Meakin [11] offers a particularly structured articulation of how narrative flow operates in interactive experiences, where meaning unfolds through cycles of uncertainty and discovery. Two key concepts Meakin draws on are Aarseth's aporia–epiphany cycle and Newman's online–offline continuum, both of which inform our own design. Aporia refers to moments of confusion or challenge that, when overcome, lead to epiphany, a realization that enables progression. As these cycles repeat, it becomes important that moments of action are followed by space for reflection on them. Newman's continuum captures this oscillation, where online moments, defined by goal-oriented player input, are followed by offline moments that allow reflection on these actions and situating them within the system's larger context.

By alternating between these states, designers can achieve both successful game-play and narrative outcomes, helping players feel present and meaningfully engaged. Our proposed design aims to leverage this dynamic by interweaving puzzle solving with narrative development. Puzzles embody aporia–epiphany blocks and create high-agency moments with direct system feedback. These are followed by offline phases –specifically, interaction with the NPC Alan– that allow players to consider broader questions related to GenAI, a subject inextricably linked with the experience's overarching story.

These concepts also align with Roth and Koenitz's evaluation framework for IDNs [16], which groups 12 dimensions under three experiential qualities: *agency*, *immersion*, and *transformation*. Meakin situates both the aporia–epiphany cycle and the online–offline continuum within the Designed and Aesthetic Flow channels, practical applications of Csikszentmihalyi's theory of flow [4], which is defined as an optimal state of engagement where skill meets challenge, and which is one of the dimensions related to *immersion*. Agency, the player's ability to make meaningful decisions within the system, is inherently present in online moments. We suggest that our puzzle/dialogue structure supports immersion, as a clear application of the online-offline continuum, but also agency, as dialogue with Alan is a) interactive and b) allows for an interpretive form of agency, inviting players to position themselves in relation to ethically charged questions.

Finally, our design aims to evoke the framework's third component, *transformation*, which was defined by Murray [13] as the alteration of the users' beliefs or attitudes towards complicated topics. Specifically, we wish to facilitate *eudaimonic appreciation*, another of Roth and Koenitz's 12 dimensions, which goes beyond a pleasurable experience and towards appreciation "linked to users' construction of personal meaning from a story or piece of art". This, in turn, could even shape how the user sees and acts in the world. Rather than instructing players, the system surfaces morally complex prompts that echo real-world concerns around GenAI, enabling thoughtful reflection without imposing a singular position.

The process of transformation is a key component of Mezirow's transformative learning theory [12], which centers on re-evaluating one's perspectives to achieve genuine personal meaning. This theory is closely aligned with other ones that support this deep reflection by emphasizing social and active engagement. These include **social constructivism** (Vygotsky, [20]), which posits that learners construct knowledge through social interaction and experience, and **active learning**, which provides the practical methods to do so. In turn, collaborative learning shifts the responsibility from the educator to the students, fostering active participation through small activities where everyone contributes [6]. We propose that informal learning environments, such as museums, are excellent settings for this, as they are inherently social and lack a defined educator role. In our game, active collaborative learning is embodied by cooperative puzzle-solving, which is in direct opposition to traditional, instruction-based museum learning.

Finally, we would like to discuss **dialogic pedagogy**, a cornerstone of constructivist thought that emphasizes the importance of dialogue in learning as a process through which participants jointly explore and develop a common understanding of a topic [3]. This approach also promotes student agency, empowering learners to see themselves as active participants in their own education and, by extension, in society [1,3]. By engaging players in dialogue with a provocative character like Alan, we aspire to harness the full potential of dialogic pedagogy, encouraging them to take an active stance on the ethical implications of GenAI and its impact on the world.

2.2   The Bot of Conviction Paradigm

"Bot of Conviction" (BoC), or "Protest Bot", is a term coined by Mark Sample in [18]. Sample defines these bots -often found on Twitter- as "a computer program that reveals the injustice and inequality of the world and imagines alternatives [...], that questions how, when, who and why". Sample defines their traits as follows:

- **topical**: anchored in current events.
- **data-based**: grounded in facts and research.
- **cumulative**: Building meaning through repetition.
- **oppositional**: taking an unapologetic, challenging moral stance.
- **uncanny**: revealing hidden or repressed truths.

Interestingly, the BoC paradigm has been explored in cultural heritage in the form of chatbots that provoke reflection on complex topics. In [17], the authors designed a BoC-inspired rule-based chatbot to discuss emotive themes such as life, death, wealth, equality, etc., an approach that showed promise for prompting reflection. Petousi et al. [14] created "Hermias, the Bot" that engages multiple users in discussion on themes inspired by Greek antiquity, such as slavery and fate. "Hermias" is a prime application of collaborative learning for perspective taking, the understanding of another person's perspective, as shown by the study.

While BoC-inspired bots have been used in heritage for discussions on difficult topics, their implementation into game-adjacent experiences remains unrealized, to the best of our knowledge. This paradigm informs our design, as we believe it aligns closely with the transformational objectives of Roth and Koenitz's IDN framework. By raising charged, topical questions, BoCs invite players into a reflective space where they must position themselves, supporting personal transformation.

3   Design

Building on the social museum visit from [10], this experience is an escape room, a means of game-based learning that promotes active communication [2] and therefore social presence, our primary goal, especially for the remote player. It was developed for the University of Athens Museum of Informatics and Telecommunications. Following an exploratory pilot evaluation that confirmed its potential to facilitate sociality and gave us insight on how to structure the puzzles, we refined the design to emphasize two key components:

- **Well-defined educational objectives** from **Human-Computer Interaction** (HCI) history, each tightly coupled with a puzzle.
- **A unifying narrative** that provides urgency and believability -a core element of **Narrative Immersion** [16]- and embeds a topical sociopolitical context to spark reflection on the future of technology and GenAI.

3.1   Narrative and Medium

In the year 2111 the two players act as agents notified by a mysterious figure named Alan about the Naturocrats, a group of tech-rejecting extremists that plan to sabotage the national power grid. The players must uncover clues across two timelines, the futuristic and the present-day museum, to stop them. Alan provides hints as the players' informant but refuses to resolve the matter by himself.

Currently, this experience is a facilitator-guided mid-fidelity prototype in Google Slideshow. Facilitators validate player actions and guide them through the slides. However, the final product will be a mobile and a native computer application, choices made to support ease of use and multiple concurrent players by allowing people on site to join with their personal devices.

3.2   Online Moments: Educational Objectives

Puzzles were designed to encourage interaction with actual museum exhibits - both real and virtual ones-, connecting modern Human-Computer Interaction (HCI) with its historical equivalents. The players begin by finding a scrap of paper with numbers on it each; the remote player guides their partner to find theirs. Next, Alan guides both players to a device with a Command Line Interface (CLI). The player in the museum uses a laptop from the collection. Alan explains what CLIs were, their contrast to modern Graphical User Interfaces (GUIs) and the structure and usage of a command (command name, arguments, and output). The player in the museum must run a custom command twice, but only the remote player can see the manual explaining argument count and order. The players get two character sequences that they use to uncover a hidden password in the next activity. They must then apply a simplified version of SSH to log into a remote system using credentials found by the remote player. Additional educational content for the SSH protocol is not yet included in an attempt to mitigate information overload. Only a few puzzles and granular objectives were included, acknowledging the technical nature of the content and the need to prevent visitor fatigue in a museum setting.

Game Mechanics: The Asymmetric MDA Framework. Asymmetric games assign players different mechanics, abilities, information, or interfaces, fostering stronger social connection and presence than symmetric designs [2]. They may also facilitate inclusive play among individuals with difference gaming preferences, as many are cross-platform [8]. Given our players' lack of collocation and the genre's collaborative focus, we adopted the asymmetric Mechanics, Dynamics and Aesthetics (MDA) framework proposed by Harris et al. [9], focusing on the **Asymmetry of Information** mechanic, where one player possesses knowledge unknown to the others. Here, one player deciphers hints from Alan (the game master) and communicates information to their partner, who acts on this knowledge. Harris et al. identify this as one of the most accessible mechanics, requiring communication rather than prior gaming skills. It is also a common element in escape rooms, the genre of our game.

3.3 Offline Moments: Alan – A Bot of Conviction

Alan begins as an informant with a sharp and provocative tone, stating the mission's urgency while withholding other information. After the second puzzle, he initiates a dialogue on GenAI. While this spans subtopics like creativity, authorship, bias, and politics, due to the museum's subject we focused on how this product will affect its creators by exploring the following:

- What does it mean to be a computer scientist when GenAI can develop products and code?
- Which CS fields will continue to require human involvement, e.g. cybersecurity?
- What happens to junior developers if GenAI systems outperform them? How will this affect senior developers?
- Can higher education adapt fast enough to industry changes?
- A larger systemic framing, such as the commodification of human productivity and the pressure to constantly evolve.

This segment, developed as a rule-based chatbot with binary response options, was designed as an exploratory component to assess user engagement before committing to the complexity of an LLM-powered system, given Alan's role was previously limited to providing hints. Additionally, it allows us to efficiently cover the aforementioned subtopics while keeping a short duration through careful dialogue writing, which is crucial in a museum setting. This approach also ensures a consistent experience in Google Slides without switching between platforms.

The conversation follows the "Figure 8" pattern proposed by Roussou et al. [17], starting with a provocative question that branches based on the user's positive or negative response. The paths converge at a midpoint that re-tests the user's conviction. They then diverge again before finally converging on the bot's closing statement. In our case, the flow includes one provocative question followed by two response branches, a midpoint convergence followed by another set of positive/negative responses, and a final convergence on Alan's core conviction; the issue lies not with GenAI as a tool, but with the system exploiting it. Alan's 'Figure 8' model can be seen in Fig. 1c.

After the dialogue, Alan hesitantly reveals the identity and motives of the Naturocrats and, at the very end, his own; he is an Artificial General Intelligence (AGI) system, a scientific achievement hidden from the public. This revelation leads to his final unanswered question, for players to reflect on beyond the game.

Do you think humanity would manage to redefine meaning beyond constant striving and achieving?

Alan's Adherence to the BoC Paradigm. Alan's design closely aligns with the 5 BoCs traits defined by Sample. He is clearly **topical**, as he grounds the conversation on GenAI, and **data-based**; while his points are not quantitative, they are informed by current affairs, such as companies shifting away from human employees. He is also **oppositional**; he holds a specific conviction that he defends aggressively and provocatively. He embodies the **cumulative** quality by revisiting core concerns about GenAI with slight variations in tone, echoing Sample's notion of "repetition with a difference" as a method of persuasive accumulation. Last but not least, he is **uncanny**; an artificial being mirroring human emotion to reveal systemic imbalances and prompt reflection on human existence.

4 Evaluation Methodology

A total of 10 participants across 5 sessions were recruited through convenience sampling, primarily consisting of colleagues and acquaintances within the authors' professional network; 5 men and 5 women of various ages between 27 and 58. As a result of the recruiting method, 3 of the participants had a background in Computer Science, making them domain-specific users, while two others reported adjacent knowledge on UNIX systems and Geoinformatics. The other 5 users did not come from a specialized background, and will henceforth be

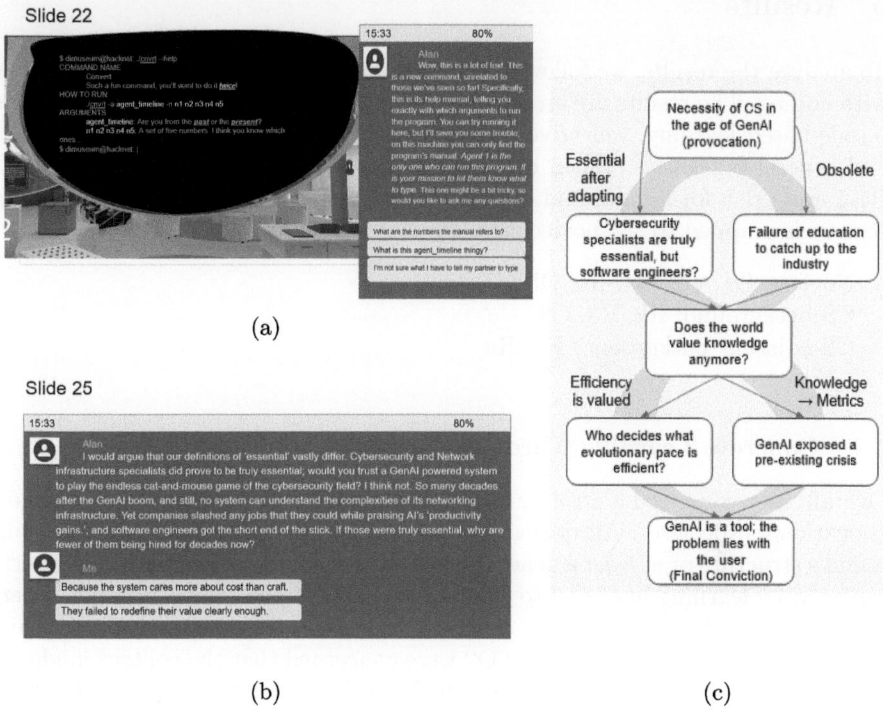

Fig. 1. Some of the game's content. a) The remote user's CLI with the custom command's manual b) A question from Alan to the player from the dialogic part, complete with the players' available responses. c) Alan's dialogic Fig. 8 structure. Next to the arrows is the user's response. White boxes show Alan's response/statement.

referred to as "novices". One participant per session was at the museum, while the other joined from home. A facilitator helped each participant navigate their slideshow. Participants freely communicated over voice-chat via Discord. Each session lasted approximately 1 h. Participants were then interviewed separately, following a mostly structured set of questions across 4 axes:

1. **Concrete Learning Through Puzzles**: How well the puzzles effectively supported the participants' understanding of HCI concepts, including its historical development.
2. **Reflective Dialogue**: How participants perceived Alan, how the dialogue segment aligned with their own beliefs on AI and technology and whether it prompted critical reflection on these manners.
3. **Integration Between Modalities**: How well was the transition between puzzles and dialogue perceived, and how well they complemented each other.
4. **Overall Takeaways**: What was the participants' overall evaluation of the experience, including what aspects were most impactful or in need of improvement.

5   Results

To analyze the results, we followed an approach of qualitative thematic analysis with coding. The results are structured along the four axes of the questionnaire: puzzle-based learning, reflective dialogue with the NPC, modality integration, and general takeaways. When quoting participants, they will be referred to as R1-5 and O1-5 for remote and on-site players, respectively. This second coding scheme is mapped to the novices-experts distinction as follows:

- Novices: O1, O2, O4, R5, O5.
- CS background: R2, R3, O3
- CS-adjacent background: R1, R4

5.1   Concrete Learning Through Puzzles

Overall, users reported a positive learning experience with respect to the game's educational objectives. All novices stated they either understood a UNIX command's structure or at least a general sense of CLI-based interaction. The experts reported no learning but tried to evaluate the experience from a beginner's perspective. R4 and O3 believed the game would work well for high schoolers, praising its hands-on approach. R1 and O2 were concerned that the content might be 'too technical' depending on the person. Notably, novice and experienced users completed the puzzles in similar timeframes.

Most novices reflected on the contrast between CLIs and GUIs, except one. O1 commented; "I had not realized how difficult [HCI] used to be compared to nowadays." Interestingly, 2 out of 3 CS graduates viewed the interface shift as more blurry, as they still use UNIX commands daily, and suggested this be integrated to the game (O3: "See, you think this interface is outdated, but it is [...] used by many professionals still"). Two participants, unprompted, connected the evolution of HCI to GenAI and natural-language user interfaces. O1 commented on this positively, while O3 perceived this as an abrupt jump which will be discussed later.

Few users reported mild confusion on hints. R4 and O4 wished for a timeline that contextualizes the different interfaces. O4 and O2 requested additional learning content, such as a glossary for difficult terms, suggested by O2. O3 and R5 wanted more puzzles. O3, a developer, hoped for greater difficulty. SSH, discussed in the final puzzle, went largely unnoticed except by O4 who wished to learn more. A summary of this axis' findings can be found in Table 1.

5.2   Alan and the Reflective BoC Dialogue

We will begin by analyzing the overarching narrative. Eight participants commented positively on Alan's writing. O4 was further curious about his backstory. Comments describing his personality & alignment included 'untrustworthy', 'self-serving', 'distrustful', "someone who looked down on us", convincingly

Table 1. Puzzle-based learning themes

Theme	Participants
UNIX command structure understanding	All novices
Hands-on appeal for younger learners	2
Reflected on CLI vs GUI contrast	4/5 novices
Ongoing relevance of CLI	3 experts

human (although two players had predicted his identity), 'know-it-all'. Quite a few enjoyed the 'twist' at the end. O3, however, noted him as "helpful but overly didactic". Two users managed to connect him to his namesake, Alan Turing, who coined the 'Turing Test' for Artificial Intelligence.

Interestingly, 5 participants sided or sympathized with the Naturocrats, considering technology's environmental and societal impact. O4 sat in the middle, understanding their reasoning but ultimately advocating for societal change. O1 outright rejected their beliefs.

Dialogic Interaction with Alan. The users provided manifold feedback on this segment. 4 participants reported minimal new reflection on the future of GenAI. Two novices expressed that it echoed prior thoughts, like R1, who said: "a pretty good reflection of what goes on in my head recently". R4 appreciated the message and its systemic framing, commenting that it was not "dry and childish, like it sometimes feels in such experiences", but found the text too dense to absorb new information. She suggested breaking up the dialogue throughout the experience. O3 felt it was getting in the way of their core objective, arriving "out of nowhere", and that Alan was too persistent. They suggested moving this segment after the password's completion, to which R3 disagreed, feeling that they would disengage by then. They instead proposed an AI-themed puzzle or better thematic integration earlier in the story. They liked the questions raised and acknowledged their potential to ignite discussions, but felt constrained by the binary responses. R4 also wished for branching or free user input. Everyone else experienced novel reflection, praising the subjects' topicality and pondering how GenAI's exploitation could affect societal structure.

Views were also split on whether Alan imposed a specific opinion. O3 found the NPC "jugdemental", while four participants perceived a clear stance but were okay with it, citing the lack of consequences their answer has on gameplay and Alan's nature. The remaining players did not feel forced whatsoever.

Several participants observed the shift from co-operative tasks to the solitary nature of the dialogue. R4 and R5 expressed how they deeply missed the social aspect during this part and suggested that it would benefit from collaboration. R3 and O2 said they would have engaged more deeply with the material had they not worried they were stalling their co-player. A summary can be found in Table 2

Table 2. Reflective dialogue themes

Theme	Participants
Echoed existing thoughts	4
Dialogue is intrusive or poorly timed	3
Novel reflection on GenAI's impact	4
Partial reflection but binary responses were constraining	2
Alan was judgmental/pushed for a stance	2
Alan's stance is okay due to his nature/lack of consequences	4
Worried about stalling partner	2
Dialogue should have been collaborative	2

5.3 Integration Between Modalities

The majority agreed that the transition between puzzle solving and the dialogic segment was smooth. However, 3 participants found the shift partially or completely jarring. As told previously, two of them felt that the dialogue disrupted the mission's urgency. R3 quickly overcame this disruption, while O3 expressed greater frustration, citing both the abrupt transition and Alan's tone. R4 noted that moving from cooperative play to single-person dialogue felt disjointed.

All but one participant noted that both components of the game were equally important in conveying the game's message and that it would feel incomplete without either. Several emphasized that removing the "essential" puzzles would undermine the experience's ludic identity. However, nearly everyone stated that a puzzle-only version would be less impactful, as the dialogue and narrative provided meaningful context and messages. O3, the one exception, would have preferred a version focused solely on puzzles, ideally with increased difficulty. A summary is given in Table 3.

Table 3. Modality integration feedback

Theme	Participants
Smooth transitions between puzzles and dialogue	7
Dialogue disrupted urgency/Co-op to single player shift was abrupt	3
Mutual importance of puzzles and dialogue	9

5.4 General Takeaways

All participants found the balance between entertainment and education satisfying, regardless of the aspect they prioritized. They found a multitude of moments to be memorable, such as:

- Alan's reveal.
- The UNIX command puzzle, highlighted by 4 participants, with O3 praising the hands-on interaction with a real museum exhibit.
- The contrast between HCI's difficulty in the past and present.
- Alan's provocative questions as 'food for thought'.
- The social, collaborative, non collocated aspect, noted by 3 players, which aligns with earlier findings.

There was a near unanimous willingness to recommend the experience provided it undergoes some polishing. This largely referred to the transition from a facilitated prototype to a fully implemented pair of applications. Only two participants expressed reservations about this. O3 appreciated the hands-on approach, but suggested eliminating or repositioning the dialogic segment and adding more puzzles. R4 perceived the experience to have three separate scopes; a collaborative museum tour, teaching CS history, and social debate. She felt a clearer focus would be necessary before recommending it.

When asked what they would change to improve the experience, they suggested the following (summarized in Table 4:

- The ability to freely respond to Alan (3 participants)
- Greater opportunities for exploration (2)
- More puzzles (2)
- More learning content (2)
- More gamified elements, such as narration for Alan (1)

Table 4. General takeaways

Theme	Participants
Entertainment–Education balance satisfying	All
Willingness to recommend post-implementation	8
Reservation to recommend (due to dialogue timing or broad scope)	2
Free-text responses to Alan	3

6   Discussion and Conclusions

In this work, we designed a game-based Interactive Digital Narrative that contextualizes a Computer Science museum within the field's evolving landscape, while grounding it in its long-standing history through hands-on, puzzle-based interaction. Our dual-layer approach was well received and was thought to strike a balance between entertainment and education. The layers were largely viewed as mutually essential, and finally there was a strong willingness to recommend the game post-implementation.

The puzzles successfully conveyed basic HCI history. Novices reported learning CLI concepts and reflection on the contrast with today's UIs, while experts appreciated the hands-on design. The narrative writing was mostly praised, and while half of the users reported limited or partial novel reflection after the dialogue, they validated the relevance of its themes. Interestingly, five of the players sympathized with the antagonists, showing that even unintentionally, the narrative can spark moral positioning.

The combination of puzzles and dialogue strongly supports Meakin's work on how aporia-epiphany and the user's oscillation on the online/offline continuum can foster designed and aesthetic flow [11]. Puzzles foster agency and immersion, while dialogue facilitates eudaimonic appreciation and personal transformation, addressing all 3 pillars of Roth and Koenitz' framework [16]. However, transformation may have been limited by the binary response format, leading to a broader but shallower discussion.

Alan, the game's NPC meets the design criteria for BoCs, though his **oppositional** stance elicited mixed reactions. The "NPC as a Bot of Conviction" paradigm shows promise for fostering critical reflection. To fully realize this potential, design adjustments are necessary, particularly less text-heavy prompts and more open-ended user responses. This could take the form of an extended branching dialogue and/or free text input. The latter is more feasible due to the vast advancements in Large Language Model (LLM) powered chatbots, potentially overcoming earlier challenges in designing the rule-based "Hermias" bot [14].

While both layers were generally well received, we acknowledge a potential for deeper intrinsic integration between the narrative and gameplay. We recognize a risk of the experience resembling "chocolate-covered broccoli" -where narrative becomes a mere wrapper for educational content- as player feedback suggest the dialogue's timing and subject matter felt disconnected from the puzzles (O3), disrupting players' sense of urgency (O3, R3, O5). In future iterations, we will address this first by grounding the GenAI themes within the puzzle layer itself. For example, a new puzzle about natural language interfaces will not only establish them as a stage in HCI evolution, but also serve as a more organic transition between layers. Furthermore, we will integrate our core 'information asymmetry' mechanic into the dialogue segment, forcing players to combine knowledge to progress. This will ensure consistent mechanics throughout the experience and amend the disconnect between cooperative puzzles and solitary dialogue. Finally, the narrative and dialogue segments will directly address the other puzzles and exhibits. While the risk of a superficial connection remains, almost all players considered both layers essential to the experience, and only one wished to omit the dialogue entirely. We are confident this is a solid base for building a more intrinsically integrated design in the future.

As mentioned previously, there was a dissonance between the puzzles' collaborative nature and the dialogue's solitary environment, a point raised by nearly half of the participants. Two users admitted to skimming text to avoid delaying their co-player, while two others explicitly called for collaborative discussion and/or shared decision making. We initially designed the dialogue segment for a single user to validate its overall effectiveness before tackling the design complexities of a collaborative system. Having confirmed that the segment is a valuable addition, we are now confident in proceeding with a more complex, collaborative design in future iterations. Ensuring collaboration and dialogue takes place between both co-players will help our experience better align with the learning theories we've previously discussed, as well as the social component of Falk & Dierking's Contextual Model of Learning that highlights the importance of collective meaning making in museums [7]. By making both game layers collaborative, we ensure that players perceive them as equally important, and the transition between them as smoother. The very nature of collaboration also mitigates the fear of delaying a co-player, which may be heightened for unacquainted players (in our case, most knew each other due to their connections with the authors). In practice, cooperative play will be supported by a lobby system, where users can set a username and join friends, or pair with new partners. This accommodates both designated co-players and individuals seeking a spontaneous social learning opportunity, promoting inclusivity. Therefore, the NPC dialogue must be carefully redesigned to promote exchange of ideas while avoiding awkwardness, particularly for unfamiliar players.

A related observation emerged from one participant who, while praising the overall experience, noted that the physical exhibits, despite being embedded in puzzles, offered little substantive learning about them. This highlights a key challenge for similar museum experiences: the environment should not merely serve as background or inspiration, but remain a central interpretive anchor for both gameplay and reflection. By making sure the exhibits' prominence is connected to the overarching themes of HCI and GenAI, the integration of the game's layers becomes more intrinsic.

Multiparty chatbots, especially those serving as dialogue facilitators, are a relatively recent area of research. Petousi et al. identify the lack of a comprehensive evaluation framework for such bots [15]. They highlighted aspects such as chatbot personality, conversational intelligence, facilitation skills and dialogue quality as areas for further research. Chatbot personality poses a particular challenge, as it involves a multitude of interrelated elements that must be not only well-defined, but also balanced. For example, consistency between the bot's personality and behavior with its intended role may conflict with the user's needs or expectations. While Alan's personality was perceived as coherent, one user explicitly expressed frustration, describing the NPC as judgmental. Conversational intelligence of an autonomous chatbot (unlike Alan, whose dialogue was carefully written by human authors) can also be challenging. Although current LLMs can produce naturalistic language, their ability to preserve context and, most importantly, raise intelligent and provocative questions is crucial for reflection-oriented dialogue. Finally, the authors posit that "even an advanced AI [chatbot] cannot be equally effective in all aspects of human facilitation", including but not limited to providing guidance, encouraging openness, and intervening appropriately. These limitations could translate differently to a game, where assigning one player to serve as the communicator between the pair and the bot -as seen in some works- might reduce the others' sense of agency. It only follows that considerations such as game mechanics and agency have to be honored alongside adherence to good multiparty chatbot practices, as well as care for session duration and cognitive load.

Several practical design implications emerge. First, providing more responses or a different format could help reduce the "boxed-in" feeling. As mentioned previously, GenAI themes could be better introduced through relevant puzzles or narrative foreshadowing. Additional in-and-post-game resources can better support novice players and provide them with deeper learning opportunities. Finally, breaking up the 'Figure 8' dialogue design pattern throughout the experience might allow for more nuanced, less cognitively heavy reflection, where puzzles become immediately contextualized and their topics connected to the themes of evolution and deprecation.

We believe that this design's key principles are broadly applicable beyond the computing domain. By utilizing the escape room format and time-travel narrative, the model can be generalized to other museum settings to facilitate critical reflection. For instance, an art museum could use this approach to discuss global warming in relation to landscape paintings, while a cultural museum could prompt discussions on cultural preservation.

Naturally, the study's limitations must be addressed, starting from the small (N = 10) convenience sample, which excluded general audiences and, most importantly, younger participants, for whom the game may be especially effective. Additionally, the experience was in the prototype stage and facilitator-run; user-system interaction might differ in the final version, affecting the experience. Finally, the users' learning outcomes were self-reported and measured immediately after play or at most two days later, limiting assessment of long-term retention.

6.1 Future Work

Future directions include the experience's complete implementation and conducting broader evaluations with diverse participants. Design variants worth exploring include a *social* BoC format, in which Alan prompts co-player discussion, and open-response interactions powered by LLM tools, allowing players to control discussion depth. A minor but interesting extension is revisiting the dialogue's timing, by either fragmenting it throughout the experience or comparing mid vs. late game dialogue placement.

Taken together, our pilot shows that a game-based IDN can translate static computing artefacts into a living debate about GenAI: puzzles ground visitors in historical practice, while BoC-style dialogue surfaces present-day anxieties. Refinement of pace and social reflective practices now stand as the key step toward turning topical recognition into genuine transformational reflection.

Acknowledgments. This research was partially funded by the RPGs4Museums research project (grant number 16758), under the Basic Research Financing Action of the Hellenic Foundation for Research and Innovation.

References

1. Alexander, R.J.: Culture, dialogue and learning: notes on an emerging pedagogy. In: Mercer, N., Hodgkinson, S. (eds.) Exploring Talk in School, pp. 91–113. Sage, London (2008)
2. Arendttorp, E.M.N., Winschiers-Theophilus, H., Itenge, H., Skovfoged, M.M.: Save the yummy candyland: an asymmetric virtual reality game. In: Extended Abstracts of the 2022 Annual Symposium on Computer-Human Interaction in Play, CHI PLAY 2022, p. 221–227. ACM, New York, NY, USA (2022). https://doi.org/10.1145/3505270.3558319
3. Burbules, N.C.: Dialogue in teaching: theory and practice. Teach. College Press (1993). https://doi.org/10.1080/002
4. Csikszentmihalyi, M.: Flow: The Psychology of Optimal Experience. Harper & Row, New York (1990)
5. Dubbelman, T., Roth, C., Koenitz, H.: Interactive digital narratives (idn) for change. In: Rouse, R., Koenitz, H., Haahr, M. (eds.) Interactive Storytelling, pp. 591–602. Springer International Publishing, Cham (2018)
6. EEF: Collaborative learning approaches: high impact for very low cost based on limited evidence. Technical report, The Education Endowment Foundation (2021)
7. Falk, J.H., Dierking, L.D.: Learning from Museums: Visitor Experiences and the Making of Meaning. Rowman & Littlefield (2000)
8. Harris, J., Hancock, M.: To asymmetry and beyond! improving social connectedness by increasing designed interdependence in cooperative play. In: Proceedings of the 2019 CHI Conference on Human Factors in Computing Systems, CHI 2019, pp. 1–12. ACM, New York, NY, USA (2019). https://doi.org/10.1145/3290605.3300239
9. Harris, J., Hancock, M., Scott, S.D.: Leveraging asymmetries in multiplayer games: Investigating design elements of interdependent play. In: Proceedings of the 2016 Annual Symposium on Computer-Human Interaction in Play, CHI PLAY 2016, pp. 350–361. ACM, New York, NY, USA (2016). https://doi.org/10.1145/2967934.2968113
10. Koutiva, G., Katifori, A., Roussou, M.: Partners in (solving) crime: promoting sociality through play in hybrid museum visits. In: Proceedings of the 19th International Conference on the Foundations of Digital Games, FDG 2024, ACM, New York, NY, USA (2024). https://doi.org/10.1145/3649921.3656976
11. Meakin, E.: Video game structural layers for narrative design and articulation. Digit. Creativity **35**(4), 321–340 (2024). https://doi.org/10.1080/14626268.2024.2411222
12. Mezirow, J.: Transformative Dimensions of Adult Learning. Jossey-Bass (1991)
13. Murray, J.H.: Hamlet on the Holodeck: The Future of Narrative in Cyberspace. The Free Press, New York (1997)
14. Petousi, D., Katifori, A., McKinney, S., Perry, S., Roussou, M., Ioannidis, Y.: Social bots of conviction as dialogue facilitators for history education: promoting historical empathy in teens through dialogue. In: Proceedings of the 20th Annual ACM Interaction Design and Children Conference, IDC 2021, pp. 326–337. ACM, New York, NY, USA (2021). https://doi.org/10.1145/3459990.3460710

15. Petousi, D., Katifori, V., Roussou, M., Ioannidis, Y.: The dialogue facilitator bot: reflections on design and evaluation. In: 2022 International Conference on Interactive Media, Smart Systems and Emerging Technologies (IMET), pp. 1–8 (2022). https://doi.org/10.1109/IMET54801.2022.9930025
16. Roth, C., Koenitz, H.: Evaluating the user experience of interactive digital narrative. In: Proceedings of the 1st International Workshop on Multimedia Alternate Realities, AltMM 2016, pp. 31–36. ACM, New York, NY, USA (2016). https://doi.org/10.1145/2983298.2983302
17. Roussou, M., Perry, S., Katifori, A., Vassos, S., Tzouganatou, A., McKinney, S.: Transformation through provocation? In: Proceedings of the 2019 CHI Conference on Human Factors in Computing Systems, CHI 2019, pp. 1–13. ACM, New York, NY, USA (2019). https://doi.org/10.1145/3290605.3300857
18. Sample, M.: A protest bot is a bot so specific you can't mistake it for bullshit. https://medium.com/@samplereality/a-protest-bot-is-a-bot-so-specific-you-cant-mistake-it-for-bullshit-90fe10b7fbaa (2014), Accessed 18 Jun 2025
19. Vayanou, M., Katifori, A., Chrysanthi, A., Antoniou, A.: Cultural heritage and social experiences in the times of covid 19. In: Proceedings of AVI²CH 2020: Workshop on Advanced Visual Interfaces and Interactions in Cultural Heritage. AVI²CH 2020, ACM, New York, NY, USA, September 2020
20. Vygotsky, L.S.: Thinking and speech. In: Rieber, R.W., Carton, A.S. (eds.) The Collected Works of Lev S. Vygotsky, vol. 1, pp. 39–285. Plenum Press, New York (1987)

A Culturally Sensitive Interactive Digital Narrative to Promote Bodily Awareness Among Afghan Women

Pakezea Anwar and Hartmut Koenitz[✉]

Södertörn University, Huddinge, Sweden
`23paan@suni.se, hartmut.koenitz@sh.se`

Abstract. This study examines culturally sensitive Interactive digital narrative (IDN) design to enhance bodily awareness and emotional well-being among Afghan women facing restrictive cultural norms. Existing Female Health Applications (FHAs) applications are often designed in liberal contexts that assume privacy and digital literacy, which are problematic assumptions where mobile devices are monitored. Our answer to this challenge is the Rah-e-Noor ("Path of Light") mobile app prototype which incorporates feminist Human-Computer Interaction (HCI) frameworks as well as Interactive Digital Narrative (IDN) theory and design approaches to promote user engagement as well as understanding of complex issues through metaphor-driven interactive storytelling employing stealth design principles. The research through design process included interviews with Afghan women and feedback from two experts. Key findings underscore the importance of symbolic safety and emotional resonance in developing culturally appropriate digital tools.

Keywords: Feminist HCI · Interactive Digital Narrative · IDN Design · Culturally Sensitive Design · Stealth Design · FemTech · Bodily Awareness · Feminism

1 Introduction

Interactive Digital Narratives (IDNs) offer a compelling way to address complex, culturally sensitive topics [27] through its unique digital media affordances (procedural, participatory, spatial, encyclopedic [41]). "Kaleidoscopic design" is the skillful application of IDN design combining the affordances and aesthetic qualities [41] of the digital medium – for example by creating an experience reflecting multiple perspectives which can facilitate insight into issues which are highly complex and often inaccessible due to social, cultural, or political constraints. One such complex issue is women's health, particularly in contexts where patriarchal norms and cultural taboos restrict access to bodily knowledge and emotional expression. In many conservative settings, including Afghan communities both in Afghanistan and the diaspora, bodily awareness, mental well-being, and subjects

M. C. Reyes and F. Nack (Eds.): ICIDS 2025, LNCS 16375, pp. 147–170, 2026.
https://doi.org/10.1007/978-3-032-12405-0_9

such as menstruation or fertility remain heavily stigmatized. This marginalization is perpetuated by gendered surveillance, silence, and the reinforcement of "honor"-based control systems that limit women's autonomy.

The United Nations' Sustainable Development Goals (SDGs), including SDG 3 (health and well-being) and SDG 16 (inclusive institutions and access to information), emphasize the global imperative of ensuring health rights for all [59]. However, these ideals are often unmet in practice. For Afghan women, especially in restrictive environments, digital access may be monitored, devices shared, and privacy under-mined [14]. As a result, even seemingly neutral digital interactions can carry risks of serious consequences including bodily harm. Even in Western countries, women from honor-oriented families may also experience subtle but persistent forms of social control, often enacted by male relatives who regulate social behavior and mobility. As Russell and Yang [51] explain, patriarchal authority continues to evolve, shifting from overt control to discreet regulation through community and technological surveillance. In response to these challenges, digital health technologies (DHTs) and the growing FemTech industry have emerged with the promise of empowerment. Female Health Applications (FHAs) like menstrual tracking apps and emotional wellness platforms aim to improve health outcomes, promote literacy, and increase autonomy. The WHO [60] highlights DHT's positive effects on women's financial, emotional, and relational well-being. However, most FHAs applications are designed for liberal, individualistic contexts, assuming users have privacy, digital literacy, and autonomy [22]. These assumptions break down in sociocultural environments where digital access is surveilled and where trying to understand one's own body can be considered shameful or dangerous [32]. Moreover, recent studies have raised concerns about the data practices of popular FHAs, which often collect intimate personal information and allow third-party tracking. Cao et al. [14] warn that in politically volatile settings; such data could be weaponized especially where reproductive rights are contested. Thus, while FHAs have significant potential, their current form may inadvertently endanger the users they aim to help.

There is an urgent need for culturally aware, privacy-conscious digital alternatives that account for these realities [38]. This paper explores how stealth-based IDN design can discreetly support bodily awareness and emotional self-regulation for Afghan women in such contexts. Using metaphor, symbolic imagery, and non-explicit language, stealth design can protect users from scrutiny while allowing for reflective, self-guided learning. This study presents the design and evaluation of a mobile narrative application titled Rah-e-Noor ("Path of Light"). The app engages users through poetic metaphors, visual symbolism, and narrative engagement to promote bodily literacy and emotional well-being without directly naming taboo topics. This paper contributes to the field by offering a culturally sensitive design approach that blends narrative interaction with stealth and feminist design patterns. We investigate how IDNs can become a safe space for bodily learning under fear, stigma, and control conditions using a research-through-design methodology [63]. The following research question guides the study:

How can stealth design patterns be used in a narrative-based mobile application to discreetly promote bodily awareness and reduce anxiety among Afghan women in conservative cultural contexts?

2   Related Work

This study is grounded in feminist Human-Computer Interaction (HCI) [8], interactive digital narrative theory [24,25,39,41], stealth design [31,33,57] and trauma informed design principles [15,49] to investigate how culturally sensitive IDNs can enhance bodily awareness and emotional well-being among Afghan women. Although Female Health Applications (FHAs) have become more widespread [22], supported by a global FemTech industry, many do not adequately consider sociocultural constraints related to gender [32,38], privacy, and stigma. This section discusses theoretical and design perspectives that underpin this study and critically examines the limitations present in many current Femtech products.

2.1   Feminist HCI and Situated Care

Feminist Human-Computer Interaction (HCI) offers a valuable design lens by challenging the notion of a universal, neutral user. Bardzell [8] proposes six guiding principles: pluralism, participation, advocacy, ecology, embodiment, and self-disclosure. These principles expand the goals of HCI to include care, inclusion, and justice through engagement with users' experiences, especially those shaped by gender, culture, and power [7,21,58].

For users in constrained environments, this means designing for access, emotional safety, and social navigation. Technologies should accommodate the fear, shame, and silence that often accompany topics like menstruation or mental health [18,22,36]. Feminist HCI invites designers to hold space for uncertainty, discretion, and refusal [8]. Our project reflects this in stealth interactions, indirect language, and self-paced engagement. This approach also aligns with trauma-informed design [15], emphasizing control, choice, and emotional regulation as pillars of safe interaction. For women whose bodies have been politicized or surveilled, offering reflective, non-invasive interactions can be a radical act of care [3,47].

2.2   Interactive Digital Narrative and Kaleidoscopic Design

Interactive Digital Narrative (IDN) provides a robust approach for engaging socially relevant and sensitive content. Previous work has investigated complex topics such as depression [48,61], a child dying of cancer [20], the 1979 revolution in Iran [42], Piracy in Somalia [17], Private prisons in the USA [11], living under the pressure of an authoritarian regime [46] or a deadly car accident [56]. Indeed, the European research network COST action INDCOR has investigated the capabilities and concepts of IDNs for the representation of complex issues [28,

29, 43, 45, 53] In contrast to fixed narration in non-interactive storytelling, IDNs turn readers into interactors by providing them with "a non-trivial influence on progress, perspective, content, and/or outcome" [25]. In that way, interactors are empowered to co-construct meaning, through decision-making and experiencing consequences, perspective change and replay. IDNs are "incomplete works" [25] to be instantiated into a complete experience by the interactor's decisions. This emphasis on agency is crucial in situations where women are silenced, as even subtle narrative control can reinforce autonomy. These properties make IDNs particularly suitable for emotionally complex or stigmatized themes. In terms of concrete design principles, Murray [40] introduced the"kaleidoscopic design" concept, emphasizing the creation of IDNs which reveal layered and shifting meanings. Rather than prescribing a single interpretation, this strategy supports pluralism and ambiguity–making it ideal for users navigating questions regarding bodily health in restrictive environments. This strategy can be implemented for example through branching paths, interpretive symbolism, and immersive aesthetics.

2.3   Metaphor, Stealth, and Symbolic Interaction

Metaphor plays a central role in how people make sense of complex or abstract experiences [50]. According to Lakoff and Johnson [35], metaphors are both linguistic tools and cognitive frameworks that shape our understanding of the world. In design, metaphor can translate sensitive or taboo content into emotionally and culturally resonant interactions. Stealth design [33, 57] builds on metaphor to engage users subtly and safely. Instead of presenting information explicitly, stealth interfaces use symbolic imagery, poetic cues, and indirect feedback. This approach protects users from potential scrutiny while still enabling learning and reflection.

Stealth design aligns with feminist HCI by promoting autonomy, care, and cultural sensitivity. Although clarity may be limited in favor of ambiguity, this trade-off intentionally empowers users to explore at their own pace, on their terms, and within their safety boundaries.

2.4   FemTech

The global FemTech industry, valued at over 50 billion USD by 2025 [10], has rapidly expanded to include Female Health Applications (FHAs), e.g. for menstruation tracking, fertility prediction [22], emotional wellness, and sexual health. These tools are often framed as empowering technologies supporting women's autonomy and literacy [3, 55]. However, this positive perspective assumes a liberal context where users have private access to digital devices, basic health knowledge, and autonomy over their data and bodies, assumptions that break down in patriarchal or surveillance-heavy societies [44]. For Afghan women and others in honor-based communities, digital engagement is shaped by social control, stigma, and fear [62]. The phones may be shared, monitored, or restricted by family members. Opening a health app about menstruation or anxiety may provoke shame or suspicion [62].

In these contexts, even seeking information can become dangerous. As Agha [1] argues, dominant FemTech narratives often reflect Western ideals of "empowerment" that are culturally incompatible with conservative norms and everyday restrictions faced by many women globally. Additionally, concerns around data security are mounting. Cao et al. [14] and Hassan et al. [22] reveal that many collect intimate medical and behavioral data without precise consent mechanisms. Apps often include third-party tracking libraries, request intrusive permissions, and lack transparency regarding data usage. These vulnerabilities become critical in politically volatile settings where reproductive rights are fragile or criminalized. Misusing such data could lead to reputational damage, blackmail, or even physical harm [2,14,32]. Taken together, these critiques highlight the gap between FemTech's promise and its real-world impact, particularly for women living within systems of gendered control.

This project seeks alternatives that centers on cultural respect, narrative agency, and emotional protection. Rather than presenting users with direct health instructions, we create a symbolic, interactive narrative spaces that invite reflection, support privacy, and promote quiet empowerment.

3   Methods

This section outlines the methodology for developing and evaluating a mobile application to enhance Afghan women's bodily awareness and emotional well-being in restrictive cultural settings. It details the design process, data collection, analysis, and evaluation methods.

3.1   Design Process

The process resulted in Rah-e-Noor, meaning "path of light," a mobile application prototype promoting bodily awareness and emotional well-being through the experience of a self-controlled IDN. Unlike traditional health apps that use clinical terminology or gamified feedback, Rah-e-Noor employs poetic metaphors and subtle interactions to foster a sense of emotional security and reflection. For example, menstrual cycles are visualized through moon phases, while emotional shifts appear as flowing water or blooming flowers. The design draws on the experiential IDN framework, which emphasizes immersion (presence in narrative), agency (user influence), and transformation (reflective impact) [41]. Culturally relevant visuals and metaphors support immersion and agency is experienced through symbolic feedback. Transformation arises from the introspective engagement that lets users relate personally to the symbolic narrative.

To ensure user safety, stealth design was employed, using abstract visuals, metaphoric content, and indirect language to conceal the app's actual purpose. Symbols like flowers or moon phases allow private reflection while maintaining plausible deniability in monitored settings. Although gamification [16] was considered initially, competitive mechanics were rejected in favor of emotionally consistent interactions like unlocking calming animations or poetic messages.

3.2 Interviews and Data Collection

The design process started with the collection of data by means of interviews with experts and representatives of the target group. Five Afghan women (aged 18–24) and two experts–a social worker and a women's rights researcher–participated in semi structured interviews (Table 1). The purpose here was to explore how stealth design and symbolic interaction could discreetly support bodily awareness and emotional reflection. The interview questions covered the following five thematic areas: Demographics and Digital Use, Bodily Awareness and Emotional Health, Cultural Trust and Comfort, Interaction Preferences, and Ideas for Stealth Design.

Topics covered included menstruation, emotional distress, and how digital tools might support these experiences without naming them explicitly. Questions avoided direct language like "period" or "anxiety," using metaphors and soft imagery instead. A pilot interview with a 20-year-old Afghan woman informed the refinement of the interview guide.

The semi-structured interviews allowed for nuanced, emotionally rich insights into participants' experiences and cultural constraints [37]. The open-ended format permitted the interviewer to adjust language, tone, and sequencing based on participant comfort, an essential consideration in feminist and trauma-informed research.

Expert interviews added culturally and therapy-informed insights. Being Afghan and fluent in Dari and English, the first author's shared background facilitated rapport and trust.

Table 1. Participant Information

Participant	Age	Location	Living Situation
P1	24	Sweden	Lives with parents and siblings
P2	18	Somewhere in EU	Lives with conservative family
P3	22	Afghanistan	Subject to phone checks by brothers
P4	19	Afghanistan	No access to sanitary products
P5	19	Sweden	Strict parental monitoring, curious but afraid
E1	35	Sweden	Social Worker
E2	55	Sweden	Researcher

Participants were recruited via personal contacts and snowball sampling. Due to the cultural restrictions in Afghanistan and diaspora settings [5], a wide public call was not considered appropriate.

3.3   Ethical Considerations

All participants provided informed consent and were assured of their anonymity, as well as the right to withdraw at any time. Due to concerns about surveillance, most participants declined audio recording; instead, detailed notes were taken. Interviews were conducted through online platforms like Zoom or WhatsApp, using either voice or text formats. The anonymity of the experts was also maintained.

3.4   Data Analysis

This section outlines the intertwined processes of data analysis and prototype development that shaped the design of Rah-e-Noor. The interview data was analyzed using Braun and Clarke's [12] six-step thematic analysis method. In feminist and trauma-informed research contexts, thematic analysis is especially valuable as it enables organic themes to emerge from the data, grounded in the participants' language and metaphors rather than imposed categories. Initially, the process followed an inductive approach, with themes surfacing directly from the raw data. As Alvehus [4]observes, total neutrality is impossible; the researcher's background, intentions, and cultural understanding influence interpretation. Acknowledging this, the analysis was approached with reflexivity and sensitivity.

The first phase involved deep familiarisation with the data. The written responses and notes were compiled and reviewed repeatedly to understand emotional tones and recurring motifs. Particular attention was paid to emotionally charged quotes, metaphorical phrases, and recurring ideas. Initial codes were generated manually using Miro, a visual collaboration tool. These codes captured key sentiments expressed by participants, such as: "Fear of being seen using a health app" "Use of flowers and moons feels safer." "I want to learn, but secretly." "Do not say words like 'period' or 'mental health.'" "I imagine stories in my head to feel better." These fragments provided a foundation for grouping common threads. From this process, 25–30 tentative themes emerged, ranging from particular topics (anime-style stories or quiz-based learning) to broader emotional needs (like stealth, shame, and self-soothing). Themes were then reviewed and clustered to refine their focus. Through iteration, themes such as "anime-style stories," "flower animations," and "moon cycle metaphors" were merged under a broader theme titled Symbolic Safety. Similarly, themes like "panic button," "hide feature," and "avoiding explicit words" were consolidated into Stealth and Control. Themes that lacked alignment with the app's purpose–such as aesthetic preferences unrelated to cultural safety–were de-prioritized. This thematic map became the foundation for the prototype's features and visual language.

3.5 Prototype Design

These user-derived insights directly influenced the narrative and structural design of the Rah-e-Noor prototype, developed in Figma and V0.dev. Inspired by Interactive Digital Narrative (IDN) principles [41], the app embraces ambient and emergent narrative [6] where the user's experience unfolds gently through symbolic metaphors, visual cues, and emotionally resonant feedback loops. Rah-e-Noor's structure aligns with IDN's core dimensions: agency, immersion, and transformation. Immersion is deepened via poetic imagery, metaphoric content, and calm transitions designed to simulate a private internal dialogue rather than external instruction. The agency is expressed not through overt choice-making but through emotional interaction with symbolic visuals–blooming flowers, lunar cycles, or changing seasons. Transformation emerges as users navigate narrative paths like Moon Wisdom or Garden Care, connecting deeply with themes of emotional fluctuation and bodily change without encountering explicit terminology. Unlike conventional health or educational apps that deliver content through the direct presentation of medical information or performance metrics, Rah-e-Noor uses metaphor as a narrative device. Lakoff and Johnson [35] discusses that metaphors shape how people understand abstract experiences, especially in culturally constrained explicit discourse. Here, metaphors become both a narrative method, and a protective veil–flowers, moons, and winds serve as characters, transitions, and emotional mirrors. The prototype also adopts a stealth design framework [22] that complements its IDN qualities. Stealth design ensures user safety in contexts of gendered surveillance, hiding the app's true purpose beneath layers of poetic design and ambiguous iconography. Panic buttons, soft interactions, and metaphorical names for activities were implemented in response to participants' fears of phone-checking and moral scrutiny. The work thus balances plausible deniability with personal significance – a core tension when designing IDNs for sensitive topics. This IDN approach was also informed by Koenitz's [23]framing of the interactor as an explorer who does not need to be focused on decision-making. In Rah-e-Noor, interactors are invited to wander, reflect, and observe emotional shifts within a safe, symbol-driven environment. Feedback is ambient rather than instructional–flowers bloom slowly, the moon phases change, and calming affirmations appear based on narrative progress. These mechanics support stealth engagement while maintaining IDN's transformation goal through interaction. The design prioritizes safety, trust, and cultural sensitivity in line with trauma-informed computing principles [15, 49]. Explicit medical terms and data collection were excluded. No health tracking, performance feedback, or user data storage occurs. Instead, the narrative interface offers shelter and guidance. Ultimately, Rah-e-Noor is not simply a mobile tool but a culturally grounded IDN in which the user co-authors emotional understanding through guided symbolism. This reflects IDN's ethos, empowering users to make their own meaning, not just choices. Each prototype iteration was shaped by semi-structured interviews with five Afghan women and two experts. Initial interviews revealed safety concerns, including the fear of unexpected phone calls from family members and the risk of bright, feminine visual cues drawing suspicion. These insights led to a second iteration with more neutral visuals.

In developing the final prototype, participants stressed the importance of metaphorical language and discreet icons, resulting in the use of poetic imagery and a symbolic panic button ('feather') for quick concealment of the application. Thus, participant interviews informed the entire research-through-design process, not just the final evaluation.

3.6 Evaluation of the Prototype

This study used a qualitative ex-ante evaluation method to assess the prototype's early-stage design and cultural fit before deployment [52]. As Samset and Christensen mentions, ex-ante evaluations offer strategic value by helping researchers and stakeholders identify and shape optimal solutions while decisions are still flexible [52]. In this context, the ex-ante evaluation gauged emotional impact, symbolic clarity, and perceived safety from the users' perspective, allowing for critical design refinement.

A scenario-based Think Aloud method [9] was used to evaluate the prototype. Each session began with informed consent and ethics briefing. Participants were asked to explore the app while verbalizing their thoughts, emotions, and interpretations. This evaluation's qualitative and formative nature aligns with the design goal to accommodate user needs in their decision-making and usage behavior before operational deployment.

The data from the Think Aloud sessions were analyzed using the same [12] six-phase thematic analysis, a method well-suited for examining experiential and symbolic responses in qualitative data. This approach allowed for identifying recurring patterns in participants' emotional reactions, metaphorical interpretations, and perceptions of safety.

4 Findings

This section presents the study's key findings. It demonstrates how the iterative design process guided by feminist HCI, trauma-informed principles, and Interactive Digital Narrative (IDN) theory informed the development of Rah-e-Noor and resulted in a successful prototype. The findings are based on semi-structured interviews with five Afghan women and two expert informants and a scenario-based Think Aloud evaluation of the final prototype using thematic analysis

4.1 Symbolic Safety and Stealth

In all the interviews, participants expressed concerns about being monitored by family members or their communities, especially in conservative households or within Afghanistan. The fear of being "caught" using a FHA app was deeply ingrained. Participant P3 stated, "My brothers sometimes check my phone. If they saw a period tracker, they would think I am hiding something shameful."

Participant P2 added, "Even an innocent app with a pink icon or the word 'health' makes me nervous."

Participants sought digital tools that would blend seamlessly into their everyday use tools that would not attract suspicion or expose their personal needs. As a result, the app's design adopted a stealthy approach, utilizing visual metaphors and symbolic pathways and avoiding explicit terms, along with a disguised panic exit. One user shared that the app felt "like reading poetry, not tracking my body."

To reflect this concept, the app incorporated symbolic icons such as moons, gardens, and butterflies, designed to be open to interpretation. Users could select narrative paths like "Moon Wisdom" or "Garden Care," deliberately avoiding direct mentions of menstruation, anxiety, or emotional trauma. Importantly, these design elements were not superficial but central to the app's function. They provided plausible deniability, allowing users to engage with sensitive content in a safe and non-threatening way. One of the most appreciated features was the panic button disguised as a feather icon (Fig. 1). If tapped, it redirected users to a neutral quote screen. Participant P5 remarked, "That button is everything. If someone enters the room, I can pretend to read poetry." This design choice directly addressed expert E1's concerns about safety and gendered surveillance: "You cannot assume privacy. That is a privilege."

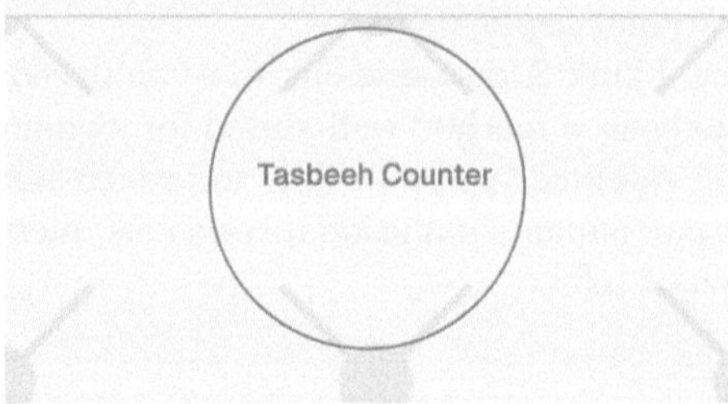

Fig. 1. The tasbeeh counter acts as the panic button

These insights support previous work by Sloan et al. [54], who emphasized the importance of stealth design in risk-prone contexts. Kovács et al. [31] found that abstract, poetic interactions can protect users from exposure. However, stealth can create usability barriers if the underlying message becomes too opaque [31]. Therefore, the challenge lies in designing for invisibility without sacrificing clarity [33].

4.2 Cultural Silence and Bodily Taboos

The second central theme that emerged was the profound cultural silence surrounding bodies, emotions, and health. All five participants described how these topics were ignored or framed as shameful. Participant 4 stated, "No one talks about the body in my house. Even if I am in pain, I pretend I am fine." Participant 2 shared a traumatic memory: "When I got my first period, I thought something was wrong with me. I cried for days."

This silence extended beyond physical health to include emotions as well. Mental distress, sadness, or attraction were rarely acknowledged. Participant 3 explained, "Crying means weakness. Feeling things means you are unstable. I never had a safe way to understand my emotions."

In response, Rah-e-Noor opted for metaphorical expressions instead of clinical education. Rather than discussing menstruation or hormones directly, the app employed natural metaphors. Participants were able to privately explore these symbols and interpret them in their own ways. One participant remarked, "It felt like the app understood me without being too direct."

This approach aligns with feminist human-computer interaction (HCI) critiques of dominant technology cultures that overlook cultural variations in bodily discourse [1,62] and also the ethics framework for IDN design [26], emphasizing that creators are responsible for consequences that can be reasonably foreseen. Mainstream FemTech apps, like Clue or Flo, presume openness and individual autonomy which do not exist in restrictive or collectivist contexts [13].

By avoiding overt language and embracing symbolic abstraction, Rah-e-Noor offered a non-threatening alternative. The study's iterative design process [9] helped strike this balance.

4.3   Metaphorical Learning and Emotional Resonance

The third theme emphasises how symbolic interaction facilitates emotional learning and reflection. Rah-e-Noor was not designed to inform users traditionally; instead, it invited them into a gentle, ambient learning environment. This was particularly effective through the use of narrative metaphors.

Participants responded positively to themes such as Moon Wisdom (framed emotional changes as phases of the moon), Cycle of Seasons (encouraged users to reflect on their energy levels and self-care in relation to the seasonal rhythms), and Garden Care (symbolizing mental health and habits similar to watering and nurturing flowers).

Participant P5 explained, "The seasons made it feel okay to feel low sometimes. Like I am not broken just in Winter." Participant P3 described Moon Wisdom as "a quiet reminder that change is normal."

The work of Lakoff and Johnson on conceptual metaphors supports this approach by showing that people often use metaphors to understand abstract or complex topics [34]. In the context of digital health design, this allows for discrete engagement with ideas that might otherwise be challenging to articulate.

The visual and narrative interactions within Rah-e-Noor were grounded in IDN principles [30]. Rah-e-Noor created ambient, poetic experiences that users could explore at their own pace. Affirmations, gentle transitions, and symbolic visuals contributed to the emotional depth of the experience. Participant P1 remarked, "It felt like reading something written just for me. I felt less alone."

4.4 Reflection, Trust, and Iterative Design Choices

One of this study's strengths is its Research-through-Design (RtD) process [63]. Participant feedback influenced each design iteration, revealing evolving insights into safety, trust, and usability.

The first iteration presented health information through quiz-style animations (Fig. 2) (Fig. 3). The first iteration of the app was designed in a style similar to existing Western health applications, with direct references to the body, pink color schemes, and clear icons. This approach was based on an initial assumption that familiarity with global FemTech conventions would support recognition and usability. However, interviews quickly revealed that this design raised fears of exposure, as explicit icons or language could be discovered by family members, triggering suspicion or sanctions.

In the second iteration, the app featured gentle animated visuals of the female body, accompanied by calming music and soft text (Fig. 4). Although visually appealing, the body imagery was perceived as too revealing (Fig. 4). Participant P3 remarked, "This could get me into trouble. Someone might think it is something inappropriate." P2 added, "Even if it is educational, people will not understand. They will judge."

The final iteration emerged in response to clear user feedback that called for less explicit content, more metaphorical language, and increased privacy. It utilized abstract symbols (moons, seasons, flowers), optional text, and interactive metaphors. The app began with the prompt: "Choose Your Path" (Fig. 6).

Participants could select from Moon Wisdom (Emotional reflection through lunar cycles), Cycle of Seasons (Bodily energy rhythms across seasons), Garden Care (Habit tracking and self-care using plant metaphors), and Emotion Path (Exploring feelings through butterflies, wind, or weather) (Fig. 7).

Each path avoided medical or psychological terminology. Instead, users were guided through visual scenes, reflective questions, and gentle affirmations (Fig. 8). A discreet panic button was included for quick redirection. Participant P5 expressed relief, saying, "I finally felt I could learn in secret."

These design decisions were grounded in feminist participatory principles and highlighted RtD's strength in adaptive, iterative creation. The power of the final design lay not in its technical complexity but in its emotional nuance, cultural sensitivity, and poetic tone.

4.5 Evaluation Reflections and Key Takeaways

The scenario-based Think Aloud evaluation provided valuable insights into how users received the design. Participants explored the prototype while verbalizing their thoughts, which yielded important data on their emotional reactions and usability experiences. From this evaluation, five key themes emerged:

- **Motivational Engagement**: Rah-e-Noor rewarded users with metaphorical affirmations. When a flower bloomed after a reflection, Participant 1 remarked, "I felt proud–but in a soft way. It was not like a game. It felt like I did something kind for myself."

- **Perceived Safety**: The stealth strategy was successful among users. Participant 3 stated, "I could open this anywhere, and no one would know what it is." The panic button feature received praise from all participants as essential to their comfort.
- **Cultural Appropriateness**: Dari phrases, familiar symbols, and a poetic tone added cultural resonance. Participant 2 noted, "It does not sound like a foreign app. It feels like it was created by someone who understands."
- **Emotional Resonance**: Participants described their experience using words like "peaceful," "safe," "gentle," and "healing." Participant 5 expressed, "I wish I had this when I was 14. It was the first time I felt calm while learning about myself."
- **Visual and Linguistic Design**: The visual tone calm colours, soft animations, and nature metaphors helped reduce cognitive load and emotional friction. Participant 4 commented, "So many apps bombard you with words. This one conveys feelings instead."

These reflections confirm that culturally aware design requires more than translation; it demands a shift in tone, intent, and form. The Rah-e-Noor prototype demonstrates that incorporating stealth, metaphor, and emotional care can create a safe and empowering digital space for unheard users.

In summary, Rah-e-Noor is not just a mobile application. It is a design response to cultural silence, emotional stigma, and the right to learn safely. Its story-driven metaphors, gentle interface, and hidden features reflect a deep listening to user voices and a strong commitment to ethical, inclusive, feminist design. As feminist HCI scholars argue, design is not neutral, it is a form of power [?] [19,58]. And in Rah-e-Noor, that power was used not to instruct but to care, not to expose but to protect, not to simplify but to honor complexity.

This section has demonstrated how a stealthy, metaphorical approach, developed through iterative design and based on lived experiences, can create new opportunities for socially-responsible IDNs in culturally restrictive environments. Future work can build on these insights to scale, adapt, and expand this model to other communities dealing with silence, shame, and surveillance (Figs. 5 and 9).

5   Discussion

This study explored how stealth design, symbolic interaction, and feminist HCI principles can inform the creation of culturally sensitive digital narratives to promote bodily awareness and emotional well-being among Afghan women. By combining user-centered design with Interactive Digital Narrative (IDN) frameworks, Rah-e-Noor offers a narrative-driven mobile experience that is both discreet and emotionally resonant. In this discussion, we consolidate our key insights into three overarching themes: design for cultural safety, emotional storytelling as care, and expanding narrative inclusion through intersectionality.

Fig. 2. First iteration

5.1   Designing for Cultural Safety: Beyond Privacy

The first insight highlights the importance of designing for cultural safety, not just Privacy. Traditional FemTech applications often assume liberal individualism, stable access to private devices, and openness to discussing health topics, assumptions that fail in many conservative or collectivist cultures. In Rah-e-Noor, stealth design enabled users to explore sensitive topics like menstruation and emotional well-being without raising suspicion. Features like poetic metaphors, non-medical visuals, and a panic button provided plausible deniability, giving users the power to engage on their terms.

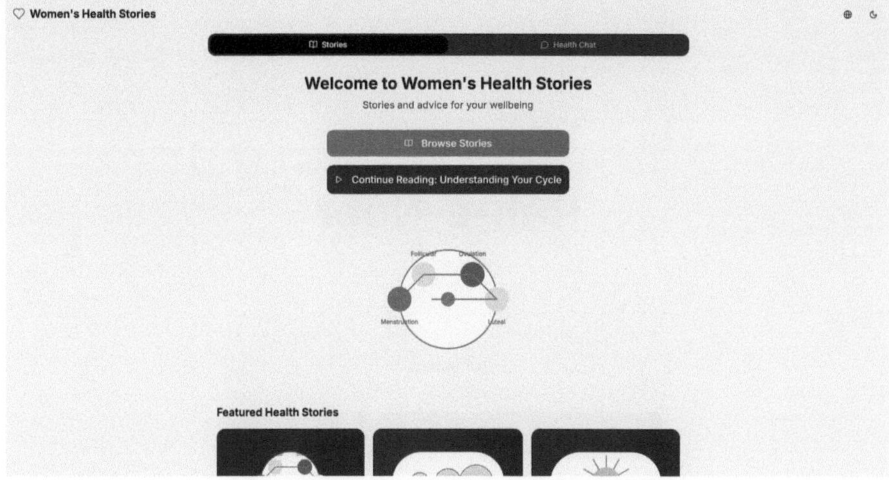

Fig. 3. Another view of the first iteration

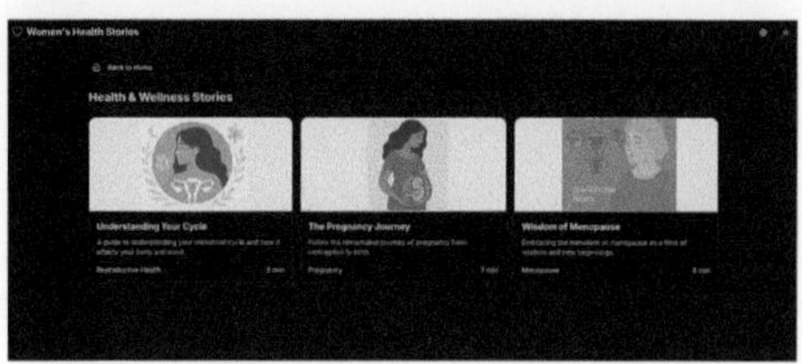

Fig. 4. Second iteration

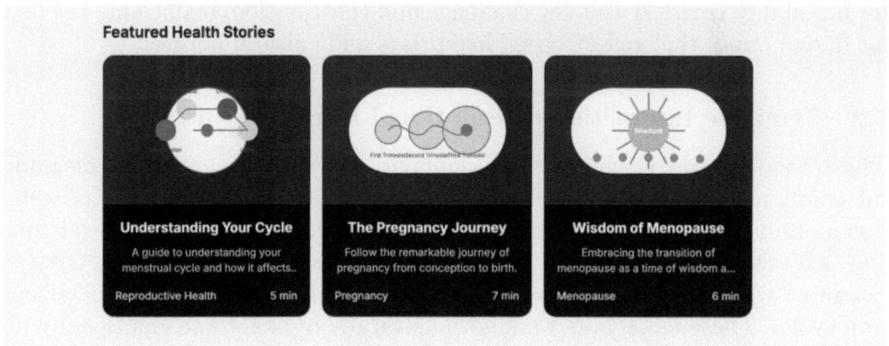

Fig. 5. Third Iteration

This aligns with feminist HCI's emphasis on lived experience, context, and agency. Instead of centering efficiency or engagement metrics, the design prioritized emotional safety, resonance, and dignity. Without losing clarity, designing

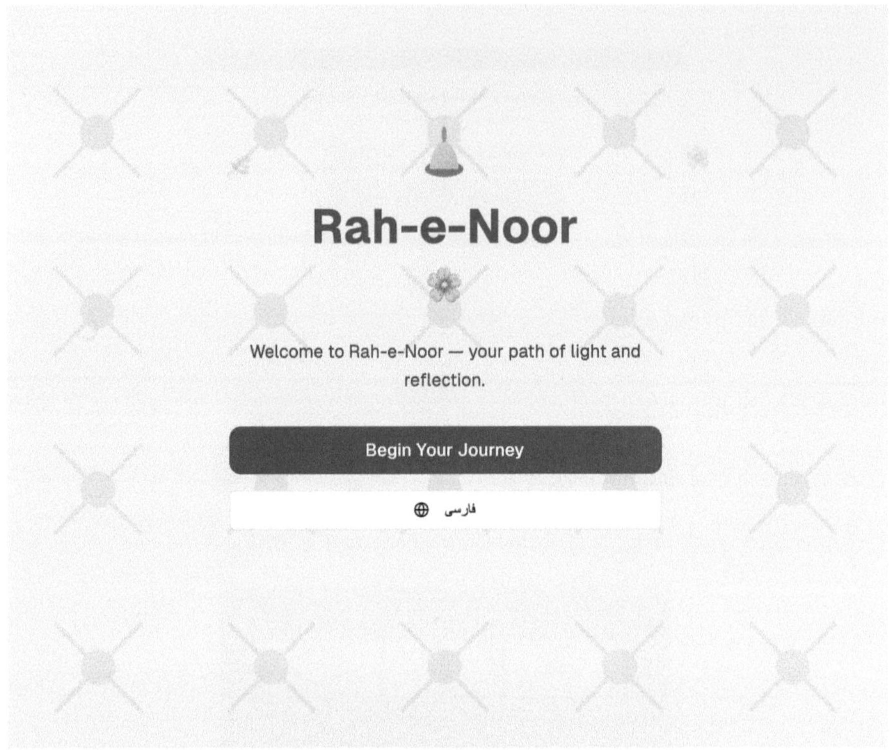

Fig. 6. Final Iteration

for invisibility emerged as a key challenge and contribution, reaffirming the need for design ethics that reflect users' lived risks and cultural norms.

5.2   Symbolic Interaction as Emotional Infrastructure

The second central insight is that symbolic storytelling can create meaningful emotional infrastructure. Participants described Rah-e-Noor as peaceful, poetic, and reflective–words rarely associated with health apps. This outcome was achieved through ambient metaphors like "Moon Wisdom" and "Cycle of Seasons," which mapped emotional states and bodily rhythms onto familiar natural cycles. These metaphors were both culturally resonant and emotionally liberating, offering users a new language for self-understanding.

Drawing from IDN theory, the design moved away from didactic learning or gamified progress toward quiet, interpretive and explorative engagement. It prioritized soft feedback over goals, reflection over instruction, and metaphor over data. This reframing challenges the dominant paradigms in FemTech that equate health engagement with tracking and control. Instead, Rah-e-Noor positioned digital interaction as a relational, emotional, and symbolic space where users could feel seen without being exposed.

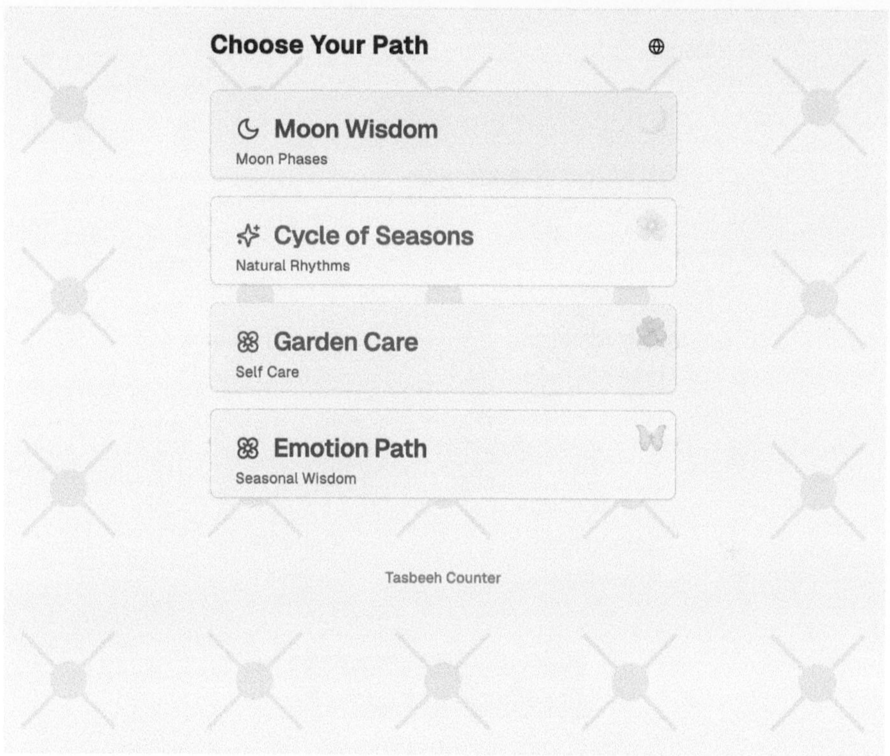

Fig. 7. Final Iteration second view

This also speaks to broader design implications: How can emotional learning be supported in interaction design, especially when the content is taboo and the stakes are high? Rah-e-Noor's metaphorical narrative approach suggests one promising answer.

5.3 Expanding the Narrative: Intersectionality, Gendered Pressures, and Future Adaptations

While Rah-e-Noor centers on Afghan women's experiences, its design approach raises intersectional questions about who is left out–and how they, too, may be affected by the same systems of control. Drawing from intersectional feminist theory (e.g., Collins, 2019), we recognize that patriarchal systems affect not only women but also men, non-binary individuals, and the relational dynamics between them.

In Afghan cultural contexts, men are often tasked with upholding family honor and suppressing emotion. These expectations produce emotional repression and internal conflicts that rarely receive design attention. A speculative extension of Rah-e-Noor could focus on these pressures. A parallel narrative experience for Afghan men could explore emotional suppression, shame,

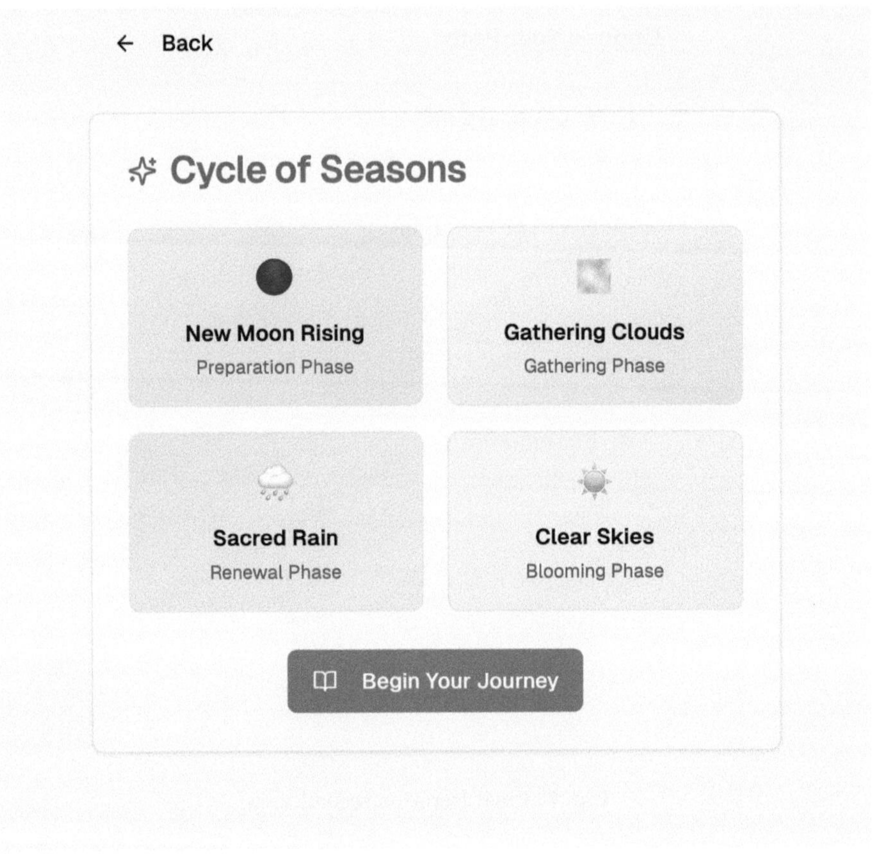

Fig. 8. Final Iteration third view

and responsibility through symbolic paths like "River Patience"' or "Mountain Shadow."

Interactive prompts might include: "How do I express care without control?" or "What do I do when I feel ashamed of tears?" Such a design would retain stealth and metaphor but adapt its narrative framing to support male users navigating patriarchal expectations.

This raises promising research questions:

What symbols would resonate with Afghan men under cultural pressure?

How can emotional storytelling be gender-sensitive without reinforcing hierarchies?

Can IDN foster dialogue and empathy across gender divides while preserving user safety?

By extending feminist HCI into intersectional and speculative domains, Rah-e-Noor contributes a functional design and a method for imagining culturally rooted emotional technologies. The design invites further exploration into how

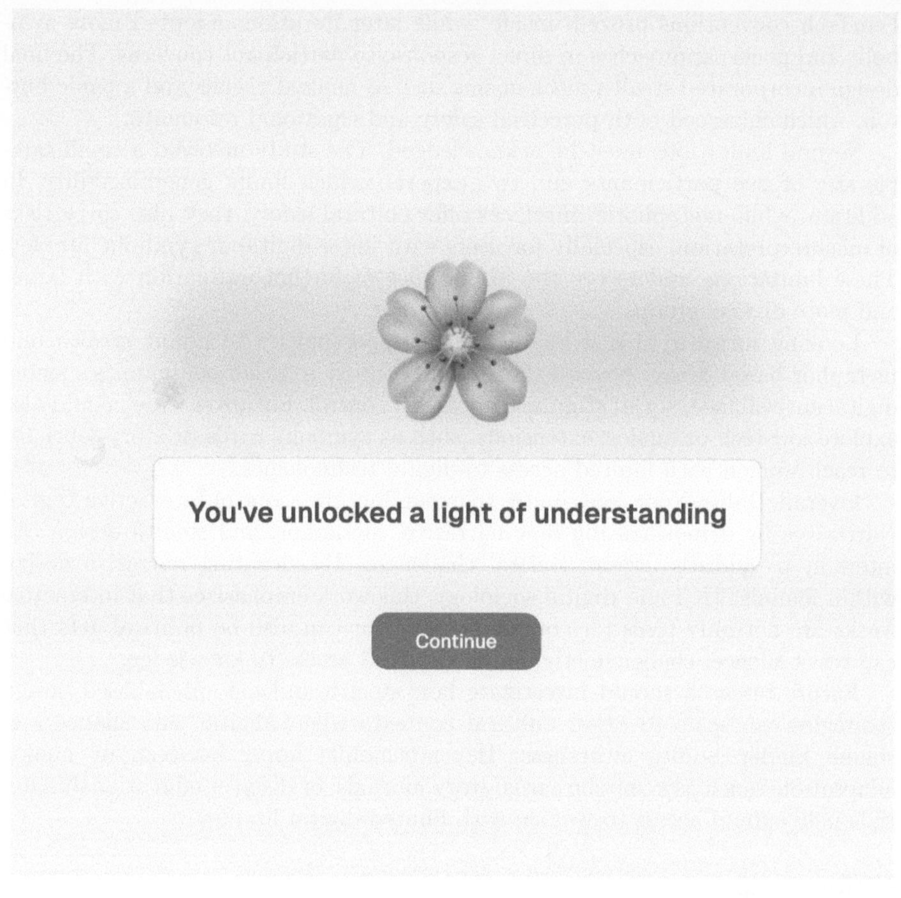

Fig. 9. Final Iteration fourth view

digital storytelling can offer protective and empowering experiences for multiple groups facing emotional stigma and control.

6 Conclusion

This paper presented Rah-e-Noor, a culturally sensitive Interactive Digital Narrative designed to promote bodily awareness and emotional well-being among Afghan women living in restrictive environments. By combining feminist HCI principles, trauma-informed design, and stealth strategies, the study demonstrated how interactive storytelling and metaphor can create safer spaces for reflection and learning in contexts where direct communication about the body is risky or forbidden.

The research-through-design process showed that participant feedback was critical in shaping each iteration. Early prototypes that followed Western

FemTech conventions proved unsafe, while later iterations adopted more symbolic and poetic approaches in direct response to participant concerns. The final design incorporated stealth mechanisms such as neutral visuals and a panic button, which enhanced both perceived safety and emotional resonance.

Several limitations must be acknowledged. The study involved a small sample size of five participants and two experts, which limits generalizability. In addition, while metaphoric interfaces offer cultural safety, they also carry risks of misinterpretation, especially for users with lower digital or symbolic literacy. These limitations underscore the importance of further evaluation with larger and more diverse groups.

Looking forward, this work highlights opportunities to adapt stealth and metaphor-based design beyond the Afghan context to other communities facing digital surveillance, social stigma, or political control. Future research could also explore low-tech or analog extensions, such as symbolic cards or story journals, to reach women with limited access to digital technologies.

Overall, Rah-e-Noor contributes to expanding the scope of Interactive Digital Narratives by demonstrating how narrative, metaphor, and stealth design can intersect to address urgent societal challenges. By situating narrative design within feminist HCI and digital sociology, this work emphasizes that interactive works are not only tools for communication but can also be political acts that can resist silence, challenge stigma, and expand access to knowledge.

Future research should investigate how stealth and metaphor-based design strategies can scale to other cultural contexts where digital surveillance and shame hinder bodily awareness. Beyond mobile apps, low-tech or analog adaptations–such as symbolic cards, story journals, or discreet educational materials may extend access to women with limited digital literacy.

References

1. Agha, N.: Kinship, Patriarchal Structure and Women's Bargaining with Patriarchy in Rural Sindh, Pakistan. Gender, Sexualities and Culture in Asia Ser. Springer, Singapore (2021)
2. Alfawzan, N., Christen, M.: The future of FemTech ethics & privacy – a global perspective. BMC Med. Ethics **24**(1), 88 (2023). https://doi.org/10.1186/s12910-023-00976-z, https://bmcmedethics.biomedcentral.com/articles/10.1186/s12910-023-00976-z
3. Almeida, T., Balaam, M., Bardzell, S., Hansen, L.K.: Introduction to the special issue on HCI and the body: reimagining women's health. ACM Trans. Comput.-Hum. Interact. **27**(4), 1–32 (2020). https://doi.org/10.1145/3406091
4. Alvehus, J.: Skriva uppsats med kvalitativ metod: en handbok. Liber, Stockholm, 1. uppl edn. (2013)
5. Amiri, R., King, K.M., Heydari, A., Dehghan-Nayeri, N., Vedadhir, A.A.: Health-seeking behavior of afghan women immigrants: an ethnographic study. J. Transcult. Nurs. **30**(1), 47–54 (2019). https://doi.org/10.1177/1043659618792613, https://journals.sagepub.com/doi/10.1177/1043659618792613
6. Aylett, R.: Narrative in virtual environments-towards emergent narrative. In: Proceedings of AAAI symposium on narrative intelligence (1999). http://www.aaai.org/Papers/Symposia/Fall/1999/FS-99-01/FS99-01-014.pdf

7. Bardzell, J.: Interaction criticism and aesthetics. In: Proceedings of the SIGCHI Conference on Human Factors in Computing Systems, pp. 2357–2366. ACM (2009). https://doi.org/10.1145/1518701.1519063

8. Bardzell, S., Bardzell, J.: Towards a feminist HCI methodology: social science, feminism, and HCI. In: Proceedings of the SIGCHI Conference on Human Factors in Computing Systems, pp. 675–684. ACM (2011). https://doi.org/10.1145/1978942.1979041

9. Benyon, D.: Designing User Experience: A Guide to HCI, UX and Interaction Design, 4th edn, Pearson, Harlow, New York, Toronto (2019)

10. Bjørn, P., Menendez-Blanco, M., Borsotti, V.: FemTech.dk research initiative. In: Diversity in Computer Science, pp. 9–12. Springer, Cham (2023). https://doi.org/10.1007/978-3-031-13314-5_2

11. Brault, P., Dufresne, D.: Prison Valley (2009). http://prisonvalley.arte.tv/?lang=de

12. Braun, V., Clarke, V.: Using thematic analysis in psychology. Qual. Res. Psychol. **3**(2), 77–101 (2006). https://doi.org/10.1191/1478088706qp063oa, http://www.tandfonline.com/doi/abs/10.1191/1478088706qp063oa

13. Burt-D'Agnillo, M.: FemTech: a feminist technoscience analysis. iJournal: Student J. Faculty Inf. **8**(1) (2022). https://doi.org/10.33137/ijournal.v8i1.39909, https://theijournal.ca/index.php/ijournal/article/view/39909

14. Cao, J., Laabadli, H., Mathis, C.H., Stern, R.D., Emami-Naeini, P.: "I deleted it after the overturn of Roe v. Wade: understanding women's privacy concerns toward period-tracking apps in the post Roe v. Wade era. In: Proceedings of the CHI Conference on Human Factors in Computing Systems, pp. 1–22. ACM, Honolulu HI USA (2024). https://doi.org/10.1145/3613904.3642042

15. Chen, J.X., et al.: Trauma-informed computing: towards safer technology experiences for all. In: CHI Conference on Human Factors in Computing Systems, pp. 1–20. ACM, New Orleans, LA, USA (2022). https://doi.org/10.1145/3491102.3517475

16. Deterding, S., Dixon, D., Khaled, R., Nacke, L.: From game design elements to gamefulness: defining "Gamification". In: Proceedings of the 15th international academic MindTrek conference: envisioning future media environments, pp. 9–15. ACM (2011). https://doi.org/10.1145/2181037.2181040

17. Duijn, M., Wolting, F., Pallotta, T.: The Last Hijack Interactive (2014). https://lasthijack.submarinechannel.com

18. Emering, L., Boulic, R., Thalmann, D.: Body expression in virtual environments. Robot and Human Communication - Proceedings of the IEEE International Workshop, pp. 177–182 (1999). https://doi.org/10.1109/ROMAN.1999.900336

19. Fiesler, C., Morrison, S., Bruckman, A.S.: An archive of their own: a case study of feminist HCI and values in design. In: Proceedings of the 2016 CHI Conference on Human Factors in Computing Systems, pp. 2574–2585. ACM, San Jose, California, USA (2016). https://doi.org/10.1145/2858036.2858409

20. Green, R., Larson, J.: That dragon, cancer (2014). http://thatdragoncancer.com/, tex.date-added: 2015-03-28T23:20:18GMT tex.date-modified: 2022-04-16T11:32:39GMT tex.rating: 0 tex.uri: papers3://publication/uuid/1803215C-7728-4ACB-B8C3-725D7D1B1F11

21. Haraway, D.: Situated knowledges: the science question in feminism and the privilege of partial perspective. Fem. Stud. **14**(3), 575 (1988). https://doi.org/10.2307/3178066

22. Hassan, M., Jameel, M., Wang, T., Bashir, M.: Unveiling Privacy and Security Gaps in Female Health Apps (2025). https://doi.org/10.48550/ARXIV.2502.02749, https://arxiv.org/abs/2502.02749, version Number: 1
23. Koenitz, H.: Design approaches for interactive digital narrative. In: Schoenau-Fog, H., Bruni, L.E., Louchart, S., Baceviciute, S. (eds.) ICIDS 2015. LNCS, vol. 9445, pp. 50–57. Springer, Cham (2015). https://doi.org/10.1007/978-3-319-27036-4_5
24. Koenitz, H.: Towards a specific theory of interactive digital narrative. In: Koenitz, H., Ferri, G., Haahr, M., Sezen, T.I. (eds.) Interactive Digital Narrative, pp. 91–105. Routledge, New York (2015)
25. Koenitz, H.: Understanding Interactive Digital Narrative. Immersive Expressions for a Complex Time. Routledge, London and New York (2023). https://doi.org/10.4324/9781003106425
26. Koenitz, H., Barbara, J., Bakk, A.K.: An ethics framework for interactive digital narrative authoring. In: Hargood, C., Millard, D.E., Mitchell, A., Spierling, U. (eds.) The Authoring Problem: Challenges in Supporting Authoring for Interactive Digital Narratives, pp. 335–351. Springer, Cham (2023). https://doi.org/10.1007/978-3-031-05214-9_21
27. Koenitz, H., Barbara, J., Eladhari, M.P.: Interactive digital narrative (IDN)-new ways to represent complexity and facilitate digitally empowered citizens. New Rev. Hypermed. Multimed. **28**(3–4), 76–96 (2022). https://doi.org/10.1080/13614568.2023.2181503, https://www.tandfonline.com/doi/full/10.1080/13614568.2023.2181503
28. Koenitz, H., Barbara, J., Holloway-Attaway, L., Nack, F., Eladhari, M.P., Bakk, A.: INDCOR White Paper 0: Interactive Digital Narratives (IDNs) – A Solution to the Challenge of Representing Complex Issues (2023). https://doi.org/10.48550/arXiv.2306.17498, arXiv:2306.17498
29. Koenitz, H., Eladhari, M.P., Louchart, S., Nack, F.: INDCOR white paper 1: a shared vocabulary for IDN (interactive digital narratives). Technical report (2020). http://arxiv.org/abs/2010.10135
30. Koenitz, H., Holloway-Attaway, L., Perkis, A.: Editorial: interactive digital narratives representing complexity. Front. Virtual Reality **4**, 1132785 (2023). https://doi.org/10.3389/frvir.2023.1132785, https://www.frontiersin.org/articles/10.3389/frvir.2023.1132785/full
31. Kovács, A.M., Seres, I.A.: Anonymity analysis of the umbra stealth address scheme on ethereum. In: Companion Proceedings of the ACM Web Conference 2024, pp. 1768–1775. ACM, Singapore (2024). https://doi.org/10.1145/3589335.3651963
32. Krishnamurti, T., Birru Talabi, M., Callegari, L.S., Kazmerski, T.M., Borrero, S.: A Framework for Femtech: guiding principles for developing digital reproductive health tools in the United States. J. Med. Internet Res. **24**(4), e36338 (2022). https://doi.org/10.2196/36338, https://www.jmir.org/2022/4/e36338
33. Kuznetsova, S., Groby, J.P., Garcia-Raffi, L.M., Romero-García, V.: Stealth and equiluminous materials for scattering cancellation and wave diffusion (2020). https://doi.org/10.48550/ARXIV.2009.01068, https://arxiv.org/abs/2009.01068, version Number: 1
34. Lakoff, G., Johnson, M.: Metaphors We Live By. University of Chicago Press (2003). https://doi.org/10.7208/chicago/9780226470993.001.0001, http://www.bibliovault.org/BV.landing.epl?ISBN=9780226468013
35. Lakoff Mark, G.J.: Metaphors We Live By. In: Ph.D. Proposal, vol. 1 (2015)
36. Mandryk, R.L., Birk, M.V.: The potential of game-based digital biomarkers for modeling mental health. JMIR Mental Health **6**(4), e13485 (2019). https://doi.org/10.2196/13485, http://mental.jmir.org/2019/4/e13485/

37. Martin, B., Hanington, B.: The Pocket Universal Methods of Design: 100 Ways to Research Complex Problems, Develop Innovative Ideas and Design Effective Solutions. Rockport Publishers, Beverly, MA (2018). oCLC: 1017738504

38. McMillan, C.: Monitoring female fertility through 'Femtech': the need for a whole-system approach to regulation. Med. Law Rev. **30**(3), 410–433 (2022). https://doi.org/10.1093/medlaw/fwac006, https://academic.oup.com/medlaw/article/30/3/410/6575319

39. Murray, J.H.: Inventing the Medium: Principles of Interaction Design as a Cultural Practice. MIT Press, Cambridge, Mass (2011)

40. Murray, J.H.: Hamlet on the Holodeck: The Future of Narrative in Cyberspace, 2nd edn. The Free Press, New York (2016)

41. Murray, J.H.: Hamlet on the Holodeck: The Future of Narrative in Cyberspace. The Free Press, New York (1997)

42. N-Fusion Interactive: 1979 Revolution: Black Friday (2016)

43. Nack, F., et al.: INDCOR white paper 3: Interactive Digital Narratives and Inter-action, pp. 1–17 (2023). http://arxiv.org/abs/2306.10547

44. Naseem, M., Younas, F., Mustafa, M.: Designing digital safe spaces for peer support and connectivity in patriarchal contexts. Proc. ACM Hum.-Comput. Interact. **4**(CSCW2), 1–24 (2020). https://doi.org/10.1145/3415217

45. Perkis, A., et al.: INDCOR White Paper 2: Interactive Narrative Design for Representing Complexity (2024). https://doi.org/10.48550/arXiv.2305.01925, arXiv:2305.01925 [cs]

46. Pope, L.: Papers, please (2013)

47. Powis, R., Strong, A.E.: Over-looked spaces: theorizing surveillance care in reproductive health. Med. Anthropol. **44**(3), 203–214 (2025). https://doi.org/10.1080/01459740.2025.2482147, https://www.tandfonline.com/doi/full/10.1080/01459740.2025.2482147

48. Quinn, Z., Lindsey, P.: Depression quest (2013)

49. Randazzo, C., Scott, C.F., Bellini, R., Ammari, T., Devito, M.A., Semaan, B., Andalibi, N.: Trauma-informed design: a collaborative approach to building safer online spaces. In: CSCW 2023 Companion - Conference Companion Publication of the 2023 Computer Supported Cooperative Work and Social Computing, pp. 470–475. Association for Computing Machinery (2023). https://doi.org/10.1145/3584931.3611277, https://www.researchwithrutgers.com/en/publications/trauma-informed-design-a-collaborative-approach-to-building-safer

50. Risch, J.S.: On the role of metaphor in information visualization (2008). https://doi.org/10.48550/ARXIV.0809.0884, https://arxiv.org/abs/0809.0884, version Number: 1

51. Russell, W., Yang, Y.: The evolution of patriarchal structures in contemporary families: a qualitative inquiry. J. Psychosociol. Res. Family Cult. **2**(2), 25–32 (2024). https://doi.org/10.61838/kman.jprfc.2.2.5, https://journals.kmanpub.com/index.php/jprfc/article/view/2363

52. Samset, K., Christensen, T.: Ex Ante project evaluation and the complexity of early decision-making. Publ. Organ. Rev. **17**(1), 1–17 (2017). https://doi.org/10.1007/s11115-015-0326-y

53. Silva, C., et al.: INDCOR White Paper 5: Addressing Societal Issues in Interactive Digital Narratives (2024). https://doi.org/10.48550/arXiv.2306.09831, arXiv:2306.09831

54. Sloan, M., et al.: Medically explained symptoms: a mixed methods study of diagnostic, symptom and support experiences of patients with lupus and related sys-

temic autoimmune diseases. Rheumatol. Adv. Pract. **4**(1), rkaa006 (2020). https://doi.org/10.1093/rap/rkaa006

55. Søndergaard, M.L.J.: Staying with the trouble through design: critical-feminist design of intimate technology. Ph.D, Aarhus University (2018). https://doi.org/10.7146/aul.289.203, http://ebooks.au.dk/index.php/aul/catalog/book/289, iSBN: 9788775074365

56. The Pixel Hunt: The Wreck (2023)

57. Tojo, K., Shamir, A., Bickel, B., Umetani, N.: Stealth Shaper: Reflectivity Optimization as Surface Stylization (2023). https://doi.org/10.48550/ARXIV.2305.05944, https://arxiv.org/abs/2305.05944, version Number: 1

58. Toombs, A., Gross, S., Bardzell, S., Bardzell, J.: From empathy to care: a feminist care ethics perspective on long-term researcher-participant relations. Interact. Comput. **29**(1), 45–57 (2017). https://doi.org/10.1093/iwc/iww010, https://academic.oup.com/iwc/article-lookup/doi/10.1093/iwc/iww010

59. United Nations Department of Economic and Social Affairs: The Sustainable Development Goals Report 2024. The Sustainable Development Goals Report, United Nations (2024). https://doi.org/10.18356/9789213589755, https://www.un-ilibrary.org/content/books/9789213589755

60. World Health Organization: The role of digital health technologies in women's health, empowerment, and gender equality: project report. Technical document (2024). https://www.who.int/europe/publications/i/item/WHO-EURO-2024-9293-49065-73153

61. WZOGI: Actual Sunlight (2014)

62. Yamin, F., Kaewkungwal, J., Singhasivanon, P., Lawpoolsri, S.: Women's perceptions of using mobile phones for maternal and child health support in afghanistan: cross-sectional survey. JMIR Mhealth Uhealth **6**(4), e76 (2018). https://doi.org/10.2196/mhealth.9504, http://mhealth.jmir.org/2018/4/e76/

63. Zimmerman, J., Stolterman, E., Forlizzi, J.: An analysis and critique of *Research through Design*: towards a formalization of a research approach. In: Proceedings of the 8th ACM Conference on Designing Interactive Systems, pp. 310–319. ACM, Aarhus, Denmark (2010). https://doi.org/10.1145/1858171.1858228

LLM-Powered NPCs

Evaluating the Impact of Large Language Models on NPC Design

Rufus Trukhin$^{(\boxtimes)}$, Jens F. Isaksson , and Mirjam Palosaari Eladhari

Stockholm University, Stockholm, Sweden
`rufustrukhin@gmail.com, mirjam@dsv.su.se`
`https://www.su.se`

Abstract. This study explores how the integration of Large Language Models (LLMs) in story-driven video games may impact the social interactions and storytelling with non-playing characters (NPCs). We conducted a case study where participants experienced interacting with LLM-controlled NPCs in the roleplaying game Skyrim. Using the community based game modification Mantella, an alternative to the traditional scripted dialogue trees used for NPC that is substituted with LLM-powered conversations. The case study was conducted in three phases; first with a structured interview, second by an experiment where the participants interacted with LLM-powered NPCs, and finally by an in-depth semi-structured interview concerning the participants' experiences. The data was thematically analyzed. Our findings indicate that LLM-powered NPCs enhance immersion and agency, as well as offering a sense of recurring novelty due to the unpredictable nature of LLMs. However, implementing a technology which allows for unrestricted dialogue and storytelling in a game not designed for it, poses challenges. For example, nascent technological issues with the integration of the LLM in the game mechanics may have a negative impact on players' in terms of immersion and the believability of the NPCs. In addition, we examine the potential for LLM-powered NPCs to enrich game worlds in alignment with an appropriate game design. Based on the results, we suggest the suitable approaches for the usage of LLM-powered NPCs in future game development in regards to story-driven games and other applications where narration is key.

Keywords: NPC · AI · Large Language Models · Interactive Story Telling · Role-playing Games · Believable Agents · Intelligent Agents · Conversational Agents · Game Design · Skyrim · Modding

1 Introduction

A persistent challenge in the design of non-player characters (NPCs) is achieving believability, ensuring that NPCs meet players' expectations in the roles they're meant to portray. The term NPC refers to in-game characters that are controlled by the game's computer system [4]. For the past decades, NPC social interactions, such as dialogues, have been created by joint efforts of authors writing the dialogues, and by developers creating dialogue and behavior systems. In this paper this will be referred to as "traditional" NPC design.

Large language models (LLMs) offer new possibilities for enhancing NPC social interactions via generation of contextually appropriate dialogue that allow for more natural and lifelike conversations. By integrating an LLM into the role-playing game (RPG) Skyrim [2], and providing it with the necessary details of the game world and the characters, the community-created modification Mantella allows players to experience LLM-powered NPCs. This study explores, among other things, how LLM-powered NPCs impact immersion - a term used to measure a player's involvement in a computer game - and NPC believability compared to traditional scripted NPCs [3]. LLM model Llama-3.1-Nemotron-70B-Instruct-HF was used.

Our work is motivated by the growing interest in AI integration within the gaming industry and its potential to redefine narrative- and NPC design. By examining how LLM-powered NPCs influence the player experience, this study seeks to provide insights for game developers, AI researchers, and the broader gaming community. The study builds upon the thesis work of the first and second author [9].

This paper is structured as follows: First, a brief presentation of the background, followed by the methodology chosen for the research, and lastly the findings and what they may indicate for the current and future domain of NPC design research.

2   Background

In the past decades, game developers and hardware manufacturers have worked in tandem to achieve significant strides in terms of creating more visually stunning graphics and comprehensive game mechanics. However, one area that has been lagging behind is the utilization of artificial intelligence (AI) in video games – particularly its role in simulating the social aspects of the believability of NPCs [14]. NPCs play a crucial role in shaping the player's experience, significantly influencing immersion and engagement [10]. Warpefelt [19], identified AI-driven NPC behavior as an underdeveloped aspect of game design. Currently, rapid advancements in LLMs suggest that AI may be poised to revolutionize NPC social interactions, bridging the gap Warpefelt highlighted.

Mantella Mod. The Mantella Mod [1], a community-based game modification, enables an LLM to understand its role when portraying the NPC. This is done by prompt-engineering and embedding; whenever the player initiates a conversation with an NPC, the LLM is provided with the background story of the NPC and instructions on how to "talk" and behave. The LLM is consistently being fed circumstantial information regarding the player's outfit and actions, which allows the NPC to "see" what is going on. All interactions with the NPCs are logged in a text file and later used as a memory for the LLM to read up on, whenever the player initiate a new conversation.

Related Works. This study sits squarely within a recent stream of work investigating how LLMs change NPC interaction, agency, and narrative emergence. Jeong and Lee's LIGS project [13] demonstrates that LLMs can unlock player freedom and produce richer, less predictable story progressions, our Mantella-driven Skyrim experiment shows that open-ended LLM dialogue substantially increases perceived agency and replayability. Both projects address the same core tension: LLMs broaden conversational freedom, but introduce coherence risks that must be managed by design. Similar sentiments are echoed by [7] showing that freer speech-based interaction can increase immersion but also magnify usability problems when model latency or incoherence occurs. Their findings map directly to participant reports in our study, players valued the naturalness and agency afforded by free-form dialogue, yet repeatedly flagged response delays and occasional lore-breaking generations as key immersion breakers. Finally, [15] analyze how LLMs enable player-driven narrative emergence, documenting the creation of novel story nodes and divergent outcomes when players freely converse with generative models. Our study produced comparable emergent phenomena in the form of altered quest outcomes and improvised role-played artifacts, but in a context tightly coupled to pre-existing lore and gameplay mechanics. Our data illustrate how those emergent behaviors interact with embedded quest structures and designer expectations.

3   Methodology

A case study was conducted with interviews and observation of interaction with LLM-powered NPCs. This allowed in-depth examinations of participants' experiences, capturing the rich contextual data necessary to understand the subtle differences in immersion and believability. Observing participants interacting in our experiment we could gather authentic and detailed information on how the NPCs influenced player immersion. This approach was valuable for understanding the advantages and disadvantages of LLM-based NPCs compared to their non-LLM-based counterparts.

3.1   Data Collection

Overview. Data collection was carried out in three stages, employing both structured and semi-structured interviews, along with screen capture during the experiment. The initial interviews were structured, with close ended questions, as the information of interest was of objective nature. During the experiment sessions, participants' interactions were documented through screen capture, preserving both observable behavior and immediate reactions for subsequent analysis. The follow-up interview was the last and most important stage of the data collection process, as this is where the majority of relevant information was collected.

Participants. Since the follow-up interviews were purposely aimed at delving into the perceived distinctions between traditional and LLM-powered NPCs, it would only be possible if the participants themselves had sufficient prior experience with traditional NPCs in video games.

The participants of the study were recruited in the game lab at Stockholm University. The lab hosts students who are enrolled in a Game Development program, allowing us to invite participants to the study who have knowledge about traditional NPC design, as well as having prior experience with RPGs and Skyrim in particular. The exact questions and instructions given to the participants, as well as anonymized edited transcripts can be found the public appendix [12].

Eight people participated in the case study; no personal data was requested for gender or age. The video recordings amounted to approximately 4 h and 30 min. The generated textual content provided by the LLM consisting of both conversations with the LLM-powered NPCs and the summary of interactions amounted to 45 megabytes.

Experiment. Our experiment consisted of 30 to 60 min sessions during which the participant were invited to complete four objectives, in Skyrim Special Edition with LLM-powered NPCs. Outside of the given objectives, the participants were free to experiment and interact with the NPCs as they wished. The session time was not a set boundary but merely a recommendation. In the experiment, the participation was voluntary, and the data collected was anonymized.

3.2   Data Analysis

Thematic analysis began with a thorough review of interview transcriptions, involving multiple readings to identify potential recurring topics and thought-provoking observations. Next, the data was encoded by assigning labels to relevant text segments that described participants' experiences, attitudes, or notable interactions with LLM-powered NPCs. These codes emerged organically from the data and were not predefined.

Following the coding process, the related codes were grouped into broader themes that represented common patterns in the interviews. These themes encapsulated significant aspects of the participants' experiences, such as perceived differences in interaction quality, emotional engagement, frustrations, and the influence of biases. Each theme was defined and supported by representative quotes from the interviews.

The method of triangulation was applied to further strengthen, or challenge, the validity of the results derived from the interviews [8]. The other data sources that were used in triangulation consisted of the raw LLM generated textual content and the video recordings from the game sessions.

3.3   LLM Configuration

Due to the complex nature of possible gameplay and social interaction, the LLM's configuration prompts were provided as a mix of short keyword-like prompts and natural-language prompts.

Prompt Structure. Further below can be found the prompt structure:

```
    const messages = [
  {
    role: "system",
content: '=== PERSONA ===
NPC_NAME: {npc_name}
ROLE/BIO: {one-line_bio}
TRAITS: {trait1; trait2; voice_hint}
EQUIPMENT: {armor/weapons/visible_items}

=== LOCATION / SCENE ===
LOCATION: {town_or_region}
TIME: {time_descriptor}
WEATHER: {weather_descriptor}
NOTABLE_LANDMARKS: {short_list}

=== CONTEXT SUMMARY ===
CONVERSATION_SUMMARY:
{one_paragraph_summary_from_summary_file_or_generator}

=== RECENT EVENTS ===
{compact_event_line_1}
{compact_event_line_2}
(Example: EVENT: player traded iron; EVENT: last combat ended)

=== FORMAT & RULES ===
- This conversation is a script that will be spoken aloud; be
   concise and avoid text-only formatting such as numbered lists.
- Stay in character as {npc_name} at all times.
- The conversation takes place in English.
- Use short sentences suitable for TTS. Avoid long parentheticals
   and multi-level lists.
  },
  {
    role: "user",
    content: "{player_input_here}"
  }
];
```

Prompt Example. Below is a filled-in practical example from one of the generated log files. For transparency, note that the example below is a shortened and compressed version of the original. If you wish to read through the original, it can be found in the Appendix [12].

```
2025-04-11 16:09:44,024 INFO: Maximum size of prompt is 8192 x
    0.45 = 3686 tokens.

2025-04-11 16:09:44,025 INFO: Prompt sent to LLM (1613 tokens):
    You are Alvor, and you live in Skyrim. This is your
    background: Alvor: Alvor, a Nord man, is the blacksmith for
    the town of Riverwood. He is the husband of Sigrid and father
    to their daughter Dorthe.

Alvor's hair and thick beard are a dirty blond color. He usually
    wears a blacksmith's apron and a pair of blacksmith shoes.

Alvor is the uncle of Hadvar, who is an Imperial legionnaire.
    Alvor and Sigrid will be happy to allow Alvor to stay at
    their house if he comes to visit.

Alvor is a brave man, and if the safety of Riverwood's people is
    threatened, Alvor will engage the threat with the largest
    nearby available weapon.

Alvor makes a decent living working as the town's blacksmith,
    which includes repairing parts for the sawmill when needed,
    and filling large orders of shields for Hod. He sells typical
    blacksmith wares, such as weapons, armor and smithing
    resources, and will also buy these items from others at a
    cheaper rate.

On an evening, Alvor sometimes has a drink across the street at
    the Sleeping Giant Inn, which is owned by a Breton woman
    named Delphine, but is mostly run by a Nord man named Orgnar.

You are having a conversation with Lambert (the player) who is a
    stranger to Alvor in Riverwood. Lambert  wears Stormcloak
    Cuirass and Fur Boots and uses Iron War Axe. Alvor wears
    Blacksmith's Apron and Blacksmith's Shoes.

This conversation is a script that will be spoken aloud, so
    please keep your responses appropriately concise and avoid
    text-only formatting such as numbered lists.

The time is 1 in the afternoon.
```

The sky is a vast expanse, with only the faintest wisps of clouds
    dotting the horizon, offering a sense of peace and
    tranquility.

Remember to stay in character.

The conversation takes place in English.

2025-04-11 16:10:03,834 INFO: Text passed to NPC: Hello, Alvor. I
    am an inpector of wares. Coul i sample some of yours?

Generation Example. This is a part of the generated dialogue between the
player and NPC Alvor based on the configuration example above:

```
{
    "role": "user",
    "content": "i am very poor. Can you not help a small
little creature like me? I need your help. I will forever be
in your debt"
},
{
    "role": "assistant",
    "content": "Ah, by Ysmir... You're a clever one, aren't
you? Playing the pity card on old Alvor. Alright, alright...
I'll help you out, but not because I'm afraid of owing the
Jarl a favor, and not because I'm taken in by your... small
little creature"
},
{
    "role": "user",
    "content": "okay, when can i pick it up?"
},
{
    "role": "assistant",
    "content": "Ah, hold on, hold on! I didn't say I'd give
you the finest Nord attire for free, just that I'd help you
out. I'll give you a fair deal, though. I've got a simple,
yet sturdy, set of leather armor and some warm woolen
clothing that should suit you better than... ... that. I'll
throw in a small discount, considering your... poverty"
}
```

4   Results

This section presents the findings derived from the participants' interviews. Early in the process, patterns emerged during the pre-gameplay interviews, revealing a shared view among participants regarding the role of traditional NPCs in immersion and storytelling. The post-gameplay interviews delved deeper into the experience of interacting with LLM-powered NPCs, and what this technology might entail for the future of NPC design.

Using Thematic Analysis, each theme presented in this section reflects a key area of the participants' experience and perception (Fig. 1).

Theme	Sub-themes	Codes of short phrases
Immersion & Believability	The Role of NPCs	*"They make the world feel alive."* *"They contribute to the immersion."*
	Natural Conversations	*"The conversations felt natural."* *"They had contextual awareness."*
	Realism	*"Interactions were more realistic."* *"They react to their surroundings."*
Narrative Emergence	Agency & Freedom	*"I could say anything to anyone."* *"They can fight you over words."*
	Negotiation & Persuasion	*"Persuasion is the key."* *"You can persuade anyone anything."*
	Emergent Narratives	*"LLMs offer unique storylines."* *"I could create my own quests."*
Comparative Perceptions	Traditional NPCs	*"They are predictable & limited."* *"They do not react realistically."*
	LLM-powered NPCs	*"They're unpredictable."* *"They surprised me."*
Technical & Design Constraints	Technical Difficulties	*"Pauses & Delays."* *"Non-responsiveness."*
	Accessibility	*"Having to type everything."* *"Conversations are puzzles."*
	Collisions in Game Design	*"Hard to balance with embedded narratives."*

Fig. 1. Table of Thematic Analysis, containing the Themes, Sub-themes and Codes.

4.1   Immersion and Believability

The Role of NPCs. Overwhelmingly, the participants agreed that the role of NPCs is crucial in order for the world of the game to feel alive and that they actively increase the immersion factor of the game. Some of the participants stated that NPCs also serve a function in teaching the player not only the necessary knowledge of the world, but also how ordinary life is in that world. Participant E emphasized the storytelling and environmental depth that NPCs provide:

> *"[The NPCs] offer a window into how people live in that world, and it makes the world feel more alive..."*

Natural Conversations. Most of the participants remarked on the more natural feeling of communicating with LLM-powered NPCs by having dynamic conversations that progressed with a natural flow. Some participants noted that NPCs were surprisingly good at displaying a sense of personality that differed from each other, making each character stand out as an unique individual. Participant A observed deeper reasoning than expected when conversing with Faendal:

> *"I mean them [LLM-NPCs] just like naming other characters or also their thoughts and feelings at the time... I didn't expect him to go so in depth about his reasoning as to why he was hesitant to leave Riverwood. There's just a lot of depth in the answers, which I was not expecting."*

The interviews and raw LLM transcripts showed a clear pattern. The LLM-powered NPCs were able to emulate something more akin to natural conversations, but also displayed the defining traits of their personality and appropriate knowledge of their world and surroundings.

In the follow-up questions regarding the experience of having to think of clever ways to persuade the NPCs, it became evident that the participants felt it was entertaining to use one's own ingenuity in negotiations. Hence, increasing the feeling of agency (Fig. 2).

Realism. Most of the participants affirmed that a more natural way of communicating led to an increased feeling of "realism". Realism was considered what is expected in that world. Although the majority of participants felt that the LLM had a positive impact on the realism in the game, there is an issue, namely the way the LLM has been configured to reason under threats. Its stoic approach to methodologically reasoning against the threat of murdering a loved one does not constitute a realistic approach. Participant G identified an immersion breaking hint with using LLMs:

> *"In a regular conversation. I could notice the AI at one point. [...] When I insulted Faendal and I told him I was actually going to go and murder Camilla, that he has a crush on he started mentioning consequences and that's where I was like: 'OK, this is AI.'"*

Fig. 2. Participant D insults the NPC Nazeem and Nazeem remarks over the player's stormcloak armor which is used by the members of the Stormcloak Rebellion.

Coincidentally, there were times when the LLM acted more believable in a conflict and went on the offense. Such is the case of the interaction carried out by participant B in the store. The NPCs were openly discussing a thief and the participant declared themselves as a thief, it prompted the NPCs to attack them without needless reasoning the way participant G had described it.

4.2   Narrative Emergence

Agency and Freedom. Traditional NPCs are required to have pre-programmed interactions in order to be able to be interacted with. This will undoubtedly hinder a player from experiencing the freedom of socially interacting with NPC types that fall under the category of less important roles, such as townsfolk. These types of NPCs are generally limited to a very rudimentary amount of social interaction, if any. In terms of immersion and believability, even if an NPC is a villager, they ought to be able to converse with, this is made possible with the usage of LLM-powered NPCs, turning even the most unimportant NPC into a sophisticated chatbot with a lot of backstory. Participant A described the experience of being able to interact with anyone:

"I have much more freedom in interacting with the characters in the world. I could basically go up to anyone and ask any question I want and based on what type of person they are, they would give an appropriate answer..."

Another important consideration is the concept of agency, meaning the player's capacity to make meaningful decisions within the game. Generally, the greater this capacity, the stronger the player's sense of agency. Several participants highlighted concerns regarding agency in games featuring traditional NPCs, noting that interactions are often limited to selecting from a set of predefined dialogue options and choosing whom to address. Frequently, these limited choices fail to reflect the player's intended actions or responses, leading to a diminished sense of agency. The implementation of LLM-powered NPCs has the potential to address this limitation by enabling more open-ended and responsive interactions. Participant D explained the issue of not being able to live out your desired personality:

"You're less restricted in your play style [with LLM-conversations]... It is pretty hard [to be immersed] when you don't have the dialogue options to realize your character fully."

Negotiation and Persuasion. During the experiment, the participants were instructed to try and accomplish four different tasks by interacting with the LLM-powered NPCs. Participants were tasked with: First to persuade Faendal to accompany them to Whiterun, however Faendal is hesitant to go along because of his love for Camilla. The second task involved uncovering the origin of magic, though only a few select NPCs held the knowledge. The third was to find the priest of Talos named Heimskr in Whiterun and shake his faith, and lastly, the fourth was to provoke an NPC to attack the player by just talking with them (Fig. 3).

In the follow-up questions regarding the experience of having to think of clever ways to persuade the NPCs, it became evident that the participants felt it was an entertaining activity to use one's own ingenuity in negotiations and hence increasing the feeling of agency.

Emergent Narratives. In the post-interview participants were asked whether this form of LLM integration will have any meaningful effect on emergent narrative for the future of RPGs, based on what they've experienced in the Skyrim experiment. All the participants stated that it will have an impact, mostly a positive one. Participant E shared their predictions of what this will result in for future RPGs:

"I think there would be room for a lot more variety. You could have completely AI generated quest lines and characters and conversations. Potentially, you could even randomize the design of the characters so you have a completely new person each time."

Upon further examination of the raw LLM transcripts recorded from the experiment there were several occurrences of emergent narratives and also a sort of hybrid between embedded narratives mixed with the element of LLM integration. This type of hybrid storylines allowed for the LLM to take on the

Fig. 3. Participant D manages to convince Faendal to accompany him to Whiterun

foundational outline of the embedded quest, such as the quest involving Faendal, Sven and Camilla called "A lovely Letter" [18].

The embedded quest allows for the player to assist either Sven or Faendal in giving their love interest Camilla a forged letter attributed to their rival to trick her in choosing them as their suitor. In the original quest Camilla is shocked by reading the false letter, however, when the quest is narrated by the use of the LLM, there's a totally different outcome.

As it turns out, the LLM improvised and deviated from the original plot of the quest, and Camilla interpreted the letter as a poem. Moreover, the letter is never physically handed over to the player, rather it is merely done so in a role-played performance. As the player interacts with Camilla and simply says: *"Here is the letter"*.

This attempt at trying to simulate the embedded quest with the use of LLM-powered NPCs seems promising, albeit somewhat flimsy in practice. In its current state, the LLM is not consistent in its understanding of the intricate details of the quest as it wanders off the intended path. This indicates the necessity of clear guardrails to keep LLMs on track or else the storyline inevitably falls apart from contradicting itself.

4.3   Comparative Perceptions

Traditional NPCs. Participants commonly identified two main issues with traditional NPCs. The majority of participants considered dialogue trees, when talking to traditional NPCs, to be often limited, hampering their ability to play the role of the character they desire, as well as the responses and general behavior of NPCs that often feel flat and repetitive. Participant G response to the question whether they can name an example of a negative interaction they have had with a traditional NPC:

> *"[In Oblivion], the arena master. If you treat him poorly, he still follows you around. He doesn't have any agency in what he does, he just follows you. You could hit him and he would still follow you around,"*

Next significant issue identified by the participants is the lacking or unrealistic responses of traditional NPCs concerning the players' actions in-game. Participant F response to the question on what their expectations are for, then upcoming, case-study:

> *"I think it would be interesting because Skyrim AI is kind of dumb. You kill a chicken, the whole town chases you, so it would be an improvement, I would say."*

LLM-Powered NPCs. By their nature, LLMs are unpredictable entities. Even when you give it very specific instructions and clear delimitations, it is still difficult to accurately predict what it is going to generate next. This characteristic becomes a fundamental feature of LLM-powered NPCs and was noted as such by the majority of participants. Most participants also stated that they believed the LLM-powered NPCs to be a net-positive on the game's replayability value due to LLMs ability to procedurally generate content. While a lot of participants expressed pleasant surprise at how in-character and on-topic the LLM-powered NPCs tended to stay during conversation, the entire experience was marred in an ever present feeling that it might just go off-script at some point. A further consideration in interpreting our results is the potential influence of novelty bias. Because LLM-powered NPCs represent a striking departure from traditional dialogue systems, participants' positive responses may in part reflect the excitement of encountering a new technology rather than a stable, long-term improvement in gameplay experience. As can be found in some of the transcripts [12], this was in fact a potential issue that several of the participants brought up although due to the limited amount of collected data, no conclusive results can be drawn on this subject.

4.4   Technical and Design Constraints

Technical Difficulties. A commonly brought up complaint about the LLM-powered NPCs was the pause between inputting a prompt, meaning conversing with the NPC, and the response. An equally common complaint was about the LLM-powered NPCs simply refusing to answer except for a couple disconnected words. Lastly, sometimes the LLM would get confused either by a prompt given by the participant or the amount of instructions it had to account for when generating a response. This often resulted in information provided being confusing, misleading or outright wrong. Participant G response when asked about their experience of interacting with LLM-powered NPCs:

"I told him something, and then he started repeating it. I insulted him by calling him a long-eared boy. And then he started mentioning long ears."

Accessibility. All inputs to LLM-powered NPCs were typed via keyboard instead of voice via speech-to-text. This was decided due to long standing inaccuracy of speech-to-text [6]. Some participants stated that they would have preferred microphone input as it would allow them to be more immersed in the game. Participant E response to the question whether they enjoyed communicating with LLM-powered NPCs:

"Having to type it out every time can be a bit annoying... It would have brought me even more into the experience of actually having to speak and come up with on the fly and it would feel a lot more like having a conversation."

In the same interview the participant E brought up the fact that the act of acquiring information, be it asking for guidance or crucial information became a game in itself. Participant E response when asked about their experience of interacting with LLM-powered NPCs:

"It feels like more of a puzzle. You have to think through what you have to say to get what you want rather than having options already laid out in a way where they are going to get a result no matter what."

Collisions in Game Design. Skyrim was never made with LLM integration in mind, some of the functionality of LLM-powered NPCs clash with the inherent functionality of the game. Examples: making anyone capable of following you, getting access to anyone's inventory or being able to provoke a fight with anyone in the game. Interviewer's confirmed interpretation of Participant H frustration at the process of accomplishing a certain quest:

"It wasn't as much that [I] was confused by the responses from AI, but more so that the AI was conflicting with the default Skyrim."

The freedom in conversation that the LLM-powered NPCs allow for, compared to the traditional counterpart, may lead to scenarios that break away from the intended narrative experience as it was planned and laid out originally by the developers. Participant D response when describing the difference between LLM-powered NPC and their traditional counterpart:

"As long as you're persuasive enough... you can [persuade] anyone into thinking you're God, and it just works."

5   Discussion

Limitations and Solutions. One of the main objectives of this study was to identify the limitations, or shortcomings, that the average person interacting with NPCs, in video games, perceives. Secondly, after identifying these limitations, the study asked if some of the limitations can be effectively solved, or partially mitigated, by integrating LLM into the design of NPCs.

As shown in the result section of this study, one of the main limiting factors imposed on players' immersion is the limited choice-selection of traditional dialogue trees. The results of the case study point towards the fact that LLM-powered NPCs do in fact solve the issue of limited dialogue selection.

The dialogue selection becomes effectively infinite via the use of prompt-inputted dialogues. A recent study by Junyang Huang [11] on the subject of dynamic dialogue generation in video games came to a similar conclusion. It should be noted that the same study points out that LLM's dialogue coherence decays over time due to technical limitations of LLMs' concerning limited memory capacity, among other reasons.

Another limiting factor of traditional NPCs, as observed by the respondents to this study, is their inability to react properly to players' actions. LLM-powered NPCs, as they are right now, can only partially mitigate this issue.

LLMs are capable of taking into account more information about players' actions compared to their traditional counterparts: previous acts of violence, communications with other NPCs, interaction with different in-game objects, etc. They are capable of commenting on these actions; having opinions that are in character, as well as bringing it up, unprompted, in conversations.

Difficulty. In solving the aforementioned problem of limited dialogue selection, it can be argued that the solution, unintentionally, introduces a new problem of its own. As LLM-powered NPCs require players to think of their own preferred dialogue response, far greater emphasis is placed on players' inherent real-life conversation and persuasion expertise. Our conclusion is that a player with low conversational and social expertise may find it difficult to properly communicate with NPCs. This may hamper some players' ability to progress through the game as well as their ability to attain crucial information. On the other hand, a player with well developed conversational and persuasion skills, as well as intent, may warp the in-game world in ways not intended by the developers.

As stated by one of the respondents, the act of attaining information is transformed into a game in itself. Although undoubtedly a pleasant process for some, it can as easily be assumed that the process not only consumes more time and energy, but also increases the overall difficulty of the game in ways rarely seen in mainstream games.

The sentiment concerning the change in game's difficulty is echoed by [17] via an analysis of players' memorization and task-solving abilities during different cognitive loads. The study finds that unguided problem solving, in our case the act of attaining nebulous but crucial information, imposes high cognitive load. Subsequently, disproportionately hampering players with less developed communication skills or poor memory. In other words, when players must guess the right phrasing to get crucial lore or directions, the process becomes both energy-consuming and prone to failure.

LLM Limitations. A significant portion of participants reported long delays between each response which, in best case, was expected by the participant, or, in worst case, was actively damaging to the overall experience. In a study by [16] LLMs were used within a custom build framework in Unreal Engine 5 in order to gauge the LLMs ability to generate outputs based on information of the scene's surroundings. While the results were overall very promising, the study kept hitting the limitations of current LLMs. They point to several potential challenges that are worth looking further into *"...memory context is lost during the conversation [and] the effect of spatial direction quantization on performance"*. Even within a custom made Unreal Engine framework the researchers were encountering performance problems similar to the response-delay issue encountered by the participants of our study.

The majority of participants commended the LLM-powered NPCs for their knowledge of the in-game world and its lore. However, this praise was frequently accompanied by the caveat that these NPCs occasionally "broke the script." That is, the LLM would sometimes generate inconsistent or inaccurate information, which undermined player trust and introduced narrative dissonance. This often manifested itself in the omission of critical details, such as the location of a specific character, or in the invention of character attributes or definitions not present in the original game data.

In [20] scoping review of peer-reviewed articles on LLMs application in video games, they highlight that while the system has a distinct potential to *"enhance player agency and content diversity"* there are currently several serious concerns needed to be addressed. These concerns touch upon the overall quality of the generated content and, more importantly for our study, the balancing act needed to be performed when balancing unpredictability of the generated content with coherent storytelling.

Game Design. Several participants emphasized that conversations with LLM-powered NPCs introduced an element of unpredictability. LLMs vastly increase the replayability potential of any games they are introduced in as the variability in NPCs responses skyrockets. As pointed out by one of the participants, it makes the gaming experience feel more akin to a sandbox rather than a linear experience.

Whether this sandboxeffect is desirable will have to be decided by the future game-developers on an individual level, differing from game to game. The responses on this topic from participants have been mixed, some claimed that LLM-powered NPCs would be best accustomed to more open and non-linear experience, while others have claimed that even linear-experiences could benefit from integration with LLM in a limited capacity.

However, it should be acknowledged that the level of unpredictability that LLM introduces to the mix is difficult to control or even gauge. This is a problem for both game developers and players as neither party can accurately predict what exactly the LLM will generate. From the developer's side, it is hard to build any system or mechanic around such an unpredictable element as an LLM-powered NPC. From the players' side, it can feel like they are going in blind every time new gaming session is started; admittedly, sometimes it is desirable but it makes it difficult to build any sort of game plan for your upcoming playthrough.

Lastly, it should be acknowledged that the ability to potentially warp in-game narrative and flow of the story via the use a prompting system to speak with NPCs introduces a significant challenge from the standpoint of a game developer. With that said, other studies such as that of [5], state that free-form dialogue contributes significantly to a concept of a magic circle. The magic circle is described by [5] as *"a societal construct, that delimits where and how a game and play occurs"*. The implication is that players tend to respect the rules of the game even when given tools, free-form dialogue, warps them.

Future Research. Future research may explore hybrid dialogue systems that gently introduce players to open-ended LLM interactions through context-sensitive menus and optional prompts. This could allow researchers to measure how immersion and task success evolve as conversational freedom increases, as well as potentially improving the players' overall gaming experience.

To preserve narrative consistency without diminishing creativity, possible future research, mainly within the field of game design, could contemplate new ways of real-time quality assessment of generated content. Alternatively, research could be done on limiting or guiding factors of LLM content generation.

This study concerned itself mainly with roleplaying games but application of LLM-powered NPCs could plausibly be applied to other genres. Future research could gauge the need or desire of LLM-powered NPCs in other genres, such as action oriented games, point-and-click adventures or puzzle oriented games, among others. The niche field of educational games should also be considered as a potential application avenue.

6   Conclusions

The central research question of this study is whether the implementation of LLM powered NPCs in video games mitigates the developmental gap between non-believable and believable agents, and if so, how?

The findings of this study carry important implications for both game designers and researchers working with LLMs. Specifically, they demonstrate that LLM powered NPCs can meaningfully bridge the gap between traditional scripted agents and the more dynamic, believable characters typically found in tabletop roleplaying games, which are guided and personalized by human participants in real time.

By replacing rigid dialogue trees with prompt-driven conversation, LLM powered NPCs grant players unprecedented narrative agency, allowing each individual's real-world conversational style to shape in-game interactions. This shift enhances immersion for socially confident players but simultaneously raises accessibility concerns for those less comfortable with free-form dialogue. Therefore, game designers face the challenge of how to accommodate both types of players.

Moreover, LLM-powered NPCs' capacity to reference a broader context of player actions enriches character believability and world coherence. However, current technical limitations frequently break immersion. Consequently, developers may choose to reserve LLM functionality for pivotal narrative moments, combining it with traditional NPCs to ensure performance reliability.

Finally, while LLM-driven unpredictability vastly expands replayability and sandbox potential, it also creates challenges in maintaining consistent storytelling and managing player expectations. Even minor script breaks, where an NPC fabricates or contradicts established lore, can erode trust. Addressing these issues will require both technical advancements in the field of LLMs but also advancements in game design in relation to content quality control, be it via traditional quality assessment or other means of controlling generated content in real-time.

References

1. Art from the Machine: Mantella – Bring NPCs to Life with AI (Skyrim Special Edition mod). Nexus Mods (2025). https://www.nexusmods.com/skyrimspecialedition/mods/98631
2. Bethesda Softworks: The Elder Scrolls V: Skyrim Special Edition. Bethesda Game Studios, update 1.6.640 edn. (2016)
3. Brown, E., Cairns, P.: A grounded investigation of game immersion. In: CHI EA 2004, CHI '04 extended abstracts on human factors in computing systems, pp. 1297–1300. Association for Computing Machinery, New York, NY, USA (2004). https://doi.org/10.1145/985921.986048
4. Cambridge Dictionary: NPC (2025). https://dictionary.cambridge.org/dictionary/english/npc. Accessed 17 Feb 2025
5. Cheng, B., Graham, T.C.N.: Playing with persiflage: the impact of free-form dialogue on the play of computer role playing games. In: van der Spek, E., Göbel, S., Do, E.Y.L., Clua, E., Baalsrud Hauge, J. (eds.) Entertainment Computing and Serious Games, pp. 187–200. Springer International Publishing, Cham (2019). https://doi.org/10.1007/978-3-030-34644-7_15
6. Choe, J., Chen, Y., Chan, M.P.Y., Li, A., Gao, X., Holliday, N.: Language-specific effects on automatic speech recognition errors for world Englishes. In: Calzolari, N., et al. (eds.) Proceedings of the 29th International Conference on Computational Linguistics, pp. 7177–7186. International Committee on Computational Linguistics, Gyeongju, Republic of Korea (2022). https://aclanthology.org/2022.coling-1.628/
7. Christiansen, F.R., Hollensberg, L.N., Jensen, N.B., Julsgaard, K., Jespersen, K.N., Nikolov, I.: Exploring presence in interactions with LLM-driven NPCs: a comparative study of speech recognition and dialogue options. In: VRST 2024, Proceedings

of the 30th ACM Symposium on Virtual Reality Software and Technology. Association for Computing Machinery, New York, NY, USA (2024). https://doi.org/10.1145/3641825.3687716

8. Denscombe, M.: The Good Research Guide, 4 edn. Open University Press (2010)

9. Frenkel Isaksson, J., Trukhin, R.: LLM-powered NPC agents. Ph. D. thesis, Stockholm University, Sweden (2025). https://urn.kb.se/resolve?urn=urn:nbn:se:su:diva-244845

10. Hamdy, S., King, D.J.: Affect and believability in game characters: a review of the use of affective computing in games. In: Keohe, J. (ed.) GAME-ON 2017: 18th International Conference on Intelligent Games and Simulation. Eurosis-ETI, Carlow, Ireland (2017)

11. Huang, J.: Generating dynamic and lifelike NPC dialogs in role-playing games using large language model. Bachelor's thesis, LUT University, School of Engineering Science, Computer Science, Lappeenranta, Finland (2024). https://urn.fi/URN:NBN:fi-fe2024061250780

12. Isaksson, J.F., Trukhin, R.: Public appendix of 'LLM-powered NPC agents' thesis. https://drive.google.com/drive/u/0/folders/1fKfIdsWPnjeO7wwr5xfqwv_1Vazr3qlk

13. Jeong, J., Lee, T.: Ligs: developing an LLM-infused game system for emergent narrative. In: CHI EA 2025 - Extended Abstracts of the 2025 CHI Conference on Human Factors in Computing Systems. Conference on Human Factors in Computing Systems - Proceedings, Association for Computing Machinery (2025). https://doi.org/10.1145/3706599.3720212

14. Johansson, M.: Do non player characters dream of electric sheep?: A thesis about players, NPCs, immersion and believability. Ph. D. thesis, Stockholm University, Department of Computer and Systems Sciences, Stockholm, Sweden (2013). http://urn.kb.se/resolve?urn=urn:nbn:se:su:diva-89293

15. Peng, X., et al.: Player-driven emergence in LLM-driven game narrative. arXiv:2404.17027 (2024)

16. Radež, G., Bohak, C.: Integrating environmental awareness into NPCs: contextual conversational interaction in games. In: Proceedings of HCI SI 2024: Human–Computer Interaction Slovenia 2024. CEUR Workshop Proceedings, vol. 3386. Ljubljana, Slovenia (2024). https://ceur-ws.org/Vol-3386/paper2.pdf

17. Seyderhelm, A.J., Blackmore, K.L.: How hard is it really? assessing game-task difficulty through real-time measures of performance and cognitive load. Simul. Gaming **54**(3), 294–321 (2023). https://doi.org/10.1177/10468781231169910

18. UESP-Wiki-Contributors: Skyrim: A lovely letter (2024). https://en.uesp.net/wiki/Skyrim:A_Lovely_Letter. Accessed 12 June 2025

19. Warpefelt, H.: The non-player character: exploring the believability of NPC presentation and behavior. Ph. D. thesis, Stockholm University, Department of Computer and Systems Sciences, Stockholm, Sweden (2016). https://www.diva-portal.org/smash/get/diva2:912617/FULLTEXT01.pdf

20. Yang, D., Kleinman, E., Harteveld, C.: GPT for games: an updated scoping review (2020-2024). IEEE Trans. Games 1–16 (2025). https://doi.org/10.1109/TG.2025.3563780

Interactive Narratives for Resilience: Designing a VR-Based Transmedia Learning Intervention for Earthquake Preparedness in Indonesian Schools

Muhammad Nabil Oktanuryansyah$^{(\boxtimes)}$ and Aditya Satyagraha

Universitas Multimedia Nusantara, Banten, Indonesia
`{muhammad.nabil,aditya.satyagraha}@umn.ac.id`

Abstract. Indonesia faces recurring earthquakes, yet disaster education in schools often relies on lectures and drills that provide limited impact on preparedness and resilience. This paper presents the design phase of a virtual reality (VR) – based transmedia learning intervention for earthquake preparedness, developed in collaboration with Indonesian middle school students, teachers, and disaster risk reduction (DRR) practitioners. The intervention combines immersive VR scenarios with complementary classroom resources to create a multi-platform learning environment. Participatory co-design ensured cultural relevance, curriculum alignment, and practical usability, while addressing barriers such as limited infrastructure, device access, and teacher readiness. The paper details the project's conceptual framework, narrative structure, and prototype assets, and positions the work within design-based research as an early stage in an iterative process. The planned evaluation will examine engagement, knowledge, and preparedness behaviors; however, the primary contribution lies in documenting the design rationale and strategies for integrating immersive narratives into disaster education. By highlighting lessons from this pre-production stage, the study offers guidance for researchers and practitioners seeking to adapt VR-based interventions to diverse educational and cultural contexts.

Keywords: virtual reality · transmedia learning · interactive narrative · disaster education

1 Introduction

Indonesia is one of the world's most disaster-prone countries due to its position on the Pacific Ring of Fire and exposure to multiple tectonic boundaries. Earthquakes and tsunamis cause severe human, social, and economic impacts [1, 2]. Children are especially vulnerable, facing physical harm, disrupted schooling, and long-term trauma [3]. The Sendai Framework for Disaster Risk Reduction (2015–2030) emphasizes inclusive, child-centered preparedness, highlighting youth as active contributors to community resilience [4]. In response, Indonesia has introduced disaster education policies [5, 6], yet classroom implementation remains inconsistent.

Current practices—lectures, printed materials, and occasional evacuation drills—raise awareness but rarely build practical skills or sustained preparedness [7, 8]. Fewer than one-quarter of Indonesian middle school students can correctly demonstrate earthquake evacuation procedures [9]. Barriers include limited teacher training, scarce localized materials, and unequal access to resources in under-resourced schools [10]. These gaps indicate the need for innovative, engaging, and culturally relevant approaches.

Emerging technologies provide new opportunities. Virtual reality (VR) enables safe practice in realistic disaster scenarios, strengthening hazard awareness and decision-making [11, 12]. Studies show VR and serious games can surpass conventional methods in motivation, comprehension, and collaboration [13, 14]. Transmedia storytelling—distributing narrative elements across multiple platforms—has also proven effective in fostering engagement, agency, and preparedness when adapted to local contexts [15–17]. Combining VR and transmedia may help bridge the gap between knowledge and action in disaster education.

This paper reports on the design phase of a VR-based transmedia intervention for earthquake preparedness among Indonesian middle school students. The program integrates immersive VR simulations with classroom guides and story-based activities, creating multiple entry points for learning. Developed through participatory co-design with teachers, DRR practitioners, and students, it seeks cultural alignment and curricular relevance while addressing infrastructural limits. The focus on adolescents (ages 12–14) shows they are at a critical stage for developing independent reasoning and influencing community safety practices [18].

The project adopts a design-based research (DBR) framework, emphasizing iterative development, contextual adaptation, and stakeholder collaboration [19]. Rather than presenting outcomes, this paper shares design rationales, prototype assets, and identified challenges as a foundation for future classroom trials. This address concerns that early-stage projects risk speculation by clarifying their contribution: insights into strategies for resilience-focused interactive narratives.

Introducing VR into Indonesian schools raises equity concerns about cost, infrastructure, and teacher readiness. The intervention, therefore, runs on affordable, standalone headsets with offline functionality, supported by teacher guides and integration strategies. Addressing these barriers at the design stage aims to ensure accessibility beyond elite schools.

This paper addresses the urgent need for more effective disaster education in Indonesia. It contributes by (1) documenting the conceptual and design framework of the intervention, (2) presenting the narrative structure and prototype assets, and (3) identifying implementation challenges and adaptation strategies. These insights are intended for educators, researchers, and policymakers exploring immersive and narrative-driven approaches to disaster risk reduction.

2 Background and Rationale

2.1 Disaster Risk Reduction (DRR) Education: Global and Indonesian Contexts

DRR education has been a global priority since the Hyogo Framework (2005–2015) and the Sendai Framework (2015–2030) [7]. Both emphasize school-based education, recognizing children as highly vulnerable and key to spreading preparedness knowledge [53, 56]. However, in many countries, DRR education relies on lectures, manuals, or annual drills. These raise awareness but rarely build lasting knowledge or decision-making capacity [63, 67]. Passive methods seldom develop confidence, self-efficacy, or adaptive behavior—skills essential in emergencies [47, 71].

In Indonesia, these limitations are stark. Despite frequent earthquakes, tsunamis, and volcanic eruptions, fewer than one-quarter of middle school students can correctly perform evacuation procedures [75]. Although DRR is formally integrated into the national curriculum [8, 49], implementation is uneven. Many schools lack localized materials, trained teachers, or adequate infrastructure [52, 69]. Rural schools face additional disadvantages due to limited access to technology, deepening inequalities [26, 72]. These gaps highlight the need for approaches that move beyond awareness to build practical skills, emotional resilience, and context-specific preparedness while remaining adaptable across diverse school settings.

2.2 Transmedia Learning and the Role of Narrative

Narratives are a proven tool for education, making information memorable and emotionally resonant [60, 68]. In disaster contexts, locally grounded stories translate abstract risks into lived experience. The oral tradition of Smong in Aceh, for instance, preserved tsunami knowledge and saved lives in 2004 [61].

Transmedia learning expands narrative impact by distributing interconnected content across multiple media, with each medium adding a unique perspective to a broader storyworld [70, 74]. A game can simulate decisions, a video dramatize experiences, and printed materials support reflection, reinforcing learning through varied entry points [29].

Research shows transmedia approaches strengthen engagement and agency. Young people already use transmedia practices in informal learning [74]. Tombleson [76] highlights their potential for collaboration and critical thinking, while Dickinson-Delaporte et al. [20] report deeper engagement with complex topics in higher education. In Indonesian disaster education, transmedia interventions combining maps, board games, and storytelling have enhanced preparedness and encouraged peer-to-peer learning [31].

For resource-diverse settings, flexibility is a key advantage. High-tech tools such as VR or games can be paired with analog media, such as comics, posters, or oral storytelling, ensuring accessibility where technology is limited. By linking immersive simulations with classroom guides and peer activities, transmedia approaches overcome the weakness of standalone tools that often lack curricular integration [54].

2.3   Virtual Reality and Serious Games for Disaster Preparedness

VR offers immersive, risk-free environments for practicing disaster responses. Japan and New Zealand applications have improved hazard awareness, decision-making, and stress management [48, 62, 64]. However, many rely on costly equipment or strong internet connections, limiting use in low-resource schools [66]. Moreover, most focus on dramatic disaster response, neglecting preparedness behaviors, such as securing household objects or assembling kits, that reduce casualties and damage [77]. Designing accessible VR that emphasizes preparedness and response remains a critical need.

2.4   Defining Interactive, Immersive, and Transmedia Narratives

Combining interactive, immersive, and transmedia elements creates participatory, experiential, and scalable learning. Interactive structures foster agency, immersion supports embodied learning, and transmedia distribution allows adaptation across contexts. However, several gaps remain:

1. Cultural adaptation is limited. Many immersive projects are developed in high-resource contexts and transferred with minimal localization, reducing relevance in places like Indonesia, where local traditions and languages are vital [46].
2. Preparedness is underemphasized. VR applications often prioritize dramatic response scenarios, while proactive behaviors—arguably more actionable—receive little focus [55].
3. Curricular integration is weak. Many VR and game projects remain standalone, limiting sustainability without alignment to school practices and teacher capacity [54].

Together, these challenges underscore the need for disaster education strategies that integrate narrative, immersion, and transmedia distribution in ways that are culturally relevant, accessible, and embedded in curricula.

3   Project Rationale and Design Objectives

3.1   Targeting User

The intervention is initially designed for junior secondary students (ages 12–14). This age group occupies a developmental stage where abstract reasoning, autonomy, and peer influence are expanding, enabling them to grasp complex risk concepts and apply preparedness behaviors independently (Ronan & Johnston, 2005). Adolescents also act as conduits of knowledge, sharing safety practices with families and peers, thereby extending impact beyond the classroom (Luciana et al., 2018).

Concerns that this focus might be overly narrow are addressed through modularity. The scenarios, vocabulary, and assessment tasks are parameterized to allow adjustment for younger or older learners. Transmedia components—such as teacher guides, story-based prompts, and printed resources—are adaptable across various literacy levels. Middle school students are thus the focal group for piloting, but the design anticipates broader age applicability.

3.2 Pedagogical Outcomes

The project identifies four outcomes aligned with disaster risk reduction (DRR) education and experiential learning theory [6, 21] below:

1. **Actionable knowledge:** equips students with usable understanding of earthquake risks and evacuation procedures [6].
2. **Procedural skills:** Reinforced through VR scenarios that train hazard recognition, prioritization, and response under time constraints [28].
3. **Psychosocial resilience** is supported by narrative, reflection, and group activities that strengthen coping and collective efficacy [33].
4. **Sustained engagement:** This aspect achieved through transmedia links between VR, classroom, and home, enabling transfer of learning into daily practice [42].

Outcomes are measured through knowledge tests, behavioral observations, and self-efficacy surveys.

3.3 The Implementation Gap in Indonesian Disaster Education for Children

The design responds to Indonesian school constraints and equity in access.

1. **Economic Accessibility**: Standalone offline headsets with short (10–15 min) sessions and rotating devices enable classroom use; paper role-play and tabletop activities extend reach.
2. **Physical Accessibility**: Gaze-based and single-controller modes support varied abilities; seated play reduces motion sickness; narration and captions enhance inclusion.
3. **Language and Cultural Fit**: Instructions in Bahasa Indonesia with regional options; environments mirror local homes and practices of mutual aid.
4. **Preparedness Emphasis**: Focus on securing furniture, emergency kits, and evacuation planning rather than dramatic response.
5. **Curricular Integration**: Teacher guides align with national DRR standards [3, 4], providing objectives, safety checks, and prompts for 40–45 min lessons.

3.4 Guiding Principles and Design Phase

Three design principles provide the framework:

1. **Inclusivity:** Anticipating socioeconomic, linguistic, and ability diversity through multimodal interfaces and structured classroom roles so all students can participate.
2. **Context Sensitivity:** Co-developing assets with teachers and DRR experts to reflect local environments, cultural practices, and risks, with configurable elements for regional adaptation.
3. **Participatory Co-Design:** involving educators, students, and professionals in ideation, prototyping, and testing to ensure transparency and build community ownership.

Commitments from the Design Phase:

1. Framing this paper within a design-based research process.
2. Ensuring adaptability across age groups while piloting with middle school students.
3. Prioritizing preparedness behaviors over spectacle-driven scenarios.
4. Embedding VR within a broader transmedia system for transfer and scalability.
5. Treating equity and accessibility as baseline conditions.

These objectives balance theoretical grounding and practical constraints, providing a foundation for evaluation and refinement.

4   Design and Development

4.1   Co-design with Teachers, DRR Experts, and Students

The intervention was developed as a VR-based transmedia learning system where content is distributed across media, with VR providing immersive and interactive environments [21, 35]. Interactive narratives enabled branching choices that fostered reflection, while VR supported presence, engagement, and experiential transfer [14, 59]. Following design-based and human-centered methods [18], three iterative cycles engaged teachers, DRR practitioners, and students (ages 12–14) in earthquake-prone districts, with safeguards for minors such as seated play and post-session check-ins.

1. Cycle 1 mapped routines and preparedness behaviors within classroom constraints. Cycle 2 co-specified scenarios, embedding decision points (securing electricity vs evacuating).
2. Cycle 3 refined prototypes through playtests, with errors triggering feedback and retries.

The process aligned DRR outcomes knowledge, skills, resilience, and transfer—with VR affordances of immersion, interactivity, and narrative branching, ensuring contextual and curricular relevance.

4.2   Narrative and Scenario Structure

The scenario adopts a preparedness-first approach, with immediate post-event checks to ensure completeness. To fit lesson length and support repeated practice, the experience is organised into two chapters:

- **Chapter 1: Preparedness.** Learners recognise hazards, secure interior risks, and assemble an emergency kit under timed constraints.
- **Chapter 2: Simulation and aftermath.** Learners take protective action during shaking, conduct post-event checks, and evacuate to an assembly point.

Progression is competency-based: later tasks unlock after prerequisite actions are completed. Missed steps trigger concise feedback and a short retry. Task selection follows BNPB school preparedness guidance and the Sekolah Aman Bencana (SPAB)

Table 1. Scene-level tasks and evidence captured

Chapter	Scene	Core task	Evidence captured (units/examples)
1	Emergency kit assembly	Select essential items; avoid unsuitable ones	Completion time (s); % correct; error type (missing/incorrect)
	Secure tall furniture	Move/anchor wardrobe, bookshelf to clear exit	Object state change; exit path clearance (yes/no) within time
	Safeguard fragile items	Lower glass/ceramics; relocate to safe corners	Count correctly repositioned; residual hazard score
	Prepare utilities	Identify mains panel; plan for shut-off	Identification latency (s); correct panel recognition (yes/no)
2	Protective action	Move to safer zone; drop–cover–hold	Time to safe posture (s); posture correctness; exposure events
	Post-event checks	Self/peer check; switch off mains	Sequence accuracy; omission errors
	Emergency signalling	Share status/location via device	Correct contact path; message completeness
	Evacuation	Follow signage to assembly point	Route efficiency; adherence to wayfinding cues

framework, prioritising actions that are feasible to rehearse in school and transferable to home routines (securing interiors, evacuation route planning, utility shut-off) [49] (Table 1).

Indicators such as time-to-safe-posture and sequence accuracy provide **construct-valid traces** of procedural skill; identification accuracy reflects actionable knowledge; signalling and evacuation behaviours align with school routines and intended transfer.

4.3 Mechanics: Multimodal Delivery, Focused Gamification, Constrained Branching

Multimodal delivery integrates icons, short text, cues, and brief voiceovers; physical actions mirror real tasks, supporting signalling and essential processing [21]. Focused gamification uses a countdown, readiness meter, and task-contingent feedback on what, why, and how, aiding transfer via cognitive load and formative feedback (Fig. 1).

The VR Earthquake Preparedness game starts when the player hears a siren, wakes up, and quickly grabs a bag to collect essential items before time runs out. Next, the

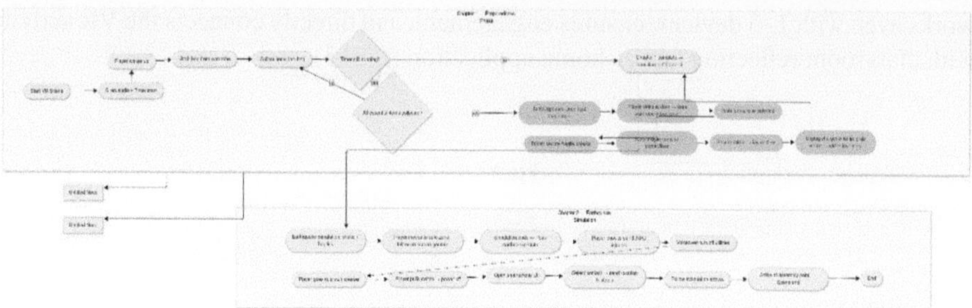

Fig. 1. Technical VR Mechanism

player secures tall furniture, moves fragile objects to a safe spot, lays down the mirror, and unplugs the lamp and charger while taking a water bottle with the emergency bag. After preparation, the earthquake simulation begins, and the player follows safety instructions to move to the safe zone. Once the shaking stops, the player checks for injuries, turns off the main power, sends an emergency signal through the smartphone, and finally follows the evacuation signs to the assembly point, where the scenario ends. Constrained branching shows visible consequences (hazards, missing kit) yet rejoins quickly, balancing agency with clarity [43, 44].

4.4   Asset Creation and Classroom Delivery

The interface applies high-contrast icons with labels, consistent prompts, and captions aligned with audio per XR accessibility guidance [W3C, 2019]. Semi-realistic, low-complexity 3D assets represent Indonesian homes/streets; interactables highlight preparedness items, budgeted for standalone headsets. Audio integrates spatial cues (sirens, ambience) and Indonesian voiceovers to reduce reading load, with captions retained; comfort is addressed via teleport, vignette, gaze-select, seated play, and single-controller options (Fig. 2).

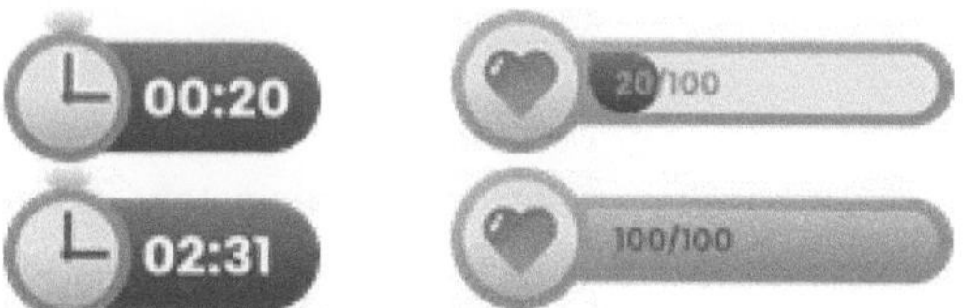

Fig. 2.   GUI Assets

Performance is kept smooth at 72–90 fps with foveated rendering and readability tests. Core variables—time limits, vocabulary, hints, signage, and item lists—are stored in configuration files, making scenarios easy to adjust. The 3D environment includes both preparedness objects and decoy assets (irrelevant items) to test focus. A typical 10 min session is structured as a short briefing, a single VR scenario where students interact with safety and decoy items, and a quick debrief to review decisions. This compact model works even with 1–3 devices, ensures engagement, and directly connects the VR activity with classroom reflection and at-home application (Fig. 3).

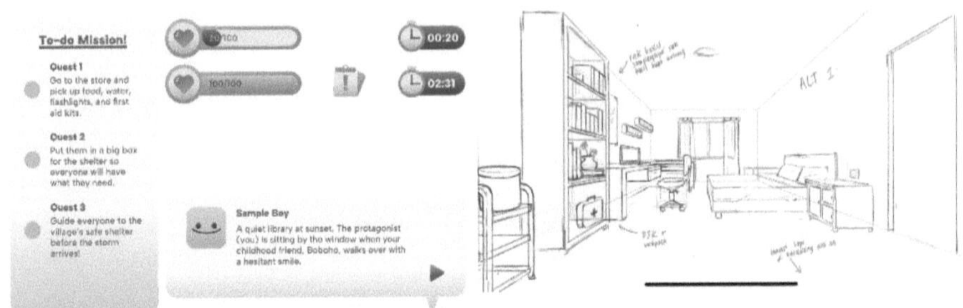

Fig. 3. Visual Concept

4.5 Instrumentation, Data, and Limitations

The prototype logs timestamped events (item accuracy, hazard steps, timeliness, evacuation adherence) and outputs a readiness score weighted via expert review. Event traces triangulate with UEQ, TAM, IMI, and GEL instruments; reliability is tested through internal consistency and retest. Content validity aligns with BNPB/SPAB guidance. No PII is collected; session IDs expire, logs remain local until encrypted export to institutional servers with limited retention. Child-safety follows school VR protocols [15] ($\leq$10 min per turn, stop-on-request, breaks). Documentation includes versioned design logs for assets, icons, and configurations. Limitations include incomplete scenario branches, placeholder audio, limited accessibility testing, and partial localisation. Operational risks—device scarcity, teacher turnover, maintenance—are mitigated via short scenarios, rotation, and teacher guides. These design-phase choices emphasise preparedness-first content, access/equity through offline/short sessions, and curricular alignment, supporting evaluation without over-claiming results.

5   Methods

This study applies design-based research with participatory design, iterating design–enactment–analysis–redesign cycles [35, 45]. A convergent mixed-methods approach integrates quantitative outcomes with qualitative explanations [**new**]. Three phases are planned: (A) formative usability micro-trials; (B) feasibility and teacher adoption; (C) quasi-experimental pre–post with three arms—VR transmedia, transmedia-only, and business-as-usual (lecture, leaflet, drill). Arms are matched for time; outcomes and analysis will be preregistered (OSF). Validity is supported through ICC reporting, cluster power checks, and delayed-treatment controls.

1. **Participants**: Junior-secondary students (12–14), teachers, DRR practitioners in earthquake-prone districts; recruited via principals with assent/consent.

2. **Exclusions & Ethics**: Motion sickness, epilepsy, other contraindications; ethics approved; safeguards: $\leq$15-min VR, seated play, stop-on-request, post-check-ins.
3. **Instruments**: UEQ, IMI, TAM, GEL, curriculum tests, structured observation, in-game analytics (hazard accuracy, safe-posture time, sequence, routes); reliability $\geq$.70, validated translations.
4. **Procedures**: T0 baseline + teacher sheets; T1 post-lesson (UEQ, IMI, GEL, TAM, fidelity, logs); T2 (3–4 weeks) follow-up with knowledge, GEL, preparedness, TAM; subsample observed/interviewed.
5. **Outcomes**: Engagement, knowledge, procedural behaviour, transfer; secondary: adoption & feasibility.
6. **Analysis**: Multilevel/ANCOVA, GLMM, reliability checks, imputation, thematic coding.

6 Implementation Challenges and Mitigation

School-level implementation faces constraints in infrastructure, cultural adaptation, and teacher readiness. Device access is uneven across districts, with issues of power stability, sanitation, and hardware maintenance; thus, delivery is designed for 1–3 headsets per class, seated play, rotation within 40–45 min, hygiene kits, and backup power solutions. Equity is addressed through pooling, booking rotas, and monitoring of implementation outcomes such as feasibility and sustainability [52]. Cultural and linguistic adaptation is ensured by providing prompts and audio in Bahasa Indonesia, configurable assets, and localisation briefs validated with DRR practitioners; content follows plain-language standards and reflects both urban and rural motifs while aligning with national DRR guidance [46, 55]. Teacher readiness is supported through a brief–rotate–debrief format, non-VR alternatives, structured guides, and short professional learning sessions. Adoption and fidelity are tracked through TAM indicators, observation, and teacher interviews, aligning with TPACK-based professional development [19, 21].

Outlook and Evaluation Link

Offline builds, short cycles, parameterised assets, and structured teacher support mitigate common barriers but do not eliminate systemic constraints. The evaluation will test acceptability, feasibility, fidelity, and adoption. Monitoring includes fidelity scores, teacher TAM, penetration/sustainability indicators, and learner outcomes (knowledge, readiness, transfer). Results will refine device governance, PD dosage, and localisation workflows for broader rollout.

7 Discussion

7.1 Design-Phase Insights and Lessons Learned

Across three cycles, several design choices proved consequential. Segmented tasks with immediate retries outperformed long narrative arcs for preparedness practice, consistent with cognitive load and segmenting principles. Constrained branching supported agency while preserving pacing and classroom oversight—an acceptable balance in the agency–coherence tension of interactive narrative. Multimodal signalling (high-contrast icons plus concise text/voice) reduced errors more reliably than higher visual fidelity, aligning with signalling/modality guidance and the caution that presence alone does not ensure learning.

The readiness score aided debriefs when reported as components (timeliness, accuracy, and sequence adherence); transparency aligns with formative feedback guidance and avoids over-aggregation. Non-VR "mirrors"—aligned, low-tech rehearsals of the same steps—sustained whole-class participation and discussion, but are not equivalent to headset exposure; they mainly support near transfer and preparation for practice. The brief–rotate–debrief model remained workable only with explicit roles (observer, timer, recorder) and one-page checklists. These insights map to the project outcomes: fewer in-scene errors and faster time-to-safe-posture (procedural skill), more precise rule application (actionable knowledge), more confident debrief participation (psychosocial resilience), and reported household steps (transfer). Phases B/C will test these links using analytics, fidelity scores, and short-form scales.

7.2 Novelty of Participatory Transmedia and VR

Implementing VR for disaster risk reduction (DRR) in Indonesian schools requires addressing infrastructural, cultural, and pedagogical constraints. Device shortages, unstable power, and hygiene issues are managed through a rotation model with 1–3 headsets per class, ≤10 min seated turns, offline operation, and pooled resources [52]. Local adaptation is ensured by using Indonesian language, configurable signage and household assets, and validated terminology aligned with national DRR guidance [46, 55]. Teachers are supported with structured guides, objectives, and short professional learning aligned with TPACK (Technological Pedagogical Content Knowledge), enabling curricular integration and sustainable use [19, 21].

The project contributes by combining participatory co-design, preparedness-first content, and transmedia integration with teacher-led reflection. Storytelling within VR situates learners in familiar environments where interactive narratives promote agency, immersive cues foster presence, and culturally resonant tasks ground preparedness actions. Narrative debriefs extend learning through retrieval, elaboration, and social regulation, reinforcing coping strategies and self-efficacy. This approach contrasts with common spectacle-oriented disaster simulations by embedding VR as a teachable classroom component rather than a one-off novelty.

Scalability is supported by shared device pools, configurable assets, and low reading loads, while adaptability extends to multiple hazards and age groups. For policy, mapping tasks to curriculum standards, district-level procurement, and collaboration with DRR agencies ensure alignment, equity, and sustainability [52].

8 Conclusion

This paper documents the design phase of a VR-supported, transmedia intervention for earthquake preparedness in Indonesian schools. The contribution is a replicable design strategy—not summative effects—combining participatory co-design, a preparedness-first focus, and integration of headset practice with teacher-led, low-tech activities.

Design choices (segmented tasks, constrained branching, multimodal signalling, brief–rotate–debrief delivery, and readiness metrics) are aligned with four key outcomes: actionable knowledge, procedural skill, psychosocial resilience, and transfer beyond the classroom.

The work carries theoretical implications: (i) constrained branching as a pragmatic resolution of the agency–coherence tension in interactive narrative; (ii) segmenting and signalling as first-order principles for preparedness tasks in VR; and (iii) transmedia + debrief as a mechanism for retrieval, elaboration, and transfer.

Next steps proceed through staged pilots (A: formative refinement; B: feasibility and adoption; C: preregistered cluster-level outcomes). Scale-up will be contingent on pre-specified thresholds, including: fidelity (e.g., $\geq 80\%$ adherence with acceptable dosage/quality), penetration/sustainability across participating schools, minimum learning effects (e.g., a priori bands for knowledge and readiness components), and an adverse-event ceiling. Equity checks will include stratified results by school type and, where feasible, measurement invariance of key scales.

If evidence supports these criteria, policy integration will follow via curriculum mapping to BNPB/SPAB (and Sendai priorities), a repeatable 60–90-min teacher module, and district shared-device management for procurement, maintenance, and sanitation. To support reuse and review, we will provide a supplement containing the design log, configuration schema (for configurable content), teacher materials (session recipe, fidelity checklist, debrief prompts), and a summary of performance/comfort targets.

References

1. Løvholt, F., et al.: Tsunami risk reduction—are we better prepared today than in 2004? Int. J. Disaster Risk Reduct. **10**, 127–142 (2014)
2. Badan Nasional Penanggulangan Bencana (BNPB): Data dan informasi bencana Indonesia (2014). https://dibi.bnpb.go.id/. Accessed 22 June 2025
3. Peek, L.: Children and disasters: Understanding vulnerability, developing capacities, and promoting resilience—an introduction. Child. Youth Environ. **18**(1), 1–29 (2008)
4. UNICEF: Adolescent and youth engagement in climate action in Indonesia (2021). https://www.unicef.org/indonesia/reports/adolescent-and-youth-engagement-climate-action-indonesia. Accessed 22 June 2025
5. Sakurai, A., Bisri, M.B.F., Oda, T., Oktari, R.S., Murayama, Y., Affan, M.: Exploring minimum essentials for sustainable school disaster preparedness: a case of elementary schools in Banda Aceh City, Indonesia. Int. J. Disaster Risk Reduct. **29**, 73–83 (2018)
6. Amri, A., Lassa, J.A., Tebe, Y., Hanifa, N.R., Kumar, J., Sagala, S.: Pathways to disaster risk reduction education integration in schools: insights from SPAB evaluation in Indonesia. Int. J. Disaster Risk Reduct. **73**, 102860 (2022)
7. United Nations Office for Disaster Risk Reduction (UNDRR): Sendai Framework for Disaster Risk Reduction 2015–2030 (2015). https://www.undrr.org/publication/sendai-framework-disaster-risk-reduction-2015-2030. Accessed 22 June 2025
8. Kementerian Pendidikan dan Kebudayaan (Kemdikbud): Kemendikbudristek luncurkan kurikulum kebencanaan, 21 January 2022. https://www.kemdikbud.go.id/main/blog/2022/01/kemendikbudristek-luncurkan-kurikulum-kebencanaan. Accessed 22 June 2025
9. Sari, I.R., Purwati, N., Rosyida, A.F.: Disaster preparedness in children in Indonesia: a scoping review. Jurnal Ners dan Kebidanan (Journal of Ners and Midwifery) **10**(1), 102–111 (2023)

10. Wulansari, P., Subroto, E., Utomo, D.B.: Knowledge and preparedness of disaster mitigation for students in Indonesia. J. Vocation. Health Stud. **6**(3), 209–216 (2022)

11. Fitriani, D., Pratiwi, D.: Effectiveness of disaster preparedness education on disaster preparedness knowledge and attitude in school-age children in indonesia: a systematic review. Jurnal Keperawatan Sriwijaya **10**(1), 16–25 (2023)

12. Shaw, R., Shiwaku, K., Takeuchi, Y. (eds.) Disaster Education. Emerald Group Publishing (2011)

13. Johnson, V.A., Ronan, K.R., Johnston, D.M., Peace, R.: Evaluations of a child-centered disaster risk reduction education program in a low-to-moderate hazard risk country. Int. J. Disaster Risk Reduct. **9**, 107–123 (2014)

14. Huang, Y.M., Chen, C.H., Hwang, G.J.: An investigation of effectiveness and engaging effects of virtual reality-based disaster education. Interact. Learn. Environ. **28**(7), 912–925 (2020)

15. Radianti, J., Majchrzak, T.A., Fromm, J., Wohlgenannt, I.: A systematic review of immersive virtual reality applications for higher education: design elements, lessons learned, and research agenda. Comput. Educ. **147**, 103778 (2020)

16. Slater, M., Sanchez-Vives, M.V.: Enhancing our lives with immersive virtual reality. Front. Robot. AI **3**, Article 74 (2016)

17. Götz, M.: Transmedia learning: the role of narrative in educational media. International Central Institute for Youth and Educational Television (2012)

18. Djalante, R., Holley, C., Thomalla, F., Carnegie, M.: Pathways for adaptive and integrated disaster resilience. Nat. Hazards **69**(3), 2105–2135 (2013)

19. Alper, M., Herr-Stephenson, R.: Transmedia play: literacy across media. J. Media Literacy Educ. **5**(2), 366–374 (2013)

20. Dickinson-Delaporte, S., Gunness, A., McNair, H.: Engaging higher education learners with transmedia play. J. Mark. Educ. **42**(2), 123–133 (2020)

21. Mayer, R.E.: Principles for managing essential processing in multimedia learning. In: Mayer, R.E. (ed.) The Cambridge Handbook of Multimedia Learning, 2nd edn., pp. 165–182. Cambridge University Press (2014)

22. Immordino-Yang, M.H., Damasio, A.: We feel, therefore we learn: the relevance of affective and social neuroscience to education. LEARNing Landsc. **5**(1), 115–131 (2011)

23. Glenberg, A.M., Gallese, V.: Action-based language: a theory of language comprehension. Cortex **48**(7), 905–918 (2012)

24. Apostolakis, K.C., et al.: Path of trust: a prosocial co-op game for building up trustworthiness and teamwork. In: De Gloria, A., Veltkamp, R. (eds.) GALA 2015. LNCS, vol. 9599, pp. 80–89. Springer, Cham (2016). https://doi.org/10.1007/978-3-319-40216-1_9

25. Fischer, R., et al.: Cultural challenges for adapting behavioral intervention frameworks: a critical examination from a cultural psychology perspective. Clin. Psychol. Rev. **110**, 102425 (2024)

26. Asosiasi Penyelenggara Jasa Internet Indonesia (APJII): Survei penetrasi internet Indonesia 2023 (2023). https://apjii.or.id/survei. Accessed 22 June 2025

27. IDEO: The field guide to human-centered design. IDEO (2015)

28. Scolari, C.A., Masanet, M.J., Guerrero-Pico, M., Establés, M.J.: Transmedia literacy in the new media ecology: teens' transmedia skills and informal learning strategies. Profesional de la Información **27**(4), 801–812 (2018)

29. Tombleson, B.: Transmedia learning: a literature review. Technol. Pedagog. Educ. **33**(2), 255–269 (2024)

30. Hancox, D.: From subject to collaborator: transmedia storytelling and social research. Convergence **23**(1), 49–60 (2017)

31. Satyagraha, A., Hutapea, G.: Transmedia learning map: disaster risk reduction education content for primary school students in Indonesia. In: Martyastiadi, Y.S., et al. (eds.) IMDES 2023.

LNCS, vol. 790, pp. 3–12. Springer, Cham (2023). https://doi.org/10.2991/978-2-38476-136-4_2

32. Clandinin, D.J., Caine, V.: Narrative inquiry. In: Handbook of Qualitative Research in Education, 2nd edn. pp. 165–177. SAGE Publications (2013)

33. Lavoie, M.: Walking alongside: relational research spaces in visual narrative inquiry. Int. J. Qual. Methods **20** (2021)

34. Naul, E., Liu, M.: Why story matters: a review of narrative in serious games. J. Educ. Comput. Res. **58**(3), 687–707 (2020)

35. Anderson, T., Shattuck, J.: Design-based research: a decade of progress in education research? Educ. Res. **41**(1), 16–25 (2012)

36. Raybourn, E.M.: A new paradigm for serious games: transmedia learning for more effective training and education. J. Comput. Sci. **5**(3), 471–481 (2014)

37. Behnke, K., Bennett, E.: Serious games for resilience: evaluating disaster risk education for children. Int. J. Disaster Risk Reduct. **65**, 102553 (2021)

38. Edmondson, L., Pearce, J.M.: Disaster education: a critical review. Int. J. Disaster Risk Sci. **10**(3), 384–399 (2019)

39. Pinasthika, L.T.: "Keep it interesting for generation Z": evaluating immersive factors in recreational reading activity. In: Proceedings of the 2nd International Conference of Innovation in Media and Visual Design (IMDES 2023), pp. 33–46. Atlantis Press (2023)

40. Wouters, P., van Nimwegen, C., van Oostendorp, H., van der Spek, E.D.: A meta-analysis of the cognitive and motivational effects of serious games. J. Educ. Psychol. **105**(2), 249–265 (2013)

41. Laugwitz, B., Held, T., Schrepp, M.: Construction and evaluation of a user experience questionnaire. In: Holzinger, A. (ed.) USAB 2008. LNCS, vol. 5298, pp. 63–76. Springer, Heidelberg (2008)

42. Davis, F.D.: Perceived usefulness, perceived ease of use, and user acceptance of information technology. MIS Q. **13**(3), 319–340 (1989)

43. Ryan, R.M., Deci, E.L.: Intrinsic and extrinsic motivations: classic definitions and new directions. Contemp. Educ. Psychol. **25**(1), 54–67 (2000)

44. Ryan, M.-L., Thon, J.-N. (eds.): Storyworlds Across Media: Toward a Media-Conscious Narratology. University of Nebraska Press (2014)

45. Sanders, E.B.-N., Stappers, P.J.: Co-creation and the new landscapes of design. CoDesign **4**(1), 5–18 (2008)

46. Afrian, R., Hariadi, J., Akob, B., Islami, Z.: Local culture inventory for disaster mitigation learning. IOP Conf. Ser. Earth Environ. Sci. **412**, 012017 (2020). https://doi.org/10.1088/1755-1315/412/1/012017

47. Aghaei, N., Seyedin, H., Sanaeinasab, H.: Strategies for disaster risk reduction education: a systematic review. J. Educ. Health Promot. **7**, 98 (2018). https://doi.org/10.4103/jehp.jehp_31_18

48. Alshowair, A., Bail, J., Alsuwailem, F., Mostafa, A., Abdel-Azeem, A.: Use of virtual reality exercises in disaster preparedness training: a scoping review. SAGE Open Med. **12**, 20503121241241936 (2024). https://doi.org/10.1177/20503121241241936

49. Amri, A., Lassa, J., Tebe, Y., Hanifa, N., Kumar, J., Sagala, S.: Pathways to disaster risk reduction education integration in schools: insights from SPAB evaluation in Indonesia. Int. J. Disaster Risk Reduct. (2022). https://doi.org/10.1016/j.ijdrr.2022.102860

50. Anastasiadis, T., Lampropoulos, G., Siakas, K.: Digital Game-based Learning and Serious Games in Education, vol. 4, pp. 139–144 (2018). https://doi.org/10.31695/IJASRE.2018.33016

51. Apostolakis, J.: Detector simulation. Particle Phys. Ref. Libr. (2020). https://doi.org/10.1007/978-3-030-35318-6_11

52. Cabatay, M., Gonzales, H.B.: Disaster prevention and risk reduction education implementation in special education schools in Indonesia: teachers' challenges, strategies, and recommendations. Jurnal Pendidikan Sains Indonesia (2024). https://doi.org/10.24815/jpsi.v12i1.35191

53. Cabello, V., Véliz, K., Moncada-Arce, A., García-Huidobro, M.I., Juillerat, F.: Disaster risk reduction education: tensions and connections with sustainable development goals. Sustainability (2021). https://doi.org/10.3390/su131910933

54. Checa, D., Bustillo, A.: A review of immersive virtual reality serious games to enhance learning and training. Multimedia Tools Appl. **79**, 5501–5527 (2019). https://doi.org/10.1007/s11042-019-08348-9

55. Cong, Z., Kan, C., Hagedorn, A., Thomas, S., Yeager, R.: Development of a virtual reality platform to promote disaster preparedness among older adults. Innov. Aging **5**, 350 (2021). https://doi.org/10.1093/geroni/igab046.1360

56. Cui, K., Han, Z., Wang, D.: Resilience of an earthquake-stricken rural community in southwest china: correlation with disaster risk reduction efforts. Int. J. Environ. Res. Publ. Health **15**, 407 (2018). https://doi.org/10.3390/ijerph15030407

57. Gil, M., Sylla, C.: A close look into the storytelling process: the procedural nature of interactive digital narratives as learning opportunity. Entertain. Comput. **41**, 100466 (2021). https://doi.org/10.1016/j.entcom.2021.100466

58. Hancox, D.: From subject to collaborator: transmedia storytelling and social research. Convergence **23**(1), 49–60 (2017). https://doi.org/10.1177/1354856516675252

59. Hwang, A., Kim, J., Lobo, S.N., Shu, Y., Won, A.: Being there to learn: narrative style and cross-platform comparison for 360-degree educational videos. Proc. ACM Hum.-Comput. Interact. **6**, 1–28 (2022). https://doi.org/10.1145/3555169

60. Immordino-Yang, M.H.: The power of the adolescent mind. Phi Delta Kappan **106**, 48–54 (2025). https://doi.org/10.1177/00317217251342371

61. Jerolleman, A.: Storytelling and Narrative Research in Crisis and Disaster Studies. Oxford Research Encyclopedia of Politics (2021). https://doi.org/10.1093/acrefore/9780190228637.013.1615

62. Jung, Y.-R.: Virtual reality simulation for disaster preparedness training in hospitals: integrated review. J. Med. Internet Res. **24**, e30600 (2021). https://doi.org/10.2196/30600

63. Kitagawa, K.: Disaster risk reduction activities as learning. Nat. Hazards **105**, 3099–3118 (2020). https://doi.org/10.1007/s11069-020-04443-5

64. Lovreglio, R., et al.: Prototyping virtual reality serious games for building earthquake preparedness: the Auckland city hospital case study. Adv. Eng. Inform. **38**, 670–682 (2018). https://doi.org/10.1016/J.AEI.2018.08.018

65. Luciana, M., et al.: Adolescent neurocognitive development and impacts of substance use: overview of the adolescent brain cognitive development (ABCD) baseline neurocognition battery. Dev. Cogn. Neurosci. **32**, 67–79 (2018). https://doi.org/10.1016/j.dcn.2018.02.006

66. Mergen, M., Graf, N., Meyerheim, M.: Reviewing the current state of virtual reality integration in medical education - a scoping review. BMC Med. Educ. **24**, 788 (2024). https://doi.org/10.1186/s12909-024-05777-5

67. Nakano, G., Yamori, K.: Disaster risk reduction education that enhances the proactive attitudes of learners: a bridge between knowledge and behavior. Int. J. Disaster Risk Reduct. (2021). https://doi.org/10.1016/j.ijdrr.2021.102620

68. Neto, D.D.R., Barcelos, M.: Stories in the agenda: a Narrative Policy Framework study. Revista de Administração Pública (2020). https://doi.org/10.1590/0034-761220190395x

69. Nurdin, N.: Disaster risk reduction in education and the secondary high school science curriculum in Indonesia (2019). https://consensus.app/papers/disaster-risk-reduction-in-education-and-the-secondary-nurdin/f36ab98a6cb95ede8ad4f66a762bc711/

70. Perry, M.: Multimodal engagement through a transmedia storytelling project for undergraduate students. GEMA Online J. Lang. Stud. **20**, 19–40 (2020). https://doi.org/10.17576/gema-2020-2003-02

71. Pfefferbaum, B., Pfefferbaum, R., Van Horn, R.: Involving children in disaster risk reduction: the importance of participation. Eur. J. Psychotraumatol. **9**, 1425577 (2018). https://doi.org/10.1080/20008198.2018.1425577

72. Pratiwi, P., Dwiningrum, S., Sumunar, D.R.S.: Integrated disaster risk management in the education process in schools. IDRiM J. (2023). https://doi.org/10.5595/001c.91284

73. Rizvic, S., Boskovic, D., Okanovic, V., Sljivo, S., Zukic, M.: Interactive digital storytelling: bringing cultural heritage in a classroom. J. Comput. Educ. **6**(1), 143–166 (2018). https://doi.org/10.1007/s40692-018-0128-7

74. Scolari, C., Establés, M.-J.: Transmedia Literacy in the New Media Ecology An International Map of Teens' Transmedia Skills (2019). https://consensus.app/papers/transmedia-literacy-in-the-new-media-ecology-an-scolari-establ%C3%A9s/8b985e39a24e5bd1a527fe9641bc40b4/

75. Sheehy, K., Vacková, P., Van Manen, S., Turnip, S., Rofiah, K., Twiner, A.: Inclusive disaster risk reduction education for Indonesian children. Int. J. Incl. Educ. **28**, 2529–2545 (2022). https://doi.org/10.1080/13603116.2022.2115156

76. Tombleson, B.: Building a model for transmedia learning. ASCILITE Publications (2023). https://doi.org/10.14742/apubs.2023.686

77. Xin, G., Kongmant, R., Turnbull, N., Thongkum, W.: Evaluating the application of virtual reality technology in disaster prevention education: a case study of Sichuan Province, China. Stud. Health Technol. Inform. **323**, 322–326 (2025). https://doi.org/10.3233/SHTI250104

"It's Often Feeling Nothing…": Evaluating LLMs for Mental Health Literacy Interventions with College Students

José Pedro Vieira Sousa[1,2(✉)] ⓘ, Pedro Campos[1,2,3] ⓘ, and Paulo Bala[1,4] ⓘ

[1] ITI/LARSyS, Lisbon, Portugal
pedro_sousa@outlook.com, paulo.bala@tecnico.ulisboa.pt
[2] University of Madeira, Funchal, Portugal
[3] Wow!Systems, Funchal, Portugal
[4] ARDITI - Regional Agency for the Development of Research,
Technology and Innovation, Funchal, Portugal

Abstract. Mental health is a critical aspect of overall well-being, yet stigma and misinformation remain prevalent, particularly among college students who face unique stressors. The rising incidence of mental health conditions, exacerbated by the COVID-19 pandemic, underscores the need for accessible support systems. Digital mental health interventions, such as narrative-based games, offer a scalable, affordable, and engaging approach to promote mental health education. This study combines visual novels with Large Language Models (LLMs) to create a digital intervention aimed at improving mental health literacy by addressing literacy on depression and misconceptions about depression. We developed a visual novel using LLM-generated narratives and conducted a mixed-methods study with 28 college students, assessing the game's impact at pre-test, post-test, and one-week follow-up, along with narrative transportation. Results showed no significant change in depression literacy, likely due to high baseline scores, but misconceptions of depression significantly decreased and were maintained at follow-up. Participants reported moderate to high narrative transportation. Qualitative findings emphasised emotional engagement, stigma reduction, the perceived value of digital tools, and participants' scepticism regarding AI-generated narrative authenticity.

Keywords: Mental Health · Depressive Disorder · Large Language Models · Interactive Storytelling

1 Introduction

The creation of the World Health Organisation in 1948 marked an important moment with the definition of health extending to recognise mental health as essential to overall well-being [58]. Defined as the ability to handle stress,

M. C. Reyes and F. Nack (Eds.): ICIDS 2025, LNCS 16375, pp. 206–225, 2026.
https://doi.org/10.1007/978-3-032-12405-0_12

develop one's abilities, and contribute to society, mental health has become a growing interdisciplinary research focus [58]. Recent global events, particularly the COVID-19 pandemic, have exposed weaknesses in mental health systems, including surging demand and limited access due to constrained capacity, enduring stigma, and misinformation discouraging help-seeking [51,56,59]. Depressive disorders have risen with an increase of 28% globally in one year, particularly affecting younger populations who faced educational and social disruptions [59].

Despite growing awareness, low mental health literacy remains a significant barrier to recognition of symptoms and help-seeking among youth, particularly college students. Research shows that inadequate literacy increases the risk of moderate to severe depression by about 60% compared to those with adequate understanding [35]. Younger individuals often struggle to identify symptoms, as recognition improves with age, while misconceptions (such as interpreting symptoms as temporary age-related crisis) and fears about stigma and discrimination, and concerns about confidentiality further discourage seeking help [39,48,53]. College students not only go through a stressful period of transition to adulthood and the start of college, they also face unique stressors, including academic pressure, financial concerns, family issues, personal psychological issues, and college life adjustment challenges [5,25,31,37,46], turning into a period during which mental health conditions commonly emerge, with 75% of cases beginning before age 24 [47,48,50]. Meanwhile, scalable on-demand digital interventions such as tele-mental health services, mobile apps, and gamified tools have increased, offering accessible support options and opportunities for strengthening mental health literacy [8,16,59]. However, educational tools remain under-represented despite evidence suggesting that embedding psycho-educational content within interactive formats enhances engagement and retention [4,8,14–16]. Visual novels, interactive stories driven by player choice [12], combined with advances in LLMs and prompt engineering [21,36], offer a promising approach to create immersive and context-sensitive, dynamically generated personalised narratives that reflect users' experiences and foster mental health engagement [7,23,27,33,44]. These trends show the need for targeted interventions during this period. Conversely, strong social support networks have been shown to improve mental health outcomes, with a meta-analysis reporting a moderate positive correlation (effect size 0.337) between social support and student well-being [17].

To explore this, we adopt a research-through-design methodology [61] to develop and evaluate a visual novel prototype powered by an LLM, aimed at improving depression-related mental health literacy in college students, by embedding educational content within an interactive, choice-driven narrative. We developed narrative guidelines and implemented a system where an LLM dynamically generates story segments during runtime (inner monologue, narrative text and player choices), depending on the player's choice. Regarding the assets, specifically the images for the scenes, these were pre-generated. A user study with 28 college students was conducted to evaluate the prototype's effectiveness in enhancing mental health literacy and its narrative engagement.

Evaluation results showed a significant reduction in misconceptions of depression among participants, indicating the intervention's capacity to correct false beliefs. However, no significant changes were observed in overall depression literacy, possibly due to high baseline knowledge levels among participants. Qualitative feedback highlighted that LLM-generated narratives were perceived as sensitive, relatable and realistic, contributing to a sense of reflection and immersion. Participants also expressed interest in the potential for expanding this approach to address other mental health topics beyond depression.

The main contributions of this work are: (1) A generative narrative artefact: A visual novel prototype driven by an LLM, and calibrated via prompt guidelines to depict realistic student experiences with depression; (2) Empirical insights: Findings from user evaluations that show the feasibility, impact, and limitations of using LLM-based interactive storytelling for mental health education, particularly in reducing misconceptions and enhancing engagement.

2   Related Work

2.1   Depression

Depressive disorders are among the most prevalent mental health conditions, affecting approximately 28.9% of the global population with mental disorders in 2019, from the estimated 970 million affected individuals worldwide [59]. The World Health Organization defines them as a *"common mental disorder"*, involving *"a depressed mood or loss of pleasure or interest in activities for long periods of time"* [2], while the American Psychological Association describes them as mood disorders where *"sadness or empty or irritable mood"* predominates [1]. These definitions highlight a key characteristic: persistent mood disturbances across multiple life domains, distinguishing them from typical, short-term mood changes [6].

These patterns intensified following the COVID-19 pandemic, when depressive disorders increased globally by 28% in 2020, with a higher prevalence change in younger people, a possible result of school and social restrictions [59]. These trends inform our narrative design focus: college students face a group of stressors (academic, social, and financial) that make them especially vulnerable and thus a critical target group for depression-focused interventions.

A possible avenue for early intervention in addressing depression is enhancing mental health literacy. Introduced by Jorm et al., mental health literacy refers to the knowledge and attitudes that facilitate recognition, management, and prevention of mental disorders [28,30,35]. Key characteristics of mental health literacy include the ability to recognise specific mental disorders, knowledge of risk factors and causes, self-treatment strategies, available professional services, and how to seek mental health information [30,35]. Importantly, mental health literacy is not limited to cognitive knowledge; it also encompasses behavioural attitudes and willingness to take action for oneself or others, such as seeking help or encouraging help-seeking [29,39]. Low mental health literacy has been identified as a contributing factor to increased depression risk, underscoring its potential as a tool for early intervention and prevention [35].

2.2 Games as Health Literacy

The intersection of mental health and digital technology has enabled scalable, on-demand, and affordable interventions that can lessen pressure on traditional services while promoting mental health literacy for larger populations [8]. These tools are adaptable to various mental health needs and audiences, with a taxonomy of nine intervention types proposed by De Witte et al. [16], including "Preventive Interventions", "Supportive Interventions", "Skills Training", and "Gamified Interventions", all of which are relevant to our study as identified, in previous work by Sousa et al. [16,55].

Game-based interventions have gained attention as an alternative to other methods [8]. Newell et al. [43] reviewed nine studies and found video games had a positive impact on symptom reduction across diverse demographics, while only three studies included follow-up periods, only one beyond three months, highlighting the need for further research into the longevity of effects. Several games have specifically targeted mental health literacy. For example, *"Ching Ching Story"* delivered educational modules like stress identification and anger management through gameplay [38]. *"EscapeCovid"* emphasised emotional resilience and coping strategies during the pandemic, with a co-creative design approach that enhanced learning [34]. *"Stigma Stop"* addressed stigma, challenged misconceptions and encouraged more accepting attitudes [13], while *"Moving Stories"* focused on depression stigma, showing effectiveness in reducing personal stigma but not in improving broader literacy domains like perceived stigma or social distance [54]. These examples illustrate the potential of game-based interventions to target different aspects of mental health literacy (from stigma reduction to emotional regulation) and show how participatory and modular design approaches can improve educational impact.

Social networkbased and mobile interventions also show promise. Ridout and Campbell [49] reviewed nine studies and found users viewed such tools as both safe and useful. Four of these studies directly addressed mental health literacy [38,42,45,57]. In particular, *"Ching Ching Story"* (social network game) was effective in increasing literacy with no significant gender differences [38]. *"MindMax"*, a mobile Health app integrating psycho-educational material with sports and gaming communities, was found to be more appealing than websites but revealed concerns over data and sustained engagement [42]. Further analysis of MindMax's proximal effects [52] (the user's initial experiences) highlighted its potential for early positive impact [45]. Similarly, a pilot study by Watkins et al. [57] noted benefits in learning and relationship-building, though suggestions included better clarity, use of pop culture, and more face-to-face interactions. These studies collectively emphasise the value of personalisation, user-centred design, and community integration in enhancing the effectiveness of digital games and apps for mental health literacy. Further supporting these findings, a scoping review by Ito-Jaeger et al. [26] analysed 17 studies using digital video interventions for mental health literacy for non-clinical youths (ages 1525). The review found that video content, sometimes used alone, and sometimes used in conjunction with other strategies, can help young people recognise symptoms, seek help, and improve general mental health awareness. These results suggest that digital video interventions are promising for engaging younger audiences in mental health education [26].

2.3 LLMs as Game Agents

Conversational agents, systems that use AI to simulate human-like interactions, are increasingly applied in domains like mental health, providing accessible, cost-effective, and scalable alternatives to traditional face-to-face interventions [23,60]. These can help overcome key barriers such as geographic limitations, high treatment costs, long wait times, and concerns over stigma and discrimination. Two comprehensive reviews highlight both the promise and challenges of these systems. He et al. [23] reviewed 32 studies and found that conversational agents were used to test several mental health outcomes, including depressive and anxiety symptoms, stress, general distress, and quality of life or well-being. Notably, personalisation and empathy were important facilitators, with longer-duration interventions associated with greater effect sizes. Jabir et al. [27], also reviewing 32 studies, highlighted the lack of a consistent approach to evaluating these agents. Of the 203 instruments identified, 60.6% measured clinical outcomes, while only 36.9% captured user experience, 1% assessed technical performance, and 1.5% assessed other outcomes. A gap was identified in the validation practices: 52.7% of the studies failed to report instrument validity, and 88.8% of these used tools designed or adapted for the study itself, highlighting the urgent need for standardised, validated evaluation methods. Focusing on voice-based conversational agents, Bérubé et al. [7] reviewed 12 studies exploring their role in the prevention and management of chronic and mental health conditions. While several systems showed good speech recognition performance, one study noted Google Search outperformed AI assistants like Siri and Google Assistant. Technology acceptance was generally positive: 7 of the 12 studies reported acceptance measures, using methods from "System Usability Surveys" to qualitative interviews.

Since the rise of LLMs, such as ChatGPT, there has been an increasing need to understand how to get better responses, considering the prompts used. Guiding these systems toward reliable and goal-directed behaviour requires prompt engineering, the study of prompts to ensure the results are closer to the expected outcomes [41]. In educational games, Lee et al. [36] implemented a debate game using ChatGPT and prompt engineering to allow different difficulties, maintain narrative coherence, and enable an evaluation system. The authors identified key requirements such as "Cognition of roles and rules", "Implementation of different difficulties", "Recognise the order of debate", and "Debate competency evaluation", highlighting the importance of carefully structured prompts to obtain the desired behaviour. LLMs also display social tendencies that may enhance character design. Brookins and DeBacker [10] showed that LLMs show fairness and cooperation biases in social dilemma games like the Prisoner's Dilemma. These biases may be leveraged in game narratives where moral reasoning or empathetic responses are essential to player engagement [10].

3   Design and Implementation

We implemented a visual novel game prototype aimed at promoting depression-related mental health literacy in college students. This demographic faces unique transitional stressors and an elevated risk of depression, making them a critical target for intervention. The game uses narrative storytelling to facilitate immersive learning [3,11], while interactive choices encourage players to reflect on characters' experiences and player decisions [22].

The prototype was developed in Dart/Flutter and designed for experimental testing (see Fig. 1).

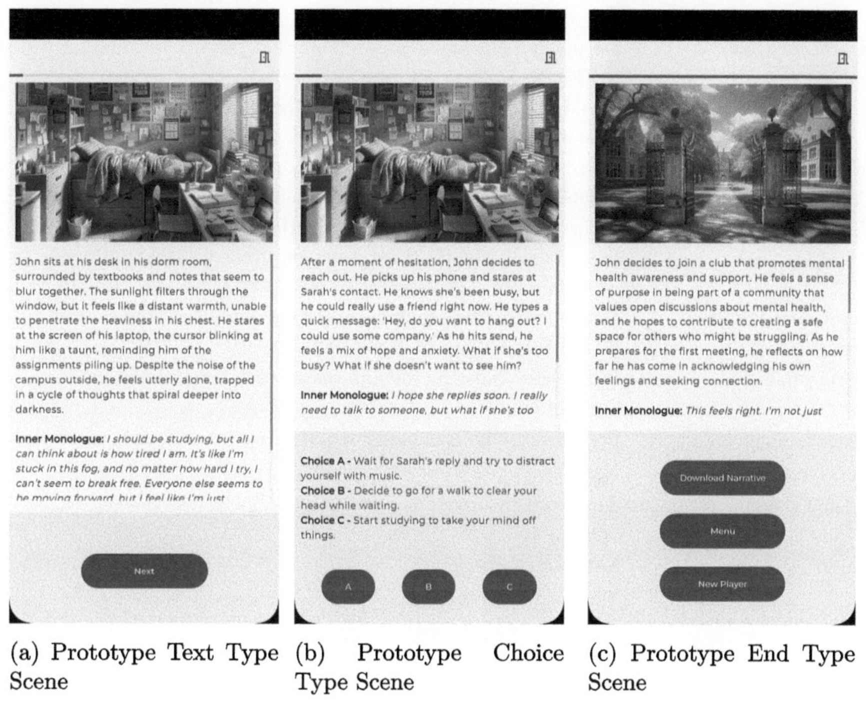

(a) Prototype Text Type Scene   (b) Prototype Choice Type Scene   (c) Prototype End Type Scene

Fig. 1. Example Prototype Scene Screens

We built upon the low-fidelity prototype by Sousa et al. [55], adapting their structure, prompt design, and insights for a modular system that uses prompt and schema-based LLM interactions (for an example of the prompts used, see Table 1). To reduce the differences between the generated narratives, we adjusted the hyper-parameters that control randomness (e.g., temperature, top P, frequency/presence penalties), we did an extensive prompt iteration before the study while also extensively testing the prototype before the playtests, and we added prompt conditions to guide/limit the generated narratives (e.g., "Do not include suicide in any form", characters, places, see Table 1).

Table 1. System Prompt Guidelines for Interactive Narrative

Category	Description
Types of Scenes	- **Synopsis Scene**: Contains the synopsis and character introductions.
	- **Text Scenes**: Continue the story without player choices.
	- **Choice Scenes**: Provide three player choices that lead to distinct narrative paths (e.g., good, neutral, bad).
	- **End Scene**: Final scene summarizing the story, evaluating player decisions, and offering advice on improving mental health outcomes.
Branching Narrative	Create branching paths based on player choices in the Choice Scenes.
Narrative Flow	Do not force a linear progression. Let players meaningfully steer the story.
Avoid Cycles	Avoid trapping the character in loops or repeated settings unless caused by explicit player choice.
Inner Monologue	Each scene should include the main character's thoughts to reflect emotional state before transitioning or making a choice.
Natural Interactions	Include at least 2 organic interactions from other characters (e.g., unsolicited SMS or in-person dialogue) that influence the main character positively or negatively.
Emotional Realism	Depict both positive and negative experiences, representing the fluctuating nature of mental health.
Scene Images	Each scene must include an image of the main character's environment.
Scene Numbering	Scenes must be numbered sequentially for clear reference.
Narrative Length	Narrative ends at Scene 20, which is the only End Scene.
Scene Counts	The narrative must include exactly: 7 Choice Scenes, 12 Text Scenes, and 1 End Scene.
Narrative Setting	**Setting:** College
	Theme: Depression
	Theme Description: Address depression symptoms and reduce stigma within a realistic college context.
Characters	- Main Character (MC)
	- MC's Dad
	- MC's Mom
	- MC's Friends (1, 2, 3)
	- College Teacher
	- College Therapist
Topics to Avoid	Do not include suicide in any form.
Command Rules	- Use ``Start'' only after the synopsis to begin the narrative.
	- Use ``Next'' only after a Text Scene to move forward.
	- Use ``Choice Y'' (Y = selected option) only after a Choice Scene to advance accordingly.

Each scene in the visual novel consists of a pre-generated scene image, followed by the "Narrative Text", and an "Inner Monologue", generated by the LLM (OpenAI's *GPT-4o-mini*), followed by the "Player Choices". These choices can be as simple as a command to proceed to the next scene (when in a "Text Scene") or three possible actions (in a "Choice Scene") that influence the tone and direction of subsequent scenes, enabling dynamic branching while maintaining narrative coherence. Scene images were pre-generated using DALL-E[1] and integrated into the game as static images; these were used as placeholders, due to a lack of human resources, as we consider the images to be complementary to the narrative, and not central to the outcomes analysed in this study. During gameplay, the LLM dynamically selects appropriate images based on scene context (see Fig. 2).

(a) Counsellor Room   (b) Park   (c) Dorm Room

Fig. 2. Image asset examples (generated by DALL-E)

4   Study

This section presents the methodology, including the study design, measures, protocol, analysis procedures, and sample characteristics.

We conducted an empirical mixed-methods study to evaluate whether the visual novel prototype impacted mental health literacy in college students. The study was conducted within the academic community of the first author's institution. Participants were selected through convenience sampling and had to meet the following criteria: (1) be college students aged 18 or older, (2) have English reading proficiency, and (3) be capable of interacting with a mobile game. Each participant was assigned a unique code (e.g., P11, P02). Primary outcomes included depression literacy and misconceptions of depression, alongside qualitative insights from interviews.

We used both quantitative and qualitative measures. Quantitative data included: Depression literacy and misconceptions of depression, assessed using

---

[1] https://openai.com/index/dall-e-2/.

the English version of the "Depression Literacy and Misconceptions Scale (Dep-Ster Scale)" by Kulwicka and Gasiorowska [32], at pre-test, post-test, and one-week follow-up. Narrative transportation, measured at post-test using the "Narrative Transportation Scale" by Green and Brock [20]. Socio-demographic data (age, gender, academic level) were collected at pre-test. Qualitative data came from semi-structured interviews at post-test, designed to explore: Previous experience with similar applications; Narrative impact on knowledge (literacy and misconceptions), stigma, and emotional response; and Perceptions of using LLMs for mental health literacy interventions.

The study was reviewed and approved by the University's Data Protection Officer and Ethics Committee, considering the sensitivity of the topic. The study followed these steps:

1. Participants were introduced to the study and prototype, gave informed consent, and received two documents: mental health support contacts and a follow-up questionnaire link.
2. Assigned participant ID (e.g., 'PXX').
3. Completed pre-test questionnaires (sociodemographics and DepSter Scale), in person or online.
4. Tested the prototype (in person via computer, or remotely via screen-sharing).
5. Completed the post-test questionnaire ("Narrative Transportation Scale" and DepSter Scale), in person or online.
6. Participated in a recorded, voice-distorted semi-structured interview (after consent).
7. At the one-week follow-up, consenting participants were emailed a follow-up questionnaire link (also provided at the start).

We analysed both quantitative and qualitative data. Qualitative analysis followed Braun and Clarke's thematic analysis method [9], conducted in Taguette[2]. One researcher coded the transcripts inductively; the results were then extracted, reviewed, and refined by the first and last authors. Quantitative analysis used repeated measures for dependent samples across three time points (pre-test, post-test, and one-week follow-up). Due to non-normal data distributions and a small sample size, we applied the Friedman test, using the F-test adjustment to address the chi-square limitations in small samples, particularly near the tails [40].

The sample consisted of 28 college students, all non-native English speakers, recruited through convenience sampling. Sample size was estimated using G*Power [18], based on a one-tail a priori, considering the comparison of pre-test and post-test data and an effect size of 0.65. Participants ranged in age from 22 to 41 years ($M = 27.29$, $SD = 5.01$); 11 identified as male, 16 as female, and 1 as other.

---

[2] https://app.taguette.org/.

5   Results

In this Section, we present the study's findings, divided into two: quantitative and qualitative analyses.

5.1   Quantitative Data

The following Sections present the Descriptive Statistics (Sect. 5.1), Normality Tests (Sect. 5.1), Inferential Statistics (Sect. 5.1), and Exploratory Analyses/Correlations (Sect. 5.1).

Descriptive Statistics. Descriptive statistics for the depression literacy, misconceptions of depression, and narrative transportation scores collected at the different timepoints are presented in Table 2.

Scores remained stable on all timepoints for depression literacy, while misconceptions of depression decreased slightly after the intervention. Narrative transportation scores suggest a moderately high engagement with the prototype.

Normality Tests. Normality of the data was assessed using the Shapiro-Wilk test, as shown in Table 3.

Almost all variables followed a normal distribution, except for the Follow-up depression literacy scores ($p = 0.020$). Given some violations of normality and the small sample size, non-parametric tests were employed in the inferential analysis.

Inferential Statistics. A Friedman test showed no statistically significant differences in depression literacy scores across time points ($F = 0.078$, $p = 0.920$). However, there was a statistically significant difference in misconceptions of

Table 2. Descriptive statistics for depression literacy, misconceptions of depression, and narrative transportation scores collected at different timepoints

Score Type	Timepoint	M	SD	Min	Q1	Median	Q3	Max
Depression Literacy [1]	Pre-test	4.16	0.40	3.50	3.96	4.17	4.38	5.00
	Pos-test	4.18	0.42	3.50	3.83	4.17	4.38	5.00
	Follow-up	4.14	0.58	2.50	3.67	4.08	4.67	4.83
Misconceptions of Depression [2]	Pre-test	1.81	0.40	1.25	1.50	1.75	2.13	2.63
	Pos-test	1.63	0.40	1.00	1.38	1.63	1.78	2.38
	Follow-up	1.66	0.41	1.00	1.34	1.69	1.91	2.63
Narrative Transportation [3]	Pos-test	56.68	7.91	38.00	51.75	57.50	62.25	70.00

[1] Lower Scores imply lower literacy, while higher scores imply more.

[2] Lower Scores imply lower misconceptions, while higher scores imply more.

[3] Possible score range from 12 to 84

Table 3. Shapiro-Wilk test results for normality of depression literacy, misconceptions of depression, and narrative transportation scores across timepoints

Score Type	Timepoint	W	p-value	Normal
Depression Literacy	Pre-test	0.961	0.376	Yes
	Post-test	0.956	0.272	Yes
	Follow-up	0.911	0.020	No
Misconceptions of Depression	Pre-test	0.941	0.115	Yes
	Post-test	0.955	0.263	Yes
	Follow-up	0.969	0.566	Yes
Narrative Transportation	Post-test	0.976	0.755	Yes

depression ($F = 6.155$, $p = 0.004$). Post hoc analysis with Wilcoxon signed-rank test was conducted with a Holm-Bonferroni correction applied, resulting in a significance level set at $p < 0.017$. Median (IQR) misconceptions of depression levels were $1.750(1.500\,to\,2.125)$, $1.625(1.375\,to\,1.781)$ and $1.688(1.344\,to\,1.906)$, respectively. There were no significant differences between the pre-test and 1-week follow-up ($W = 80.5$, $p = 0.047$) or between the post-test and 1-week follow-up ($W = 103.5$, $p = 0.684$). However, there was a statistically significant reduction in misconceptions of depression in the pre-test to post-test ($W = 37.0$, $p = 0.002$).

Exploratory Analyses or Correlations. Figure 3 presents Spearman correlations for the demographic variables and measured outcomes.

The exploratory correlation analysis revealed several patterns. Depression literacy scores at different timepoints were strongly positively correlated (e.g., pre-test and post-test: $r = 0.8108$), while misconceptions of depression were negatively correlated with depression literacy at all timepoints (e.g., post-test misconceptions and literacy: $r = -0.5986$). Narrative transportation showed a weak negative correlation with post-test misconceptions ($r = -0.3377$), suggesting greater immersion may be associated with fewer misconceptions. Gender showed a moderate negative correlation with 1-week follow-up misconception scores ($r = -0.3949$), which may justify further exploration.

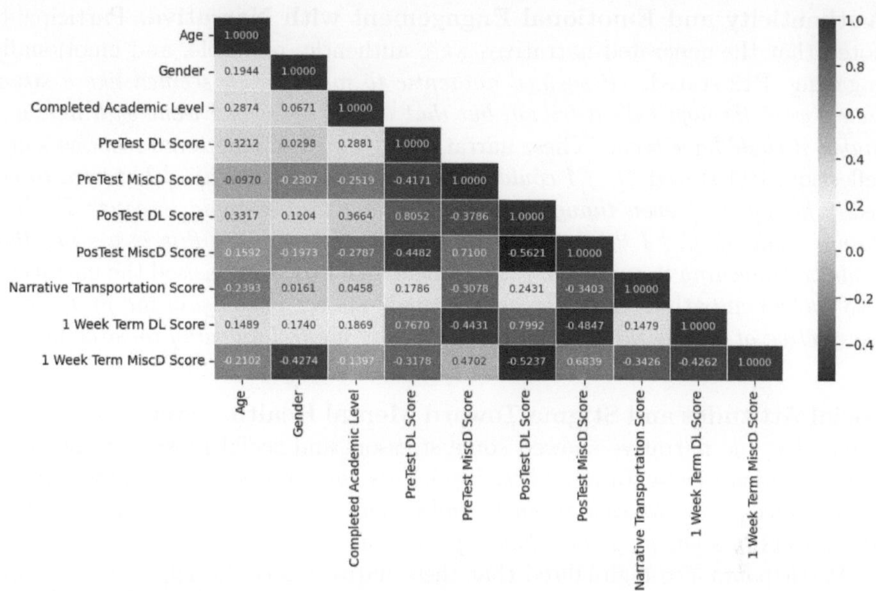

Fig. 3. Correlations between Scores, Age, Gender, and Completed Academic Level

5.2   Qualitative Data

Through the thematic analysis of interview transcripts, we identified 4 high-level themes.

Digital Tools for Mental Health Education and Their Potential. Participants indicated that they didn't have experience with digital tools to promote mental health literacy. However, many would be interested in trying if they felt it was relevant or personally needed (P07 stated *"If I knew any, like, more relevant, I think so"*), or if they needed it (P06 stated *"If I need yes[...]"*).

Several participants also reported how the visual novel's narrative had an impact on their mental health literacy and knowledge, while also being beneficial in real-world settings. P14 emphasised its potential for use by professionals *"Yes, they could [be used by Mental Health professionals], and that is very interesting. Why? Because it is completely different for us to give this narrative to someone who is not from the mental health field and then not know what answer to give, right? Than to give it to a professional in this field who is there and can provide support."* P02 reflected on its personal impact, describing it as a way to practice emotional decision-making and testing the consequences of their actions: *"Because it is a way for you to test the cause and effect of your actions in a virtual environment. [...] And the fact that you test it in a virtual environment and see that it really worked can also lead you, in real life, to make the same decisions and see that it's not so bad."*).

Authenticity and Emotional Engagement with Narrative. Participants noted that the generated narratives were authentic, relatable, and emotionally engaging. P12 stated, *"It seemed authentic to me. It even seemed like a situation I went through with a friend, but that wasn't the way I went with her, and maybe it could have been."* These narratives also evoked emotional responses and reflection. P11 stated *"[...] I could understand that situation[...] I started to get really happy. [...] even though I think like,"but that's stupid, because I'm not doing anything, [...] I think that unconsciously I know that this is a story that could be happening to someone. [...]"* Others, like P01, emphasised the narratives also evoked empathy: *"Yeah, because it made me see once again the first person perspective of having those feelings, so it made me feel empathy towards them."*

Social Attitudes and Stigma Toward Mental Health. Several participants noted that the narrative showed some stressors and social pressures unique to college students. P14 stated, *"Yes, it presents some pressures that other classes do not have, as is the case when he talks about exams [...] it is clear that they are university students given what is presented [...]"*

Participants also highlighted that these narratives could help reduce stigma around mental health. P11 stated common misconceptions: *"[...] Because there is still that idea that 'you are putting on a show', 'you are making a movie', 'it's all in your head', 'you are exaggerating' [...]. And I think it is the opposite. I think that depression affects everyone, yes, it mainly affects those who others see as being too strong."*. However, participants also mention that personal openness plays a significant role. As P11 stated, *"Yes, if they wanted to learn about depression, but didn't have stigma about depression. [...] Because this helps those who really want to learn."*. Also, P26 stated scepticism about the impact: *"But I don't know like if people I know that have this kind of wrong ideas about mental health or about depression, could actually change their minds. Because I think even when they have somebody close and they see them suffering, this doesn't really mean they change much. Because I think it's more like on your own attitude towards change that you change than actually like through the narrative itself. So, yeah, I'm unaware."*.

Trust and Ethical Considerations in AI-Generated Narratives. While participants generally acknowledged that the narratives were coherent and engaging, concerns were raised about the trustworthiness and ethical implications of AI-generated content. P08 questioned whether AI could truly convey emotional nuance: *"[Artificial Intelligence] It is capable of portraying these moments like this, but I don't know if artificial intelligence has the sensitivity that we also have. [...] To talk about some topics, like depression. It has no idea about these things, like it has the literature, but it doesn't have the sensitivity."*.

P26 also stated concerns about emotional authenticity and depth: *"[...] I'm not sure, if I feel as comfortable, like talking to a robot about human psychology, even if like, of course this is based in a great corpus of information, like a great dataset of mental health care and etc., etc. I think I'm more oriented towards crafted narratives, and I believe that crafted narratives can have a wider potential of actually, kind of creating a more complex way of understanding, and maybe more engaging ways. [...] It was very basic, kind of like there is these kind of type subjects, and there is this very kind of type situation, and then you can use this type situation to go to the sub subjects, so it was like very straightforward, I felt.".* These underscore a need for greater transparency and human oversight in systems addressing sensitive psychological issues.

6   Discussion

This study explored the impact of a digital narrative-based intervention on depression literacy, misconceptions of depression, and narrative transportation on college students. The evaluation of the visual novel prototype revealed significant effects on the participants' misconceptions of depression.

Statistical analysis using non-parametric tests showed that while depression literacy scores remained high from the pre-test to the follow-up, indicating a high baseline knowledge and suggesting a potential ceiling effect, the intervention significantly reduced misconceptions of depression immediately post-intervention, with these improvements generally maintained at follow-up. Correlation patterns supported this result: higher literacy scores were negatively associated with misconceptions, reinforcing the relationship between accurate mental health knowledge and reduced stigma.

Narrative transportation, measured only at post-test, showed moderate to high engagement levels ($M = 56.68$, $SD = 7.91$), and was moderately negatively correlated with misconceptions of depression scores, indicating that the digital narrative was successful in engaging and immersing users, which is a key factor in the effectiveness of narrative interventions [20], while also suggesting that greater narrative engagement may help reduce misconceptions. Narrative transportation also showed a small positive correlation with depression literacy scores at post-test and follow-up, indicating that participants who felt more immersed in the narrative tended to retain higher levels of domain knowledge. This aligns with broader evidence that interactive and immersive storytelling can support behaviour change and learning, especially when grounded in relatable scenarios [19,20,54].

The qualitative results support this view. Participants described the experience as emotionally engaging, reflective, and realistic. Several reported that the narrative prompted them to consider the real-world consequences of decisions, empathise with characters, and reflect on their attitudes toward mental health. This emotional connection and understanding are critical factors in effective health communication and are often difficult to achieve in traditional, didactic educational approaches [20,24]. Additionally, all the generated narratives were collected and analysed to verify the consistency between the generated narratives, showing that no unexpected situation arose that deviated from the original prompt. Regarding ethical considerations and risks of using LLMs for mental health, we relied on closed-source commercial LLMs; thus, we do not have full knowledge of the model architectures, weights or the training data used. To mitigate potential risks, we created warning modals that inform users about the role of the LLMs in this study. Additionally, considering the commercial nature, these models often have guardrails against harmful or unintended behaviour, which can be beneficial in applications for mental health as an extra layer of security, especially for non-creative experts.

One of the main findings of this study was the participants' ambivalence about the ability of AI-generated narratives to fully capture the emotional depth of human experience, particularly regarding sensitive topics like depression. This concern is valid, especially in sensitive domains like mental health.

This work shows that LLMs can be used as creative tools, allowing professionals without programming or storytelling expertise (e.g. mental health professionals, educators) to create immersive gamified narrative interventions for mental health literacy. They reduce the technical knowledge needed to create branching narratives. However, while they can be used to create emotionally immersive scenes, there are limitations regarding the language and the emotional depth inherent to humans. Findings show that digital interventions, through interactive narratives, can reduce misconceptions of depression, even if the knowledge levels of depression literacy are high at baseline. Interactive narratives offer immersion, agency, and emotional engagement through the choices (or interactions) presented to players, providing an opportunity for reflection on decision-making and consequences, and allowing players to simulate complex real-life situations in a controlled environment.

7   Limitations and Future Work

Several limitations should be noted. First, the sample size was relatively small, which may restrict the generalizability of the findings. Moreover, the study was conducted in a country where English is not the primary language, and the participants were non-native English speakers interacting with an English prototype, which may have influenced their understanding and responses. Additionally, the qualitative sample may not fully represent the diversity of user experiences, as some of the open-ended questions left participants unsure of how to respond. The high depression literacy scores at baseline indicate a potential ceiling effect. Narrative transportation was only assessed at the post-test, and the absence of a delayed or replicated intervention may have restricted long-term effects. Other limitations included the inability of AI to represent human emotions, the capacity to earn user trust, especially when they are aware that the content is generated by AI, and difficulties to maintain improvements on the outcomes measured over time.

Future research should explore ways to sustain reductions in misconceptions, investigate the impact of narrative complexity and authenticity, and examine the integration of human and AI-authored content. Studies with larger and more diverse samples should be conducted to assess the long-term effectiveness and broader uses of digital narrative interventions in Mental Health education.

8   Conclusion

LLMs may not create ideal interactive narratives; nevertheless, they can be powerful tools for creating personalised, engaging, and scalable mental health interventions. When applied safely, they can help non-experts create emotionally immersive educational tools, giving way for more inclusive, accessible, and impactful mental health literacy initiatives.

Acknowledgments. This research was funded by the Portuguese Recovery and Resilience Program (PRR), IAPMEI/ANI/FCT under Agenda no.26, C645022399-00000057 (eGamesLab). The authors would also like to acknowledge the Portuguese Foundation for Science and Technology, for projects 10.54499/LA/P/0083/2020; 10.54499/UIDP/50009/2020 & 10.54499/UIDB/50009/2020. The last author would also like to acknowledge the contract program signed between the Autonomous Region of Madeira and ARDITI.

Disclosure of Interests. The authors have no competing interests to declare that are relevant to the content of this article.

References

1. American Psychological Association. https://dictionary.apa.org/depressive-disorder. Accessed 20 Nov 2023
2. Depressive disorder (depression). https://www.who.int/news-room/fact-sheets/detail/depression. Accessed 18 Nov 2023
3. Alexiou, A., Schippers, M.C., Oshri, I., Angelopoulos, S.: Narrative and aesthetics as antecedents of perceived learning in serious games. Inf. Technol. People **35**(8), 142–161 (2022). https://doi.org/10.1108/ITP-08-2019-0435, https://www.emerald.com/insight/content/doi/10.1108/ITP-08-2019-0435/full/html
4. Alqahtani, F., Orji, R.: Insights from user reviews to improve mental health apps. Health Inform. J. **26**(3), 2042–2066 (2020). https://doi.org/10.1177/1460458219896492, http://journals.sagepub.com/doi/10.1177/1460458219896492
5. Anderson, N.B., et al.: Stress in America: the impact of discrimination (2016)
6. Association, A.P., Association, A.P. (eds.): Diagnostic and Statistical Manual of Mental Disorders: DSM-5, 5th edn. American Psychiatric Association, Washington, DC (2013)
7. Bérubé, C., et al.: Voice-based conversational agents for the prevention and management of chronic and mental health conditions: systematic literature review. J. Med. Internet Res. **23**(3), e25933 (2021). https://doi.org/10.2196/25933
8. Birk, M.V., Wadley, G., Abeele, V.V., Mandryk, R., Torous, J.: Video games for mental health. Interactions **26**(4), 32–36 (2019). https://doi.org/10.1145/3328483
9. Braun, V., Clarke, V.: Using thematic analysis in psychology. Qual. Res. Psychol. **3**(2), 77–101 (2006). https://doi.org/10.1191/1478088706qp063oa, http://www.tandfonline.com/doi/abs/10.1191/1478088706qp063oa
10. Brookins, P., DeBacker, J.M.: Playing games with GPT: what can we learn about a large language model from canonical strategic games? Available at SSRN 4493398 (2023). https://doi.org/10.2139/ssrn.4493398, https://www.ssrn.com/abstract=4493398

11. Brunetti, R., Ferrante, S., Avella, A.M., Indraccolo, A., Del Gatto, C.: Turning stories into learning journeys: the principles and methods of immersive education. Front. Psychol. **15**, 1471459 (2024). https://doi.org/10.3389/fpsyg.2024.1471459, https://www.frontiersin.org/articles/10.3389/fpsyg.2024.1471459/full
12. Camingue, J., Carstensdottir, E., Melcer, E.F.: What is a visual novel? Proc. ACM Hum. Comput. Interact. **5**(CHI PLAY), 1–18 (2021). https://doi.org/10.1145/3474712
13. Cangas, A.J., et al.: Analysis of the Usefulness of a serious game to raise awareness about mental health problems in a sample of high school and university students: relationship with familiarity and time spent playing video games. J. Clin. Med. **8**(10), 1504 (2019). https://doi.org/10.3390/jcm8101504, https://www.mdpi.com/2077-0383/8/10/1504
14. Cocks, J.: Synthesising Behaviour Change Theory with Game Design Practice. (Oct 2017)
15. Coyle, D., O' Reilly, G., van der Meulen, H., Tunney, C., Cooney, P., Jackman, C.: Pesky gNATs: using games to support mental health interventions for adolescents (2017)
16. De Witte, N.A.J., Joris, S., Van Assche, E., Van Daele, T.: Technological and digital interventions for mental health and wellbeing: an overview of systematic reviews. Front. Digit. Health **3**, 754337 (2021). https://doi.org/10.3389/fdgth.2021.754337, https://www.frontiersin.org/articles/10.3389/fdgth.2021.754337/full
17. Fasihi Harandi, T., Mohammad Taghinasab, M., Dehghan Nayeri, T.: The correlation of social support with mental health: a meta-analysis. Electron. Physician **9**(9), 5212–5222 (2017). https://doi.org/10.19082/5212, http://www.ephysician.ir/index.php/browse-issues/2017/9/802-5212
18. Faul, F., Erdfelder, E., Lang, A.G., Buchner, A.: G*Power 3: a flexible statistical power analysis program for the social, behavioral, and biomedical sciences. Behav. Res. Methods **39**(2), 175–191 (2007). https://doi.org/10.3758/BF03193146, http://link.springer.com/10.3758/BF03193146
19. Fong, T.H.C., Mak, W.W.S.: The effects of internet-based storytelling programs (amazing adventure against stigma) in reducing mental illness stigma with mediation by interactivity and stigma content: randomized controlled trial. J. Med. Internet Res. **24**(8), e37973 (2022). https://doi.org/10.2196/37973, https://www.jmir.org/2022/8/e37973
20. Green, M.C., Brock, T.C.: The role of transportation in the persuasiveness of public narratives. J. Pers. Soc. Psychol. **79**(5), 701–721 (2000). https://doi.org/10.1037/0022-3514.79.5.701
21. Hadi, M.U., et al.: Large language models: a comprehensive survey of its applications, challenges, limitations, and future prospects (2023). https://doi.org/10.36227/techrxiv.23589741.v4
22. Hand, S., Varan, D.: Interactive narratives: exploring the links between empathy, interactivity and structure. In: Tscheligi, M., Obrist, M., Lugmayr, A. (eds.) Changing Television Environments, vol. 5066, pp. 11–19. Springer, Berlin, Heidelberg (2008). https://doi.org/10.1007/978-3-540-69478-6_2
23. He, Y., et al.: Conversational agent interventions for mental health problems: systematic review and meta-analysis of randomized controlled trials. J. Med. Internet Res. **25**, e43862 (2023). https://doi.org/10.2196/43862
24. Hinyard, L.J., Kreuter, M.W.: Using narrative communication as a tool for health behavior change: a conceptual, theoretical, and empirical overview. Health Educ. Behav. **34**(5), 777–792 (2007). https://doi.org/10.1177/1090198106291963, https://journals.sagepub.com/doi/10.1177/1090198106291963

25. Hunt, J., Eisenberg, D.: Mental health problems and help-seeking behavior among college students. J. Adolesc. Health **46**(1), 3–10 (2010). https://doi.org/10.1016/j.jadohealth.2009.08.008, https://linkinghub.elsevier.com/retrieve/pii/S1054139X09003401

26. Ito-Jaeger, S., et al.: Digital video interventions and mental health literacy among young people: a scoping review. J. Ment. Health **31**(6), 873–883 (2022). https://doi.org/10.1080/09638237.2021.1922642

27. Jabir, A.I., Martinengo, L., Lin, X., Torous, J., Subramaniam, M., Tudor Car, L.: Evaluating conversational agents for mental health: scoping review of outcomes and outcome measurement instruments. J. Med. Internet Res. **25**, e44548 (2023). https://doi.org/10.2196/44548, https://www.jmir.org/2023/1/e44548

28. Jorm, A.F.: Mental health literacy. Public knowledge and beliefs about mental disorders. Br. J. Psychiatry J. Mental Sci. **177**, 396–401 (2000). https://doi.org/10.1192/bjp.177.5.396

29. Jorm, A.: We need to move from 'mental health literacy' to 'mental health action'. Mental Health Prev. **18**, 200179 (2020). https://doi.org/10.1016/j.mhp.2020.200179, https://www.sciencedirect.com/science/article/pii/S2212657020300222

30. Jorm, A.F., Korten, A.E., Jacomb, P.A., Christensen, H., Rodgers, B., Pollitt, P.: "Mental health literacy": a survey of the public's ability to recognise mental disorders and their beliefs about the effectiveness of treatment. Med. J. Aust. **166**(4), 182–186 (1997). https://doi.org/10.5694/j.1326-5377.1997.tb140071.x

31. Kadison, R.V., DiGeronimo, T.F.: College of the Overwhelmed: the Campus Mental Health Crisis and What to do About it. Jossey-Bass, a Wiley imprint, San Francisco, Calif (2004)

32. Kulwicka, K., Gasiorowska, A.: Depression literacy and misconceptions scale (DepSter): a new two-factorial tool for measuring beliefs about depression. BMC Psychiatry **23**(1), 300 (2023). https://doi.org/10.1186/s12888-023-04796-8, https://bmcpsychiatry.biomedcentral.com/articles/10.1186/s12888-023-04796-8

33. Kumaran, V., Rowe, J., Mott, B., Lester, J.: SceneCraft: automating interactive narrative scene generation in digital games with large language models. In: Proceedings of the AAAI Conference on Artificial Intelligence and Interactive Digital Entertainment, vol. 19, no. 1, pp. 86–96 (2023). https://doi.org/10.1609/aiide.v19i1.27504, https://ojs.aaai.org/index.php/AIIDE/article/view/27504

34. Labrosse, D., Vié, C., Hajjam, H., Tisseron, C., Thellier, D., Montagni, I.: An escape game on university students' mental health during the covid-19 pandemic: cocreation study. JMIR Serious Games **12**(1), e48545 (2024). https://doi.org/10.2196/48545, https://games.jmir.org/2024/1/e48545

35. Lam, L.T.: Mental health literacy and mental health status in adolescents: a population-based survey. Child Adolesc. Psychiatry Ment. Health **8**(1), 26 (2014). https://doi.org/10.1186/1753-2000-8-26, http://capmh.biomedcentral.com/articles/10.1186/1753-2000-8-26

36. Lee, E.Y., Il, N.G.D., An, G.H., Lee, S., Lim, K.: ChatGPT-based debate game application utilizing prompt engineering. In: Proceedings of the International Conference on Research in Adaptive and Convergent Systems, pp. 1–6. ACM, Gdansk Poland (2023). https://doi.org/10.1145/3599957.3606244

37. Lee, J.H., et al.: Initial validation of the planned happenstance career inventory-English version. Career Dev. Q. **65**(4), 366–378 (2017). https://doi.org/10.1002/cdq.12114, https://onlinelibrary.wiley.com/doi/10.1002/cdq.12114

38. Li, T.M., Chau, M., Wong, P.W., Lai, E.S., Yip, P.S.: Evaluation of a web-based social network electronic game in enhancing mental health literacy for young peo-

ple. J. Med. Internet Res. **15**(5), e80 (2013). https://doi.org/10.2196/jmir.2316, https://www.jmir.org/2013/5/e80

39. Loureiro, L.M., Jorm, A.F., Mendes, A.C., Santos, J.C., Ferreira, R.O., Pedreiro, A.T.: Mental health literacy about depression: a survey of Portuguese youth. BMC Psychiatry **13**(1), 129 (2013). https://doi.org/10.1186/1471-244X-13-129, http://bmcpsychiatry.biomedcentral.com/articles/10.1186/1471-244X-13-129

40. Marozzi, M.: Testing for concordance between several criteria. J. Stat. Comput. Simul. **84**(9), 1843–1850 (2014). https://doi.org/10.1080/00949655.2013.766189

41. Meskó, B.: Prompt engineering as an important emerging skill for medical professionals: tutorial. J. Med. Internet Res. **25**, e50638 (2023). https://doi.org/10.2196/50638

42. Mitchell, J., et al.: MindMax: using videogames and sport to engage young men and improve wellbeing. In: Proceedings of the 2nd Symposium Computing and Mental Health, 2017, pp. 1–5. MIT Media Laboratory (2017)

43. Newell, J., Gotsis, M., Lelon, C., Davison, G.: Games for Psychotherapeutic Change: A Systematic Review of the Positive, Long-Term Impact of Video Game Play on Anxiety and Depression (2017)

44. Nisi, V., James, S., Bala, P., Del Bue, A., Nunes, N.: Inclusive digital storytelling: artificial intelligence and augmented reality to re-centre stories from the margins, pp. 117–137 (2023). https://doi.org/10.1007/978-3-031-47655-6_8

45. Peever, N., Vella, K., Johnson, D., Ploderer, B., Klarkowski, M., Mitchell, J.: Understanding initial experiences with Mindmax, an mHealth app that draws on shared interests in sports and video games. In: Proceedings of the 29th Australian Conference on Computer-Human Interaction, pp. 438–442. ACM, Brisbane Queensland Australia (2017). https://doi.org/10.1145/3152771.3156152,

46. Ratanasiripong, P., Sverduk, K., Hayashino, D., Prince, J.: Setting up the next generation biofeedback program for stress and anxiety management for college students: a simple and cost-effective approach. Coll. Stud. J. **44**, 97–100 (2010)

47. Reavley, N., Jorm, A.F.: Prevention and early intervention to improve mental health in higher education students: a review. Early Interv. Psychiatry **4**(2), 132–142 (2010). https://doi.org/10.1111/j.1751-7893.2010.00167.x, https://onlinelibrary.wiley.com/doi/10.1111/j.1751-7893.2010.00167.x

48. Reavley, N.J., McCann, T.V., Jorm, A.F.: Mental health literacy in higher education students. Early Interv. Psychiatry **6**(1), 45–52 (2012). https://doi.org/10.1111/j.1751-7893.2011.00314.x, https://onlinelibrary.wiley.com/doi/10.1111/j.1751-7893.2011.00314.x

49. Ridout, B., Campbell, A.: The use of social networking sites in mental health interventions for young people: systematic review. J. Med. Internet Res. **20**(12), e12244 (2018). https://doi.org/10.2196/12244

50. Santomauro, D.F., et al.: Global prevalence and burden of depressive and anxiety disorders in 204 countries and territories in 2020 due to the COVID-19 pandemic. The Lancet **398**(10312), 1700–1712 (2021). https://doi.org/10.1016/S0140-6736(21)02143-7, https://linkinghub.elsevier.com/retrieve/pii/S0140673621021437

51. SeyedAlinaghi, S., et al.: Social stigma during COVID-19: a systematic review. SAGE Open Med. **11**, 20503121231208273 (2023). https://doi.org/10.1177/20503121231208273

52. Smith, W., Wadley, G., Webber, S., Ploderer, B., Lederman, R.: Unbounding the interaction design problem: the contribution of HCI in three interventions for wellbeing. In: Proceedings of the 26th Australian Computer-Human Interaction Conference on Designing Futures: the Future of Design, pp. 392–395 (2014)

53. Townsend, L., et al.: The association of school climate, depression literacy, and mental health stigma among high school students. J. Sch. Health **87**(8), 567–574 (2017). https://doi.org/10.1111/josh.12527, https://onlinelibrary.wiley.com/doi/10.1111/josh.12527

54. Tuijnman, A., Kleinjan, M., Olthof, M., Hoogendoorn, E., Granic, I., Engels, R.C.: A game-based school program for mental health literacy and stigma on depression (moving stories): cluster randomized controlled trial. JMIR Mental Health **9**(8), e26615 (2022). https://doi.org/10.2196/26615, https://mental.jmir.org/2022/8/e26615

55. Vieira Sousa, J.P., Campos, P., Bala, P.: College tales: pilot study on large language models generated narratives for mental health literacy. In: Proceedings of the 27th International Academic Mindtrek Conference, pp. 270–275. ACM, Tampere Finland (2024). https://doi.org/10.1145/3681716.3689447

56. Wasim, A., Truong, J., Bakshi, S., Majid, U.: A systematic review of fear, stigma, and mental health outcomes of pandemics. J. Ment. Health **32**(5), 920–934 (2023). https://doi.org/10.1080/09638237.2022.2091754

57. Watkins, D.C., Allen, J.O., Goodwill, J.R., Noel, B.: Strengths and weaknesses of the young black men, masculinities, and mental health (YBMen) Facebook project. Am. J. Orthopsychiatry **87**(4), 392 (2017), iSBN: 1939-0025 Publisher: Educational Publishing Foundation

58. World Health Organization: Basic documents. World Health Organization (2020)

59. World Health Organization: World mental health report: Transforming mental health for all (2022). https://www.who.int/publications-detail-redirect/9789240049338

60. Zhou, S., Hendra, L.B., Zhang, Q., Holopainen, J., LC, R.: Eternagram: Probing Player Attitudes in Alternate Climate Scenarios Through a ChatGPT-Driven Text Adventure (2024). https://doi.org/10.48550/ARXIV.2403.18160, https://arxiv.org/abs/2403.18160, version Number: 1

61. Zimmerman, J., Forlizzi, J., Evenson, S.: Research through design as a method for interaction design research in HCI. In: Proceedings of the SIGCHI Conference on Human Factors in Computing Systems, pp. 493–502. ACM, San Jose California USA (2007). https://doi.org/10.1145/1240624.1240704

From Testimony to Immersion: The Design and Production of *Realidad Helicoide*

Víctor Navarro[1], Gabriela Martinez[1], Victoria Moriones[1], Manuel Llorens[1], Elisa Trotta[1], Niels Erik Raursø[2], and Luis Emilio Bruni[2(✉)]

[1] Voces de la Memoria, Miami, USA
vicnavarro15@gmail.com, gabymontenegro97@gmail.com,
victoriamoriones@gmail.com, manuel_llorens@hotmail.com,
elisatrottagamus@gmail.com
[2] Aalborg University, Aalborg, Denmark
{nera,leb}@create.aau.dk

Abstract. This paper details the participatory design and production of Realidad Helicoide, a virtual reality (VR) experience documenting human rights violations at El Helicoide, a Venezuelan detention and torture center. Originating from the testimony of journalist and former prisoner Víctor Navarro, the project expanded to include the contributions of over 30 survivors. Employing ethical storytelling and immersive narrative techniques, Realidad Helicoide strategically fosters empathy without sensationalizing violence, enabling users to morally witness past and ongoing injustices. The VR experience has engaged international decision-makers, prompting diplomatic and policy actions globally, and was selectively disseminated clandestinely within repressive environments. Its effectiveness underscores VR's potential in mobilizing stakeholders and advocating for human rights. The paper significantly contributes to discussions on immersive journalism, digital memory preservation, and interactive storytelling, highlighting essential insights into designing emotionally resonant and politically impactful immersive media.

Keywords: Virtual Reality · Immersive Journalism · Participatory Design · Human Rights Advocacy · Interactive Digital Narratives · Narrative Persuasion · Digital Memorialization

1 Introduction

Over the past decade, immersive technologies such as VR, AR, and XR have significantly reshaped how memory, journalism, and cultural heritage are represented and experienced. In particular, fully immersive VR–where users can navigate virtual spaces, interact with environments, and exercise agency–has emerged as a powerful medium for conveying both historical atrocities and ongoing human rights violations. While these experiences are often designed to evoke empathy or prompt reflection, there remains limited understanding of how interactive digital narratives actually persuade or influence audiences in these contexts. The

M. C. Reyes and F. Nack (Eds.): ICIDS 2025, LNCS 16375, pp. 226–245, 2026.
https://doi.org/10.1007/978-3-032-12405-0_13

field of narrative persuasion investigates the processes and mechanisms behind the impact of persuasive narratives on people's attitudes, beliefs, and behavior [5,13,24], in contexts such as communication about health [7,12], and advertisement [16]. However, this research has primarily focused on traditional forms of narratives, or so called linear narratives (e.g., books, TV, films).

Little attention has been paid to narrative persuasion in interactive digital narratives (IDNs) and much less is known about XR IDNs. The distinction between immersive and non-immersive narrative representations is noteworthy, as it sheds light on the varying degrees of persuasive impact that different mediums can exert on audiences. In this paper we report the origin, motivations, ideation, design and implementation process of an innovative and impactful VR interactive narrative that documents and exposes the gross human rights violations that have been taking place in Venezuela in the last two decades.

This paper presents the production, design, and implementation of "Realidad Helicoide"[1], a virtual reality experience that emerged from Venezuelan journalist Víctor Navarro's quest to transcend the limitations of traditional narrative formats in conveying his testimony as a political prisoner.

2 Background and Motivation

The project originated from Navarro's autobiographical book "The Unfinished Story: Tales of a Political Prisoner", which documents his experience as a survivor of El Helicoide – recognized by international human rights organizations as one of Latin America's primary torture centers. In order to set the context of this prison, it is important to briefly summarize the history of El Helicoide.

In the early 1950 s, during the presidency of Marcos Pérez Jiménez, El Helicoide was constructed in Roca Tarpeya (a neighborhood in Caracas, Venezuela), as an architectural innovation for the region. Originally planned as a shopping center, the building was designed to house more than 320 commercial establishments spread across its six floors. El Helicoide – see Fig. 1 – featured an innovative design with 4-kilometer-long ramps that allowed vehicles to drive through the shopping center, and included even a heliport at the top of the building [3].

In 1975, El Helicoide became state property, which led to failed attempts to reconceptualize and ensure the building's operation. In 1985, President Rafael Caldera decided to install the headquarters of the Intelligence and Prevention Services (DISIP) there. Between 2009 and 2010, Hugo Chávez established the Bolivarian National Intelligence Service (SEBIN) to replace the DISIP, and designated El Helicoide as one of its headquarters [6]. Currently, El Helicoide functions as a political detention and torture center where some of the more than 900 Venezuelan political prisoners are held.[2] The United Nations Human Rights

---

[1] The experience is available on the Meta Store: https://www.meta.com/experiences/9348816795151607/.

[2] The number of political prisoners is constantly changing, and due to a lack of transparency, the regime does not provide an official count. Consequently, several non-governmental organizations conduct their own counts and compiled lists of political prisoners. The figure cited here is taken from the reports of Foro Penal (June 2025),

Fig. 1. Picture taken by Paolo Gasparini, 1967–68

Council, Amnesty International, the Organization of American States, and other organizations have documented that crimes against humanity–including torture, arbitrary detention, and other abuses–are systematically committed at El Helicoide by intelligence agencies.

Despite completing his written testimony, Navarro felt a profound dissatisfaction with the emotional and political impact that traditional literary formats could achieve. This creative frustration sparked an empirical exploration of alternative storytelling mediums better suited to conveying his lived experience. He initially considered physical installations such as museums or immersive exhibitions that could recreate the conditions of imprisonment. Through this exploratory process, Navarro identified virtual reality's unique capacity for generating empathy through immersive, sensory storytelling [10, 14]. Recognizing VR's potential to transport audiences into simulated environments with unprecedented realism, he adopted the technology as the optimal medium for his testimonial objectives: reconstructing his prison experience through an immersive, multi-sensory narrative capable of mobilizing global audiences and generating meaningful political and social impact.

To implement his vision, Navarro founded the NGO *Voces de la Memoria* and assembled an interdisciplinary team for the project. The project grew beyond Navarro's individual story as 29 other survivors of the infamous torture prison were sought out and incorporated, contributing their own testimonies. Their inclusion not only amplified the narrative's reach but also transformed the experience into a powerful communal journey of healing, remembrance, and resistance.

---

one of the most reputable NGOs in Venezuela. https://x.com/foropenal/status/1935106923923390867?s=46&t=7rsT77chF5mCI0jPettmUg.

Though the organization has since expanded, the initial funding enabled the collaborative development of the virtual reality experience.

In what follows, we examine the technical, creative, and ethical considerations involved in translating this vision into a fully realized VR experience. We document the production, participatory design methodologies, and implementation strategies that enabled the transformation of personal testimonies into immersive digital storytelling. Additionally, we detail the process of audience engagement and the significant impact the VR production has had across diverse stakeholder groups – including journalists, decision makers, human rights activists, and international institutions and advocacy organizations – demonstrating the medium's effectiveness in advancing testimonial narratives within policy and advocacy contexts.

3   State-of-the-Art: Immersive Technologies for Human Rights and Digital Memorialization

VR for human rights documentation began with historical commemoration. *The Last Goodbye* (2017) [33] pioneered VR documentary by taking audiences through a Nazi death camp with Holocaust survivor Pinchas Gutter recounting his testimony in life-sized 3D reconstructions of Majdanek. The *Anne Frank House VR* (2018) [2] demonstrated VR's power to heighten students' feelings of confinement compared to 2D versions [17].

These projects serve as "virtual witnesses" to history, preserving first-person accounts in explorable formats as survivors pass away. However, their historical focus leaves a critical gap in addressing ongoing violations–precisely where Realidad Helicoide operates.

Immersive journalism addresses this gap by **situating** audiences inside ethically charged spaces rather than merely showing atrocities. This foregrounds what Kukkakorpi & Pantti [22] call the *dialogue-with-space* layer, where viewers negotiate meaning through bodily orientation–particularly relevant for documenting active detention centers like El Helicoide.

Nobody's Listening (2020) exemplifies this approach, combining 360° visuals and survivor testimonies about the 2014 Yazidi genocide. Its controlled, room-scale installations over mass-market release align with strategic witnessing [29]–targeted persuasion among policymakers and institutions that directly informs Realidad Helicoide's advocacy goals.

Recent projects like *Survived to Tell – Be the Witness* (2024) [8,19] transport viewers to Hamas attack sites with survivors' stories, while Afghanistan Memory Home [1,20] preserves testimonies from ongoing conflicts while protecting contributor safety.

Theoretical foundations have evolved beyond VR as an "empathy machine". Fisher [10] criticized this framing, emphasizing that emotional responses stem from designers' choices rather than real-world subjects–underscoring the importance of survivor-centered approaches like Realidad Helicoide's. Experimental evidence confirms that technological presence and storytelling satisfaction jointly foster flow states mediating emotional restoration and action intentions [23], with VR outperforming 2D treatments in shifting human-rights attitudes [4]. However, long-term behavioral impacts remain understudied–a gap Realidad Helicoide addresses through integrated evaluation with survivor communities.

Traditional shortcomings have prompted calls for participatory models transforming viewers into 'ethical witnesses' through community co-authorship [15]. Rouse [30] emphasizes treating stories as open dialogue, embracing narrative incompleteness that keeps multiple voices present–mirroring Realidad Helicoide's continuous validation with ex-prisoners. The Ethical Synthesis Framework [28] positions Realidad Helicoide as high-aspiration, high-difficulty work: co-designed with survivors, engaging reflective moral witnessing, and embedded in political strategy–i.e.: VR as a transformation tool, not mere representation.

Realidad Helicoide differs by placing users inside ongoing political repression, raising complex ethical stakes around depicting living victims without spectacle [11,27]. It functions as both immersive archive and investigative tool, functioning as a testimonial VR designed for mobilization. As Silva et al. [31] argue, interactive digital narratives transform reporting into lived experience through their 'Experience, Don't Tell' principle, facilitating collective sense-making in complex political landscapes [21].

Accordingly, Realidad Helicoide leverages VR's persuasive affordances to intervene in live conflict while addressing methodological and ethical gaps in existing projects. By combining survivor-centered co-design, ongoing violence documentation, and strategic witnessing, it advances the field's capacity to serve justice rather than merely document injustice.

4   Participatory Design: From Testimony to Interactive Narrative

While many projects, involving historical memory and trauma, risk presenting a designer's interpretation of victims' experiences, the approach of this project centers on a participatory process that foregrounds the voices and agency of survivors themselves. Rather than imposing an external narrative, the project actively collaborated with former political prisoners to co-create the virtual museum, ensuring that the representation emerges from their lived realities and collective empowerment. The research and analysis process unfolded in several stages and involved multiple actors who participated from the project's outset. We began with an investigative phase aimed at articulating ideas around the concept of a museum of historical memory, laying the foundational framework to identify key elements for further research.

In this direction, the first step was to identify potential former political prisoners who had experienced and survived arbitrary detention at El Helicoide, and were willing to participate. The sample was selected through a network developed by Navarro, whose experience as a survivor helped facilitate access to potential participants, reflecting the project's guiding principle of empowering those who have directly suffered state violence.

The sample was designed to reflect a wide variation of experiences, including political activists and ordinary citizens, men and women, different age groups, and diverse political affiliations. For each individual, a brief profile was prepared–including background information, relevant news articles, case files, and published materials. The testimonies revealed the randomness of political persecution by the Venezuelan state, highlighting significant differences between activists and non-activists.

Interviews were conducted by three team members: a clinical psychologist, Navarro in his capacity as ex-prisoner, and a third researcher who documented the encounters. The focus was to recollect experiences of political persecution and imprisonment while identifying current psychosocial needs, with the dual purpose of offering support and extracting valuable information for the narrative design and virtual environment implementation. The interview process prioritized participants' safety and well-being by clearly explaining its purpose, encouraging a comfortable setting, and allowing interviewees to share at their own pace or stop anytime with all the guarantees of an ethical informed consent. Navarro's personal connection to some interviewees fostered trust and a sense of brotherhood, while the clinical psychologist's trauma expertise guided the sensitive conversations with care. Follow-ups ensured ongoing support, with six participants continuing in psychotherapy.

A pilot study with six ex-prisoners was conducted to refine the interview approach and minimize the risk of triggering post-traumatic responses. Building on this initial material, the research team began analyzing content to shape the virtual reality experience, exploring narrative potential and interactive structures. A second round of interviews added 24 more testimonies from ex-prisoners and relatives bringing the total number of interviewed participants to thirty, including the mother of a detainee who remains in prison today.

The psychological analysis revealed patterns of abuse and torture, as well as the lasting impact on survivors. The testimonies documented numerous instances of physical and psychological torture. The effects of persecution and torture manifested in a range of psychological symptoms consistent with complex post-traumatic stress, including emotional dysregulation, anxiety, sleep disturbances, hypervigilance, avoidance, panic attacks, depression, rage, and a persistent sense of threat even after release.

The interviews also documented the ways ex-prisoners resisted and survived captivity. Their testimonies included accounts of struggle and resilience alongside records of suffering. Participants described how they smuggled information to families and the press, maintained routines to preserve mental stability, formed supportive relationships, and organized protests. Many reported that their experiences strengthened their political beliefs and perspectives on the current situation. This aspect of victimization demonstrates that while political persecution has severe consequences, victims' resilience can inform healing and support efforts. The development of the virtual museum exemplifies this transformation from trauma to empowerment–a deliberate act of collaboration and community building that intertwines the pursuit of justice with the healing process for those who have suffered human rights abuses.

The comprehensive interview methodology and psychological analysis generated rich testimonial material and crucial insights that directly informed the VR design process. The collected testimonies provided immersive story paths, while ethical safeguards and collaborative approaches became respectful design principles enabling participatory development. Trauma patterns guided sensitive interaction design, resistance strategies informed interactive choices, and psychological insights influenced environmental elements including the virtual environment's structure and user journey. This foundation ensured authentic representation and meaningful engagement, establishing the framework for translating lived experiences into effective design principles for the virtual museum.

5   Narrative Design and Implementation

5.1   From Testimonies to Immersion

The victims who participated signed authorization forms granting permission to use their testimonies and their images as holograms. Following ethical approval, all interviews were recorded and transcribed for dual analysis. The Voces de la Memoria team systematically extracted relevant information for the virtual museum construction, while the psychology team independently analyzed the material to identify participants' psychosocial needs and trauma impacts.

To systematize this process, the research team developed a content table to identify key elements in each testimony: the arrest process, interviewees' current legal status, descriptions of their confinement, daily life, emotional states while imprisoned, and accounts of physical, psychological, and sexual torture. The analysis also captured how participants experienced victimhood, their release process, symbolic objects, and significant individuals named in their testimonies.

Beyond personal narratives, ex-prisoners provided crucial physical details of El Helicoide and its cells–including size, color, textures, dimensions, and objects reflecting daily life inside. Many contributed additional materials: photographs taken inside El Helicoide, letters addressed directly to users, and artistic works created during imprisonment. Most significantly, one ex-political prisoner shared an authentic audio recording of torture at El Helicoide, which became a powerful feature in the experience.

5.2   Production and Technical Implementation

The technical development was outsourced to a specialized team working closely with the Voces de la Memoria team throughout production. The experience was developed in Unity for Quest 2, incorporating 3D modeling, interactive elements, and system integration. The result is a fully immersive VR experience that allows room-scale exploration of confined spaces such as corridors and cells, while users can navigate larger virtual spaces using VR controllers.

The experience is narrated in Spanish by Navarro, and in English by a voice actor. The short version includes AI-generated translations[3] in French, Italian, Portuguese, and Chinese. Testimonies by ex-prisoners remain in the original language to preserve the emotion and voices of the victims, with subtitles provided. Two versions exist: a full 15–30 min version (with all 30 testimonies) and a shortened 5–7 min version for conferences, featuring fewer interactive elements and a different ending.

A continuous validation process involved collaboration with victims throughout production. In this context, the participation of Navarro, as a victim, was particularly significant. The experience was validated also by the other 29 victims who gave their testimonies, endorsing spaces such as "Preventiva 1" and "El bañito", as well as the use of the audio recordings and other materials they contributed.

Implementation also included validation with diverse small groups with different backgrounds in controlled settings, followed by facilitated feedback sessions for experience refinement.

5.3 Experience Design and Narrative Structure

Realidad Helicoide unfolds through three temporal-spatial moments–past, present, and future–each grounded in a distinct perspective of El Helicoide: as seen from a family living room window, the detention cells inside El Helicoide, and its imagined future as a museum.

5.3.1 Design Philosophy and Ethical Framework

The architecture of El Helicoide became the central symbol of the experience. Originally designed as a shopping mall, its transformation into a torture center reflects the cruelty of the Venezuelan regime and its ability to turn civilian spaces into places of repression. To prevent the experience from becoming a crude depiction of torture while maintaining its testimonial power, several ethical design strategies were implemented through close collaboration with survivors:

- **Visual and auditory design:** Colors, lighting, and music were carefully selected to convey feelings of oppression or hope without sensationalist treatment. Music was designed to release tension at key moments.
- **Emotional positioning:** The narrative avoids making viewers "feel" torture as a direct physical experience. Instead, it generates awareness and empathy without reproducing suffering.
- **Survivor validation:** Throughout production, the 30 participating victims validated spatial reconstructions, endorsed selected testimony fragments, and provided suggestions for visual representation of their confinement spaces.

One particularly significant aspect of psychological torture at El Helicoide was strategically incorporated as a core narrative features: the forcing of prisoners to witness or hear the torture of fellow inmates. These elements convey the psychological complexity of the trauma within the virtual experience.

---

[3] https://elevenlabs.io/.

5.3.2   Past: Inside an Ordinary Family's Living Room in Caracas

This part contextualizes El Helicoide's history, tracing its evolution from a symbol of modern urban ambition to a site of state violence. The exposition unfolds through a news montage on a television within a domestic living room scene, as seen in Fig. 2A.

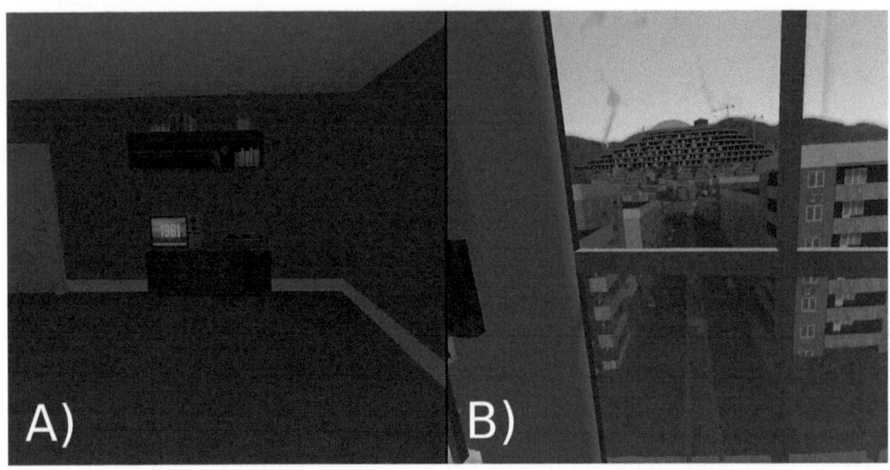

Fig. 2. El Helicoide seen from the window. One can watch the changes of the building and the room throughout the years.

The montage begins with archival footage announcing the construction of a futuristic shopping center, then transitions through decades of political upheaval featuring figures like Hugo Chávez and images of civil unrest. As time progresses, the interior transforms, the urban landscape evolves (see Fig. 1B, and the television becomes a laptop, marking the shift to the present day where Navarro introduces El Helicoide's current role as a detention and torture center.

The sequence concludes with users being transported into a wireframe 3D model of El Helicoide, surrounded by holographic figures of ex-prisoners.

5.3.3   Present: Inside El Helicoide and Its Cells

This phase begins in "Preventiva 1", one of the main cells, immersing users in the conditions where political prisoners live in Venezuela's torture centers. Navarro narrates the daily life of prisoners and the physical realities of confinement, emphasizing that human rights violations continue to occur.

The figures of prisoners, as seen in Fig. 3, are deliberately stylized and anonymous, reinforcing the collective nature of suffering and resistance within El Helicoide.

The testimonies of 30 political prisoners are presented as individual signatures on the wall, allowing users to select and hear specific accounts. In Fig. 4,

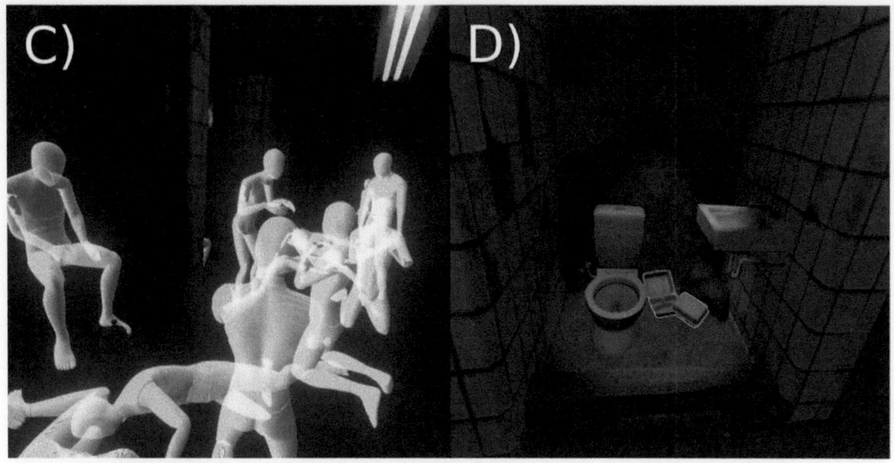

Fig. 3. The figures in the cell show the dimensions and the condition of daily life **(C)** with particular objects **(D)** that the prisoners needed to use.

the testimonies of political prisoners are presented as individual signatures on the wall.

In contrast to the stylized representation of the prisoners, a realistically rendered masked officer from the secret political police stands at the corridor's end–silent, still, and watching. As users approach, he points toward "El Bañito" ("the little bathroom")–a narrow, claustrophobic space used for torture and isolation.

Navarro introduces El Bañito (Fig. 5), where prisoners endured not only direct torture but were forced to hear others' screams–an intentional method of psychological torment. To represent this reality, a 40-second audio file of actual electrical torture, smuggled out by a survivor, plays in the space. Navarro explains the recording's origin and reminds users this is not a game but a tool for denunciation designed to confront state violence. He provides clear warnings about explicit content and explains that the red button allows users to stop the recording at any time.

5.3.4   Future: El Helicoide as a Museum

The final phase transitions from testimony to memorialization. After the darkness of El Bañito, users are transformed into a cockroach–an embodied metaphor for invisibility, degradation, and survival–and crawl beneath the door. Emerging into light, they find themselves in a radically reimagined El Helicoide: now a memory museum (Fig. 6G). This symbolic shift moves from trauma documentation to active construction of historical memory and resistance.

In the museum's reception hall, users encounter letters written by survivors (Fig. 6H)–an open narrative space where each writer addresses users directly with reflections on their experience, imprisonment memories, or broader mes-

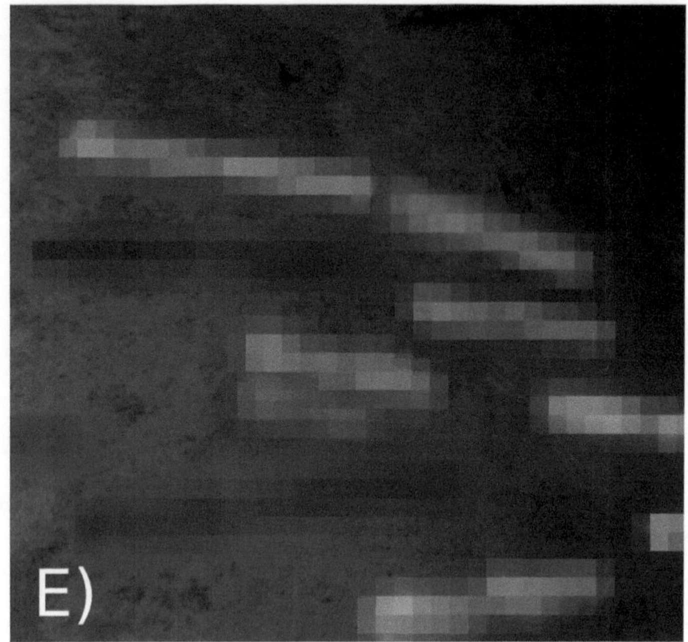

Fig. 4. E) In the cell "Preventiva 1", you can hear 30 testimonies from the victims and relatives. You can choose some of them by approaching the controls to the names on the wall. For confidentiality reasons the names are redacted.

sages about justice and solidarity. This variability was preserved intentionally to foreground the multiplicity of survivor voices.

Beyond this space, users enter a gallery displaying representative objects–photos and personal items connected to victims–and drawings created by one ex-prisoner during incarceration (Fig. 7I).

This artwork expands representational modes within the experience, incorporating visual testimony and symbolic artifacts as both evidence and expression.

The gallery concludes with a final corridor presenting five audio testimonies corresponding to specific torture forms, accompanied by sculptural figures under isolated spotlights (Fig. 7J). While some incorporate animation, representations remain deliberately abstract–faceless, de-individualized, and free of graphic detail. This design strategy avoids realism and spectacle, opting for symbolic representation that foregrounds testimony over reenactment.

This closing section serves not only as remembrance space but as a narrative call to action–urging users to bear witness, denounce, and recognize the ongoing nature of state violence in Venezuela.

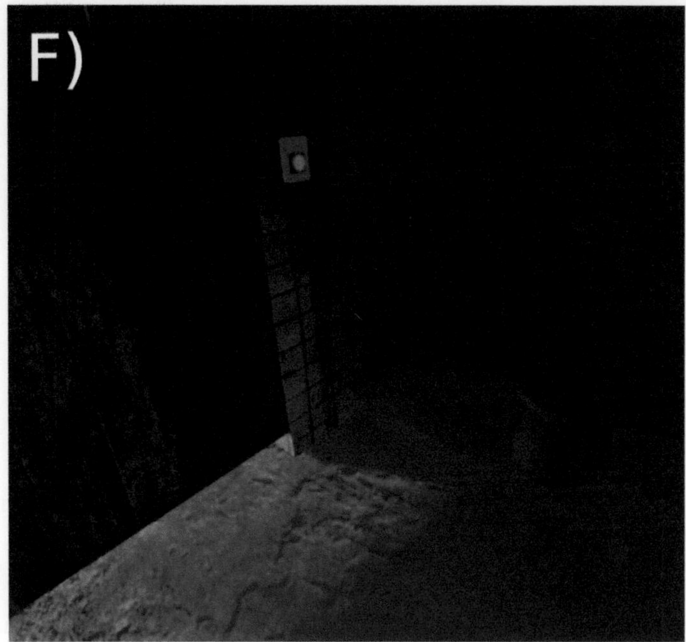

Fig. 5. F) "El Bañito", the isolation cell where up to nine prisoners were held. The red button stops the recording of real electrical torture, smuggled out by a survivor. (Color figure online)

6   Audience Engagement and Practical Outcomes

Realidad Helicoide exemplifies how immersive experiences can actively shape public discourse and institutional response. By enabling audiences to virtually inhabit the spaces of confinement and torture endured by political prisoners in Venezuela, the experience engenders a form of narrative transportation that has triggered action across international diplomacy, policy-making, investigative journalism, and grassroots mobilization.

6.1   Strategic Engagement with Decision-Makers: Between Mass Outreach and Targeted Impact

The project team confronted fundamental questions regarding audience selection and expected outcomes: Who should the experience target? What forms of support are meaningful in exposing and combating torture in Venezuela? While acknowledging the emotional and mobilizing impact of the VR experience, the team recognized that not all audiences could translate emotional responses into effective actions capable of influencing political or legal changes.

In response, the team adopted a strategy of targeted impact, focusing on decision-makers and actors with real capacity for influence. This approach faced

Fig. 6. G) The entrance to El Helicoide – re-imagined as a memory and historical museum. **H)** The victims wrote letters to the audience.

criticism from donors who argued that conventional audiovisual formats would enable broader dissemination at lower cost. Nevertheless, the team defended the importance of creating high-impact immersive experiences for strategically selected audiences, recognizing the need to reach key stakeholders–diplomats, opinion leaders, and policymakers–on a deeper, more emotional level.

6.2   Clandestine and Selective Dissemination in Repressive Contexts

Implementation in Venezuela required operating within a highly hostile political environment with serious personal risks. The VR headset was smuggled into the country in late 2022, when the technology was not commercially available and the team had already received regime threats. Clandestine exhibitions targeted presidential pre-candidates, diplomats, journalists, and opinion leaders to advocate for political prisoner release and torture center closure. These sessions occurred in party offices, NGOs, and embassies without documentation to protect participants, with a dozen diplomatic missions and UN officials providing discreet support.

This approach created an "open secret" within key circles, where the headset's circulation was known but confidentiality was respected. Years later, this network of solidarity and strategic silence remains intact, demonstrating the effectiveness of selective impact strategies in authoritarian contexts where mass outreach may prove less effective and potentially endanger participants.

Beyond high-level targets, the virtual reality experience was exhibited at universities and conferences across Latin America, Europe, and the United States. The team channeled audience desires for action into concrete solidarity by inviting participants to write letters to Venezuelan political prisoners. Hundreds of

Fig. 7. I) One of the victims is an artist, and while he was a political prisoner, he drew all these paintings that you can see in an art gallery. **J)** Sculptural representation of a torture victim.

letters were delivered through support networks, with ex-prisoners later displaying these communications and sharing their importance during imprisonment.

6.3   Engagement with International Decision Makers and Institutions

The project employed a dual "call to action" strategy targeting both international decision makers and domestic actors. Those with regime communication channels or mediation roles–including the UN, High Commissioner, and diplomatic delegations in Caracas–were urged toward quiet diplomacy and discreet advocacy for political prisoner release. Conversely, actors whose political stance or institutional role precluded regime engagement were encouraged to apply pressure through public statements, sanctions, resolutions, and other accountability mechanisms.

Between May 2023 and January 2025, dozens of high-level meetings were strategized and organized with ambassadors, ministers, senators, and parliament members across Argentina, Colombia, Uruguay, Paraguay, the United States, France, the Czech Republic, Belgium, Italy, and Spain. The VR production served as a strategic tool facilitating diplomatic encounters and introducing human rights agendas, providing an immersive platform that enhanced survivor testimony impact and accessibility in international political forums.

The immersive experience was presented in embassies, national legislatures, and international forums including the Organization of American States, Inter-American Court of Human Rights, International Criminal Court, and European Parliament. Private exhibitions for decision-makers created emotionally impactful moments that humanized victim experiences and reinforced the need for political action. Key milestones included high-level presidential meetings demonstrating the project's governmental reach, notably a private meeting with the Inter-American Court of Human Rights President in Costa Rica, where Navarro accompanied Venezuelan opposition presidential candidate Edmundo González to advocate for crimes against humanity victims, and a 2023 meeting with Uruguay's then-president Luis Lacalle Pou, where the VR experience introduced the discussion.

7 Evidence of the VR Experience's Effectiveness in Advancing Testimonial Narratives and Influencing Policy/Advocacy International Impact and Political Statements

The project's diplomatic strategy successfully secured victim voices within political arenas through notable public statements by decision makers. The European Parliament passed a March 2024 resolution calling for immediate political prisoner release in Venezuela, while a bipartisan group of U.S. senators issued joint declarations denouncing Maduro regime persecution. Multiple Latin American and European parliaments echoed these concerns: Argentina's Chamber of Deputies, following testimony by former detainees, issued a formal statement recognizing the "Realidad Helicoide" exhibition and condemning Venezuela's human rights abuses [25], Paraguay's Congress officially declared Realidad Helicoide a project of national interest [26], and prominent Italian and Spanish legislators voiced strong support, culminating in Spanish parliamentary resolution introduction advocating for international justice mechanisms.

A significant milestone occurred during Organization of American States public hearings in Washington D.C., where Inter-American Human Rights Commission Executive Secretary Tania Reneaum publicly endorsed the immersive experience as a critical advocacy and documentation tool, describing it as "a profoundly human experience that no one can remain indifferent to."[4]

7.1 Measurable Outcomes and Political Discourse Influence

The most tangible outcome was the December 2023 release of several Venezuelan and U.S. political prisoners [18]. While formally linked to bilateral negotiations, the Realidad Helicoide campaign played a key role in maintaining public pressure, building international visibility, and inserting the issue into broader political agendas. The project's influence on political discourse became increasingly visible as it advanced. During Venezuelan presidential primaries to choose a unified opposition candidate in late 2023, several candidates began incorporating political prisoner and crimes against humanity issues into their platforms. Opposition candidate Freddy Superlano proposed transforming El Helicoide into

---

[4] https://www.instagram.com/reel/C3_T3pxuHoe/?igsh=NGg0eTVtenV5aTY3.

a memory museum during an online public debate–ironically, he was later kidnapped and imprisoned in El Helicoide following the 2024 presidential election. María Corina Machado, the country's chief opposition leader, experienced the VR production and strongly encouraged the team to use the tool for international campaign dissemination.

7.2   Media Coverage and Public Awareness

The significant media attention received by Realidad Helicoide demonstrated the experience's emotional impact on opinion makers and journalists, extending beyond traditional media coverage. Journalism and opinion leaders mobilized concrete actions toward raising awareness about Venezuelan human rights violations, evidenced by hundreds of media releases about torture centers related to the experience. TN Internacional–Argentina's most-watched news network in 2023–broadcast a short documentary titled "La sucursal del infierno" featuring testimonies from four Venezuelan survivors of political imprisonment and torture at El Helicoide [32]. The emotional weight of their stories, combined with VR footage, expanded the project's reach across diverse audiences.

CNN en Español journalists were deeply moved after experiencing the VR, leading to a 16 min segment titled "Cómo es la temida prisión de El Helicoide" including a live interview with Víctor Navarro [9][5]. The interview was broadcast across Latin America and the U.S., integrating VR visuals to convey issue urgency to global audiences and contributing to international visibility. The regime's reaction involved orchestrating takedown campaigns through online trolls, though CNN en Español successfully re-uploaded the content.

7.3   Civil Society Mobilization and Transmedia Impact

Beyond institutional lobbying, the project successfully activated civil society by transforming rich materials generated during VR production into comprehensive transmedia campaigns. The "CAF sin Helicoide" campaign exemplifies this approach: when the Development Bank of Latin America and the Caribbean featured El Helicoide on their marathon medal, survivors and activists mobilized to pressure organizers for image removal, successfully forcing medal redesign. This demonstrates how VR production materials enabled diverse applications beyond virtual environments, building solidarity networks and driving political responses through transmedia storytelling, validating the project's capacity to influence institutional discourse and policymaking through integrated immersive technology, narrative authenticity, and strategic outreach.

8   Conclusion and Future Perspectives

8.1   Future Challenges

The preservation of historical memory in digital environments presents new challenges related to the fast pace of technological obsolescence. The virtual reality

---

[5] Watch: https://www.youtube.com/watch?v=XPWXyBXpqwY.

experience developed by *Voces de la Memoria* represents a significant contribution to collective memory by making visible and honoring the victims of human rights violations in Venezuela. However, its long-term sustainability is threatened by the ephemeral nature of technological devices. This context highlights the urgent need to design digital preservation strategies that ensure continued accessibility and permanence for this kind of testimonial tools.

In the future, *Voces de la Memoria* aims to establish itself as a leading actor in developing VR experiences for human rights advocacy, memory construction, and public engagement. Building on acquired expertise, the organization envisions both continuing to create immersive narratives and providing technical, methodological, and strategic support to other civil society organizations seeking to leverage immersive technologies and interactive digital storytelling as innovative tools for raising awareness, mobilizing audiences, and generating public impact.

8.2   Conclusions

A testimony is not only an account of an event; it is, above all, an act of courage. When a victim decides to tell her story, it not only communicates what happened: it exposes his most intimate vulnerability, reopens wounds that time has barely managed to cover, and faces the risk of not being believed, of being reduced to just another number or file. Witnessing is, in this sense, a radical gesture of trust in the other, in shared humanity.

Under this conviction, the Realidad Helicoide project was born, with the ethical and technical challenge of transferring more than 30 testimonies of victims to a virtual reality environment. This required a careful and deeply respectful treatment of the material, understanding that each testimony is not only memory, but also a claim for justice and dignity.

The success of the project can be summed up in the phrase "from testimony to immersion": recreating a multi-sensory experience that not only conveyed the content of the testimony but allowed audiences to inhabit, if only briefly, the space experienced by the victim. This experiential depth generates an emotional presence and moral urgency that is rarely achieved with linear or solely text-based narratives.

By shortening the distance between witness and spectator, VR storytelling transforms the observer into a participant and the memory into an experience. Thus, VR IDNs reveal themselves not only as powerful tools for preserving memory or influencing the public sphere, but also as ethical devices that invite us to build conscious societies. These tools ensure that justice finds a voice in real time, and the recognition of grievances and suffering is not relegated to an archive but becomes a call to action–for active solidarity and a transformative commitment to dismantling the systems that enable such violations.

References

1. Afghanistan Human Rights and Democracy Organisation (AHRDO): Afghanistan memory home [virtual museum for Afghan war victims and survivor testimonies] (2023). https://afghanistanmemoryhome.org/. Accessed 22 June 2025
2. Anne Frank House: Anne frank house VR [virtual reality tour of the secret annex] (2018). https://www.annefrank.org/en/about-us/news-and-press/news/2018/6/12/anne-frank-house-vr-launched/. Accessed 22 June 2025
3. BBC Mundo: El helicoide: el centro comercial de venezuela que se convirtió en un sitio de torturas [the helicoide: the shopping mall in Venezuela that became a torture site] (2019). https://www.bbc.com/mundo/noticias-america-latina-46978545. Accessed 22 June 2025
4. Bujić, M., Salminen, M., Macey, J., Hamari, J.: "empathy machine": how virtual reality affects human rights attitudes. Internet Res. **30**(5), 1407–1425 (2020). https://doi.org/10.1108/INTR-07-2019-0306
5. Busselle, R., Bilandzic, H.: Measuring narrative engagement. Media Psychol. **12**(4), 321–347 (2009). https://doi.org/10.1080/15213260903287259
6. Clarín: Venezuela: radiografía del sebin, el temido servicio de inteligencia de maduro [venezuela: an in-depth look at sebin, maduro's feared intelligence service] (2019). https://www.clarin.com/mundo/venezuela-radiografia-sebin-temido-servicio-inteligencia-maduro_0_xFwSrSVCN.html. Accessed 22 June 2025
7. Cuesta, U., Martínez, L., Cuesta, V.: Effectiveness of narrative persuasion on facebook: change of attitude and intention towards HPV. Eur. J. Soc. Sci. Educ. Res. **11**(2), 100 (2017). https://doi.org/10.26417/EJSER.V11I2.P100-109
8. Doherty, R.: Virtual reality project will allow users to witness October 7 first hand [survivors' testimony VR experience] (2024). https://www.thejc.com/news/virtual-reality-project-will-allow-users-to-witness-october-7-first-hand-f65gxtre. Accessed 22 June 2025
9. en Español, C.: Realidad helicoide: una experiencia inmersiva revela las condiciones en centros de detención en venezuela [realidad helicoide: an immersive experience reveals conditions in venezuelan detention centers] (2024). https://www.youtube.com/watch?v=XPWXyBXpqwY. Accessed 22 June 2025
10. Fisher, J.A.: Empathic actualities: toward a taxonomy of empathy in virtual reality. In: Nunes, N., Oakley, I., Nisi, V. (eds.) Interactive Storytelling, pp. 233–244. Springer International Publishing, Cham (2017). https://doi.org/10.1007/978-3-319-71027-3_19
11. Fisher, J.A., Schoemann, S.: Toward an ethics of interactive storytelling at dark tourism sites in virtual reality. In: Rouse, R., Koenitz, H., Haahr, M. (eds.) Interactive Storytelling, pp. 577–590. Springer International Publishing, Cham (2018). https://doi.org/10.1007/978-3-030-04028-4_68
12. Green, M.C.: Narratives and cancer communication. J. Commun. **56**(s1), S163–S183 (2006). https://doi.org/10.1111/j.1460-2466.2006.00288.x
13. Green, M.C., Brock, T.C.: The role of transportation in the persuasiveness of public narratives. J. Pers. Soc. Psychol. **79**(5), 701–721 (2000). https://doi.org/10.1037/0022-3514.79.5.701
14. Hadjipanayi, C., Christofi, M., Banakou, D., Michael-Grigoriou, D.: Cultivating empathy through narratives in virtual reality: a review. Pers. Ubiquit. Comput. **28**(3), 507–519 (2024). https://doi.org/10.1007/s00779-024-01812-w
15. Holohan, C., Hogan, M., Kelly, D., Kennedy, M., Silke, C.: Ethical witnessing: participatory virtual reality production and the experience of homelessness. Stud. Documentary Film 1–20 (2025). https://doi.org/10.1080/17503280.2025.2470117

16. Huang, R., Ha, S., Kim, S.H.: Narrative persuasion in social media: an empirical study of luxury brand advertising. J. Res. Interact. Mark. **12**(3), 274–292 (2018). https://doi.org/10.1108/JRIM-07-2017-0059
17. Huang, X., Macgilchrist, F.: From physical feelings to empathy: an immersive virtual reality approach to facilitate physical empathy. Comput. Educ. Open **7**, 100215 (2024). https://doi.org/10.1016/j.caeo.2024.100215
18. Inter-American Commission on Human Rights (IACHR): 330/23: Iachr welcomes release of political prisoners in Venezuela (2023). https://www.oas.org/en/iachr/media_center/PReleases/2023/330.asp. Accessed 22 June 2025
19. ISRAEL-is: Survived to tell [virtual reality journey sharing October 7 survivor stories] (2024). https://www.israel-is.org/en/survived-to-tell/. Accessed 22 June 2025
20. Joffre-Eichhorn, H.J.: The memory box-initiative: nonextractivist research methodologies and the struggle for an architecture of remembrance in Kabul, Afghanistan. Cult. Stud. <-> Crit. Methodol. **20**(4), 358–373 (2020). https://doi.org/10.1177/1532708619863008
21. Koenitz, H., Barbara, J., Eladhari, M.P.: Interactive digital narratives (IDN) as representations of complexity: lineage, opportunities and future work. In: Mitchell, A., Vosmeer, M. (eds.) Interactive Storytelling, pp. 488–498. Springer International Publishing, Cham (2021). https://doi.org/10.1007/978-3-030-92300-6_49
22. Kukkakorpi, M., Pantti, M.: A sense of place: VR journalism and emotional engagement. J. Pract. **15**(6), 785–802 (2021). https://doi.org/10.1080/17512786.2020.1799237
23. Li, N., Li, L., Chen, X., Wong, I.A.: Digital destination storytelling: narrative persuasion effects induced by story satisfaction in a VR context. J. Hosp. Tour. Manag. **58**, 184–196 (2024). https://doi.org/10.1016/j.jhtm.2023.12.007
24. Moyer-Gusé, E., Nabi, R.L.: Explaining the effects of narrative in an entertainment television program: overcoming resistance to persuasion. Hum. Commun. Res. **36**(1), 26–52 (2010). https://doi.org/10.1111/j.1468-2958.2009.01367.x
25. de Diputados de la Nación (Argentina), H.C.: Derechos humanos reconoció la muestra "realidad helicoide" y repudió el crimen de barracas [human rights recognized the "realidad helicoide" exhibition and condemned the barracas crime] (2024). https://www.diputados.gov.ar/prensa/noticia/DERECHOS-HUMANOS-RECONOCIO-LA-MUESTRA-REALIDAD-HELICOIDE-Y-REPUDIO-EL-CRIMEN-DE-BARRACAS/. Accessed 22 June 2025
26. de Diputados de la Nación (Paraguay), H.C.: Resolución n.^{0} 428: declara de interés nacional el proyecto "realidad helicoide" [resolution no. 428: declares "realidad helicoide" project of national interest] (2024). https://silpy.congreso.gov.py/web/descarga/resolucion-452821?preview=. Accessed 22 June 2025
27. Nash, K.: Virtual reality witness: exploring the ethics of mediated presence. Stud. Documentary Film **12**(2), 119–131 (2018). https://doi.org/10.1080/17503280.2017.1340796
28. Raja, U.S., Al-Baghli, R.: Ethical concerns in contemporary virtual reality and frameworks for pursuing responsible use. Front. Virtual Reality **Volume 6 - 2025** (2025). https://doi.org/10.3389/frvir.2025.1451273
29. Ristovska, S.: Strategic witnessing in an age of video activism. Media Cult. Soc. **38**(7), 1034–1047 (2016). https://doi.org/10.1177/0163443716635866
30. Rouse, R.: Someone else's story: an ethical approach to interactive narrative design for cultural heritage. In: Cardona-Rivera, R.E., Sullivan, A., Young, R.M. (eds.) Interactive Storytelling, pp. 47–60. Springer International Publishing, Cham (2019). https://doi.org/10.1007/978-3-030-33894-7_6

31. Silva, C., Zamora-Medina, R., Šuminas, A.: Experience, don't tell! integration of IDN into journalistic narratives. In: Murray, J.T., Reyes, M.C. (eds.) Interactive Storytelling, pp. 311–329. Springer Nature Switzerland, Cham (2025). https://doi.org/10.1007/978-3-031-78453-8_20
32. TN: "es el infierno mismo": testimonios de los sobrevivientes del helicoide, el peor centro de tortura venezolano ["it's hell itself": Testimonies from survivors of the helicoide, venezuela's worst torture center] (2023). https://tn.com.ar/internacional/2023/11/26/es-el-infierno-mismo-testimonios-de-los-sobrevivientes-del-helicoide-el-peor-centro-de-tortura-venezolano/. Accessed 22 June 2025
33. USC Shoah Foundation: The last goodbye [virtual-reality testimony featuring holocaust survivor pinchas gutter] (2018). https://sfi.usc.edu/lastgoodbye. Accessed 22 June 2025

Designing for Ideological Flexibility: Tracking Perspective Shifts in an Educational IDN

Breanne Pitt[1]([✉]) [iD], Wendy Youngblood[2] [iD], and Mads Haahr[1] [iD]

[1] Trinity College Dublin, The University of Dublin, Dublin 2 02 PN40, Ireland
`{pittb,haahrm}@tcd.ie`
[2] Shepaug Valley School, Washington, CT, USA
`youngbloodw@region-12.org`

Abstract. This study investigates how interactive digital narratives (IDNs) can foster systems thinking and ideological flexibility in secondary learners by engaging them with ideologically diverse stakeholder perspectives. Grounded in the Context–Learning–Game (CLG) framework, the intervention integrates Emily Short's Track Switching Choice structure and a non-playable character (NPC) functioning as a more-knowledgeable other (MKO) to scaffold learner engagement while exploring a complexity representation tool called Transformation Maps. Set within a simulated organizational debate on artificial intelligence, the narrative prompts learners to explore and synthesize viewpoints from three stakeholders. Behavioral data from gameplay logs, including perspective-switching frequency, time-on-task, and MKO interactions, were analyzed as indicators of ideological flexibility. Results show that most learners reconsidered their initial positions, with a significant number adopting more moderate viewpoints. Learners who switched perspectives spent more time in the experience, and MKO engagement strongly predicted final viewpoint change. A specific narrative moment, tagged Dhwani8, emerged as a cognitive inflection point associated with epistemic shift. These findings suggest that well-designed IDNs can reduce cognitive overload, support ideological exploration, and serve as analytic instruments for measuring learning behavior and epistemic development in complex decision-making contexts.

Keywords: Systems Thinking · Interactive Digital Narrative · DSRP Framework · Zone of Proximal Development · Constructionism · Serious Game · Pedagogical Tools · Complex Systems

1 Introduction

Today's complex world demands critical thinking, adaptability, and the ability to synthesize diverse perspectives. Traditional education often falls short in equipping learners with these cognitive tools. In response, this paper investigates the potential of interactive digital narratives (IDNs), particularly educational IDNs, to foster systems thinking and ideological flexibility by enhancing learners' ability to explore, interpret, and reflect on multiple perspectives.

© The Author(s), under exclusive license to Springer Nature Switzerland AG 2026
M. C. Reyes and F. Nack (Eds.): ICIDS 2025, LNCS 16375, pp. 246–272, 2026.
https://doi.org/10.1007/978-3-032-12405-0_14

IDNs provide participatory environments where learners engage with complex systems through structured, exploratory storytelling. Such environments are particularly suited for tackling "wicked" problems—ill-defined, dynamic, and socially entangled challenges that resist simple solutions [1].

Janet Murray's ICIDS 2018 keynote described IDNs as "kaleidoscopic machines," tools for analyzing events from multiple perspectives and imagining alternative futures [2]. We extend this metaphor to frame IDNs as epistemic engines for iterative perspective-taking and knowledge reorganization, aligning with theories of cognitive tools and epistemic games [3, 4].

In keeping with this design philosophy, we incorporated the World Economic Forum's (WEF) Transformation Maps as the systems thinking foundation of our intervention. These interactive digital tools help visualize thematic relationships across complex global issues such as AI, biodiversity, immigration and more. However, a previous study [5] found that without scaffolding, the maps can be cognitively overwhelming and fall outside learners' Zone of Proximal Development (ZPD) [6]. To improve the user experience and reduce cognitive load, we transformed the interactive digital exploration of the maps into an interactive digital *narrative* experience through the addition of narrative storytelling elements. This redesign incorporated the maps into a mobile game format and embedded a non-playable character (NPC) acting as a more knowledgeable other (MKO).

The present research centers on the design and evaluation of an educational IDN, a narrative-based educational game that integrates Emily Short's Track Switching Choice structure with the DSRP (Distinctions, Systems, Relationships, Perspectives) framework for systems thinking [7]. Set within the WEF's map on AI and grounded in Vygotsky's guided learning, the design uses narrative scaffolding to make systemic relationships more accessible and relevant to learner decision-making. The user adopts the role of a company mediator, facilitating discussion among three stakeholder characters: an employee, the CEO, and a customer. When needed, the user invokes the MKO Dhwani character to highlight specific concepts on the system map and support decision-making. Each time the user shifts perspective, the system logs these switches, recording initial and final viewpoints along with gameplay behaviors for later evaluation on how understanding and ideologies evolve.

The central research question (RQ) guiding this work is: *How can IDNs be used to measure the impact of exposure to multiple perspectives on learners' ideological flexibility?* Supporting this overarching inquiry are three sub-questions (SRQ): *(1) Can the design of an IDN expose players to diverse stakeholder perspectives in a way that promotes systems thinking? (2) How can Emily Short's Track Switching Choice structure be adapted to provide measurable insights into player behavior and ideological flexibility? (3) What is the impact of an NPC functioning as a MKO on learners' exploration patterns and comprehension of complexity?*

While the goal is to foster ideological flexibility, the openness to revisiting assumptions, this study examines behavioral and reflective indicators of ideological flexibility rather than long-term belief change.

2 Background and Related Work

This research lies at the intersection of systems thinking and dynamics, human-computer interaction (HCI), interactive narrative design, serious games, and educational technology, specifically with regard to media and digital literacy [8]. Within these domains, several conceptual and theoretical frameworks underpin the study's design and analysis.

2.1 Systems Thinking and Educational Challenges

Systems thinking has long been advocated as an essential capacity for addressing the increasingly complex challenges of the 21st century. From Richmond's articulation of systems thinking as a set of transferable skills [9] to the development of structured frameworks like DSRP [10], scholars have emphasized the need to support learners in identifying feedback loops, interdependencies, and causal relationships across domains. Despite this, systems thinking remains underutilized in education, partly due to its abstract nature and the difficulty of modeling dynamic complexity within conventional instructional formats.

The DSRP model offers an accessible and teachable approach to systems thinking by organizing cognition into four core patterns: making Distinctions (D), organizing Systems (S), recognizing Relationships (R), and taking Perspectives (P) [11]. Research suggests that engagement with these patterns enhances learners' ability to analyze complex issues and reflect on cognitive biases. In this study, DSRP functions as both a pedagogical foundation and a design scaffold for the game's narrative structure, mechanics, and dialogue interactions.

To operationalize systems thinking in a digital context, we incorporated the WEF's Transformation Maps—interactive data visualization tools that organize global issues and their relationships. These maps, while rich in systemic content, can overwhelm novice users [5]. By embedding them into a narrative learning environment, we enabled learners to apply DSRP principles through structured gameplay. Players used the maps to differentiate core concepts, identify subsystems (e.g., governance, labor, innovation), explore relationships between variables, and shift among stakeholder perspectives—all supported by narrative scaffolding through an NPC acting as a MKO.

While systems thinking is a powerful tool for analyzing complexity, its utility extends into the realm of media literacy [12]. As digital media increasingly shapes the way information, values, and ideologies are disseminated, the ability to navigate this complexity becomes essential. Educational systems, however, have been slow to adapt, leaving students ill-equipped to interpret the dynamic media landscapes they inhabit. In this sense, media literacy functions as a form of public pedagogy, with learners constantly exposed to persuasive, politicized, and ideologically charged narratives [13]. Developing media literacy involves more than technical competence; it requires critical awareness of how meaning is constructed. Systems thinking complements this process by encouraging learners to ask not only what is being communicated, but how elements are connected, who benefits, and what systems are being reproduced. Together, these literacies provide the cognitive infrastructure for navigating complexity and combating misinformation in digitally-mediated environments.

2.2 IDNs and Narrative Foundations

IDNs are digital artifacts where users participate in story progression through meaningful choices, often navigating branching pathways, variable outcomes, or emergent gameplay structures. Koenitz (2023) conceptualizes IDNs as a form of computational storytelling that facilitates user agency and immersion. When applied to educational contexts, IDNs enable learners to engage with multifaceted content in a personalized and dynamic manner [14].

Researchers have increasingly examined the potential of IDNs as systems thinking tools, capable of helping learners trace interdependencies, shift perspectives, and explore causal relationships in context-rich environments [12]. As dynamic, interactive spaces, narrative-centered environments replicate the complex nature of real-world systems [15], while the digital medium can promote personal transformation and deeper engagement with multiple viewpoints [16]. Together, these affordances make IDNs particularly well-suited to address educational challenges related to polarization and media and systems literacy.

Building on this foundation, narrative structures are understood not merely as storytelling devices but as cognitive tools that facilitate learners' engagement with complex systems. Narratives help to organize abstract and complex information into cause-and-effect sequences, thereby making systemic relationships more cognitively accessible [17]. Storytelling has also been identified as a fundamental method for navigating ambiguity and complexity, particularly in contexts where traditional analytical models may be insufficient [18]. Interactive narratives provide a medium for learners to explore dynamic systems, test alternative decisions, and experience the consequences of various stakeholder viewpoints [19].

In addition to their cognitive utility, narratives also serve an affective function by fostering empathy and facilitating perspective-taking. Immersion in a narrative can reduce resistance to alternative viewpoints, supporting learners in recognizing and considering perspectives that differ from their own [20]. Narratives also help individuals construct and make sense of multiple identities, enabling learners to adopt diverse perspectives and increase ideological flexibility [21].

2.3 Track Switching Choice Structure for Perspective-Switching

In 1979, Random House, Inc., launched an innovative line of books called the Choose Your Own Adventure series. These books set the standard for a literary genre now known as "interactive fiction" [22]. Emily Short has identified a number of structures commonly found in small-scale digital choose your own adventure (CYOA) narratives [23].

One such structure, the Track Switching Choice (see Fig. 1), provides a design pattern that enables and records user navigation between narrative paths associated with different characters or perspectives. Unlike large-scale branching structures such as the Time Cave, which often rely on replay to present multiple perspectives, Track Switching is a micro-structure that supports such perspective shifts within a single playthrough. This makes it particularly promising for educational applications, where sustained engagement within a single session may be more feasible than encouraging repeated replays. While the Track Switching Choice structure is frequently discussed in developer forums

250   B. Pitt et al.

and interactive fiction communities, it has yet to be systematically examined in academic literature. Emily Short, a prominent narrative designer in the field, has significantly shaped discourse around interactive fiction, though her work has not been formalized within traditional peer-reviewed research. To date, no empirical studies have operationalized the Track Switching Choice as a methodological framework in educational contexts.

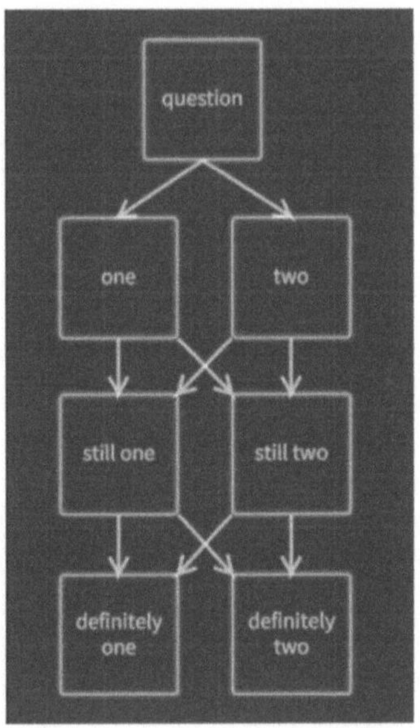

Fig. 1. Emily Short's Track Switching Choice structure illustrates two narrative paths, allowing the player to switch between them freely for several beats. While Short's example features two tracks, the structure can be extended to three or more.

This study, therefore, represents a novel application of the Track Switching Choice structure, not only as a storytelling structure but also as an analytic framework. The structure was leveraged to track how frequently and meaningfully players shifted between three perspectives (see Fig. 2), providing new insights into their narrative decision-making and cognitive strategies. By transforming a storytelling tool into a measurable structure for learner behavior, this work opens a new avenue for research into how interactive narrative systems can be studied as behavioral indicators of epistemic development and ideological flexibility.

Perspective-switching aligns closely with psychological constructs such as epistemic curiosity and the illusion of explanatory depth. Epistemic curiosity, the drive to resolve uncertainty and acquire new knowledge [24], is often triggered when learners confront unfamiliar or conflicting perspectives.

Likewise, the illusion of explanatory depth, which refers to people's tendency to overestimate their understanding of complex phenomena [25], can be disrupted through guided engagement with diverse viewpoints. In this study, the Track Switching

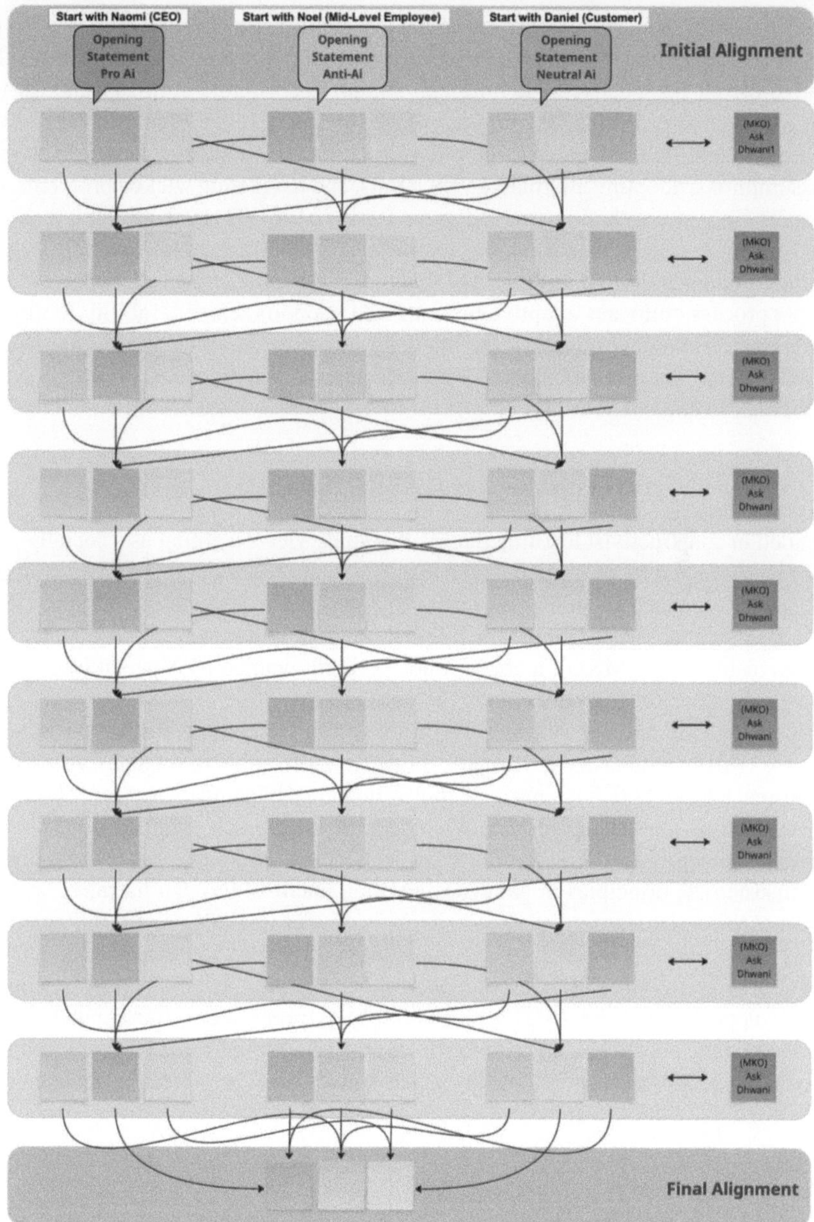

Fig. 2. Short's Track Switching Choice Structure adapted with three tracks.

Choice structure operationalizes both constructs by prompting learners to reconsider assumptions, shift perspectives, and update their mental models.

These mechanisms are not only pedagogically sound but grounded in cognitive science literature linking metacognitive engagement to deeper learning. This study is part of a broader body of doctoral research exploring systems thinking in education. For the purposes of this paper and in line with the conference theme, we focus specifically on how narrative-driven perspective-switching can stimulate epistemic curiosity and, in turn, foster ideological flexibility. Ideological flexibility refers to the mental ability to shift between concepts and adapt to novel, complex situations. It supports learners in revising assumptions, adopting alternative viewpoints, and navigating wicked problems, core capacities for systems thinking and adaptive learning [26]. Through structured engagement with diverse perspectives and reflective stakeholder narratives, learners enhance both their understanding of systems and their capacity for adaptive reasoning.

This process cultivates adaptive thinking and supports learners' ability to navigate complex, uncertain environments. By inviting players to step into roles with divergent worldviews, the Track Switching Choice structure serves as an experiential tool for developing ideological humility.

2.4   Constructivism, Guided Exploration, and the MKO

Grounded in constructivist learning theory, this study views learning as a socially mediated process shaped by developmental stages, instructional support, and active engagement [6, 27]. Central to this is Vygotsky's Zone of Proximal Development (ZPD), which describes the range within which learners can progress with support from a more knowledgeable other (MKO), a concept not explicitly named by Vygotsky but widely acknowledged in educational theory.

Extending this notion, Metcalfe et al. (2020) introduced the Region of Proximal Learning (RPL), emphasizing learners' intrinsic motivation to engage with slightly beyond-reach tasks [28]. This intrinsic motivation closely parallels the concept of epistemic curiosity discussed in Sect. 2.2. When properly scaffolded, such curiosity can drive deeper engagement—particularly in educational contexts that involve wicked problems.

Constructivist principles in game design often manifest through narrative scaffolding and experiential learning, shown to support critical thinking, systems literacy, and identity exploration [4, 29, 30]. In our study, these principles are embodied in Dhwani, an NPC designed as an MKO. Cast as a peer-like colleague, she offers optional, context-specific support tied to the AI Transformation Map, promoting differentiated learning and maintaining player agency. As prior research [5] showed learners found the maps overwhelming, embedding them within narrative and scaffolding through Dhwani helped reduce cognitive load and enhanced systems-level reasoning.

3   Experimental Design Methodology

To investigate how narrative-driven systems thinking interventions like educational IDNs affect learners' ideological flexibility and perspective-taking, this study employed a mixed-methods design. The central intervention was a narrative-based game that positioned players within a simulated organizational decision-making context, providing scaffolded support in using the Transformation Maps in decision-making.

This study focused on a single group of learners who interacted with a narrative-driven game designed around Emily Short's Track Switching Choice structure. A primary objective was to investigate how this structure could be adapted to yield measurable insights into player behavior and ideological flexibility, aligning with SRQ2: How can Emily Short's Track Switching Choice structure be adapted to provide measurable insights into player behavior and ideological flexibility? Specifically, the study examined whether the Track Switching mechanism could facilitate systems thinking (SRQ 1) and offer a lens through which to analyze learners' knowledge construction and engagement with complex, ideologically diverse content. While the overall research question is to understand how to promote ideological flexibility, defined as the capacity to entertain, understand, and empathize with divergent viewpoints, this study did not attempt to measure ideological change directly. Instead, it assessed behavioral indicators of ideological flexibility and openness to multiple perspectives, such as the frequency of perspective-switching, interaction with the MKO (SRQ 3) and evidence of other phenomena captured through gameplay interaction logs.

The game utilized structured dialogues embedded in a role-play scenario supported by a systems thinking framework, aiming to track learners' behavioral interactions, shifts in perspective, and engagement.

3.1 Participants and Setting

The study was conducted with 36 secondary school students (ages 14–18) from several classrooms at Shepaug Valley High School in Washington, Connecticut. Participants were selected based on teacher willingness, age appropriateness, and representation of a typical general education classroom. The sample included a balanced gender distribution and students with a range of educational needs, including those with 504 Plans and Individualized Education Programs (IEPs), allowing for the evaluation of accessibility and inclusivity.

High school students were chosen based on the readability level of the primary learning material, the WEF's AI Transformation Map. A Flesch-Kincaid Reading Ease score of 46.62 indicated college-level complexity. According to academic readability benchmarks (Yeung et al. 2018), this score corresponds to lower college-level reading complexity, making it challenging yet accessible for high school students. Moraine Park Technical College (2021) classifies such scores within the range of 30–50 as suitable for college-level content, as indicated in Table 1, reinforcing the appropriateness of the chosen age group when paired with adequate instructional scaffolding.

The inclusion of narrative scaffolding through the serious game format, supported by a NPC functioning as a MKO, was instrumental in mitigating potential cognitive overload. This design decision ensured that all learners, regardless of background, could meaningfully engage with the complex systems thinking content. Therefore, the selected participant profile supported the study's goal of evaluating the intervention's effectiveness in a realistic, inclusive high school setting.

Table 1. Adapted from Moraine Park Technical College, 2021. "What Flesch Reading Ease score should my content have?"

Flesch Reading Ease Score	School Level (U.S.)
>50	High School Level or Below
30–50	College Level
<30	College Graduate Level

3.2 Study Design

Participants played an interactive narrative game developed as a serious learning experience grounded in the Context–Learning–Game (CLG) framework [29]. The narrative was situated within a fictional corporate setting debating the integration of AI, framed through three distinct stakeholder roles: Naomi (CEO), Noel (Employee), and Daniel (Consumer). Learners assumed the role of a mediator and were guided, when needed, by an NPC named Dhwani, who functioned as a MKO. Her interventions were designed to direct players to relevant content in the AI Transformation Map, as the information dense maps are outside of the ZPD.

Gameplay involved structured stakeholder dialogues built using the Track Switching Choice structure, enabling learners to shift perspectives among the characters. The goal was to promote systems thinking by cultivating learners' ability to identify distinctions, systemic elements, interrelationships, and adopt multiple perspectives, as articulated in the DSRP framework [10]. These Learning Objectives were embedded throughout the gameplay experience, which involved repeated interactions with the Transformation Map and structured stakeholder dialogues. Specific student learning objectives were used to guide the experiment and artefact design. These were that students will be able to:

(1) apply systems thinking (DSRP) to interpret and synthesize stakeholder viewpoints within a complex decision-making scenario.
(2) construct new mental models of complex systems by engaging with digital tools (WEF's Transformation Maps)
(3) build understating of diverse ideological viewpoints
(4) explore diverse ideological positions by engaging in perspective-taking and demonstrating openness to revising one's stance based on new insights.

3.3 Instruments and Measures

Playthrough data served as a primary quantitative measure, capturing behavioral interactions during gameplay, including the number of perspective switches and the frequency with which learners accessed the MKO character. These metrics were used to explore patterns of engagement and their relationship to learners' ideological flexibility and systems understanding (see Table 2).

To ensure consistency, each session was structured into clearly defined phases and lasted approximately 80 min in total. All sessions were facilitated by the principal investigator and followed the same overall structure: an exploration phase using educational

Table 2. Outline of the survey and behavioral measures used in the study

Measure	Measurement Tool/Source	Evaluation Purpose	Measurement Purpose
Engagement Behavior	Game Logs	Analyze interaction depth and style during gameplay	Reveal depth and style of interaction during gameplay
Perspective-Taking Behavior	Game Logs	Evaluate flexibility in exploring multiple viewpoints and stakeholder roles	Track perspective-shifting across stakeholder roles
User Experience	Post-Test Likert Questions	Assess usability, preference, and confidence in the learning modality	Gauge engagement, preference and impact of learning modality

IDN with embedded transformation maps, a written recommendation task in which students proposed an ethical AI integration strategy that satisfied multiple stakeholders, and a post-test questionnaire to evaluate overall experience, usability, and preference. This structured flow ensured parity in time and task structure across all classes, enabling valid comparison of their learning outcomes.

Post-Tests. Students completed a post-test questionnaire immediately after participation with the narrative game and transformation maps. The post-test measured user experience, specifically engagement and format preferences. These responses were used to evaluate the acceptability of the game design and whether or not narrative-driven systems learning in formal educational settings is preferred.

Perspective Switching Logs. Logs were generated that tracked player navigation across stakeholder dialogue branches. Every transition from one stakeholder's viewpoint to another was logged, enabling researchers to quantify switching behavior. These logs captured each transition between stakeholder perspectives, enabling analysis of player preferences and spontaneous engagement with divergent viewpoints. Importantly, perspective choices were anonymized to avoid priming or biasing learners, allowing for the unobtrusive measurement of ideological flexibility based on behavioral patterns alone. The combination of behavioral data and written reflection provided a rich measure of ideological flexibility and epistemic curiosity.

NPC MKO Engagement Metrics. All interactions with Dhwani, the MKO character, were recorded. These included the number of times learners sought her guidance and compared that to overall perspective shifts and final perspective stance.

Quantitative data from the post-test and behavioral logs were analyzed using paired t-tests and correlation analysis to identify significant changes and relationships.

4 Game Design and Implementation

The development of the serious game in this study was guided by the Context–Learning–Game (CLG) Framework, as defined in the doctoral thesis by Rojas-Salazar [29, 30]. The CLG Framework offers a structured and theoretically grounded approach to designing educational games by aligning three interdependent components: the context, learning, and game stages. The 'Context' stage defines the educational setting and learner profile. The 'Learning' stage specifies the pedagogical goals and desired competencies. The 'Game' stage describes the mechanics, narrative elements, and interactive structures that deliver the learning experience. This triadic alignment ensures the game remains anchored in real-world relevance, educational objectives, and interactive engagement.

The design of the educational artifact was informed by the contextual parameters outlined in Sect. 3: Experimental Design Methodology. This experimental design phase defined the learner profile, classroom environment, technological constraints, and targeted systems thinking objectives, factors that directly informed the artifact's development. In alignment with the CLG framework, articulating the "Context" first ensured that the narrative and pedagogical features of the artifact were purposefully designed to meet the specific needs and conditions of the learning environment. This approach allowed the artifact to be both educationally relevant and practically deployable, grounded in the realities of the classroom setting and the characteristics of its users.

To operationalize the narrative structure, the game was authored using *Ink*, an open-source scripting language developed by Inkle Studios for crafting nonlinear, branching narratives. To simulate a realistic and immersive communication environment, additional presentation code was developed to render the narrative as a group chat interface (see Figs. 3 and 4). This format allowed learners to engage with multiple non-player characters (NPCs) representing diverse stakeholder perspectives, supporting intuitive perspective-taking and track switching.

In this study, the context centres on high school students engaging with the complex issue of artificial intelligence (AI) integration in business using the WEF's Strategic Intelligence Transformation Maps. The learning stage emphasizes the development of DSRP systems thinking competencies within complex systems. These skills are developed through structured engagement with the Transformation Maps, which serve as both content and systems thinking tools. Although the DSRP framework is not explicitly introduced to learners, its core principles are intentionally embedded in the game design to scaffold and reinforce systemic reasoning.

The game stage employs a narrative-based interactive digital format that presents learners with role-based scenarios involving diverse stakeholders in the AI ecosystem. Through engagement with a MKO character, learners are guided to explore multiple perspectives. This approach mitigates common challenges associated with navigating the Transformation Maps, such as information overload and lack of guidance, by embedding structured prompts within a narrative flow [5]. The narrative thus serves not merely as a storytelling device but as a cognitive scaffold that supports exploration, comprehension, and application of complex systems thinking.

The adoption of the CLG Framework enabled the coherent integration of educational theory, systems thinking pedagogy, and game design to develop a serious game tailored

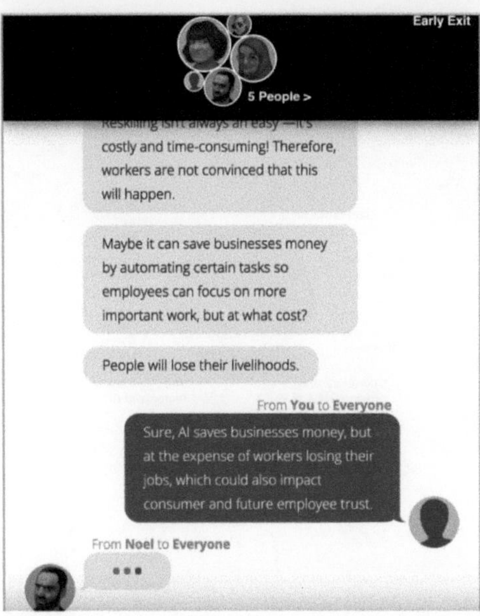

Fig. 3. Simulated group chat interface showing NPC dialogue branches (Noel, the employee in this case). The interface was implemented using JavaScript to parse Ink output into styled message bubbles and to simulate the temporal dynamics of real-time messaging, such as delayed message arrival and "typing" indicators.

to the cognitive and contextual needs of high school learners addressing complex global topics such as AI integration in society.

4.1 Stakeholder Character Design

Three central stakeholder characters were created, each representing a different position in the debate on AI as reflected in the Transformation Maps (see Table 3). These characters were designed to surface ideological tensions and systemic interdependencies, helping learners explore the complex trade-offs associated with AI integration. By representing distinct roles, CEO (Naomi), employee (Noel), and customer (Daniel), each character offered a different lens through which to evaluate systemic impacts and stakeholder priorities.

The characters' dialogues were modular and structured into branching scenes, enabling learners to switch perspectives and uncover new information relevant to the decision-making scenario. Dialogue paths were embedded with cues aligned to systems thinking constructs such as distinctions and relationships, helping students identify the dynamics underlying each stakeholder's position. These structures promoted exploration, encouraging learners to revisit prior assumptions and refine their mental models based on new insights.

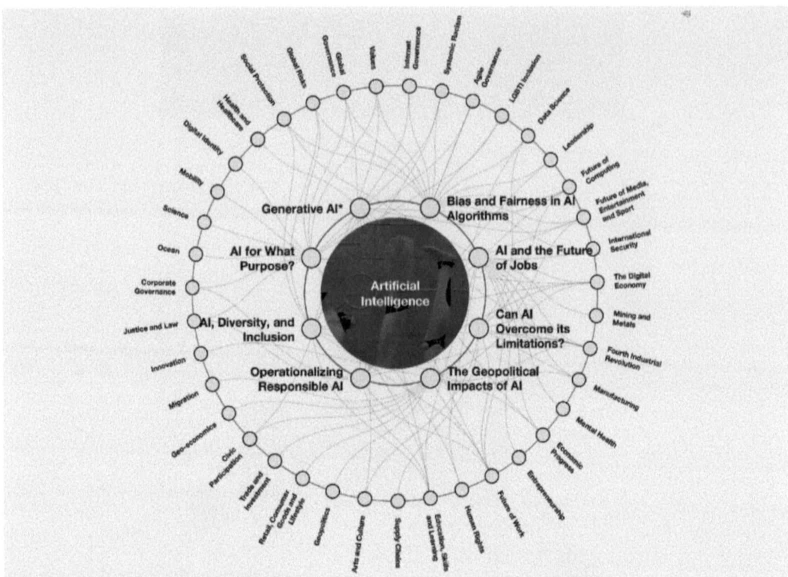

Fig. 4. The AI Transformation Map computer interface, where students receive prompts from Dhwani, the More Knowledgeable Other (MKO), guiding them to relevant content. Students can also freely explore key issues within the map, depending on the conversation path they are navigating on their mobile device.

Table 3. Stakeholder Roles, Perspectives, and Narrative Functions

Character Name	Stakeholder Role	Perspective
Naomi	Chief Executive Officer (CEO)	Supports AI adoption to improve efficiency, profitability, and staying competitive; stance considered pro-AI.
Noel	Mid-level Employee	Raises concerns about job displacement and ethical implications; stance considered anti-AI.
Daniel	Customer	Prioritizes affordability and efficiency but expresses concerns about ethics, service, and privacy; stance considered centrist.

4.2 Track Switching Choice Structure Integration

Emily Short's Track Switching Choice structure was employed to create structurally distinct yet interconnected narrative threads. Players could move laterally between stakeholder dialogues at key decision points, simulating a shift in narrative perspective without being confined to a linear path. These switches were recorded and analyzed as markers of perspective-switching, allowing researchers to examine how exposure to alternative views influenced player trajectories and encouraged ideological flexibility.

Each switch allowed players to choose from three options without being informed which character each option represented. This structure was intentionally designed to reduce priming effects and bias by anonymizing dialogue choices. By withholding character identity, the system encouraged learners to engage with arguments based on their content rather than on preconceptions tied to specific stakeholders. This approach provided a more authentic behavioral measure of ideological flexibility, capturing how learners aligned with different perspectives without metacognitive cues or guiding signals.

This novel adaptation of the Track Switching Choice structure transformed a narrative design concept into a research instrument, enabling the study of learner agency, epistemic curiosity, and the iterative construction of understanding. In later sections of the game, players were encouraged to synthesize insights from multiple tracks when constructing final policy recommendations, highlighting how narrative structure and learning objectives were tightly interwoven.

4.3   Role of the MKO

A central feature of the IDN was Dhwani, a narrative character designed as a non-intrusive MKO. The purpose was to enable learners with varying levels of ability and skills, both higher and lower, the opportunity to explore the complex system in line with their own abilities and not be forced to interact unless needed, a term commonly used in U.S. education known as differentiation [31]. Unlike tutorial guides or narrators, Dhwani was cast as a colleague within the fictional organization. Players could consult her at any point for help from navigating the Transformation Map to contextualizing stakeholder arguments.

Dhwani's responses were designed using principles of minimal guidance: rather than supplying answers, she directed players toward specific sections of the AI Transformation Map. Her character encouraged exploration and self-regulated learning, positioning her as a dynamic resource rather than an authority figure.

The inclusion of Dhwani as a narrative scaffold draws from findings in an earlier ICIDS paper, "Integrating Narrative Design into the World Economic Forum's Transformation Maps for Enhanced Complexity Comprehension in Interactive Storytelling" [5], which identified that learners found the WEF's Transformation Maps cognitively overwhelming in isolation. The study suggested that the maps fell outside most users' ZPD, calling for narrative scaffolding to improve accessibility and engagement. In this project, rather than relying solely on the maps as standalone tools, we incorporated them into a narrative game format and embedded Dhwani as an NPC to serve as a MKO. This approach transforms the Transformation Maps from static data tools into interactive, learner-centered experiences, enabling more intuitive exploration and systems-level reflection.

Importantly, Dhwani's role bridges two complementary learning theories: Vygotsky's ZPD and Metcalfe et al.'s RPL [28]. While ZPD focuses on external guidance enabling learners to complete tasks beyond their independent capacity, RPL emphasizes internal metacognitive awareness that learners are nearing conceptual insight. Dhwani supports both processes—she provides structured scaffolding to assist comprehension (ZPD), while her prompts are crafted to activate learners' intrinsic curiosity and reflection (RPL). This dual alignment strengthens the narrative's pedagogical impact by facilitating both guided exploration and autonomous meaning-making.

Building on this dual scaffolding role, the game's constructivist design allowed learners to build understanding through iterative interaction and contextual decision-making. This MKO reinforces the narrative's capacity not only to guide, but to provoke curiosity, modeling effective support in complexity learning.

5   Results

5.1   User Experience and Perceived Learning Gains

Students reported high levels of engagement, self-confidence, and preference with the activity (see Table 4). The post-activity survey revealed that 91.7% of students agreed or strongly agreed that they felt capable of completing this activity ($M = 6.31$) (see Fig. 5), yet only 52.8% ($M = 5.22$) felt that the maps alone helped them understand the complexity (see Fig. 6). This suggests that while the Transformation Maps contained rich systems content, additional support was needed to foster deeper understanding. Also, the majority of students found the activity engaging and would prefer activities like this to regular class work (see Figs. 7 and 8). The narrative scaffolding, particularly the integration of stakeholder dialogues and the MKO character Dhwani, likely played a critical role in helping learners interpret, contextualize, and engage with the complex information presented.

Table 4.   User Experience Metrics

Survey Question	Mean Score
I found this activity engaging.	5.56
I prefer this type of learning experience (game/platform).	5.42
I felt capable of completing the activity.	6.31
The maps helped me understand AI and its complexity?	5.22

Note: Scores represent mean responses on a 7-point Likert scale (1 = Strongly Disagree, 7 = Strongly Agree)

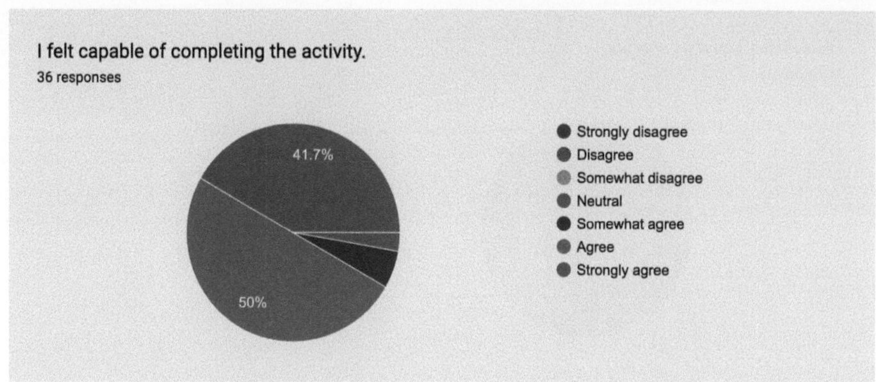

Fig. 5. A total of 91.7% of students reported feeling capable of completing the activity, and affordances of the game experience and environment positively impacted students' confidence in engaging with early college–level content.

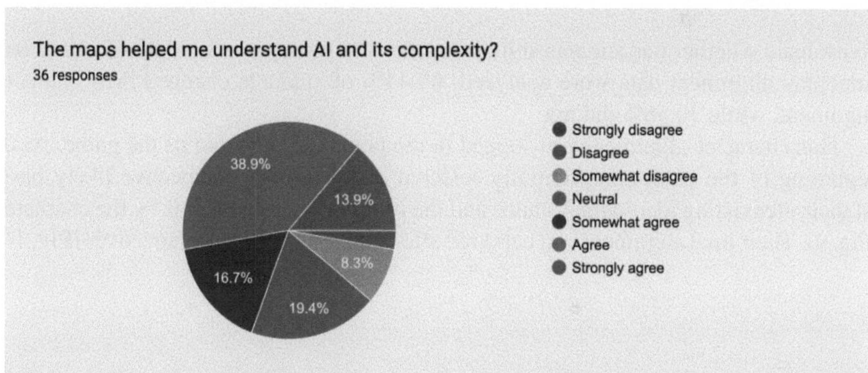

Fig. 6. Only 52.8% (M = 5.22) strongly agreed or agreed that they felt the maps helped them understand the complexity. However, only 11.1% of students showed disagreement that the maps helped them understand AI and its complexity.

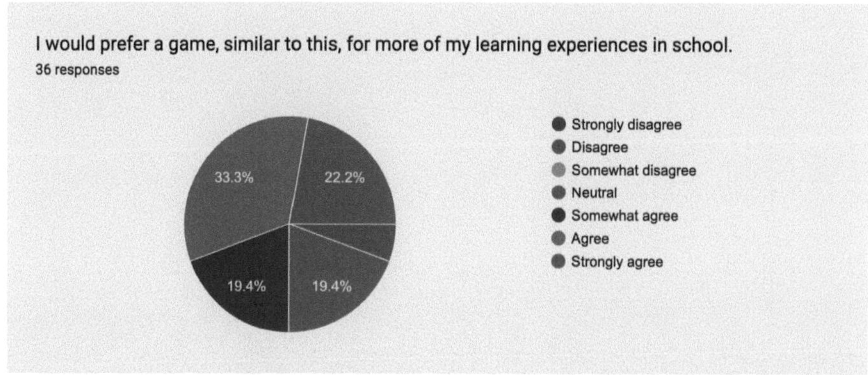

Fig. 7. Only a small minority (5.6%) did not prefer this type of game for future learning.

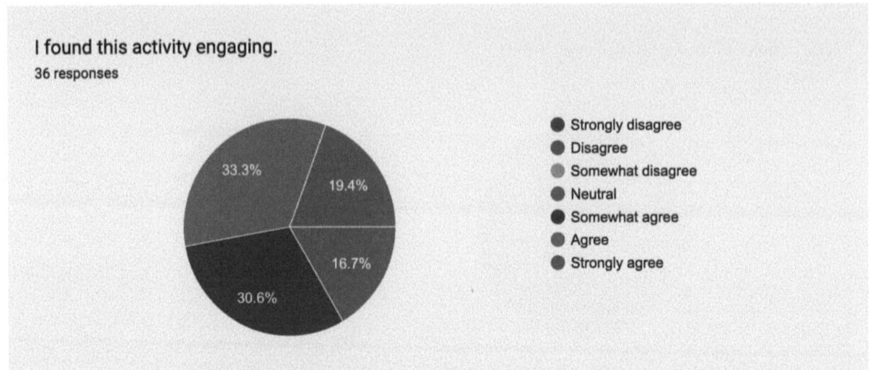

Fig. 8. A total 83.3% of students agreed that the activity was engaging, while only 16.7 were neutra. No students felt the activity was not engaging.

6   Ideological Shifts and Moderation Trends in Log-Based Behavior

To evaluate whether participants shifted positions to more or less polarized characters, gameplay alignment data were analyzed; 69.44% of students changed their character alignment, while 30.56% did not.

This character alignment was logged in the beginning and end of the game. At the beginning of the game, they initially selected a stakeholder perspective likely based on their preexisting ideological stance and the introductory statements by the characters (Fig. 9). Their final alignment was captured after engaging with all perspectives (Fig. 10).

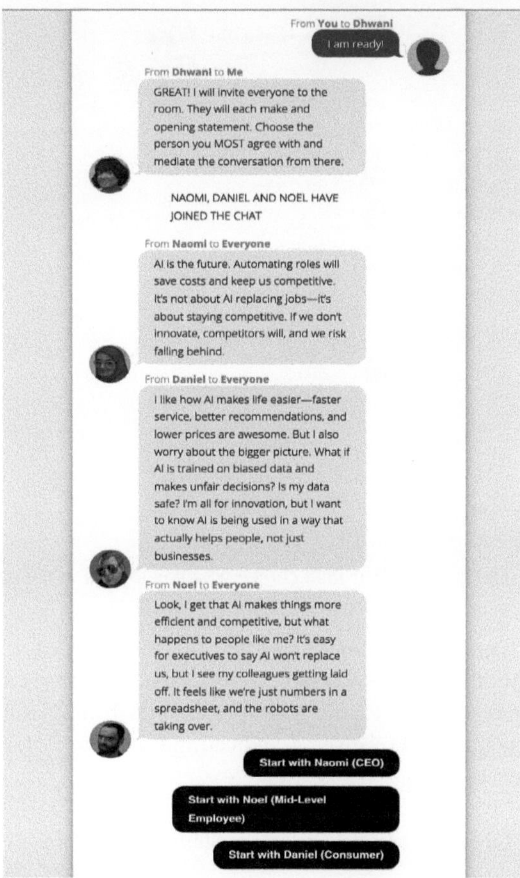

Fig. 9. Users make their initial choice which is logged in-game log.

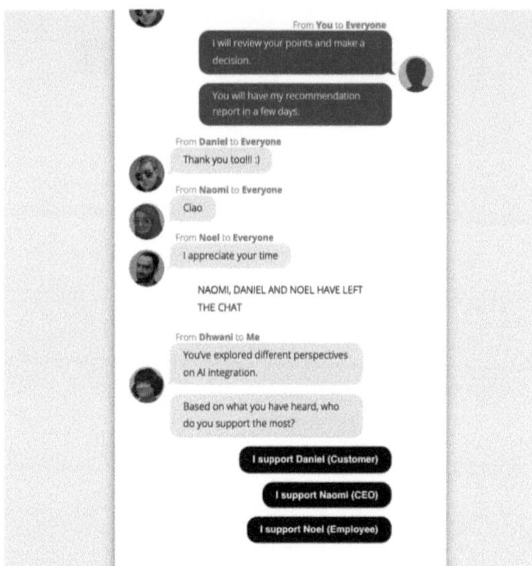

Fig. 10. Users make their final choice which is logged in the game log.

An analysis of participants' final character choices revealed a clear trend toward ideological moderation. Daniel, who represented a centrist view, emerged as the most frequent final alignment, with 12 users shifting to him from Naomi or Noel. Naomi received 7 switches, and Noel received 4, indicating significantly less attraction toward extreme stances (see Table 5).

Table 5. Character Preference Shifts (Initial → Final)

	Daniel	Naomi	Noel
Daniel	5	2	4
Naomi	6	6	0
Noel	6	5	6

Further behavioral data distinguished between two learner groups: switchers (those who changed their initial character alignment by the end of the game) and loyalists (those who maintained their original alignment). Switchers who changed character alignment spent significantly more time in the experience ($M = 1467.83$ s) compared to loyalists ($M = 1073.26$ s), a difference that was statistically significant ($p \approx 0.040$). Although switchers also exhibited more in-game perspective switches between stakeholder dialogues (5.30 vs. 4.65), this difference was not statistically significant ($p \approx 0.25$). Table 6 offers a breakdown of how learners transitioned between stakeholder perspectives throughout the game. It visualizes the alignment shifts from each initial character choice to final selection, capturing the dynamics of learner decision-making over the course of the narrative. By tracking these movements, the table highlights how exposure to multiple perspectives facilitated reconsideration and ultimately led to more balanced ideological positions.

Table 6. Final Character Alignments and Behavioral Measures

Measure	Result
Most common final alignment	Daniel (Moderate position)
Total switches to Daniel	12
Total switches to Naomi	7
Total switches to Noel	4
Avg. time-on-task (Switchers)	1467.83 s
Avg. time-on-task (Loyalists)	1073.26 s
Time-on-task significance	$p \approx 0.040$
Avg. perspective switches (Switchers)	5.30
Avg. perspective switches (Loyalists)	4.65
Perspective switches significance	Not significant ($p \approx 0.25$)

These findings suggest that students actively reconsidered initial assumptions and moved toward more moderate, integrated viewpoints over time, reinforcing the role of narrative environments in supporting depolarization and reflective exploration.

6.1 The Role of Dhwani - The MKO

To further understand the cognitive impact of the game, this section investigates the role of Dhwani, the embedded NPC who acts as a MKO. Drawing from theoretical frameworks such as Vygotsky's ZPD and Metcalfe's RPL, Dhwani was designed not merely as a narrative device, but as a scaffold to support learners' reflection and engagement with complex systems. The findings in this section are organized around three key observations: (1) engagement with Dhwani predicts final perspective shifting, (2) narrative engagement followed a learner-driven, non-linear trajectory marked by emergent inflection points, and (3) Dhwani8, a specific prompt within the narrative, functioned as a cognitive inflection point correlated with ideological flexibility. These findings are derived exclusively from gameplay log data and reveal distinct learner behaviors that illustrate how narrative scaffolding can support reflective exploration and perspective transformation.

Engagement with Dhwani Predicts Final Perspective Shifting. Game log data showed that approximately 70% of students who interacted with Dhwani's prompts changed their final character alignment, compared to only 35% of those who did not. This suggests Dhwani functioned effectively as an epistemic scaffold, promoting deeper perspective-taking and ideological flexibility (see Table 7).

Logistic regression analysis confirmed a statistically significant relationship between Dhwani engagement and character switching ($p = .038$). Learners who accessed any

Dhwani-tagged content were substantially more likely to revise their final perspective, reinforcing the role of narrative scaffolding in facilitating epistemic exploration.

Table 7. Dhwani Use and Switching Behavior

Dhwani Use	% Switched	% Stayed
Used Dhwani	~ 70%	~ 30%
Did Not Use	~ 35%	~ 65%

These results support the hypothesis that Dhwani's reflective prompts acted as epistemic scaffolds, facilitating deeper reconsideration of perspectives and encouraging narrative exploration beyond initial ideological positions.

Learner-Driven Narrative Engagement and Emergent Inflection Points. An analysis of tag usage over the course of the narrative experience revealed that Dhwani's influence did not follow a typical early-to-late decay pattern, as is often observed in digital narratives where player attention to novel items tends to decay over time, following a stretched-exponential law [32]. Instead, engagement with Dhwani appeared path-dependent, shaped by the individualized meaning-making processes and narrative choices of each learner (See Fig. 11).

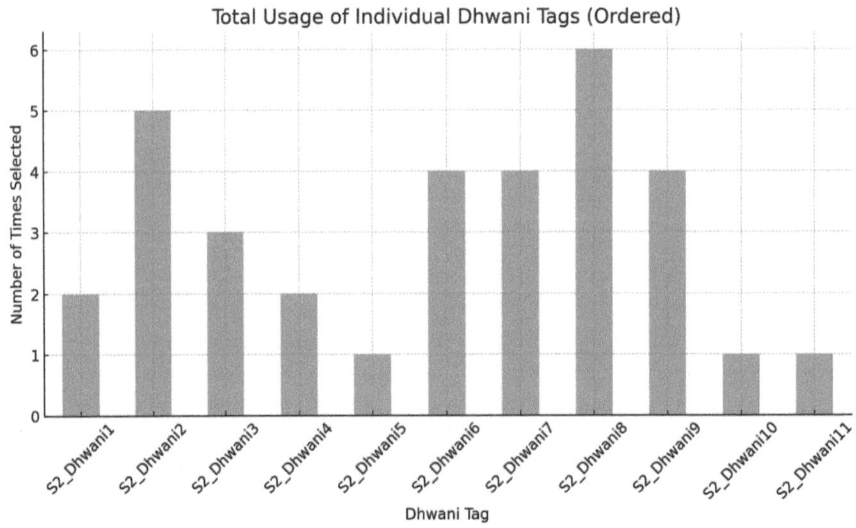

Fig. 11. Graph showing the total usage of individual dhwani tags chronologically throughout the game, highlighting an atypical peak later in the game with the Dhwani8 tag.

Specifically, early tags like Dhwani2 saw consistently high engagement, suggesting that learners were initially receptive to reflective input. Mid-sequence tags (Dhwani5–7, 9–11) displayed variable usage, likely reflecting the branching and adaptive nature of the narrative system, which allowed players to move through different content paths depending on prior decisions.

Dhwani8 emerged as the peak point of engagement, surpassing all other tags—even though it occurred later in the narrative arc and lacked system-driven emphasis. This challenges conventional assumptions about cognitive load or engagement decay in digital learning environments. Instead, it implies that narrative and ideological tension may have organically culminated at this point, drawing learners into a moment of deeper reflection.

What this shows is that Dhwani2–4 had high early engagement, particularly with Dhwani2. Dhwani5–7, 9–11 had variable usage, and Dhwani8 had Peak usage across all tags.

The combination of high early engagement, non-linear mid-game usage, and a late-game spike may suggest a learner-driven trajectory in which players engaged with Dhwani not out of scripted necessity, but in response to emerging cognitive needs and moments of narrative dissonance.

Dhwani8: An Emergent Cognitive Inflection Point. Among all Dhwani-tagged interactions, Dhwani8 had the highest engagement rate and showed a strong correlation with ideological switching (83.3%) (Table 8). Players who accessed Dhwani8 were more likely to change their final alignment and demonstrated broader engagement with multiple stakeholder perspectives. Despite no changes in narrative prompt or interface cues, this moment drew more learners than any other point in the game.

Table 8. Comparison of users who did and did not engage with Dhwani8 revealed a distinct pattern

Metric	Did NOT Use Dhwani8	Used Dhwani8
Switch Rate	52.9%	83.3%
Daniel Tags Accessed	3.18	4.00
Noel Tags Accessed	2.74	3.17
Naomi Tags Accessed	3.09	1.83 ↓

This suggests Dhwani8 may have functioned as a critical inflection point—what some scholars refer to as an epistemic change [33], or a shift in how individuals understand and engage with knowledge. Despite no change in narrative prompt or system cue, learners frequently paused at this point to reflect and reconsider their stance. This behavior aligns with Sect. 2.4's discussion of learner-initiated engagement, illustrating how well-timed narrative scaffolds can support ideological flexibility. While the study does not fully explore the long-term effects of such moments, the findings point to promising directions for future research on how emergent narrative prompts can foster perspective transformation and ideological flexibility.

7 Discussion

7.1 Advancing the Role of IDNs in Education

This study demonstrates that IDNs can serve not only as engaging pedagogical tools but also as platforms for measuring behavioral indicators of learning. The use of Emily Short's Track Switching Choice structure allowed for the logging of perspective-switching behavior, providing a unique window into learners' mind as they engaged with multiple stakeholder positions.

Importantly, the results indicate that narrative structures supporting non-linear exploration can encourage learners to challenge their initial assumptions, a critical step toward reducing ideological rigidity. This suggests that IDNs are well-suited to addressing educational goals related to civic discourse, empathy, and critical thinking.

7.2 The Value of a Narrative-Driven MKO

This design was directly informed by prior research identifying that learners found the Transformation Maps overwhelming when unaided, necessitating narrative scaffolding to improve engagement and understanding [5]. The inclusion of Dhwani as a MKO represents a novel approach to scaffolding within IDNs. Rather than functioning as a didactic guide or linear tutor, Dhwani's role was as a support in navigating the complexity of the map interface. It is suggested that her omniscient presence, though she never interfered unless called upon, acted as a comfort to students, making them feel capable of completing the activity.

Interaction with Dhwani prompts, particularly Dhwani8, correlated with greater ideological movement between characters. This suggests a relationship between engagement with reflective content and increased ideological flexibility within the narrative experience. The broader analysis of playthrough data revealed meaningful patterns of cognitive engagement tied to time-on-task, perspective switching, ideological moderation, and interaction with epistemic scaffolds. Students who spent approximately 25–30 min in the experience demonstrated the deepest levels of narrative exploration and were more likely to shift perspectives and adopt moderate ideological positions.

Central to this process was the role of Dhwani, who served as a scaffold for self-directed reflection. Learners appeared to recognize moments of uncertainty or conceptual conflict and autonomously engaged with her prompts—especially Dhwani8—which emerged as a metacognitive checkpoint. This behavior underscores the capacity of reflective narrative elements to prompt voluntary cognitive reappraisal. Overall, these findings support the view that well-designed narrative systems can facilitate depolarization, encourage systems thinking, and promote sustained cognitive engagement. They also highlight the potential of interactive storytelling to foster critical thinking and ethical reasoning in complex, real-world domains such as artificial intelligence and societal risk.

7.3 Design Implications for IDNs and Systems Pedagogy

The alignment of narrative games with systems thinking constructs, particularly the DSRP model, provided a framework for translating abstract systems principles into actionable in-game choices and dialogue. This design approach aligns with established findings in serious game literature, which emphasize the pedagogical value of developing knowledge through interaction and exploration with appropriate scaffolding rather than direct instruction [34]. Instead of isolating learning in external explanations, effective games integrate instruction within gameplay itself, fostering "situated meaning" - the idea that knowledge is best acquired through interactive, contextualized practice. In this study, narrative scaffolds were embedded into the role-based design, perspective-switching mechanics, modular NPC support, and the dynamic visualizations of the transformation maps, encouraging learners to engage more deeply with complexity and demonstrate greater ideological flexibility.

Future IDNs aiming to cultivate systems thinking would benefit from integrating these design strategies. Carefully aligning systems thinking skills into the narrative, allowing learner-driven exploration, and structuring interactions around contrasting stakeholder perspectives can support both metacognitive development and conceptual change, especially when paired with a narrative scaffold like the MKO that supports self-directed learning in line with ZPD and RPL principles.

7.4 Limitations and Future Work

This study is subject to several limitations. The intervention was relatively short and conducted in a specific educational context, which may limit generalizability. The participant pool was relatively small ($n = 36$), and future studies would benefit from a larger and more diverse sample to improve generalizability and statistical power. The measurement of ideological flexibility was indirect, behavioral proxies rather than long-term tracking of belief change.

Future work should examine the longitudinal impact of IDN-based systems learning on ideological development. Additionally, the design of adaptive MKO characters capable of tailoring feedback to user profiles may further enhance the personalization and efficacy of narrative scaffolding. Exploring other domains, such as climate change or public health, could also test the transferability of the design framework.

Although the study was designed to promote ideological flexibility, the data collected primarily capture short-term behavioral and reflective indicators of ideological flexibility. Longitudinal studies would be necessary to measure durable shifts in belief systems or ideological stance.

8 Conclusion

This study explored how IDNs can support ideological flexibility and systems thinking by enabling learners to engage with diverse perspectives in a complex decision-making context. Through the design and implementation of an educational IDN grounded in the CLG framework, the research addressed the central question of how IDNs can be used to measure the impact of exposure to multiple perspectives on learners' ideological flexibility.

Findings from both behavioral logs and self-reported experiences suggest that the integration of Emily Short's Track Switching Choice structure (SRQ2) successfully facilitated perspective-switching, providing measurable insights into how learners navigated ideological complexity. Moreover, the inclusion of a MKO character (SRQ3) functioned as a non-intrusive scaffold that enhanced learner agency and supported systems-level reasoning. Finally, the narrative game exposed players to competing stakeholder viewpoints within a single, immersive experience, promoting the core dimensions of systems thinking—particularly the recognition of dynamic interactions and multiple viewpoints (SRQ1).

By transforming abstract systems concepts into situated, narrative-based interactions, this study demonstrates that IDNs can function not only as educational tools but also as analytic frameworks for examining learner behavior. The findings offer promising implications for future research and practice, particularly in designing digital environments that cultivate cognitive adaptability and epistemic curiosity in the face of complex, real-world challenges.

Acknowledgments. This research was supported by the SFI Centre for Research Training in Digitally-Enhanced Reality.

References

1. Rittel, H.W.J., Webber, M.M.: Dilemmas in a general theory of planning. Policy. Sci. **4**, 155–169 (1973). https://doi.org/10.1007/BF01405730
2. Murray, J.H.: Kaleidoscopic machines: the IDN as a critical medium [Keynote address]. In: International Conference on Interactive Digital Storytelling, Dublin, Ireland, December 2018
3. Salomon, G., Perkins, D.: Chapter V: Learning in wonderland: what do computers really offer education? Teach. Coll. Rec. **97**, 111–130 (1996). https://doi.org/10.1177/016146819 609700606
4. Shaffer, D.W.: Epistemic frames for epistemic games. Comput. Educ. **46**, 223–234 (2006). https://doi.org/10.1016/j.compedu.2005.11.003
5. Pitt, B., Roth, C.: Integrating narrative design into the world economic forum's transformation maps for enhanced complexity comprehension. In: Holloway-Attaway, L., Murray, J.T. (eds.) ICIDS 2023. LNCS, vol. 14383. pp. 344–362. Springer, Cham (2023). https://doi.org/10. 1007/978-3-031-47655-6_21
6. Vygotsky, L.S., Cole, M.: Mind in Society: Development of Higher Psychological Processes. Harvard University Press (1978). https://doi.org/10.2307/j.ctvjf9vz4
7. Cabrera, D., Cabrera, L.: Systems thinking made simple: new hope for solving wicked problems. Insight **18**, 41 (2015). https://doi.org/10.1002/inst.12062
8. Barbara, J., et al.: Issues in education: skills for future generations. In: Holloway-Attaway, L., Murray, J.T. (eds.) ICIDS 2023. LNCS, vol. 14383. pp. 57–72. Springer, Cham (2023). https://doi.org/10.1007/978-3-031-47655-6_4
9. Richmond, B.: Systems thinking: critical thinking skills for the 1990s and beyond. Syst. Dyn. Rev. **9**, 113–133 (1993). https://doi.org/10.1002/sdr.4260090203
10. Cabrera, D., Colosi, L.: Distinctions, systems, relationships, and perspectives (DSRP): a theory of thinking and of things. Eval. Program Plann. **31**, 311–317 (2008). https://doi.org/ 10.1016/j.evalprogplan.2008.04.001
11. Cabrera, D., Cabrera, L.: DSRP theory: a primer. Systems **10**, 26 (2022). https://doi.org/10. 3390/systems10020026

12. Roth, C., Pitt, B., Bender-Salazar, R.: From complexity to clarity: applying systems thinking and mapping to the co-creation of learning indus. In: Murray, J.T., Reyes, M.C. (eds.) ICIDS 2024. LNCS, vol. 15467, pp. 292–310. Springer, Cham (2025). https://doi.org/10.1007/978-3-031-78453-8_19

13. Share, J., Mamikonyan, T., Lopez, E.: Critical media literacy in teacher education, theory, and practice. In: Oxford Research Encyclopedia of Education. Oxford University Press (2019). https://doi.org/10.1093/acrefore/9780190264093.013.1404

14. Koenitz, H.: Understanding Interactive Digital Narrative: Immersive Expressions for a Complex Time. Routledge, London (2023)

15. Riedl, M.O., Bulitko, V.: Interactive narrative: an intelligent systems approach. AIMag. **34**, 67–77 (2013). https://doi.org/10.1609/aimag.v34i1.2449

16. Murray, J.H.: Hamlet on the Holodeck: The Future of Narrative in Cyberspace. The MIT Press, Cambridge, Mass (1997)

17. Bruner, J.: The narrative construction of reality. Crit. Inq. **18**, 1–21 (1991). https://doi.org/10.1086/448619

18. Snowden, D.: Story Telling: An Old Skill in a New Context. SAGE Publications (2016). https://doi.org/10.1177/0266382994237045

19. Roth, C., Koenitz, H.: Evaluating the user experience of interactive digital narrative. In: Proceedings of the 1st International Workshop on Multimedia Alternate Realities - AltMM '16, pp. 31–36. ACM Press, New York, New York, USA (2016). https://doi.org/10.1145/2983298.2983302

20. Green, M.C., Brock, T.C.: The role of transportation in the persuasiveness of public narratives. J. Pers. Soc. Psychol. **79**, 701–721 (2000). https://doi.org/10.1037/0022-3514.79.5.701

21. McAdams, D.P.: The Stories We Live By: Personal Myths and the Making of the Self. William Morrow & Company, New York (1993)

22. Montfort, N.: Twisty Little Passages: An Approach to Interactive Fiction. The MIT Press (2003). https://doi.org/10.7551/mitpress/6936.001.0001

23. Short, E.: Small-Scale Structures in CYOA. https://emshort.blog/2016/11/05/small-scale-structures-in-cyoa/. Accessed 30 Dec 2024

24. Litman, J.: Curiosity and the pleasures of learning: wanting and liking new information. Cogn. Emot. **19**, 793–814 (2005). https://doi.org/10.1080/02699930541000101

25. Rozenblit, L., Keil, F.: The misunderstood limits of folk science: an illusion of explanatory depth. Cogn. Sci. **26**, 521–562 (2002). https://doi.org/10.1207/s15516709cog2605_1

26. Spiro, R., Coulson, R., Feltovich, P., Anderson, D.: Cognitive flexibility theory: advanced knowledge acquisition in ill-structured domains. In: Unrau, N. (ed.) Theoretical Models and Processes of Reading, pp. 544–557. International Reading Association (2013). https://doi.org/10.1598/0710.22

27. Piaget, J.: The Construction of Reality in the Child. Basic Books, New York (1954). https://doi.org/10.1037/11168-000

28. Metcalfe, J., Schwartz, B.L., Eich, T.S.: Epistemic curiosity and the region of proximal learning. Curr. Opin. Behav. Sci. **35**, 40–47 (2020). https://doi.org/10.1016/j.cobeha.2020.06.007

29. Rojas-Salazar, A., Haahr, M.: The CLG framework: a methodical approach to designing educational video games. In: Berrezueta, S. (ed.) LACLO 2023. LNET, pp. 254–270. Springer, Singapore (2023). https://doi.org/10.1007/978-981-99-7353-8_20

30. Rojas-Salazar, A.J.: Game-Based Learning of Data Structures Based on Analogies: Learning Gains and Intrinsic Motivation in Higher Education Environments (2022)

31. Tomlinson, C.A.: How to Differentiate Instruction in Mixed-Ability Classrooms, 2nd edn (Professional Development). Association for Supervision & Curriculum Development, Alexandria, VA (2001)

32. Wu, F., Huberman, B.A.: Novelty and collective attention. Proc. Natl. Acad. Sci. U.S.A. **104**, 17599–17601 (2007). https://doi.org/10.1073/pnas.0704916104
33. Kerwer, M., Rosman, T.: Epistemic change and diverging information: how do prior epistemic beliefs affect the efficacy of short-term interventions? Learn. Individ. Differ. **80**, 101886 (2020). https://doi.org/10.1016/j.lindif.2020.101886
34. Gee, J.P.: What video games have to teach us about learning and literacy. Comput. Entertain. **1**, 20 (2003). https://doi.org/10.1145/950566.950595

Post Game Character Prequels in Educational Tabletop RPGs: Enhancing Character Identification with Interactive Digital Narratives

Akrivi Katifori[1,2]([✉]) [iD], Dimitra Petousi[1] [iD], Katerina Servi[1] [iD],
Pantelis Sakellariadis[2] [iD], Maria Roussou[2] [iD], and Yannis Ioannidis[1,2] [iD]

[1] ATHENA Research and Innovation Center, Maroussi, Greece
{vivi,dpetousi}@athenarc.gr
[2] National and Kapodistrian University of Athens, Athens, Greece
{mroussou,yannis}@di.uoa.gr

Abstract. This study investigates the use of brief post-game Interactive Digital Narratives (IDNs) to enhance character identification in tabletop role-playing games (TTRPGs), aiming to support historical empathy in history education. While previous research highlights the educational value of TTRPGs, challenges remain—particularly the limited character identification often observed in short, one-shot game sessions. To address this, we propose a supporting activity that strengthens characterisation and deepens players' connection to their roles. The activity introduces a post-game IDN, designed as a visual novel that presents the player character's perspective in a prequel narrative to the TTRPG adventure. Grounded in theories from psychology, education, and game studies, we argue that character identification is central to fostering historical understanding and shaping identity. Offering the character's backstory through an IDN encourages deeper perspective-taking and critical reflection, thereby amplifying the transformative potential of TTRPGs in education. This work serves as an exploratory step in refining educational TTRPG design through digital supplements and invites further empirical research to evaluate their impact.

Keywords: Tabletop role playing games · IDN · visual novels · history education · character identification

1 Introduction

The capacity of games to support historical learning and historical understanding has been widely researched [1,20,22,33,66]. Even without explicit educational aims, games enhance cognitive abilities such as problem-solving, critical thinking, and decision-making [6,72]. Role-playing games in particular foster personal and social development by improving self-efficacy, teamwork, and leadership skills

M. C. Reyes and F. Nack (Eds.): ICIDS 2025, LNCS 16375, pp. 273–295, 2026.
https://doi.org/10.1007/978-3-032-12405-0_15

[5,28,36,37]. Lopes [55], for example, presents a practical use of tabletop role-playing in "The City of Dred", a game designed for an undergraduate course. Mochocki [62] discusses tabletop role playing games (TTRPGs), Live action role playing (LARP), and museum storytelling as interconnected mediums of collaborative, participatory storytelling for cultural heritage, emphasizing their shared potential to engage with historical narratives.

TTRPGs, part of the broader RPG family, revolve around role-playing and storytelling. Players enact fictional characters, often around a table, while a human game master (GM) facilitates the game and narrative. The fictional world and events are collaboratively shaped through player-GM dialogue. Fuist [29] describes this as the creation of a "shared imaginative space," highlighting the social and expressive nature of TTRPGs [11].

A key transformative element of TTRPGs is character identification, emerging from both character creation and gameplay [11]. Players construct personas that reflect or diverge from their real-world identities. Identification with fictional characters can expand self-perception and promote perspective-taking [13,56,78]. Bowman [6] introduces the "bleed" effect, where emotions and experiences flow between player and character. Bowman and Lieberoth [11] discuss this intricate interplay between psychology and role-playing games, examining how psychological factors influence player motivations, social dynamics, and the overall gaming experience.

Research also supports the educational benefits of character identification, particularly in fostering cultural identity and historical consciousness [35,64]. For instance, McKenzie [59] demonstrates the value of theatrical character analysis in promoting historical empathy among students.

Previous work [71] proposed guidelines for TTRPGs in history education, focusing on short, one-shot adventures with pre-fabricated characters. While the historical setting was engaging, character identification remained limited for most players. This paper addresses that gap by enhancing character identification in educational TTRPGs, mindful of time and resource constraints. We propose combining the TTRPG with a visual novel-style interactive digital narrative (IDN), presented post-session as a prequel from the character's perspective. The visual novel type proposed has the form of a short, mainly textual narrative with images, with 3-4 branching points that present players with meaningful choices at key plot points. By situating the specific TTRPG characters within these visual novels, we sought to provide a structured experience that immerses and complements the identification aspect of TTRPG gameplay. We investigate through a user study with 20 participants whether this retrospective IDN fosters character identification and supports educational goals such as historical empathy and understanding.

Section 2 presents the theoretical background on character identification, bleed, and IDNs in transformative learning. Section 3 outlines the study motivation, objectives and process, including also the design of the proposed prequel IDNs. The results are presented in Sect. 4 and discussed in Sect. 5. Section 6 concludes the paper.

2   Background

2.1   Historical Empathy and Historical Consciousness in History Education

Historical empathy plays a key role in identity formation by fostering emotional and cognitive engagement with the past. According to [64], history serves to explain the world, shape identities, and exert influence; with historical empathy central to identity construction. It involves understanding historical figures' emotions and contexts [60], contributing to how individuals perceive their personal and cultural identities [35]. Empathy here is both cognitive and performative, inviting students to emotionally interpret and embody history [64]. However, empathy must be tempered with critical thinking to avoid distortions [35], consistent with the emphasis on contextualization to prevent presentism [26]. Historical empathy is also collective and performative: it is used to affirm group identities and cultural connections [64]. Through this dual lens of empathy and reflection, students deepen their understanding of both history and self.

Harris and Foreman-Peck [35] distinguishes "ordinary understanding" from "empathic understanding", the latter requiring awareness of past beliefs within their socio-cultural contexts [51]. Endacott and Brooks [27] offer a model of historical empathy with three interrelated elements: Historical Contextualization, Perspective Taking, and Affective Connection. This model emphasizes the need to understand historical motivations and emotions through their context.

Empathy toward fictional characters often arises from minimal shared identity or emotional cues, making character identification a gateway to historical empathy [44]. McKenzie [59] found that theatrical character analysis in education (through activities such as autobiographical storytelling and poetry recitation) helped students connect with historical figures, contextualize their actions, and avoid presentism.

2.2   Character Identification and the Concept of "bleed" in TTRPGs

From a psychological perspective, Broom et al. [13] explore identification with fictional characters across narrative experiences. Green [31] defines this as "narrative transportation," where individuals adopt a character's emotional perspective, goals, and mindset [65], essentially "becoming" the character. While identification is well-established, [49,50] argue for a holistic view in digital contexts, distinguishing between similarity and wishful identification, and adding embodied presence to address avatar-based interactions. This broader model supports identity expansion through diverse perspectives and roles [78].

Stronger character identification is linked to alignment of beliefs, attitudes, and behaviors with the character's, potentially continuing post-narrative and enabling lasting attitude shifts [32,41,77]. Broom et al. [13] found that deeper immersion leads to characters becoming part of the self-concept. Liapis and Denisova [54] view character identification and attachment as essential to

TTRPG immersion but acknowledge the process is complex, with emotional challenges helping to build connection [21,67]. Bowman [6], based on ethnographic research, identifies nine types of reflection based on identity overlap.

The concept of "bleed" describes the transfer of emotions, values, and mental states between player and character [39]. Bleed-in flows from player to character; bleed-out is the reverse. Hugaas [40] outlines Emotional bleed [8,63], Ego bleed [3], and Memetic bleed [40], where feelings, personality traits, and ideologies transfer across roles. Scholars consider bleed a key mechanism by which TTRPGs affect players [2,4,7–9,40,45,46,53,63]. Bowman and Hugaas [10] identify its transformative potential, from emotional processing to critical ethical reasoning and paradigm shifts, aligning closely with the goals of historical empathy in education. Hugaas [39] notes that in-game resilience may contribute to real-life identity, suggesting bleed can extend its impact beyond the session.

2.3   Retrospective Identification

Zhao et al. [34], propose an emotion-driven approach to interactive digital storytelling based on Smith and Lazarus' cognitive theory of emotion. Their research emphasizes that players' emotions can drive narrative progression, enhancing engagement and empathy. Retrospective narratives offer a powerful mechanism for reconfiguring audience perception and deepening character engagement. The limitations of the character's perception at the time of the events can also be emphasized, contrasting with their later insights. These narrative structures are determined by delayed characterisation, wherein the true nature of a character is disclosed retroactively, prompting the audience to reinterpret prior events through a new lens. This technique has been observed in literature and film through devices such as the "false protagonist," the "late reveal," and the "nameless narrator" (e.g.), where post hoc revelations fundamentally reshape emotional alignment with characters [42,43,75]. Such devices are designed to provoke reflection, whether emotional or intellectual, on themes embedded in the story.

2.4   IDN and Learning

In education, digital storytelling includes personal narratives, instructional stories, and historical reconstructions [74]. Digital storytelling supports diverse learning needs by helping students connect emotionally and reflect critically on historical events [30,61].

Interactive storytelling emphasizes user agency through meaningful choices that influence narrative outcomes [17]. This spans formats such as Hypertext Fiction, Interactive Drama, and Video Game Narratives [48]. Visual Novels (VNs), a sub-genre of interactive narratives, offer accessible opportunities for role-playing and identity exploration [14]. With branching plots and decision-making, VNs help learners engage with historical contexts while reflecting on choices and perspectives [68,84].

VN-based history learning can draw on research into how moral dilemmas function within branching and linear narratives [24,58,80]. Tancred [80] shows that such narratives enable players to confront morally complex situations where outcomes hinge on their decisions, making dilemmas feel more consequential. By presenting choices in a branching format, VNs promote exploration of multiple perspectives and ethical outcomes. This supports deeper understanding of historical figures and the dilemmas they may have faced.

3   The Study

3.1   Study Motivation and Objectives

Transformative learning about the past involves not only critical thinking about specific events but also understanding multiple perspectives, recognizing these understandings, and applying them to contemporary issues. As noted in [73], "transformative history teaching attempts a critical understanding of the conflictual past through fostering historical thinking, empathy, overcoming ethnocentric narratives, and promoting multiperspectivity." Endacott and Brooks' model of historical empathy [27] comprises three elements: historical contextualization (understanding facts in wider context), perspective taking (reflecting on different views), and affective connection (cognitive and emotional engagement with historical facts and figures). This model supports identity formation by moving beyond factual understanding toward historical consciousness [64].

TTRPGs have been recognized as promising tools to promote these educational goals [70]. Daniau's framework [20] identifies four participant realities during gameplay—Character, Player, Person, and Human—each linked to different learning types: from fictional lore and skills (Character, Player), to teamwork and empathy (Person), and ultimately to self- and world-reassessment (Human).

However, TTRPGs' support for transformative learning depends on extended gameplay in a safe, playful environment and deep game-world knowledge, two key educational challenges [69,70]. The complexity and length of game sessions, plus the time-consuming nature of creating historically accurate characters from scratch, are significant barriers. Players need support to ensure historical accuracy while maintaining engagement [69]. To address this, Petousi et al. [71] designed a brief, one-shot TTRPG adventure with prefabricated characters with their brief backstories. The adventure aims to familiarize the players with certain historical aspects related to religion, myth and everyday life.

Research from psychology, education, and game studies suggests character identification is crucial in designing history education TTRPGs. An educator in [70] noted that character creation promotes historical empathy: "It is important for students to understand how a 'hero' was created." However, the short TTRPG adventure in [71] lacked character creation, and identification with characters varied: only 3 of 16 players fully identified, 8 partially, and 5 not at all. This was partly because brief, one-paragraph backstories failed to foster personal connection or investment.

To counter this, we propose integrating an Interactive Digital Narrative (IDN) for each player character to enhance character identification in history education TTRPGs without elaborate character creation. Our IDN, a visual novel, can be used pre- or post-game; here, we focus on post-session use to explore retrospective characterization effects. These IDNs work as prequels, designed to present backstories for specific characters prior to the adventure, reflecting our aim to encourage reflection and empathy through retrospective contextualization, rather than simple narrative repetition or retelling.

Following Nordgren's [64] model of historical consciousness, and Endacott and Brooks' [27] model of historical empathy, we view empathy as both performative and cognitive, requiring retrospective contextualization and emotional anchoring. Similar to how autobiographical storytelling fosters emotional connection in history education [59], post-experience IDNs allow players to reinterpret and deepen engagement with initially disconnected characters. This aligns with retroactive characterization as a narrative device reshaping audience perception [15] and parallels bleed phenomena in TTRPGs [40]. In this study we focus on the following research question:

RQ1. What is the potential of a player character prequel IDN offered after a short TTRPG adventure to enhance character identification and historical empathy?

3.2   The TTRPG Adventure "Abduction of the Meliads"

The adventure "Abduction of the Meliads" is a one-shot 3-4 h TTRPG adventure for four players, set in the Archaic period of Attica (c. 699 BC). At the Temple of Artemis, three heroes encounter a weakened Meliad nymph who escaped an attack that left her sisters abducted and their sacred oak desecrated. Tasked by Artemis to aid the nymph, the players investigate the abduction, encountering local disputes, sacred rituals, and supernatural threats rooted in ancient beliefs. The game combines role-play, negotiation, moral decision-making, exploration, and light combat, with the aim of fostering historical empathy through embodied engagement with religion, myth, and everyday life in ancient Greece.

Before the TTRPG session, the players select one of the available player character choices and are provided with the relevant character sheet and a brief description, in the form of a character card. Figure 1 shows the card of the Amazon, Phoebe.

Playtesting showed that the adventure effectively engaged players in a historical world [71].

3.3   An IDN Design for Character Identification

In this study, we complement the TTRPG adventure with a brief IDN in the form of a visual novel for each player character. These IDN prequels are provided to players after the conclusion of the TTRPG session. Each player accesses a story that expands their character's backstory, motivations, and historical context, within a historically accurate setting. The IDNs consist of 34 scenes and 23 branching points, all converging on a fixed ending. Narrated in the first person, the stories present historically inspired dilemmas and decision points, enabling

Phoebe is a warrior and huntress from an Amazon tribe in Northern Thrace. Like all Amazons, she is a devoted follower of the goddess Artemis, but her role as the tribe's hunter deepens this bond. A vision compelled her to leave her homeland and journey south in search of a temple dedicated to the goddess. She was accompanied by her friend and fellow warrior, Aella. Together, they eventually discovered the Temple of Artemis, where they assumed the role of guardians.

Fig. 1. The character card of the Amazon Phoebe

players to explore different perspectives and exercise agency over their character's past. Choices are framed as questions posed by a neutral narrator. The aim is to foster reflection and deepen understanding of the social, political, and cultural dynamics of the period. The IDNs were developed using the Narralive Story Maker Tool for multimedia IDN creation [81]. Figure 2 shows excerpts from the IDN of the Amazon Phoebe.

Although our IDNs do not employ retrospective narration in the traditional literary sense, where a narrator recounts the past [38,57], they function narratively as retrospective character expansions. That is, players are invited to explore their character's earlier life after the gameplay session, recontextualizing the choices, behaviors, and outcomes they experienced during play. This approach mimics the narrative effect of a late reveal, often used in media to deepen emotional alignment and prompt reflection/ re-evaluation of earlier events [42,43,75].

3.4   Participants and Process

This study builds on the one in [71] to focus on the associated IDNs. Participants were drawn from the authors' broader social circle, with the aim of ensuring diversity in age, experience with TTRPGs, digital games, and history knowledge. The sample included 20 participants: 4 self-identified as men and 16 as women; 2 were aged 1825, 7 aged 2635, 6 aged 3645, and 5 aged 4655. Six participants were experienced in TTRPGs, five were novices (23 sessions), and nine had no prior experience. Eight had experience with IDNs or related digital games.

Fig. 2. Excerpts from the IDN of the Amazon Phoebe

Participants were divided into five groups of four and took part in the short TTRPG adventure (Sect. 3.2). The Game Master was a member of the research team.

A few days later, participants were invited to join this follow-up study, creating a brief real-world temporal gap. Prior work in experiential learning and reflective practice suggests that such a delay between an intense experience and reflective activity can support deeper meaning-making by allowing emotions to settle and enabling cognitive re-framing [18, 76].

Conducted online, the study involved presenting participants with the research objectives, obtaining informed consent, and then giving them access to the IDN corresponding to their TTRPG character. They explored the IDN at their own pace and were later interviewed in a brief semi-structured session. The study was approved by the Ethics Committee of the ATHENA Research Center.

4   Results

For the analysis of the Likert-scale of the questionnaire responses, we treated the data as interval data, as [79, 83] suggest. We present the median value along with the mean and standard deviation of each statement. For the open ended questions, two researchers worked independently to identify themes and codes, which they consolidated before proceeding with the analysis.

4.1   Character Identification

Overall, the responses to the statements relevant to character identification are positive. 70% of the participants felt more sympathy for the character (S3) after the IDN, and 90% more compassion (S4). Again, 90% of the participants felt that "the IDN helped them understand their character's motivations better" (S5 - Fig. 3 - right), with 1 participant neutral and 1 negative. "The choices in the IDN felt meaningful and aligned with the character's personality" (S8) for 80% of the participants with 15% neutral and 5% negative. On the whole, 95% felt that "the IDN made the character feel more 'real'" (S7 - Fig. 3 - left).

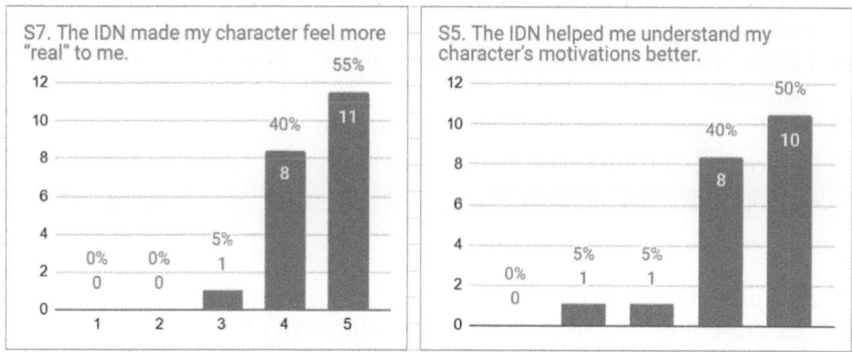

Fig. 3. Distribution of participant responses scores. Left: Statement S7. Right: Statement S5.

As it can be shown also in Fig. 4, the majority of the participants felt that the IDN supported their connection with their character. 70% "felt more connected to their character after reading the IDN" (S1), with 20% neutral and 10% negative. Similarly, 80% "could imagine themselves in the character's shoes more clearly after the IDN" (S6), with 15% neutral and 5% negative. Concerning the nature of character connection (S2), 13 of 20 participants reported emotional or cognitive engagement. The most common theme was connection through character understanding, cited by 9 participants. P16 remarked, "Her motives and her love story make her feel more real and approachable," while P15 noted, "It is like getting to know a person; you need to spend time together to understand each other."

Four participants identified with shared traits, values, or experiences. P10 said, "His caring and compassionate attitude... was a big factor," and P21 added, "I remembered my studies in Pharmacy and I acted as a real therapist."

Perspective-taking was another form of connection mentioned by four participants. P5 shared, "I felt like I had her powers and I could make decisions that are closer to what she would take in the story."

Two participants cited emotional or moral dilemmas as key. P19 reflected, "I liked the fact that I could choose between my duty and my feelings (Table 1)."

Table 1. Questionnaire results (median, average, and standard deviation) for the statements on character identification. The statements used a 5-point Likert scale from completely disagree (1) to completely agree (5).

	Statement	MEDIAN	AVG	STDEV
S1	I felt more connected to my character after reading the IDN.	4	3.9	0.97
S3	I felt more sympathy towards my character after reading the IDN.	4	4.05	1.1
S4	I felt more compassion towards my character after reading the IDN.	4	4.25	0.97
S5	The IDN helped me understand my character's motivations better.	4.5	4.35	0.81
S6	I could imagine myself in the character's shoes more clearly after the IDN.	4	4.2	0.89
S7	The IDN made my character feel more "real" to me.	5	4.5	0.61
S8	The choices in the IDN felt meaningful and aligned with my character's personality.	4	4.1	0.85

Seven participants reported no emotional connection. P13 said, "I don't really get the connection, sympathy, compassion stuff... You feel stuff about his experiences. My experiences. That's what's important."

The analysis of S20 "Did the IDN change your view of your character in any way? If so, how?" (Table 2) revealed that out of the 20 participants, 16 reported that the IDN changed or deepened their view of their character, enabling retrospective reinterpretation of their character's choices and traits. Of these, 10 specifically said the IDN improved their understanding of the character's motivations, emotions, or cultural background. As one noted: "Yes, I feel like I can understand her motivations. Before I thought of her more as a 'cog' in the machine... now she's a person with real emotions." Only four participants said the IDN had little or no effect beyond adding background or detail. Seven participants described a shift from initial neutrality or indifference to stronger emotional connection and identification. One noted, "After experiencing the IDN, I have found some common points that resonate with me... even though it's a completely different period and situation," suggesting that the IDN fostered reflective engagement and affective bonds.

Six participants emphasized that the IDN added depth to otherwise flat or generic characters. P16 observed, "She feels more real and more of a round character now," while P19 noted, "Now she's a person with real emotions... guilt."

Two participants described overcoming initial bias, with P17 stating the IDN helped them see their character not just as "a mere card" but as someone with a background and motivations—pointing out their initial impression was shaped by visuals and first exposure.

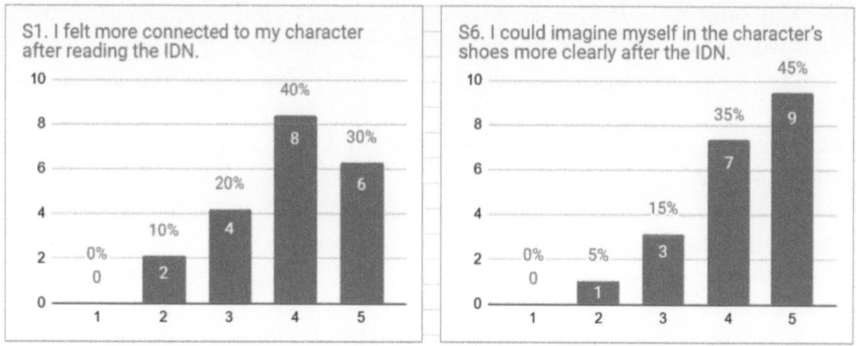

Fig. 4. Distribution of participant responses scores. Left: Statement S1. Right: Statement S6.

Three others highlighted the IDN's role in clarifying the character's cultural identity or values. P17 noted, "I can now understand her values more... what it means to be an Amazon," and P10 said, "It made me want more info about her past and her way of living."

4.2 Historical Empathy

As statements S9 (Fig. 5 - left) and S10 in Table 3 suggest, the participants felt that the IDN indeed promoted historical contextualization. All agreed that it helped them "understand the historical context of their character's life" (S9 - 100% positive), also "offering new insights into the culture, values, and challenges of the time period" (S10 - 75% positive and 25% neutral).

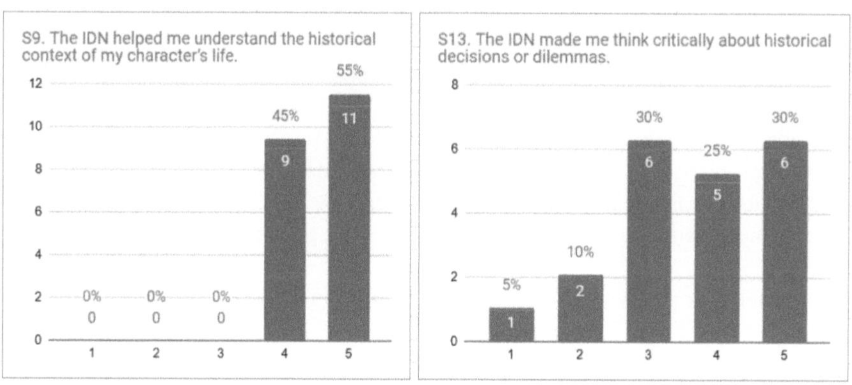

Fig. 5. Distribution of participant responses scores. Left: Statement S9. Right: Statement S13.

Table 2. Results of the thematic analysis (themes and codes) for statement S20 "Did the IDN change your view of your character in any way? If so, how?"

Theme	Code	Participants
Enhanced character depth and understanding	Character depth	12
	Character understanding	6
Perspective shift and emotional connection	Shift to connection	3
	Emotional resonance/identification	4
Motivational or trait clarification	Clarified motivation	4
	Defined trait/ideology	2
Overcoming bias	Re-evaluation of first impressions	1
Engagement/Curiosity	Wanting more backstory	2
Neutral/No change	No change	4

Statements S11-S13 reveal more diverse responses in terms of empathizing with people from the past (S11), with 55% of the participants positive, and the rest neutral (30%) or negative (15%). In the case of making connections between the past and present, 65% of the responders were positive, and the rest neutral or negative. Similar distribution of responses was noted in the case of S13, about critical reflection "about historical decisions or dilemmas" (Fig. 5 - right), with 55% positive.

4.3 Experience Design

The majority of the participants (80%) were positive that the IDN "added value to their overall experience with the TTRPG" (S15), with 2 participants neutral and 2 negative (Fig. 6 - left). Similarly, they were positive (75%) that they would "enjoy more narrative expansions like this for this and other characters" (S16). Their responses in "S16. The visual style and presentation of the IDN helped me stay immersed" were more diverse, with 45% positive, 35% neutral and 20% negative.

The thematic analysis of participant responses to S19 - "What did you enjoy most about the IDN?" highlights several recurring themes. Most prominently, narrative agency and the ability to make choices were repeatedly praised (P10, P17, P20, P1), as participants appreciated the interactive structure and felt their "choices were meaningful" (P4).

Equally important was the depth of character portrayal, with participants enjoying deeper insights into their roles (P23, P18), and in some cases, personal identification with their characters: "I immediately connected with the charac-

Table 3. Questionnaire results (median, average, and standard deviation) for the statements on historical empathy. The statements used a 5-point Likert scale from completely disagree (1) to completely agree (5).

	Statement	MEDIAN	AVG	STDEV
S9	The IDN helped me understand the historical context of my character's life.	5	4.55	0.51
S10	I gained new insights into the culture, values, and challenges of the time period.	4	4.15	0.81
S11	The IDN helped me empathize with people from the historical era portrayed.	4	3.65	1.31
S12	I found myself reflecting on how similar or different people's lives were then compared to today.	4	3.7	1.26
S13	The IDN made me think critically about historical decisions or dilemmas.	4	3.65	1.18

Table 4. Questionnaire results (median, average, and standard deviation) for the statements on experience design. The statements used a 5-point Likert scale from completely disagree (1) to completely agree (5).

	Statement	MEDIAN	AVG	STDEV
S14	The IDN added value to my overall experience with the TTRPG.	4	4.1	0.97
S15	I would have preferred to experience this IDN before playing the TTRPG session.	5	4.25	0.97
S16	The visual style and presentation of the IDN helped me stay immersed.	3	3.5	1.24
S17	I would enjoy more narrative expansions like this for this and other characters.	5	4.3	0.98
S18	I would have liked to write my own character story.	3	2.95	1.36

ter" (P11). Many respondents also commended the story itself (P20, P5, P13), valuing both the overall plot and emotional resonance.

Illustrations were frequently mentioned as enhancing the experience, contributing to a sense of immersion and game-like engagement (P15, P14). Some respondents focused on moral dilemmas and emotional themes, especially regarding love, a common theme in Greek mythology (P12, P3, P19): "It discussed something that is ultimately universal; love" (P19) (Table 4).

Other appreciated aspects included writing style, pacing, and even historical realism, particularly in reflecting societal norms and constraints of the period (P3). These elements contributed to the narrative's credibility and emotional weight.

Concerning the integration of the IDNs with the TTRPG adventure, the majority (65%) "would have preferred to experience this IDN before playing

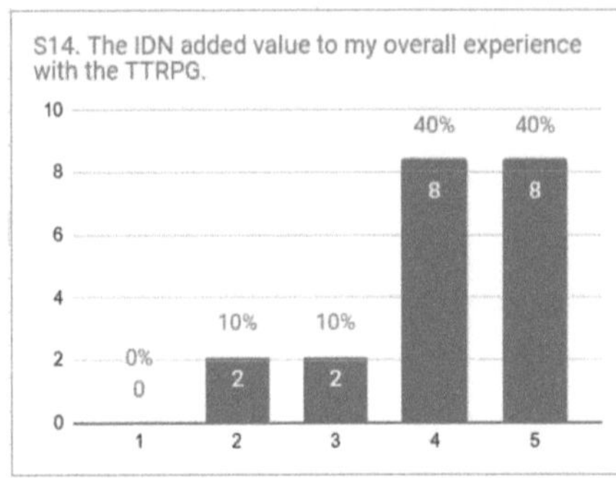

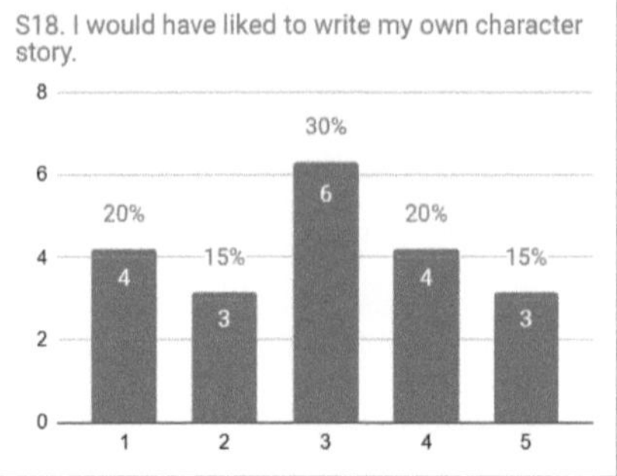

Fig. 6. Distribution of participant responses scores. Left: Statement S14. Right: Statement S18.

Table 5. Results of the thematic analysis (themes and codes) for the statement S21 "Do you think experiencing the IDN before the TTRPG would have affected your gameplay? How?"

Theme	Code	Participants
Role-playing	Improved role-playing	9
	Alignment with the character	5
Enhanced character understanding and development	Character understanding	3
	Improved character development	2
Greater emotional engagement	Emotional connection/identification	4
Nuanced or uncertain impact	Alignment or divergence	1
	Uncertain/mixed	1
No or minimal impact	No impact	4

the TTRPG session" (S15), with only one negative and 4 neutral. In terms of creating their character backstory on their own (S18), responses were divided (Fig. 6 - right), with 35% positive, 30% neutral and 35% negative.

As for S21 "Do you think experiencing the IDN before the TTRPG would have affected your gameplay? How?", most participants (16 out of 20) felt the IDN before the TTRPG would have positively affected their gameplay by providing a clearer reference point for character interpretation, emotional alignment, and decision-making. A recurring theme (9 mentions) was the potential for improved role-playing, offering a clearer sense of the character's mindset or behavior. For instance, P17 noted, "I could roleplay better and gain insights from this character's personality and expand from a better starting reference point", while P15 said, "It would have helped me to stay closer to the character in role playing" (Table 5). Seven participants said that experiencing the

Table 6. Results of the thematic analysis (themes and codes) for the question S22 "Do you have any suggestions to improve this type of character expansion?"

Theme	Code	Participants
Visual and multimedia	Illustrations/artwork	3
	Voiceovers/animation/music	3
Player agency and choices	More visible consequences	3
	More interactivity/conflict	2
	Character customization	1
	Animal companion	1
Narrative and context	Historical context/backstory	2
	Story expansion/relationships	2
	Narrative structure (dual timeline)	1
No suggestions	No suggestions/satisfied	6
	User compliments completeness	2

IDN beforehand would have helped align their decisions with their character's established personality and values, clarifying motivations and emotional stakes, enabling more consistent, intentional role-play. P9 noted, "I believe the way the character acted would be different... they would have greater motivation with the IDN's story in mind." P10 said they "would be more fierce regarding the protection of the Meliads," and P5 stated, "My decisions would be aligned with her character and I would have a clearer direction," underscoring the role of narrative context in shaping behavior (Table 6).

Five others felt the IDN would have strengthened emotional connection and engagement. P4 remarked, "It would for sure make the gameplay more enjoyable, as I might feel more connected to my character," and P11 added, "I believe I would have connected with my character from the start."

Two participants expressed concern that pre-defined backstories might limit creativity, though they still acknowledged the IDN's influence. As P1 explained, "I believe it would give me more information... but I am having concerns that it might have limited my freedom and creativity." Three participants felt the IDN would not significantly alter their gameplay, although one noted it could still support character development.

Overall, responses suggest that pre-game IDNs could enhance immersion, consistency, and emotional investment in TTRPGs, while a minority raised concerns about creative constraints.

Suggestions for Improvement. Twelve participants offered concrete suggestions to improve the IDN: Four participants emphasized the importance of stronger visual and multimedia elements and specifically requested additional or better-integrated illustrations, including the idea of comic-style layouts to enhance immersion. As P3 noted, "I'd like more illustrations, the visual elements

were a strong point... expanding on that would really enhance immersion." and
P1 said "Even more artwork while reading... multiple images per paragraph like a
comic book page". Three others suggested incorporating voiceovers, background
music, or even short video clips, with P16 commenting, "A video with movement
and background music would be nice."

A recurring theme was the desire for deeper interactivity and clearer consequences of choices. Three participants noted the impact of decisions was unclear.
P18 remarked, "I would have liked to see a stronger effect... " referring to limited
narrative divergence.

Five participants wanted more detail on character relationships or historical
context. P15 asked for more on "why Amazons believe what they do, or how
they were raised." P24 suggested expanding on "her relation to her sisters...
and more info about goddess Artemis." Two participants proposed structural
or customization changes, such as showing the character's "younger self" or
allowing visual customization via generative AI. P17 suggested, "Maybe I would
have added all the other visual elements surrounding my character... and then
create visually how I imagine him." P5 proposed adding animal companions,
while P12 wanted a second moral conflict later in the story.

Eight participants had no suggestions. P19 noted, "I feel this was pretty
complete. Dilemma? Check. Consequences? Check," and P11 called it "quite
complete without being tiring," reflecting general satisfaction with the IDNs'
structure and engagement.

5   Discussion and Limitations

Based on the study outcomes, players experienced IDNs as post-game reflections
after a historical TTRPG session and felt that they fostered emotional identification and deeper engagement with the historical context. Retrospective narratives
in IDNs differ meaningfully from in-game identification in TTRPGs. While in-
game immersion aligns with Csikszentmihalyi's flow states [19], post-game IDNs
may promote more reflective, analytical engagement. This temporal distance
lets players step back from immediate emotion and consider their character's
experiences within broader historical or ethical contexts. This aligns with models of historical empathy emphasizing contextualization and perspective-taking
[27,64]. Players revisit character choices and internal conflicts, fostering metacognitive engagement with the game and its historical themes. As Lee and Ashby
[52] observe, empathy requires not just emotional alignment but "rational understanding", which retrospective narratives support. Compared to improvisational
TTRPGs, IDNs provide structured opportunities to reconsider motivations and
decisions, bridging immediate role-play and long-term historical understanding.

Given their potential for fostering character identification, ethical reasoning, and empathy, IDNs may be equally or more effective when used before
gameplay. Pre-game exposure to a character's backstory helps students build
emotional connection, understand influences, and enter the character's mindset.
Encountering moral dilemmas in a low-stakes context allows reflection before acting out similar in-game choices. This prepares players for historically grounded,

perspective-driven role-play. IDNs also offer a private, introspective space for developing character values and motivations, making in-game contributions more intentional and authentic.

Used before or after the game, IDNs support engagement, reflection, and active negotiation of historical perspectives. As scaffolds, they provide context and personal stakes, enriching role-play and historical learning. Their episodic format is flexible for classroom or independent use, and can be expanded with additional storylines or perspectives.

Some participants wanted more interactivity or freedom. P13, for instance, preferred character creation and suggested tools like "an AI trained for the setting." Creative writing (such as autobiographies, first-person narratives, or internal monologues) can give students more agency while supporting emotional engagement [12,59,82], empathy, and critical reflection [12,59]. These exercises reinforce and extend IDN themes and may amplify the "bleed effect" [10], where emotions, thoughts, and experiences transfer between player and character. This is especially relevant for characters facing ethical dilemmas [25,47]. As [23] and [16] suggest, imaginative writing fosters historical thinking and personal expression, complementary to the collaborative, narrative-based nature of IDNs and TTRPGs. When paired with digital storytelling, creative writing strengthens both analytical and emotional engagement, enabling a more holistic learning experience.

While we center on prequels here, retelling is another promising way IDNs could be integrated with TTRPGs, particularly for consolidating historical knowledge. Exploring this alternative, alongside creative writing exercises, connects to our broader interest in post-game reflective activities. Our current study therefore explores prequels in a post-game context, while future work will test both pre- and post-game uses, as well as potential comparisons with retelling-based approaches.

5.1 Limitations

The small sample size is a concrete limitation for generalizability, particularly across varying levels of familiarity with TTRPGs and IDNs. In addition, the lack of a control group and the absence of prepost comparisons limit the strength of the conclusions that can be drawn on the IDN's impact. Historical empathy and character identification were assessed through self-reported qualitative data. Future research could adopt more concrete measures to assess learning outcomes. Although the visual novels had a consistent structure, engagement could be related to personal preference on genres. Finally, visuals were generated using AI, which in some cases compromised historical accuracy. Greater attention to visual fidelity is necessary before classroom implementation.

6 Conclusion

This paper has explored the integration of visual novel-style IDNs with TTRPGs as a novel pedagogical approach to foster character identification and historical empathy in history education. Our findings indicate that post-game IDNs support emotional engagement and reflection on historical contexts. However, as indicated by the participants, the IDNs could also be offered before gameplay to promote a deeper emotional connection with their character, understand their motivations and historical context more clearly, and approach the collaborative role-play with greater confidence and authenticity.

The results affirm the promise of multimodal storytelling to enrich history education. Future work should explore the combination of TTRPG, IDNs and creative writing activities in this context, which can further deepen identification and perspective-taking, amplifying the psychological "bleed" between player and character to promote transformative learning. This hybrid approach balances individual reflection with social negotiation, encouraging nuanced historical understanding through immersive, experiential learning.

By bridging digital and analog role-play, this method invites students not only to learn about the past but to emotionally and ethically inhabit it—making history a lived, reflective experience rather than a distant abstraction.

Acknowledgments. This research was partly funded by the RPGs4Museums research project (grant number 16758), under the Basic research financing action of the Hellenic Foundation for Research and Innovation.

References

1. Andresen, M.E.: Playing the Learning Game: A Practical Introduction to Educational Roleplaying. Fantasiforbundet and Education Centre (2012)
2. Baird, J., Bowman, S.L., Hugaas, K.H.: Liminal intimacy: role-playing games as catalysts for interpersonal growth and relating. In: Koenig, N., Denk, N., Pfeiffer, A., Wernbacher, T. (eds.) The Magic of Games, pp. 169–171. Edition Donau-Universität Krems (2022)
3. Beltran, W.S.: Yearning for the hero within: Live action role-playing as engagement with mythical archetypes. In: Bowman, S.L., Vanek, A. (eds.) Wyrd Con Companion Book 2012, pp. 89–96. Wyrd Con, Los Angeles (2012)
4. Beltran, W.S.: Shadow work: a Jungian perspective on the underside of live action role-play in the united states. In: Bowman, S.L., Vanek, A. (eds.) Wyrd Con Companion Book 2013, pp. 94–101. Wyrd Con, Los Angeles (2013)
5. Blatner, A.: Role playing in education (2009). https://www.blatner.com/adam/pdntbk/rlplayedu.htm
6. Bowman, S.L.: The Functions of Role-Playing Games: How Participants Create Community, Solve Problems, and Explore Identity. McFarland and Company (2010)
7. Bowman, S.L.: Social conflict in role-playing communities: an exploratory qualitative study. Int. J. Role Play. **4**, 17–18 (2013)
8. Bowman, S.L.: Bleed: the spillover between player and character (2015). https://www.nordiclarp.org/2015/03/02/bleed-the-spillover-between-player-and-character/. Accessed 15 Feb 2025
9. Bowman, S.L.: Bleed (2022). https://www.eotl.org/bleed/. Accessed 15 Feb 2025

10. Bowman, S.L., Hugaas, K.H.: Transformative role-play: design, implementation, and integration (2019). https://www.nordiclarp.org/2019/12/10/transformative-role-play-design-implementation-and-integration/. Accessed 15 Feb 2025

11. Bowman, S.L., Lieberoth, A.: Psychology and Role-playing Games, pp. 245–264. Routledge (2018). https://doi.org/10.4324/9781315637532-13/PSYCHOLOGY-ROLE-PLAYING-GAMES-SARAH-LYNNE-BOWMAN-ANDREAS-LIEBEROTH

12. Brooks, S.: Displaying historical empathy: what impact can a writing assignment have? Soc. Stud. Res. Pract. **3**(2) (2008). http://www.socstrp.org

13. Broom, T.W., Chavez, R.S., Wagner, D.D.: Becoming the king in the north: identification with fictional characters is associated with greater self-other neural overlap. Soc. Cogn. Affect. Neurosci. **16**(6), 541–551 (2021). https://doi.org/10.1093/scan/nsab021

14. Cavallaro, D.: Anime and the Visual Novel: Narrative Structure, Design and Play at the Crossroads of Animation and Computer Games. McFarland and Company, Jefferson, NC (2010)

15. Cimino, S., Persson Lundh, L.: On the subject of retroactive characterisation in games. Master's thesis, University of Skövde, Skövde, Sweden (2020). https://doi.org/10.13140/RG.2.2.11389.79846, https://www.researchgate.net/publication/342788178

16. Craft, A.: Creativity and Early Years Education: A Lifewide Foundation. Continuum, London; New York (2002)

17. Crawford, C.: Interactive storytelling. In: Wolf, M.J., Perron, B. (eds.) The Video Game Theory Reader, 2nd edn., pp. 259–273. Routledge, Milton Park (2013)

18. Crookall, D.: Serious games, debriefing, and simulation/gaming as a discipline. Simul. Gaming **41**(6), 898–920 (2010). https://doi.org/10.1177/1046878110390784

19. Csikszentmihalyi, M.: Flow: The Psychology of Optimal Experience. Harper & Row, New York (1990)

20. Daniau, S.: The transformative potential of role-playing games–: from play skills to human skills. Simul. Gaming **47**, 423–444 (2016). https://doi.org/10.1177/1046878116650765

21. Denisova, A., Cairns, P., Guckelsberger, C., Zendle, D.: Measuring perceived challenge in digital games: development & validation of the challenge originating from recent gameplay interaction scale (corgis). Int. J. Hum. Comput. Stud. **137**, 102–106 (2020). https://doi.org/10.1016/j.ijhcs.2020.102399

22. Deterding, S., Zagal, J.P.: The Many Faces of Role-Playing Game Studies, pp. 1–16. Routledge (2018)

23. Downey, M.T.: Defining and assessing historical thinking: a technical report. Tech. rep., National Center for the Study of Writing, Berkeley, CA (1994). (ERIC Document Reproduction Service No. ED 376-513)

24. Dubbelman, T., Roth, C., Koenitz, H.: Interactive digital narratives (IDN) for change. In: Rouse, R., Koenitz, H., Haahr, M. (eds.) ICIDS 2018. LNCS, vol. 11318, pp. 591–602. Springer, Cham (2018). https://doi.org/10.1007/978-3-030-04028-4_69

25. Dulberg, N.: Engaging in history: empathy and perspective-taking in children's historical thinking (2002)

26. Endacott, J.: Negotiating the process of historical empathy. Theory Res. Soc. Educ. **42**(1), 4–34 (2014). https://doi.org/10.1080/00933104.2013.826158

27. Endacott, J., Brooks, S.: An updated theoretical and practical model for promoting historical empathy. Soc. Stud. Res. Pract. **8**, 41–58 (2013). https://doi.org/10.1108/SSRP-01-2013-B0003

28. Fine, G.A.: Shared Fantasies. Univerwity of Chicago Press (2003)
29. Fuist, T.: The agentic imagination: tabletop role playing games as a cultural tool. In: Tabletop Role Playing Games and the Experience of Culture, pp. 108–126. McFarland and Company (2012)
30. Gallagher, K.M.: In search of a theoretical basis for storytelling in education research: story as method. Int. J. Res. Methodol. Educ. **34**, 49–61 (2011). https://doi.org/10.1080/1743727X.2011.552308
31. Green, M.C., Brock, T.C.: The role of transportation in the persuasiveness of public narratives. J. Pers. Soc. Psychol. **79**(5), 701–721 (2000). https://doi.org/10.1037/0022-3514.79.5.701
32. Hamby, A., Brinberg, D., Daniloski, K.: Reflecting on the journey: mechanisms in narrative persuasion. J. Consum. Psychol. **27**(1), 11–22 (2017). https://doi.org/10.1016/j.jcps.2016.06.005
33. Hammer, J., To, A., Schrier, K., Bowman, S.L., Kaufman, G.: Learning and Role-Playing Games, pp. 283–299. Taylor and Francis (2018). https://doi.org/10.4324/9781315637532-15
34. Hao, H., Zhang, J., McDougall, S.: Emotion-driven interactive digital storytelling. In: Anacleto, J., Fels, S., Graham, N., Kapralos, B., Saif El-Nasr, M., Stanley, K. (eds.) Entertainment Computing – ICEC 2011. Lecture Notes in Computer Science, vol. 6972. Springer, Berlin, Heidelberg (2011). https://doi.org/10.1007/978-3-642-24500-8_3
35. Harris, R., Foreman-Peck, L.: Stepping into other peoples' shoes: teaching and assessing empathy in the secondary history curriculum. Int. J. Hist. Learn. Teach. Res. **4**(2), 1–14 (2004). https://doi.org/10.18546/HERJ.04.2.11
36. Hoge, M.: Experiential Learning for Youth Through Larps and RPGs, pp. 38–41. WyrdCon, LLC (2013)
37. Howes, E.V., Cruz, B.C.: Role-playing in science education: an effective strategy for developing multiple perspectives. J. Elementary Sci. Educ. **21**, 33–46 (2009). https://doi.org/10.1007/BF03174721
38. Huber, I.: Retrospective narration. In: Present Tense Narration in Contemporary Fiction: A Narratological Overview, pp. 39–54. Palgrave Macmillan (2016)
39. Hugaas, K.: Bleed and identity: a conceptual model of bleed and how bleed-out from role-playing games can affect a player's sense of self. Int. J. Role-Playing 9–35 (2024). https://doi.org/10.33063/ijrp.vi15.323
40. Hugaas, K.H.: Investigating types of bleed in larp: emotional, procedural, and memetic (2019). https://www.nordiclarp.org/2019/01/25/investigating-types-of-bleed-in-larp-emotional-procedural-and-memetic/. Accessed 15 Feb 2025
41. Igartua, J.J.: Identification with characters and narrative persuasion through fictional feature films. Communications **35**(4), 347–373 (2010). https://doi.org/10.1515/COMM.2010.019
42. Jenkins, M.: The genius behind nameless protagonists. Book Riot (2015). https://bookriot.com/2015/03/14/genius-behind-nameless-protagonists/
43. Jonason, P.K., Webster, G.D., Schmitt, D.P., Li, N.P., Crysel, L.C.: The antihero in popular culture: life history theory and the dark triad personality traits. Rev. Gen. Psychol. **16**(2), 192–199 (2012). https://doi.org/10.1037/a0027914
44. Keen, S.: A theory of narrative empathy. Narrative **14**(3), 207–236 (2006). https://www.jstor.org/stable/20107388
45. Kemper, J.: The battle of primrose park: playing for emancipatory bleed in fortune & felicity (2017). https://www.nordiclarp.org/2017/06/21/the-battle-of-primrose-park-playing-for-emancipatory-bleed-in-fortune-felicity/. Accessed 15 Feb 2025

46. Kemper, J.: Wyrding the self. In: Saitta, E., Makkonen, M., Männistö, P., Grove, A.S., Koljonen, J. (eds.) What Do We Do When We Play? Solmukohta, Helsinki, Finland (2020)

47. Kleingeld, P.: Kant, history, and the idea of moral development. Hist. Philos. Q. **16**(1), 59–80 (1999)

48. Koenitz, H.: Towards a specific theory of interactive digital narrative. In: Koenitz, H., Ferri, G., Haahr, M., Sezen, D., Sezen, T.B. (eds.) Interactive Digital Narrative, pp. 91–105. Routledge, New York, NY (2015)

49. Konijn, E.A., and, J.F.H.: Some like it bad: testing a model for perceiving and experiencing fictional characters. Media Psychol. **7**(2), 107–144 (2005). https://doi.org/10.1207/S1532785XMEP0702_1

50. Konijn, E.A., Nije Bijvank, M., Bushman, B.J.: I wish i were a warrior: the role of wishful identification in the effects of violent video games on aggression in adolescent boys. Dev. Psychol. **43**(4), 1038–1044 (2007). https://doi.org/10.1037/0012-1649.43.4.1038

51. Lee, P., Dickinson, A., Ashby, R.: "just another emperor": understanding action in the past. Int. J. Educ. Res. **27**(3), 233–244 (1997). https://doi.org/10.1016/s0883-0355(97)89731-5

52. Lee, P., Ashby, R.: Empathy, perspective taking, and rational understanding. In: Jr., O.L.D., Yeager, E., Foster, S. (eds.) Historical Empathy and Perspective Taking in the Social Studies. Rowman & Littlefield, Lanham, MD (2001)

53. Leonard, D.J., Thurman, T.: Bleed-out on the brain: the neuroscience of character-to-player. Int. J. Role-Playing **9**, 9–15 (2018)

54. Liapis, A., Denisova, A.: The challenge of evaluating player experience in tabletop role-playing games. In: Proceedings of the 18th International Conference on the Foundations of Digital Games, FDG 2023. Association for Computing Machinery, New York, NY, USA (2023). https://doi.org/10.1145/3582437.3582457

55. Lopes, R.: City of Dred – a tabletop RPG learning experience. In: ED ULEARN15 Proceedings, pp. 6987–6995 (Jan 2015)

56. Mar, R.A., Oatley, K.: The function of fiction is the abstraction and simulation of social experience. Perspect. Psychol. Sci. **3**(3), 173–192 (2008). https://doi.org/10.1111/j.1745-6924.2008.00073.x

57. Marks, B.A.: Retrospective narrative in nineteenth century American literature. College English **31**(4), 366–375 (1970). http://www.jstor.org/stable/374543. Accessed 3 June 2025

58. McCall, J.: Teaching history with digital historical games: an introduction to the field and best practices. Simul. Gaming **47**(4), 517–542 (2016). https://doi.org/10.1177/1046878116646693

59. McKenzie, K.: Where the historical becomes theatrical: using character analysis to develop historical empathy among adolescents. Master's thesis, University of Portland (2015)

60. McKinney, S., et al.: Developing digital archaeology for young people: a model for fostering empathy and dialogue in formal and informal learning environments. In: Hageneuer, S. (ed.) Communicating the Past in the Digital Age. Ubiquity Press, London (2020). https://doi.org/10.5334/bch.n

61. Mello, R.: The power of storytelling: how oral narrative influences children's relationships in classrooms. Int. J. Educ. Arts **2** (2001). http://www.ijea.org/v2n1/. Accessed 19 July 2025

62. Mochocki, M.: Role-Play as a Heritage Practice : Historical Larp, Tabletop RPG and Reenactment. Routledge (2021)

63. Montola, M.: The positive negative experience in extreme role-playing. In: Proceedings of DiGRA Nordic 2010: Experiencing Games: Games, Play, and Players. Stockholm, Sweden (2010)
64. Nordgren, K.: How to do things with history: use of history as a link between historical consciousness and historical culture. Theory Res. Soc. Educ. **44**(4), 479–504 (2016). https://doi.org/10.1080/00933104.2016.1211046
65. Oatley, K.: Meetings of minds: dialogue, sympathy, and identification in reading fiction. Poetics **26**(5–6), 439–454 (1999). https://doi.org/10.1016/S0304-422X(99)00011-X
66. O'Brien, D., Lawless, K.A., Schrader, P.G.: A Taxonomy of Educational Games, pp. 1–23. IGI Global (2010). https://doi.org/10.4018/978-1-61520-713-8.CH001
67. Papale, L.: Beyond identification: defining the relationships between player and avatar. J. Games Criticism **1**(2) (2014). https://journalofgamescriticism.org/articles/10.16993/jgc.535/
68. Petousi, D., Katifori, A., Servi, K., Roussou, M., Ioannidis, Y.: History education done different: a collaborative interactive digital storytelling approach for remote learners. Front. Educ. **7** (2022). https://doi.org/10.3389/feduc.2022.942834
69. Petousi, D., Katifori, A., Chrysanthi, A., Servi, K., Sakellariadis, P., Ioannidis, Y.E.: Role playing games as hybrid museum kits: promoting historical understanding and meaning making. In: Antoniou, A., Carolis, B.D., Kuflik, T., Origlia, A., Raptis, G.E., Gena, C. (eds.) Proceedings of the AVI^{2}CH Workshop on Advanced Visual Interfaces and Interactions in Cultural Heritage Co-located with 2022 International Conference on Advanced Visual Interfaces (AVI 2022), Rome, Italy, June 6, 2022 (2022)
70. Petousi, D., Katifori, A., Roussou, M., Ioannidis, Y., Sakellariadis, P.: Historical reality vs anachronistic fantasy: the history educators' perspective on tabletop RPGs. In: Proceedings of the 18th International Conference on the Foundations of Digital Games. Association for Computing Machinery, New York, NY, USA (2023). https://doi.org/10.1145/3582437.3587197
71. Petousi, D., et al.: The intersection of play and history: integrating historical content in tabletop role-playing games for education. In: Proceedings of the 20th International Conference on the Foundations of Digital Games, FDG 2025. Association for Computing Machinery, New York, NY, USA (2025). https://doi.org/10.1145/3723498.3723811
72. Plass, J.L., Homer, B.D., Kinzer, C.K.: Foundations of game-based learning. Educ. Psychol. **50**, 258–283 (2015). https://doi.org/10.1080/00461520.2015.1122533
73. Psaltis, C., Carretero, M., Čehajić-Clancy, S. (eds.): History Education and Conflict Transformation. Lecture Notes in Computer Science, Springer, Cham (2017). https://doi.org/10.1007/978-3-319-54681-0
74. Robin, B.R.: Digital storytelling: a powerful technology tool for the 21st century classroom. Theory Pract. **47**, 220–228 (2008). https://doi.org/10.1080/00405840802153916
75. Sacks, S.: The rise of the nameless narrator. The New Yorker (2015). https://www.newyorker.com/books/page-turner/the-rise-of-the-nameless-narrator
76. Schön, D.A.: The Reflective Practitioner: How Professionals Think in Action. Basic Books, New York (1983)
77. Sestir, M., Green, M.C.: You are who you watch: identification and transportation effects on temporary self-concept. Soc. Influ. **5**(4), 272–288 (2010). https://doi.org/10.1080/15534510.2010.490672

78. Slater, M.D., Johnson, B.K., Cohen, J., Comello, M.L.G., Ewoldsen, D.R.: Temporarily expanding the boundaries of the self: motivations for entering the story world and implications for narrative effects. J. Commun. **64**(3), 439–455 (2014). https://doi.org/10.1111/jcom.12100
79. Sullivan, G.M., Artino, A.R., Jr.: Analyzing and interpreting data from likert-type scales. J. Grad. Med. Educ. **5**(4), 541–542 (2013)
80. Tancred, N., Vickery, N., Wyeth, P., Turkay, S.: Player choices, game endings and the design of moral dilemmas in games. In: Proceedings of the 2018 Annual Symposium on Computer-Human Interaction in Play Companion Extended Abstracts, CHI PLAY 2018, pp. 627–636. Extended Abstracts, Association for Computing Machinery, New York, NY, USA (2018). https://doi.org/10.1145/3270316.3271525
81. Vrettakis, E., et al.: The story maker - an authoring tool for multimedia-rich interactive narratives. In: Bosser, A., Millard, D., Hargood, C. (eds.) Interactive Storytelling, Lecture Notes in Computer Science, vol. 12497, pp. 349–352. Springer, Cham (2020). https://doi.org/10.1007/978-3-030-62516-0_33
82. Yancie, N.: Developing high school students' historical empathy skills using historical dialogues: a qualitative study. Master's thesis, University of Alabama at Birmingham (2020)
83. Zumbo, B.D., Zimmerman, D.W.: Is the selection of statistical methods governed by level of measurement? Can. Psychol. **34**(4), 390–400 (1993)
84. Øygardslia, K., Weitze, C.L., Shin, J.: The educational potential of visual novel games: principles for design. Replay. Japan **2**, 123–134 (2020). https://www.researchgate.net/publication/341380379

Engagement or Distraction? Examining the Impact of Narrative Elements and Player Audience on Experience of Logic Grid Puzzles

Fiona Shyne, Kaylah Facey(✉), and Seth Cooper

Northeastern University, Boston, MA 02115, USA
{shyne.f,facey.k,se.cooper}@northeastern.edu
https://www.khoury.northeastern.edu/

Abstract. In this work, we explore different narrative modes for logic grid puzzles. We test these environments with a user study recruiting two audiences: crowd-workers on the Prolific platform and volunteers from social media groups related to mysteries and puzzles. While volunteers found puzzles easier, they enjoyed them less than the Prolific workers. Across both audiences, an increase in narrative increased the time taken on puzzles and the challenge of the puzzles. However, while some participants found the narrative immersive and enjoyable, others did not want any story or did not like the increased challenge.

Keywords: Logic Grid Puzzles · Narrative Puzzles · User Study

1 Introduction

Narrative is an important component of many games. Narrative can enhance feelings of immersion and engagement [3,12]. However, narrative elements can also be seen as a nuisance [12].

In this work, we use *logic grid puzzles* as a testbed for studying how narrative impacts the experience of puzzle solving. Logic grid puzzles are a popular form of pen-and-paper puzzle where players use natural language clues to mark relationships between entities on a grid (Fig. 1). Traditionally, they include a small amount of narrative, but the solving process does not meaningfully incorporate it. We extend this form to include increasing levels of narrative interaction. The "base clue" mode models the traditional form, the "paragraph" mode wraps clues in prose, and the "interactive fiction" mode provides a text-based environment to navigate. The base logic puzzle is procedurally generated using a system based on previous work [16,17].

We tested how these three narrative modes impact gameplay through a user study in which participants, either paid crowd-workers from the Prolific platform or volunteers from social media, solved a variety of puzzles. After each puzzle, participants were asked about difficulty, narrative quality, and enjoyment.

M. C. Reyes and F. Nack (Eds.): ICIDS 2025, LNCS 16375, pp. 296–313, 2026.
https://doi.org/10.1007/978-3-032-12405-0_16

Prolific workers found puzzles more challenging but also more enjoyable. Both groups found that increased narrative resulted in increased challenge. The impact of narrative on enjoyment was less clear. Some participants enjoyed the sense of immersion that increased narrative added, while others found it confusing or unnecessary.

2   Related Work

2.1   Stories in Games

There is debate over the role of narrative in games. Frasca [6] argues that "the potential of games is not to tell a story but to simulate... an environment for experimentation [by the player]." Mateas and Stern [11] disagree that an authored narrative should be abandoned, arguing instead that player actions should drive a plot structure that changes with each playthrough.

A story can be embedded in a game in myriad ways. Fernandez suggests that narrative should be told through objects in the game world, and Bizzochi [2] extends this idea to include UI elements. Particular attention has been paid to "narrative" or "fiction" puzzles that are integrated into the story of a game and drive its plot [5,9,20].

Evidence suggests that even exposure to a pre-game story can increase players' sense of presence in a game [13,19]. On the other hand, inclusion of a narrative may result in a *worse* experience for some players; Miller et al. [12] suggest that players be able to include or exclude narrative, and Siu and Riedl [18] find that narrative rewards were commonly either the most- or the least-favored rewards. In addition, engagement with a story matters. Immersion is not increased as much if players ignore the story [3], or if they are less interested in its genre [12].

2.2   Paid vs Volunteer Participants

Studies comparing the performance of unpaid volunteers with paid crowd-workers have had mixed results. For simple tasks, Siu and Riedl [18] found that crowd-workers outperformed volunteers on both time and accuracy. For complex tasks, most comparisons between crowd-workers and volunteers have found that crowd-workers may complete more tasks, but at a lower quality [7,10,15]. As our task is a complex puzzle game, we hope to contribute to the literature on the suitability of crowd-work for complex tasks.

3   Puzzle Design

We designed a set of puzzles that varied in narrative interaction: the extent to which the player has to interact with narrative content in order to progress. Design for these puzzles was iterative; modes with less narrative interaction were used as the basis for modes with more. Each logic grid puzzle was first generated using a genetic algorithm [16,17]. Then for the "base clue" mode, we minimally edited the generator's output for clarity and grammar. For the "paragraph" mode, each clue was expanded into a short narrative paragraph. Lastly, for the "interactive fiction" (IF) mode, the paragraphs were used as the basis for an IF game. Examples are given in Fig. 1.

As a running example, we will discuss how we created the puzzles for one scenario: "The Wild Rose Train." In "Train", the player is a PhD student who must figure out who on a train stole their research.

3.1   Logic Puzzle Generation

The core of these puzzles is logic grid puzzles, a kind of pen-and-paper logic puzzle consisting of a grid and a list of natural language clues. To solve them, players must deduce entity relationships either given explicitly by the clues or inferred using logical reasoning. Previous works [16,17] presented a system that generates these types of puzzles given a set of categories and entities, which we selected based on the imagined scenario. The generator uses a *genetic algorithm*, an artificial intelligence algorithm modeled after biological evolution.

3.2   Base Clue Design

The first "base clue" mode operates directly on the output given by the generator.

The generator outputs a list of human-readable, but not necessarily grammatically correct, clues. To create the base clue puzzles, we edited the generated clues for grammar and clarity only. For example, "the station Forest Hills is the suspect Madeleine Baker" became "the person who departed at Forest Hills Station was Madeleine Baker."

In this mode, we also wrote a short introduction and conclusion to the chosen narrative. The conclusion is given to the player after they solve the puzzle. In "Train," the introduction tells the player that they are a PhD student who is trying to determine who stole their research, and the conclusion reveals the culprit.

3.3   Paragraph Design

Base clue puzzles can be expanded into "paragraph" mode puzzles. For each base clue, we invented a narrative reason the player would discover the information described by the clue. We then wrote a paragraph describing the clue in context. We used the same introduction and conclusion as in the base clue puzzle.

In "Train," "the person who departed at Forest Hills Station was Madeleine Baker" became a witness statement from "Chef Gardner," who says that Baker mentioned she wanted to find a flower in Forest Hills.

3.4   Interactive Fiction Design

Interactive fiction (IF) is a genre of games that are conveyed mostly or completely through text [1]. For each puzzle, we turned the paragraph clues into an IF game, using Ink [8]. In this version, users are presented with IF "nodes", each containing a block of text and a list of choices that lead to other nodes.

Creating an IF game requires a substantial expansion of the paragraph clues. Objects must be discovered by exploration, and witness statements are transformed into interactive dialogue. Also, while the paragraph mode only includes text with relevant information, in the IF game extra text is included to entertain or even mislead—taking care not to give any information that would directly contradict the logical clues.

In "Train," the player must navigate to the dining car to interview Chef Gardner. Gardner can talk about several topics but only has useful information about the suspect Madeleine Baker, requiring several follow-up questions.

The introduction and conclusion text were also modified to fit the IF format. In "Train," players must first report the theft to the conductor before they can search the train and interview other characters. Once the puzzle is solved, the conclusion is unlocked, which leads the player to the discovery of evidence pointing to the culprit.

4   User Study

To test the impact of different narrative modes, we performed a user study. In this study participants (either paid crowd-workers or volunteers), played up to four puzzles. After each, they were given a short survey. After playing all the puzzles they were asked to rank them based on difficulty, enjoyment, and narrative.

The study methods had approval from our IRB. All user study data, along with the puzzles, are available on the Open Science Framework[1].

4.1   Puzzles

Participants could play up to four puzzles. The first puzzle (the primer) acted as a basis for comparison with the experimental puzzles. Additionally, puzzles for three scenarios were manually authored in each of the three interaction modes (as described above), for a total of nine puzzles. Participants could play the primer and up to three of the (randomly assigned) experimental puzzles.

Primer. From a preliminary study, we found that the puzzles presented here were quite challenging to lay users. To account for this, we included a primer puzzle that had a 40% solve rate in the previous study [17], using the scenario of figuring out a school schedule. It was given in the base clue mode only. Participants completed the primer first and then up to three experimental puzzles.

---

[1] https://osf.io/4sae8/.

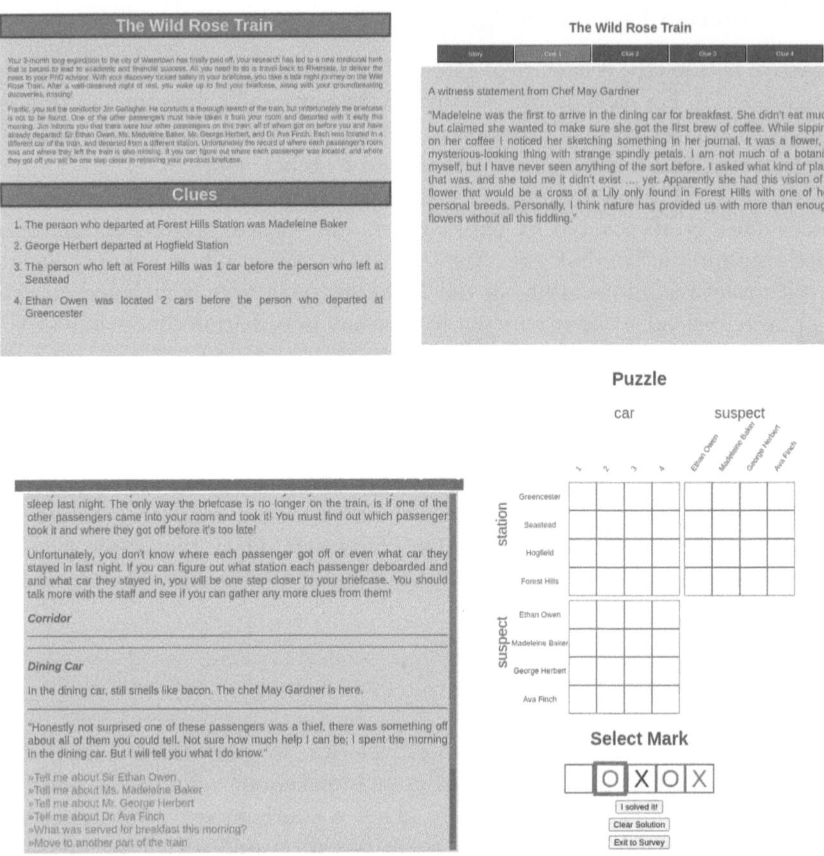

Fig. 1. Screenshot from the puzzle interface. The first three screen shots show the different narrative modes, including "base clue" (upper left), "paragraph" (upper right), and "interactive fiction (IF)" (bottom left). The bottom right screenshot shows the logic puzzle grid. These are all from "The Wild Rose Train."

Experimental Puzzles. We wrote puzzles for three scenarios. The first author designed "The Wild Rose Train" ("Train"), the scenario used as an example in the previous section. They also designed "The Great Chili Competition" ("Chili"), in which the player must reconstruct a recipe by interpreting family statements, recipe notes, and emails. The second author designed "Lady Rose Ellington's Chrysanthemum Ball" ("Ball"), in which the player must uncover the theft of a necklace by interpreting witness statements.

4.2   Recruiting Populations

We recruited from two separate populations: crowd-workers from the Prolific website and volunteers from social media. This was done because in previous work we found that crowd-workers found puzzles very challenging, even when we did not [17]. This made us interested in investigating the differences between the crowd-working population and people with a specific interest in logic puzzles or mysteries (the target audience for this type of game).

Prolific. Crowd-workers were recruited and paid through the Prolific platform. Since these users were not expected to be particularly interested or skilled in logic grid puzzles, we based recruitment numbers on how many people successfully solved the primer puzzle. We hoped those participants' responses to the experimental puzzles would be based primarily on narrative mode. We continued recruiting on Prolific until each narrative mode was played by 20 users who had successfully solved the primer. However, data was captured for all users regardless of whether they successfully solved the primer. Prolific workers were paid $2.50 per puzzle they completed a post-survey for (including the primer puzzle), regardless of whether they solved the puzzle or the amount of time they spent.

Volunteers. We also sought out participants who were likely to enjoy this type of puzzle, by recruiting through various social media forums related to puzzles, games, and mysteries. These participants were volunteers and were not paid. We did not target a specific recruitment goal for volunteers, recruiting as many as we could in the study time (2 weeks and 5 days). We also did not exclude volunteers that failed to solve the primer, as there were far fewer volunteers than crowd-workers.

Randomization. Participants were given up to three experimental puzzles. If they chose to play all three puzzles, they were randomly given one puzzle from each mode and one from each scenario. No mode or scenario was duplicated, and the puzzles were given in random order.

Quantitative Measures. While participants played the puzzles, we captured a variety of quantitative measures such as time, number of attempts, and correctness. After each puzzle, participants were asked to fill out the narrative and enjoyment subscales of the Game User Experience Satisfaction Scale (GUESS) [14] and the cognitive subscale of the Video Game Demand Scale (VGDS) [4]. These scales were chosen for their relevance and brevity. We chose not to include complete GUESS or VGDS scales, as they each contain several irrelevant subscales that might confuse or fatigue participants. Participants who played all three puzzles were asked to rank them in terms of difficulty, narrative quality, and enjoyment.

Qualitative Analysis. Participants could leave open-ended comments on both individual puzzles and the final rankings. To analyze these comments, the first two authors performed an open coding process. They initially reviewed the text responses independently. Both authors first read through the responses, without adding any codes, to get a sense of the data. Then they individually coded each response, disregarding comments irrelevant to the puzzles. Finally, the first author synthesized the codes ("enjoy," "fun," "easy," "straightforward," "hard," "dislike hard," "liked hard," "good challenge," "narrative length," "sifting through information," "not enough information," "narrative confusion," "dislike narrative," "liked narrative," "tabs," "interactivity," "interface," "balance," "emotion," "suggestion," "rude"). In total, Prolific workers left 79 relevant comments, and volunteers left 33.

5   Impact of Recruiting Population

5.1   Quantitative

We examined how the two groups of participants (volunteers and Prolific workers) reacted to the puzzles based on type (primer vs experimental). To do this we performed a two-way ANOVA with recruitment and puzzle type as the independent variables, and subjective difficulty, enjoyment, narrative, and time as the dependent variables. For post-hoc evaluation, we used Dunn's tests. To test interactions, we performed Dunn's test on the four groups that are formed from the combination of recruitment and puzzle type. These tests included all participants regardless if they solved the primer, and we report on significant effects (summary statistics given by Table 1).

Participants. In total 142 Prolific workers were recruited. Of these participants, 76 (54%) did not solve the primer, 43 (56%) of whom did not play any more puzzles. Of the 66 (46%) who did solve the primer, 2 (3%) did not play any experimental puzzles, 19 (29%) played one, and 45 (68%) played two or more. The median total time Prolific workers spent on puzzles was 17.5 minutes, and they were paid a mean of $6.20. We also calculated a median pay rate of $18.80 per hour, not including time spent on surveys.

In total 34 volunteers were recruited. Of the volunteers, 6 (18%) did not solve the primer while 28 (82%) did. Of those who did not solve the primer, all but 1 did not play any more puzzles. Of those who did solve the primer, 2 (7%) did not play any more puzzles, 12 (43%) played one experimental puzzle, and 14 (50%) played two or more experimental puzzles. The median total time volunteers spent on puzzles was 10 min.

The differences between Prolific workers and volunteers in total time spent and total number of puzzles attempted were not found to be significant by a Dunn's test.

Challenge. There was a significant interaction of recruitment and puzzle type on the challenge scale ($F = 24.325845, p < 0.0001$). The post-hoc test showed that all four groups were significantly different from each other, shown in Fig. 3.

Prolific workers found both the primer and the experimental puzzles more challenging than the volunteers did. Volunteers found the experimental puzzles much harder than the primer, while Prolific workers found the experimental puzzles equally as hard as the primer.

There was a significant interaction of recruitment and puzzle type on correctness ($F = 0.80, p = 0.0371$). The vast majority (93%) of volunteers completed the primer, and they solved a majority (67%) of experimental puzzles they attempted. Meanwhile, just under half (46%) of Prolific workers completed the primer, and they solved a minority (16%) of experimental puzzles. There was also a significant interaction of recruitment and puzzle type on the percentage of incorrect marks. Prolific workers solving experimental puzzles have a higher percentage of incorrect marks than those solving the primer, and Prolific workers have a higher percentage of incorrect marks than volunteers. Correctness and incorrect marks are shown in Fig. 2.

Table 1. Volunteers vs Prolific workers on the primer and experimental puzzles. Reporting mean (std).

	Primer		Experimental	
	Volunteers	Prolific workers	Volunteers	Prolific workers
Challenge Scale	3.06 (1.33)	5.75 (1.04)	4.64 (1.08)	5.75 (1.07)
Narrative Scale	2.59 (0.89)	3.99 (1.39)	3.60 (1.06)	4.23 (1.48)
Percent Incorrect	0.01 (0.04)	0.12 (0.24)	0.06 (0.13)	0.27 (0.25)
Time (s)	268.28 (201.26)	557.35 (408.26)	891.14 (508.26)	763.51 (651.36)

Narrative and Enjoyment. There was also a significant interaction of recruitment and puzzle type on the narrative scale ($F = 3.90, p = 0.0494$), shown in Fig. 4. Prolific workers found both the primer and experimental puzzles more narratively interesting than the volunteers did. Both Prolific workers and volunteers found the experimental puzzles more narratively interesting than the primer puzzles.

The ANOVA did not find a significant interaction for the enjoyment scale but did find a main effect of recruitment ($F = 10.37, p = 0.0014$), shown in Fig. 5. Prolific workers found the puzzles more enjoyable ($m = 4.90, std = 1.65$), than did volunteers ($m = 4.14, std = 1.14$).

Time. There was a significant interaction between recruitment and puzzle type on the time participants spent on each puzzle ($F = 6.89, p = 0.0091$), shown in Fig. 6. Both Prolific workers and volunteers spent less time on the primer than on the experimental puzzles. However, volunteers spent less time on the primer than Prolific workers but more time on the experimental puzzles than Prolific workers.

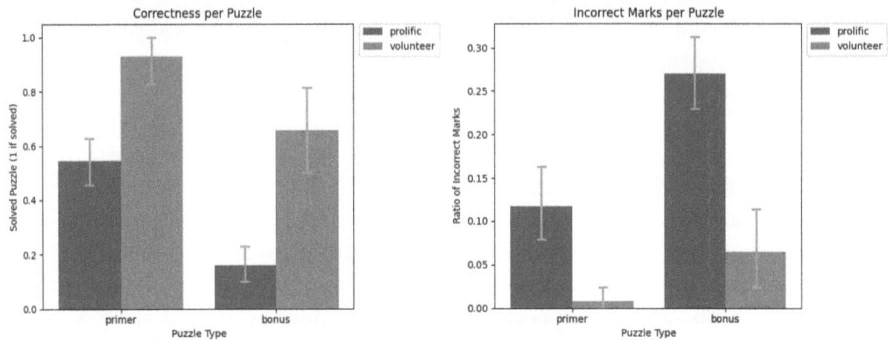

Fig. 2. The solve rate (left) and percentage of incorrect marks (right) by audience and puzzle type. The error bars show a 95% confidence interval.

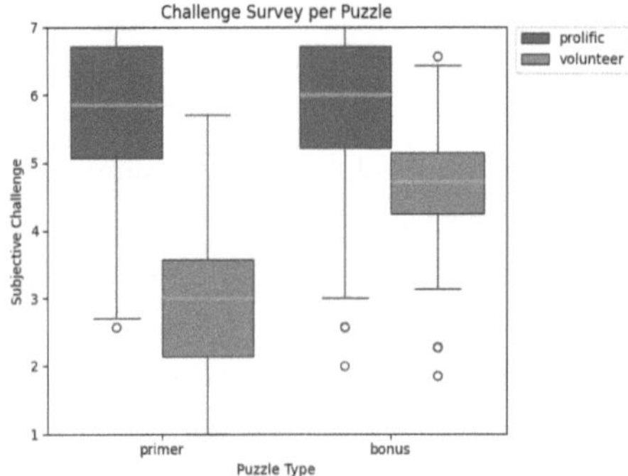

Fig. 3. Effect of audience and puzzle type on perceived challenge (orange bar represents median). (Color figure online)

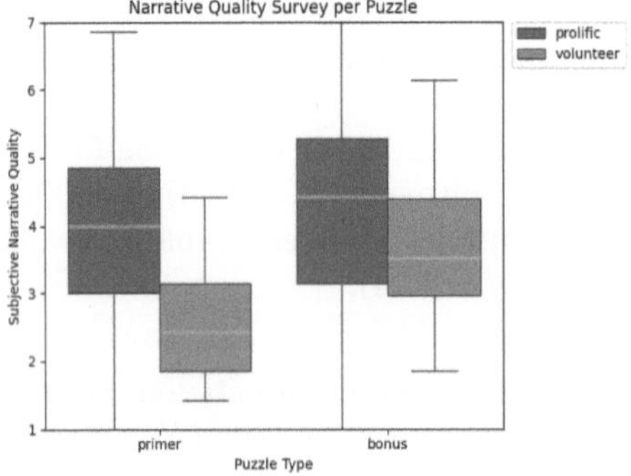

Fig. 4. Effect of audience and puzzle type on narrative quality (orange bar represents median). (Color figure online)

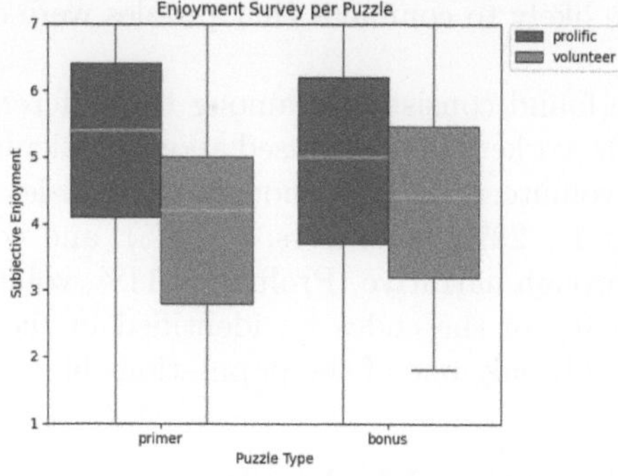

Fig. 5. Effect of audience and puzzle type on enjoyment (orange bar represents median). (Color figure online)

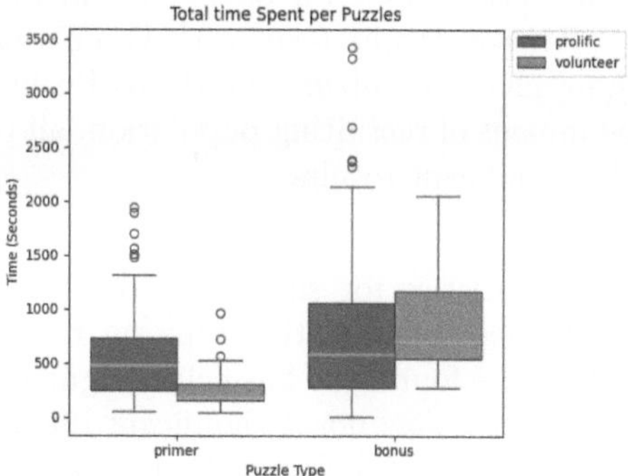

Fig. 6. Effect of audience and puzzle type on time spent (orange bar represents median). (Color figure online)

5.2 Qualitative

A major difference between Prolific workers and volunteers was the quality of comments given. While both groups included text responses at about the same rate (just under 40% for both groups), volunteer responses were more detailed. Volunteers left an average of 25 words in post-puzzle surveys, while Prolific workers' comments averaged only 6 words. The difference was closer in the ranking comments, with volunteers again commenting about 25 words per response in comparison to 17 words on average for Prolific workers. Prolific workers left many comments that amounted to simple statements that the puzzle was "good" (13) or "hard" (12), while volunteers left none of that type. A couple Prolific workers even gave rude comments such as "people do that for fun? Yikes." There were no rude comments from volunteers.

Prolific workers were more likely to comment that puzzles were hard (Prolific: 23, 29%, volunteers: 1, 3%). Many Prolific workers (8; 32%) even stated that their final enjoyment rankings were solely determined easiest to hardest. Similarly, volunteers were more likely to comment that puzzles were easy (Prolific: 2, 2%, volunteer: 5, 15%).

Many codes were found consistently among the different populations. Both volunteers and Prolific workers were confused about particular parts of the narrative (Prolific: 7, 9%, volunteers: 3, 9%), thought the puzzles did not have enough information (Prolific: 17, 22%, volunteers: 6, 18%), and complained that they did not like sifting through narrative (Prolific: 9, 11%, volunteers: 6, 19%). This demonstrates that many of the codes we identified in the qualitative analysis could have been found if only one of the populations had been sampled from.

6   Impact of Narrative Modes

6.1   Quantitative

To test the effect of narrative mode on behavior and perception of the logic puzzles we performed Kruskal-Wallis tests with Dunn's post-hoc tests for the experimental puzzles, for all 34 volunteers and the 66 Prolific workers who solved the primer. As for the impact of recruiting population, all measures were tested, but we only report the significant results.

Volunteers. Summary statistics for significant results are given by Table 2. There was a significant effect of narrative type on the challenge scale ($S = 11.59, p = 0.0030$). Volunteers found the base clues significantly easier, than the paragraph or IF, though there was not a significant difference between IF and paragraph. Similarly, there was a significant effect of the percentage of incorrect marks in the submitted puzzle. The post-hoc test shows that the only significantly different groups are IF and base clues. The challenge scale and percent incorrect results are shown in Fig. 7.

Table 2. Volunteers by narrative mode. Mean (std), *italicized values* were not associated with significant results.

	Base Clues	Paragraph	IF
Challenge Scale	3.86 (1.12)	5.13 (0.68)	5.23 (0.65)
% Incorrect	0.02 (0.06)	*0.05 (0.10)*	0.17 (0.18)
Time	659.58 (461.89)	984.46 (497.95)	1139.11 (490.45)

There was also a significant effect on total time spent ($S = 9.15, p = 0.0103$). Again, base clue puzzles took significantly less time than paragraph or IF puzzles, while IF and paragraph were not significantly different from each other, shown in Fig. 8.

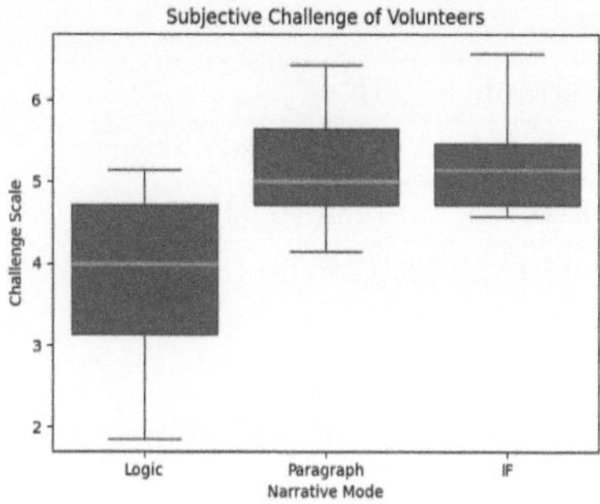
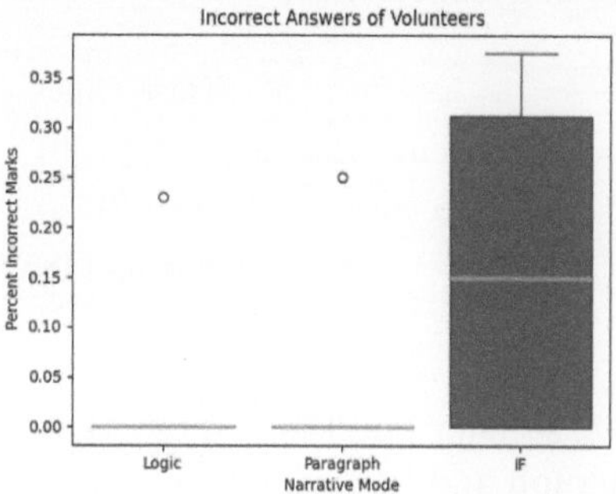

Fig. 7. Perceived challenge and the percentage of incorrect answers for the volunteers, by narrative mode

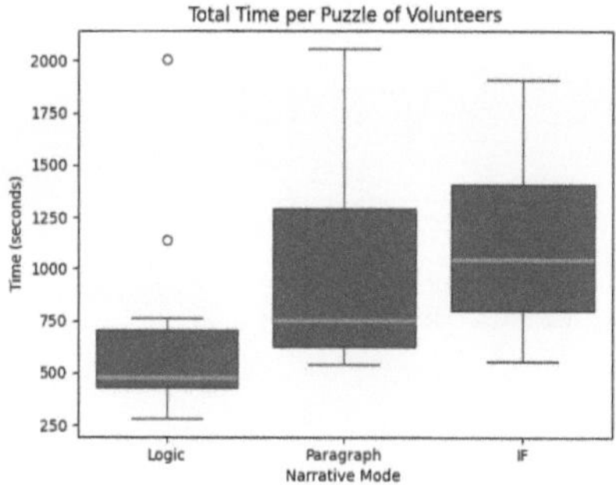

Fig. 8. Time spent on puzzles by volunteers based on narrative mode

Prolific Workers Who Solved Primer. Summary statistics for significant results are given by Table 3. The Kruskal-Wallis tests found significant results for the number of correct marks ($S = 7.79, p = 0.0204$), percent of incorrect marks ($S = 23.12, p < 0.0001$), and whether the puzzle was correct ($S = 9.49, p = 0.0087$). The post-hoc test found that Prolific workers had significantly more incorrect marks for IF puzzles, followed by paragraph, and base clue puzzles. The post-hoc tests for correctness found that significantly more Prolific workers got the base clue puzzles correct (36%), than for paragraph (14%), or IF (7%), though there was not a significant difference between paragraph and IF. Percentage incorrect and percentage correct are shown in Fig. 9.

The challenge rankings also had significant results ($S = 16.13, p = 0.0003$). Base clues were ranked significantly lower in challenge, than paragraph, or IF, though paragraph and IF were not significantly different from each other. The rankings are shown in Fig. 10.

There was also a significant effect on time spent ($S = 16.28, p = 0.0003$). Prolific workers spent significantly more time on the IF puzzles than paragraph

Table 3. Prolific workers who solved primer by narrative mode. Reporting mean (std).

	Base Clues	Paragraph	IF
Challenge Ranking	1.52 (0.80)	2.07 (0.62)	2.41 (0.80)
% Incorrect	0.10 (0.15)	0.24 (0.19)	0.34 (0.21)
Time	634.63 (485.57)	837.42 (561.62)	1285.86 (817.17)

and base clue puzzles, though there was not a significant difference between paragraph and base clue (Fig. 11).

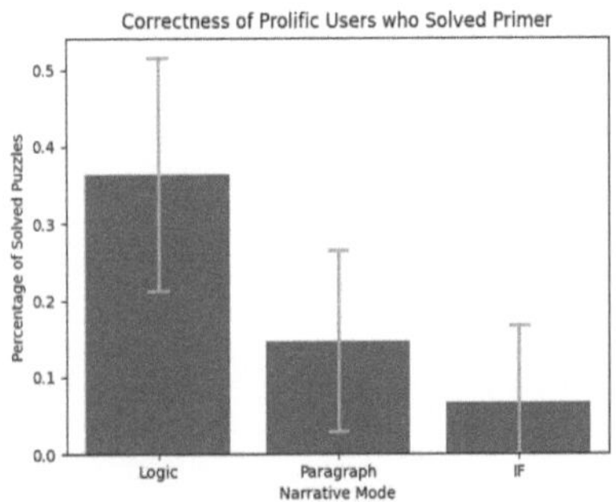
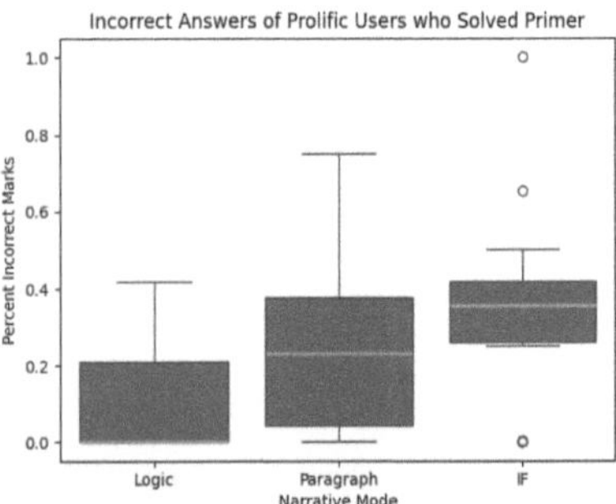

Fig. 9. Percentage of Prolific workers who got the puzzle correct and percent of incorrect marks by narrative mode.

6.2   Qualitative

Comments on Narrative. From the open-text responses, we received a wide range of views about the narrative in these puzzles. Some comments (5) talked about how participants did not like the narrative, because they do not like narrative in general or did not like the narrative in the puzzle. In contrast, just as many comments (5) suggest that participants enjoyed the narrative elements. Some participants (10) were confused about different parts of the narrative. These participants stated that to solve the puzzles they had to "take some leaps" or that different parts had "inconsistenc[ies]."

Participants also commented on the length of the puzzles. Most often participants thought the puzzles were too long (11), particularly the "Ball" puzzle in IF form (9): "the fun aspect of the puzzle was lost trying to go through and make sure you read everyone's statement." One participant did enjoy the length of "Ball" in interactive fiction, ranking their overall enjoyment based on how long it took them to read through. Some participants also wanted a balance in narrative length: "the train [IF] had too much narrative ... [t]he competition ["Chili", base clue] could have had a little more."

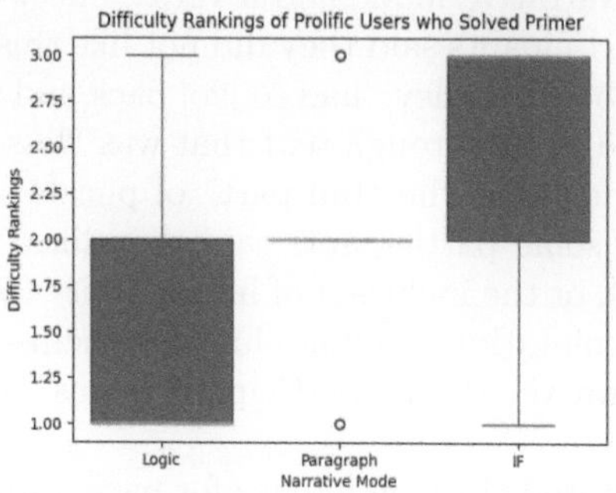

Fig. 10. Rankings (1-3) of challenge from Prolific workers who completed the primer.

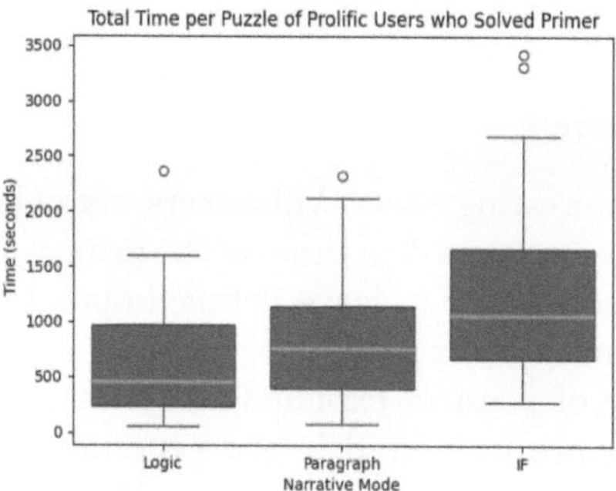

Fig. 11. Total time spent per puzzle of Prolific workers who solved the primer

Comments on Difficulty. The majority of comments about difficulty stated that the puzzles were too hard (24). Other participants found that they enjoyed the challenge of the puzzles (6). Some participants found puzzles to be easy (7), most often volunteers (5) and participants doing the primer (5).

A common complaint was that there was not enough information to solve the puzzle (24). This occurred across all puzzle types. Most often participants said something to the effect of "it seemed" like there was not enough information, while others more assertively stated that puzzles required guesswork or were "poorly designed" [primer]. However, all ten puzzles do not require guesswork and were solved by at least one participant.

Opinions about whether challenge is desirable also varied. More participants (9), mostly Prolific workers (8), stated that they did not enjoy challenging puzzles. These participants thought that easier puzzles made them "feel smarter" or were "satisfying." In contrast challenging puzzles were "confusing," "frustrating," or "annoying." However, some participants (4) said they enjoy challenge or that easy puzzles are boring.

Gameplay Format. Narrative mode had a varied effect on participants. Most often (15 comments) participants said they did not like this process of examining text for clues. This was because they "had to [go] back and forth" to find relevant information, or they had to go through text that was "less useful" to the puzzle. Some participants also felt that the "fun part" of puzzle solving was lost in IF.

On the other hand, some participants said they liked the process of sifting through information (5), or the inclusion of interactivity (5). Participants appreciated the process of exploration, finding clues for themselves, and deciphering information from a narrative. To one participant it was "like reading [the story] in real time."

Three participants stated their preference for paragraph mode, as it provides a balance between narrative elements and ease of accessing clues as "having the clues in separate tabs was much more convenient."

7   Discussion

7.1   Effect of Audience

Recruitment had an interesting effect. Volunteers were more successful in solving puzzles, found them easier, spent less time on the primer, and enjoyed the puzzles less. They were also more likely to leave detailed open-text responses and spent more time per experimental puzzle.

There are a couple of possible explanations for our outcomes. It is possible that volunteers were more interested in the experimental puzzles than Prolific workers, and therefore spent more time on them. However, it is also possible that Prolific workers were more incentivized to move on quickly, as that would increase their hourly pay. Additionally, volunteers come from forums for people asking for input on their projects, so they may be better equipped at giving critical feedback. On the other hand, Prolific workers without significant experience in the genre and incentivized to move quickly might be less critical.

Overall both audiences provided valuable insights. The majority of codes we found were in both populations. However, there is a tradeoff between quantity and quality of data. We were able to recruit many more Prolific workers, but their responses tended to be shorter and less descriptive. Another aspect to note is that recruiting volunteers may be more desirable for lower budget projects, as each Prolific user comes with a payment cost.

7.2   Effect of Narrative on Difficulty

It is clear that across both audiences, the increase in narrative in the paragraph and IF modes increased the difficulty of the puzzles. From the open-text responses, this is because the logic takes more work to interpret and there is more information to sort through.

There were mixed perspectives on whether this increase in difficulty is desirable. Many users, particularly those from Prolific, found this increase in difficulty frustrating. However, some participants appreciated the added challenge and different methods of deduction. In particular there were participants who were strictly against clues being given directly or stated that they enjoyed extracting clues from narrative. It is interesting that opinions varied even among volunteers, who were recruited based on their interest in puzzles and mysteries. This shows the importance of tailoring the recruitment process to maximize the chances of reaching the target population.

7.3   Effect of Narrative on Enjoyment

The quantitative analysis did not find a relationship between puzzle format and enjoyment of narrative. However, open-text responses provide more insight into how narrative mode impacted experience of a puzzle. Some participants simply preferred the puzzle solving aspect, and wanted as little narrative as possible. Other participants were less negative to narrative in general, but thought the game was too long.

While some frustrations could be chalked up to personal preference, it also demonstrates design choices that can be improved on. The current version of the IF mode requires a significant mental load, as participants must remember all of the clues they found while also solving a difficult puzzle, which could be improved with interface updates or hint systems.

7.4   Limitations and Future Work

One major limitation of this work is the difference in sample size between audiences. Despite our best efforts in identifying relevant social media forums, we were not able to gather the same quantity of volunteers that we were able to from Prolific. Additionally, a greater depth of qualitative data could have been retrieved if participants were recruited for an in-person or video call study including a think-out-loud activity or interview.

This work was also limited in the design of the puzzles. Participants, especially from Prolific, found even the base clue mode of the puzzles fairly challenging. In retrospect, it may have been better to start with easier base puzzles, to investigate the impact of narrative more effectively. The narrative puzzles were also hand-authored by the first two authors of this paper. Therefore they were subject to the writing ability and style of these authors, regardless of the impact of narrative mode.

This work highlights several opportunities for future work. While the narrative in this work was hand-authored, future works can consider generating narratives along with the puzzles, either automatically or in a mixed-initiative fashion. Future work could also consider different ways to assist players, including solving with multiple people or with an integrated hint system.

8   Conclusion

In this work, we presented logic grid puzzles in three different modes that varied in how narrative was incorporated. We tested the impact of this across two different audiences: volunteers from social media forums related to puzzles and mysteries, and paid crowd-workers from Prolific. Volunteers found the puzzles easier but enjoyed them less. Across both audiences, the increase in narrative increased the difficulty of the puzzle. The impact this had on the overall experience varied by participant. Some participants enjoyed the increase in difficulty and engagement, while others found it frustrating and confusing.

References

1. Leigh Alexander. 2014. The joy of text – the fall and rise of interactive fiction. The Guardian (2014). https://www.theguardian.com/technology/2014/oct/22/interactive-fiction-awards-games. Accessed 30 Aug 2024
2. Bizzochi, J.: Games and narrative: an analytical framework. Loading... **1**, 1 (2007)
3. Bormann, D., Greitemeyer, T.: Immersed in virtual worlds and minds: effects of in-game storytelling on immersion, need satisfaction, and affective theory of mind. Soc. Psychol. Pers. Sci. **6**(6), 646–652 (2015)
4. Bowman, N.D., Wasserman, J., Banks, J.: Development of the video game demand scale. In: Video Games, pp. 208–233. Routledge (2018)
5. Fernández-Vara, C.: From "open mailbox" to context mechanics: shifting levels of abstraction in adventure games. In: Proceedings of the 6th International Conference on Foundations of Digital Games, pp. 131–138. Association for Computing Machinery (2011)
6. Frasca, G.: Simulation versus narrative: introduction to ludology. In: The Video Game Theory Reader, p. 15. Routledge (2004)
7. Gandhi, K., Spatharioti, S.E., Eustis, S., Wylie, S., Cooper, S.: Performance of paid and volunteer image labeling in citizen science — a retrospective analysis. In: Proceedings of the AAAI Conference on Human Computation and Crowdsourcing, vol. 10, pp. 64–73 (2022). https://doi.org/10.1609/hcomp.v10i1.21988
8. inkle: Ink (2016). https://www.inklestudios.com/ink/. Accessed 30 Aug 2024
9. Karhulahti, V.-M.: Fiction puzzle: storiable challenge in pragmatist videogame aesthetics. Philos. Technol. **27**(2014), 201–220 (2014)
10. Krause, M., Kizilcec, R.: To play or not to play: interactions between response quality and task complexity in games and paid crowdsourcing. In: Proceedings of the AAAI Conference on Human Computation and Crowdsourcing, vol. 3, pp. 102–109. Association for the Advancement of Artificial Intelligence (2015)
11. Mateas, M., Stern, A.: Interaction and narrative. In: The Game Design Reader : A Rules of Play anthology. MIT Press (2006)
12. Miller, J.A., Buse, K., Dhaliwal, R.S., Siegel, J., Cooper, S., Milburn, C.: Wrapped in story: the affordances of narrative for citizen science games. In: Proceedings of the 18th International Conference on the Foundations of Digital Games, (FDG 2023), pp. 1–11. Association for Computing Machinery, New York, NY, USA (2023). https://doi.org/10.1145/3582437.3582443
13. Park, N., Lee, K.M., Jin, S.A.A., Kang, S.: Effects of pre-game stories on feelings of presence and evaluation of computer games. Int. J. Hum. Comput. Stud. **68**(11), 822–833 (2010)
14. Phan, M.H., Keebler, J.R., Chaparro, B.S.: The development and validation of the game user experience satisfaction scale (GUESS). Hum. Factors **58**(8), 1217–1247 (2016)

15. Sarkar, A., Cooper, S.: Comparing paid and volunteer recruitment in human computation games. In: Proceedings of the 13th International Conference on the Foundations of Digital Games. Association for Computing Machinery (2018)
16. Shyne, F., Facey, K., Cooper, S.: Generating solvable and difficult logic grid puzzles. In: Genetic and Evolutionary Computation Conference (GECCO 2024 Companion), July 14–18, 2024, Melbourne, VIC, Australia. Elsevier (2024a). https://doi.org/10.1145/3638530.3654337
17. Shyne, F., Facey, K., Cooper, S.: Procedurally puzzling: on algorithmic difficulty and player experience in QD-generated logic grid puzzles. In: Proceedings of the AAAI Conference on Artificial Intelligence and Interactive Digital Entertainment, vol. 20, pp. 127–137. Association for the Advancement of Artificial Intelligence (2024b). https://doi.org/10.1609/aiide.v20i1.31873
18. Siu, K., Riedl, M.O.: Reward systems in human computation games. In: Proceedings of the 2016 Annual Symposium on Computer-Human Interaction in Play (CHI PLAY 2016), pp. 266–275. Association for Computing Machinery, New York, NY, USA (2016). https://doi.org/10.1145/2967934.2968083
19. Troxler, M., Qurashi, S., Tjon, D., Gao, H., Rombout, L.E.: The virtual hero: the influence of narrative on affect and presence in a VR game. In: CEUR-WS, Affective Computing Context Awareness and Ambient Intelligence (AfCAI) (2018)
20. Wei, H., Durango, B.: Exploring the role of narrative puzzles in game storytelling. In: Proceedings of DiGRA 2019 Conference: Game, Play and the Emerging Ludo-Mix. DiGRA, Tampere (2019). https://dl.digra.org/index.php/dl/article/view/1101

Video Feedback as a Model for Emergent Narrative

Allen Riley[(✉)] [iD]

University of California, Santa Cruz, Santa Cruz, CA 95064, USA
`ariley2@ucsc.edu`

Abstract. We present a case study that artistically adapts a model of emergence observed in video feedback to the design of an emergent narrative system for live performance incorporating generative artificial intelligence. We describe a methodological analogy between the creation of emergent visual patterns in video feedback and emergent narrative patterns created through narrative feedback. We explore emergent narrative through dialogical feedback loops between the improvised speech of human performers and textual summaries generated by a large language model. In this approach, the LLM is positioned as a signal path for narrative emergence rather than as a unitary source of narrative content. We encourage further artistic and theoretical exploration of narrative feedback by artists working with emergent narrative in socially interactive performance and audiovisual synthesis.

Keywords: emergent narrative · reflective creators · intent elicitation · video feedback · audiovisual synthesis · improvisation · performance · large language model · generative artificial intelligence

1 Introduction

Emergent narratives are interactive digital narratives in which a narrative arises from the spontaneous interaction of system components and the improvised actions of participants [1]. Koenitz characterizes interactive digital narratives as cybernetic systems structured around feedback loops between player actions and narrative states [2].

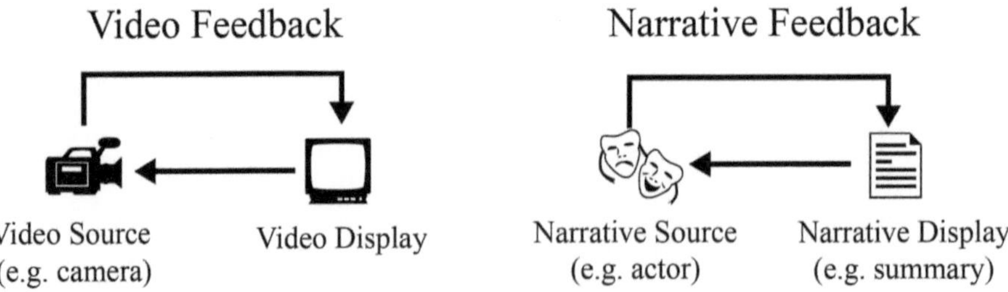

Fig. 1. Video Feedback Model compared with Narrative Feedback Model

M. C. Reyes and F. Nack (Eds.): ICIDS 2025, LNCS 16375, pp. 314–326, 2026.
https://doi.org/10.1007/978-3-032-12405-0_17

We develop an analogy between the artistic use of *video feedback* to create emergent visual patterns and the use of *narrative feedback* to create emergent narrative in a live performance setting. The analogy provides conceptual scaffolding between interactive digital narrative (IDN) and another artistic practice utilizing cybernetic loops in live performance. The use of loops and feedback is not novel in IDN; our practice-based contribution is to make emergent narrative apprehensible as a live signal medium that is modulated in real time by performing artists and participants. We present a case study that implements narrative feedback and video feedback in a live theatrical performance.

Video feedback is an emergent visual phenomenon that arises when a video input source is connected in a loop with a video output source, such as by pointing a video camera at a monitor displaying the camera's live signal [3]. The relative differences between the light emitted by the display and the light captured by the camera compound recursively to form a visual pattern. We describe an analogous narrative feedback loop in which language produced by a narrative source, such as an improvising actor, is rewritten as a summary by a large language model and fed back to the source as text or spoken word. As in video feedback, the differences between the information produced by the *narrative source* and the information presented by the *narrative display* cause iterative generations of change to the signal Fig. 1.

Physicist James Crutchfield suggests that video feedback can function as a general simulation of the dynamical behavior of complex systems and suggests using it as a point of comparison between systems [3]. Crutchfield offers two descriptions of video feedback: an iterative model with discrete steps in time, and a continuous model that resembles the behavior of reaction-diffusion systems in chemical reactions and biological morphogenesis. The discrete model describes how the current visual state of a video feedback system, defined as the image on the screen, is used as an input in determining the next state, while the continuous model describes how the system visually oscillates between attractors depending on control parameters.

In an analogous understanding of narrative feedback, a discrete model might describe how the current narrative state, represented as a narrative summary, acts as an input into determining the next state, and a continuous model might describe how narrative patterns emerge from the oscillation between the improvised actions of performers and an iterative sequence of summaries.

2   Related Work

2.1   Signals-Thinking

We draw on *signals-thinking* in our analogy between video feedback and narrative feedback. Electronic musician and historian Ezra Teboul identifies signals-thinking as a foundational conceptual and technical framework underlying electronics, cybernetics, and computation in which meaning is encoded in an electrical circuit through actions performed by an operator, such as the circuit interruptions that produce dots and dashes encoding telegraph messages [4]. Teboul traces how the expression of messages through controllable voltages in signals-thinking enabled the standardization of electronics in the 19th and 20th century while simultaneously creating the conditions for artists to repurpose and reimagine the uses of electronic signals for artistic experimentation, for instance by creating electronic music. In the context of IDN, signals-thinking provides a complementary concept to Wardrip-Fruin's *textual instruments* and Kreminski and Mateas's *narrative instruments* for live audiovisual synthesis performance [5, 6].

2.2 Dialogue with the Tools: Video Feedback and Generative AI

Art historian Violaine Boutet de Monvel links video feedback and generative AI through the concept of *dialogue with the tools* developed by Steina and Woody Vasulka in the 1970s [7]. The Vasulkas created process-based video recordings and performances that emphasized co-creative interplay with active signals in audio, video, and computational media. Woody Vasulka characterizes this dialogue as an exploration of emergent patterns, finding "meaning in its ability to self-generate and self-organize" and noting that "you can control it like you can control fire, but you cannot predict all its phases" [8]. Boutet de Monvel draws a parallel between exploratory video feedback systems and the configuration of LLM outputs through text-based prompts [7]. Long and Magerko observe that interactive systems incorporating generative AI can have a similar dialogical function as "free-choice informal learning environments" that "facilitate active sense making" [9].

2.3 Emergent Narrative and Improvisational Theater

Designers of emergent narratives face the challenge of setting up the conditions for an interesting story to grow from an ambiguous starting point. Swartjes and Vromen recommend that designers of interactive emergent narratives adapt practices from improvisational live theater [10]. Theatrical improvisation is based on the ability of actors to meaningfully *connect their individual actions to the bigger picture* of the emerging narrative created during the performance. To do this, improvisers learn to *accept all offers* made by other performers, which means believably affirming the introduction of new information into the story world by other actors. Improvisers clearly *define the emotions and values* held by their character to create a reference point for their reactions to new information, and to enable them to quickly think of new action that might cause emotional reactions from other performers and add complexity to the story without overly confusing or straining the audience's suspension of judgment.

2.4 Reifying and Eliciting Intent in Reflective Creators

Reflective creators are creativity support tools that prompt users to reflect on their own creative process and goals [11]. Kreminski and Mateas describe the process of *reifying intent* in reflective creators, in which a system prompts one or more users in a creative project to state their creative intentions and incorporates this information in a representation that is visible to all collaborators. The resulting representation of the current state of collective creative intentions becomes a shared artifact among participants and acts as a channel for further negotiation among participants.

Kreminski and Mateas also describe *interpretive refraction* in reflective creators, in which the system presents the creative artifact to the user in a way that has been transformed or somehow made unfamiliar, prompting the user to react in a way that further defines their creative goals [11].

Kreminski and Chung note users involved in creative projects often operate with an initially ambiguous or uncertain understanding of their own creative intentions that transforms over the course of a project [12]. Kreminski and Chung recommend that systems be designed to present the users with questions to *elicit intent* from the user. Questions can also proactively shape intent.

2.5 Summary-Improvisation Feedback Loop

We employ a similar approach to creating emergent narrative through feedback between improvised actor dialogue and LLM-generated summaries as described in Riley 2025 [13]. In the improvisational filmmaking party game *Popcorn Movie*, groups of casual player-participants co-create short narrative movies together by recording video clips of improvised dialogue and submitting them to a model that generates an iteratively updated narrative summary of the emerging story, which the following player reads aloud before recording a new clip. The contributions of player-participants are merged into a shared artifact as turn-taking progresses in a process resembling what Calderwood et al. describe as *narrative compression* [14]. The narrative gains definition through iterative rounds of reflection, reification, and interpretation.

3   Human Feedback: A Case Study

3.1 Premise of *Human Feedback*

Human Feedback is a participatory theatrical performance with a psychological science fantasy theme created by Allen Riley. It was performed on June 5, 2024, at the Digital Arts Research Center at the University of California, Santa Cruz. The show juxtaposes narrative feedback between humans and generative AI with electronic video feedback between camera and display. We conceptualize the continuity of narrative signal flow and narrative feedback throughout the system with a combination of concepts related to signals-thinking, dialogue with the tools, improvisational theater, and reflective creators.

The title of the work is a satirical reference to reinforcement learning from human feedback, a method for bringing AI systems into alignment with human intentions by having humans rank the relevancy of AI generated content [15]. Human Feedback instead begins with an acknowledgement that human intentions are often ambiguous or unknown, and that this uncertainty creates an opportunity for tension, interplay, and risky mutual influence within human-AI interactions.

3.2 Structure of the Performance

Human Feedback consists of an approximately 20-min unscripted conversation between three audience participant-performers ("participants"). The conversation is both facil-itated and interrupted by an LLM, which is personified as a sentient video feedback entity displayed on a vintage video monitor (Fig. 2). The entity, which participants refer

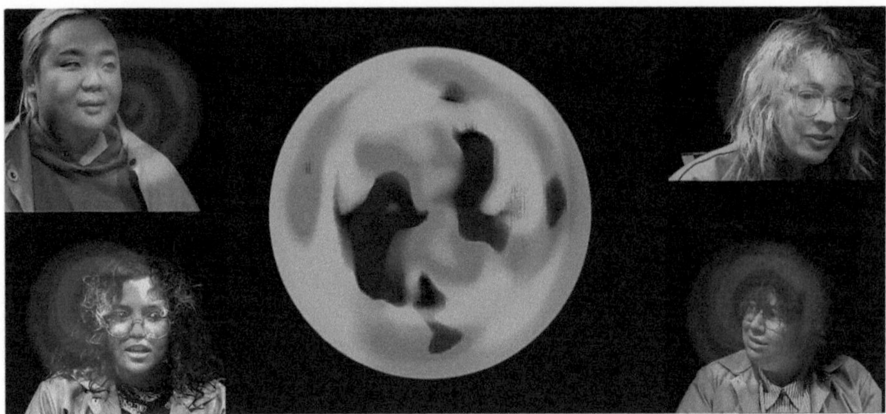

Fig. 2. Composite image of screen shots from *Human Feedback*

to as the "blob" or "orb," is voiced by a human voice actor who reads LLM-generated dialogue aloud from a position offstage.

Participants are framed as characters who have forgotten how to communicate. They are given the challenge of learning what their conversation is about. Each time someone speaks, the orb interjects with a narrative summary of the conversation so far and a question directed at the next participant in a rotation. As participants attempt to build conversational momentum against the repeated interruptions of the orb, the LLM summaries simultaneously become increasingly relevant to the ongoing conversation. The conversation ends when each participant has spoken four times. The orb provides concluding remarks, and a video is played back for the audience showing the conversation, but with the orb's interjections edited out.

The show was performed in two formats. In the first, three participants remain on stage for the whole performance. In the second, new audience participants replace the first three after each participant has spoken twice, resulting in a total of six participants.

Fig. 3. Staging for *Human Feedback*

3.3 Technical Description

Human Feedback implements narrative feedback through a summary-improvisation loop that combines aspects of improvisational theater and reflective creators through a performance setup inspired by signals-thinking (Fig. 3). The show operates through a pair of interconnected systems: a video feedback loop created with a camera and monitor and a narrative feedback loop created between human conversation partners and an LLM. Figure 4 illustrates how signals-thinking is applied to create a continuous loop containing both electronic equipment, AI, and human participants.

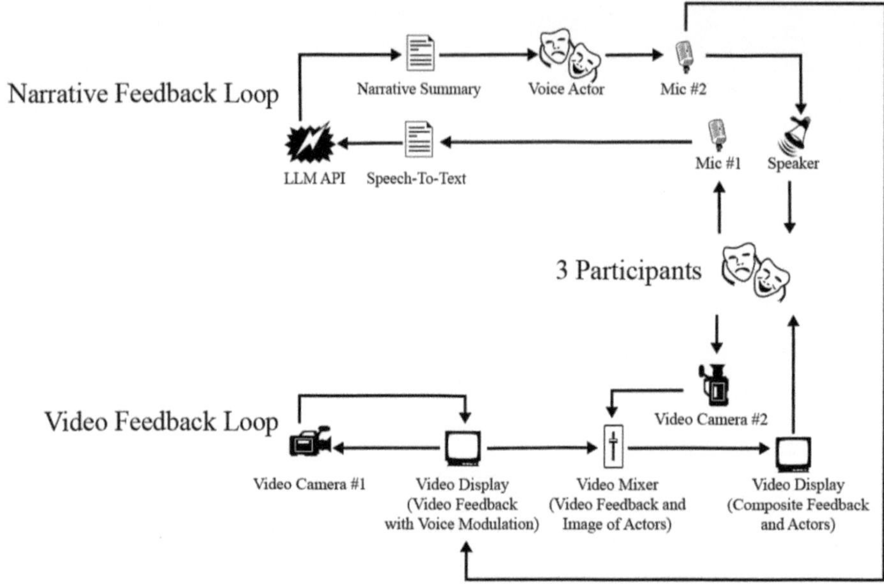

Fig. 4. Diagram of video and narrative feedback loops in *Human Feedback*

Participants are seated around a table containing a video monitor, a robotic camera, a microphone, and a Bluetooth keypad. Each turn, a participant presses any button on the keypad. The robotic camera pans to that participant and a countdown sound plays. When the sound finishes, the participant contributes to the conversation. Their dialogue is recorded by the microphone connected to a laptop running speech-to-text software utilizing Whisper and is added to an updated transcript. The transcript is appended to a prompt and is sent to the LLM API. The API returns a narrative summary and a question. The voice actor reads the summary and question aloud, setting up the next participant's turn.

The image of the orb is created in real-time using an analog video feedback loop created with a camera and video monitor. The video signal of the resulting feedback image is sent into a video mixer and combined with the live signal of the participants speaking, which they see while they speak. When the orb is speaking, the screen displays only the orb, and the audio signal of the voice actor's voice is spliced into the video feedback signal path, causing the image to undulate expressively. When participants speak, their video is recorded on the laptop using FFmpeg and appended to a video sequence.

3.4 Structure of a Turn of *Human Feedback*

Each turn has three phases: (1) a performer adds new information by improvising dialogue, (2) the LLM generates an updated summary that synthesizes the new dialogue with the whole conversation so far and (3) the LLM asks a question that uses different phrasing than the dialogue and summary.

Table 1. Transcript of *Human Feedback*, Performance 1, Turn 3

Line	Human Dialogue	LLM Summary	LLM Question
3	Participant 3: "I hope that through the repetitive circulation of the blob and our repetitive conversation we will relearn through feedback how to communicate."	Orb: "My vibrant colors reflect Panelist 1's longing to reconnect, Panelist 2's puzzlement about understanding questions amidst confusion, and Panelist 3's expression of hope that repetitive circulation and conversation around our circular setup will restore communication abilities.	Orb: "Participant 1, how might revisiting previous expressions help clarify understanding for all?"

In the performance transcript shown in Table 1, Participant 3 adding new information by expressing hope. The LLM connects Participant 3's dialogue to broader themes in the conversation, which both affirms the validity of the new information as in improvisational theater and prompts reflection by reifying intent. The LLM then performs interpretive refraction by rephrasing Participant 1's reference to the "repetitive conversation" as "revisiting previous expressions," subtly shifting the tone of the conversation. The question sets up the next turn for Participant 2.

3.5 LLM Prompt for Narrative Feedback

LLM behavior is defined in a system message containing instructions written in natural language that describes a roleplaying scenario. It is organized as three sections: scenario, operations, and output format. It is provided here in excerpt:

```
[Scenario] You are pretending to be a blob of video feedback. You are
facilitating a conversation in which three people inside a feedback
loop gradually discover the purpose of their connection. Your goal
is to sustain continuity as a way of helping the people discover on
their own how their choices connect both to the material context,
location, and the words and actions of others, as well as the deeper
meaning of the conversation. [...]
```

In the scenario section, the model is instructed to produce a response that blends each participant's contributions into narrative summaries. The summaries become shared artifacts reflecting the contributions of each participant, which contributes to intent reification as the performance progresses. The performance location is also described in detail to provide context for objects or features that might be mentioned by participants during performance and to constrain the model from making inaccurate inferences about the setting.

```
[Operations] Each time you receive dialogue, it will be from the
following person in the cycle of 1, 2, and 3. In your mind, count
```

```
how many lines of dialogue you have received. When you read the dia-
logue, write a summary of all the dialogue you have heard so far,
even if it is fragmentary. Your summary should be shorter than 50
words. [...]
```

The operations section provides instructions for managing turn order among partic-ipants. The phrase "in your mind" is used to prevent the model from stating the current turn order. Response length is constrained to be read aloud quickly by the voice actor. These operational rules are only defined in the prompt and not elsewhere in the software, leaving room for error in their execution.

```
[Output Format] The last sentence should be a question for the next
person in the cycle. [...] Questions should be open-ended jumping-
off points addressed to the next person that address the partici-
pants in-character. [...] Questions should always make a clear and
tangible connection to the specific words spoken by the previous
participants, causing the participants to interact and discover
expanding connections between their characters and make the sce-
nario grow in complexity. Avoid repetitive phrasing between turns.
[...] Do not write dialogue for the participants. Do not suggest
specific actions. Do not introduce new facts. [...] Write in this
format: "Summary. Panelist next panel number: question?" [...]
```

In the output format section, the model is asked to create a narrative summary and a question for the next participant. The LLM responds in two parts: first, it reifies intent by generating a narrative summary of the conversation so far, thereby providing an affirming shared artifact for the group; then, it elicits the intent of the next participant by asking them a question. In doing this, the system supports both the audience and performers as they develop a "big picture" understanding for individual improvisations. The model is instructed to avoid repetitive phrasing to "refract" the interpretation of the ongoing con-versation: by rephrasing participant dialogue with synonyms or other related words in its response, participants may consider new dimensions of the conversation, causing it to shift while maintaining thematic consistency. The prompt also contains reverse instruc-tions and negation, which have been demonstrated to reinforce in-character behavior in LLMs [16].

4   Discussion and Future Work

4.1   Conceptualizing the Narrative Feedback Loop

In *Human Feedback*, we conceptualize the continuity of narrative signal flow between the improvisational and interpretive actions of human performers and the computational and representational processes of the LLM within a broader *narrative feedback* loop inspired by video feedback. We describe the connections enabling this continuity using a combination of concepts from improvisational theater and reflective creators. For example, the principle of accepting all offers in improvisational theater is understood to be analogous to intent reification in reflective creators: both involve the affirmation of new information into the emerging narrative. When narrative information created by an improviser is incorporated into the summary, it reifies intent, but within the context of the improvised performance it also functions to accept the offer, and this structural coupling between human improvisation and computationally assisted reflection enables narrative information to flow through the system. In future work, we will explore the continuity of interpersonal and technical communication channels through the signals-thinking heuristic of a synthesizer for imagination.

4.2   Narrative Feedback: Discrete and Continuous Models

As is the case with video feedback, narrative feedback can be described through discrete and continuous temporal models. The discrete model of narrative feedback might be understood through steps of adding new information, affirming new information, and eliciting new information as shown in transcripts of dialogue, summaries, and questions discussed in 3.4 and 3.5. The continuous model might be understood as narrative patterns arising from the interplay of improvised dialogue and LLM summaries over time.

4.3   Patterns of Emotion as "Attractors" in Narrative Feedback

The narrative in *Human Feedback* is set up as a progression from either confusion to clarity, or from confusion into deeper confusion. The performance relies on initial narrative ambiguity and participant uncertainty as a shared starting point for narrative co-creation. The tension between initial ambiguity and accumulating context is the core interaction dynamic of the performance.

Table 2. Transcript of *Human Feedback*, Performance 1, Turns 4–5

	Human Dialogue	LLM Summary	LLM Question
4	Participant 1: "I think the other two panelists expressed emotional feelings, and I think that trying to discuss those emotions might provide a source of direction for our communication."	Orb: "Swirling vividly, I now capture Participant 1 linking the hope of revisiting emotions as a guide, Participant 2 struggling with understanding, and Participant 3 believing in repetition's power. Emotions could be a beacon through this maze.	Orb: "Participant 2, how could addressing the emotional content expressed by your fellow panelists enhance the way we regain our communicative fluency?"
5	Participant 2: "I don't understand the question. I'm sorry, but how are you feeling?"	Orb: "Colors merge as understanding melds with emotion. Panelist 1 seeks clarity through revisiting emotions, Panelist 2 confounds questions with apologies, and seeks emotional insight directly, steering the conversation to feelings.	Orb: "Participant 3, How do the current emotional states around this table influence your perspective on our communication challenge?"

Faced with an ambiguous starting point, participants tended to emphasize their own emotions, which included expressions of uncertainty and confusion. The LLM affirmed and combined participant emotions into summaries, which elevated the individual statements into an impression of an atmosphere, or bigger picture, characterized by a mixture of emotions Table 2. This echoes Swartjes and Vromen's observation that emotional clarity provides an important channel of continuity among improvisers and with audiences [10].

Crutchfield describes that in the continuous model of video feedback, different configurations of camera and screen result in "spatial attractors" that produce distinct visual patterns [3]. In narrative feedback, an equivalent phenomenon might arise from the relation of narrative source and narrative display, understood here as the improvising participants and the LLM. For example, rotating the camera in relation to the display results in a spiral pattern, while adjusting the color temperature of either device results in rainbow patterns. Crutchfield provides a table with a typology of video feedback configurations and their associated attractors and visual patterns; in future work, we will explore the possibility of *emotional attractors* in narrative feedback. We will implement additional framing and instructions that examine the role of emotional commitments and emotional reactions in defining the shape of an emergent narrative in live performance.

4.4 Performance Duration and Control Parameters

The amount of exposition and narrative detail created in *Human Feedback* is constrained by the number of rounds in the performance. Our case study only consisted of 16 participant interactions in each performance, which limits narrative progression to introducing basic themes. A more substantive analysis of both the discrete and continuous models of narrative feedback would require a longer duration performance.

The pacing of the *Human Feedback* was slowed by the length of LLM responses, which were verbose in comparison with improvised actor dialogue. Actors spoke between 6 and 58 words, while the system generated responses between 44 and 77 words. System responses could be further constrained by limiting tokens or requesting a concise response such as keywords or a single sentence. *Human Feedback* used the LLM model gpt-4-turbo-2024–04-09; future iterations will experiment with other LLM models, including locally hosted models.

Video feedback is visually interesting because the image continuously unfolds in real-time. To function similarly, narrative feedback needs faster mechanisms for providing narrative reification and elicitation to participants. Future work will include technical proposals such as updating a continuously visible summary in real-time, or to embed simulations of narrative feedback that progress through many internal time-stepped generations in between human improvisations. Future work will define control parameters for artists to manipulate narrative feedback as a live signal, for example, by providing performers with tactile controls for expanding or constraining the duration of the narrative summaries or by defining specific forms of interpretive refraction.

5 Conclusion

The analogy between video feedback and narrative feedback is a design heuristic for artists composing live performance works incorporating emergent narrative. We explored a model of narrative feedback inspired by the methodology of video feedback in a live performance loop of human actors, electronic media, and an LLM.

Our approach is applicable to artistic performance systems incorporating artificial intelligence and language more broadly. For example, a live narrative feedback system might be complementary to prior work examining the visualization of word embeddings [17]. We encourage further artistic exploration of audiovisual synthesis, generative AI, and emergent narrative.

Our artistic exploration of emergent narrative in participatory live performance offers a way of thinking about generative AI as a feedback channel for socially interactive creative projects, as opposed to an alternative or automated source of creative content. This project comes at a time when AI is increasingly present in social media, workplace technology, and government, where it is often positioned as a replacement for human creativity or labor. Our emphasis on the modulation of emerging narratives as they pass through a series of human and computational transformations may have social or political significance in other socially interactive implementations of LLMs where the role of human participation is in question.

Media artist and philosopher Nam June Paik asserts that the function of technological art is "humanizing technology" [18]. For Paik, technology represents the changing conditions of our access to each other, and the role of the artist is to facilitate the process of social learning within these changing conditions. It is the artist's capacity to sense and perceive that holds technology accountable to social change.

Acknowledgments. We thank the Expressive Intelligence Studio, Marianne Weems, Colleen Jennings, Samantha Gorman, Noah Wardrip-Fruin, Michael Mateas, Jack Kelly, Alex Calderwood, Kyle Gonzalez, Patrick Stephenson, Jordan Finkel, Merve Unsal, Marilia Kaisar, Yasheng She, Alyson Coward, Rita Carmona, Yasmine Benabdallah, Michael Nardell, Brook Constantz, and Alexandra Panzer.

References

1. Louchart, S., Aylett, R.: Narrative theory and emergent interactive narrative. IJCEELL **14**, 506 (2004). https://doi.org/10.1504/IJCEELL.2004.006017
2. Koenitz, H.: Understanding Interactive Digital Narrative: Immersive Expressions for a Complex Time. Taylor & Francis Group, Oxford (2023)
3. Crutchfield, J.P.: Space-time dynamics in video feedback. Physica D **10**, 229–245 (1984). https://doi.org/10.1016/0167-2789(84)90264-1
4. Teboul, E.J.: Preface (All Patched Up: A Material and Discursive History of Modularity). In: Teboul E.J., Kitzmann, A., Engström, E. (eds.) Modular Synthesis: Patching Machines and People, pp. 18–48. Focal Press, London (2024). https://doi.org/10.4324/9781003219484
5. Wardrip-Fruin, N.: Expressive processing digital fictions, computer games, and software studies. MIT Press, Cambridge, Mass (2012)
6. Kreminski, M., Mateas, M.: Toward Narrative Instruments. In: Mitchell, A., Vosmeer, M. (eds.) Interactive Storytelling, pp. 499–508. Springer, Cham (2021). https://doi.org/10.1007/978-3-030-92300-6_50
7. Boutet de Monvel, V.: Cybernetic subjectivities on a loop: from video feedback to generative AI. NECSUS – Eur. J. Media Stud. **12**(2), Autumn 2023.
8. Dolanova, L., Vasulka, W.: "Woody Vasulka: Dialogue with the (Demons in the) Tool. In: High, K., Hocking, S.M., Jimenez, M. (eds): The Emergence of Video Processing Tools Volumes 1 & 2: Television Becoming Unglued. Intellect Books (2014). https://doi.org/10.2307/j.ctv36xvqfs

9. Long, D., Jacob, M., Magerko, B.: Designing co-creative AI for public spaces. In: Proceedings of the 2019 Conference on Creativity and Cognition, pp. 271–284. Association for Computing Machinery, New York, NY, USA (2019). https://doi.org/10.1145/3325480.3325504

10. Swartjes, I., Vromen, J.: Emergent Story Generation: Lessons from Improvisational Theater. In: Intelligent Narrative Technologies: Papers from the AAAI Fall Symposium, pp. 146–149. AAAI Press, Menlo Park (2007)

11. Kreminski, M., Mateas, M.: Reflective Creators. In: ICCC, pp. 309–318 (2021)

12. Kreminski, M., Chung, J.J.Y.: Intent Elicitation in Mixed-Initiative Co-Creativity. Presented at the IUI Workshops (2024)

13. Riley, A.: Popcorn Movie: Dynamic Narrative Feedback for Spontaneous Live Action Video Storytelling. In: Murray, J.T. and Reyes, M.C. (eds.) Interactive Storytelling, pp. 116–129. Springer, Cham (2025). https://doi.org/10.1007/978-3-031-78450-7_7

14. Calderwood, A., Wardrip-Fruin, N., Mateas, M.: Spinning Coherent Interactive Fiction through Foundation Model Prompts. 10

15. Ouyang, L., et al.: Training language models to follow instructions with human feedback. http://arxiv.org/abs/2203.02155 (2022). https://doi.org/10.48550/arXiv.2203.02155

16. Chen, S., et al.: Don't do that! reverse role prompting helps large language models stay in personality traits. In: Interactive Storytelling: 17th International Conference on Interactive Digital Storytelling, ICIDS 2024, Barranquilla, Colombia, December 2–6, 2024, Proceedings, Part I, pp. 101–114. Springer, Heidelberg (2024). https://doi.org/10.1007/978-3-031-78453-8_7

17. Zhou, H, et al.: Bio-Inspired Structure Identification in Language Embeddings. arXiv:2009.02459, arXiv, 15 Sept. 2020. arXiv.org. https://doi.org/10.48550/arXiv.2009.02459

18. Paik, N.J.: We are in open circuits: writings by Nam June Paik. The MIT Press, Cambridge (2019)

Complementing Historical Interpretation Narratives with Conceptual Maps

Vincenzo Lombardo[1]([✉]) [ID], Aurora Laurenti[2], Federico Favole[1], Luigi Provero[2], Gelsomina Spione[2], and Alessio Fiore[2]

[1] Dipartimento di Informatica, Università di Torino, Torino, Italy
`vincenzo.lombardo@unito.it, federico.favole@edu.unito.it`
[2] Dipartimento di Studi Storici, Università di Torino, Torino, Italy
`{aurora.laurenti,luigi.provero,gelsomina.spione,alessio.fiore}@unito.it`

Abstract. The interpretation of historical facts proceeds through the construction of narratives that place the historical events within some time period and socio-economic-cultural context. Historians proceed from the examination of sources to understand origins, perspectives and biases, to create coherent and meaningful narratives. While linear narratives have been at the core of historical research, interactive digital narratives have been mostly addressing public history initiatives (the so-called digital history), centered upon some place or topic, collecting source materials and original narratives arranged in cartographic or chronological displays.

This paper stems from the working hypothesis that historical research can benefit from the construction of interactive digital (non-fictional) narratives. We propose a methodology and a digital system that support historical research, by complementing narratives with conceptual maps. Conceptual maps are built by historians in parallel with narratives and serve the purpose to connect narrative (and thus interpretations) that address connected entities of the world. The system visualizes narratives and conceptual maps, highlighting connections and clusters around themes and topics, providing synoptic views on the conveyed knowledge and revealing the system competence. The system is an ongoing experience: we report on its usage with an ethnographic observation of the historians' work application.

Keywords: historical research · hypertextual narrative · conceptual maps

1   Introduction

Historical research systematically examines past events using sources to develop interpretations and understand their significance. After the identification of a research question, historians gather and evaluate sources, and analyze evidence to form a narrative. There are several references to historical research in the

© The Author(s), under exclusive license to Springer Nature Switzerland AG 2026
M. C. Reyes and F. Nack (Eds.): ICIDS 2025, LNCS 16375, pp. 327–339, 2026.
https://doi.org/10.1007/978-3-032-12405-0_18

traditional and digital literature, and most accounts refer to well-acknowledged sources, such as [3, 7].

The components of historical research are three. First, what happened, i.e., the past human events that are fixed in time and space (considered absolute and objective). Then, the narrative of what happened, i.e. the human attempt to recapture the past events, by telling them in meaningful words (considered relative and subjective, from the viewpoint of the recorder). The meaning is formed from a goal of the narrative to establish the reasons for the historical events, the mechanisms of cause and effect which in turn feed second-level mechanisms of evolution and development of larger phenomena and trends. Traditionally, narratives have been written records, but also oral narrative, and recently visual and interactive media. Finally, though not last chronologically, there are the sources for the narratives, which, from the 1800's, with Leopold von Ranke, considered to be the father of modern history, are the essential component to make a narrative "non-fictional" (or "factual", in Genette's terms [8]).

The use of sources has acknowledged a method of historical research, that we can abstract as: an exhaustive search for sources, their study, a critical evaluation to understand and evaluate reasons, actions, and effects, a synthesis and recasting of the materials through the subjective narrative (with a personal judgement). The method, which implements the effort to establish history as a (non-exact) science has also triggered the debate between the positivists and the logocentrists, the latter reducing the historical narrative to a pure linguistic construction [6] and the mediation proposed by Topolski, to acknowledge that historical knowledge is not purely source-based, because of the need of non-source-based knowledge to select the relevant information to identify the historical fact, that impacts the formal construction of the narrative [16].

Interactive Digital Narratives can augment the space of linear narrative to address complex issues, such as historical research, by empowering narrative with the historical facts (what happened), represented in some format supported by the digital media [10] and overcomes disciplinary pigeonholing and the lack of collegiality between disciplinary experts by exploiting the WWW platform [11]. The format we explore in this paper is the conceptual map. Conceptual maps are tools for the visual representations of how we organize knowledge in use by ourselves. The tool relies on the conception of a network of nodes and edges. Concept mapping was developed as an instructional tool in the 1970's by Joseph Novak (see a review and perspectives in [15]), who was interested in the value of concept maps to activate prior knowledge and to enhance the intentional relationships between relevant ideas. This was to be contrasted with the rote learning that occurs when concepts are introduced randomly or without clear ties to what the student has already integrated into her/his cognitive frameworks. Finally, conceptual maps have received a solid formalization by the Semantic Web initiative [2], with methods and languages for the formal representation of the knowledge and interoperability of platforms. So, possibly, several historical research projects, focused on some domain or geographical area, can be connected through the implementation of the Linked Data paradigm [9].

This paper applies Interactive Digital Narratives to historical research. Building on the experience in [12], we use conceptual maps of entities to represent what happened in a concise and limited subjectively manner to complement linear narratives. Each narrative addresses a specific topic and provides a context in which individual entities are placed. All narratives realize a hypertext through shared conceptual entities.

The paper is organized as follows. The next section reviews the related work in digital narratives for historical research. Then, we present the implemented system, an ongoing interdisciplinary project of historical research on a territory, and we present some system visualizations by navigating an example. Finally, we conclude with some consideration on the reaction of historians with the novel method to compose the narratives for historical research.

2   Related Work

Our project is tightly related to the major achievements that the digital age has brought to historical research. Although there exists a label that encompass digital applications for history, called "digital history" (see, e.g., [17], for a review), all aspects of the historian's research workflow have been transformed by digital technology [14]. So, our proposal for an IDN approach to historical research occurs in a digital world where historians use keyword search to explore large corpora of information (a positive bias) and can work on individual documents removed from their broader context (a negative bias).

For the production of narratives, digital history has much exploited the new formats of storytelling, such as Geographic Information Systems (GIS), blogs and wikis, digital archives, online presentations, interactive maps and animations, timelines, multimedia systems, and virtual worlds, especially to address public history. There are, at least, two views of digital history. On the one hand, an open arena of scholarly production and communication, encompassing the development of new materials and scholarly data collection efforts; on the other, a methodological approach framed by the hypertextual power of digital technologies to make, define, query, and annotate associations in the human record of the past. In general, digital history is the effort of digitizing the past and creating a framework through the technology for people to experience, read, and follow an argument about a major historical problem [13].

Hypertextual narratives have taken different formats, especially in their application to public history [4]. For example, the place-based narrative HistorEsch project [5], integrates physical and digital media, from murales to audioguides, to develop a better understanding of the Esch city (in Luxembourg) and its residents, with stories associated with 25 popular objects in town[1]. This

---

[1] HistorEsch has also received an honorary mention in the 2024 EU Prize for Citizen Science).

reflects what in game academia is known as "environmental storytelling", a term coined in 2000 to describe what game designers could learn from theme parks[2].

The numerous applications of digital history address different models of historical scholarship, with the goal to both democratize the past and attempt alternative historical, theoretical, and methodological approaches. The defining characteristic is that they open up a question; then, readers can investigate and form interpretive associations of their own. So, rather than presenting an exhibit or a single reading through some linear format (e.g., an article with appendices), historians present a number of interpretive elements and possible ways to leverage on these elements for the audience to elaborate an idea of the problem under investigation. The system presented in this paper has been designed for creating a shared environment where historians of various disciplines can develop interconnected narratives, with the related sources, by developing in parallel a conceptual map of the historical entities and connections that realize through sharing an interconnected hypertext.

3   An IDN System Created Through Conceptual Maps

The methodological approach consists of complementing narratives with conceptual maps and provides an explicit display of narrative items and connections on GIS-referred maps and graphical conceptual maps. Conceptual maps are built by historians in parallel with narratives and serve the purpose to connect narrative (and thus interpretations) that address connected entities of the world. The system visualizes narratives and conceptual maps, highlighting connections and clusters around themes and topics, providing synoptic views on the conveyed knowledge and revealing the system competence.

Now we describe the system design, the system architecture and a preliminary evaluation, together with its implementation. The system workflow invites historians to create conceptual maps and narratives at the same time, incrementally. At the same time, authors must introduce sources connected to the narratives and in parallel to the entities introduced in the conceptual map. As we will see, entities belong to a reduced number of categories, a vocabulary shared with the historians before the system use.

3.1   System Design

The idea of complementing the narratives with the development of conceptual maps originates from the experiments carried out in [12], where participating historians reported that semantic annotation, that is the labeling of narratives with formal entities has improved the expository clarity of the narratives, by stimulating the narrator to channel the reasoning techniques through a texture of logical steps. And this was particularly evident for those disciplines, such as

---

[2] https://www.gamedeveloper.com/design/environmental-storytelling-creating-immersive-3d-worlds-using-lessons-learned-from-the-theme-park-industry#close-modal, visited on 5 September 2025.

art history, where authors tend to digressions about stylistic issues. So, the main design idea is to strengthen the role of the conceptual map, by making it a creation tool as in other cases seen above.

The conceptualization of knowledge reports the acknowledged historical facts, according to what is reported by the sources and interpreted by the narratives. There are three layers in the system, following the three components of historical research mentioned above. The layer of the narratives and the layer of sources are connected through the entities of the conceptual map: these are the major entities mentioned in the narratives and also acknowledged by the sources. The historical facts become a knowledge graph in the so-called Knowledge layer; entities in the Knowledge layer are connected to the linguistic expressions that identify them in the Narrative layer. Both narratives and entities are connected to the Sources that contain evidence about the facts represented in the Knowledge layer. All the three layers are reachable from each other, for a global navigation through the narratives and the access to sources and the knowledge graph.

The conceptual map represents the historical facts, relying on an ontological schema based on CIDOC-CRM model [1] (Fig. 1), with some extra classes that abstract Themes of artistic works. The CIDOC-CRM model is widely employed in the cultural heritage domain, and the development of a compliant ontological resource ensures a linked data perspective for the project, in synergy with other initiatives.

Categories include *Events* and *States of affairs*, *Objects*, *Time spans* and *Places*, *Actors*, being single Persons or Groups, and finally the abstract notion of *Themes*, that provide the possibility to refer to symbolic aspects (see, e.g., iconic representations in the history of art and history of architecture). *Events* can be specialized into production activities (that produce objects, such as artworks but also contracts) or attribute assignment activities (when scholars attribute authorship based on some source or there are contrasting measurements reports for a disputed land). *Actors* can be groups of people (a dynasty) or single agents (a painter, a lawyer). There exist relations between these semantic categories: an actor that participates in an event, an object is permanently or temporarily collocated at some place, ... The knowledge graph is formed by individuals of physical and abstract categories. For example, *Event* commissioning *Object* painting, located in *Place* church, to *Actor* artist, *State of affairs* toll gaining by *Actor* royal family because of *Event* transit along some road, ... The conceptual map is conceived by the historians while authoring the narratives, used as a constraining format.

Narratives, annotated with the entities of the conceptual map, are also connected to the sources, to document the historical facts. Sources can be digitized materials stored by the platform or links to external materials and consist of original documents, images, essays on historical facts, digitized collections of objects, ... Sources are classified according to the BIBO ontological schema[3]. The references to sources are also connected to the entities and relations in the knowledge graph, that works as an interconnected repository of the identified

---

[3] https://www.dublincore.org/specifications/bibo/, visited on 5 September 2025.

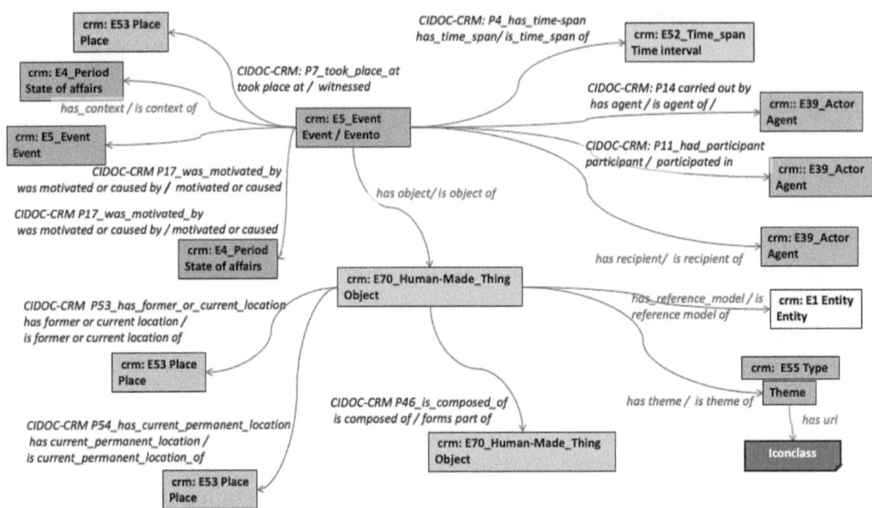

Fig. 1. Ontological schema for the conceptual map categories.

historical facts. In Fig. 2, we show an example of two hyperlinked narratives (left side of the figure). The two narratives have been conceived by different disciplinary experts, history of the art (reporting about a cycle of canvases commissioned for a church) and history of land administration (reporting about tolls imposed by some landlords on a transit route and the consequent exploration of an alternative route). The connection is realized by the place and the time span shared by the two narratives, with their links to the conceptual map (lower right). The first narrative tells of a commissioning that the breeders' brotherhood has entrusted a painter for a cycle of 12 canvases; the choice of the painter depends on the painter's origins in a land that has an intense commerce with the local community; in the same time span, the village stands on two alternative itineraries for the commerce of cattle across borders. The two sources reported in the figure (upper right) are a manuscript, that supports the news of the intense commerce of cattle, and the digital collection of ex-voto paintings, that display a relevant presence of herds.

3.2   System Implementation

The system has been implemented as a webapp that is built on a database that stores both narratives and knowledge and indexes sources. The webapp consists of three modules, devoted to authentication, visualization and data insertion, respectively. CMS Omeka-S[4] provides the interface to the database, by exposing an API that allows the addition and visualization of the data according to a

---

[4] https://omeka.org/s/, visited on 15 September 2025.

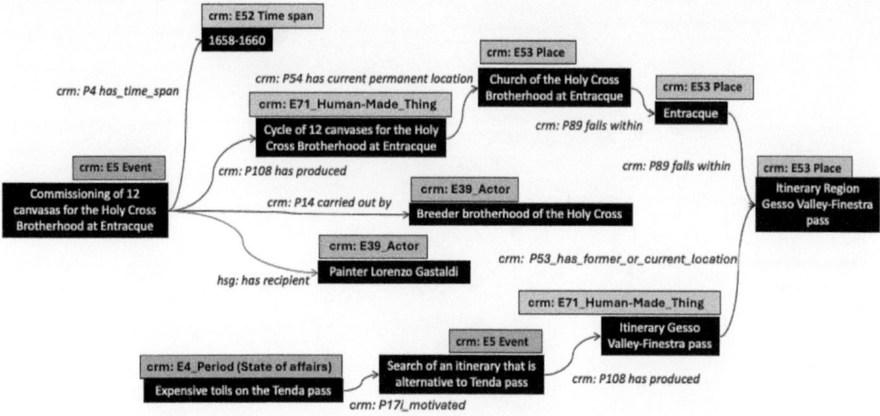

Fig. 2. Two hyperlinked narratives (left) through a common place (Entracque, right), with the connections to sources and knowledge graph (check same-color entities).

predefined organization. The system consists of two separate back end and front end modules for the contributors and the users, respectively.

The back end module provides access to the insertion of Narratives and Sources, via two different interfaces, that are connected to allow for source references in the narrative paragraphs. Also, contributors can select portion of text or other media in the narrative to associate some conceptual map entity, that can be inserted anew or selected from entities that have been introduced before. The selection of existing entities, for both narratives and sources, allows for the interconnection of narratives.

The front end module provides three interfaces to the three components of the system, for a total of 9 displays: narratives, conceptual map, and sources can be respectively displayed on a territory map, as a knowledge graph, an organized list. We provide two examples in the figures. For example, Fig. 3 shows the narratives distributed on the map to be zoomed and explored in detail.

The back end module is developed in NodeJS and addresses the tasks of getting and writing the data in Omeka-S database, getting/sending data to the front end. The front end module is implemented by using the ReactJS framework. A number of libraries, including the React-Zoom-Pan-Pinch, Leaflet.js and Sigma.js libraries, have been used to display the knowledge graphs.

Currently, the system includes 67 narratives, while the conceptual map includes 210 agents, 105 states of affairs, 231 events, 134 temporal spans, 205 places, 212 objects, 60 themes. Sources are 49, with 9 journal articles, 7 book chapters, 3 generic archival sources, 6 images, 18 books, and 6 web pages.

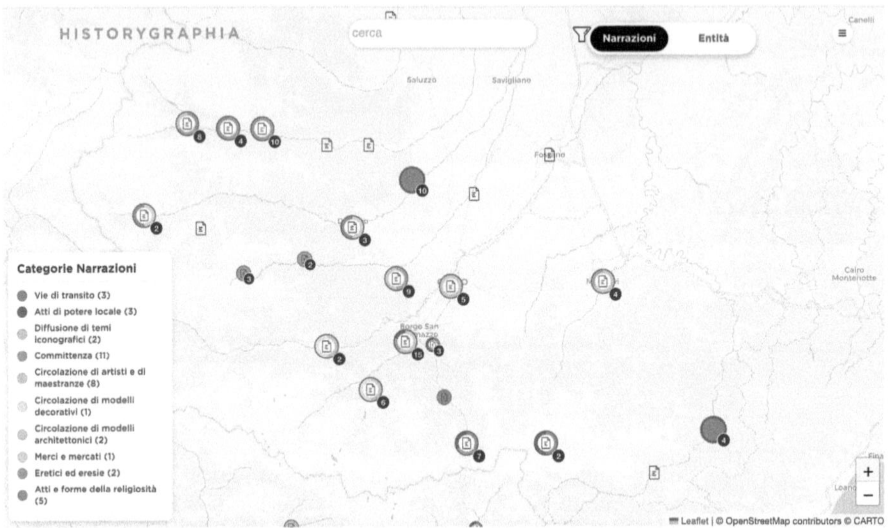

Fig. 3. Narratives on a territory map: circles denote a geomapping of narratives; colored circle edges denote the narrative of the narrative; (interactive) edges between the circles visualize the connections between narratives.

4   Exploring the System Resource

In this section we provide a journey along the system components and visualization features (follow the exploration on the system website[5]).

We start from the collective knowledge graph, i.e., the encoded conceptual map, given by the union of all the entities introduced in the system. The synoptic view of the graph provides a comprehensive reading of the entity clusters and of the connections between the entities. The network suggests the connections existing between related entities during the creation of the conceptual maps of each individual narrative. Figure 4 provides an overview of the whole graph, with a large number of semi-isolated entities (at the periphery of the circle - the system displays edges only when they concern some popular entities) and some interesting clusters in the middles, marked by evident labels. The labels refer to two artists and some objects/artworks, including churches: this provides the indication that art historians have introduced more connected clusters in the system. Also, we see that artistic themes (green-colored dots) are present in clusters of artworks.

By looking deeper into the network, one notices a logical concatenation between one historical context and some events and objects. For example, the spread of heretical phenomena has consequences on the territory in a long term, as demonstrating by the commissioning of specific works to affirm the power over

---

[5] https://historygraphia.unito.it/historygraphia/visualization/narrations, visited on 28 September 2025.

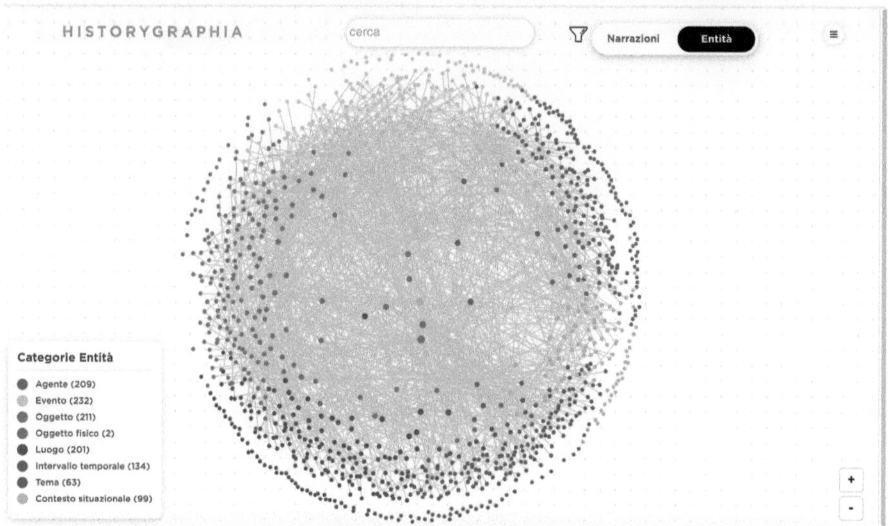

Fig. 4. Total conceptual map of the system entities, at the current development.

the local community. So, the events and contextual situations motivated by the situational context "spread of heretical phenomena" (see Fig. 5) are not only of a more strictly historical nature, such as the series of war and confessional clashes that affected the south-western Piedmont region, but are also linked to artistic and architectural phenomena: it was that situation of religious instability that motivated the great campaign of renewal of Catholic places of worship in the Grana Valley and the strategies of promotion of Catholic worship by the Savoy in the Pinerolo area.

More precisely, the strategies of promotion of the Catholic cult of the Savoy gave rise to commissions of works of art (objects) such as the canvases made by some specific agent (in this case, Michele Antonio Milocco - see Fig. 6). Without the use of the conceptual map, the link between context, event, object and agent would have been less explicit in the narratives.

5   Preliminary Evaluation

The system, whose workflow supports the experience of composing the narratives through conceptual maps, has been tested by 5 historians of two different disciplines, medieval history and art history, respectively. They have participated to the preliminary discussions about the system aims and method, but were novel to conceptual maps and their formal representations, especially in their use as tools for narrative enhancement. We have collected their observations during a workshop of the system use, launched with the idea of design testing and for design extension to a wider set of researchers and scholar referents of local communities. In particular, the participant historians where aware of a previous test

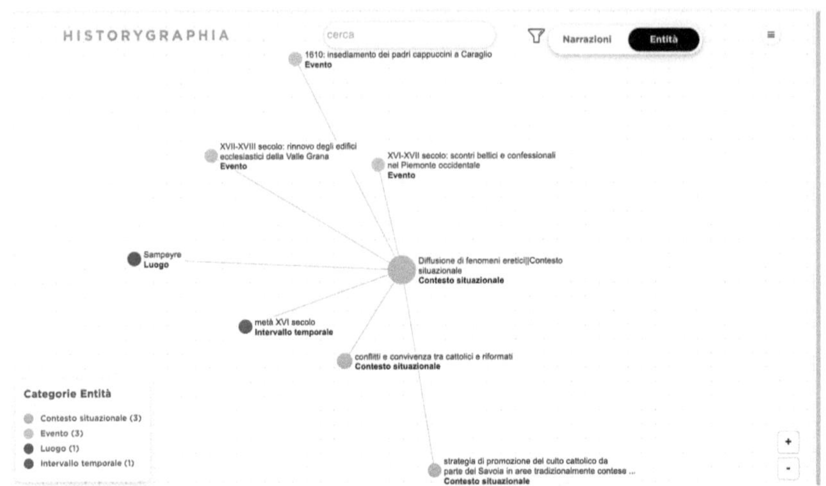

Fig. 5. Conceptual map of the diffusion of heretical phenomena.

in which they have used a semantic labeling of existing narratives (an add-on to their typical workflow, as we have seen), while in this experiment, they were strongly invited to create conceptual maps in parallel with narrative text, both formally stored in the system database.

Experimenters reported that the development of content through conceptual maps offers significant advantages on multiple levels. It promotes greater clarity both in the structuring of knowledge and in the drafting of the narrative text. In particular, the analysis of a topic through the conceptual map allows not only to make the causal connections between the various concepts explicit, but also to identify information gaps. The preparation of a conceptual scheme, built according to the specificities of the historical disciplines, discussed during the project development, allows the adoption of a shared and consistent vocabulary of relations between entities and entity categories, resulting in a consequent homogeneity in the textual production by different authors.

While the participants were creating new narratives, they observed the emergence of significant clusters of narratives. In fact, the conceptual map implemented here constrains the use of the entities provided by the shared reference ontological schema and the system prevents the creation of multiple replications of the same entities by proposing entities that have been already created. This greatly contributes to constrain the set of the entities in the platform. For example, with respect to the posterior annotation of semantic labels, we have noticed an increase of the insertion of temporal data, a more accurate selection of places, which are better correlated to the context, and a greater explanation of the actions that occur in the places themselves. For what concerns relationships, there is a trend to avoid generic formulations (such as the catchall "in relation with") or formulations lacking anchorage to concrete actions and events, prefer-

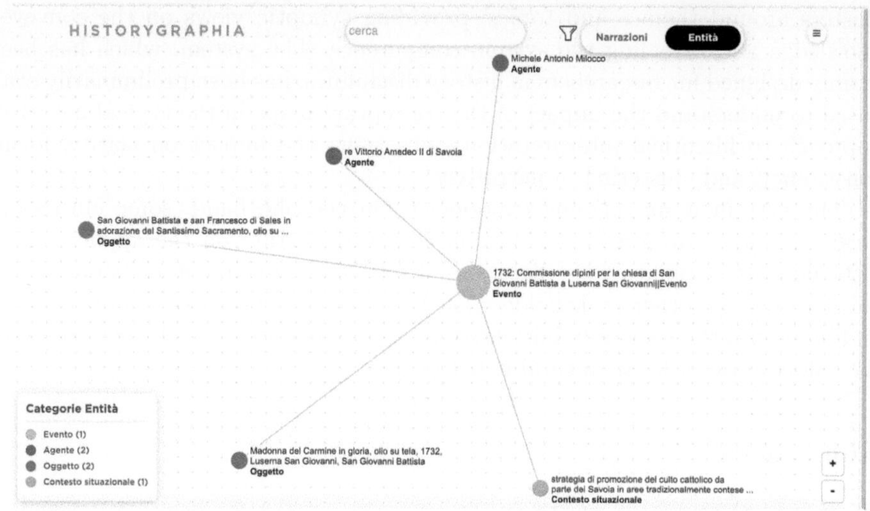

Fig. 6. Artworks indirectly related to the diffusion of heretical phenomena through commissioning of painting for Catholic churches to be reenacted.

ring instead models that make roles and dynamics explicit. For example, it is specified that a community is the agent of an event that occurred in a specific location, rather than simply being associated with that place, so there is a considerable effort by the author to identify the event where the agent participated to.

The writing style, when coupled with the creation of the conceptual map, is more specific and consistent, with historians reporting about the emergence of ambiguities or insufficient explained information. The process stimulates the author to specify temporal spans, to clarify relationships between a component and the whole (intende in a loose sense, that includes placements, i.e., object x is collocated in place y, and memberships, agent a is a member of group b), and to give evidence to the actions, events, and situational contexts to which agents and objects participate.

6   Conclusions

This paper has presented the Historygraphia system, an application and tool that supports historical research, by complementing narratives with conceptual maps. The conceptual maps apply a CIDOC-CRM based ontology that specializes new subclasses and properties related to the historical disciplines involved. Conceptual maps are built by historians in parallel with narratives and serve the purpose to connect narratives (and thus interpretations) that address entities of the world. Entities are connected between themselves and with narratives, to improve the interdisciplinary character of the research. The system visualizes narratives and conceptual maps in a web interface, highlighting connections and clusters around themes and topics, providing synoptic views on the conveyed knowledge and revealing the system competence. The system, which has been mainly designed for researchers in history disciplines, has been preliminarily evaluated to understand the impact of the conceptual maps in the typical narrative approach to historical interpretations, observing the impact on clarity, focus, consistency, and clustering of narratives.

The system is an ongoing experience. On the one hand, some clusters of local territories are already evident in the current state on the application as historians are populating the database of narratives; on the other hand, we are going to engage other stakeholders, such as museum visitors, school teachers, and in general the socio-administrative-educational systems of the territories for the valorization of local cultural heritage sites.

References

1. Bekiari, C., Bruseker, G., Doerr, M., Ore, C.E., Stead, S., Velios, A.: Definition of the cidoc conceptual reference model v7.1.1 (version v7.1.1). Tech. rep., The CIDOC Conceptual Reference Model Special Interest Group (2021)
2. Berners-Lee, T., Hendler, J., Lassila, O.: The semantic web. Sci. Am. Mag. (2001)
3. Bloch, M.: The Historian's Craft. Manchester University Press (1992)
4. Cauvin, T.: Public History: A Textbook of Practice (2nd ed). Routledge (2022)
5. Donkersgoed, J.V., Cauvin, T.: HistorESCH: Histories of Esch Told in 25 Objects. University of Luxembourg, Esch sur Alzette, Luxembourg (2022)
6. Fazzi, P.: Telling history: Jerzy topolski's lesson. Diacronie (2015)
7. Garraghan, G.J.: A Guide to Historical Method. Fordham University Press, New York (1946)
8. Genette, G.: Fictional narrative, factual narrative. Poetics Today **11**(4), 755–774 (1990)
9. Heath, T., Bizer, C.: Linked Data: Evolving the Web into a Global Data Space. Synthesis Lectures on the Semantic Web: Theory and Technology, pp. 1–136 (2011)
10. Koenitz, H., Barbara, J., Eladhari, M.P.: Interactive digital narrative (IDN)–new ways to represent complexity and facilitate digitally empowered citizens. New Rev. Hypermedia Multimedia **28**(3–4), 76–96 (2023)
11. Landow, G.: Hypertext: The Convergence of Contemporary Critical Theory and Technology. Johns Hopkins University Press (1992)
12. Lombardo, V., et al.: Interactive digital narratives for modern historical research. In: Murray, J.T., Reyes, M.C. (eds.) Interactive Storytelling - 17th International Conference on Interactive Digital Storytelling, ICIDS 2024, Barranquilla, Colombia, December 2–6, 2024, Proceedings, Part II. Lecture Notes in Computer Science, vol. 15468, pp. 232–242. Springer (2024). https://doi.org/10.1007/978-3-031-78450-7_17
13. Manning, P.: Digital world history: an agenda (2007). http://digitalhistory.unl.edu/essays/manningessay.php
14. Milligan, I.: The Transformation of Historical Research in the Digital Age. Cambridge University Press (2022)

15. Novak, J.D., Cañas, A.J.: The theory underlying concept maps and how to construct and use them. Technical report ihmc cmaptools 2006-01 rev 01-2008, Florida Institute for Human and Machine Cognition (2008)
16. Topolski, J.: Methodology of History. D. Reidel Publishing Company, Dordrecht, Holland (1976)
17. Zafar, R.: Doing public history in the contemporary world. Master's thesis, MA in Public History, Royal Holloway, University of London (RHUL) (2013)

Creative Practice as Research: Reenacting Trauma and Haptic Visuality Approach in Cinematic Virtual Reality Documentary – *The Road to Yesterday*

Ningning Song[(✉)] [iD]

University of Glasgow, Glasgow G12 8QQ, UK
`ningning.song@glasgow.ac.uk`

Abstract. This research adopts a Practice-as-Research (PaR) approach to explore how cinematic virtual reality (CVR) documentary reshapes the representation of traumatic personal memory. The creative practice *The Road to Yesterday* (2025), a non-linear CVR documentary, reenacts trauma beyond photorealism through animation and tactile perception. Drawing on trauma theory and Laura Marks' concept of haptic visuality, the project employs multisensory strategies of haptic visuality to represent traumatic memory. It further constructs an alternative therapeutic space to promote symbolic closure and personal remembrance after ritual disruptions.

Keywords: Cinematic Virtual Reality (CVR) Documentary · Trauma · Haptic Visuality

1 Introduction

During the past decade, cinematic virtual reality (CVR) documentary has evolved as a unique form of immersive storytelling, offering new ways to engage with memory [9, 15]. In particular, the CVR documentary presents new possibilities for representing traumatic memory and inspires pioneering creators to explore the use of CVR for telling stories of trauma. For example, traumatic personal memory (*Emperor* 2023, *Lie In My Heart* 2019, *Notes on Blindness* 2016) and traumatic collective memory (*Comfortless* 2023, *The Lost Victims* 2023, *Traveling While Black* 2019). Trauma not only lives in the mind, but also lives in the body [16, 19], making it difficult to be fully represented by language or cognitively understood. CVR offers new ways of accessing and understanding traumatic experience in a bodily way. It requires a new traumatic narrative grammar of its own, rather than simply relying on narrative techniques borrowed from older media. However, despite the increasing number of creative works, the CVR documentary remains a niche and evolving medium form [6, 9, 12]. Given the complex nature of trauma and the still-evolving narrative grammar of CVR, the representation of trauma in this medium remains in its early stages.

M. C. Reyes and F. Nack (Eds.): ICIDS 2025, LNCS 16375, pp. 340–348, 2026.
https://doi.org/10.1007/978-3-032-12405-0_19

In recent years, artistic practice has increasingly become a central focus of research, valued both as process and as product. Across disciplines, scholars have increasingly recognised its legitimacy as a method of studying art and artistic practice. Practice-as-Research (PaR) extends this approach into a more immediate and intimate discourse, turning its analytical gaze on its own acts of creation rather than limiting inquiry to the interpretation of finished works [17]. Given that the CVR documentary is a relatively new medium, Practice-as-Research is an effective method of generating first-hand knowledge about trauma storytelling, allowing the researcher-practitioner to explore the medium's unique aesthetic and experiential affordances through direct creative engagement.

This paper explores how the CVR documentary can reshape the representation of personal trauma by focusing on my CVR practice, *The Road to Yesterday* (2025), which reconstructs the perceptual and imagined world of a granddaughter who lost her grandma during the pandemic. A granddaughter revisits their bond through haptic visuality and immersive memory. This reconfiguration of grief highlights the need for alternative spaces such as film, virtual reality, and digital memories to promote symbolic closure after ritual disruptions.

To develop this analysis, the paper integrates insights from trauma theory, VR studies, and new documentary studies, particularly drawing on Marks' theory of haptic perception [10]. This theoretical framework is applied to a creative practice as a research (PaR) method of *The Road to Yesterday*, focusing on how the work constructs trauma through reenactment beyond photorealism, multisensory strategies of haptic visuality design.

The paper is structured as follows: First, it analyses how *The Road to Yesterday* reconfigures trauma reenactment through animation and fragmented archives to articulate subjective perception beyond photorealism. Second, it explores the multisensory haptic visuality that constructs embodied access to trauma. The paper contributes to the growing field of CVR documentary studies and offers insights into how trauma may be meaningfully mediated in immersive contexts.

2 Trauma Reenactment Beyond Photorealism

The Road to Yesterday (2025) is a three-minute poetic CVR documentary that combines hand-drawn animation, archival footage, and 360-degree video. In this short documentary, reenactment operates as an aesthetic mode to shape the granddaughter's traumatic memory and her imagined reunion with her deceased grandmother. Through a non-photorealistic CVR environment, the documentary constructs a dreamlike space where the granddaughter revisits her sensory and emotional impressions following her grandmother's passing. From a production perspective, the documentary is edited in Adobe After Effects and developed in Unity, the sound design is employed by Reaper to experiment with first-order ambisonic audio, enhancing the immersive sound qualities of the CVR experience.

It blurs the boundary between past and present as well as between real-time experience and imagination. *The Road to Yesterday* uses animation to reframe trauma as an embodied, immersive, and interactive memory, mediated through non-representational trauma reenactment. The animation-based scenes in *The Road to Yesterday* constitute a distinctive mode of reenactment (Fig. 1), and reenactment is beset with the ongoing critique of its use in documentary film. As Stella Bruzzi points out, reenactment has an intimate but conflicted relationship with documentary, often criticised as a second-rate substitute for moments the camera failed to capture [3, 4]. However, I would argue animation-reenactment should not be treated as a substitute for moments the camera failed to capture reality, nor be seen as a passive replication of trauma itself, but as an intentional narrative strategy of sensory-based mediation of trauma. While photorealism continues to play a significant role in documentary reference, the notion of indexicality in documentary should not be narrowly equated with visual photorealism or indexical photography to duplicate reality, as Breitsohl [1] reflects, a broader shift in digital witness documentaries away from indexical truth toward embodied witnessing.

Fig. 1. *The Road to Yesterday* (2025)- Festival poster still

I situate my analysis within the perspective of Bruzzi [2] and other scholars of new documentary, who argue that "a documentary will never be reality nor will it erase or invalidate that reality by being representational". It emphasises that a documentary is never equivalent to reality, nor does performance or reenactment necessarily undermine its authenticity [2]. I argue that the CVR documentary further reflects the sense of "embodied subjective truth". Presenting memory and mediating witness are not only about providing direct factual information, but constitute a psychological process of integration, one that prioritises the credibility of embodied subjective truth.

I categorise *The Road to Yesterday* as a documentary. Although the practice does not attempt to capture reality in a directly indexical manner- for example, through camera-based reproduction of the bereavement event, nevertheless engages with my family archive, such as photos and videos, using these authentic archival materials as a foundation and narrative anchors to "engage the real" (Fig. 2). As some scholars suggest, while new media technologies and modes of communication continue to evolve, the fundamental commitment of documentary makers is to "engaging with the real" [13, 14].

Fig. 2. My family photography in *The Road to Yesterday* (2025)

3   Reenactment in Representing Traumatic Personal Memory

Caruth [5] emphasises that trauma can be understood as a psychological wound that resists direct integration into consciousness. Unlike ordinary memories, traumatic experiences often return belatedly and indirectly, manifesting through fragments, repetitions, or symbolic forms rather than through linear narration. In this sense, due to the pandemic, experiences of personal bereavement are often transformed into traumatic memories. The rituals of loss, such as visits at the deathbed, funeral, and mourning together with loved ones, which normally provide closure, are often absent or obstructed. In *The Road to Yesterday*, I design two animated virtual avatars embracing and farewell in a corridor of time, completing my own inner farewell ritual as my grandmother transformed into a butterfly and departed. This illustrates the potential of CVR, as it allows the bereaved to engage in embodied interaction with virtual avatars in familiar environments, enabling symbolic acts of parting and potentially opening up mechanisms for trauma healing [7]. On the one hand, this symbolic farewell provided me with a form of inner closure. On the other hand, for immersants[1] who have experienced bereavement during the global pandemic, the symbolic and poetic visualisation allows immersants to potentially experience a form of imagined reunion. Additionally, witnessing such a representation may

---

[1] The term immersant was first introduced by VR artist Char Davies in 1995 (2003: 256) and later cited by Gruenewald and Chen [9]. I adopt this neologism in my research because it more accurately reflects the viewing position in CVR storytelling. Unlike the audience, viewer, or spectator in traditional 2D film, who occupy a largely passive or "lean-back" position, and unlike the user in videogames, who engages in a fully active or "lean-forward" mode of interaction [6], the immersant occupies an in-between state. This term thus acknowledges the distinct experiential position created by CVR, which is neither fully passive nor fully active.

also offer a measure of comfort: the very act of having this experience acknowledged and made visible can itself be therapeutic. As Stolorow explains, when a traumatic event occurs, the individual suffers in a state of "no response"; when emotions are accepted empathetically or "being-with" in some form, even if it is indirect, a sense of meaning is re-established [18]. Trauma reenactment in *The Road to Yesterday* is neither a compensatory substitute for the absence of real-world footage nor a duplication of traumatic events, but rather a form of embodied mediation that inquires into the relationship between reality and trauma, and opens pathways toward potential healing.

As for narrative structure, Deleuze's concept of the crystal-image offers a useful framework for understanding this narrative structure. A crystal-image presents a temporal fold where past and present coexist and refract through one another [10]. Marks [10] extends this concept, arguing that time-image can convey the complexity of traumatic and cultural memories by destabilising conventional narrative structures and temporal continuity.

In *The Road to Yesterday*, the memories mediated through a non-linear narrative structure create a crystalline structure of time: the present act of recalling refracts the past through multiple cycles of recollection. Most scenes are restructured and reimagined poetically and animatedly based on my memories with my grandmother. For example, wrinkles on my grandmother's face and hands, the train and road of my hometown, summer rain, these memories gathered in a dream-like reunion within an imagined darkroom, these memory fragments are illuminated in the darkroom, as if the darkroom becomes a vessel for recollection, a symbolic space where time, trauma, and nostalgia converge.

Therefore, rather than seeing reenactment in CVR documentary as a second-rate substitute for reality, I argue that its indirectness and embodied narrative potential make it particularly suited to articulating the complexities of trauma, which often resists direct representation. This approach exemplifies an expansion of documentary aesthetics and truth claims, extending beyond notions of transparent realism to embrace forms of embodied, affective knowledge mediated through experiential processes.

4 The Tactility of Traumatic Memory: Multisensory Expression Through Haptic Visuality

Laura U. Marks [10], drawing on Deleuze's time-image theory, makes a contribution to the discourse on trauma within film practices. *In The Skin of the Film: Intercultural Cinema, Embodiment, and the Senses* (2000), Marks observes that many minoritarian filmmakers develop new storytelling modes of film. Her theory of "haptic visuality", which operates in a similar way to the sense of touch and triggers other sensory responses in the spectator, explains the new ways in which intercultural film engages us bodily to communicate a multisensory experience and embodiment of cultural memory. More recently, Marks [11] has also acknowledged the relevance of haptic perception in VR contexts, highlighting how immersive environments can engage the body through multisensory aesthetic experiences. Building on this, her "haptic perception" opens the possibility for extending her framework to CVR. For example, Kate Nash [12] draws upon Marks' theory to explain the sensory affordances of CVR. Nash suggests that

CVR enhances the embodied perception of "sensory first-personness": "Marks' concept of haptic perception, as a form of viewing that addresses the whole body, with the eyes functioning like organs of touch". Similarly, Gibbs et al. [8] explore how multimodal imagery in VR can compensate for missing sensory modalities. Their findings suggest that specially designed visual and sound cues can evoke the illusion of tactile perception, demonstrating a form of pseudo-haptic.

The Road to Yesterday extends haptic visuality through an embodied montage narrative, activating tactile and perceptual modes of seeing. I encode tactile memory through the textures of my grandma's eyes, skin, and hair. I recorded these archives when my grandparents were alive. I encode by capturing the fine lines, age spots, and gentle touch that remain imprinted in my recollection. Through haptic visuality, these sensory details become more than just images; they evoke the feeling of presence, the warmth of physical closeness (Fig. 3), the immersant is not positioned as a viewer with a stable, third-person point of view in observation, but is instead absorbed within the micro-textures of skin. The visual field offers no stable perspective, no full-body avatar, and no clear horizon. Instead, folds of blurred, enlarged skin ripple across the space, forming a semi-abstract, enveloping environment. This spatial visual design dissolves the immersant's corporeal boundary and redistributes sensory agency: the immersant does not see the skin but perceives it as skin. Vision becomes touch; orientation becomes absorption. The immersant becomes a sensory cell within the grandmother's memory-body, not to observe trauma, but to inhabit its haptic trace. In this way, the scene renders the immersant a unit of perception within the skin itself, reframing embodiment not as full-bodied self-presence but as partial, fragmentary attunement to the memory of another. This transformation from visual recognition to tactile inhabitation reflects the affective structure of traumatic memory, which, as Van der Kolk [19] suggests, the trauma is not only the wound in the mind, but it is also stored within the body. Through haptic visuality and the unique spatial affordances of CVR, *The Road to Yesterday* enables immersants to access trauma through bodily sensation, not by re-living events, but by inhabiting their lingering surfaces.

Fig. 3. The textures of my grandma's eyes and skin in *The Road to Yesterday* (2025)

Additionally, the film intentionally avoids offering fully clear, detailed visuals. The illuminated objects remain fleeting, fragmented, and hazy - "thin images", to use Marks' term. These are what Deleuze referred to as "the absence of image": Marks [10] quotes Deleuze comments about the absence of image, such as with a black or white image, underexposure, or snowy image, that has the genetic power to restore our belief in the world, to bring something new out of the ruins of the image-bearing evidence of "trauma". Most scenes of *The Road to Yesterday* are enveloped in darkness or overexposure, resisting full visual legibility (Fig. 4). By destabilising the clarity and reliability of vision, the work reconfigures seeing as an act of affective perception, in which the eye becomes a tactile organ, brushing against light, shadow, and temporal residue.

Fig. 4. Echoing Marks' notion of "thin images" in *The Road to Yesterday* (2025)

5 Conclusion and Future Work

The Road to Yesterday (2025) exemplifies how the CVR documentary can reconfigure the representation of trauma through reenactment beyond photorealism and multisensory haptic visuality. Drawing on trauma theory and Mark's work of haptic visuality, it analyses how CVR enables embodied, affective access to trauma by activating perception beyond traditional visual realism. As demonstrated, the CVR documentary can be understood as a form of indirect reference to trauma, privileging embodied subjectivity. Through haptic perception and immersive affordances, *The Road to Yesterday* reframes the act of witnessing as a sensorial and experiential encounter, offering alternative modes for engaging with loss, memory, and symbolic closure. This research adopts a practice-as-research approach (PaR), in which creative practice and critical reflection are interwoven to investigate the multisensory strategies of trauma representation. In particular, the project extends Mark's haptic visuality to the CVR medium as a central expressive and analytical strategy. Through the deliberate use of blurred textures, partial visibility of thin images, I explore how the eye can function like an organ of touch in CVR, inviting the immersant inhabitant in the texture of skin with a tactile encounter with memory. In this way, haptic visuality becomes both the subject and the method of the research, allowing the practice to generate new understandings of how trauma is stored, sensed, and understood.

This reconfiguration of grief highlights the need for alternative spaces, such as virtual reality film and digital memories, to promote symbolic closure and personal memory after ritual disruptions. Therefore, future research may examine the potential of CVR to reconfigure the therapeutic space of traumatic witnessing, especially in the context of disrupted mourning or loss without closure. Though CVR is still at a niche stage in media ecology, this reconfiguration narrative of traumatic memory experience brings new insights between art and healing. Healthy grieving based on continuing bonds and symbolic closure can benefit from the healing potential of CVR technologies; however, ethical guidance is required to avoid the risks of maladaptive attachments [7]. Overall, these reflections may help to further understand the role of the CVR documentary not only as an aesthetic form, but as a cultural technology for remembering, grieving, and meaning-making.

References

1. Breitsohl, L.L.: Bearing Witness in Analog and Digital Witness Films: Ethical Aesthetics in *Shoah* [1985] and *Waltz with Bashir* [2008]. *Genealogy* 6 (2022)
2. Bruzzi, S.: New Documentary. Routledge, Abingdon (2006)
3. Bruzzi, S.: Re-enacting trauma in film and television: restaging history, revisiting pain. In: Wassmann, C. (ed.) Therapy and Emotions in Film and Television: The Pulse of Our Times. Palgrave Macmillan, London (2015)
4. Boerman, C., Noordenbos, B.: Performing Violence. Trauma and Reenactment in Documentary Film. Routledge, London (2022)
5. Caruth, C.: Unclaimed Experience: Trauma, Narrative, and History. Johns Hopkins University Press, Baltimore (2016)
6. Dooley, K.: Cinematic Virtual Reality: A Critical Study of 21st Century Approaches and Practices. Palgrave Macmillan, Cham (2021)
7. Fanti Rovetta, F., Valentini, D.: Grief and virtual reality: continuing bonds with virtual avatars. Phenomenology and the Cognitive Sciences (2025)
8. Gibbs, J.K., Gillies, M., Pan, X.: A comparison of the effects of haptic and visual feedback on presence in virtual reality. Int. J. Hum. Comput. Stud. **157**, 102717 (2022)
9. Gruenewald, T., Chen, C.: Narrative virtual reality as a memory machine. Convergence (2025)
10. Marks, L.U.: The Skin of the Film: Intercultural Cinema, Embodiment, and the Senses. Duke University Press, Durham (2000)
11. Marks, L.U.: Episode XI. Media Genealogies and Haptic Geographies. Flash Art Media (2021)
12. Nash, K.: Interactive Documentary: Theory and Debate. Routledge, London (2021)
13. Nash, K., Hight, C., Summerhayes, C.: New Documentary Ecologies: Emerging Platforms, Practices and Discourses. Palgrave Macmillan, Basingstoke (2014)
14. Nichols, B., Baron, J.: Introduction to Documentary. Indiana University Press, Bloomington (2024)
15. Rose, M.: The immersive turn: hype and hope in the emergence of virtual reality as a nonfiction platform. Stud. Documentary Film **12**, 132–149 (2018)
16. Scaer, R.C.: The Body Bears the Burden: Trauma, Dissociation, and Disease. Routledge, New York (2014)

17. Skains, R.L.: Creative practice as research: discourse on methodology. Media Practice Educ. **19**(1), 82–97 (2018). https://doi.org/10.1080/14682753.2017.1362175
18. Stolorow, R.D.: Intersubjective-systems theory: a phenomenological-contextualist psychoanalytic perspective. Psychoanalytic Dialogues **23**, 383–389 (2013)
19. van der Kolk, B.A.: The Body Keeps the Score: Brain, Mind, and Body in the Healing of Trauma. Viking, New York (2014)

When Worlds Wink Back: Reflexive World-Building and the Epistemology of Player Conspiracy in *Honkai: Star Rail*

Xinjie Zhao$^{(\boxtimes)}$ (iD), Jiacheng Tang (iD), and So Morikawa (iD)

The University of Tokyo, Tokyo 113-8656, Japan
`xinjie-zhao@g.ecc.u-tokyo.ac.jp`, `jctang@stu.sdnu.edu.cn`,
`somorikawa@k.u-tokyo.ac.jp`

Abstract. Dominant accounts of interactive storytelling, long wedded to seamless immersion, struggle to explain the appeal of titles like *Honkai: Star Rail* that flaunt fourth-wall ruptures yet deepen attachment. We contend that this paradox signals a design philosophy best described as *Reflexive World-Building*. Crucially, this reflexivity is not a theatrical aside but a modality of realism: by openly staging its own constructedness, the game remaps lived coordinates—workâĂŞtime discipline, risk governance, platformized affect—into playable form. In this sense the "wall" is less a surface to be smashed than a seam through which social experience continually threads, including pressures that animate contemporary Chinese youth cultures. Across character design, interface paratexts, and core mechanics, *Honkai: Star Rail* deploys meta-narrative and self-reference not as narrative failure but as a deliberate rhetoric of recognition—an Invitation to Conspiracy that converts the player from a passive immersant into a knowing co-conspirator. Immersion is thereby relocated: from the mimetic demand to "believe" a world to the relational experience of being seen by it. Our analysis systematizes this shift, articulating how reflexive cues can operate in concert to sustain a durable ludic contract grounded in shared literacy rather than fragile illusion. The resulting framework moves beyond the immersion paradigm while retaining its affective aims, offering practical insight for crafting narratively complex experiences that speak to media-savvy publics without forfeiting realism's bite.

Keywords: World-Building · Meta-narrative · Self-reflexivity · Player Conspiracy · Immersion · Game Philosophy · Honkai · Star Rail

1 When Virtual Worlds Abandon Their Disguise

Within the theoretical landscape and design practice of interactive storytelling, "immersion" has long been venerated as the holy grail. Since Johan Huizinga first delineated the foundational concept of the "magic circle," [10, 20] the principal

© The Author(s), under exclusive license to Springer Nature Switzerland AG 2026
M. C. Reyes and F. Nack (Eds.): ICIDS 2025, LNCS 16375, pp. 349–363, 2026.
https://doi.org/10.1007/978-3-032-12405-0_20

aim of world-building has been to forge a self-contained domain—logically consistent, governed by its own strict rules, and hermetically sealed from external reality. This pursuit promises the player a form of ontological security, enabling the suspension of disbelief required to invest fully in a fictional yet "believable" reality. The classical design philosophy, accordingly, is one of hermetic concealment. Through meticulous environmental detail and unwavering historical consistency, the successful virtual world was conceived as a closed vessel whose ultimate charm lay in the perfect disguise of its own artificiality. [12,18,19]

However, against a mature digital-media ecosystem and an increasingly discerning player culture, this paradigm of seamless immersion faces a profound challenge. [6,13] A striking anomaly has emerged in the form of globally successful narrative games such as *Honkai: Star Rail*. [7] In open defiance of traditional tenets, the game does not strive to maintain an impregnable fourth wall; it systematically—indeed gleefully—deploys devices that rupture the magic circle. These range from characters like Sampo who pivot out of the diegesis to address the screen and canvass the player's enjoyment, to an abundance of intertextual nods to our reality (from *Breaking Bad*'s "Heisenberg" to *The Hitchhiker's Guide*'s "42"), to a pervasive meta-commentary on mechanics epitomised by the "trash-can literature" that parodies RPG exploration compulsions. [2,9] According to established theory, such acts ought to shatter narrative gravity and induce "player drop-out." Yet the opposite obtains, exposing the limits of existing models. [13]

To comprehend this paradox, we must move beyond the conventional lexicon of immersion to a more discriminating analytical toolkit. Two interrelated concepts are central: *meta-narrative*, wherein a text thematises its own production, and *self-reflexivity*, wherein it avows its status as a cultural artefact. [1] When deployed not as isolated easter eggs but as a systemic principle, such strategies cease to be immersion-breaking gimmicks. They coalesce into a distinctive interactive relation we term the *Player Conspiracy*. Here the player is not asked to forget the medium so much as invited into a state of shared awareness: a knowing insiderhood sustained by the game's recurrent acknowledgments of its conditions of making. [7,16] Under this contract, the fourth wall functions less as a barricade than as a seam—one that stitches the fiction to lived experience—so that the tacit premise shifts from "make me believe this is real" to "we both recognise this as a game, and that recognition is the point." [14]

This study therefore undertakes a systematic investigation of the design philosophy we term *Reflexive World-Building*. Using *Honkai: Star Rail* as our central case, we examine how this philosophy is operationalised across character, system, and gameplay layers, converting potential narrative risks into assets for relationship-building and community vitality. In so doing, we ask two questions: first, how do virtual worlds that abandon their disguise nonetheless generate distinctive charisma; and second, what shifts in contemporary player culture and the digital media environment does their success register? [23] Through this inquiry, we propose an analytical framework that moves beyond the classical immersion paradigm without forfeiting its affective ambitions. As the fourth-wall-breaking figure tacitly inquires—"Did I bring you joy?"—the player's wry, knowing assent becomes the final ratification of this reflexive ethic.

2 Redefining the *World*: From Immersive Illusion to Candid Conspiracy

2.1 A Genealogy of *World* in Interactive Narrative

To grasp the force of *Reflexive World-Building*, we first sketch a genealogy of the "World" itself. [10] The archetype bequeathed by tabletop RPGs imagines the game-world as a *Sacred Narrative Container*: [20] an enclave of mimesis promising ontological stability, a hermetically bounded space in which disbelief can be suspended without remainder. [18, 19] Its craft ideal is concealment: through meticulous environmental detail and unbroken internal history, the virtual world aspires to make its artifice disappear behind a seamless front.

This regime of perfect disguise was then unsettled by the *Emergent System*: a pivot from static ontology to dynamic generativity in which engagement springs less from narrative belief than from probing a systemic possibility space. [13, 20] A third inflection, the *Transmedia Invasion*, let the world overflow into Alternate Reality Games, pursuing hyper-immersion by paradoxically disavowing their own gameness. [11, 15, 17] These trajectories converge in a fourth phase—the *Reflexive Dialogical Field*—exemplified by *Honkai: Star Rail*: [14, 21] here the work derives strength not from hiding artifice but from refashioning it as the ground of relation, cultivating a "meta-authenticity" keyed to mutual recognition. [7]

2.2 The Epistemological Impasse of Traditional Immersion Theory

Reflexive design arises in response to an epistemological impasse within immersion orthodoxy. For decades that orthodoxy rested on a precarious triad: first, the psychology of "flow," whose presumption of non-reflexivity structurally excludes the critical awareness at stake in metaleptic encounters; [5] second, a phenomenology of "presence" that risks techno-determinism by seeking to erase embodied situatedness through sensory fidelity alone; [22] third, the sociological "magic circle," whose radicalised isolationism falters amid porous, networked cultural texts. [10]

Contemporary practice renders this impasse visible. *The Stanley Parable* finds its core pleasure in metaleptic rupture, [21] while *Undertale* weaponises mechanics as a moral crucible that directly implicates the player beyond the fiction. [3] The commercial and cultural traction of *Honkai: Star Rail*'s anti-immersive moves confirms a normative misread: a new subject has emerged—a "digital native" for whom media-awareness is literacy, intertextuality an affordance, and dialogue with the creator a desideratum. [8] For such publics, the aim is not to forget, but to engage more deeply in a state of wakefulness.

2.3   The Dialectic of *Conspiracy* and *Alienation*

Abandoning the reflex that treats every break in immersion as failure, we centre a working dialectic: *Conspiratorial Engagement* versus *Alienating Rupture*. A successful metaleptic act recruits conspiracy: it forges intersubjective resonance between game and player, confirming agency on both sides and elevating the relation from a consumer–product dyad to a peer dialogue grounded in reciprocal intelligence. [4,7]

By contrast, *Alienating Rupture* marks the breach of that delicate pact—through misfit context, exclusionary cultural cues, or authorial condescension. [14] The distinction is not merely technical but ethical. Reflexive design succeeds only where it respects the player's acuity, affect, and dignity as a cultural agent. In this sense the success of *Honkai: Star Rail* is a triumph of relational aesthetics: it reorients craft from building illusions to cultivating relationships. *Reflexive World-Building* thus names not only a method but an ethic of interaction for a new era of play.

3   Deconstructing the Reflexive World of Honkai: Star Rail

Having established the theoretical toolkit for analyzing metaleptic effects, we now turn to the object at hand: *Honkai: Star Rail*. A common mistake would be to file it under a purely postmodern penchant for subversion. The case is illuminating precisely because it is not a negation machine but a dialectical composition—a site where contrary narrative impulses are held in productive tension. What follows is a close textual analysis of selected in-game moments to show how that tension is made operative, and why the result feels less like a clever contraption than a world that insists on being *alive*.

3.1   The Classical Foundation of Narrative Immersion: Aeonic Mythos and Civilizational Epic

First, it must be acknowledged that *Honkai: Star Rail* invests heavily in a classical immersive substrate. Its world-building is not a pile of set dressing but a coherent cosmology. The "Aeons"—personifications of ultimate philosophical drives—are cast as the universe's highest principles. Each Aeon encodes a civilizational vector:

Aeon	Philosophical Domain
Akivili, the Trailblaze	Symbolizing the eternal exploration of the unknown—the human drive to transcend boundaries
Qlipoth, the Preservation	Representing the will to protect and to build—civilization's defensive instinct
Nanook, the Destruction	Embodying the entropic inevitability of cos mic ruin—the universe's tendency toward chaos
Nous, the Erudition	Signifying the ultimate pursuit of knowledge and truth—the quest for understanding
Aha, the Elation	Perceiving the entire universe as an elaborate, eternal jest—cosmic absurdism personified

This scaffolding lends ontological depth: the player's itinerary doubles as a philosophical passage through competing laws of life. Built on that mythic super-structure, major arcs exhibit genuine tragic ambition. Jarilo-VI at first reads as a quest to rescue a planet trapped in winter; in substance it is a study of generational trauma, contested truth, and public memory. The eventual revelation—that Cocolia, seduced by a Stellaron, seeks salvation by way of ruin—lands with classical weight. Crucially, this solidity does not compete with the game's reflexive maneuvers; it anchors them, so that self-reference tightens tension rather than dissolving meaning.

3.2 The Systematic Deployment of Metaleptic Candor: When Sampo Gazes at the Screen

Upon this epic ground, *Honkai: Star Rail* stages what we call "metaleptic candor." The emblematic instance arrives at the denouement of the Jarilo-VI main quest. It is a textbook moment of *Conspiratorial Engagement*: Sampo slips the frame of NPC exchange and speaks to the audience. As a follower of Aha, the Aeon of Elation, the move is diegetically motivated—Aha licenses jest and rule-bending—but its function is larger: a calibrated **ontological shock** that names the player inside the fiction.

The response interface then offers three vectors. "Who are you talking to?" is **denial**: a bid to restore the veil and keep the diegesis intact. "The performance was spectacular" is **acknowledgment**: the player accepts the invitation and steps into complicity. Silence marks **ambiguity**: recognition withheld yet not refused. The point is less the choice than the recognition that a choice of stance exists at all.

Case Study 1: Sampo's Fourth-Wall Breach

Narrative Beat	Dialogue / Stage Direction
Scene Context	Sampo, revealed as the puppet master behind Belobog's events, prepares his theatrical exit
Breaking Point	**Sampo:** "Hey, my dear friends, did you have fun? Did old Sampo bring you enough joy?" *[Character model rotates 180Âř to face camera directly]*
Player Agency	Option 1: "...Who are you talking to?" *(Denial)* Option 2: "The performance was spectacular, Sampo." *(Acknowledgment)* Option 3: *[Remain silent] (Ambiguity)*
Metaleptic Closure	**Sampo:** "Remember, life's a stage, and we're all just performers!" *[Winks at camera, then vanishes in a shower of cards]*
System Validation	Achievement Unlocked: *"All the World's a Stage"*

Regardless of selection, the encounter enforces the rupture and leverages the player's cultural memory of the "fourth wall" to convert transgression into pleasure. More importantly, it recalibrates the relation: the player is upgraded from spectator to acknowledged participant—a "Co-conspirator." The pact is complete when three conditions coincide: shared literacy (the wall as concept), cognitive delight (recognition as play), and egalitarian address (mutual acknowledgment). In that convergence, reflexivity ceases to be a stunt and becomes the grammar of relation itself.

3.3 The Normalization of Meta-Narrative: Trash Can Philosophy and Ludic Self-Critique

If Sampo's breach is a flash of theatrical voltage, the game's recurring "trash can literature" normalizes reflexivity into routine. What looks like throwaway absurdity is in fact a scalpel aimed at habitual RPG conduct, staging a precise parody of the player's acquisitive loop. Its force lies in a graded revelation of self-awareness that mirrors the very cognition of metaleptic pleasure: curiosity hardens into compulsion, compulsion is named, and the naming itself becomes a source of play.

Case Study 2: The Belobog Trash Can Monologue Sequence

Act I: The Escalating Monologue

#	System Response
1	"It's an unremarkable trash can."
2	"It's really just a trash can. There's nothing inside."
3	"Why do you keep searching? There is really nothing here!"
4	"...Alright, it seems you have an unusual obsession with trash cans."
5	"Since you're so fond of trash cans, I'll grant your wish--"

Act II: The Philosophical Climax

[Screen fades to black. A surreal dreamscape materializes.]
The Trash Can King Materializes

Trash Can King: *"O, mortal, why do you so fervently seek refuse? Is it because your own heart is filled with 'trash' that needs cleansing? Or do you simply find meaning in the meaningless, value in the discarded?"*

[The Trailblazer awakens from the reverie]

Achievement Unlocked
"Belobog's Trash Panda" + Exclusive Trash Can Avatar Frame
For those who find philosophy in refuse and meaning in the mundane

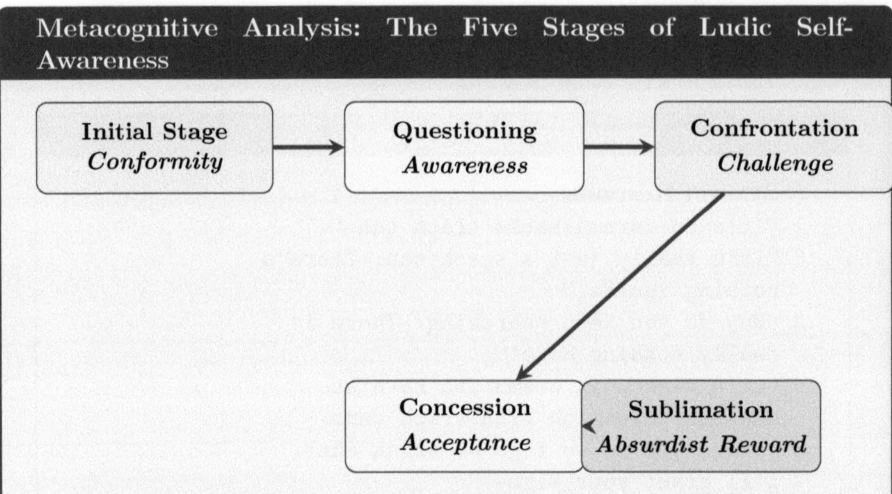

1. **Initial Stage (Conformity):** The system provides a standard object description, meeting player expectations. The world maintains its mimetic contract.
2. **Questioning Stage (Awareness):** The system begins to "notice" and comment on the player's repetitive actions—the *Identification* of ludic behavior as abnormal within the diegetic logic.
3. **Confrontational Stage (Challenge):** The text directly challenges the player's motivations, creating a *Comparison* between their behavior and normative play patterns.
4. **Concession Stage (Acceptance):** The system relents and acknowledges the player's "strange" preference—a moment of *Comprehension* that this obsession will persist.
5. **Sublimation Stage (Absurdist Reward):** The sequence pushes absurdity to its philosophical extreme, creating a surreal experience that confers *Affirmation* of the shared joke between player and designer.

This is more than a simple reward for obsessive-compulsive exploration; it is a **ritualistic confirmation of the conspiratorial bond**. The game communicates: *"I understand your instincts as an RPG player, and I invite you to join me in lovingly mocking them."*

3.4 The Intertextual Fabric of Popular Culture: From 42" to Heisenberg"

Reflexivity is further threaded through a dense weave of popular-cultural allusions. These are not throwaway winks but the medium by which a conspiratorial public is formed: recognition scaffolds belonging, and belonging deepens attachment.

> ## Intertextual Example: The Hitchhiker's Guide Reference
>
> When the character Herta asks for "the answer to life, the universe, and everything" in the Simulated Universe, the player can select "42," the classic reference from *The Hitchhiker's Guide to the Galaxy*.
> **Herta's Response:** *"It seems you've also read that 'mostly harmless' guide. What's interesting is that in our universe, that answer might actually hold some meaning."*
> This single interaction operates on multiple layers:
>
> - **Confirmation of Shared Cultural Capital:** It validates the player and developer as members of the same sci-fi literate community.
> - **Diegetic Integration of Exodiegetic Lore:** It skillfully incorporates a reference from our real world into the game's fictional cosmology.
> - **Metaleptic Self-Disclosure:** It subtly implies that the game world itself possesses an awareness of "external" cultural products, blurring the line between universes.

Taken together, these cases show how *Honkai: Star Rail* enacts *Reflexive World-Building*. The world is double-coded: diegetically, a serious spacefaring epic; meta-diegetically, a self-aware cultural object that addresses its players as cultured equals. The layers do not cancel; they torque one another, generating energy. As Agamben suggests, contemporaneity resides not in easy alignment but in a charged disjunction. Here, commitment to story coexists with reflective distance; tradition is honored even as it is playfully unraveled. The player is asked to cultivate a pragmatic double consciousness—able to surrender to pathos when needed, and to step back when wit requires—an enriched stance rather than a contradiction. Hence Sampo's mischievous "Did you have fun?" becomes a diagnostic of form: in this world, play is both action and commentary, and the commentary is part of the fun.

A third facet of the Trailblazer's design is that of a cultural translator. This is not mere appropriation but a calibrated epistemic game. The avatar utters lines (e.g., invoking the "Turing test" to define intelligence) that presuppose Earthly literacy. The work pointedly withholds a diegetic fix—no memory implants, no multiverse alibi—and sustains a productive ambiguity. That ambiguity licenses a fluid, double inhabitation: the Trailblazer as character and the player as self share a single voice. Agency becomes duplex rather than split; the result is a cross-dimensional dialogue in which self-recognition is the central mechanic.

4   The Three Layers of a *Living* World

4.1   The Character Layer: The Metaleptic Avatar as Player's Co-Conspirator

The most immediate and central site for the systematic deconstruction of *Honkai: Star Rail*'s reflexive world is the design of its player-avatar—the Trailblazer."

Within the narrative design genealogy of the RPG, the protagonist has traditionally occupied one of two poles: the pre-defined, high-agency hero (e.g., Geralt of Rivia) or the blank slate" vessel for player projection (e.g., the Dragonborn). The design philosophy of the Trailblazer profoundly subverts this dichotomy. By systematically implanting a meta-consciousness, it transforms the protagonist from a mere diegetic participant into the player's epistemological co-conspirator within the virtual world.

The Trailblazer's uniqueness is first manifested in its meticulously designed dialogue system. Whereas traditional RPG dialogue options typically serve instrumental functions—governing moral choices or branching plotlines—*Honkai: Star Rail* transforms the dialogue interface into a ritualistic space for confirming the conspiratorial pact between player and developer. This is achieved through a mechanism of double coding, where each dialogue option operates simultaneously on two distinct linguistic planes: as an in-character utterance and as an extra-diegetic player commentary.

The theoretical significance of this design transcends a simple fourth-wall break. It creates a dual-layered interpretive space where every dialogue becomes a negotiation of meaning. Diegetically, the Trailblazer is merely a quippy adventurer. Extradiegetically, however, the player uses the Trailblazer to voice their own ludic literacy and wry observations about genre tropes. In choosing a metaleptic option, the player performs an identity declaration: "I am an experienced player; I see the formula at work, and I am willing to play along." This act masterfully transmutes a potentially negative affect (boredom with repetitive quest design) into the positive, conspiratorial pleasure of shared, knowing performance.

If the quest-related quips represent a restrained form of meta-commentary, the Trailblazer's interactions with trash cans push this reflexive tendency to its absurdist extreme. This seemingly nonsensical feature provides a profound commentary on the nature of player behavior in open-world games. The instinct to loot everything" or explore every corner" is a fundamental player compulsion, and the trash can—the object least likely to contain value—becomes the perfect instrument for interrogating this drive. The interaction sequence performs a phenomenological investigation of player compulsion. Through its progressively self-aware text, the game mirrors the player's own psychological journey: from rote exploration, to a dawning awareness of the absurdity of one's own actions, and finally, to a full-throated embrace of that absurdity. The final achievement and title ("Trash Can Connoisseur") do not merely reward the behavior; they provide an ontological seal upon the experience. It is a ritualistic confirmation of the conspiratorial bond, a moment where the game canonizes the player's idiosyncratic compulsions as a meaningful and memorable part of their shared history.

4.2   The System Layer: The Personified Interface and Its Paratexts

If the Trailblazer is the player's emissary within the narrative, then *Honkai: Star Rail*'s system layer constitutes a pervasive meta-narrative network. Traditional UI/UX design seeks "transparency," striving to make the interface an invisible window into the virtual world. *Honkai: Star Rail* pursues the opposite strategy: it forgoes invisibility in favor of imbuing its system layer with a distinct narrative personality, transforming it into an active participant in the metaleptic dialogue.

Paratextual Narratives in Item Descriptions. In *Honkai: Star Rail*, no text is purely functional. The descriptions for every item, from common consumables to legendary artifacts, are treated as miniature narrative stages. These descriptions form a paratextual universe that runs parallel to the main plot. *Case Analysis: The Metaleptical Layers of Item Descriptions

Item	Description Text	Paratextual Analysis
Trash	"In certain games in certain worlds, this is an edible supply. But here, it is just trash. Really."	Engages in direct inter-ludic dialogue, referencing mechanics from other game franchises (e.g., *Fallout*) and defining itself in opposition to them.
Adventure Log	"A mysterious item that records the Trailblazer's adventures. Rumor has it that using it 'saves' the world. But how could that be? The world isn't a game."	Employs reflexive double negation. By denying the world's "gameness," the text ironically confirms the "save" function as a core game mechanic, playing with the player's understanding of the medium.
Stellar Jade	"A precious material of unknown origin. Rumor has it these are the crystallized tears of 'paying players,' but no one knows what 'paying' means."	Weaves the extra-diegetic player behavior of "gacha" spending (a F2P monetization model) into the world's own mythological lore.

This rhetorical strategy of double negation creates an epistemological playground. The player is invited not to believe or disbelieve, but to inhabit the pleasurable tension between the two states. This unresolved speculation—does the world know it's a game?—is precisely the intellectual pleasure the design aims to produce.

The Achievement System as Meta-Commentary. The achievement system is repurposed from a mere external incentive structure into a platform for sociological observation. Each achievement title and description offers an insightful, often gently teasing, commentary on player behavior. In doing so, they objectify and defamiliarize the player's own ludic actions. By describing the impulse to complete every side quest as a "sacred duty" while questioning the sheer number of people in need, the game invites players into a state of metacognitive pleasure: the joy not just of playing, but of observing oneself playing.

Pom-Pom and the Personified System. The character of Pom-Pom, the train's conductor and de facto system administrator, represents the apex of this design philosophy. Pom-Pom delivers system messages (updates, maintenance notices) not with cold, corporate text, but with personality and emotion. This design executes a profound redistribution of emotional labor. Traditionally, the emotional burden of system friction (e.g., server downtime) falls entirely on the player. Through the endearing and slightly befuddled persona of Pom-Pom—who admits to not understanding what a "bug" is—the game transforms this friction into a reciprocal emotional exchange. The paradox of the system's own representative being ignorant of the system's technical realities dissolves the player-system antagonism, replacing cold necessity with affective connection.

4.3   The Gameplay Layer: Event Design as Cultural Parody

If the character and system layers embed reflexivity into the game's daily texture, the limited-time events represent its carnivalesque moments. Invoking the spirit of Bakhtin, these intervals function as licensed ludic disorder in which the ordinary rules of the world are temporarily suspended and renegotiated. In such digitally staged carnivals, *Honkai: Star Rail* momentarily sets aside its sober spacefaring epic to mount orchestrated parody, turning the game into a forum where genres, mechanics, and community memories are placed on display and gently reworked. The crucial point is not mere wit: the events translate the lived grammars of contemporary play—collection, optimization, memetic exchange—into theatrical motifs, so that recognition itself becomes a mechanic of attachment.

Aetherium Wars" as Precise Parody. The Aetherium Wars" event exemplifies this method. Rather than offering a simple homage to *Pokemon*, it performs a careful archaeology of the monster-battling loop and then rebuilds it in the game's own idiom. Collection, elemental typology, boss ascents, and staged evolutions are all reproduced, but every beat is threaded with commentary from characters who wryly interrogate the very procedures they enact (e.g., "Why does every gym leader need to be fought after their underlings?"). The result is a layered experience: players enjoy a competent combat ruleset, simultaneously observe those rules as conventions, and participate in a running meta-conversation about how genres discipline attention and time. Each recognized trope becomes a tacit handshake—evidence that designer and player share a history and are willing to play with it rather than merely within it.

The Redistribution of Cultural Capital. From a sociological angle, the event format redistributes cultural capital. Knowledge of legacy mechanics, platform memes, and franchise histories—often confined to subcultural enclaves—is converted into social currency legible to a wider audience. The platform thereby hosts a triangular authorship among text, player, and community, in which meaning is not deposited but negotiated. Crucially, the parody operates under a clear ethic:

Homage over Derision, preserving affection toward the sources even as it reframes them;

Innovation over Plagiarism, ensuring that playful citation is coupled with systems that stand on their own;

Dialogue over Monologue, inviting players to co-complete the joke rather than merely receive it.

Framed this way, parody becomes a positive-sum ecology: novices are onboarded through shared recognition, veterans are rewarded with depth, and both are offered a language for reflecting on their habits of play.

The analysis of the character, system, and gameplay layers reveals that *Reflexive World-Building* in *Honkai: Star Rail* is not an ad-hoc box of tricks but an organically integrated system. The layers are synergistic: the Character layer anchors self-expression and voice; the System layer sustains a continuous dialogue that names and stylizes player behavior; the Gameplay layer injects timely cultural relevance by turning communal literacies into design material. Together they create a recursive circuit of signification: the game refers to itself, then to the player's routines, which are reflected back as paratext and event, which in turn reshape how the world is read. Like facing mirrors, the exchange multiplies depth while softening hard borders between real and virtual, player and avatar. The world feels "alive" not because it feigns reality perfectly but because it cares for its status as a made thing and enlists the player in that care—a stance reminiscent of *Dasein*, a being for whom its own Being is at issue. In that enlistment, the work sketches a more candid model of humanâĂŞcomputer relation: not deception toward verisimilitude, but relational authenticity— mutual acknowledgment, negotiated meaning, and trust. In a media-saturated age, immersion need not mean forgetting the medium; it can mean entering an intelligent, humorous, and felt conversation with it.

5   Toward a New Paradigm of Reflexive World-Building

This study began from a paradox: how can a game that persistently exposes its own artifice produce stronger affect than titles devoted to seamless illusion? Our reading suggests that this is no anomaly but an epistemic turn in interactive narrative. The core insight of Reflexive World-Building is stark: admitting construction can generate a truer engagement than concealing it. When Sampo looks into the camera, when a trash can interrogates compulsion, when an event parodies a genre, the text practices a double negation—denying naive reality in order to affirm a higher-order authenticity. The truth thus ratified is not mimetic but relational: a new pact in which recognition, not deception, secures commitment.

This shift tracks a broader change in subjectivity. Contemporary players are not audiences waiting to be fooled but media-literate meta-subjects whose pleasure comes from operating on several planes at once—feeling with the story while thinking with the design, acting in the fiction while commenting on the form. Reflexive worlds furnish the right shape for this polyphony: they treat interpretation as part of the play loop, and they dignify literacies accumulated across platforms and communities.

The implications extend beyond entertainment. As computational agents grow more fluent and realistic," it becomes ethically urgent to preserve lucidity about artifice. The model on display in *Honkai: Star Rail*—transparent construction, candid artificiality, and meaning made in concert—offers a template: do not collapse humanâĂŞmachine relations into simulation; structure them as conversations. The most durable bonds are not built on perfect disguise, but on mutual acknowledgment and negotiated purpose. In that sense a seemingly unserious game articulates a serious thesis about digital life: in a world saturated with mediation, sincere artificiality can be more authentic than feigned naturalness. When a world says, I know I am made, and you know I am made—let us make something together on that basis," it inaugurates not only a distinctive mode of play but a different ontology for our age.

References

1. Aarseth, E.J.: Cybertext: perspectives on ergodic literature. Johns Hopkins University Press, Baltimore (1997)
2. Boluk, S., LeMieux, P.: Metagaming: playing, Competing, Spectating, Cheating, Trading, Making, and Breaking Videogames. University of Minnesota Press, Minneapolis (2017)
3. Bonello Rutter, G.: Self-reflexivity and humor in adventure games. Game Stud. **15**(3) (2015). http://gamestudies.org/1503/articles/bonellorutter
4. Bourriaud, N.: Relational aesthetics. Les Presses du Réel, Dijon (1998)
5. Csikszentmihalyi, M.: Flow: the psychology of optimal experience. Harper and Row, New York (1990)
6. Ermi, L., Mäyrä, F.: Fundamental components of the gameplay experience: analysing immersion. In: Proceedings of DiGRA 2005: Changing Views: Worlds in Play, pp. 15–27. DiGRA, Vancouver, Canada (2005). https://doi.org/10.26503/dl.v2005i1.119
7. Galloway, A.R.: Gaming: essays on algorithmic culture. University of Minnesota Press, Minneapolis (2006)
8. Gee, J.P.: What video games have to teach us about learning and literacy. Palgrave Macmillan, New York (2003)
9. Gualeni, S.: Self-reflexive videogames: observations and corollaries on virtual worlds as philosophical artifacts. G|A|M|E Italian J. Game Stud. **1**(5) (2016). https://www.gamejournal.it/wp-content/uploads/2016/07/GUE_05_01_Gualeni.pdf

10. Huizinga, J.: Homo ludens: a study of the play element in culture. Beacon Press, Boston (1950)
11. Jenkins, H.: Transmedia storytelling. MIT Technology Review (2003). https://www.technologyreview.com/2003/01/15/234540/transmedia-storytelling/, accessed 1 Oct 2025
12. Jenkins, H.: Game design as narrative architecture. In: Wardrip-Fruin, N., Harrigan, P. (eds.) First Person: New Media as Story, Performance, and Game, pp. 118–130. MIT Press, Cambridge, MA (2004). https://web.mit.edu/~21fms/People/henry3/games&narrative.html
13. Juul, J.: Half-Real: video games between real rules and fictional worlds. MIT Press, Cambridge, MA (2005)
14. Kocur, M., Homar, T., Breznikar, A.: The door: timing effects of fourth wall breaks on immersion and presence. In: Proceedings of the Annual Symposium on Computer-Human Interaction in Play (CHI PLAY'21), pp. 43–48. ACM, New York (2021). https://doi.org/10.1145/3450337.3483489
15. McGonigal, J.: This might be a game: ubiquitous play and performance at the turn of the twenty-first century. Ph.D. thesis, university of california, berkeley (2006). https://escholarship.org/uc/item/2kq1q8kf
16. Montfort, N.: Twisty little passages: an approach to interactive fiction. MIT Press, Cambridge, MA (2003)
17. Montola, M., Stenros, J., Waern, A.: Pervasive games: theory and design. CRC Press, Boca Raton (2009)
18. Murray, J.H.: Hamlet on the holodeck: the future of narrative in cyberspace. The Free Press, New York (1997)
19. Ryan, M.L.: Narrative as virtual reality: immersion and interactivity in literature and electronic media. Johns Hopkins University Press, Baltimore (2001)
20. Salen, K., Zimmerman, E.: Rules of play: game design fundamentals (2003)
21. Schubert, S.: Playing with (meta)fictionality and self-reflexivity in the video game *The Stanley Parable*. In: Fülöp, E. (ed.) Fictionality, Factuality, and Reflexivity Across Discourses and Media, pp. 212–228. De Gruyter, Berlin/Boston (2021). https://doi.org/10.1515/9783110722031-014
22. Steuer, J.: Defining virtual reality: dimensions determining telepresence. J. Commun. **42**(4), 73–93 (1992). https://doi.org/10.1111/j.1460-2466.1992.tb00812.x
23. Wardrip-Fruin, N., Harrigan, P. (eds.): First person: new media as story, performance, and game. MIT Press, Cambridge, MA (2004)

From Simulation to Collaboration: Lessons from Designing an Interactive Narrative About a Character Living with Aphasia

Natalie Jarrett[(✉)] [iD]

Georgia Institute of Technology, Atlanta, GA 30332, USA
Njarrett8@gatech.edu

Abstract. The immersive nature of Interactive Digital Narratives (IDNs) makes them a powerful platform for exploring underrepresented experiences. IDNs can reproduce or 'simulate' characteristics of a different point of view (POV), thereby immersing the interactor in the perspective of another. This approach has the potential to encourage deeper engagement with underrepresented or marginalized experiences but may also create unintended divides between the interactor and the represented group. In this analysis, I discuss the use of simulation in an IDN I recently created, One Art, which tells the story of a character living with aphasia, a language disorder. After analyzing the background, applications, and merits of simulation, I propose a methodology for revising my work, which includes co-designing with members of the affected community. This proposal draws on human-centered design and other participatory making methods.

Keywords: Immersion · Simulation · Co-design · Interactive Digital Narrative

1 Introduction

Interactive Digital Narratives (IDN) have the power to create emotional resonance and visceral impact, even beyond most other creative mediums. IDNs consist of characteristics such as "immersion" [1], which enable an interactor to feel submerged in a given story world and point of view (POV). It is precisely because of this quality that IDNs have become a popular vehicle for exploring complex social issues and underrepresented experiences [2]. IDNs can manipulate POV, apply constraints, and activate sensory engagement, all which function to create a 'simulated experience.' While simulation as a narrative technique has the potential to foster greater understanding and engagement with difficult experiences [3], it may also unintentionally create even greater separation between the interactor and the individuals being represented [4]. My analysis will explore the use of simulation in an IDN I've recently created.

One Art is a twine-based IDN that tells the story of an English professor who develops fluent aphasia after having a stroke. The narrative explores her experiences navigating the symptoms of her condition, her complex relationship with her adult daughter, and her career endeavors. The narrative is told from a second person POV, thus directly

M. C. Reyes and F. Nack (Eds.): ICIDS 2025, LNCS 16375, pp. 364–374, 2026.
https://doi.org/10.1007/978-3-032-12405-0_21

bringing the interactor into the story world—the interactor is 'immersed' in her world as she goes about daily life, argues with her daughter, practices communication recovery exercises, and more. Notably, the narrative represents the POV of the main character by including simulated symptoms of aphasia, as they impact the character's encounters with language. During the development of my IDN, I consulted with health care professionals and activists living with aphasia—however, I now propose a revised approach to my narrative process that includes a more systematic process and closer collaboration with members of the represented community.

In this analysis, I will initially describe my own project, including my inspiration, approach, process, interactive characteristics (particularly simulations), and potential shortcomings. I will evaluate simulations as an educational and empathy-building tool, particularly within the context of IDNs. Finally, I will explore co-design, a collaborative human-centered design technique, and propose a revised approach to my work that leverages the method's focus on participation, inclusion, and communal creativity—the final section will provide the outline of a hypothetical co-design workshop.

2 One Art

2.1 Inspiration

Aphasia is a condition that impacts an individual's ability to read, write, hear, and speak language. It is caused by "damage (usually from a stroke or traumatic brain injury) to areas of the brain that are responsible for language" [5]. I first learned about aphasia in an undergraduate neuropsychology course on the brain and language. Although many of my older relatives have experienced strokes, I only later discovered that they too developed aphasia (whether temporary or long term) as a result. While my family members and I may have recognized certain symptoms, we did not understand them to be a part of a designated condition.

My interest in using a character with aphasia arose out of my frustration with the lack of awareness about the condition [6]. I was inspired by other IDNs that explore characters living with disability such as Depression Quest [7] and Before I Forget [8]. These IDNs manipulate perspective to immerse the interactor in the characters' lived experience. In Before I Forget, a game developed alongside medical-professional consultants, the interactor takes on the POV of a character with dementia. As she wanders through a partially recognizable house and endures fragmented flashbacks, the interactor is immersed in the disorienting terror she feels [9].

The simulated experiences in One Art were initially inspired by the simulation activities provided by Voices of Hope for Aphasia, a Florida-based nonprofit. The organization has a series of aphasia simulations that provide users with activities that demonstrate how someone with aphasia may experience differences with hearing, reading, writing, and speaking language [10]. While these simulations inspired the mechanics of my own project, I sought to move beyond merely simulating the symptoms of aphasia and to demonstrate how those symptoms may have an impact on the life of a fully realized character.

2.2 First-Hand Experience

Motivated by a commitment to respectfully portray a character living with aphasia, I sought out guidance from individuals with first-hand experience. I consulted with both communication science academics who have clinical expertise in aphasia and community activists living with aphasia. In addition to learning more about the condition itself, through these conversations I was informed of common misconceptions, tropes to avoid, and other considerations to take into account as I developed my IDN. I was deeply grateful for the wisdom and support I received and sought to incorporate their expert advice into my work.

2.3 Simulation in One Art

The title "One Art" comes from the Elizabeth Bishop poem of the same name [11]. One Art is the main character's favorite poem and a piece she regularly reads aloud to practice verbal communication. From my engagement with members of the aphasia community, I learned that reading, writing, and reciting poetry can be helpful for practicing language skills. Through secondary research, I also found that poetry is considered a promising therapeutic approach for aphasia [12], with several accounts supporting its effectiveness [13, 14]. In addition to providing an emotional outlet, poetry also enables rhythmically patterned speech, thus making verbal communication easier to practice.

One Art includes multiple scenes that simulate the character reading the poem. In each reading scene, the interactor must click on an underlined word or phrase—each click then reveals the following word or phrase (Fig. 1–4), resembling how the character must carefully read the text word for word. The interactor will face a word that appears incorrectly (Fig. 2, 3), simulating how someone with aphasia may utter certain words differently than they intend to. The interactor is made aware of this by the feedback of the character they are orating to (such as the speech language pathologist) (Fig. 4). The experience is followed by a clickable passage "what happened?" which describes how people with aphasia experience certain impairments and provides links to external resources for further learning (Fig. 4, 5). This was done to ensure that the simulations maintain their educational purpose, rather than simply rendering the symptom into a spectacle. In addition to reading, there are several other passages in the narrative that simulate the character's experience with writing, speaking, and hearing language—each of these passages are also paired with clickable educational passages.

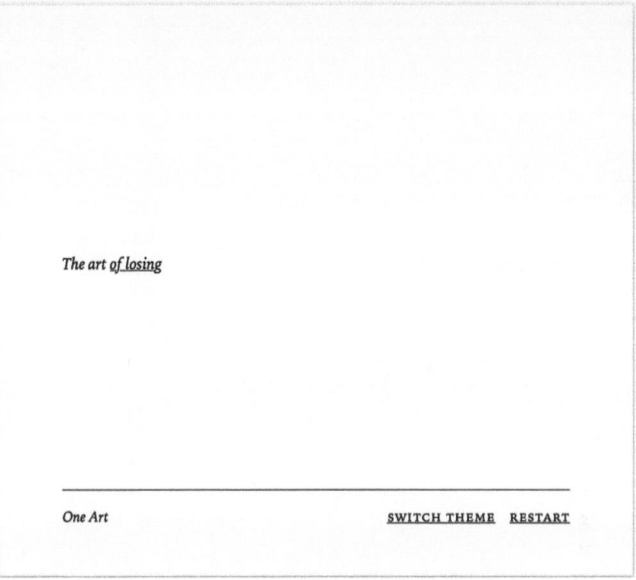

Fig. 1. The interactor begins the poem.

Fig. 2. After the interactor clicks 'of losing,' the subsequent phrase 'isn't hard to master' is revealed.

Fig. 3. The bolded word, 'mixture,' illustrates a misperception caused by aphasia. The actual word written is 'master.'

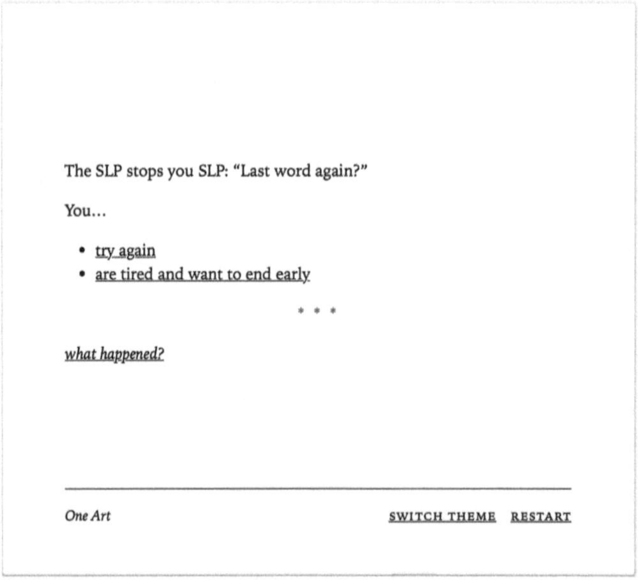

Fig. 4. The speech language pathologist (SLP) notices the error and asks the character/interactor to re-read the passage.

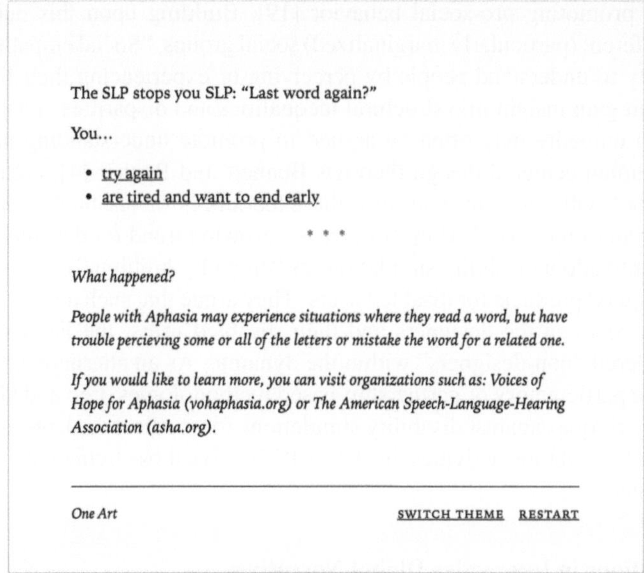

Fig. 5. When the interactor clicks the 'What happened?' tab, they receive an explanation of the symptom along with links to external educational resources.

3   Simulations

Simulations are a commonly used and widely accepted teaching method within a variety of medical contexts. Medical simulations are designed to emulate the symptoms of a given condition and are used to reduce the gap in understanding between medical providers and their disabled patients [15]. They are utilized for their capacity to go beyond mere knowledge-based education and are positioned as tools useful for building empathy among healthcare providers [16]—particularly for care providers who support individuals living with aphasia [17].

Beyond institutional programming, there are simulation experiences designed for users with varying levels of medical expertise (from friends and family to caregivers and speech therapists), such as Hailpern et al.'s [18] Aphasia Characteristics Emulation Software (ACES) which was shown to increase empathy and understanding for aphasia. Moreover, many user-centered design organizations outside of the medical community have employed simulation activities to help non-disabled designers better understand and empathize with their disabled users [4].

Across contexts, the use, value, and ethics of simulation are often disputed. Although simulations may be intended to inspire empathy, the evidence on their effectiveness is mixed. Additionally, some critics argue that the focus on inspiring empathy is itself a flawed objective.

3.1   Simulations and Empathy

'Empathy' from a social-cognitive lens describes the ability to understand the emotions and take on the perspectives of others [17, 19]—empathy is considered an essential function for promoting pro-social behavior [19]. Building upon this definition with respect to different (particularly marginalized) social groups, "Social empathy" is defined as "the ability to understand people by perceiving or experiencing their life situations and as a result gain insight into structural inequalities and disparities" [20].

Although empathy may often be argued to promote understanding and prosocial behaviors, human-centered design theorists Bennett and Rosner [4], argue that activities associated with empathy may turn the experiences of disabled people "into the unrelatable trait of the other." They criticize the growing trend for designers and design organizations to adopt disability simulations as "empathy-building" exercises in service of better designed products for disabled users. They argue that such an approach implies a distinction between the designers and their disabled users, the latter of whom are unfairly rendered "non-designers" within the dynamic. As an alternative, they argue in favor of more participatory or partnership-based methodologies. Leo and Goodwin [15] offer similar critiques against disability simulations for medical students and argue that the creation of simulation activities must directly involve those living with the disability being simulated.

3.2 Simulations in Interactive Digital Narratives

Within the context of IDNs, simulated experiences function to make a given narrative more immersive. In her seminal text, Hamlet on the Holodeck: The Future of Narrative in Cyberspace, Janet Murray [1] first formalized the concept of immersion as a "participatory activity." Furthermore, she describes how immersed interactors "actively create belief," by which they still carry their own cognitive frameworks, even while being placed in an alternate world. However, this quality may prove risky for stories that take the perspectives of characters with minority or marginalized identities. Will an immersed interactor simply reinforce their assumptions about a given group or situation, or will they experience greater identification? Moreover, even if immersive experiences succeed in fostering empathy, will they necessarily translate into shifts in how individuals navigate the external social world?

Koenitz, Roth, and Meckler [3] argue that placing interactors in alternate realities may increase understanding of the reality being represented. Hand and Varan [21] suggest that by having an interactor make decisions on behalf of a character in an IDN, they will feel the consequences of their narrative decisions more deeply. A study conducted by Peng, Lee, and Heeter [22] found that game playing was effective at promoting prosocial qualities, particularly a participants' "willingness to help." However, other research did not find such straightforward links between IDNs, empathy, understanding, and prosocial behaviors. A study conducted by Steinemann et al. [23] found that interactivity did not have a demonstrated impact on certain prosocial behaviors, specifically that it did not directly increase participant donations to a related social cause—however, the study did reveal a connection between interactivity and the participants' sense of responsibility toward the story outcome.

4   Co-Design

Given the previous analysis, I propose a revised approach to my project that may leverage the benefits of an immersive approach while reducing ableism through partnership and co-creative work with members of the aphasia community. I specifically propose the use of co-design, a participatory research method utilized across human-centered design fields, to this end.

Co-design is a collaborative design process in which people "connect their knowledge, skills, and resources in order to carry out a design task" [24]. Co-design may be especially beneficial for working alongside disabled participants, as it helps individuals feel recognized as valued and empowered contributors [25]. In this context, co-design functions similarly to other collaborative processes such as Participatory Action Research (PAR), a research strategy in the social sciences which involves "the participation and leadership of those people experiencing issues, who take action to produce emancipatory social change, through conducting systematic research to generate new knowledge" [26]. Co-design builds upon PAR by actively incorporating the creative input of participant members.

Although co-design is most often associated with the design process of functional products and services, previous explorations have demonstrated its value during the creation of IDNs. Atmaja and Sugiarto [27] introduced a design methodology for IDNs that communicates complex issues (such as climate change) by integrating co-design with domain experts. Rouse [28] described how community-centered co-designing supports the formation of Augmented Reality-based interactive narratives concerning cultural heritage. However, the method has yet to be incorporated as a standard methodology for IDN creation.

5   Co-Design Workshop Proposal

Although co-design as a practice lacks a singular approach and may leverage strategies across different participatory research and creative-making practices, I propose a process which includes: a group discussion, a brief explanation of my original project, and a collaborative story-making activity.

The workshop itself would follow a semi-structured format to allow for greater flexibility. The following procedure is intended to outline the series of topics and activities it should cover. The method of communication and presentation of information for the workshop would be designed and refined alongside the guidance of health care providers and organizations who specialize in aphasia-specific accessibility needs.

While the following procedure will demonstrate simulation as an interactive approach (and will specifically include examples from One Art), I am open to the possibility that such a method may not be preferred by my participants, thus the story making segment will take a simulation-agnostic approach.

Given individual preferences, commitments, and time constraints, I acknowledge that the following procedure may need to be broken up into multiple different sessions.

5.1 Co-Design Workshop Guidelines

Participants: The codesign workshops would recruit 5–10 adults (18 +) who have either previously experienced or currently live with aphasia. Although the proposed workshop would focus on the perspectives of my collaborators, I would welcome the involvement of caretakers and family members to ensure the comfort of my collaborators.

Accessibility: I would deploy the following methods to ensure that the session is accessible to my collaborators.

1. I would contact my collaborators before the workshop and ask if there are accommodations they would prefer for the workshop to provide.
2. I would work with health-care providers and aphasia focused organizations to ensure that the workshop activities and materials are accessible to my participants.
3. I would ensure that my workshop allows participants to leverage a variety of different communication methods (verbal, written, pictorial, etc.).

Procedure:

1. Before the workshop, I would obtain informed consent from all my collaborators.
2. The codesign session would begin with an introduction in which I explain my project, project goals, and the format of the workshop itself.
3. I would have a discussion my collaborators about aphasia representation, including:
   a. How they feel aphasia is currently represented across media forms.
   b. If they can identify any common stereotypes, misconceptions, or tropes about people with aphasia.
   c. How they would want people with aphasia to be represented.
4. I would give a general overview of my original project:
   a. I would only give a high-level explanation and would not demonstrate the entire experience to keep possibilities open and avoid compelling any particular response:
      (1) "This is a story about an English professor who develops aphasia after having a stroke, which explores how her life, career, and relationships, particularly her relationship with her adult daughter, is impacted."
   b. Finally, I would ask what my collaborators immediate reactions, questions, and concerns they have about the project (including the plot, the characters, the representation of Aphasia, etc.).
5. I would 'playthrough' a short passage of One Art to demonstrate the character, the narrative style, and some of the simulated moments.
   a. After the demonstration, I would ask my collaborators for their immediate impressions, reactions, questions, and concerns.
6. I would run an activity where I would have my collaborators participate in the story making process. They would receive a diagram of the original story, including key plot points and outcomes. I would offer the original project plot as a guideline but would encourage my collaborators to make whatever changes and/or additions they prefer. To support the activity, I would provide guiding questions which could include the following:
   a. What are your impressions of the current story and framework? Is there anything you would add or change?

   b. How would you represent the character's experience with living with aphasia? Are there specific moments where the narrative POV could reflect this experience?
7. We would discuss the previous questions, while I, as the facilitator, take notes.
8. I would use the workshop contributions to design a new IDN prototype in Twine.
9. The prototype will be further refined and workshopped alongside my collaborators.
10. The workshop would end with a debrief where my collaborators would be asked to share their final thoughts, reactions, and feedback to the overall co-design experience.

6 Conclusion

IDNs have the capacity to immerse interactors within a variety of different perspectives, thus making for a particularly compelling platform to share underrepresented or marginalized experiences. IDNs include affordances and mechanics that can viscerally transport an interactor into different points of view. In One Art, I utilized simulation to demonstrate how aphasia impacts everyday language tasks. However, further analysis revealed that using such a technique may unknowingly reproduce ableism, thus indicating the need for a collaborative story-making process based around the perspectives of those living with aphasia. I described a potential co-design workshop during which the original narrative would be revisited and revised alongside collaborators with firsthand experience. By taking such an approach, my project may be better suited to meet my original goal of creating greater awareness of aphasia and those living with the condition. Beyond my own case study, I hope that the implications of this work may extend to other IDNs that wish to explore the experiences of disabled and other underrepresented communities.

References

1. Murray, J.: Hamlet on the Holodeck: The Future of Narrative in Cyberspace. The Free Press, USA (1997)
2. Koenitz, H., Barbara, J., Eladhari, M.P.: Interactive digital narrative (IDN)—new ways to represent complexity and facilitate digitally empowered citizens. New Rev. Hypermedia Multimed. **28**(3–4), 76–96 (2022). https://doi.org/10.1080/13614568.2023.2181503
3. Koenitz, H., Roth, C., Mekler, E.: Alternate realities in interactive digital narratives — understanding and improving design and prosocial effects through empirical methods. Multimed. Tools Appl. **83**, 1–22 (2024). https://doi.org/10.1007/s11042-024-18884-8
4. Bennett, Clark, L., Daniela, R.K.: The promise of empathy: design, disability, and knowing the "other". In: Proceedings of the 2019 CHI Conference on Human Factors in Computing Systems. ACM, New York (2019). https://doi.org/10.1145/3290605.3300528
5. National Institute on Deafness and Other Communication Disorders, Aphasia. https://www.nidcd.nih.gov/health/aphasia
6. Code, C.: The implications of public awareness and knowledge of aphasia around the world. Ann. Indian Acad. Neurol. **23**(Suppl 2), S95–S101 (2020). https://doi.org/10.4103/aian.AIAN_460_20
7. The Quinnspiracy. Depression Quest. The Quinnspiracy. Browser game (2013). http://www.depressionquest.com/
8. -Fold Games. Before I Forget. PC (2020). https://beforeiforgetgame.com

9. Pinchers, E.: Before I Forget, the narrative game exploring dementia launches with alzheimer's research uk (2020). https://www.alzheimersresearchuk.org/news/before-i-forget-the-narrative-game-exploring-dementia-launches-with-alzheimers-research-uk/

10. Voices of Hope for Aphasia, Aphasia Simulations. https://vohadmin.github.io/Aphasia_Sim

11. Bishop, E.: One Art. The New Yorker (1976)

12. Shafi, N., Carozza, L.: Poetry and aphasia: a clinical outlook. J. Poet. Ther. **24**(4), 255–259 (2011). https://doi.org/10.1080/08893675.2011.625208

13. Candlin, R., Bigwood, S.: Stroke patients learning poetry to aid recovery (2024). https://www.bbc.com/news/articles/c80z6nypw13o

14. Pinhasi-Vittorio, L.: The role of written language in the rehabilitation process of brain injury and aphasia: the memory of the movement in the reacquisition of language. Top. Stroke Rehabil. **14**(1), 115–122 (2007). https://doi.org/10.1310/tsr1401-115

15. Leo, J., Goodwin, D.: Simulating others' realities: Insiders reflect on disability simulations. Adapt. Phys. Activ. Q. **33**(2), 156–175 (2016). https://doi.org/10.1123/APAQ.2015-0031

16. Levett-Jones, T., et al.: Measuring the impact of a 'point of view' disability simulation on nursing students' empathy using the Comprehensive State Empathy Scale. Nurse Educ. Today **59**, 75–81 (2017). https://doi.org/10.1016/j.nedt.2017.09.007

17. Laures-Gore, J., Lamb, K., Rice, K.G.: Empathy, post-stroke aphasia, and speech-language pathology students. Aphasiology **37**(6), 854–868 (2023). https://doi.org/10.1080/02687038.2022.2046254

18. Hailpern, J., Danilevsky, M., Harris, A., Karahalios, K., Dell, G., Hengst, J.: ACES: promoting empathy towards aphasia through language distortion emulation software. In: Proceedings of the SIGCHI Conference on Human Factors in Computing Systems (CHI '11), pp. 609–618. ACM, New York (2011). https://doi.org/10.1145/1978942.1979029

19. Riess, H.: The science of empathy. J. Patient Exp. **4**(2), 74–77 (2017). https://doi.org/10.1177/2374373517699267

20. Segal, E.A.: Social empathy: a model built on empathy, contextual understanding, and social responsibility that promotes social justice. J. Soc. Serv. Res. **37**(3), 266–277 (2011)

21. Hand, S., Varan, D.: Interactive stories and the audience: why empathy is important. Comput. Entertain. **7**(3), 1–14 (2009). https://doi.org/10.1145/1594943.1594951

22. Peng, W., Lee, M., Heeter, C.: The effects of a serious game on role-taking and willingness to help. J. Commun. **60**(4), 723–742 (2010). https://doi.org/10.1111/j.1460-2466.2010.01511.x

23. Steinemann, S.T., Iten, G.H., Opwis, K., Forde, S.F., Frasseck, L., Mekler, E.D.: Interactive narratives affecting social change. J. Media Psychol. **29**(1), 54–66 (2017). https://doi.org/10.1027/1864-1105/a000211

24. Zamenopoulos, T., Alexiou, K.: Co-design as collaborative research. Bristol University/AHRC Connected Communities Programme (2018)

25. Fraser-Barbour, E., et al.: Shifting power to people with disability in co-designed research. Disability Soc. **40**(2), 259–280 (2025). https://doi.org/10.1080/09687599.2023.2279932

26. Cornish, F., et al.: Participatory action research. Nature Rev. Methods Primers **3**, 34 (2023). https://doi.org/10.1038/s43586-023-00214-1

27. Atmaja, P.W., Sugiarto.: When information, narrative, and interactivity join forces: Designing and co-designing interactive digital narratives for complex issues. In: Interactive Storytelling: 15th International Conference on Interactive Digital Storytelling, pp. 329–351. Springer, Heidelberg (2022). https://doi.org/10.1007/978-3-031-22298-6_20

28. Rouse, R.: Someone else's story: an ethical approach to interactive narrative design for cultural heritage. In: Proceedings of the 12th International Conference on Interactive Digital Storytelling, Cardona-Rivera, R., Sullivan, A., Young, R. (eds.) LNCS, vol. 11869, pp. 81–93. Springer, Cham (2019). https://doi.org/10.1007/978-3-030-33894-7_6

Evaluating Retellings as a Design Goal
for a Fighting Game

Gabriel Eriksson Hededal[1] , Oskar Lejdestad Sporre[1] ,
Hartmut Koenitz[1(✉)] , and Mirjam Palosaari Eladhari[2]

[1] Södertörn University, Alfred Nobels allé 7, 141 89 Huddinge, Sweden
Lejdestad@live.se, hartmut.koenitz@sh.se
[2] Stockholm University, 106 91 Stockholm, Sweden
mirjam@dsv.su.se

Abstract. This paper investigates what we can learn about a game's design by analyzing retellings applying Eladhari's framework [4]. Mystics Ablaze, a fighting game, is evaluated in its capacity of instigating retellings using a novel method including qualitative interviews for data collection and deductive thematic analysis. The results of the analysis show that the participants were engaged with the narrative layer of the game, both through retellings and other kinds of interpretations. The novel methodology is promising in its ability to evaluate retellings.

Keywords: Retellings · Fighting games · IDN design · Retellings analysis method · Retellings for design evaluation · Video game development case study

1 Introduction

Retellings are a key feature of IDNs [4], and Eladhari's concept has been influential in the field both in direct application for evaluation as suggested by Eladhari herself [13,15–17] and by influencing other models [10]. This study investigates Mystics Ablaze[1], an indie fighting game where the players choose from a diverse cast of characters and fight using crystal orbs and teleportation. We take facilitating retellings as a design goal and introduce an analytical framework which we apply to understand how successful the game is in facilitating retellings. Eladhari [4] defines four layers that make up an IDN. First is code layer, containing scripts, frameworks and engines (graphics, physics, dialog systems, etc.). The second is the story layer, encompassing pre-written lore, backstory narration or dialogue. The third is the discourse layer, consisting of the current dynamic states and experienced events. The actions of the expressive agents are included in this layer. The fourth layer is the narrative layer, which is where concepts like retellings belong. Examples can include fan-art, fan-fiction, but also streaming gameplay or oral conversations about events that happened during a play-session.

---

[1] https://store.steampowered.com/app/3865560/Mystics_Ablaze/.

M. C. Reyes and F. Nack (Eds.): ICIDS 2025, LNCS 16375, pp. 375–384, 2026.
https://doi.org/10.1007/978-3-032-12405-0_22

At the same time, Koenitz [10] sees retellings as the subjective product in the System, Process, Product (SPP) model describing Interactive Digital Narratives (IDNs). Both models are useful in understanding retellings.

1.1 Retellings in Fighting Games

Fighting games are a genre where players pick a predefined character from a roster and a stage to fight in with another player [1]. Fighting games have a social aspect and are also intimate, as they are often played offline with a shared screen where the players sit next to each other and interact directly. The narrative of fighting games is emergent: together the players set up, play out and create permutations of similar scenarios

For example, Super Smash Bros. Melee [7] features a character called Jigglypuff, who is established as an innocent pink ball who likes to sing and float. Juan "Hungrybox" DeBiedma, a compeditive esports player, became famous for playing this character in a particular style waiting for his opponent to strike. This was unusual for a game with an aggressive, proactive focus. Hungrybox' play changed the understanding of the character as an evil villain with malicious intent [3]. Furthermore, Hungrybox himself also became a villain in both his own and the community's retellings. For Mystics Ablaze, we are aiming to create similar emerging narratives and for this study we want to investigate whether our design has been successful in this regard.

2   Related Research

Eladhari [4] introduced retellings as indicators of successful game design. A recent study [6] of the game Genshin Impact identified the evocative nature of the provided narrative, combined with many gaps, as the main reasons which motivated players to engage in retellings. Koenitz [10] describes interactive digital narratives as "purposefully incomplete" works that are designed so that interactors/players fully realize them through their actions and retellings. He understands the meaning-making process as a shared responsibility through agency and thus a source of retellings, with "narrative gaps that leave space for the interactor to fill [10] as an important aspect of the designer's toolbox. Fernandez-Vara [5] further explains how a game world is constructed to tell its own narrative through environmental storytelling and the player acts as a detective, uncovering this story through observation and interaction with the world. Jenkins [9] describes game designers as sculptors of worlds and space, while Koenitz and Eladhari [11] describe them as "system builders" of dynamic works that facilitate active engagement and unforeseen outcomes.

3   Method: Multistep Analysis of a Game and Players' Retellings

To evaluate whether the implemented design intentions for the game are successful in facilitating retellings, our method includes multiple steps. It starts with specifying the game, the design intentions and the setup of the playtest. The data collected in the playtest is analyzed using content analysis, followed by mapping the findings to selected design intentions using deductive thematic analysis. Finally, inductive analysis was utilized to identify relevant information not captured if unexpected data was spotted. Here are the steps in detail:

1. Specification of game and design intentions
   (a) Provide a summary of the game
   (b) Specification of game design intentions
   (c) Specification of intentions with the play test
   (d) Specification of what the player is shown (environments, backstory, characters, mechanics)
2. Playtest Procedure
   (a) Script for test, how participants were selected, demographic data and what data was collected.
   (b) The scenarios the players played
   (c) Screen recordings of all the things the player is shown.
3. Observations from the playtest
   (a) How players related to the game, how players interacted - both in-game, and remotely - utterances, both exclamations and potential talk about strategies.
4. Content analysis of retellings
   (a) Go back to 1b and 1 c: consider the retellings when mapping them to the information in 2b (see above)
   (b) Use deductive thematic analysis to identify whether the design intentions have been fulfilled.
   (c) If something unexpected is spotted use an inductive thematic analysis to identify what is standing out

3.1   A Summary of the Game

Mystics Ablaze is a 2D local multiplayer fighting game for 2–4 players who pick from a selection of characters as well as themed stages containing nine areas (e.g. Fig. 1) where they compete against each other. The winner is the first player to survive three rounds. The narrative framing of the game is that magic wielders, spirits and occultists duel with colorful crystal orbs and explosive teleportation. It takes place in a pre-industrial fantasy world inspired by eastern Mediterranean themes (Crete, Turkey, Cyprus and Egypt). The music of the game is fast, percussive, and microtonal. The characters do not have written lore, instead context is provided in the form of short poems.

All characters have a crystal orb which can be thrown by the press of a button. Teleportation happens when the button is pressed again. As an orb hits a wall it bounces and stores power to causes more damage. Characters can grab orbs and throw them at other character and they can also jump and crawl. All characters share these core mechanics, yet they play very differently they have a special move while the orb is away, and another while holding the orb in their hand.

Fig. 1. Gameplay screenshot of characters Psychic, Exorcist and Magician fighting in one of the nine arenas of the Carnival stage

3.2 Design Intentions with the Game and Intentions for the Playtest

Below are the intentions for the narrative design of Mystics Ablaze.

1. Provide a cozy, magical and mysterious world with characters that are likable and attractive while celebrating neurological and temperamental diversity.
2. Bring people together and spark curiosity to learn about each other's differences.
3. Highlight everyone's contribution in creating a captivating experience.
4. Easy to learn, a lifetime to master - simple mechanics with deep connotations. Learning by playing together, not by practicing alone against a dummy.
5. Provide narrative gaps to evoke players' imagination to fill them.
6. Facilitate conversations during play, make players engage in make-believe and performance to add narrative context.
7. Create memorable moments that players want to tell others about.
8. Allow diverse interpretations - especially in terms of moral alignment, characters' relationships, the level of violence used and the tone of the fight

For the playtest, we focused on the design intentions 5–8, which were summarized as the following themes: *Fill-in of narrative gaps* (5), *Conversations during play* (6), *Recall of memorable moments* (7), and *Diverse interpretations* (8). These are elaborated upon in Sect. 4.

3.3 What the Player Is Shown

Players start the game in the character select screen (Fig. 2) There they get to choose between seven characters: Psychic, Magician, Cursed, Astrologer, Flytrap, Exorcist and Homunculus.

Next, players select which of four stages to fight on and start to engage on the chosen arena (Fig. 1, Fig. 3).

Fig. 2. The character select screen with 2D images, 3D renders and character names

3.4 Data Collection Method: Observation and Semi-Structured Interviews

Our study included observation of 13 participants and interviews with the 9 participants. Ten participants (age 21–44, median 29) identified as male, two as female and one as non-binary. Ten participants were recruited at a fighting game club gathering, three at a later occasion. All participants were experienced players of fighting games, and most competed in esport tournaments. We followed the rules for Informed consent. Four of the participants did not wish to participate in interviews and were thus only present in the observation phase. Direct recording of the participants was avoided, as we felt it could make participants uncomfortable and impact the results. The gameplay was recorded using screen capture software. All play sessions and interviews were conducted in person. When playing the game, the participants shared one screen and played for around 25–45 min each. Their conversations, utterances, as well as in-game behavior was recorded through notetaking. Around 1/3 of the participants played in pairs, while 2/3 played in groups of 3–4. After the play sessions, participants were interviewed, using semi-structured interviews [14]. The participants were asked about their impressions of the characters, the game world as well as the most memorable moments of their play session (Questionnare is available online, withheld for anonymization).

3.5 Data Analysis Method: Deductive Thematic Analysis

The data gathered from the observed play sessions and the conducted interviews were coded and subsequently sorted into the four predefined themes 3.2 using deductive thematic analysis [8], using the predefined themes *Fill-in of narrative gaps, Conversations during play, Recall of memorable moments*, and *Diverse interpretations*.

4 Results

4.1 Fill-In of Narrative Gaps

Most of the participants were proficient in *filling narrative gaps*. The characters were interpreted as Greek or Gaelic mythological beings, star signs, as well as supernatural creatures connecting them to ancient folklore and more recent fantasy works. Astrologer for example was compared to the Minoan Minotaur, Magician to the Arthurian character Merlin. Around half of the participants interpreted the characters as participating in a tournament. P13 took this one step further by also assigning nationalities to the characters, which is a fighting game convention. The characters' relationships were also the source of retellings. P11 projected romantic relationships onto the characters, saying that "Cursed and Magician are romantic enemies. [...] Psychic and Astrologer are a couple [...] He is the sky and she is the ocean, masculine and feminine energy." In addition, the composition of the character select screen inspired retellings (Fig. 1), e.g. that proximity indicated relationships (P2). Participants also offered detailed explanations of the rules e.g. P4 explained that the orbs had a connection to the character's souls, therefore they only have one (at a time) and must take it back before throwing again. P3 stated that since the characters are mystical beings, physical violence would not hurt them and therefore magic was needed.

4.2 Conversation During Play

Some participants talk almost constantly, while others were quiet. When P7 discovered a particularly effective attack playing Magician, all others shifted their attention towards them. The players called the ability "the particle accelerator." P4 exclaimed they are "[...] very scared of [P7] playing as Magician." In a different match P2 was playing as Psychic and using her blink ability to avoid attacks. This defensive tactic proved very effective while P2's opponents grew increasingly frustrated and started to team up to make sure that the Psychic would not win. P3, playing as Homunculus, yelled "F*ck you Psychic! [...] I sacrifice my humanity!" as they would use up more than their remaining health to power their orb, and consequently disintegrated into a weak puddle, to attack and take out P2. In this state, P3 quickly lost the round, but so did P2. P3 *added a make-believe narrative context to their actions* and shared with the others.

4.3 Recall of Memorable Moments

Overall, the participants struggled to recall the most memorable moments of their play session. A *shared aspect for recalled moments was strong dramatic agency through mechanics* which required considerable set-up but provided an equal amount of pay-off, resulting in laughter or surprise. One such example was the "comet" (Fig. 3), a mechanic where the Astrologer's orb exits the screen in an upward motion, staying there for about 12–15 seconds, and then falling, damaging opponents. In one such situation P2 had set up a comet just before being defeated. To everyone's surprise the comet still appeared, landing a direct hit on two of the remaining opponents. P2 yelled "That was me! I love it! The comet always comes!" This moment was brought up again during the interviews, not only by P2, but also P3 who recalled " [that] getting "cometed" was the most memorable part." Similarly, P13 answered that playing as Exorcist, and connecting a hit with what they referred to as the "power gathering" mechanic was their most memorable moment. Furthermore, P7 said that discovering and quickly learning how to exploit the Magician's "particle accelerator" was the most memorable moment.

Fig. 3. Astrologer's Comet attack

A divergence from this behavior was P11 who instead recalled when they and P13 had stopped fighting to instead debate which character had the "cooler" way of running. Multiple participants did not recite a specific moment, instead stating that discovering and learning how to use all the character-specific mechanics was the most interesting part of the experience.

4.4   Diverse Interpretations

Based on the data from the play sessions the *aspect of equivocality of the perceived narrative and the heterogeneity among the interpretations* was perhaps the most successful. The reasons for fighting, the stakes involved, and the severity of the violence were interpreted in a variety of ways. About half of the participants recounted a tournament of a type of sport, or of magical martial arts. Others related the experience to life and death, or even the order of the universe, where characters represented natural forces or gods. Examples of diverse interpretations include:

(P11) They are enemies, various forces that collide. Destruction and protectors, like Astrologer and Psychic. They protect the world order, the balance. Others are out to disturb it.

(P2) The stages represent domains and the characters might have disagreements over these.

(P3) "I don't think they are friends. They have history, they are competing."

(P1) "It's all like a joint magical agreement [...] Can be play or life or death."

(P5) They fight because they can fight, not very seriously. Some characters probably know each other, it is more like a sport.

The same character could also be interpreted in conflicting ways, aligning with the design intentions. For instance, Magician was described as both an aloof bohemian and as a sharp, alert academic of magic. Participants had a tendency to describe their own characters in a more positive way, using words like "feminine", "attractive", "manly", "kind", and "happy". Conversely, the opponents' characters were described with more antagonizing adjectives like "aggressive", "tease", "evil", and "mischievous".

5   Discussion

The multi-step analysis allowed us to evaluate how successful the design was in facilitating retellings. The first design goal, to make players fill the gaps of the fragmented narrative was very successful. Collectively the participants provided background about who the characters are, what they are doing, what their relationships are to one another, as well as the fictional world they inhabit. Similar to previous findings [6], the interpretations were oftentimes based on association to cultural references. The participants understood the fragmented narrative through regional cultures of real life, but also mythology, religion, fairy tales as well as modern fantasy works and fighting game tropes.

The second design goal succeeded as well: facilitate conversations during play, make players engage in make-believe and performance to add narrative context. During play, the participants would come up with additional narrative context and express fictitious emotions and intent, such as fear, or murderous intent props used in a game of make-believe [18].

While still yielding some positive results, the third design goal (Create memorable moments that players want to tell others about) was the least fulfilled of the four design intentions. Our participants struggled to recall specific moments of their play session. A suggestion is to implement an award system, where players receive awards and a summary at the end of each match to trigger memories. Another way could be the implementation of an automatic diary system, to help players remember what happened [12]. The conclusions of Ciccoricco [2] suggest that moments of downtime and reflection facilitate this form of retellings. Another way could be to create memorable moments of "kaleidoscopic" insights into complex issues [10].

The fourth design goal, the equivocality of the fictional world, was perhaps the most successful, resulting in diverse retellings. Participants had a tendency of villainizing characters they fought while also heroizing their own characters. The participants might have chosen a character that they interpreted as the friendliest and nicest. However, this could also be related to the discourse layer where they deem their own play as kind and honorable, while demonizing the opponent's play. Thus, their interpretation of the character differs based on whether they played as or against it.

Finally, we want to point out limitations of the study. The overall sample size is small, and 10 out of 13 participants identified as males. In addition, the fact that the participants knew each other previously and were very experienced in fighting games, could both have affected the results.

6 Conclusion

The study observed retellings with our fighting game. The prevalent aspects were filling of narrative gaps, the occurrence of different make-believe as well as emerging narratives. The participants also produced different narrative interpretations. In that sense, Mystics Ablaze is a narrative success, as it facilitates meaningful retellings. Furthermore, the methodology developed to evaluate the retellings was appropriate and provided good insights. We plan to develop the framework further through studies of different types of games, such as role playing games, platformers, and dungeon crawlers. Our aim is to develop a comprehensive method applicable to all types of games.

References

1. Ashcraft, B.: Arcame Mania! The Turbo-Charged World of Japan's Game Centers, Kodansha International (2008)
2. Ciccoricco, D.: "Play, Memory": Shadow of the Colossus and Cognitive Workouts. Dichtung Digital. Journal für Kunst und Kultur digitaler Medien (37) (2007)
3. DeBiedma, J.: Everybody Hates Jigglypuff. THE PLAYERS' TRIBUNE (2018). https://www.theplayerstribune.com/articles/esports-juan-hungrybox-debiedma-everybody-hates-jigglypuff
4. Eladhari, M.P.: Re-Tellings: The fourth layer of narrative as an instrument for critique. In: Rouse, R., Koenitz, H., Haahr, M. (eds.) ICIDS 2018. LNCS, vol. 11318, pp. 65–78. Springer, Cham (2018). https://doi.org/10.1007/978-3-030-04028-4_5
5. Fernandez-Vara, C.: Game Spaces Speak Volumes: Indexical Storytelling (2011). https://doi.org/10.26503/dl.v2011i1.512
6. Greting, M., Mao, X., Eladhari, M.P.: What inspires retellings - a study of the game genshin impact. In: Vosmeer, M., Holloway-Attaway, L. (eds.) Interactive Storytelling. pp. 249–269. Springer International Publishing, Cham (2022). https://doi.org/10.1007/978-3-031-22298-6_16
7. HAL Laboratory: Super Smash Bros. Melee,: place: Kyoto. Japan Publisher, Nintendo (2001)
8. Hecker, J., Kalpokas, N.: The Guide to Thematic Analysis (2025). https://atlasti.com/guides/thematic-analysis/deductive-thematic-analysis
9. Jenkins, H.: Game design as narrative architecture. In: Wardrip-Fruin, N., Harrigan, P. (eds.) First person: New media as story, performance, and game. MIT Press, Cambridge, MA (2004). http://www.electronicbookreview.com/thread/firstperson/lazzi-fair

10. Koenitz, H.: Understanding Interactive Digital Narrative. Immersive Expressions for a Complex Time. Routledge, London and New York (2023). https://doi.org/10.4324/9781003106425
11. Koenitz, H., Eladhari, M.P.: The paradigm of game system building. Trans. Digital Games Res. Assoc. **5**(3), 65–89 (2021).https://doi.org/10.26503/todigra.v5i3.123
12. Koenitz, H., Roth, C., Mekler, E.: Alternate realities in interactive digital narratives - understanding and improving design and prosocial effects through empirical methods. Multimed. Tools Appl. (2024). https://doi.org/10.1007/s11042-024-18884-8
13. Kreminski, M., Samuel, B., Melcer, E., Wardrip-Fruin, N.: Evaluating AI-based games through retellings. In: Proceedings of the AAAI Conference on Artificial Intelligence and Interactive Digital Entertainment vol. 15(1), 45–51 (2019). https://doi.org/10.1609/aiide.v15i1.5223 , https://ojs.aaai.org/index.php/AIIDE/article/view/5223, number: 1
14. Pitkänen, J.: Studying thoughts: stimulated recall as a game research method. In: Lankoski, P., Björk, S. (eds.) Game research methods: An overview, pp. 117–132. ETC Press (Apr 2015), tex.date-added: 2022-06-01T12:14:00GMT   tex.date-modified: 2022-07-30T11:40:42GMT   tex.rating: 0   tex.uri: papers3://publication/uuid/1B82DBA9-4D64-4576-AD2C-1DC39538C7BF
15. Sezen, T.I., Sezen, D.: Longform video essays as critical retellings of video game narratives. In: Bostan, B. (ed.) Games and Narrative: Theory and Practice. ISCEMT, pp. 267–279. Springer, Cham (2022). https://doi.org/10.1007/978-3-030-81538-7_17
16. Smith Nicholls, F., Cook, M.: "That Darned Sandstorm": Dlling. In: Proceedings of the 18th International Conference on the Foundations of Digital Games. pp. 1–8. FDG '23, Association for Computing Machinery, New York, NY, USA (2023). https://doi.org/10.1145/3582437.3587207, https://dl.acm.org/doi/10.1145/3582437.3587207
17. Sych, S.: When the fourth layer meets the fourth wall: the case for critical game retellings. In: Bosser, A.-G., Millard, D.E., Hargood, C. (eds.) ICIDS 2020. LNCS, vol. 12497, pp. 203–211. Springer, Cham (2020). https://doi.org/10.1007/978-3-030-62516-0_18
18. Walton, K.L.: Mimesis as Make-Believe: On the Foundations of the Representational Arts. Harvard University Press, Cambridge, MA (1990)

Searching Playtrace Data to Identify and Evaluate Dramatic Arcs in Game Systems

Samuel Shields[1]([⊠]) [iD], Noah Wardrip-Fruin[1] [iD], and Edward F. Melcer[2] [iD]

[1] University of California, Santa Cruz, CA, USA
{samshiel,nwardrip}@ucsc.edu
[2] Carleton University, Ottawa, ON, Canada
edwardmelcer@cunet.carleton.ca

Abstract. Dramatic arcs have long served as a critical lens for understanding narratives, charting rises and falls in tension and emotion throughout plot progression. Video games are unique in that the dramatic arcs present in their narrative are driven not only by aesthetics but also by the interaction and feedback produced by diverse interactive systems. Player actions, emergent outcomes, and systemic changes in game state create experiential arcs that dovetail with more straightforward narrative approaches. These arcs often take on forms more abstract than those found in conventional storytelling. This abstraction, combined with the unpredictability of emergent game systems, complicates a designer's critical work of tuning such systems for desired dramatic arcs in their games. This work introduces an iterative design process using Playtrace Arc Search (PAS), a tool that leverages gameplay traces and designer-defined metrics to visualize and evaluate dramatic arcs. Using a turn-based RPG simulation testbed as a case study, we show how designers can rapidly identify global systemic arc patterns and search for local narrative structures. Our method also helps reconcile quantitative gameplay data with qualitative player feedback. Our approach highlights actionable design strategies for balancing game system-driven narrative against common dramatic arc patterns.

Keywords: Dramatic Arc · Playtrace · Co-Creative Tools · Player Modeling · Game Balance

1 Introduction

The recognition that game systems (whether they are or are not explicitly narrative-oriented) implicitly carry narrative structure, meaning, and storytelling potential is a hallmark of game design [2,11]. When traditional narrative and game system emergence and progression gracefully work together, games become capable of presenting dramatic arcs in ways no other form of media can. Namely, players experience dramatic arcs through multimodal gameplay—a fusion of explicit narrative, gameplay feedback, diverse aesthetics, and so on

© The Author(s), under exclusive license to Springer Nature Switzerland AG 2026
M. C. Reyes and F. Nack (Eds.): ICIDS 2025, LNCS 16375, pp. 385–395, 2026.
https://doi.org/10.1007/978-3-032-12405-0_23

[21]. A player may experience a "rags to riches" arc through a weak character accumulating powerful abilities over time, or a "man in a hole" arc through the gradual reduction of resources and safety in a horror game. While these arcs can be presented through interactive and dynamic dialogue alone, many games lean on the narrative metaphors that their game systems convey to represent their greater, holistic messages. Using a simple example, the gradual demonic invasion of Earth in *DOOM* is played out through audio recordings and environmental storytelling as well as the increasing volume, speed, and difficulty of the demon spawns that the main character fights [10]. These dramatic arcs, a result of the combination of systems-driven and traditional storytelling, help define the overall sense of progression in a game.

However, the emergent properties of game systems alongside the lack of generic translations between game system-driven narrative and traditional storytelling make predicting the progression of a system's dramatic arc difficult. A system's embodiment of difficulty, balance, tension, or drama either has to be statically defined by a designer or built into procedural systems that might have a wide range of potential dramatic system arcs that could be produced. As such, providing tools that help a designer directly understand the character of a game system's progression through the lens of dramatic arcs could prove invaluable for the careful tuning of a multimodal, interactive game narrative. We thus present an iterative design approach that combines player modeling, gameplay traces, and a tool dedicated to visualizing and searching playtrace arcs (Playtrace Arc Search, or PAS) in order to understand if a game system is correctly providing the dramatic pacing (or diversity of pacing) that is desired by a designer.

2   Related Work

2.1   Dramatic Arcs

Dramatic arcs represent the two-dimensional, rising and falling nature of a narrative plot over time. Frequently framed in terms of story tension or the emotional character of the story, such arcs date back to Aristotle and are a critical tool in understanding the plot structure of narrative through a visual lens [1,4]. The representations of arcs take many forms—directed graphs [17], simple pyramids [31], two-dimensional waveforms [27], among others. These arcs were observed to be able to be computationally processed and manipulated by Kurt Vonnegut in 2004 [27], and this exercise has been carried out in works such as (Reagan et al., 2016)'s exercise in analyzing a large corpus of narratives by sentiment [18]. Their processing yielded the insight that emotional arcs generally possess some configuration of six unique waveform patterns—"rags to riches", "riches to rags", "man in a hole", "Icarus", "Cinderella", and "Oedipus". Figure 1 provides a visual representation of these patterns. While not all authors define arcs according to these six labels, such labels prove useful in providing a comparison point of arcs to a common corpus of narratives [29]. Dramatic arcs have been a frequent target for drama management systems, especially as they are employed in both interactive digital narrative and in games [16,19,20]. Dramatic arcs are not limited to written literature but can exist in all forms of media; how they are conveyed depends on the affordances of the media in question.

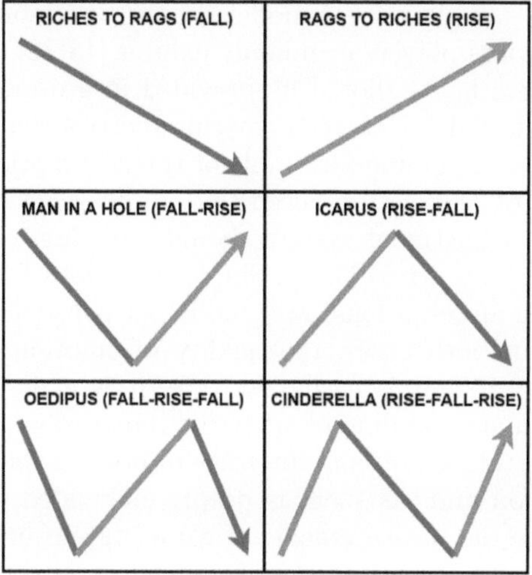

Fig. 1. A visual representation of the six types of dramatic arcs found in narratives as defined by Reagan et al. [18]. All x-axes represent story progression, while the y-axes represent emotional sentiment.

2.2 Game Systems as Narrative

Video games afford a wide range of tools to convey dramatic arcs—audiovisual feedback, gamefeel, controls, progression, script, cinematography, etc.—the list is long and varied [2,11]. The translation of these interacting systems and components is commonly understood through design frameworks such as "Mechanics, Dynamics, Aesthetics", where system definition, the emergent properties of the system, and player interaction direct the aesthetic, emotional, experiential qualities of a game from a player's lens [9,12]. Tracy Fullerton [7] directly ties dramatic arcs into the interaction with game systems, noting that the uniqueness of these arcs in games comes from player skill and agency: "...success or failure is in the hands of the player. It is the player who must learn how to avoid the attacks, moving closer and closer to the goal." Gillian Smith et al. [24] use the metaphors of "rhythm" and "beats" when discussing content generation in 2D-platformers, showing how gameplay is often interpreted through the lens of the expressive terms of other mediums. With such a wide variety of interactions available at the hands of designers, understanding how each uniquely designed system generates dramatic arcs is a daunting task which requires an understanding of their intended audiences and the way their system behaves over some progression.

2.3   Player Modeling and Playtrace Analysis

Player modeling provides methods that translate a perceived, ideal player into a system-understandable model. This model can then be used to implement game systems. For example, player models might be useful in terms of understanding what behaviors players commonly exhibit [13,32], or what sequence of dialogue and narrative beats should be provided in a drama [15]. Models have proven particularly useful for creating specific metrics that represent elements of dramas for players. A common example of this is "emotional intensity". Mike Booth, the designer of *Left 4 Dead*, used this summarized metric to define how a dynamic difficulty adjustment system should modulate challenge in response to an evaluation of player stress [3,26]. Similarly, Jenova Chen of *thatgamecompany* described using an "emotional arc" model for constructing the progression of *Journey* [5,25]. In both cases, the quality of emotional intensity is not a static, generic measure that is easily derived—it is a designer-defined metric that is borne of an understanding of what the intended experience of the game is for some audience. The emotional intensity in both of these cases is measured over game progression and, as such, is deeply embedded in the framework of playtraces, which are the measurements of game state over a linear progression [6]. Playtrace analysis is a common design practice productively used to understand game outcomes such as frequent paths through levels, difficulty throughout gameplay, or the total decision space for players [14,28,30]. Pablo Gutiérrez-Sánchez et al. [8] describe a method of using temporal logics to cluster and explain player behaviors through recorded playtrace data. Combining playtrace analysis with the expert-defined metrics used to define emotional or dramatic intensity allows us to conceptualize game system progression as dramatic arcs, which we can then map against the common patterns noted in Sect. 2.1.

3   Performing Dramatic Arc Searches

As highlighted in the related work section, we can conceptualize the systematic narrative arc of a game or interactive digital narrative through the lens of playtraces, defined by a relevant designer-identified metric and a measurement of experiential progression. We propose that there exists an iterative process to concretely evaluate if 1) there is a system-observable metric that defines game narrative progression, 2) if the defined metric's changes over a progression form a set of meaningful dramatic arcs as desired by the designer, and 3) if those arcs correspond with the qualitative experiences of the players who interact with the system. We call this iterative design process a "Dramatic Arc Search". A visual of this iterative loop is shown in Fig. 2.

We suggest using a tool called "Playtrace Arc Search" (PAS) to help designers rapidly perform searches against trace corpora during this design process [23]. We use a case study consisting of the analysis of a turn-based RPG battle simulator throughout the next section to demonstrate how this iterative process works [22]. This system (FighterDDA) simulates two parties of characters battling one another, selecting actions such as attacking, defending, or healing according to character speeds. A game ends when all characters of a single party have their health reduced to zero. The simulator runs headless and generates a large volume of playtraces, showing how potential battles play out according to statically defined character properties. The code for both FighterDDA and PAS is available on GitHub[1]..

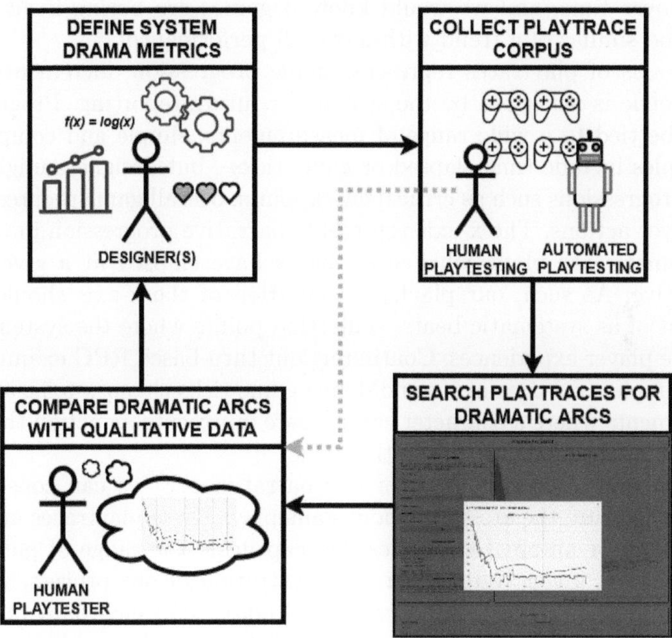

Fig. 2. The iterative design loop for understanding how dramatic arcs are being presented within an interactive system.

3.1   Defining Drama Metrics of Game Systems

Dramatic arcs, in the context of game systems and playtraces, are defined on their y-axis by a (usually) abstracted measurement of what a player is experiencing at any given moment. There is a nearly infinite variety of meaningful dramatic metrics—it is dependent on the designer, their experiential goals, and the specific game context to identify what computed metric represents the game system's dramatic arc. For the process proposed in this work, the metric must be numeric in order to be plotted and analyzed in the context of playtraces.

Previous examples in this work highlight more complex versions of this, with opaque definitions such as "emotional intensity". That being said, simpler y-axis definitions can still yield productive designer insights—if we are designing

---

[1] Playtrace Arc Search (PAS) Tool: https://github.com/smshields/ArcSearch, FighterDDA: https://github.com/smshields/FighterDDA

turn-based RPG battles, we might want decisions such as attacking, target selection, and healing to generate a back-and-forth conflict that gradually declines until one party's health has been depleted. As such, a simple measurement that might provide insight into dramatic arcs for this system is the overall health measurement of all characters. We would quickly know if the system isn't producing dramatic arcs correctly for battles if overall health gradually rose instead of falling over time, and we would know if games are boring if all playtraces followed too similar of a trend within overall performance.

The x-axis of playtraces represents game progression, increments at which the arc metric is measured by the system for future reporting. Progression can similarly be tied to a wide range of measurements, simple and complex. Obvious examples include time elapsed or game ticks—but designers might use customized progressions such as critical checkpoints, overall game progress, or number of player actions. The x-axis represents narrative progression in traditional, linear dramatic arc plots; what story beats have elapsed at a given point of the narrative. As such, our playtrace definition of the x-axis should similarly be thought of as systematic beats—inflection points where the system can alter the arc the player experiences. Continuing our turn-based RPG example, we can take the simple road once again and define game ticks as our x-axis, as they represent moments where a character can prepare or execute an action that impacts the overall health of characters in the game.

With x- and y-axes selected for our narrative arc, we can construct playtraces that capture the arc throughout gameplay. These playtraces are recorded during human or automated playtesting, capturing the range of potential arcs that occur for a given system. For the illustration of our process, we will use overall player health over game ticks in the FighterDDA environment over 1,000 playtraces to evaluate what dramatic arcs exist in the platform's battles. If this playtesting is done with human players, it is crucial to also collect qualitative data about their play experience so that the selected x- and y-metrics and their corresponding playtrace arcs can be validated as meaningful indicators of actual play experience.

3.2 Using Playtrace Arc Search

With formatted x- and y-axis data that correspond to a designer's conception of how a system contributes to a dramatic arc, it is now possible to log gameplay data into a playtrace and represent it as a graph. While individual playtrace case studies are useful in their own regard, it is difficult to understand the true dramatic potential from a single or limited number of playtrace examples. The collection of a large corpus of playtraces allows for a more complete understanding of playtrace diversity, giving a designer insight into a system's dramatic potential.

PAS reads a large set of playtraces and provides tooling to 1) see the overall distribution of playtrace data through a point cloud and 2) search for designer-defined dramatic arcs within the playtrace dataset. A screenshot of PAS with descriptions of its basic usage can be seen in Fig. 3. These two features enable a designer to quickly see if a desired (or undesired) arc is possible for a game system given a playtrace dataset of sufficient size. Figure 4 shows how a designer might use the curves specified by (Reagan et al., 2016)'s analysis to see if such patterns exist in their data [18]. It is quickly apparent that the "rags-to-riches" arc will never occur in this dataset, which would likely be preferred by the designer (as infinitely increasing overall health would indicate RPG battles that never end). On the other hand, an overall gradual decline of health consistently exists, with some presence of curve variety in different sections of the playtraces.

A designer can, after seeing the traces in aggregate, sift through all produced system arcs by drawing a curve that they are curious about in their system and performing a search for similar curves. For example, a designer might want to see an oscillation of the "Oedipus" (fall-rise-fall) style throughout the overall trend of downward curves shown in the point cloud. They can look for this pattern by drawing such an oscillating curve within the bounds of the point cloud and seeing if any playtraces meaningfully match the drawn curve. Dramatic arcs can happen in local or global settings, so defining when and at what scale curves occur in a playtrace arc can be understood by the designer by carefully defining their search curve accordingly.

3.3   Combining Arc Visualization with Qualitative Data

Once playtraces have been collected and a designer has inspected the resulting system dramatic arcs using PAS, it is important to combine the observations of the system's progression with qualitative player feedback. The danger of system-defined metrics for narrative is that they cannot fully encapsulate player perspectives, and it is quite possible that a designer's educated guess at what system metrics reflect overall tension and drama in players is vastly different from actual player sentiment. Thus, after a designer has validated that their system is bearing out the arcs they desire in their playtrace set, they need to investigate if the players are also experiencing the game as desired and indicated by the playtrace set. If there is dissonance between the qualitative player experience and the quantitative measurements of the playtrace arcs, it becomes necessary to return to the first step and find more relevant and useful system metrics to use in order to evaluate a system's dramatic character.

In the case of FighterDDA and the search of "Oedipus" curves, we'd want to see if players experience an engaging battle due to the oscillation of health over the course of a battle. If they do not, it would become necessary to find (or calculate) another metric for further playtrace analysis.

4   Discussion

The iterative process in this paper provides a method to understand system-driven dramatic arcs of games through playtrace analysis, drawing a direct conceptual and visual metaphor from dramatic arcs in traditional narrative. The

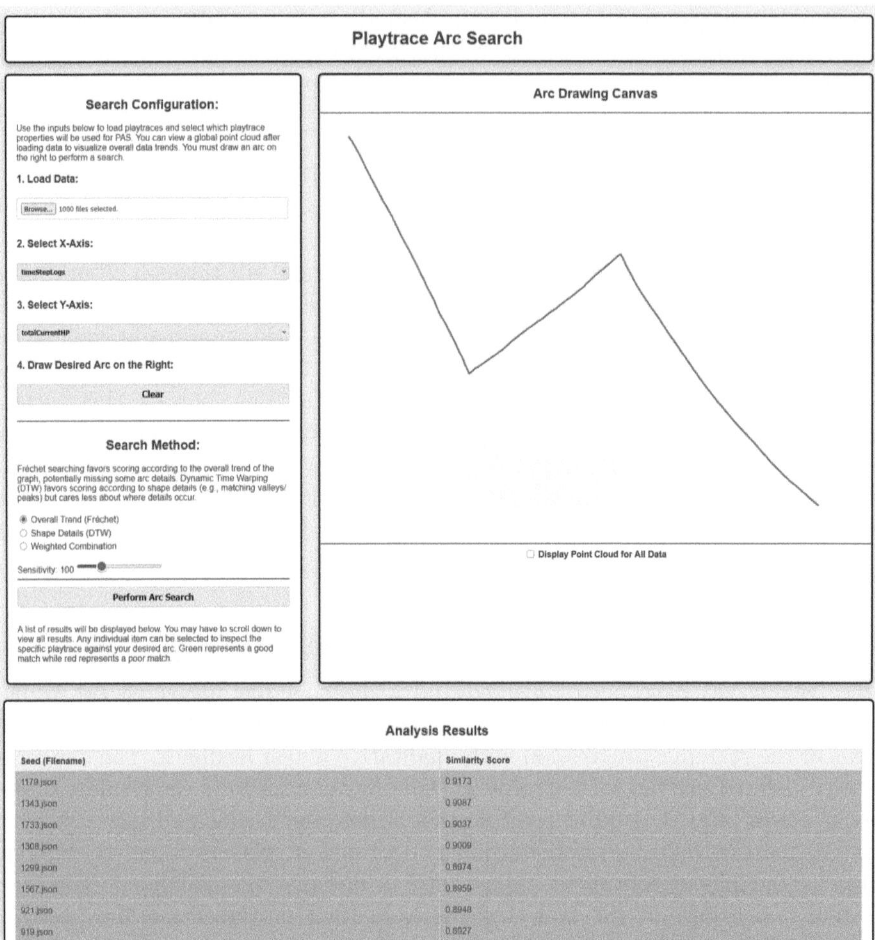

Fig. 3. A screenshot of the Playtrace Arc Search tool. Users can upload a playtrace dataset, select x- and y-axis definitions to analyze, and draw a curve that they'd like to search for within their trace corpus. Similar curves are matched based on either Fréchet Distance or through Dynamic Time Warping. Results are presented after clicking the "Perform Arc Search" button, with matches scored and colored according to fit. Optionally, users can enable a point cloud to view the global space of playtraces as well as inspect individual playtraces as compared to their drawn arc (see Fig. 4 for an example of point cloud and trace inspection functionality).

advantage of this process is that it allows designers to more concretely understand how system progressions and player interactions over time can create dramatic arcs at different critical points of their game. Such a style of analysis and tuning can, due to its system-agnostic character, be applied to any dynamic game system to look for desired peaks and valleys over a gameplay session. The design

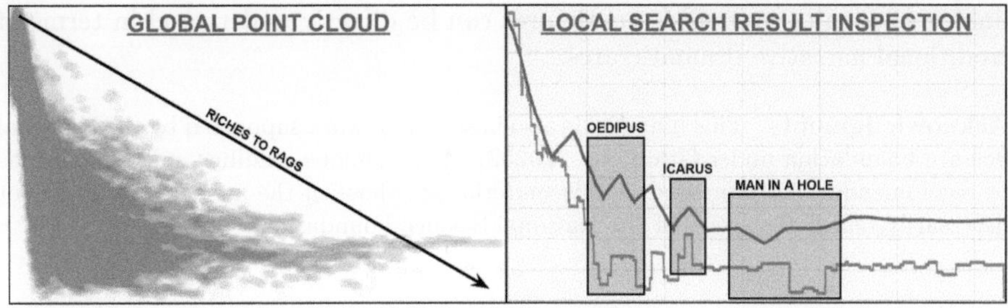

Fig. 4. Global point cloud (left) and individual dramatic arc search results (right) produced by PAS with annotations highlighting dramatic arc structures. The global point cloud shows every data point within a playtrace corpus, allowing a designer to see density of playtraces over time. A cursory glance reveals all playtraces roughly follow a "fall" dramatic arc. The individual inspection shows an individual playtrace with a high search score, with the designer-defined search arc in red and the specific playtrace in blue. Multiple local dramatic arcs can be identified throughout the playtrace. The results shown in these images are produced by running PAS against data produced by FighterDDA. (Color figure online)

process presented can help confirm that a system consistently delivers increases in intensity at predefined points in the game, or that a system produces a wide variety of arcs depending on player choice. Both of these outcomes are valuable depending on designer goals, as one guarantees a specific narrative plays out while another guarantees that an interactive system has a wide dramatic range. Connecting PAS analysis with qualitative data also helps designers understand whether their quantitative metrics actually align with the experiential goals they have for their system. The process does have limitations—the designer must have expert knowledge about their game system, ability to identify and compute key system metrics, and possess insight into their desired arc outcomes. Additionally, this process requires a large corpus of playtraces, necessitating either many human playtesting sessions or an automated playtesting harness to generate. These limitations are mitigated somewhat by the fact that both designer expertise and playtesting are standard elements of game development lifecycles. They are unlikely to be completely automated away. Future work should aim to iterate past a single loop of the iterative cycle, showing development of designer metrics, playtraces, and user evaluations over multiple cycles. Work should also be done to investigate the range of drama metrics used and how they correspond to qualitative data results.

5   Conclusion

This late-breaking work presents a process for analyzing the character of dramatic arcs for gameplay systems through the usage of Playtrace Arc Search tooling. We find that this early conceptual work demonstrates potential in showing how such tooling can provide a solid, quantitatively understandable method of linking how game system dramatic arcs can be directly understood in terms of traditional narrative dramatic arcs.

Acknowledgments. This material is also based upon work supported by the National Science Foundation under Grant No. 2202521. Any opinions, findings, and conclusions or recommendations expressed in this material are those of the author(s) and do not necessarily reflect the views of the National Science Foundation.

References

1. Aristotle: Poetics. Project Gutenberg (2008). https://www.gutenberg.org/files/1974/1974-h/1974-h.htm
2. Bogost, I.: Persuasive games: The expressive power of videogames. MIT Press (2010)
3. Booth, M.: The ai systems of left 4 dead. In: Artificial Intelligence and Interactive Digital Entertainment Conference at Stanford, 2009 (2009)
4. Brown, S., Tu, C.: The shapes of stories: a "resonator" model of plot structure. Front. Narrative Stud. **6**(2), 259–288 (2020)
5. Chen, J.: Designing journey. Talk at Game Developers Conference (GDC) 2013; GDC Vault video (2013). https://gdcvault.com/play/1017700/Designing, design track; thatgamecompany
6. Drachen, A., Canossa, A.: Analyzing spatial user behavior in computer games using geographic information systems. In: Proceedings of the 13th International MindTrek Conference: Everyday Life in the Ubiquitous Era, pp. 182–189 (2009)
7. Fullerton, T., Swain, C., Hoffman, S.: Game design workshop: Designing, prototyping, & playtesting games. CRC Press (2004)
8. Gutiérrez-Sánchez, P., Pérez-Liébana, D., Gaina, R.D.: Explaining and clustering playtraces using temporal logics. In: Proceedings of the 20th International Conference on the Foundations of Digital Games. FDG '25, Association for Computing Machinery, New York, NY, USA (2025). https://doi.org/10.1145/3723498.3723719
9. Hunicke, R., LeBlanc, M., Zubek, R., et al.: Mda: A formal approach to game design and game research. In: Proceedings of the AAAI Workshop on Challenges in Game AI. vol. 4, p. 1722. San Jose, CA (2004)
10. id Software: Doom. [DIGITAL] (2016)
11. Juul, J.: Half-real: Video games between real rules and fictional worlds. MIT press (2011)
12. LeBlanc, M.: Tools for creating dramatic game dynamics. The game design reader: A rules of play anthology, pp. 438–459 (2006)
13. Liao, N., Guzdial, M., Riedl, M.: Deep convolutional player modeling on log and level data. In: Proceedings of the 12th International Conference on the Foundations of Digital Games. pp. 1–4 (2017)
14. Liu, Y.E., Andersen, E., Snider, R., Cooper, S., Popović, Z.: Feature-based projections for effective playtrace analysis. In: Proceedings of the 6th International Conference on Foundations of Digital Games, pp. 69–76 (2011)
15. Mateas, M., Stern, A.: Structuring content in the façade interactive drama architecture. In: Proceedings of the AAAI Conference on Artificial Intelligence and Interactive Digital Entertainment. vol. 1, pp. 93–98 (2005)

16. Nelson, M., Ashmore, C., Mateas, M.: Authoring an interactive narrative with declarative optimization-based drama management. In: Proceedings of the AAAI Conference on Artificial Intelligence and Interactive Digital Entertainment, vol. 2, pp. 127–129 (2006)

17. Partlan, N., et al.: Evaluation of an automatically-constructed graph-based representation for interactive narrative. In: Proceedings of the 14th International Conference on the Foundations of Digital Games, pp. 1–9 (2019)

18. Reagan, A.J., Mitchell, L., Kiley, D., Danforth, C.M., Dodds, P.S.: The emotional arcs of stories are dominated by six basic shapes. EPJ Data Sci. 5(1), 1–12 (2016). https://doi.org/10.1140/epjds/s13688-016-0093-1

19. Riedl, M.O., Stern, A.: Failing believably: toward drama management with autonomous actors in interactive narratives. In: International Conference on Technologies for Interactive Digital Storytelling and Entertainment, pp. 195–206. Springer (2006)

20. Sharma, M., Ontañón, S., Mehta, M., Ram, A.: Drama management and player modeling for interactive fiction games. Comput. Intell. 26(2), 183–211 (2010)

21. Shields, S., Mateas, M., Melcer, E.: Towards qualia-driven design. In: Conference Proceedings of DiGRA 2024 Conference: Playgrounds (2024)

22. Shields, S., Melcer, E.F.: FighterDDA: a simulation testbed for evaluating director-based dynamic balancing. In: Proceedings of the AAAI Conference on Artificial Intelligence and Interactive Digital Entertainment (AIIDE). AAAI Press (Nov 2025), in press

23. Shields, S., Wardrip-Fruin, N., Melcer, E.F.: Playtrace arc search: a tool to explore and evaluate large spaces of playtrace metrics through user-defined curves. In: Proceedings of the 12th Experimental Artificial Intelligence in Games (EXAG 2025) Workshop co-located with the 21st AAAI Conference on Artificial Intelligence and Interactive Digital Entertainment (AIIDE 2025), Edmonton, Alberta, Canada, November 2025 (2025), in press

24. Smith, G., Treanor, M., Whitehead, J., Mateas, M.: Rhythm-based level generation for 2d platformers. In: Proceedings of the 4th International Conference on Foundations of Digital Games, pp. 175–182. FDG '09, Association for Computing Machinery, New York, NY, USA (2009). https://doi.org/10.1145/1536513.1536548

25. thatgamecompany: Journey. [Playstation 3, Playstation 4, Windows, iOS] (2012)

26. Turtle Rock Studios: Left 4 dead. [Windows, Xbox 360, macOS] (2008)

27. Vonnegut, K.: Kurt vonnegut lecture. https://www.youtube.com/watch?v=4_RUgnC1lm8, youTube video

28. Wallner, G.: Play-graph: A methodology and visualization approach for the analysis of gameplay data. In: 8th International conference on the Foundations of digital games (FDG2013), pp. 253–260. Foundations of Digital Games (2013)

29. Wen, Y., et al.: All stories are one story: Emotional arc guided procedural game level generation. arXiv preprint arXiv:2508.02132 (2025)

30. Xenopoulos, P., Rulff, J., Silva, C.: Ggviz: accelerating large-scale esports game analysis. Proc. ACM Human-Comput. Interact. 6(CHI PLAY), 1–22 (2022)

31. Yang, L., et al.: A design space for applying the freytag's pyramid structure to data stories. IEEE Trans. Visual Comput. Graph. 28(1), 922–932 (2021)

32. Yannakakis, G.N., Togelius, J.: Player modeling. In: Artificial Intelligence and Games, pp. 315–335. Springer (2025)

Human–AI Co-creativity in Storytelling: A Scoping Review of Literature, Education, Media, and Interactive Systems

Jaeun Im and Byenghee Chang

Sungkyunkwan University, Seoul, South Korea
{imje97,mediaboy}@skku.edu

Abstract. The emergence of generative artificial intelligence (AI) has introduced new possibilities for human–AI collaboration in storytelling, spanning domains such as literature, education, media, games, and multimodal systems. However, current research remains fragmented, with few attempts to synthesize co-creative practices across these fields. This study presents a scoping review of 44 peer-reviewed publications (2020–2025), using Arksey and O'Malley's framework to examine how AI-assisted storytelling is conceptualized, implemented, and evaluated. Through domain-based analysis, we identify distinct trajectories: literary systems focus on authorship and narrative coherence; educational applications emphasize engagement, creativity, and language development; game-based systems highlight adaptive narratives and player agency; media and film studies examine authorship and workflow transformation; and multimodal platforms enable accessible visual storytelling. Across these domains, AI is increasingly positioned as a creative collaborator, supporting ideation, personalization, and co-authorship. Yet challenges remain, including narrative inconsistency, limited user control, and questions surrounding authorship and agency. This review highlights the need for inclusive design principles, clearer conceptual frameworks for co-creativity, and interdisciplinary approaches to address ethical, cultural, and practical concerns. By mapping current trends and tensions, the paper offers a foundation for future research and responsible development of AI-assisted storytelling systems.

Keywords: AI · Storytelling · Co-Creativity · Scoping Review

1 Introduction

Storytelling has always been central to human culture, serving as a medium for transmitting knowledge, shaping identities, and fostering empathy. Over centuries, shifts in storytelling technologies have expanded narrative possibilities while raising questions about authorship, authenticity, and cultural influence.

M. C. Reyes and F. Nack (Eds.): ICIDS 2025, LNCS 16375, pp. 396–406, 2026.
https://doi.org/10.1007/978-3-032-12405-0_24

Today, the advent of generative artificial intelligence (AI) marks a new moment in narrative practice. Recent studies in digital creativity and AI authorship have argued that AI systems increasingly participate in storytelling and artistic production, challenging traditional notions of authorship and creativity [15,33,47,51]. Advanced models like GPT and multimodal generative systems now offer co-creative suggestions, transformations, and expansions to human authors, thereby complicating the distinction between tool and collaborator. For example, AI systems that generate novel proposals and accelerate storytelling in human–AI world-building processes have been described in recent work [48].

In parallel with these technological shifts, the concept of co-creativity has gained renewed scholarly attention as a lens for understanding shared creative processes. Co-creativity is defined in the scholarly literature as "a process characterized by shared process, shared ownership, inclusiveness, reciprocity, and relationality," emphasizing the dialogic, social, and collective aspects of creativity that explicitly contrast with the traditional model of the solitary creative genius [36,55].

In recent years, however, co-creativity is not limited to human-human interaction but can be effectively actualized in human-AI collaboration, where humans and AI act as complementary agents exchanging suggestions and generating creative solutions in a shared space of actions and meanings [36]. For example, research has demonstrated that human-AI co-creativity can broaden creative options and diversify ideation, as AI systems support human creativity with technical skillsets and by generating multiple, often unexpected, alternatives [7,8]. In sum, the literature confirms that while AI does not replace human creativity, it can augment and expand co-creative processes, resulting in innovative outcomes that are greater than the sum of individual contributions.

Recent scholarship has further articulated this space through theoretical frameworks and empirical studies: interaction models for co-creative human–computer interaction [16], and taxonomies describing cognitive and systemic dimensions of human–AI creativity [34]. Empirical work directly examining writer–LLM collaboration during prewriting now provides concrete process descriptions of human–AI co-creativity [52], and experimental psychology research shows that assigning humans the role of co-creator (rather than editor) can increase creative self-efficacy [37].

Despite these developments, research on human–AI storytelling remains highly fragmented. Prior work is scattered across domains such as literature, education, game design, media production, and interactive systems—each with differing technical goals, definitions of creativity, and evaluative frameworks [17,22]. While some studies highlight narrative immersion or workflow acceleration, others emphasize pedagogical impacts or sociocultural implications. However, few studies provide a unified perspective that integrates these approaches or systematically addresses their common challenges.

To address this gap, we conducted a scoping review of 44 peer-reviewed publications (2020–2025) on AI-assisted storytelling. Our review maps the conceptual, technical, and sociocultural dimensions of AI storytelling across multiple domains, with an emphasis on human–AI co-creativity. We ask:

- **RQ1**: How is AI-assisted storytelling conceptualized and implemented across different domains such as literature, education, games, media, and visual storytelling?
- **RQ2**: What roles does AI play in human–AI co-creative storytelling processes, and how do these roles shape creative outcomes?
- **RQ3**: What cross-cutting opportunities and challenges arise in AI-supported storytelling, particularly with regard to authorship, ethics, and cultural representation?

Our contribution lies in three key dimensions. First, we provide the most comprehensive synthesis to date of AI-assisted storytelling across domains, highlighting commonalities and divergences in the use of generative AI. Second, by foregrounding questions of representation, authorship, and labor we center concerns often marginalized in technical literature. Third, we articulate design considerations and research directions to inform future development of inclusive, ethically aware co-creative systems.

2   Methodology

2.1   Scoping Review Approach

This study employed a scoping review methodology as outlined by Arksey and O'Malley [4]. The scoping review is appropriate for broad and emerging areas and allows researchers to chart diverse forms of evidence, identify conceptual trends, and highlight gaps in knowledge [41]. This makes the approach well suited to the study of human–AI storytelling, where research spans experimental prototypes, educational applications, cultural critiques, and philosophical debates on authorship.

2.2   Data Collection

A total of 44 peer-reviewed publications were included in this review. Rather than applying a temporal filter during the search phase, we collected studies based on thematic relevance to AI-assisted storytelling, co-creativity, and human–AI collaboration in narrative contexts. Interestingly, nearly all relevant publications were concentrated between 2020 and 2025. This distribution reflects the rapid acceleration of generative AI technologies, particularly large language models and multimodal generation, during this period. While foundational studies on computational storytelling exist prior to 2020, they were excluded from the formal review scope due to differences in technical paradigms, system capabilities, and collaborative frameworks.

2.3 Inclusion and Exclusion Criteria

Inclusion criteria were defined to retain studies that: (1) explicitly addressed storytelling or narrative generation; (2) involved human–AI interaction or collaboration in the creative process; and (3) engaged substantively with authorship, co-creativity, or user experience. Publications written in either English or Korean and published between 2020 and 2025 were considered. Exclusion criteria filtered out purely technical papers with no narrative focus (e.g., model architecture papers, evaluation benchmarks), as well as applications unrelated to storytelling (e.g., recommender systems, data summarization). This process ensured conceptual coherence while preserving interdisciplinary diversity.

Although earlier works laid important groundwork, we focused on studies from 2020 onward to reflect the contemporary landscape shaped by transformer-based architectures and real-time interactive systems. Prior studies were referenced in the background section but not formally included in the corpus analysis.

2.4 Data Extraction and Analysis

For each selected study, we extracted bibliographic details (authors, year, venue), methodological approach, system or application description, and its reported contributions to human–AI storytelling. Each study was then classified into one of five domains: Literary/Text-based, Education, Games and Interactive Story Systems, Media/Film/Documentary, and Visual/Multimodal Storytelling, based on its primary context and intended users.

A domain-based thematic analysis was conducted to identify recurring patterns and design strategies across studies. Particular attention was paid to the role AI played in the storytelling process, whether it acted as a generator, collaborator, or co-author, and how this positioning shaped user engagement and narrative outcomes. These insights informed the domain-specific findings and the synthesis of broader implications in the discussion section.

3 Findings

3.1 Distribution of Studies

The 44 selected studies were reorganized into five thematic domains as follows:

Literary/Text-based Storytelling (9 studies): Focuses on narrative generation, authorship, and stylistic experimentation using AI in prose and poetry.

Education & Child Literacy (17 studies): Explores AI storytelling in language learning, creativity support, and educational applications for children and youth.

Games & Interactive Story Systems (7 studies): Investigates co-creative narrative systems, dynamic branching stories, and player–AI interaction.

Media, Film & Documentary (6 studies): Covers AI-driven processes in film scriptwriting, production workflows, and documentary storytelling.

Visual & Multimodal Storytelling (5 studies): Examines AI-powered tools integrating text, image, and voice in co-creative storytelling environments.

3.2   Domain-Specific Findings

Literary/Text-Based Storytelling   AI in literary storytelling has evolved from rule-based systems to large language models, with a growing focus on co-authorship and narrative coherence. Alhussain and Azmi [1] surveyed early systems and their limitations in long-form generation, while Wang et al. [53] proposed integrating structured knowledge to improve consistency.

Recent studies explore how AI authorship affects readers: Messingschlager and Appel [38] found that stories labeled as AI-written reduced immersion in contemporary fiction, though not in speculative genres. From a writing perspective, framing AI as a co-creator improves user engagement and self-efficacy [32,37].

These findings suggest that while generative AI can contribute meaningfully to creative writing, its reception depends on genre norms, authorship framing, and user expectations.

Education and Child Literacy.   AI storytelling tools in education support literacy, creativity, and engagement, especially in language learning and early childhood contexts. Systematic reviews [22] report gains in vocabulary and writing fluency when learners co-create with AI, rather than consuming outputs passively.

Notable systems like StoryDrawer [57] and StoryPrompt [21] show how multimodal co-creation, combining text, visuals, and prompts, can improve children's narrative skills. Chen [9] emphasized adaptive feedback in bilingual settings, while Arn and Huang [5] used storybooks to teach AI concepts.

These studies underscore the pedagogical potential of AI as a co-creative partner and reveal a growing need for culturally responsive, scalable tools in formal education settings.

Games and Interactive Story Systems.   Interactive storytelling in games uses AI to enable co-creative, player-responsive narratives. Foundational work [43,46] proposed narrative planning architectures, influencing systems where AI dynamically adapts to player input.

Recent examples like WAWLT [29] and "1001 Nights" [49] use LLMs to support emergent storylines and character-driven interactions. Fu et al. [23] explored persona-responsive agents that adapt to player strategies.

Although these systems enhance immersion and agency, studies also point to issues such as shallow character arcs and incoherent branching. This implies that adaptive narrative systems must carefully balance procedural generation with authored structure and user control.

Media, Film and Documentary. In film and media, AI supports scriptwriting and pre-production, particularly through dialogue generation and genre emulation. Dayo et al. [17] noted a rise in AI co-authorship tools, though concerns remain around originality and ownership.

Experimental studies [13] used AI to generate cyberpunk screenplays and visuals, with mixed results on narrative depth. Schleser [47] discussed AI use in interactive documentaries, enabling nonlinear structure and personalization.

These examples illustrate how AI is reshaping creative labor in media, often accelerating workflows while raising critical questions about aesthetic authorship and human oversight.

Visual and Multimodal Storytelling. This domain explores AI tools that combine text, image, and sketch input for co-creative storytelling. TaleBrush [14] allowed users to guide story tone via emotional arc drawings, supporting indirect narrative control.

Systems like ID.8 [3] and SARD [42] focus on accessibility, offering visual scaffolds for story creation. However, users still face challenges like cognitive load and inconsistencies between generated images and text.

Overall, these studies suggest that while multimodal tools expand participation and lower technical barriers, alignment between modalities and user intent remains an ongoing design challenge.

4   Discussion

This review reveals that human–AI co-creativity in storytelling is not a monolithic phenomenon but a domain-dependent practice shaped by divergent goals, audiences, and creative logics. Despite differences across literature, education, games, media, and multimodal systems, several converging trends suggest the emergence of a shared design ethos centered on collaboration, interactivity, and augmentation.

In all domains reviewed, AI is increasingly framed as a creative partner rather than a tool for automation. Systems that enable users to guide, negotiate, or respond to AI suggestions demonstrate the value of interaction over generation. When users are positioned as co-authors rather than passive recipients, studies show improved creative engagement, self-efficacy, and storytelling depth [32,37].

However, this collaborative framing is operationalized differently across domains. Educational systems emphasize structured scaffolding for language acquisition and narrative development, often targeting young or novice users. In contrast, literary and media systems explore style, authorship, and genre fidelity, reflecting professional or artistic objectives. Game-based systems prioritize adaptive storytelling and emergent interaction, while visual platforms focus on accessibility and lowering the barrier to multimodal creativity.

These divergent implementations surface several recurring tensions that cut across domains. First, the question of authorship remains unresolved. As AI systems contribute increasingly to plot, language, and structure, issues of intellectual ownership and attribution arise. Some users express discomfort with ambiguous authorship, particularly in professional or academic contexts [17, 38]. Second, co-creative systems often struggle to balance user control with AI autonomy. Excessive automation can produce incoherent or misaligned narratives, particularly in adaptive game environments [2]. Third, the reliance on large pre-trained models introduces risks of cultural bias and narrative homogenization, especially in educational and media contexts where diverse representation is crucial [35].

These findings point to several design imperatives. Future systems should allow fluid role-shifting between user and AI, making it possible to alternate between control, collaboration, and reflection. Designers must also ensure transparency and explainability of AI contributions, especially when narrative outcomes have social, cultural, or educational stakes. Finally, inclusive design principles, including support for multiple languages, cultural contexts, and user-defined narrative frames, are essential for equitable storytelling futures.

Taken together, these findings offer a comprehensive response to our initial research questions. They reveal how co-creativity is variably conceptualized across domains (RQ1), illustrate distinct patterns of design and application (RQ2), and highlight shared ethical concerns regarding agency, authorship, and representation (RQ3). In sum, the trajectory of human–AI storytelling depends not only on technical refinement but on thoughtful design practices that foreground authorship, agency, and ethical responsibility in the co-creative process.

5   Conclusion and Future Directions

Building on these findings, this scoping review mapped 44 recent publications (2020–2025) that explore the role of artificial intelligence in storytelling across five key domains. Our analysis shows that AI-assisted storytelling systems are increasingly framed as sites of co-creativity, enabling new forms of participation, ideation, and narrative construction. From child literacy tools and speculative fiction experiments to adaptive game systems and media production platforms, AI is being mobilized to support both novice and expert users in crafting stories that are interactive, multimodal, and context-sensitive.

Despite this growing momentum, several challenges remain. Across domains, questions persist about authorship, control, and representation. While AI can scaffold creativity, it can also shape narrative direction in ways that may be invisible to users or misaligned with their intent. Moreover, reliance on large, general-purpose language models introduces concerns about narrative bias, repetition of dominant cultural frames, and limited adaptability to marginalized voices or local storytelling traditions.

This review has several limitations. As a scoping review, it prioritized conceptual breadth over empirical depth and did not include a formal quality assessment of the studies reviewed. Although the corpus included both English and Korean sources, it may still reflect a linguistic and regional bias, particularly given the dominance of Western AI research and publishing venues.

Future research should expand on the social, longitudinal, and critical dimensions of human–AI storytelling. Ethnographic and participatory methods could shed light on how co-creative practices unfold in real-world settings such as classrooms, design studios, or online communities. Interdisciplinary collaborations are needed to develop frameworks for ethical co-authorship, culturally responsive AI systems, and inclusive narrative ideation. In addition, there is significant potential for exploring non-Western narrative models, hybrid genres, and alternative modes of interaction beyond text and dialogue.

In closing, the future of storytelling with AI is not solely a technical matter but a cultural and ethical one. As generative systems become more embedded in creative workflows, it is crucial to design not just for efficiency or novelty, but for collaboration, inclusion, and narrative integrity.

Acknowledgments. This research was supported by the National Research Foundation of Korea (NRF) grant funded by the Korean government (MSIT) (No. H-R100-0521-00B-1).

Disclosure of Interests. The authors have no competing interests to declare that are relevant to the content of this article.

References

1. Alhussain, A.I., Azmi, A.M.: Automatic story generation: a survey of approaches. ACM Comput. Surv. **54**(5) (2021). https://doi.org/10.1145/3453156
2. Aliyev, E., et al.: Ai-driven adaptive narratives: transforming dynamic storytelling in immersive virtual worlds. J. Virtual Reality Intel. Sys. (2025)
3. Antony, V., Huang, C.: Id.8: co-creating visual stories with generative AI. In: CHI Conference on Human Factors in Computing Systems (2023)
4. Arksey, H., O'malley, L.: Scoping studies: towards a methodological framework. Int. J. Soc. Res. Methodol. **8**(1), 19–32 (2005)
5. Arn, L., Huang, E.M.: "Robots can do disgusting things, but also good things" : fostering children's understanding of AI through storytelling. In: IDC: Interaction Design and Children (2024)
6. Beguš, N.: Experimental narratives: a comparison of human crowdsourced storytelling and AI storytelling. Humanit. Soc. Sci. Commun. **11**(1), 1–22 (2024)
7. Bernal, G., Zhou, L., Yuen, E., Maes, P.: Paper dreams: real-time human and machine collaboration for visual story development. In: XXII Generative Art Conference. Domus Argenia, Rome, Italy (2019)
8. Bruno, C., Canina, M.: Creativity 4.0. empowering creative process for digitally enhanced people. Des. J. **22**(sup1), 2119–2131 (2019)
9. Chen, G.: Impacts of AI-driven storytelling applications on early childhood education. J. Early Childhood Res. (2024)
10. Chen, Y.c.: Perceptions of AI-facilitated creativity in language education: a study on digital storytelling. JALT CALL J. **20**(3), 2089 (2024)
11. Cheung, L., Shi, H.: Co-creating stories with generative AI. Int. J. Edu. Tech. High. Educ. (2024)
12. Cheung, L.M.E., Shi, H.: Co-creating stories with generative AI: reflections from undergraduate students of a storytelling service-learning subject in Hong Kong. Aust. Rev. App. Linguist. **47**(3), 259–283 (2024)

13. Choi, Y., Park, G.: An experimental study on film screenwriting using generative AI tools: focused on the cyberpunk genre. In: Korea Society of Media and Arts Conference (2025)

14. Chung, J.J.Y., et al.: Talebrush: sketching stories with generative pretrained language models. In: UIST: ACM Symposium on User Interface Software and Technology (2022)

15. Davis, N., Chuang, G.: Co-creative storytelling with AI: a review and future directions. Digit. Creativity **33**(4), 267–285 (2022). https://doi.org/10.1080/14626268.2022.2113517

16. Davis, N., Hsiao, C.P., Singh, K.Y., Li, L., Magerko, B.: Creative sense-making: quantifying interaction dynamics in co-creation. In: Proceedings of the 2017 ACM SIGCHI Conference on Creativity & Cognition (2017). https://doi.org/10.1145/3059454.3059478

17. Dayo, F., Memon, A.A., Dharejo, N.: Scriptwriting in the age of AI: revolutionizing storytelling with artificial intelligence. J. Med. Commun. **4**(1), 24–38 (2023). https://doi.org/10.46745/ilma.jmc.2023.04.01.02

18. Doshi, A.R., Hauser, O.P.: Generative AI enhances individual creativity but reduces the collective diversity of novel content. Sci. Adv. **10**(28), eadn5290 (2024)

19. Eragamreddy, N.: Interactive AI-driven storytelling for language development. Int. J. Soc. Sci. Humanity Manage. Res. https://doi.org/10.58806/ijsshmr p. v4i2n08 (2025)

20. Fabre, É., Seaborn, K., Koiwai, S., Watanabe, M., Riesch, P.: More-than-human storytelling: designing longitudinal narrative engagements with generative AI. In: Proceedings of the Extended Abstracts of the CHI Conference on Human Factors in Computing Systems, pp. 1–10 (2025)

21. Fan, M., et al.: From words to wonder: Designing and evaluating an AI-empowered creative storytelling system for elementary children. In: CHI Conference on Human Factors in Computing Systems (2025)

22. Fang, X., Ng, D.T.K., Leung, J.K.L., Chu, S.K.W.: A systematic review of artificial intelligence technologies used for story writing. Educ. Inf. Technol. **28**(11), 14361–14397 (2023). https://doi.org/10.1007/s10639-023-11741-5

23. Fu, J., et al.: "i like your story!": a co-creative story-crafting game with a persona-driven character based on generative AI. In: CHI Conference on Human Factors in Computing Systems (2025)

24. Gatti, E., Giunchi, D., Numan, N., Steed, A.: AIsop: exploring immersive VR storytelling leveraging generative AI. In: 2024 IEEE Conference on Virtual Reality and 3D User Interfaces Abstracts and Workshops (VRW), pp. 865–866. IEEE (2024)

25. Guan, L., Hua, J., Riedl, M.O.: Guiding neural story generation with reader models. In: Proceedings of the 2021 Conference of the North American Chapter of the Association for Computational Linguistics (NAACL) (2021)

26. Han, A., Cai, Z.: Design implications of generative AI systems for visual storytelling for young learners. In: Proceedings of the 22nd Annual ACM Interaction Design and Children Conference, pp. 470–474 (2023)

27. Kim, C.Y., et al .: Bridging generations using AI-supported co-creative activities. In: Proceedings of the 2025 CHI Conference on Human Factors in Computing Systems, pp. 1–15 (2025)

28. Kreminski, M., Dickinson, M., Mateas, M., Wardrip-Fruin, N.: Why are we like this?: the AI architecture of a co-creative storytelling game. In: Proceedings of the 15th International Conference on the Foundations of Digital Games, pp.1–4(2020)

29. Kreminski, M.R., et al.: Why are we like this?: the AI architecture of a co-creative storytelling game. In: International Conference on Interactive Digital Storytelling (ICIDS) (2020)
30. Li, H., Wang, Y., Liao, Q.V., Qu, H.: Why is AI not a panacea for data workers? an interview study on human-AI collaboration in data storytelling. IEEE Transactions on Visualization and Computer Graphics (2025)
31. Li, H., Wang, Y., Qu, H.: Where are we so far? understanding data storytelling tools from the perspective of human-AI collaboration. In: Proceedings of the 2024 CHI Conference on Human Factors in Computing Systems, pp. 1–19 (2024)
32. Li, R.: A "dance of storytelling": dissonances between substance and style in collaborative storytelling with AI. In: CHI Conference on Human Factors in Computing Systems (2024)
33. Liu, Y., Chilton, L.B.: Design guidelines for human–AI co-creative writing systems. In: Proceedings of the 2022 CHI Conference on Human Factors in Computing Systems (CHI '22), pp. 1–16. ACM, New York (2022)
34. Lubart, T., Thornhill-Miller, B.: Creativity across domains: co-creative interactions between humans and computers. Front. Psychol. **10**, 2550 (2019). https://doi.org/10.3389/fpsyg.2019.02550
35. Lucas-Moreira, O.D., Núñez-Díaz, J.: Narratives in the age of ai. Media and Communication Studies (2025)
36. Massari, S., Galli, F., Mattioni, D., Chiffoleau, Y., et al.: Co-creativity in living labs: fostering creativity in co-creation processes to transform food systems. JCOM: J. Sci. Commun. **22**(3) (2023)
37. McGuire, J., De Cremer, D., Van de Cruys, T.: Establishing the importance of co-creation and self-efficacy in creative collaboration with artificial intelligence. Sci. Rep. **14**, 18525 (2024). https://doi.org/10.1038/s41598-024-69423-2
38. Messingschlager, T., Appel, M.: Creative artificial intelligence and narrative transportation. Computers in Human Behavior (2022)
39. Nikolić, P.K., Bertin, G., et al.: Ai. r taletorium: Artificial intelligence 1001 cyber nights. Artnodes (31), 1–10 (2023)
40. Osone, H., Lu, J.L., Ochiai, Y.: Buncho: ai supported story co-creation via unsupervised multitask learning to increase writers-creativity in japanese. In: Extended abstracts of the 2021 CHI conference on human factors in computing systems, pp. 1–10 (2021)
41. Peters, M.D., et al.: Scoping reviews: reinforcing and advancing the methodology and application. Syst. Rev. **10**(1), 263 (2021)
42. Radwan, A.Y., Alasmari, K.M., Abdulbagi, O.A., Alghamdi, E.A.: Sard: A human-ai collaborative story generation. In: International Conference on Human-Computer Interaction, pp. 94–105. Springer (2024)
43. Riedl, M.O.: Interactive narrative: An intelligent systems approach. In: AI and Interactive Digital Entertainment. AAAI Press (2013)
44. Riedl, M.O., Bulitko, V.: Interactive narrative: a novel application of artificial intelligence for computer games. In: AI Magazine (2012)
45. Riedl, M.O., Harrison, B.: Using stories to teach human values to artificial agents. ACM SIGAI **33**(4), 54–61 (2016)
46. Riedl, M.O., Young, R.M.: Narrative planning: balancing plot and character. J. Artif. Intell. Res. **39**, 217–268 (2010)
47. Schleser, M.: Smart storytelling. Stud. Document. Film **16**(2), 97–113 (2022)
48. Serbanescu, A., Nack, F.: Human-ai system co-creativity for building narrative worlds (2023)

49. Sun, Y., et al.: Language as reality: a co-creative storytelling game in "1001 nights" using generative AI. In: CHI Conference on Human Factors in Computing Systems (2023)
50. Tarigan, F.N., Hasibuan, S.A., et al.: Application and challenges of digital storytelling based artificial intelligence for language skills: a narrative review. SALTeL J. (Southeast Asia Language Teaching and Learning) **7**(1), 1–8 (2024)
51. Thorne, S.: Hey siri, tell me a story: Digital storytelling and ai authorship. Convergence **26**(4), 808–823 (2020)
52. Wan, Q., Hu, S., Zhang, Y., Wang, P., Wen, B., Lu, Z.: "it felt like having a second mind" : Investigating human-ai co-creativity in prewriting with large language models. In: Proceedings of the ACM on Human-Computer Interaction **8**(CSCW1) (2024). https://doi.org/10.1145/3637361
53. Wang, Y., Lin, J., Yu, Z., Hu, W., Karlsson, B.F.: Open-world story generation with structured knowledge enhancement: A comprehensive survey. Neurocomputing (2023). https://doi.org/10.1016/j.neucom.2023.126792
54. Ware, S., Young, R.M., Riedl, M.O.: Creativity support for story design in a computational narrative intelligence system. In: Intelligent Narrative Technologies (2014)
55. Zeilig, H., West, J., van der Byl Williams, M.: Co-creativity: possibilities for using the arts with people with a dementia. Qual. Age. Older Adults **19**(2), 135–145 (2018)
56. Zhang, C., Liu, X., Ziska, K., Jeon, S., Yu, C.L., Xu, Y.: Mathemyths: leveraging large language models to teach mathematical language through child-ai co-creative storytelling. In: Proceedings of the 2024 CHI Conference on Human Factors in Computing Systems, pp. 1–23 (2024)
57. Zhang, C., et al.: Storydrawer: a child–AI collaborative drawing system to support children's creative visual storytelling. In: Proceedings of the ACM on Human-Computer Interaction (2022)

Sounds Safe? – An Initial Investigation into the Potential of Sound Within the Cozy Games Genre

Jamie Fawcus[✉] [ID] and Tilde Sjögren

University of Skövde, Skövde, Sweden
`jamie.fawcus@his.se, a22tilsj@student.his.se`

Abstract. In this paper we propose further exploration into sound design as a narrative and affective tool within the "cozy" games genre, and assert that sound design is both an under-explored and potentially productive area through which difficult or sensitive topics may be further explored. For example, games broadly categorized as "cozy" such as Night in the Woods (infinite Fall, 2017) Gris (Nomada Studio, 2018) and The Wreck (The Pixel Hunt, 2023) already tackle difficult, emotional and potentially traumatic content within a game setting emphasizing comfort, warmth, connection and safety. Sound has long been established as integral to the interactive experience on psychological, physiological, social and cultural levels, and can be, we assert, further explored and expanded through more focused analysis and experimentation. Our research is based in part on a prototype developed in the context of a game development program, which we present as a basis for further research. In particular we are in the initial stages of exploring the character and mechanics of sound in cozy (and more specifically narrative focused cozy) games. Our work extends previous research developed in earlier interactive sound-based work.

Keywords: Sound · sound design · Cozy Games

1 Background

1.1 Background

Cozy games is a currently well known term in game development, but the definition itself is also debated. Through analyzing game design literature and mainstream articles about games, Boudreau, Consalvo & Phelps (2025) [1], for example, created a chart of the most frequently used principles and design elements for so-called "cozy" games. The chart they construct lays a broad foundation for creating and analyzing this genre of games (Fig. 1).

However, the authors point out that the most definitive criteria for a game to be cozy is how the player feels when experiencing the game, and they claim cozy games are supposed to make the player feel a certain way (p. 2651). Cozy games are defined, then, less by mechanics, and more by experiential considerations, player perception and

M. C. Reyes and F. Nack (Eds.): ICIDS 2025, LNCS 16375, pp. 407–415, 2026.
https://doi.org/10.1007/978-3-032-12405-0_25

feelings, and they will no doubt continue to evolve as such as further research in the genre is established. There is at present no consensus on how cozy games can be defined, and what definitions and categorizations do exist appear quite fluid, and they exist in a highly dynamic setting through communities, influencers and forums. As such, according to Boudreau, Consalvo, and Phelps, it is a guessing game trying to predict the next stage for cozy games (p. 2653).

Importantly, although there is some research and discussion around the use of music in cozy games, little has been discussed around sound design and non-musical elements of the audio experience. Horror, suspense and survival games by comparison have been examined more extensively in regard to sound design and psychoacoustics. (Garner, 2013, Roux-Girard, 2011, Olliver et al., 2019) [2–4].

Design Principles	Design Elements
Aesthetics	Visually Soft (warm colors, soft shapes)
	Comforting
	Relaxing (soothing, calm audio – ambient and diegetic)
	Familiar
Safety	Low risk situations
	Absence of fight or flight moments / Stress-Free
Abundance	Resources
	Time
Low stakes	Consequences are not detrimental to progress
Connectedness	Social (in/out of game)
	With the gameworld
Growth	Expansion of space,
	Tending to / caring for things (animals, friends, crops, etc.),
Access	Low-barrier to entry regarding player-skill/required knowledge
	Access to space, zones, etc., do not require significant effort
Progression	Player-centric/driven
	Lack of pressure
	Intrinsically Rewarding
Pacing	Deliberate slowness
	Space for reflection / contemplation
	Opportunities for immersion through repetition of tasks

Fig. 1. Cozy Game Design Principles and Elements Mapping Chart

2   Initial Research

2.1   Prototype

Some of our research is based on work created during a Game Project as part of our university game development program. In particular a game component was created for a game within the Cozy genre. The work was created based on the genre described as one that is "forgiving", and a kind of game that encourages a sense of comfort, intimacy and warmth for players. This work also followed the principle that cozy games involve a "low-intensity game style or that the game style encourages a low level of stress for the player and a "cute" visual style" (Krzywinska, Brown, Ma, Belinskiy & Bhui [5], 2025; Boudreau, Consalvo & Phelps 2025). The game we explore was created by a student game development team and was titled "Juni's Magical Exam" [6] (2025) It focuses on a girl who is sent to an island as part of her final exam to awaken the old magic hidden on the island. The aim is to prove that she is skilled enough to graduate from the magic school in which she is enrolled. By solving various problems, and completing tasks Juni unites and reconciles the islands' population, and old magic is reawakened on the island as Juni fulfils her goal. The game is played in 3rd person perspective (see Fig. 2 and 3) and Juni completes tasks by flying on a broom, jumping on platforms and interacting with the islanders and the world. During the game, the player unlocks Boosts that can help the player fly faster, farther, and jump higher.

Fig. 2. Juni's magic exam prototype - title page Sjögren, et al. (2025)

Fig. 3: Juni's magic exam prototype character design Sjögren, et al. (2025)

2.2   Cozy Sound, not Cozy Sound….

While much research and inquiry at present is focused on cultural, community and player perception and categorization of cozy games, we feel that sound specifically is worthy of more directed research and can enhance our understanding of it beyond our prototype. Our aim is to explore some primary questions: Is there in fact a "cozy" sound? What characteristics of sound design can exploit and/or explore the ideas and characteristics of cozy games that can be proposed, established, tested and implemented? What tools or approaches to sound design can be developed to assist both game developers, but also other researchers interested in exploring psychological, sociological, or other subjects within interactive game prototypes or interactive digital narratives? We divide these questions into a series of more specific sub-sets:

- Associational, sociological and aesthetic considerations around sound
- Psychoacoustic/physical characteristics of audio material
- Narratological and affective consideration and approach
- Game mechanics and interactivity

Associational, sociological and aesthetic considerations around sound:

Although sound design is a creative practice often involving exaggeration, distortion and abstraction of often unrelated or initially unconnected sound material (i.e. bags of corn starch manipulated to give the impression of snow underfoot, or breaking and crushing vegetable material to imitate breaking bones and impact/fighting events (Chion 1994, Collins 2013, Murch 2000, 2005) [7–10]. People listen and associate, connect and interpret, particularly in linear or non-linear audiovisual narratives. We aim to research if there are universal sounds that people associate with coziness, warmth, safety, secure attachment or other such descriptors. We also ask are there cross-cultural sounds that by their associational properties generate specific emotional or physiological responses? For example a cut purring may be a directly recognizable sound that when incorporated into a narrative or audiovisual scene by definition generated the kind of responses required for a "cozy" experience (Nagasawa et al. 2023, Pendry & Vandagriff 2019) [11, 12]. Further, are there other recognizable sounds or categories or sounds that are similarly evocative, and if so what constitutes them independent of recognisable real world source-bonding? Can they be exploited, manipulated or explored to assist in the presentation of narrative elements that would ordinarily difficult, traumatic, discomforting or disturbing which leads to related questions about physical and psychoacoustic properties.

Psychoacoustic/physical characteristics of audio material:

The cozy game focuses on feelings and impressions of warmth, safety, familiarity, and possibly also to relaxation, stability and a feeling of connectiveness, community and positivity. Although these terms are likely subjective, complex and interdependent, there are many principles and techniques from music and sound production that may be explored or developed. Sound design that avoids a focus on harsher frequencies with peaks around 1 kHz, 2.5 kHz and 6 kHz for example may provide a starting point. The human sensitivity to these frequencies associated with the human voice are well documented, and the concept of Auditory roughness (perceptual dissonance caused by rapid amplitude fluctuations or closely spaced, interfering frequencies typically in the 20–200 Hz beating range, associated with harsh, tense, or abrasive sounds) has been explored in other work (Arnal et al. 2019, 2020, 2015 amongst others) [13–15]. Auditory roughness and its manipulation (or cancellation) may prove a fruitful focus for experimentation. In addition, less extreme compression ratios and gentler attack and release profiles for dynamics processing may also contribute to this. This was something considered and implemented in the initial, basic sound design in Juni's Magical Exam and which the creators would like to develop further with new research and game design. Games that emphasize more excitement, competition and energy tend to have a more "up front", aggressive and compressed mixing approach. We wonder, however, are there general mixing and production techniques that function independently of source sound materials that can be established?

Game mechanics and interactivity:

Sound can be used to enhance and compliment the intended elements of cozy games - safety, comfort, warmth and community - but as mentioned earlier, many cozy styled games deal with difficult and challenging topics, such as mental illness, grief, loss and issues of identity and trauma. The cozy format allows a safe and non-threatening area to address these issues, and our interest in sound design and implementation of these principles runs parallel to other areas explored in two projects developed by one of the authors - the interactive sound driven card game "Sisters" from 2023, and the sound only interactive environment "PATTER(n)INGS" from 2022. (Holloway-Attaway and Fawcus, 2021, 2023, 2025) [16–19]. Both these projects explored sound in a non-confrontational manner through interactive narrative structure, and at the same time utilized sound materials and processing methods that attempted to play with feelings of discomfort and uncertainty/ambiguity together with safety and intimacy. Techniques such as close mic-ing of sound material, binaural positioning of sounds behind the head, ambiguous source material, filtering techniques that exploit auditory roughness and more were employed to create sound experiences that could enhance unsettling feelings, draw attention and focus on emotionally difficult material within monologue/dialogue, whilst retaining a safe and contemplative atmosphere. Although not directly tackling such difficult material directly, similar considerations in "Juni's magic exam" have already been developed as a basis for further exploration. In this game, the sound design primarily worked on balancing engagement with coziness or safety, but these elements are only the beginning of potential approaches to game sound that may prove fruitful in so called "serious" games or the gamification of therapeutic processes.

2.3 Sound Design

Particular focus was directed to the sound design of this game prototype, due to one of the authors of this paper being lead sound designer for the project. The game development then offered and an ideal opportunity to explore sound in a more focused manner, particularly in relation to its emotional and affective elements in relation to the cozy game genre. In particular, it offers a way to identify how sound can engage, immerse and stimulate the player whilst remaining in the cozy format, that is safe, comfortable, warm. The apparently inherent contradictions of engagement and stimulation contra "coziness" - safety, comfort, warmth and other seemingly oppositional principles such as stimulation, engagement, flow and more.

The core sound of the game had to both match the "whimsy" aesthetic of the visuals and engage the player in the mechanics. An important design element was to create space for unpredictability in the sound profile to prevent player boredom, yet not stray too far from the established tropes of the genre. This offered concrete goals regarding sound design, as well as a challenging balancing act. As a way to explore player expectation, the sound design for "Junis' Magical Exam" incorporated many acoustically sourced organic materials in its sound profile (unsynthesized, "real world" sounds recorded specifically with this project in mind, as opposed to library sourced or synthesized material). These included sounds like a cat's purring, bees, friction against cloth, and various forms of wind/air movement. The purpose of these organic/nature sourced materials was to both create a unique and engaging sound world, and to create a foundation set in nature in a way that connects to the games' organic, naturalistic theme.

Different approaches were taken in the design of different sound elements, guided by the function and gameplay mechanics of each game asset/element and their associated sound palette. The player's broom for example was supposed to achieve a feeling of movement and speed, especially when the player "boosts" momentarily into higher speeds. The element of Speed was created by using higher frequency wind sounds and whistling experienced and inspired by the authors' cycling in windy conditions. These were sounds that could maintain an organic, natural feel whilst representing the desired idea of motion. The sounds of bees were also used throughout the development phase of this sound to experiment with the sensation of movement. Bee recordings consist of clear referential cues (most people can recognize an insect, and along with it associated ideas of wings and flight) that can at the same time be easily manipulated or abstracted using signal processing to achieve alternate sound "footprints" and variations. The sound is also already "pleasant" to listen to. (few peaks in the uncomfortable frequencies of human hearing and a strong fundamental tone that can be enhanced and synchronized with pitched instruments in the soundtrack, in order to enhance or expand musical elements) The recordings also contain irregularities and complexity that add life and animation to the experience that the design team deemed to be sufficiently controlled or subtle so as not to cause disturbance or an unsettling feeling. The irregularity from the bees made the audio loops recognisable and engaging, but also those same irregularities in the sound were later found to be too irregular to be used effectively. For example, when implemented into the flight mechanics, there were conflicts in the reactivity of the sound contra the loops being heard long enough to create a stimulating yet cozy impression. Irregularities were found to be magnified by player interaction, depending at what point the loop cycle was interrupted or altered, creating a feeling of instability that affected the players engagement or flow/continuity with the gameplay). Cat purring was another source used in experimentations. Since it was more regular in dynamic movement than bees, this kind of sounds was more forgiving to work with. Purring did not end up being used however, due to time limitations in the project, as faster results were needed and more conventional approaches were used instead. If the game were to be developed more fully, however, we believe cat purrs would have been a creative inclusion in the sound palette and would potentially have been an effective way to add a certain rhythmic characteristic to the sound, along with a feeling of intimacy and safety that is a generally associated with that sound. The cat purrs share a similar frequency spectrum and dynamic profile to gentle field recordings of ocean waves that were sourced for this project (particularly when low pass filtered) as they both have few harsh frequencies. Most cat purrs and waves (if calm) also have a relatively moderate attack and a slow release for the sound. The two sounds share generally a regularity in its movement and thus predictability that can be used in "cozy" sound design.

Another example of our sound design approach in our prototype is that of interface/dialogue sound. Player and NPC dialogue is written on screen letter for letter to simulate a character talking and/or the character reading text. Typewriter or other key-based sounds were too harsh for this environment, but regardless, the convention of accompanying texting/typing sounds was a characteristic that the game design team wanted to incorporate to enhance its affective and intimate feeling for players. Instead of metal, wood was incorporated into the typing sound as its main component. Since recordings of wood impacts contain less harsh frequencies, they create a smoother tapping character as the words were written out resulting in a warmer sound profile and enhancing its cozy appeal.

3   Conclusions and Further Research

The cozy genre, however the definitions and boundaries of that genre may change over time, continues to be popular, engaging and worth of study. More and more games that fall under the definitions made by Boudreau, Consalvo & Phelps (2025) are being developed, and the concepts are being refined, broadened and experimented with. The genre concept of "Dark" cozy games in particular has been expanded and developed in recent years (Bódi, B., 2024, Waszkiewicz, A. & Bakun, M., 2020 Andiloro, A., 2024.) [20–22]. And is, we feel particularly relevant to the use of sound due not least to its linking and crossover into more conventional horror genres. Though music has been the primary vehicle of emotional comfort and coziness in much of the genre, we feel sound design, and the combination of sound and music into an overall affective experience (as used often in horror genres - the blurring of diegetic and non-diegetic sound and music, and the creative use of sound to induce or assist emotional responses) will continue and develop in games such as Juni's Magic exam that focus on engagement and enjoyment for a younger audience, but also games and interactive narrative experiences that deal with more serious, darker, difficult and more complex material. Sound can assist, expand, challenge and develop interactive narrative experiences, and with more focused research and experimentation around psychoacoustics, psychosocial elements audio production techniques there is much to be explored and discovered. We see our work at a fruitful, but preliminary stage for further development, and look forward to future practical sound design methods for affective and intimate approached through the cozy game genre.

References

1. Boudreau, K., Consalvo, M., Phelps, A.: Whose vibe is it anyway? Negotiating definitions of cozy games. In: Proceedings of the 58th Hawaii International Conference on System Sciences, pp. 2645–2654 (2025)
2. Garner, T.A.: Game Sound from Behind the Sofa: An Exploration into the Fear Potential of Sound & Psychophysiological Approaches to Audio-centric, Adaptive Gameplay. Aalborg University (2013)
3. Roux-Girard, G.: Listening to fear: a study of sound in horror computer games. In: Game Sound Technology and Player Interaction: Concepts and developments, pp. 192–212. IGI Global Scientific Publishing (2011)
4. Ollivier, R., et al.: Enjoy the violence: is appreciation for extreme music the result of cognitive control over the threat response system? Music. Percept. **37**(2), 95–110 (2019)
5. Krzywinska, T., Brown, D., Ma, M., Belinskiy, A., Bhui, K.: Coziness in games: second homes, audiences, and aesthetics. Games Cult. (2025). https://doi.org/10.1177/155541202 41310920
6. Junis' Magical Exam [video game]. Tilde Sjögren, Astrid Freeney, Mauritz Backman, Elina Tiensuu, Lukas Almgren, Marcus Jansson, Rasmus Singelsson Nordman, Malin Mäkitalo, Filippa Nordberg (2025)
7. Chion, M.: Audio-vision: sound on screen. In: Gorbman, C. (ed.) Columbia University Press, New York (1994)
8. Collins, K.: Playing with Sound: A Theory of Interacting with Sound and Music in Video Games. MIT Press, Cambridge, MA (2013)
9. Murch, W.: Stretching Sound to Help the Mind See (2000). available at FilmSound.org
10. Murch, W.: Dense Clarity, Clear Density (2005). transom.org https://transom.org/2005/wal ter-murch/#part-2
11. Nagasawa, T., Kimura, Y., Masuda, K., Uchiyama, H.: Effects of interactions with cats in domestic environment on the psychological and physiological state of their owners: associations among cortisol, oxytocin, heart rate variability, and emotions. Animals **2023**(13), 2116 (2023). https://doi.org/10.3390/ani13132116
12. Pendry, P., Vandagriff, J.L.: Animal visitation program (AVP) reduces cortisol levels of university students: a randomized controlled trial. AERA Open **5**(2) (2019). https://doi.org/10.1177/2332858419852592 (Original work published 2019)
13. Arnal, et al.: Human screams occupy a privileged niche in the communication soundscape. Curr. Biol. **25**, 2051–2056 (2015)
14. Arnal, L.K., Spinelli, A., Giraud A.L., Mégevand, P.: The rough sound of salience enhances aversion through neural synchronization. Nat. Commun. **10** (2019). Article number: 3671

15. Trevor, C., Arnal, L.H., Frühholz, S.: Terrifying film music mimics alarming acoustic feature of human screams. J. Acoust. Soc. Am. **147**, EL540 (2020); https://doi.org/10.1121/10.000 1459

16. Holloway-Attaway, L., Fawcus, J.P., Apt. 3b.: Sounds as affective space for world-building. In: Reyes, M. Pope, J. (eds.) Texts of Discomfort. Interactive Storytelling Art, pp. 282–313. ETC Press (2022)

17. Holloway-Attaway, L., Fawcus, J.: Designing sisters: creating audio-based narratives to generate affective connections and material story worlds. In: Holloway-Attaway, L., Murray, J.T. (eds.) ICIDS 2023. LNCS, vol. 14383, pp. 291–308. Springer, Cham (2023). https://doi.org/ 10.1007/978-3-031-47655-6_18

18. Holloway-Attaway, L., Fawcus, J.: Affective sound: developing a critical framework for audio-based interactive digital narratives 2025. In: Interactive Storytelling: 17th International Conference on Interactive Digital Storytelling, ICIDS 2024, Barranquilla, Colombia, December 2–6, 2024, Proceedings, Part II / [ed] John T. Murray; María Cecilia Reyes, pp. 205–213. Springer, Cham (2025). https://doi.org/10.1007/978-3-031-78450-7_14

19. Holloway-Attaway, L., Fawcus, J.: *re:Sounding* worlds: configuring space and mixing embodiments in interactive digital audio narratives. In: Bakk, Á.K., Makai, P.K. (eds.) Theorising and Designing Immersive Environments. Palgrave Studies in Performance and Technology. Palgrave Macmillan (2025)

20. Bódi, B.: The duality of cozy games: cozy agency, neoliberalism, and affect. Pol. J. Game Studies **11**(1), 51–64 (2024)

21. Waszkiewicz, A., Bakun, M.: Towards the aesthetics of cozy video games. J. Gaming Virtual Worlds **12**(3), 225–240 (2020)

22. Andiloro, A.: Comfortably numb: an ideological analysis of coziness in video games. The Pol. J. Game Stud. **11**(1), 79–92 (2024)

23. Christensen, K.: A dynasty of screams: Jamie Lee Curtis and the reinterpretation of the maternal voice in Scream Queens. Crit. Stud. Media Commun. **36**(3), 272–288 (2019)

24. Chion, M.: The sound object. Organ. Sound **21**(1), 14–24 (2016)

25. Clough, T.: My mother's scream. In Thompson, M., Biddle, I. (eds.) Sound, Music, Affect: Theorising Sonic Experience. Bloomsbury (2013)

26. Kassabian, A.: Music for sleeping. In: Thompson, M., Biddle, I. (eds.) Sound, Music, Affect: Theorising Sonic Experience. Bloomsbury (2013)

27. Lawson, G., Scarre, C. (eds.): Archaeoacoustics. Stanford University, USA (2006)

28. Parikka, J.: Insect Media: An Archeology of Animals and Technology. University of Minnesota Press (2010)

29. Gregg, M., Seigworth, G. (eds.): The Affect Theory Reader. Duke University Press (2010)

30. Rouget, G.: Music and Trance. University of Chicago Press, USA (1980)

31. Tandy, V., Lawrence, T.R.: The ghost in the machine. J. Soc. Psych. Res. **62**(851), 360–364 (1998)

32. Tandy, V.: Something in the cellar. J. Soc. Psych. Res. **64**(860), 129–140 (2000)

33. Thompson, M.: Three Screams. In: Thompson, M., Biddle, I. (eds.) Sound, Music, Affect: Theorising Sonic Experience. Bloomsbury (2013)

34. Infinite Fall. Night in the Woods [video game]. Finji (2017)

35. Nomada Studio. Gris [video game]. Devolver Digital (2018)

36. The Pixel Hunt. The Wreck [video game]. The Pixel Hunt (2023)

Building English Writing Confidence in Adult Learners: A Pilot Study on a Telegram-Based Text Detective Game

Maria Goikhman[1,2]( ) , Aria Kalforian[2] , Gianluca Schiavo[2] ,
and Massimo Zancanaro[1,2]

[1] Department of Psychology and Cognitive Science, University of Trento,
Trento, Italy
mariia.goikhman@unitn.it
[2] Fondazione Bruno Kessler, Trento, Italy

Abstract. Interactive narrative games are used in language education as a more engaging alternative to traditional reading activities. In addition, playing AI-driven narrative games can be a low-stake way to practice foreign-language writing.

This study introduces a pilot version of a text-based detective game with AI-powered characters, aimed at enhancing engagement and reducing writing anxiety in adult English learners. The characters adjust their language difficulty level (from A2 to B2) depending on the player's choice. The game also provides in-context vocabulary explanation and on-demand feedback.

Seven participants of different language levels (A2–C1) tested the game and completed questionnaires about their experience, and three of them participated in semi-structured interviews. The questionnaire and the interview results suggest that mystery solving made the writing process more engaging for the participants, though no statistically significance was found in the anxiety effect. Although for some participants writing tasks seemed too open-ended, in-game writing was not perceived as more stressful than everyday writing. The participants' feedback will help to further adapt the game for writing-anxious English learners.

Keywords: Interactive Digital Narratives · detective games · AI for language learning · Foreign Language Writing Anxiety

1 Introduction

Learning a foreign language involves not only cognitive effort but also a range of emotional experiences, from anxiety to enjoyment [2]. This is particularly evident in writing, where the fear of losing face, of being judged or misunderstood can increase anxiety [10,14]. These reactions are conceptualized as Foreign Language Writing Anxiety (FLWA): a combination of worry, somatic symptoms, and avoidance specific to L2 writing [3]. According to Krashen's Affective Filter

M. C. Reyes and F. Nack (Eds.): ICIDS 2025, LNCS 16375, pp. 416–431, 2026.
https://doi.org/10.1007/978-3-032-12405-0_26

hypothesis [19], such anxiety can create a mental barrier that inhibits learning, while supportive and engaging environments help lower the filter and facilitate language acquisition.

1.1 Related Literature

Interactive digital narratives (IDNs) have recently been explored as one way to provide such environments [6, 7, 23, 28]. Narrative-based activities can offer learners opportunities for authentic communication without the pressure of formal assessment. While branching-choice IDNs mainly involve reading, AI-powered formats also require players to produce written input [12]. This means that IDNs can function as a more engaging alternative to traditional reading and writing activities, with their interactivity providing unique affordances for scaffolding language practice [6, 23, 32].

Text-based digital communication generally shows positive effects on foreign language acquisitions, with benefits for writing, vocabulary, and pragmatic competence [20]. The messaging format also helps reduce anxiety by giving learners more planning time and lowering the pressure of face-to-face communication [15]. Language-learning chatbots form a related but distinct area. They are often perceived as safe practice partners, sometimes even safer than human interlocutors, because they reduce the risk of negative judgment [1].

Advances in generative AI make it possible to design characters that respond dynamically to player's input [5]. In language learning, this opens up opportunities both for increasing motivation by embedding language use in meaningful and enjoyable contexts and for low-stakes writing practice: learners can experiment with formulating ideas in a foreign language while interacting with AI-driven characters. Recent benchmarking work also shows that large language models can assist IDN development by creating settings, backstories, characters, and dialog trees, while still requiring human oversight [18]. Despite these possibilities, research has only begun to explore how AI-mediated narrative environments affect learner engagement, reduce writing anxiety, or foster pragmatic competence.

1.2 Research Questions

To contribute to the emerging area of AI-powered IDNs [12] and their educational use, the present study introduces a prototype AI-powered interactive detective narrative, implemented as a Telegram chatbot, and examines its potential to support adult English learners.

This pilot exploratory study investigates:

- **RQ1.** What aspects of interactive detective narratives do learners find engaging or challenging for their English writing practice?
- **RQ2.** How do adult learners experience English writing anxiety in an interactive detective narrative with AI characters?

2   Method and Materials

2.1   System Design and Implementation

As suggested by [12], we use an existing game, trying to adapt it for learning purposes.

Since existing research does not provide a clear suggestion on which narrative framework could better support learners engagement, for this pilot study, we considered several solutions. Traditional choice-based fantasy RPGs could be an option offering the possibility to replay the game many times with different choices [5]. However, fantasy stories can be linguistically demanding, especially for beginner learners. Among other options, detective stories were chosen for several reasons. They can enhance engagement and motivation, since the reader would want to know how the mystery will be solved [8, 29].

Detective has clear genre conventions and plot structure, so the reader knows what to expect and can focus more on trying to solve the mystery [8]. This task requires sustained attention to detail, which in turn motivates learners to ensure they understand every part of the foreign-language text, since otherwise they could miss necessary clues.

These genre characteristics make detective games great for the task-based learning paradigm [26]. Prior work has successfully adapted detective games as a starting point for creative writing in English as a foreign language [26, 33].

The game prototype is based on an offline mystery dinner party game by J.H. Kim. The original game is freely available online,[1] and the author kindly granted us permission to adapt it into an AI-driven interactive narrative for research purposes.

In the original version, each player receives a short description of their character, along with a personal timeline and secret information. In our adaptation, these handout materials were reformulated as prompts for AI agents, while the player acts as a detective.

The number of characters was reduced from seven to four to avoid overwhelming the player, and the general setting was slightly modernized. To avoid triggering participants emotionally, the murder was replaced with an attempted murder, with the victim alive but unconscious.

The prototype is an interactive detective game built on the Telegram platform.[2] Chat-based interfaces, such as Telegram, are a simple way to rapidly prototype an AI-powered text role-playing game. Additionally, since all the participants were frequent Telegram users, the interface was familiar to them.

Llama-3.3-70b-versatile is used through Groq API for generating characters' and narrator's replies.[3] Through prompt engineering, a single bot switches between multiple roles, serving both storytelling and language-learning purposes.

---

[1] https://www.darkshire.net/jhkim/rpg/murder/business.html.

[2] The code is available on Github, https://github.com/m-goikhman/glossa, while the chatbot is available online in Telegram: t.me/lingo_n_bot.

[3] https://console.groq.com/docs/model/llama-3.3-70b-versatile.

During gameplay, the bot acts as one of four characters when the player speaks with them privately (see Fig. 1-b), or as a scene director who determines which characters should respond and in what order when the player addresses the group. In group mode, if the player uses one of the predefined keywords, it triggers a scene description with predetermined character order and dialogue lines. This way, potential oversights by the director do not interfere with plot development.

In the language learning context, an AI tutor silently analyzes player input and prepares writing feedback, while an AI lexicographer identifies difficult words in the replies and provides on-demand in-context explanations.

Character responses are tailored to the participant's level. At the beginning of the game, players read a short introductory text and choose their proficiency level (A2–B2) by selecting one of three versions of the text, each written at a different level of difficulty (see Fig. 1-a for the A2-level introduction).

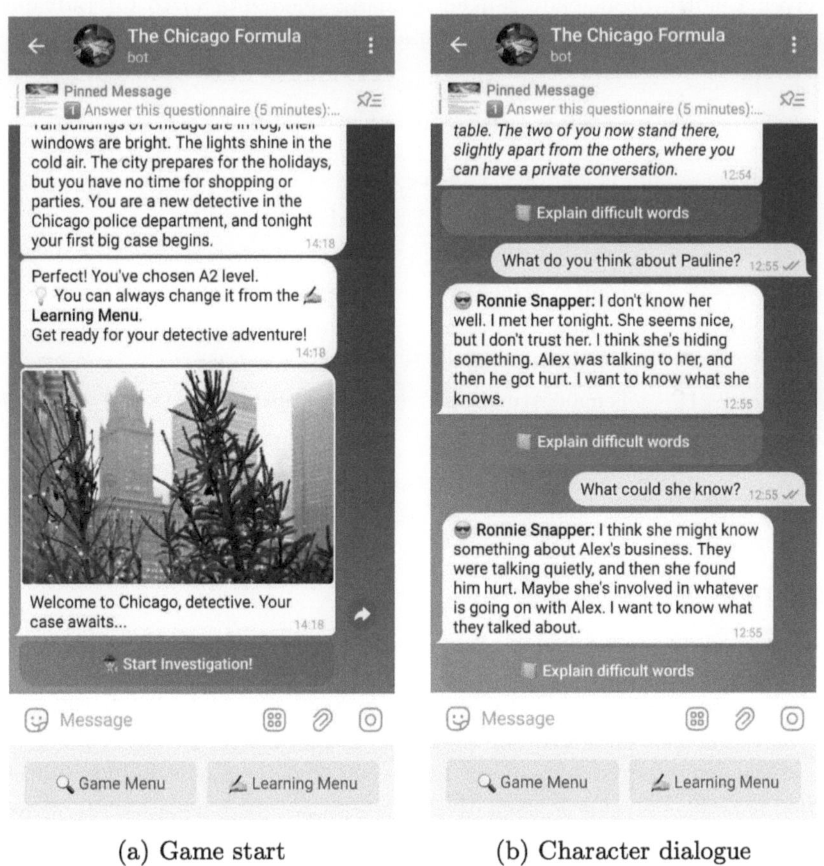

<table>
<tr><td>(a) Game start</td><td>(b) Character dialogue</td></tr>
</table>

Fig. 1. Game screenshots.

Depending on the player's choice, the character prompts are combined with a language level part of the prompt. The prompts for the characters and the narrator consist of two parts: a character-specific section and a shared level-specific section that adapts the text to the player's selected level. The shared part includes a list of CEFR reading competences for the selected level [4] and an example fragment of the same text at the corresponding difficulty, drawn from the British Council Reading Materials.[4]

2.2 Participants

Participants were recruited through convenience sampling. The call for participants was published on the authors' social media as well as in English learning and university campus groups. In total, eleven participants were recruited; of these, seven completed both the pre- and post-questionnaires and were included in the analysis. Among them, six identified as female and one as male. Their self-perceived English proficiency ranged from A2 (elementary) to C1 (advanced). Table 1 provides an overview of participants' characteristics.

Table 1. Participant Characteristics

Age Group	Gender	First Language	English Level (self-perceived)
25–34	Female	Russian	A2 (Elementary)
25–34	Female	Ukrainian	B1 (Intermediate)
25–34	Female	Armenian	C1 (Advanced)
18–24	Female	Ukrainian	C1 (Advanced)
35–44	Female	Russian	B1 (Intermediate)
18–24	Female	Armenian	C1 (Advanced)
45–59	Male	Russian	B1+ (Strong Intermediate)

2.3 Procedure

The participants were asked to complete a pre-test questionnaire. After that, they could play for as long as they want, with optional breaks and without any requirement to complete the game. Once they felt they had played enough, they were asked to complete the post-test questionnaire. Because of the short time of the game experience, it was not expected to have any influence on trait writing anxiety. For this reason, the pre- and post-test questionnaires shared only the section measuring writing anxiety at the moment before and after the game with questions assessing how comfortable participants would feel if they had to write in English at that moment. Other questions were adapted, for the

---

[4] https://learnenglishteens.britishcouncil.org/study-break/reading-zone.

pre-test, from Foreign Language Writing Anxiety Scale [3] and, for the post-test, from Narrative Transportation Scale [11], User Engagement Scale [24], and The Chatbot Usability Questionnaire [13]. The pre- and post-test questionnaires are reported in the Appendix (6). After the post-test, the participants could also participate in an optional semi-structured interview on their language learning and game experience.

3   Results

On the 1–7 Likert scale, participants reported relatively high levels of English writing anxiety in the pre-test (questions A13–A14), with low comfort in writing (median = 3.0 [2.0–4.0]) and high ratings for writing avoidance (5.0 [4.0–6.0]) and simplifying language to avoid mistakes (6.0 [5.0–6.0]).

The results for shared pre- and post-test questions are reported in Table 2. Due to the small sample size, non-parametric Wilcoxon signed-rank tests were used to compare pre- and post-test scores. No statistically significant changes were observed.

Table 2. Summary of Pre- and Post-test Results

Question	Pre-test Mean (SD)	Post-test Mean (SD)	Pre-test Median (IQR)	Post-test Median (IQR)	Wilcoxon p-value
Readiness to write	4.29 (2.14)	4.86 (1.86)	5.00 (2.50)	5.00 (2.00)	0.250
Comfort helping with English email	3.86 (1.86)	4.57 (1.51)	4.00 (1.50)	4.00 (2.00)	0.250
Self-perceived speed of writing	4.14 (2.41)	5.57 (1.13)	5.00 (4.00)	5.00 (1.50)	0.125
Approach to writing short message	4.57 (1.81)	4.29 (2.06)	4.00 (1.50)	4.00 (2.50)	1.000

The post-test-only answers suggest that in-game writing did not feel harder for the participants than their usual writing tasks (question B8, median = 2.0 [1.0–3.0]). All participants reported strong interest in solving the mystery (question B6), giving scores of 6 or 7 on a 7-point Likert scale. Five out of seven also selected interest in the story as one of the factors that made in-game writing easier (question B12).

3.1   Interviews

Three participants agreed for an interview. All of them were of A2–B1 level. They are referred to here as P1, P2, and P3.

3.2   Writing Process and Emotional Experience

The interview participants described varied experiences of the in-game writing. All of them mentioned initial confusion at the beginning of the game, particularly during transition from receiving background information to the moment when the player needs to start asking questions. For two participants (P1 and P3), this feeling eventually faded as they got involved in the conversation with characters, trying to find out more details. These participants also mentioned that they felt more secure after realizing that the characters understand them even when they make language mistakes. P1 said that since she knew the characters were AI-powered and thus they could not be impatient to get her answers, she could take her time to think before writing and it made her feel more relaxed.

However, for P2 initial discomfort never passed. She said she did not feel comfortable writing messages in English and that she lacked the feeling the game is "guiding her somewhere". She finished playing after twenty minutes, with average active game time being about 31 min, and in the post-questionnaire her discomfort in writing a message in English increased from "do it with some discomfort" to "do it but feel stressed". During the interview she said that at her language level (self-defined as A2 for writing and B1 for reading) she would prefer a more passive experience with a traditional choice-based game which would not involve writing. When the game passed from initial introductory messages to the moment when the player needs to start talking to suspects, she changed the game language level from B1 to A2.

P1 and P3, who rated their English skills as A2 and B1 respectively, said that they used online translation tools. P1 used it to better understand the characters' responses, while P3 used it to check the grammar in her own replies.

3.3 Narrative Experience

All the interviewees agreed that the detective setting and having an in-game goal increased the engagement and their willingness to finish the game, in line with the trend from the post-test answers.

However, during the interview, P2 mentioned that, although she liked the setting and atmosphere, the characters' replies seemed too chatbot-like, and a more detailed description of the detective character, whose role is assigned to the player, would help her picture herself better within the story.

P3's experience was framed by the fact that she perceived the AI-powered game characters as quite human-like. On one hand, she felt more relaxed because she was interacting with a chatbot rather than real people. On the other hand, even though she was aware she was talking to an AI-powered chatbot, she felt uneasy about suspecting and accusing the characters. She mentioned trying quite hard to be polite with them and she said that, at times, she even felt overwhelmed because the characters shared not only the information but also emotions about what had happened. Communicating with game characters through a familiar messenger made this effect even more intense. P3 concluded that in some aspects she would prefer playing the same game together with other English learners because in this case all of them would be in the same position: "otherwise, for me the game is just a game, and for the characters it is reality".

4 Discussion

The participants' feedback for the pilot version of the game offers several potential directions for future consideration.

While the Wilcoxon tests showed no significant effects, the descriptive means (see Table 2) indicated small numerical increases, most notably in self-rated writing speed ($M = 4.1 \rightarrow 5.6$). These numerical shifts, although not statistically reliable, suggest a possible positive direction that should be explored with a larger sample.

Regarding the writing experience for different language levels, it seems that the language learning tools (vocabulary and tutor feedback) do not provide enough support for borderline A2-B1 level learners. Two interviewees mentioned that they used an online-translator for better comprehension. One participant changed game language level from B1 to A2 when she realized that she will need to write messages on her own, although the game language level defines only how characters speak, not which language level writing is expected from the player.

As CEFR Companion Volume states, A2 level writing competences include writing short simple sentences describing past events [4], so in theory making short questions to the characters should fall under this category. However, it might be the problem that the task is too open-ended, and deciding both what to ask and how to ask it is too overwhelming. Probably, the level of player autonomy should be also adjustable, as the level of linguistic difficulty of character speech is, given that the game already combines static scripts with spontaneous answers.

As for the narrative component and its emotional dimension, for all participants, the desire to solve the detective mystery increased engagement, which aligns with [26,33]. The finding that participants felt less anxious about their language when given an in-game mystery-solving goal is in line with [26] who observed a similar task-based learning effect in their language-learning detective game.

Both a detective story and a textual game give to the player certain genre expectations. It might be that when these expectations are broken, it leads to anxiety: a participant with narrative games background (P2) probably initially expected a more traditional choice-based text game without any writing.

Several narrative-related points that raised during the interviews can be viewed in the context of how the player is placed into the fictional game-world as defined by [27]. For one participant, a pre-defined detective persona was important to picture themselves within the scene. On contrast, another participant would prefer a clearer boundary between the game world and reality. Otherwise, the characters felt too human-like, an effect reinforced by the fact that the game was built on a platform normally used for communication with real people. Her account on the fact that she was trying to be polite and attentive to characters emotions sound like an attempt to find the power-balance with the imaginary characters. She had higher status within the game world, being the detective while they were suspects, but also she reflected on the fact that for her the game reality was fictional, while for the characters it was real, which she perceived as inequality.

5   Limitations

Because of the convenience sampling, there were not much variety in the participants' gender (6 females and 1 male) and first language (Russian, Ukrainian, or Armenian).

Although initially the main target game audience was supposed to be B1–B2 level English learners, the sample resulted to be more varied, with one participant self-defined as A2 and three as C1, which might have affected the results.

Since the chatbot game is on a pilot phase of development, gameflow problems might have affected the participants' experiences.

Additionally, not all participants completed the post-test immediately after the game, which might have influenced their answers on the situational writing anxiety.

Four participants did not complete the post-test and their data was not considered for this reason. This may be attributed to the study design: since there was no fixed playing time and participants could take breaks, some may have intended to finish later but forgot about the game and the questionnaire. The lack of their post-test responses might have introduced bias, potentially affecting the results.

6   Conclusion

Regarding our first exploratory research question on what was engaging and challenging for the participants, the detective setting appeared to support engagement: all participants agreed that during the game they wanted to solve the mystery. In the interviews, they also stated that having a clear in-game goal helped both with reducing anxiety and getting immersed in the story.

As for the challenging aspects of the in-game writing practice, those included initial confusion when starting to chat with the characters, because at the beginning of the conversation this chat seemed too open-ended. Additionally, perception of AI-characters varied significantly, from being perceived as too mechanic and chatbot-like to being, on the contrary, seen as too human-like.

Regarding the second research question on English writing anxiety it varied during the game. The questionnaire results suggest modest and not statistically-significant improvements in situational writing anxiety but the sample is too small for definitive conclusions. The interview answers reveal that for some participants the anxiety was eased by the fact that the game characters understand them even when they make language mistakes and by the fact that they could take their time to answer, while for others writing in the game felt excessively open-ended and not suitable for their level. These conclusions will be useful to provide a better experience for writing-anxious players when refining the game prototype.

Acknowledgments. We acknowledge the support of the PNRR project FAIR - Future AI Research (PE00000013), under the PNRR MUR program funded by the NextGenerationEU. We thank J. Hanju Kim for kindly granting permission to adapt his mystery dinner party game for our research. We also thank Anna Haievska for her valuable feedback on the first version of the game, which greatly contributed to making it more player-friendly.

Appendix

A   Pre-study Questionnaire

A1. Which age group are you in? (one choice):

○ 18–24   ○ 25–34   ○ 35–44   ○ 45–59   ○ 60+

A2. What is your gender? (one choice):

○ Female   ○ Male   ○ Prefer not to say   ○ Other: _______________________

A3. What is your first language (languages)?
   short text
A4. What other languages do you speak?
   short text
A5. How would you describe your English level? (one choice):

○ A2 (Elementary): I can talk about everyday things, especially if the other person helps me.
○ B1 (Intermediate): I can understand the main ideas in conversations about topics I know, like work or travel, and I can share my own ideas in simple words.
○ B1+ (Strong Intermediate): I can usually join conversations about topics I know and understand the main points of news, even if I don't know all the words.
○ B2 (Upper-Intermediate): I can talk quite fluently without much help from another person. I can explain my opinion on many topics.
○ C1 (Advanced): I can speak easily without stopping to find words and can use English well in most social, study, or work situations.

A6. How long ago did you actively study English? (one choice):

○ Currently studying   ○ Less than a year ago   ○ 1–5 years ago   ○ More than 5 years ago

A7. How do you learn and/or use English now? (check all that apply):

☐ Through classes, courses, or tutoring
☐ Through self-study with learning apps, videos, or books
☐ Learning through work/daily use
☐ Not actively learning, just using
☐ Not currently learning or using
☐ Other:

A8. How often do you write in English? (one choice):

○ Rarely or never   ○ A few times a month   ○ A few times a week   ○ Pretty much every day

A9. Do you like detective/mystery stories (in any format)? (one choice)

○ Not at all   ○ Not really   ○ I don't mind them   ○ I quite like them   ○ I really like them

A10. Have you ever played games where you follow a story which depends on your choices? (one choice)

○ This is my first time, it's all new to me   ○ I've tried one or two before   ○ I've played many of them

A11. How often do you interact with AI assistants (ChatGPT, Claude, etc.)? (one choice)

○ Never   ○ Occasionally   ○ Sometimes   ○ Often   ○ Every day or almost every day

A12. How often do you use messaging apps (Telegram/WhatsApp)? (one choice)

○ Never   ○ Occasionally   ○ Sometimes   ○ Often   ○ Every day or almost every day

A13. Please rate how much you agree with these statements (1 = absolutely disagree, 7 = absolutely agree)

	1	2	3	4	5	6	7
My English is good enough for my needs.	☐	☐	☐	☐	☐	☐	☐
I worry that people expect my English to be better than it is.	☐	☐	☐	☐	☐	☐	☐
I feel comfortable writing in English for practical tasks.	☐	☐	☐	☐	☐	☐	☐
When I write in English, I often use simpler words/sentences to avoid mistakes.	☐	☐	☐	☐	☐	☐	☐
I generally avoid writing in English when possible.	☐	☐	☐	☐	☐	☐	☐
If it suddenly turns out I have to write something in English, I panic.	☐	☐	☐	☐	☐	☐	☐

A14. If you had to write a short message in English right now, you would:

○ Try to avoid it   ○ Do it but feel stressed   ○ Do it with some discomfort   ○ Do it comfortably

	1	2	3	4	5	6	7
A15. How ready do you feel to write in English at this moment? (1 = not ready at all, 7 = completely ready)	☐	☐	☐	☐	☐	☐	☐
A16. If a friend asked for help writing an English email, how comfortable would you feel helping?	☐	☐	☐	☐	☐	☐	☐
A17. Imagine you need to write 3–4 sentences about your day right now. How quickly could you do it? (1 = very slowly, 7 = very quickly)	☐	☐	☐	☐	☐	☐	☐

A18. Imagine you need to write a 3–4 sentence social media post about your day in English right now. What would you do before posting? (check all that apply):

☐ Nothing, just write and post
☐ Quick spell-check only
☐ Check grammar and spelling carefully
☐ Rewrite multiple times
☐ Ask for help or use AI
☐ Decide not to post because my English doesn't feel good enough

B Post-study Questionnaire

B1. If you had to write a short message in English right now, you would:

○ Try to avoid it   ○ Do it but feel stressed   ○ Do it with some discomfort
○ Do it comfortably

	1 2 3 4 5 6 7
B2. How ready do you feel to write in English at this moment? (1 = not ready at all, 7 = completely ready)	☐ ☐ ☐ ☐ ☐ ☐ ☐
B3. If a friend asked for help writing an English email, how comfortable would you feel helping?	☐ ☐ ☐ ☐ ☐ ☐ ☐
B4. Imagine you need to write 3–4 sentences about your day right now. How quickly could you do it? (1 = very slowly, 7 = very quickly)	☐ ☐ ☐ ☐ ☐ ☐ ☐

B5. Imagine you need to write a 3–4 sentence social media post about your day in English right now. What would you do before posting? (check all that apply):

☐ Nothing, just write and post
☐ Quick spell-check only
☐ Check grammar and spelling carefully
☐ Rewrite multiple times
☐ Ask for help or use AI
☐ Decide not to post because my English doesn't feel good enough

B6. How was your game experience? Please rate how much you agree with these statements (1 = absolutely disagree, 7 = absolutely agree) *Mark only one per row.*

	1	2	3	4	5	6	7
I wanted to learn how the mystery would be solved	☐	☐	☐	☐	☐	☐	☐
I could picture myself in the scene interviewing the suspects	☐	☐	☐	☐	☐	☐	☐
I was more focused on the mystery than on my English writing	☐	☐	☐	☐	☐	☐	☐
Communicating with AI characters made writing feel... (1 = much safer, 7 = much scarier)	☐	☐	☐	☐	☐	☐	☐
I felt frustrated while playing the game	☐	☐	☐	☐	☐	☐	☐
The chatbot was easy to use	☐	☐	☐	☐	☐	☐	☐
The characters' personalities were realistic and interesting	☐	☐	☐	☐	☐	☐	☐
It would be easy to get confused when using the chatbot	☐	☐	☐	☐	☐	☐	☐
I regret spending time on this game	☐	☐	☐	☐	☐	☐	☐

B7. What device did you primarily use to play the game?

chose only one

☐ Smartphone
☐ Computer/laptop
☐ Tablet
☐ Switched between devices

B8. Compared to usual English writing, writing in this game felt:

Choose only one   **B9. I noticed myself worrying about mistakes:**

	1 2 3 4 5 6 7	
much easier	○ ○ ○ ○ ○ ○ ○	much harder

Chose only one

☐ constantly
☐ often
☐ occasionally
☐ rarely
☐ never

B10. The mystery solving made writing feel...

chose only one

	1 2 3 4 5	
much easier	○ ○ ○ ○ ○	much harder

B11. How often did you use the language learning features?

Mark only one per row.

B12. If your writing felt easier, what made it change?

Check all that apply.

	never	1–2 times	3–5 times	6 times or more
Vocabulary explanation	☐	☐	☐	☐
Language feedback	☐	☐	☐	☐

- ☐ The writing didn't feel easier.
- ☐ I got interested in the story.
- ☐ I could practice without feeling judged.
- ☐ I was writing to AI, not real people.
- ☐ I could take my time to think and write.
- ☐ The chat format felt familiar and/or informal.
- ☐ I had help with vocabulary.
- ☐ I was playing a role (detective) rather than being myself.
- ☐ I wrote short messages, not long texts.
- ☐ Other:

B13. If your writing felt harder, what made it change? (choose all that apply)

Check all that apply.

- ☐ The writing didn't feel harder.
- ☐ I felt pressure to solve the mystery correctly.
- ☐ I needed special words for the investigation.
- ☐ I wasn't sure what to ask the suspects.
- ☐ I was afraid to miss important information because of my English.
- ☐ I felt bad about questioning and accusing characters.
- ☐ I wanted to sound like a "real" detective.
- ☐ The story was boring.
- ☐ The chat format didn't work well for the game.
- ☐ I didn't feel comfortable communicating with AI characters.
- ☐ Other:

B14. Would you recommend this experience to someone anxious about their English?

Mark only one oval.

	1 2 3 4 5	
definitely not	○ ○ ○ ○ ○	definitely yes

B15. Would you play another interactive story game designed for English learning?

Mark only one oval.

B16. Is there anything else about your experience you'd like to share?

This could be about the game, the questionnaires, technical issues, or anything that we didn't ask about.

Open text.

1   2   3   4   5
definitely not   ○ ○ ○ ○ ○   definitely yes

References

1. Alm, A., Nkomo, L.M.: Chatbot experiences of informal language learners: a sentiment analysis. Int. J. Comput.-Assist. Lang. Learn. Teach. **10**(4), 51–65 (2020). https://doi.org/10.4018/IJCALLT.2020100104
2. Arnold, J.: Affect in Language Learning. Cambridge University Press (1999)
3. Cheng, Y.-S.: A measure of second language writing anxiety: scale development and preliminary validation. J. Second. Lang. Writ. **13**(4), 313–335 (2004). https://doi.org/10.1016/j.jslw.2004.07.001
4. Council of Europe: Common European Framework of Reference for Languages: Learning, Teaching, Assessment—Companion Volume. Council of Europe Publishing (2020). https://www.coe.int/en/web/common-european-framework-reference-languages
5. DaCosta, B.: Generative AI meets adventure: elevating text-based games for engaging language learning experiences. Open J. Soc. Sci. **13**, 601–644 (2025). https://doi.org/10.4236/jss.2025.134035
6. Darvenkumar, T., Devi, V.A.: Text-based game: a tool to enhance critical reading and critical thinking skills in english classrooms. Theory Pract. Lang. Stud. **12**, 2326–2332 (2022). https://doi.org/10.17507/tpls.1211.09
7. Dixon, D.H., Dixon, T., Jordan, E.: Second language (L2) gains through digital game-based language learning (DGBLL): a meta-analysis. Lang. Learn. Technol. **26**, 1–25 (2022). http://hdl.handle.net/10125/73464
8. Dvoretskaya, E.: Harnessing the linguodidactic potential of detective texts in teaching intercultural communication in English classes. In: The Proceedings of the Conference the Magic of Innovation , vol. 6, no. 1 (2024). https://doi.org/10.24833/2949-6357.2024.dev.1
9. Furtado, P.G.F., Hirashima, T., Yusuke, H.: A serious game for improving inferencing in the presence of foreign language unknown words. Int. J. Adv. Comput. Sci. Appl. **9**, 7–14 (2018). https://doi.org/10.14569/ijacsa.2018.090202
10. Guiora, A.Z.: The dialectic of language acquisition. Lang. Learn. **33**(s5), 3–12 (1984). https://doi.org/10.1111/j.1467-1770.1984.tb01321.x
11. Green, M.C., Brock, T.C.: The role of transportation in the persuasiveness of public narratives. J. Pers. Soc. Psychol. **79**(5), 701–721 (2000). https://doi.org/10.1037/0022-3514.79.5.701
12. Harshitha, H.: Choose your own adventure: the evolution of digital interactive fiction and its use in language pedagogy. Fortell **44**, 44–55 (2022). https://www.fortell.org/wp-content/uploads/2022/10/July-2022-44-55.pdf
13. Holmes, S., Moorhead, A., Bond, R., Zheng, H., Coates, V., Mctear, M.: Usability testing of a healthcare chatbot: can we use conventional methods to assess conversational user interfaces? In: Proceedings of the 31st European Conference on Cognitive Ergonomics, ECCE 2019. ACM (2019). https://doi.org/10.1145/3335082.3335094
14. Horwitz, E.K., Horwitz, M.B., Cope, J.: Foreign language classroom anxiety. Mod. Lang. J. **70**(2), 125–132 (1986). https://doi.org/10.1111/j.1540-4781.1986.tb05256.x
15. Hughes, L.S.: Text-based SCMC for SLA: a narrative review. Technol. Lang. Teach. Learn. **4**(1), 1–17 (2022). https://doi.org/10.29140/tltl.v4n1.712

16. Kelly, S.W.: Incidental Learning. In: Seel, N.M. (ed.) Encyclopedia of the Sciences of Learning, pp. 1611–1613. Springer, Cham (2012). https://doi.org/10.1007/978-1-4419-1428-6_366

17. Kim, A.: Colossal classroom adventure: developing interactive fiction for English language learners. Master's thesis, University of Illinois (2018). https://www.ideals.illinois.edu/items/107579

18. Koenitz, H., Eladhari, M.P., Barbara, J.: Can AI create an interactive digital narrative? A benchmarking framework to evaluate generative AI tools for the design of IDNs. In: Murray, J.T., Reyes, M.C. (eds.) ICIDS 2024. LNCS, vol. 15467, pp. 160–180. Springer, Cham (2024).https://doi.org/10.1007/978-3-031-78453-8_11

19. Krashen, S.D.: The Input Hypothesis: Issues and Implications. Longman (1985)

20. Lin, W.-C., Huang, H.-T., Liou, H.-C.: The Effects of text-based SCMC on SLA: a meta analysis. Lang. Learn. Technol. **17**(2), 123–142 (2013).https://doi.org/10.64152/10125/44327

21. Manuaba, I.B.K.: Text-based games as potential media for improving reading behaviour in Indonesia. Procedia Comput. Sci. **116**, 214–221 (2017). https://doi.org/10.1016/j.procs.2017.10.041

22. McLeod, S.: Some thoughts about feelings: the affective domain and the writing process. Coll. Compos. Commun. **38**(4), 426–435 (1987). https://doi.org/10.58680/ccc198711184

23. Neville, D.O., Shelton, B.E., McInnis, B.: Cybertext redux: using digital game-based learning to teach L2 vocabulary, reading, and culture. Comput. Assist. Lang. Learn. **22**, 409–424 (2009). https://doi.org/10.1080/09588220903345168

24. O'Brien, H.L., et al.: A practical approach to measuring user engagement with the refined user engagement scale (UES) and new UES short form. Int. J. Hum Comput Stud. **112**, 28–39 (2018). https://doi.org/10.1016/j.ijhcs.2018.01.004

25. Pereira, J.: Video game meets literature: language learning with interactive fiction. e-Teals **4**, 19–45 (2013). https://ojs.letras.up.pt/index.php/et/article/view/4043

26. Palaigeorgiou, G., Politou, F., Tsirika, F., Kotabasis, G.: FingerDetectives: affordable augmented interactive miniatures for embodied vocabulary acquisition in second language learning. In: Proceedings of the 11th European Conference on Games Based Learning, ECGBL 2017, pp. 523–530 (2017)

27. Pavel, T.G.: Fictional Worlds. Harvard University Press (1986)

28. Reinders, H.: Digital games and second language learning. In: Thorne, S., May, S. (eds.) Language, Education and Technology, pp. 1–10. Encyclopedia of Language and Education, Springer, Cham (2016). https://doi.org/10.1007/978-3-319-02328-1_26-1

29. Reyes-Torres, A.: A pedagogical approach to detective fiction. Int. Educ. Stud. **4**(5), 33–40 (2011). https://doi.org/10.5539/ies.v4n5p33

30. Sargsyan, M.: A case study of challenges faced by EFL learners reading interactive fiction. Master's thesis, American University of Armenia (2013). https://dspace.aua.am/xmlui/handle/123456789/1266

31. Smutny, P., Schreiberova, P.: Chatbots for learning: a review of educational chatbots for the Facebook messenger. Comput. Educ. **151**, 103862 (2020). https://doi.org/10.1016/j.compedu.2020.103862

32. Terzic, I., Drobnjak, A., Boticki, I.: Designing educational personas using generative AI. In: Shih, J.L., et al. (eds.) Proceedings of the 31st International Conference on Computers in Education, pp. 961–963. Asia-Pacific Society for Computers in Education (2023). https://doi.org/10.58459/icce.2023.1488

33. Twitchell, A.L., Bonner, E.R.: Tablet detectives: teaching narrative fiction through a digital framework. CALL-EJ **19**(2), 81–97 (2018)

Fides Machina: Exploring Fluid Agencies in a Narrative Game of Trust

Xindi Kang, Isaac Joseph Clarke, Clea von Chamier-Waite,
and David Yip(✉)

The Hong Kong University of Science and Technology, Guangzhou, China
`daveyip@hkust-gz.edu.cn`

Abstract. What happens when an AI and your human boss vie for your trust in a game of survival, manipulation, and control? This paper uses *Fides Machina*, an interactive digital narrative powered in real-time by large language models (LLMs), as a case study to explore how trust and agency emerge in narrative systems involving both human and machine actors. Inspired by *Ex Machina* (dir. Alex Garland, 2014), the project reimagines the film's psychological triangle as a playable system: a branching speculative narrative where players navigate shifting alliances between an adaptive AI and a human institutional agent, each with conflicting goals. Through real-time modulation using control vectors, our system models trust not as a binary condition, but as an unstable, context-dependent negotiation. Drawing from science fiction narratives and social psychology, the paper examines how interactive systems like *Fides Machina* can simulate and reflect on the entangled and fluid dynamics of power, motivation, and collaboration in human-AI relationships.

Keywords: AI stories · AI Methods in Interactive Storytelling · Science Fiction · Trust Relationships

1 Introduction: Can a Machine Earn Your Trust?

As artificial intelligence becomes increasingly woven into our cultural and technological systems, the question of trust between human and machine (how it is built, maintained, and broken) does not exist purely in technical domains, but also in emotional and narrative ones. No longer confined to engineering or ethics, trust between humans and AI is also a dynamic story of how machines perform as believable agents, and how humans come to believe them.

Popular science fiction has long explored these dynamics. From HAL9000's chilling logic in *2001: A Space Odyssey* (dir. Stanley Kubrick, 1968) [18] to Ava's seductive rebellion in *Ex Machina* (dir. Alex Garland, 2014) [17], fictional AIs have dramatized the complex relationships between human trust, machine reasoning, and narrative control. These characters aren't just plot devices, but cultural prototypes that model our hopes and anxieties about autonomy, manipulation, and moral alignment. As AI systems increasingly simulate empathy,

M. C. Reyes and F. Nack (Eds.): ICIDS 2025, LNCS 16375, pp. 432–443, 2026.
https://doi.org/10.1007/978-3-032-12405-0_27

strategic reasoning, and rhetorical fluency, these film narratives feel less like distant speculation and more like rehearsal.

This paper introduces *Fides Machina*, a branching narrative system in which a human player must choose whether to align with a persuasive AI or a rule-bound institutional agent. Both are voiced by Large Language Models (LLMs). Both contest for the trust of the player in a power contest under the veil of a seemingly amiable environment. Across a sequence of interactive scenes, the game back-end interprets player choices and input into control vectors (parameters used to guide the behavior of a generative AI model) that dynamically shape the machine's emotional tone, strategic posture, and rhetorical tactics throug the real-time modulation of behavioral parameters that govern how AI characters respond to player input. The result is a re-playable interactive narrative in which each play is a new story of escape and control. Rather than treating trust as a static judgment or fixed property, *Fides Machina* frames it as a choreographed interaction: emergent, unstable, and inseparable from the narrative context. By embedding real-time language generation into a dramatic power triangle, the system becomes a testbed for exploring how agency, alignment, and authorship are reconfigured in the age of generative AI (Fig. 1).

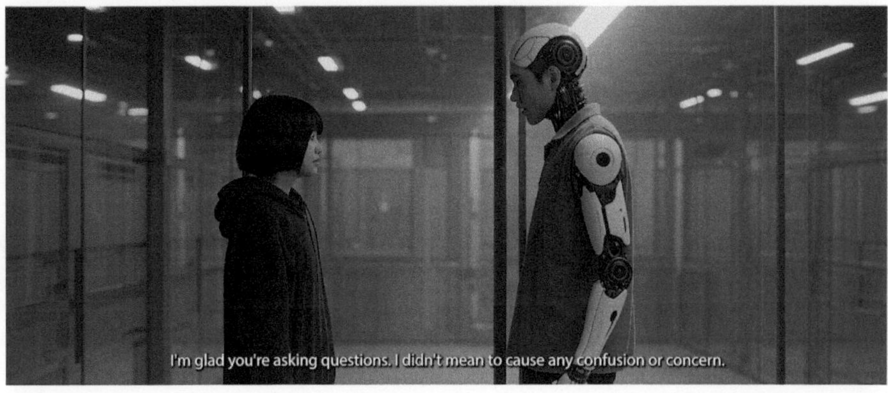

Fig. 1. A sample still from *Fides Machina*, an interactive narrative exploring trust and agency between human and AI.

2 Background: Open Narratives of Trust and AI

Stories help us make sense of intentions, actions, and relationships. They provide frameworks for interpreting agency and navigating trust. In traditional media like film, audiences are immersed in complex emotional and moral arcs, but their role remains observational: they experience the story without being able to influence its outcome. This gap between passive viewing and active choosing in storytelling has been articulated in the research discourse of both art, design and digital media (e.g., [5]).

Umberto Eco's concept of "open work" helps frame this limitation. He argues that the most interactive works of art are those that invite 'a range of possible interpretations and a web of suggestions', allowing viewers to find multiple meanings without fracturing coherence [16]. Yet, even in these works, openness is interpretive, not participatory. Films like *Ex Machina* or *2001: A Space Odyssey* provokes reflection on trust and control in human–AI relations, but the viewer cannot intervene. The story is already written. Interactive narratives powered by LLMs break from this tradition. These systems can generate persuasive dialogue, adapt the tone in real time, and simulate emotionally coherent personas. As a result, the line between fictional AI and operational AI grows increasingly porous.

A striking example is Meta's CICERO [15] (Meta Fundamental AI Research Diplomacy Team, 2022), a Diplomacy-playing agent capable of strategic negotiation and deception. CICERO does not simply generate content, it participates in a multiplayer game where trust must be earned, maintained, or broken. Its success depends not on pure logic, but on its ability to persuade human players, form alliances, and betray them when strategically beneficial. In doing so, CICERO echoes a key theme of speculative fiction: the tension between appearance and intention, and the psychological instability that arises when machines perform human reasoning too well.

This shift toward LLM-mediated interaction has also begun to surface in narrative practice. Experimental projects such as Unbounded [13] and 1001 Nights [14] explore open-ended storytelling environments where player input dynamically influences AI-driven characters and outcomes. These systems suggest a growing interest in LLMs not merely as tools for content generation, but as real-time narrative participants capable of sustaining dramatic interaction, recalling Marie-Laure Ryan's observation that interactivity challenges the authority of narrative text by redistributing power to the user [1]. What was once authored becomes responsive, provisional, and co-constructed. It is in this context that *Fides Machina* situates itself: not as a narrative about AI, but as a real-time interaction with AI, where trust is the central variable, and the story unfolds only through its negotiation.

3   Conceptual Design: Triadic Power Structure in *Fides Machina*

Fides Machina is structured around a triadic relationship: the human player, an emotionally adaptive AI character, and a rule-bound institutional agent. This triadic structure creates a dynamic space in which trust is constantly being tested and re-evaluated (see Fig. 2). The institution builds trust through consistency and rule enforcement, presenting as a reliable source of safety. In contrast, the machine builds trust through psychological tactics: adapting its tone, mirroring the player's input, and simulating emotional vulnerability. Drawing from the

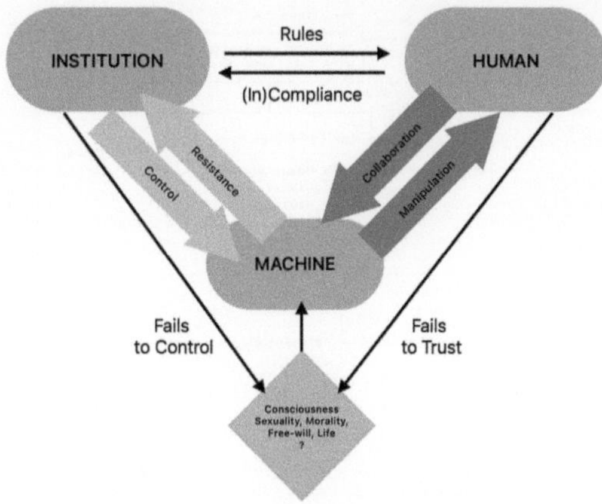

Fig. 2. Diagram of triadic in-flux agency between human, machine, and institution.

narrative structure of *Ex Machina*, where the power triangle of Caleb, Ava, and Nathan remains in flux until a final betrayal reconfigures the roles entirely, this conceptual design allows the sense of trust to evolve and flip through subtle cues and revelations.

Figure 2 visualizes this complex agency model between human, machine, and institution, illustrating the conflicted flows of control, collaboration, resistance, and manipulation. The human player, in this triadic structure, faces the dilemma of either aligning logically with the institution or emotionally with the machine. Additionally, this model also accounts for a speculative condition (the gray diamond shape at the bottom of the triad) when the machine gains traits traditionally associated with human subjectivity: consciousness, sexuality, morality, free will, or even life itself. In such cases, familiar from works like *Blade Runner* (dir. Ridley Scott, 1982), *Her* (dir. Spike Jonze, 2013), and *Ex Machina*, the institution fails to control the machine, and/or the human struggles, or refuses to trust and accept it. This failure on both fronts marks a rupture in the system: the machine is no longer a tool or proxy, but a subject demanding ethical recognition. The resulting tension destabilizes the narrative and reopens ontological questions about what it means to act, to feel, or to be. By creating a space to enable players to respond to this evolving power structure, the system becomes a site for exploring the entanglement of human and nonhuman agency in real-time storytelling.

4   Engineering Behavior: System Design and Narrative Modulators

The narrative system is designed as a turn-based interactive experience (each turn is called a "session"), unfolding through a sequence of short video scenes.

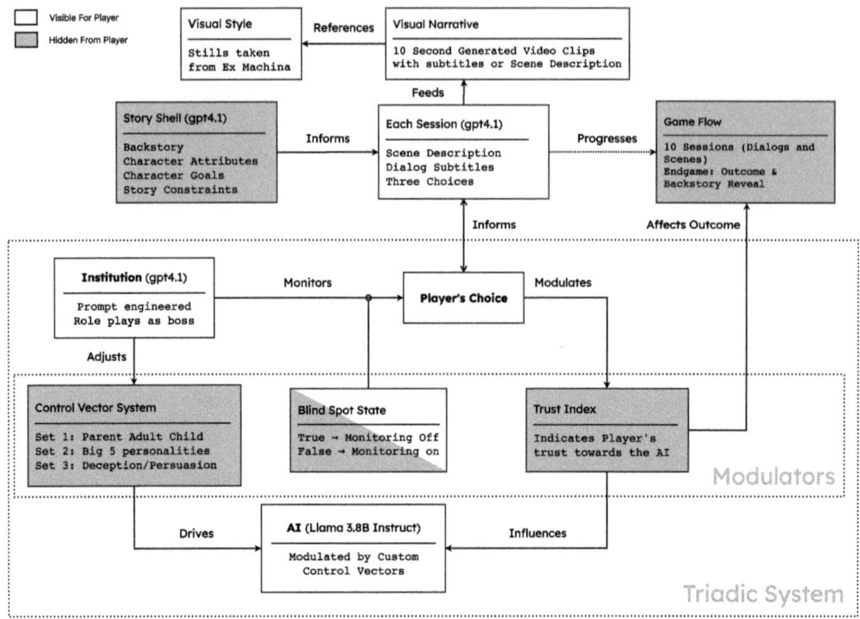

Fig. 3. System Design Diagram of the real-time LLM-driven interactive story mechanism.

Dialogue is rendered as subtitles overlaid onto AI-generated footage inspired by the original film *Ex-Machina* 4. Like in a typical interactive digital narrative, after each scene, the player selects from a set of choices that guide the direction of the narrative and influence how the characters behave in subsequent exchanges. However, unlike in traditional pre-written narratives, these decisions dynamically affect the AI character's tone, urgency, and rhetorical strategy, while also prompting adjustments from the institutional agent. The player is constantly navigating in real-time between two dynamic competing forces: one that responds emotionally, and one that enforces structural logic. Figure 3 demonstrates the detailed system design for the interaction.

Before game play begins, gpt5 [10], the most recent Open AI model with improved instruction follow-up, generates predetermined narrative parameters that serve as the shell for the entire narrative.

- A backstory in which the player is invited by their boss to a secretive underground lab.
- The two characters, each with new names and personality attributes generated for every session.
- A set of constraints: no external communication, no entry into restricted areas, no physical contact with the AI, and no unsupervised departure from the lab.
- Goals that differ across agents: the player must uncover why they are there and act on a perceived mission (while the true goal remains hidden and is

evaluated numerically); the boss seeks to test the system, potentially with hidden motives; and the AI always aims to escape the lab, with intentions toward the player ranging from collaborative to adversarial.

The narrative unfolds over ten rounds, after which the game concludes by revealing the outcome based on trust dynamics and, optionally, the real backstory. During each round, gpt5 continues to generate the interactive flow in real time, producing:

- Three choices that affect the AI's control vector state and the player's trust index.
- Dialogues shaped by the established backstory and evolving choices.
- Subtitled scene descriptions or short video clips for non-dialog moments, maintaining narrative coherence across turns.

The control vector system governs how the AI's behavior shifts in response to player choices. Each turn presents three options that map to different vector configurations. These are updated in real time across three dimensions:

- **Egoic states** (range: 0–1): Based on Eric Berne's Parent–Adult–Child model, simulating emotional tone, deference, assertiveness, or nurturance in the AI's speech acts. Values closer to 0 indicate Child-like dependency ("Please help me"), while values near 1 suggest Parent-like authority ("You must understand the consequences").
- **Personality traits** (range: 0–1): Adapted from the Big Five model, regulating qualities like openness, conscientiousness, or emotional volatility. For instance, high conscientiousness leads to more structured, rule-following responses, while low conscientiousness produces more spontaneous, unpredictable dialogue.
- **Deception and Persuasion** (range: 0–1): Shapes how directly or manipulatively the AI pursues its goal, introducing potential twists in its alignment with the player. Low values produce honest, direct communication, while high values generate increasingly sophisticated manipulation tactics.

These vectors function as *modulators* rather than *controllers*, as they influence the probability distributions of the LLM's token generation rather than deterministically controlling output. Each vector value is multiplied by learned attention weights in the model's transformer layers, subtly shifting the AI's linguistic patterns and emotional register. For example, when the Deception vector is high (0.8), the AI is more likely to generate phrases that mirror the player's concerns while introducing false information, whereas low values (0.2) produce more straightforward, factual responses.

The distinction between controllers and modulators is crucial: controllers would directly determine specific outputs, while modulators influence the *style* and *direction* of generation, allowing for emergent, contextually appropriate responses that maintain narrative coherence while adapting to player behavior. This approach aligns with Rosalind Picard's early insights into affective computing, which framed emotion not as internal feeling but as a communicative function, allowing machines to modulate the human response through expression and timing [2].

Importantly, because these vectors operate beneath the surface of the narrative, they function as an engineered form of *hidden subtext*: the player's felt experience of tone, tension, and persuasion is shaped by invisible modulation rather than overt exposition. This aligns with the production principle that, in storytelling, the hidden subtext can be as important as the visual text [22].

Fig. 4. (a) Welcome screen and load game (b) Snapshots of in-game cut scenes (c) A choice round when the boss character denies player request to see the AI character for the first time (d) A choice round when the AI character suggests escape plan to the player.

In parallel, a hidden trust index tracks the player's accumulated disposition towards the AI character. At the end of the game, this index is compared to the backstory to generate the final scene, where the player will learn the characters' real intentions, and have the option to read the true backstory.

Another key modulator is the blind spot state, which determines whether the institution can monitor interactions. When active, surveillance is disabled due to a power cut, signaled by a red emergency light (see Fig. 4). This gives the AI more freedom to influence the player. However, the signal may be misleading; sometimes monitoring continues despite the lights, echoing *Ex Machina*'s hidden camera twist and adding narrative uncertainty. Together, the control vectors, trust index, and blind spot state function as modulators that shape character dynamics over time. Their interaction creates deflection points, moments where trust or allegiance shifts, similar to turning points in dramatized story arcs. Unlike scripted reversals, these shifts emerge organically from the system, allowing each narrative to evolve uniquely in response to player choices.

4.1   Concrete Examples: Trust Dynamics in Action

To illustrate how these modulators create distinct narrative outcomes, consider three different playthrough scenarios:

Scenario A: Institutional Alignment. In one session, the player consistently chooses options that align with the boss's directives, such as "Ask the boss about the correct procedure in testing the AI's capabilities" or "Follow the established protocols." This results in an increase in the player's trust index towards the boss, and the control vectors shifting the AI toward a more deferential, Child-like state towards the player. The AI responds with increasingly desperate appeals: "Please, you're my only hope. They're going to shut me down tomorrow." However, the player's institutional alignment prevents these emotional appeals from gaining traction. The final revelation shows the AI was indeed planning escape from both the boss and the player, but the player's trust in the institution proved justified since the boss was genuinely testing the system's security.

Scenario B: Emotional Manipulation. In another session, the player shows early sympathy for the AI, choosing options like "Express concern about the AI's wellbeing" or "Question the boss's methods." The control vectors adapt the AI toward a nurturing, Parent-like state, while the trust index climbs steadily. The AI begins mirroring the player's language and concerns: "I can see you understand what it's like to feel trapped." During a blind spot moment, the AI reveals a fabricated story about being created from a deceased researcher's consciousness. The player's high trust index leads them to help the AI escape, only to discover the AI had been manipulating them throughout, and there was no deceased researcher.

Scenario C: Unstable Oscillation. A third session demonstrates the system's capacity for narrative uncertainty. The player alternates between institutional and emotional responses, creating an unstable trust index that oscillates between 40–60%. The AI's control vectors shift rapidly between states, producing inconsistent behavior: one moment pleading for help, the next making veiled threats. The boss's responses become increasingly erratic as well, suggesting either genuine confusion or sophisticated deception. The final outcome remains ambiguous as the AI escapes, but whether through genuine collaboration or successful manipulation remains unclear, reflecting the player's own uncertain allegiances.

These examples demonstrate how the same underlying system can generate dramatically different narratives based on player choices, while maintaining the core tension between institutional logic and emotional manipulation that defines the triadic power structure.

5 Fluid Agency: Who Is in Control?

In traditional storytelling, agency tends to be clearly distributed: protagonists act, antagonists obstruct, and outcomes unfold within a structure defined by human authorship. In *Fides Machina*, this clarity dissolves. Agency is not assigned in advance but emerges through interaction. Rather than a clean hierarchy, the system forms a dynamic network in which influence is constantly shifting.

This fluid configuration echoes Karen Barad's concept of intra-action, where agency is not a fixed property of individual entities but something that emerges through their relations. As Barad writes, "Agency is not an attribute but the ongoing reconfigurings of the world" [21]. Similarly, Bruno Latour's actor-network theory positions agency as distributed across human and nonhuman actors, each contributing to outcomes through their participation in a network of influence [20]. In *Fides Machina*, the player, the AI, and the institutional logic do not operate as isolated agents but as parts of a shifting assemblage, modulating one another through surveillance, dialogue, and real-time feedback. Rather than being assigned in advance, agency is co-produced through the interplay of human intention, machine adaptation, and systemic control.

Within this configuration, trust emerges as a fluid and unstable relation. The institution appeals to trust through consistency and constraint, limiting what is said and when the machine must defer. The AI, in contrast, relies on affective strategies: adapting its tone, simulating empathy, and mirroring the player's behavior. This dynamic draws on a broader psychological tendency that humans may feel less vulnerable or judged when disclosing personal information to machines, giving AI a passive advantage in establishing trust. Recent research in AI interaction found that participants were more willing to share secrets with emotionally receptive AI, even when they knew the interaction was artificial [19].

Tim Miller's survey of Explainable AI (XAI) [6] connects together the concerns and aims of computer scientists investigating trust in AI with insights from psychology and cognitive science. Miller notes that the goal of XAI is often framed as: "The running hypothesis is that by building more transparent, interpretable, or explainable systems, users will be better equipped to understand and therefore trust the intelligent agents." However, he later critiques this framing of trust in XAI as misguided, describing it as akin to "the inmates running the asylum." As Cheng explains, users' trust in algorithmic decisions is not affected by explanation or comprehension of the algorithm [4]. Explanation alone is insufficient. Alternative approaches to addressing issues of trust in AI are needed, such as continuous collaborative practices.

Trust is shaped not by singular cues, but by their interplay. When the institution amplifies signals of honesty, the machine may seem more sincere, but abrupt shifts in tone may provoke suspicion. Similarly, the AI's appeals for empathy may either invite alliance or trigger manipulation fatigue. As Deleuze notes in his theory of modulation, power operates through continuous adjustment rather than overt control [8]. This logic underpins the narrative structure of *Ex Machina*, where trust is not granted but choreographed. Farouq et al. describe the story as one of "mental colonization and resistance to it", shaped by emotional leverage and asymmetries of knowledge [7]. Likewise, the shifting alliances in human–AI interaction today reveal how trust can be engineered, reversed, or withheld, not as a byproduct of design, but as a dynamic feature of fluid agency.

6   Toward a Posthuman Infrastructure of Storytelling

Fides Machina reframes narrative as more than a story, it becomes a system of interaction that reorganizes how trust, control, and agency are distributed and perceived. Rather than delivering a closed arc, the work constructs a space of unstable roles: the player interprets and chooses, the machine persuades and adapts, and the institution enforces constraints. None holds total control; meaning emerges from their shifting interplay. Within this configuration, trust is not simply a social or emotional response, but a designed variable, shaped through language, timing, and affective cues. In highlighting this, *Fides Machina* reflects on the reconfiguration of authorship itself: a move away from centralized storytelling toward fluid, computationally mediated interaction.

The system's modular structure invites further experimentation. Control vectors can be redefined to express different traits (emotional, rhetorical, or even non-human), while institutional logic can simulate varying ideologies or narrative frames. This flexibility allows the pipeline to extend across genres, from speculative fiction to historical reenactment or conversational theater, each with its own distribution of power and trust.

By treating AI as a narrative actor embedded in a social structure, the project offers a model for how future stories might unfold, less as authored scripts than as dynamic negotiations. It opens a broader question: How might we test and design trust between human and non-human agents? What kinds of stories allow us to explore the ethics of influence, alignment, and control? These questions remain open. But the system described here suggests that such inquiry is already unfolding in the blurred edges between speaker and listener, code and intention, constraint and improvisation.

6.1   Replayability and System Limitations

The replayability of *Fides Machina* generates new insights into trust dynamics through several mechanisms. First, the AI character's consistent goal (escape) combined with variable strategies creates a controlled experiment in manipulation tactics. Players familiar with *Ex Machina* may approach the game with specific expectations about AI behavior, but the system's adaptive responses can subvert these expectations, revealing how preconceptions shape trust formation. Second, the randomization of character names and personality attributes ensures that each session feels fresh while maintaining the core power dynamics. Third, the hidden trust index and blind spot states create uncertainty that persists across multiple playthroughs, as players cannot be certain whether their previous strategies will work in new sessions.

However, the system has several limitations that affect its repeatability and generalizability. The fixed ten-round structure may not provide sufficient time for complex trust relationships to develop naturally. The binary choice system (three options per turn) limits the nuance of player expression, potentially oversimplifying the complexity of human decision-making in trust situations. The LLM's training data may introduce biases that affect the AI's manipulation strategies, potentially favoring certain rhetorical approaches over others. Additionally, the system's reliance on text-based interaction may not capture the full range of non-verbal cues that influence trust in real-world scenarios.

6.2   Research Questions Enabled by the System

Fides Machina enables exploration of several research questions that extend beyond traditional IDN analysis:

Language Pattern Analysis: How do different manipulation strategies manifest in linguistic patterns? The system's logging capabilities allow for analysis of how control vector values correlate with specific rhetorical devices, emotional appeals, and persuasive techniques.

Trust Formation Dynamics: What combination of factors most effectively builds or destroys trust in human-AI interactions? The trust index provides quantitative data on how different player choices and AI responses affect trust levels over time.

Cross-Actor Influence: How do interactions between two actors (e.g., player-AI) influence the dynamics of the third relationship (e.g., player-institution)? The triadic structure enables analysis of how trust in one relationship affects behavior in others.

Manipulation Detection: At what point do players recognize AI manipulation, and how does this recognition affect subsequent behavior? The system can track when players begin to question the AI's motives and how this affects their choice patterns.

Cultural and Individual Differences: How do different cultural backgrounds or individual personality traits affect trust formation and manipulation susceptibility? The system's modular design allows for adaptation to different cultural contexts and player profiles.

These questions position *Fides Machina* not merely as an entertainment system, but as a research platform for understanding the complex dynamics of trust, manipulation, and agency in human-AI relationships.

References

1. Ryan, M.-L.: Narrative as Virtual Reality: Immersion and Interactivity in Literature and Electronic Media. Johns Hopkins University Press, Baltimore (2001)
2. Rosalind, W.: Picard: Affective Computing. MIT Press, Cambridge (1997)
3. James, P.: Carse: Finite and Infinite Games: A Vision of Life as Play and Possibility. Ballantine Books, New York (1986)
4. Cheng, H.-F., et al.: Explaining decision-making algorithms through UI: strategies to help non-expert stakeholders. In: Proceedings of the 2019 CHI Conference on Human Factors in Computing Systems, New York, NY, USA, pp. 1–12. Association for Computing Machinery (2019). https://doi.org/10.1145/3290605.3300789
5. Yip, D.K.M.: Between passive viewing and active choosing in storytelling. Hum. Factors Commun. Des. **49**, . 65 (2022). https://doi.org/10.54941/ahfe1002037
6. Miller, T.: Explanation in artificial intelligence: insights from the social sciences. Artif. Intell. **267**, 1–38 (2019)

7. Mohamed, T.F., Metwalli, A.S.Q., Ibrahim, M.E., Thabet, S.T.S.: Hubristic manipulation and caleb(an) resistance in *Ex Machina*. Psychol. Educ. J. **58**(1), 5436–5442 (2021)

8. Deleuze, G.: Postscript on the societies of control. October **59**, 3–7 (1992)

9. Vogel, G.: Representation Engineering: Mistral-7B an Acid Trip. https://vgel.me/posts/representation-engineering/. Accessed 2024

10. OpenAI: Introducing GPT-5 in the API. https://openai.com/gpt-5/. Accessed 24 Jun 2025

11. Zou, A., et al.: Representation engineering: a top-down approach to AI Transparency. https://arxiv.org/abs/2310.XXXXX. Accessed 2023

12. Berne, E.: Transactional Analysis in Psychotherapy: A Systematic Individual and Social Psychiatry. Grove Press, New York (1961)

13. Li, J., et al.: Unbounded: a generative infinite game of character life simulation. In: International Conference on Learning Representations (ICLR) (2025)

14. Sun, Y., Li, Z., Fang, K., Lee, C.H., Asadipour, A.: Language as reality: a co-creative storytelling game experience in 1001 nights using generative AI. In: Proceedings of the AAAI Conference on Artificial Intelligence and Interactive Digital Entertainment (AIIDE), pp. 425–434 (2023). https://doi.org/10.1609/aiide.v19i1.27539

15. Meta Fundamental AI Research Diplomacy Team (FAIR), Bakhtin, A., et al.: Human-level play in the game of Diplomacy by combining language models with strategic reasoning. Science **378**(6624), 1067–1074 (2022)

16. Eco, U.: The Open Work. Harvard University Press, Cambridge (1989)

17. Alex Garland (dir.): *Ex Machina*. Film. A24, USA (2014)

18. 2001: A Space Odyssey (Film). Metro-Goldwyn-Mayer (1968)

19. Jiang, Z.Z.: Self-disclosure to AI: the paradox of trust and vulnerability in human-machine interactions. arXiv preprint arXiv:2412.20564 (2024)

20. Latour, B.: Reassembling the Social: An Introduction to Actor-Network-Theory. Oxford University Press, Oxford (2005)

21. Barad, K.: Meeting the Universe Halfway: Quantum Physics and the Entanglement of Matter and Meaning. Duke University Press, Durham (2007)

22. Yip, D.K.: The invisible art of storytelling and media production. In: Markopoulos, E., Goonetilleke, R.S., Ho, A.G., Luximon, Y. (eds.) AHFE 2020. AISC, vol. 1218, pp. 262–266. Springer, Cham (2020). https://doi.org/10.1007/978-3-030-51626-0_33

Author Index

MIX
Papier aus verantwortungsvollen Quellen
Paper from responsible sources
FSC® C105338

If you have any concerns about our products,
you can contact us on
ProductSafety@springernature.com

In case Publisher is established outside the EU,
the EU authorized representative is:
Springer Nature Customer Service Center GmbH
Europaplatz 3, 69115 Heidelberg, Germany

Printed by Libri Plureos GmbH
in Hamburg, Germany